Date Due

Oct 6 43			
Nov 3			
Oct. 17			
Nov 15			
MAY 2 0			
MAR 30			
NOV 1 5			
DEC 2 0			
JUL 9			
MAY 1			

No. 293   DEMCO

FINANCIAL ORGANIZATION
AND THE
ECONOMIC SYSTEM

BY

HAROLD G. MOULTON, Ph.D., LL.D.

FIRST EDITION

McGRAW-HILL BOOK COMPANY, Inc.

NEW YORK AND LONDON

1938

Published by arrangement with The University of Chicago Press

THE MAPLE PRESS COMPANY, YORK, PA.

PREFACE

In 1921 the author published a broad integrated analysis of the functions performed by the various financial institutions which comprise the modern financial system, under the title "The Financial Organization of Society." Succeeding editions, appearing in 1926 and 1930, took account of the significant changes and developments which had occurred in the intervening years. After 1930, modifications of the monetary and credit system were made in such rapid succession that for some years it became impossible to present anything resembling a "still picture," or to describe an "existing" financial organization. When at last the new pattern had become sufficiently set to permit at least a tentative appraisal of the significance of recent developments, it was evident that the changes which had taken place had been so numerous, and their implications so far reaching, that something more than a revised edition of the former treatise was essential. While the present volume builds on the structural foundations of the former, and follows the same central theme, the earlier book has been largely rewritten and greatly amplified. The new title is believed to convey more adequately than the former one the scope and character of the analysis as a whole.

This volume is designed not only to reveal the functional significance of the various separate financial institutions, but also their interrelations as parts of a complex financial organization which largely controls the operation of the economic system as a whole. All of our private financial institutions and agencies owe their existence to the requirements of an evolving economic system for liquid capital resources. These funds could be obtained only through borrowing operations, the carrying out of which was facilitated by the organization of varied types of credit agencies. These institutions, by virtue of their control over credit, came in due course to assume a position of dominant importance in directing and allocating the flow of productive energy in the economic system as a whole. As we point out in this study, however, one of the most significant developments of recent years has been a substantial transfer of such power from private financiers to government officials.

In view of the vast mass of material pertaining to the history, organization, and regulation of monetary and credit institutions that is now available, the problem of selection and emphasis has become of the utmost importance. If, as the decades pass, we are to keep on top of the data and maintain perspective with reference to the financial organization as a whole, it is necessary to eliminate obsolete, irrelevant, and unimportant details and to reduce the historical material to the indispensable minimum. It has been interesting to the author to note how much compression has been possible, especially on the historical side, without sacrifice of essentials.

This volume not only includes a discussion of the numerous modifications of monetary and credit regulations of recent years and of the many new public credit agencies which have been organized, but it also includes certain important subjects not covered at all in the earlier volume—namely, the financial systems of other countries and the factors and forces involved in the fluctuations of prices under modern conditions. It is hoped that the approach used in connection with the latter may shed new light on a very old economic issue.

In the preparation of this volume I have received invaluable aid from friends intimately connected with various types of financial operations, notably Dudley Cates of New York and Wilfred Goodwyn and Lew Coit of Washington. I am also deeply indebted to Professors James D. Magee of New York University and George W. Edwards of the College of the City of New York, who have not only read portions of the manuscript but have made numerous constructive suggestions with respect to the scope, content, organization, and emphasis of the volume. I am also under enduring obligation to Dr. Edwards for the invaluable assistance which he has rendered in the furnishing of materials in a number of fields with which he is especially familiar. I am also indebted for aid and suggestions to Dr. Frieda Baird of the Farm Credit Administration and to numerous colleagues at the Brookings Institution, including Leo Pasvolsky, Edwin G. Nourse, Charles O. Hardy, Daniel T. Selko, and Laurence F. Schmeckebier. Government agencies have been uniformly helpful in furnishing current data.

It is difficult for me to convey adequately the extent of the assistance given by my daughter Barbara. She has not only served as assistant in the gathering of data but she has prepared practically all of the illustrations, collaborated on certain sections, and served as editor and critic of the entire manuscript.

HAROLD G. MOULTON.

WASHINGTON, D. C.,
August, 1938.

CONTENTS

	PAGE
PREFACE	v
LIST OF ILLUSTRATIONS	xiii
LIST OF TABLES	xv
EDITOR'S FOREWORD	xvii

CHAPTER I
THE NATURE AND FUNCTIONS OF A PECUNIARY UNIT

I. Definition and Origin of the Pecuniary Unit	3
II. An Index for Business Policies	4
III. A Basis of Family Budgets.	7
IV. A Guide to Economic Organization	8
V. Effects on Social Standards	10

CHAPTER II
THE STANDARD FOR DEFERRED PAYMENTS

I. Why Gold Came to be the Standard	12
II. Fluctuations in the Price Level.	14
III. Consequences of Price Changes.	16

CHAPTER III
OTHER FUNCTIONS AND SERVICES OF MONEY

I. Money as a Medium of Exchange.	20
II. Money as a Store of Value.	21
III. Money in Relation to Production.	21
IV. Money Income and Economic Organization	24

CHAPTER IV
THE EVOLUTION OF THE MONETARY SYSTEM

I. Coinage Problems.	28
II. Gresham's Law and Bimetallism	31
III. The Adoption of the Gold Standard	36
IV. Forms of Money in the United States.	38
V. An International Monetary System.	42

CHAPTER V
RECENT CHANGES IN THE AMERICAN MONETARY SYSTEM

I. America's Departure from the Gold Standard	45
II. Other Monetary Legislation	49
III. Gold Devaluation and the Price Level.	51

PAGE

IV. The "Gold Clause" Cases. 53
V. A "Provisional" Gold Standard 60

CHAPTER VI
THE FOREIGN EXCHANGES

I. The Exchange Mechanism. 63
II. The Significance of Credit Operations. 67
III. War-time Disruption of Exchanges 70
IV. Restoration of Stable Exchanges, 1924–1929 73
V. Breakdown of Exchanges During Depression. 75
VI. Recent Trends and Current Problems. 80

CHAPTER VII
GOVERNMENT FINANCE AND MONETARY STABILITY

I. Methods of "Manufacturing" Money. 84
II. The Lessons of Experience. 85
III. Recent Trends in the United States. 90
IV. The Inflation Issue 95
V. Interrelations in the Financial System. 97

CHAPTER VIII
THE NATURE AND FUNCTIONS OF CREDIT

I. The Nature of Credit 99
II. The Various Kinds of Credit. 100
III. The Basis of Credit. 102
IV. Economic Significance of Credit 103

CHAPTER IX
CREDIT INSTRUMENTS

I. Investment Credit Instruments. 106
II. Commercial Credit Instruments 111
III. The Use of Credit Instruments in Transferring Wealth 114

CHAPTER X
THE EVOLUTION OF CREDIT INSTITUTIONS

I. The Corporation as a Device for Raising Capital 123
II. Stages of Modern Development. 126
III. Problems Arising from Corporate Organization. 130
IV. The Modern Financial Structure 132

CHAPTER XI
CAPITAL REQUIREMENTS AND SOURCES OF CAPITAL

I. Raising Capital for Private Business 137
II. Raising Public Capital. 149

CHAPTER XII
MARKETING SECURITIES THROUGH INVESTMENT HOUSES

I. History of Investment Banking. 153
II. Functions of Investment Banking Institutions 156

CONTENTS   ix

                                                 PAGE
  III. Investigation and Analysis. 157
  IV. Underwriting. 162
   V. Distribution 166
  VI. Sundry Services of Investment Banks. 168
 VII. Capital Requirements and Profits of Investment Banks 170
VIII. Investment Banks and the General Economic Organization 171

CHAPTER XIII

INTERMEDIARY INVESTMENT INSTITUTIONS

   I. The Investment Trust. 175
  II. Savings Institutions. 181
 III. Insurance Companies as Savings Institutions. 188
 IV. The Economic Significance of Savings Institutions 190

CHAPTER XIV

TRUST COMPANIES AND THE MODERN FINANCIAL SYSTEM

   I. The Scope of Trust Company Operations 194
  II. Services to Individuals and Estates. 196
 III. Services Performed for Corporations. 198
 IV. The Trust Company as a Custodian. 206
  V. The Economic Significance of Trust Companies. 210

CHAPTER XV

THE STOCK EXCHANGE AND CAPITAL RAISING

   I. History of Stock Exchanges 212
  II. The Organization of the Stock Exchange. 216
 III. Economic Functions of the Stock Exchange 221

CHAPTER XVI

THE REGULATION OF THE INVESTMENT CREDIT SYSTEM

   I. Regulations applied to Corporations. 228
  II. Limitations on Government Financial Issues. 231
 III. Controlling Investments of Intermediary Institutions 232
 IV. Regulation of Trust Functions 234
  V. Supervision of the Marketing of Securities. 235
 VI. Control of the Stock Exchange. 237

CHAPTER XVII

THE PRACTICAL OPERATIONS OF THE COMMERCIAL BANK

   I. Incidental Services of Commercial Banks 240
  II. Analysis of Commercial Banking Operations 242
 III. Various Types of Commercial Bank Loans. 247
 IV. Commercial Banks and Foreign Trade. 261

CHAPTER XVIII

SUPPLEMENTARY COMMERCIAL CREDIT INSTITUTIONS

   I. The Marketing of "Commercial Paper". 264
  II. The Discount of Accounts Receivable. 269
 III. Financing Installment Sales 270
 IV. Significance of Installment Credit Institutions 274

CHAPTER XIX
CONSUMPTIVE CREDIT AGENCIES

I. The Magnitude of Consumer Credit. 279
II. Illegal Lenders 280
III. The Business of Pawnbroking 282
IV. Personal Finance Companies and Remedial Loan Societies. 283
V. Cooperative Credit Unions and Axias 285
VI. Industrial Banks 288
VII. Personal Loan Departments of Banks. 289
VIII. The Significance of Consumer Credit 290

CHAPTER XX
THE COMMERCIAL BANKING SYSTEM

I. Clearing-house Associations 292
II. Relations Between Banks in Different Cities. 298
III. Clearings and Collections under the Federal Reserve System 300
IV. The Commercial Banking System and the Manufacture of Credit
Currency 303
V. The Central Position of Commercial Banking in the Economic System 308

CHAPTER XXI
THE CHANGING CHARACTER OF COMMERCIAL BANKING

I. The Growth of Investment Operations. 312
II. The Problem of Liquidity 316
III. Commercial Banking Trends in Recent Years 321

CHAPTER XXII
THE EVOLUTION OF AMERICAN BANKING REGULATION

I. Banking before the Civil War 325
II. National and State Banking Systems, 1863–1913 327
III. The Broadened Scope of Regulation in 1913 341
IV. Banking Developments Since 1930 354
V. The Lesson of Experience 361

CHAPTER XXIII
THE FEDERAL RESERVE SYSTEM

I. Administrative Framework of the System 363
II. Creating an Elastic Bank Note Currency 368
III. The Control of Credit. 374
IV. The Shifting Character of Reserve Bank Assets. 382
V. Federal Reserve Banks As Government Depositaries 385

CHAPTER XXIV
THE RESERVE SYSTEM IN OPERATION

I. Financing the World War 390
II. The Crisis of 1920 392
III. Experience in the Twenties. 396
IV. The Reserve System Since 1929. 407

CHAPTER XXV

THE BANKING AND CREDIT SYSTEMS OF OTHER COUNTRIES

I. Foreign Credit Systems 418
II. Central Banking Experience and Trends. 427
III. International Aspects of Financial Organization. 430

CHAPTER XXVI

AGRICULTURAL CREDIT INSTITUTIONS

I. Short-Term Credit 435
II. Long-Term Credit 442
III. Intermediate Credit. 449
IV. Significance of Agricultural Credit Organization. 454

CHAPTER XXVII

FINANCING URBAN REAL ESTATE

I. Building and Loan Associations. 456
II. Financing Through the "Old Line" Mortgage 460
III. Financing Through the First Mortgage Bond. 463
IV. Government Participation in Urban Real Estate Financing. 467

CHAPTER XXVIII

THE POSITION OF THE GOVERNMENT IN THE CREDIT SYSTEM

I. Sources of Treasury Funds. 472
II. The Uses of Government Funds 476
III. The Shifting Balance of Power. 483

CHAPTER XXIX

THE PECUNIARY SYSTEM AND PRICE CHANGES

I. The Economic Setting. 485
II. Long-Term Price Trends and Economic Progress 486
III. Price Changes and the Business Cycle. 492
IV. Modifications of the Standard and Price Changes. 494
V. The Traditional Approach to the Price Problem 495
VI. Lessons of Recent Experience. 501

INDEX. 505

LIST OF ILLUSTRATIONS

	PAGE
Movement of Prices, 1801–1937	16
The Flow of Money Income	23
The Allocation of Income in Relation to Economic Organization	25
Commercial Ratio of Gold and Silver, 1800–1937	35
Price Movements of Gold, All Commodities, and Foreign Trade Commodities, 1933–1938	52
Balance of International Payments of the United States	69
Dollar Exchange Value of the Franc, 1914–1937	72
Distribution of World Gold Supply, 1913–1937	74
Breakdown of the International Monetary System, 1931–1937	79
German Small Change in 1923	90
Receipts and Expenditures of the Federal Government, Fiscal Years, 1915–1938	91
Aggregate Federal Debt, Fiscal Years, 1915–1938	93
Institutions Utilized in Financing Corporate Enterprise	133
Methods of Raising Long-term Capital, 1919–1937	149
Fluctuations of Prices, 1900–1938	226
Growth of the Credit Structure of National Banks, 1864–1937	306
Loans and Investments of National Banks, 1900–1937	314
Number of National Banks, State Banks, and Trust Companies, 1865–1935	333
Average Capital, Including Surplus and Undivided Profits of National Banks, State Banks, and Trust Companies, 1865–1935	335
Fluctuations in Business Activity, 1877–1938	342
The Organization of the Federal Reserve System under the Banking Act of 1935	365
Map of the Federal Reserve Districts	366
Reserve Position of Federal Reserve Banks, 1915–1937	398
Reserve Position of Member Banks, 1930–1938	411
The Agricultural Credit Structure	437
The Treasury and the Credit System	475
Movements of Wholesale Prices and Weekly Wage Rates, 1801–1937	489

LIST OF TABLES

PAGE

Production of Gold and Silver in the World since the Discovery of America   34

Stock of Money at the End of Each Fiscal Year   39

Money in Circulation at the End of Each Fiscal Year.   40

Exchange Fluctuations, 1918–1924   71

Exchange Stabilization, 1925–1929   73

Disintegration of the Gold Standard System.   78

German Currency Inflation, 1913–1923   89

Growth of Public Debts, 1932–1937.   95

Security Issues by Types of Business 148

Federal Government Expenditures for Capital Construction. 151

Net Debt of All Local Governments, 1912–1932 151

Assets of American Life Insurance Companies 189

Mortgage Holdings of Life Insurance Companies, December 31, 1936 . . . 189

Balance Sheet of a National Bank 246

Consumer Credit by Types of Lending Agencies, 1936. 279

Investments of National Banks, June 30, 1937. 315

Demand and Time Deposits of National Banks 316

Bank Suspensions, 1930–1937 356

Changing Character of Federal Reserve Operations, 1915–1937. 383

Assets and Liabilities of the Federal Reserve Banks, December 31, 1937 . . 384

Number of Depositaries of Each Class, and Amount of Deposits Held, June
    30, 1937. 388

Balance Sheet of a Joint Stock Bank 419

Loans Made by Farm Credit Administration Agencies 453

Reconstruction Finance Corporation Activities, February 2, 1932 to March
    31, 1938. 477

Sources and Ownership of Capital of Government Credit Agencies . . 479–481

EDITOR'S FOREWORD

Financial Organization and the Economic System is the second title to appear in the series of Business and Economics Publications. While in one sense it is a revision of Mr. Moulton's *The Financial Organization of Society*, which was originally published in 1921, the present work is far more than a mere revision of the former. In the earlier publication Mr. Moulton did pioneer work in the field of economics in placing emphasis upon the fact that the business order is a financially organized scheme for producing goods and services. He placed even greater emphasis upon the fact that many financial institutions besides banking institutions play important roles in the economic system, and indicated how these financial institutions are employed by businessmen in the management of their affairs.

Although, as the author points out in his preface, "the present volume builds on the structural foundations of the former, and follows the same general theme," the present treatise goes beyond the first book, as is indicated by the adoption of the new title, and shows the delicate interrelations of the various separate financial institutions "as parts of a complex financial organization which largely controls the operations of the economic system as a whole."

The former publication was prepared with the needs of college and university students primarily in view. The wide acceptance which the original treatise has had throughout the nation during the past fifteen years or more testifies to its usefulness for this purpose. The present revised edition should serve even more effectively than the previous one as the basis for instruction in departments of economics and in schools of business.

The present book, however, has a broader objective than the former one. It is prepared with the needs of the lay reader and businessmen in view also. During the past ten or fifteen years the public mind as never before has been drawn to the importance of financial institutions and their relationships to the operations of the economic system. Businessmen, too, have come to a realization of the complicated relations between financial institutions and business management. Both the lay reader and the practical businessman will find in this treatise excellent discussions of these important subjects.

This treatise, as well as others projected in the series of Business and Economics Publications, emphasizes the changing relationship between the government and business. Whether one agrees or disagrees with the flood of legislation which has swept over the nation during the past ten years, the fact is that it is here and business must make an adjustment to it. Although much of this legislation may be revised as time goes on and some of it may be repealed in its entirety, it is safe to predict that the major portion of it will continue as a part of our national social policy. Both businessmen and students of business must have an appreciation of the new standards of business conduct and the new administrative machinery that the government has established, the operation of which profoundly conditions modern business management. Mr. Moulton in this revision of his original treatise has effectively integrated recent legislation relating to the financial system to a fundamental discussion of our financial organization and the economic system.

WILLIAM H. SPENCER.

CHICAGO,
August, 1938.

FINANCIAL ORGANIZATION
AND
THE ECONOMIC SYSTEM

CHAPTER I

THE NATURE AND FUNCTIONS
OF A PECUNIARY UNIT

The complex social and industrial system of the present day is commonly said to be organized on the basis of a pecuniary unit of calculation called, according to the country, the dollar, pound sterling, franc, mark, crown, etc. In this chapter it is our purpose to consider the precise nature of the monetary unit and to disclose the various ways in which it is of service to society. It will help to avert misunderstanding on the part of the reader if it is stated at the outset that the function of a pecuniary unit of calculation is quite different from that of a medium of exchange, discussion of which is reserved for the third chapter.

I. DEFINITION AND ORIGIN OF THE PECUNIARY UNIT

The nature of the monetary unit may best be appreciated if it is thought of as a certain definite weight and fineness of metal. For instance, the unit in the United States, the gold dollar, is composed of 15$\frac{5}{21}$ grains of metal, of which nine-tenths is gold and one-tenth copper (or 13.72 grains of pure gold).[1] This monetary unit need not be used as a circulating medium; indeed it need not even be coined. The American dollar, for example, has never been coined because it would be too small for convenience. In former times larger gold coins were extensively used as media of exchange; but today, in both the United States and other countries, gold has ceased to be used as a means of payment except in international transactions.

The pecuniary unit is a sort of language device—a final step, as it were, in the development of means of communicating ideas. Because of restricted vocabulary primitive man found great difficulty in exchanging ideas with his fellows, with the result that both intellectual and material progress were seriously retarded. Trading operations were early impeded, moreover, not only because of inadequate *word* symbols for the communication of ideas, but also because of the lack

[1] Congress has the power to change either the weight or the fineness of the dollar. For reasons discussed in chap. V, an act of 1934 reduced the weight from 23.22 grains of gold (25.8 grains of metal nine-tenths fine), to the present figure. It had previously been unchanged since 1834.

of *numerical* symbols for reckoning quantities. It was necessary for a system of notation to be developed before trading could be conducted on any considerable scale; for it is apparent that without a means of quantitative measurement of the goods to be purchased or sold, the risk involved in trading operations would be so great as to prevent all except the simplest transactions.

But the development of a system of notation was not sufficient of itself to lay the basis for extensive trading operations. A still further step in the development of the language of trade and business was necessary, namely, to express a variety of quantitative units in terms of some qualitative, or *value*, unit. It is very difficult to trade yards of cloth for tons of coal, or bushels of wheat for skins of animals, without some means of reckoning the relative values of physical quantities of unlike goods.

It is probable that the use of money as a pecuniary unit, in terms of which the values of unlike quantities are measured, developed earlier than its use as a medium of exchange. The word "pecuniary" comes from the Latin word for money, *pecunia*, and it is generally believed that *pecunia* is derived from *pecus*, meaning cattle. Now cattle were obviously ill-adapted for use as media of exchange; but since their approximate value was a matter of common knowledge, they could serve very well as a means of measuring values. Among barbaric tribes wealth has often been expressed in terms of shells, precious stones, skins, or whatever commodity was most widely known. Wherever they were found in sufficient quantity the precious metals, gold and silver, naturally came to be used for the same purpose. But gold and silver, shells, etc., unlike cattle, were also serviceable as media for effecting actual exchanges of goods.

It would seem that the use of money as a medium of exchange was necessarily of later development than its use as a common denominator of values; for it is difficult to conceive of an exchange of goods for money where there had not already been a pre-existing evaluation of the goods in terms of a pecuniary unit. In any event, the development of a pecuniary unit gave the necessary commensurability to pounds, quarts, and bushels—and to wheat, cattle, and cloth—and was thus one of the most significant developments in history. It was the final vital step in the evolution of means of communicating ideas. It made language and numbers intelligible for the purposes of business.

II. AN INDEX FOR BUSINESS POLICIES

We have pointed out that without a unit for measuring values exchange operations would involve such risks as to be practically prohibitive. We shall see now that a pecuniary unit is also of vital importance from the standpoint of the organization of productive activities. Let us illustrate with a unit such as the dollar.

Mr. X is a manufacturer. He finds that he has 10,000 yards of finished cloth on hand, 12,000 pounds of raw cotton in his warehouse, and 5,000 yards of cloth in process of manufacture. He has supplies in his shop, consisting of so many gallons of oil, rolls of packing, etc. He has a building that is 100 feet long and 60 feet wide, with two stories, each 14 feet high. The building is made of reinforced concrete material. His power and heating plant is five years of age, with five years of wear remaining. He owns two automobiles and three trucks, all somewhat the worse for wear and tear. He manufactures 50,000 yards of cloth per year, of which 30,000 yards are of grade A, 10,000 yards of grade B, and 10,000 yards of grade C. Without a means of measuring all these units in terms of a common denominator of value, it is apparent that it would be impossible for Mr. X to ascertain from his books whether his business is successful or unsuccessful. It is also obvious that the chances of failure would be very great.

The choice of a business is guided by analysis of pecuniary accounts. We may note first how X was aided in choosing this particular line of business. Having capital at his disposal, he naturally would wish to employ it in that line of industry which would yield him the largest income. Let us assume that at the period when Mr. X must decide where to invest, the typical establishment is receiving a return of two per cent on the capital invested in line A; five per cent in line B; seven per cent in line C; and ten per cent in line D. If other things were equal, Mr. X would as a matter of course choose line D. But other things are not as a rule exactly equal. There may be more risk involved in line D, and hence a greater chance of failure in the event of untoward developments. It may well be, however, that the risks in line D are not proportionately greater than in line A and line B. The demand for the produce of line A may have been declining, or perhaps D is at present enjoying an extraordinary demand. In either event, a larger margin of profit can for the present be secured in line D than in line A. Since Mr. X is looking for employment of his funds in the most profitable branch of industry, he will therefore probably choose line D, provided of course there are no personal or other reasons which might prevent his success in that line.

The question now arises, How can the business man ascertain the rate of profits in different industries? In brief, by a study of the general market conditions in the different industries and of the financial returns actually received by existing companies in the various lines of industry. The quotations of securities on the stock exchange serve, as we shall later see, as a fairly reliable index to the relative profits of different industries. If, however, one is thinking of venturing as a pioneer into a new line of industry, he can of course rely only upon a study of general market conditions. But in any case the estimated relative costs of production in this and other lines will serve as an important index to the probabilities of success.

The pecuniary unit aids those who participate in the financing of business enterprise. Business is nowadays commonly organized on a corporate basis, and the fixed capital is raised largely by the sale of bonds and stock through the intermediation of investment bankers, whose support is necessary to the success of the enterprises. Individual investors also study, with the aid of pecuniary accounts, the prospective value of the securities.[2] It is usually necessary to borrow some of the working capital required to operate the business, in which case the commercial banker passes judgment on the feasibility of the enterprise. And once more the financial standing of the business, as shown by accounts that are expressed in pecuniary terms, affords the criterion for reliable judgment.

Managerial decisions are rendered on the basis of pecuniary data. In the building of a manufacturing establishment there is, for instance, a question of the types of materials to be used in the construction. Shall it be of wood, of steel, or of concrete? The cost of each, the varying rates of fire insurance with the respective types of materials, the relative durability for the purposes in hand of the different materials, all must be taken into consideration. And in every case the decision revolves around the question of relative costs, computed in terms of dollars.

Similarly, in equipping the establishment, there is the choice between machine A and machine B. Machine A costs $1,000; machine B costs $1,200. Machine A, however, would turn out only three-quarters as much product as machine B. On the other hand, machine A would require $50 more per year for maintenance; while machine B would last five years longer. The problem of deciding which type of machine to use under these conditions is not a simple one at best. But it is much simpler by virtue of the dollars-and-cents computation than it would be in the absence of any such guide.

Let us suppose that the decision is for the purchase of machine B. Presently there appears upon the market a new machine, which can perform the same work at one-half the cost per unit of product. Machine B has, however, ten years of wear remaining in it. Should it

[2] See chap. XII.

be discarded now as obsolete, or should it be used until worn out?
There is here involved a delicate balancing of costs; and a decision
necessarily carries with it a certain element of risk. But again it is
clear that the pecuniary basis of reckoning greatly lessens the chances
of error and thereby increases the probability of business success.

This factory employs a large number of laborers. The management
finds that there is a possibility of a considerable substitution of
machinery for labor. The question arises, When is it wise to substitute machinery for labor, or vice versa, as the case may be? The
decision is made, as in the other cases, on the basis of pecuniary
calculations.

Instances of this sort might be multiplied indefinitely. In fact,
virtually every decision that is made by the business manager today
involves a careful consideration of costs and returns; practically all of
modern business is organized on the basis of pecuniary computations.
The enormous size of the business unit nowadays, and the complex
relationships that obtain between the business man and those from
whom he buys and to whom he sells, require not merely the keeping
of records of transactions that are entered into, but also the development of elaborate financial accounting systems from which cost and
profit data may be obtained. It should be repeated here that without
the monetary unit accounting records would be lifeless; while with the
dollar unit the business man may use his accounts both as an indication of past business achievement and as a guide to future policy.

III. A BASIS OF FAMILY BUDGETS

The pecuniary unit also provides the basis for an intelligent apportionment of the income of individuals. When family incomes, which
in a pecuniary society are initially received in the form of money
rather than in the form of goods, are carefully considered, a formal
budget is prepared by means of which the income is apportioned in
such a way as to bring the largest satisfaction of family wants.

Let us assume, first, a family income of $150 per month, an income
sufficient to buy only the ordinary necessities of life. This $150 must
provide for food, clothing, shelter, light, heat, and miscellaneous
expenses. Since this income should be so apportioned among these
various needs that the family will enjoy the largest measure of comfort, the expenditure in each direction must be considered in comparison with the expenditures in every other direction. Will $50 for rent
and $100 for the remaining necessities give as large a measure of
satisfaction as $25 for rent and $125 for the remaining items? Should
$75 be spent for food and $20 for clothing, or should it be $85 for food

and $10 for clothing? The arrangement of a family budget in this fashion is difficult enough at best, and precision in measurement is of course not to be expected. The dollar unit, however, provides a rough measuring stick by means of which a larger satisfaction may be derived from a given income than would otherwise be possible.

With an income of $1,000 a month the problem of family expenditures is in some ways less difficult, because the adequacy of the income to meet the bare necessities of life is no longer in question. From another standpoint, however, it is more difficult, because a wider range of expenditures for luxuries is now possible. After necessities are provided for, how shall the remainder be spent? Shall it be for a chair, a picture, or other household decoration? Shall it be for more extravagant clothes, for a pleasure trip, or for a new automobile? The family would no doubt prefer to enjoy all these luxuries rather than to choose between them; but if the income is not adequate to provide for all of them, the question of selection inevitably presents itself. The cost of the automobile must then be compared with the cost of a pleasure trip, and, in fact, with all the additional things that might be purchased if the automobile were foregone. The dollar unit comes to stand for a certain amount of "generalized purchasing power," and the task of making a wise apportionment of the family income is thus greatly simplified.

The monetary unit is also a guide to savings requirements. Every family has the problem of making provision for the proverbial rainy day, for old age, and for dependents. By reckoning in terms of dollars, one may compute with a fair degree of accuracy how large a fund of savings is necessary to provide, upon retirement, an income sufficient to insure one's self and dependents against want. Let us assume that in a given case this is $3,000 a year. To make sure of a perpetual income of $3,000 a year it is therefore necessary to accumulate, assuming the interest rate to be 4 per cent, a fund of $75,000, or less if the principal as well as the interest is to be used in the form of an annuity. One must save each year such proportion of one's income as will provide in a given period of time the fund required. Insurance tables, worked out on the basis of the dollar unit, serve as a reliable guide to the saving that is necessary in given cases to make adequate provision for old age, sickness, etc.

IV. A GUIDE TO ECONOMIC ORGANIZATION

Thus far we have been considering the pecuniary unit in its relation to the making of business and personal decisions. We may now look for some of the broader economic and social consequences of the decisions that are made on the basis of pecuniary computations. In the first place, the conduct of international trade has been facilitated. The development of the pecuniary unit in the various commercial nations has given rise to an international denominator of values. A merchant who wishes to sell goods in a foreign country may ascertain the profits from such sales by simply translating dollars into pounds sterling, francs, or marks, as the case may be. The actual settlement of these international financial obligations, however, has required the development of a rather complex financial mechanism known as the foreign exchanges (see chapter VI).

It should be noted here that with narrowly restricted trading operations little division of labor was possible and small-scale, inefficient production therefore necessarily prevailed. A large volume of output is absolutely dependent upon wide markets—national and international; hence division of labor and large-scale efficient production had to wait, among other things, upon the development of the pecuniary unit and the extensive trading operations which it made possible.

The monetary unit also serves as a ready means of indicating the relative productive advantages of different regions and thus directs and hastens the spread of population to the areas where a given expenditure of effort will produce the greatest possible productive output. Analogous to the spread of population has been the flow of capital from the older to the newer portions of the world. Investors seek to place their funds where the income return will be highest. The pecuniary unit makes possible a fairly accurate directing of capital to the sections of the world where it will be most productive. Within any given country the flow of capital from one region to another is of course guided in a similar manner.

Pecuniary accounting facilitates the satisfaction of human wants. The directing of labor and capital into the various lines of industry, guided, as we have seen, by the pecuniary unit of calculation, has likewise important social results. The reason why any given line of industry becomes more profitable than do others is that the demands for the products of such industry are not so adequately met by existing production as is the case in other lines. The pecuniary unit of calculation, which hastens the diversion of labor and capital into lines where the demand is greatest, thereby serves to satisfy human wants more quickly and more adequately than would otherwise be possible.

Similarly, if any given line of industry is waning, owing to a decrease in the power of its product to satisfy human wants, the losses expressed in dollars and cents on a profit and loss statement force labor and capital out of that line of industry much more quickly than would otherwise be the case. Hence misdirected labor and capital remain misdirected for a shorter time, with the result that the losses incident to such industrial maladjustment are minimized.

Again, in the internal organization of any business, pecuniary calculations cause improvements in machinery, labor organization, and administrative methods to be adopted more quickly than would be the case in the absence of an accurate index of profits. There is a continual process of elimination, by means of which antiquated industrial organization is rapidly supplanted, the changes being super-induced by a fear of pecuniary loss, on the one hand, and by the incentive to pecuniary profit, on the other. Every such improvement means elimination of waste in production and hence a larger output with a given expenditure of human energy.

V. EFFECTS ON SOCIAL STANDARDS

Like most important things the pecuniary system based on money is not without its disadvantages. Since it constitutes a general fund of purchasing power—a veritable key to things desired—money is by many people regarded as an end in itself, the *summum bonum* of human endeavor; while by others it is deemed at least a very superior form of wealth, a plentiful or scanty supply of which renders a nation rich or poor, powerful or impotent. The confusion of money with welfare has, moreover, been responsible for many ill-judged movements for social reform.

More articles and books have been written and more discussions held on money than on any other subject in the entire realm of political economy. At the same time monetary controversies have developed more extreme enthusiasm and greater bitterness of denunciation than those in any other field. In the somewhat exaggerated phraseology of William Jennings Bryan, "Brother has been arrayed against brother, father against son. Warmest ties of love, acquaintance and association have been disregarded; old leaders have been cast aside . . . and new leaders have sprung up to give direction to the cause of truth."

The extraordinary importance that has been attached to money throughout the ages may be appreciated by reference to the following classical quotations. They also suggest the influence of the pecuniary calculus upon ethical standards:

Horace: Make money, money, man;
Well, if so be,—if not, which way you can.

Timocles: Money's the life and soul of mortal man. Who has it not, nor has acquited it,
Is but a dead man, walking 'mongst the quick.

Milton:	Money brings honour, friends, conquest, and realms.
Pope:	There London's voice, 'Get money, money still, And then let virtue follow if she will.'
Tennyson:	But the jingling of the guinea helps the hurt that honour feels.
Paul of Tarsus:	For the love of money is the root of all evil.

The perversion of social ideals that has attended the development of a pecuniary system is well expressed by Herbert J. Davenport in the following language:[3]

All economic comparisons are made in money terms, not in terms of subsistence, or of beauty, or of artistic merit, or of moral deserving. This same standard tends to become also the test and measure of human achievement. Men engage in business, not solely to earn a livelihood, but to win a fortune in a pecuniary sense. To win by this money test is to certify one's self tangibly and demonstrably as having scored in the most widespread and absorbing of competitions. Is one a great artist—what do his pictures sell for? Or what is the income of this leading advocate? or of that famous singer? How great are the author's royalties? The pecuniary standard tends to be carried over into non-pecuniary fields.

It is almost past belief how far both in degree and in direction money valuations pervade all our thinking. Cheapness is prone to be synonymous with ugliness, richness with beauty, elegance with expensiveness. No one can tell for himself where the really aesthetic begins and the sheer pecuniary ends. In the field of morals, also, the so-called cash-register conscience is an actual thing. And one might go still further and note that almost all great political issues, and almost all absorbing social problems, and almost all international complications, rest upon a pecuniary basis.

The importance that individuals in a pecuniary society necessarily attach to their monetary incomes lies at the basis of the prevailing idea that the quantity of money possessed by a nation is always of paramount importance. If the more money an individual has the wealthier he is, why is it not also true that the greater the quantity of money within a nation the richer is the nation? This belief that nations, like individuals, are well-off in proportion to the amount of their wealth or income as expressed in monetary terms lies at the basis of the so-called mercantilist system of the seventeenth and eighteenth centuries; and it explains in large part the persistent belief that our economic ills are largely attributable to an insufficient quantity of money. It is the philosophy underlying most of the monetary controversies of the past, among which may be mentioned the cheap money experiments of Colonial days and the greenback and free-silver movements of our later history.

[3] *The Economics of Enterprise*, pp. 22–23.

CHAPTER II

THE STANDARD FOR DEFERRED PAYMENTS

It was the purpose of chapter I to show the relation of the pecuniary unit to financial accounting, and thereby to the organization of both business and household economics. It should be noted that the discussion related mainly to the rendering of decisions at a given moment; it was not concerned with transactions where the time element was a factor. The present chapter will consider the function of the monetary unit in connection with credit operations or obligations involving payment at some date in the future.

A standard for deferred payments is of use not merely in the purchase and sale of actual commodities. It is quite as important in connection with the lending of funds. Business is largely conducted in the modern world by means of borrowed capital, represented by credit instruments in the form of stocks, bonds, notes, and bills of exchange. All these financial borrowing operations involve risks of loss incident to economic changes during the life of the loans; and it is accordingly important that the standard for deferred payments be a commodity possessing a high degree of value stability.

I. WHY GOLD CAME TO BE THE STANDARD

In modern times gold has been the standard of value and of deferred payments in nearly all of the leading countries of the world. The *single* gold standard was first adopted by Great Britain in 1816; in the latter part of the nineteenth century other nations followed suit. The reasons why gold rather than silver came to be used as the single standard will be considered in chapter IV. For the moment our interest is in noting the advantages of gold over other commodities, such as shells, beads, fish, iron, wheat, or other products, which have been or might be used as money.

The outstanding quality of gold has been its comparatively stable value. Qualities of durability, homogeneity, divisibility, and cognizability served to make gold coins satisfactory media of exchange; but it was its relative stability of value that commended gold above other commodities as a standard of deferred payments.

Gold, as a commodity, is subject to the forces of supply and demand just as is any other commodity. The supply of gold is influenced directly by the conditions of production at the mines. The discovery of a "bonanza" mine tends to depress the exchange value of gold as a metal, while, conversely, the exhaustion of a rich vein of ore tends to raise its value.

However, until comparatively recent times changes in the cost of producing gold did not have very much effect upon the quantity produced, owing to the speculative character of gold mining. It has been stated that the cost of producing gold has probably, on the whole, exceeded its value, that the losses sustained by the many who have searched in vain have outweighed the gains made by the fortunate few. But in recent years, with the rapid disappearance of placer mining and the development of machine production of gold, the cost of production has come to be very carefully considered. There are marginal mines where it barely pays to take out the gold, just as there are marginal farms and marginal factories. The increased cost of producing gold during the World War, for instance, resulted in the closing of many mines where production had formerly been profitable. On the other hand, during the world depression after 1929 gold production was greatly stimulated.

Gold differs from most other commodities in that the supply at any given time is not merely the output of a previous year's mining operations; it is a stock that has been accumulated through centuries of production. Gold is a highly durable commodity, and as a result the world supply becomes larger each year, even though the annual production may be rapidly decreasing. The greater part of the gold mined in modern times is still in existence, quite as though it were fresh from the mines of the Klondike. The result of this accumulated world supply is to render any yearly change in output relatively ineffective in influencing the value of the whole mass. Obviously, however, a great increase in gold production continued over a period of years may have a substantial effect upon the exchange value of the accumulated mass. The world production of gold since the discovery of America is shown on page 34.

The demand for gold is twofold: (1) for use as a commodity in the manufacturing and industrial arts; and (2) for employment as a medium of exchange (now virtually an obsolete function) and as the basis of monetary systems. The demand for gold as a commodity is, of course, subject to the same general conditions as is the demand for any other commodity. It has utility in the satisfaction of human desires, and this utility is affected by degree of scarcity, change of custom, possibility of substituting other commodities, etc., in the same way that the utility of other commodities is affected. For monetary uses, however, the demand for gold, where free coinage exists, is sometimes said to be unlimited—since all the gold produced may be taken to the mints and converted into dollars or sovereigns.

Gold has been chosen as the standard for deferred payments, not because it is absolutely stable in value but because it has been more nearly stable than have other commodities which might conceivably be used. As a matter of fact, gold leaves much to be desired as a standard for deferred payments, and its abandonment has often been urged. Indeed, in a sense gold has ceased to be a standard of value, for as the result of the world depression of 1929–1933 and attendant financial disturbances other forms of currency have ceased to be convertible into gold. Nevertheless, gold remains the underlying basis of paper money systems, the apparent assumption being that at some time in the future redeemability of other currencies in gold will be reestablished. Discussion of the gold situation in the world today must, however, be postponed; we are for the moment interested only in its historical position as the standard of value.

A distinction is to be made between the value of gold and the price of gold. The latter is the number of dollars that a given quantity of gold, say an ounce, will make when coined at the weight prescribed by law. At present the number of grains of pure gold prescribed for the American dollar unit is 13.72; hence an ounce would be the equivalent of $35. The price of gold can, of course, change only as the law prescribing the weight of the dollar changes.

The *value* of a dollar, on the other hand, represents merely the exchange ratio of the dollar and other commodities. It fluctuates with every change in conditions affecting either gold or other commodities.

These relative values are expressed in terms not of the price of gold but of the price of other commodities as expressed in gold. Thus, if a bushel of wheat exchanges for a dollar, we say that its price is a dollar; while if it requires two bushels to equal a dollar the price is 50 cents a bushel. The value of each particular commodity expressed in dollars gives us the price of that commodity. The average of individual prices is referred to as the general price level.

II. FLUCTUATIONS IN THE PRICE LEVEL

In the case of obligations involving payment at a subsequent date, both parties to the contract assume the risk of price changes. If a lender parts with $1,000 having a purchasing power over other commodities amounting to x, and later receives the principal back when prices are higher, he gets x minus, in terms of buying power. The borrower gains the difference, for with higher prices it is proportionally easier to get possession of the $1,000. If prices fall the situation as between lender and borrower is reversed. That the gold standard has not given us a stable basis for time contracts is apparent from the data with respect to price movements.

Variations in the price level are shown by means of an index number. "An index number of any given article at any given date is the percentage which the price of that article at that date is of the price of the same article at a date or period which has been selected as base or standard." There are numerous index numbers in use; and the base that is employed varies. For example, the index number of the *London Economist* took as its base the average price of the commodities included for the years 1845 to 1850. The official index number in the United States, that published monthly by the United States Bureau of Labor Statistics, has been reconstructed from time to time, and is now based on the average actual prices for the year 1926.

The method of computing index numbers may be illustrated as follows: The average price of each commodity for the base period is considered as 100. Then every month the prices of the various commodities are turned into "relatives" on that scale. Thus if wheat sold in the base year, say 1926, at $1.00 a bushel, and in June 1927, at $1.25 a bushel, the relative price of wheat is then 125. If, on the other hand, the price of any commodity should drop from 50 cents to 40 cents a yard, the relative price would be 80. To ascertain the change that has occurred from month to month in the general level of prices, it is necessary merely to strike an average of these relative prices.

It is obvious that if the index number is to be truly representative of general changes in prices, a large number of commodities must be used. The present index number of the United States Bureau of Labor Statistics is based upon 550 separate commodities classified in eleven groups. The commodities chosen are, moreover, weighted in accordance with their relative importance, the reason assigned for this choice being that "great staples like bituminous coal, yellow pine lumber, beef, and cement exercise much more influence upon the final results than articles like horsehair, hickory, cinnamon, and bone buttons." In order to make the price level reflect the greater importance of such commodities, they are weighted by multiplying the monthly price of each commodity by the quantity marketed in the United States.

The level of prices fluctuates more or less continuously and at times violently. The diagram presented on the next page shows the fluctuations in the United States from 1801 to 1937. The broken line from 1862 to 1878 indicates what the gold price would have been during the

period when paper currency—in which the actual prices were made—
was irredeemable and hence depreciated as compared with gold. It
will be observed that there have been many minor fluctuations and
several longer term trends. The phenomenal effects of war are indicated in the peaks of 1814, 1865, and 1920. Similarly, the effects of
depressions are clearly manifested, especially in the severe and pro-

MOVEMENT OF PRICES, 1801–1937[a]

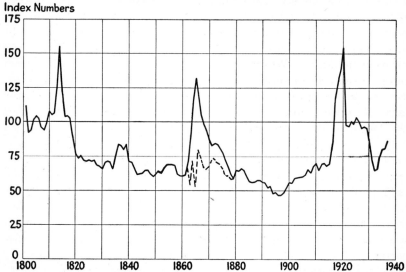

[a] Heavy black line shows index of wholesale prices. Dotted line shows gold prices during period
of greenback depreciation, 1862–1878. The data are taken from revised index numbers of the United
States Bureau of Labor Statistics. 1926 = 100.

tracted recessions of the seventies, nineties and nineteen thirties. The
sharpest decline on record was that of 1920–1921.

III. CONSEQUENCES OF PRICE CHANGES

Price fluctuations, if extensive or long continued, are always dis-
ruptive in their effects upon the general economic organization. Rapid
price changes render more difficult the pecuniary calculations of
business men, thereby greatly increasing the risks of industry and
acting as a serious deterrent to business enterprise. The accumulation
of capital is discouraged, lending or credit operations are deterred,
speculation is induced, and international financial relations are
deranged. The utterly disastrous social consequences of extreme currency inflation will be illustrated in chapter VII by reference to historical examples.

Price changes disrupt the equity between debtors and creditors. For example the general fall in prices following the Civil War period (see chart on page 16) was bitterly opposed by the debtor group; but it was looked upon with composure, not to say with satisfaction, by the creditor classes. The reason for this was that a fall in prices impaired the economic position of debtors and improved the economic position of creditors. It should be understood here that by debtors is meant not merely the ne'er-do-wells, people who are poverty stricken, shiftless, and hopelessly in arrears. The debtor class is composed most largely of individuals and corporations who have borrowed capital for use in business enterprises of various sorts. For instance, the farms of the Middle West were in many cases purchased on borrowed funds. A small accumulation was sufficient to make an initial payment, a mortgage being given for the balance. Out of the income from the farm, the owner paid interest on his mortgage and gradually reduced the principal, thus eventually acquiring complete ownership.

The fall in the prices of farm products after the Civil War made it very difficult to pay mortgages as they fell due, with the result that a large percentage of them were extended again and again. Since a falling price did not increase the number of bushels grown per acre, the farmer found his actual income reduced. Falling prices thus meant hard times—inability to get ahead in the world. The consequence was a great popular resentment against a contraction of the volume of currency, which was deemed responsible for the fall in prices; and for more than a generation the money question overshadowed all other issues in American politics.

When the upward movement of prices began in 1896, the interests of the debtor and creditor classes were reversed. The rise in the general level of prices meant that it became increasingly easy for those who had borrowed funds to meet interest payments and to reduce the principal when the obligations matured. For instance, when the price of wheat was advancing farmers did not need to raise so many bushels in order to meet their obligations. On the other hand, lenders who received this interest and principal found that the dollars received in payment would not go so far as formerly in purchasing commodities. The real return on the money invested was thus diminished; moreover, the shrinkage in the value of the investment itself often produced serious consequences.

By the creditor class we do not mean merely "capitalists" with large investments. The term includes anyone who deposits money in savings banks, takes out insurance, or invests in bonds. All who depend on fixed incomes from investments find their annual purchasing power steadily reduced. A larger amount of insurance is required to afford the necessary protection to one's dependents, and the volume of savings that must be set aside for old age must be increased.

Similar difficulties accompanied the inflation of the World War period and the deflation which followed. Farmers who had bought land at war prices were again especially handicapped. Throughout the twenties the agricultural industry as a whole suffered and vast losses were sustained by financial institutions associated with agricultural enterprise.

The drastic price recession following 1929 not only created further distress for agricultural debtors, but it so seriously embarrassed railroad, public utility, and industrial corporations, and government debtors, as to appear to necessitate either cancellation or wholesale reduction of debts, an arbitrary reduction of interest rates, moratoria on debt payments for a period of years, or an artificial stimulation of new price advances. It was this situation which was largely responsible for the dollar devaluation and other acts by which the first Roosevelt Administration attempted to restore prices to the 1926 level.

Changes in prices also produce variations in real wages and salaries. When prices increase, the salaried man or wage earner can escape a fall in real income only provided his money income is increased in proportion to the price advances. But the truth is that salaries almost never advance in step with an increase of prices. There are numerous reasons for this.

First, there is a great deal of inertia to be overcome. Second, salaried men are seldom organized and they can therefore bring no concerted pressure to bear. Third, there are many cases where the employer cannot raise salaries without serious financial consequences. This is particularly true in the case of institutions whose income is largely derived from fixed investments, themselves subject to the adverse effects of rising prices. Fourth, there is usually the hope, if not the expectation, that prices will shortly recede again; and since salaries once raised are difficult to lower, it is regarded as the part of wisdom to make no premature salary advances.

Wages show more of a tendency to rise with prices than do salaries. However, there has usually been a considerable lag in the adjustment of wage rates, owing to the same forces that operate to prevent an increase in salaries. But where laborers are strongly organized, an early increase of wage rates is usually secured—sometimes even beyond the increase in prices. A factor of great importance in connection with the wage situation in a period of advancing prices is that in the early stages of a price advance there is usually very active business, and hence steady, as opposed to intermittent, employment.

Even though wage rates do not rise so rapidly as do prices, the aggregate annual wage may nevertheless for a time keep pace with, or even rise faster than, the cost of living. There is always an end to this compensating advantage, however, and eventually the laborer inevitably feels keenly the effects of a rapid advance in prices.

During a period of falling prices results opposite to those described above tend to work out. Salaries are usually not reduced as prices fall, and the real income of the salaried man therefore increases. While wages fall, they do not as a rule decline so rapidly as do prices; and the laboring class also would accordingly find its standard of living raised were it not for the fact that a period of falling prices is usually a period of dull times, during which the employer endeavors to minimize his losses by reducing the number of men on the pay-roll. As business recovers, however, unemployment diminishes and organized labor groups are sometimes able to consolidate the gains resulting from their resistance to wage decreases.

The failure of metallic standards to provide a stable standard for deferred payments has led to various proposals for a substitute standard in which time contracts would be settled. Among these the most important is the so-called multiple or tabular standard. With such a standard, gold would still perform the function of a pecuniary unit, but time contracts would be adjusted to the degree that prices changed. Concretely, if during the life of a $1,000 debt the index number of prices showed an advance of 10 per cent, the borrower would be obliged to pay back $1,100. Similarly, if prices declined by 10 per cent, he would repay only $900. Thus the effects of price change would be nullified as far as debtor-creditor relations are concerned. It is of course possible under present laws for contracts to be made in such terms. Proposals to make the method compulsory have never been given serious consideration by legislative bodies.

The causes or forces responsible for changes in the general level of prices have long been the subject of discussion and controversy; and even today there remain wide differences of opinion on the subject. Moreover, numerous plans for controlling price movements have been advanced; and some of them have been unsuccessfully tried. The issues involved in this general problem cannot, however, be advantageously discussed at this place for two reasons; first because the money supply includes, besides gold, other forms of currency and credit instruments; and second, because price changes are intimately related to fluctuations in general business conditions. Hence consideration of this problem must be postponed to the final chapter.

CHAPTER III

OTHER FUNCTIONS AND SERVICES OF MONEY

"Money is a medium of exchange." This is the definition of money usually found in the dictionaries; it is the essence of the layman's thought on the subject; and it is the function upon which most emphasis has been placed by writers on monetary theory. Treatises on money, indeed, commonly begin with a statement of the inconvenience of barter, or direct exchange of one commodity for another, and then proceed to show the advantages of money as a medium for effecting exchanges.

I. MONEY AS A MEDIUM OF EXCHANGE

The inconvenience of making exchanges by means of barter is obviously very great. It is not only necessary for an individual who wishes to trade a commodity to find someone who has the very article which he desires; he must also find someone who wishes the particular commodity that is offered in exchange. And even when two individuals, each having a commodity desired by the other, are brought together, it is still often impossible to effect an exchange, because the commodities may be of substantially different value.

Money as a medium of exchange eliminates the inherent difficulties of barter. The seller disposes of his goods for money, and with the money purchases, at such times and in such quantities as he desires, the goods which he needs. This function of money as a medium of exchange really divides barter into three parts as follows:

(1) Selling goods for money, (2) keeping the money until other goods are needed, and (3) using the money to buy other goods. It is further evident that in these three phases, looked at from the standpoint of the man who starts out with goods to sell, money plays three different parts. In the first, its role is that of a thing which can *be obtained* with any goods whatsoever. In the second, its business is to *keep*—store—this power to obtain other goods. In the third, its part is that of a thing which can *obtain* any goods whatsoever.[1]

Exchange makes possible large-scale production. The service of money as a medium of exchange is not merely that it saves time in effecting exchanges. Of infinitely greater significance is the fact that

[1] F. M. Taylor, *Some Chapters on Money*, pp. 14, 16.

it makes possible a specialized exchange society, and hence large-scale production. Without a transfer medium business transactions would necessarily be confined to local areas, and production would have to be conducted on a small-scale basis. In fact, without a medium of exchange the modern system of specialized production and exchange, by means of which industrial establishments are enabled to produce in tremendous quantities at a low cost per unit, and to sell their products throughout the civilized world, would be out of the question.

II. MONEY AS A STORE OF VALUE

Before the development of modern banking and credit institutions, wealth was usually stored up for future use by hoarding precious metals. Gold and silver, comprising large value in small bulk, and being of universal acceptability in exchange for commodities, constituted the best available means for accumulating wealth; hence the hidden treasures of history and fable. Under modern conditions, money is not ordinarily stored in the sense of being hoarded. While it may be held for a brief interval it is, as a rule, quickly invested through the machinery provided by credit institutions.

However, in periods of economic and political instability, hoarding of the precious metals may assume large proportions. In time of war it has usually been found necessary to suspend the convertibility of paper money into specie. Similarly it has often been deemed advisable in periods of economic disturbance to suspend specie payments. During the world depression of 1929–1933 hoarding became an almost universal phenomenon and assumed such proportions that nearly everywhere governments found it necessary to place an embargo upon gold payments in both domestic and international transactions. (For further discussion see pages 44–45 and 75–80.)

III. MONEY IN RELATION TO PRODUCTION

When money is spoken of as a medium of exchange, one usually has in mind the exchange of consumers' goods. For convenience of exposition, economic treatises have commonly been divided into four parts, devoted respectively to consumption, production, exchange, and distribution. Money is treated under exchange, and its chief function is usually regarded as that of effecting the exchange of goods that have already been produced and are in the market awaiting transfer to the hands of those who are to consume them.

But if one is to appreciate fully the significance of money under a capitalistic industrial régime it is necessary to consider the part that it plays in the productive as well as in the exchange process. Exchange of consumers' goods is not to be excluded; but the rôle of money in getting goods ready to be exchanged as completed products must be included.

Modern business is almost universally conducted through the use of money. With money the manufacturer purchases the materials needed for the construction of his plant; with money he employs an administrative staff to manage his business; and with money he purchases the raw materials and supplies and employs the labor force required to operate the business. In a similar way producers of raw materials, transportation agencies, and wholesalers and retailers employ money in connection with every phase of their business operations; under modern conditions even the farmer makes an extensive use of money.

In short, practically the entire productive process is nowadays organized and operated through the use of money. All the capital used in modern business is expressed in terms of money; is, in a sense, made possible by money. Indeed, the business man usually thinks of capital as money, or funds, available for business purposes. The business man's attitude is readily explained by the fact that stock or bond subscriptions are received in the form of liquid funds, as are also short-term loans procured from banking institutions. With this liquid capital, or money, the business man constructs plant and equipment and purchases the materials and supplies required in producing, manufacturing, or marketing goods. Upon reflection he will, of course, realize that money is only a handmaiden of production—that the things with which wealth is really created are concrete capital instruments in the form of plant and equipment. Money is nevertheless a *prerequisite*; it is indispensable to the process of wealth production.

Because of the great importance that has always been attached to money as *capital*, the economist has been wise in laying emphasis upon the fact that real capital consists of tangible properties. However, this emphasis has in turn tended to minimize the significant part that money plays in a capitalistic society. Productive instruments cannot be made effective in the service of society unless liquid capital is available with which to assemble raw materials and labor power in producing organizations.

Government enterprise, also, is made possible by the use of liquid funds. The functions performed by government are carried out through the use of money derived from taxes, from borrowing operations, or from the manufacture of currency. Historically the needs of government for money have for the most part grown out of the exigencies of war. Its significance in this connection may be illustrated by the statement of Napoleon that three things are necessary if a war is to be

THE FLOW OF MONEY INCOME

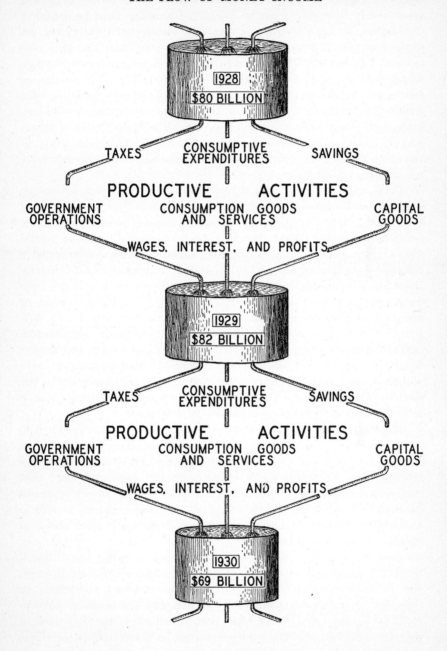

waged successfully: money, more money, and still more money. To be sure, money here as elsewhere is but a means to an end; but it is indispensable for assembling, under the control of government, the men, materials, and munitions required for the conduct of war.

The activities of government in times of peace are constantly expanding. Our government, for instance, provides funds for education, charitable organizations, public health, highways and parks, national defense, and a large amount of scientific and social investigation in connection with such departments as agriculture, interior, labor, etc. Moreover, governments are now expected to cushion the shock of great economic dislocations in the field of private enterprise. In the recent world depression every government was required to provide relief for both distressed individuals and distressed businesses; and in most cases they sought to promote recovery through an expansion of public enterprise. Since taxation revenues shrink in time of depression such government outlays require extensive credit operations on the part of government. As we shall note later, there are various credit devices which governments may use; and, as we shall also see, the abuse of government credit may undermine the entire monetary and credit system.[2]

IV. MONEY INCOME AND ECONOMIC ORGANIZATION

We have seen in chapter I that the distribution of productive energy is guided by the relative profits to be obtained in different lines of industry. It is now to be noted that money expenditures in the markets provide the effective demands which call forth the production of the various types of commodities and services.

Money outlays not only serve to allocate productive energy among the different industries engaged in the production of consumers' goods; they also govern the apportionment between consumer goods and capital goods. The creation of additional capital goods usually requires the borrowing of liquid capital in the form of monetary instruments. Hence the saving of a portion of the annual money income is necessary if funds are to be available in the hands of investment banking institutions for the uses of capitalists who are seeking to develop new enterprises.

Moreover, families and individuals desiring to accumulate for the future must set aside a portion of their money incomes for investment through the facilities provided by the financial markets. To become productive these money savings have to be utilized by business managers in the construction of new plant and equipment. The

[2] See chap. VII.

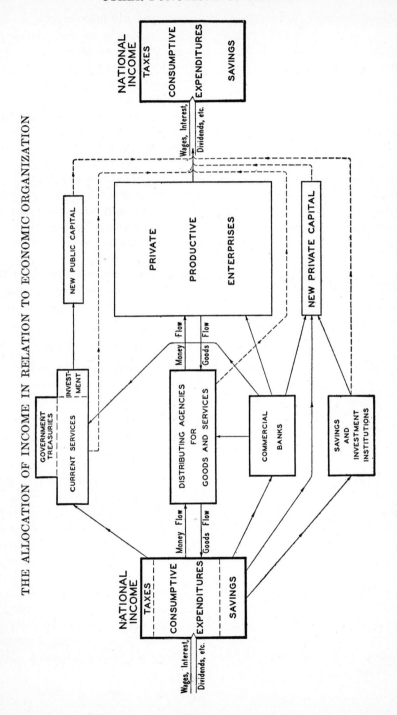

THE ALLOCATION OF INCOME IN RELATION TO ECONOMIC ORGANIZATION

allocation of money income as between consumption expenditures and savings thus directly affects the allocation of our productive facilities as between the creation of consumers' goods and capital goods. The problem of economic adjustment here involved is one of the most difficult and important in the entire field of economic organization.[3]

While we cannot here enter into further discussion of the flow of money in relation to economic activities in the modern world, its ramifying importance may be illustrated by means of diagrams. The diagram on page 23 indicates the flow of money income from year to year in its general relation to economic organization. In order to indicate the magnitude of the income flow for a given time period, it is necessary to impound this income, for the moment, in a series of reservoirs, each of which represents the entire income for a year's time. It goes without saying, however, that what we have is a continuous flow rather than a periodical impounding and release of income. As individuals receive wages, salaries, or other income from week to week or month to month they make payments for current requirements.

The money income shown in the top reservoir for the year 1928 was about 80 billion dollars. It represented the amount of wages, salaries, interest, profits, etc., received by the American people as a whole during the course of that year. This monetary income was disbursed in three directions, or for three major purposes. Some of it was expended for consumption goods and services, some of it was saved and rendered available for additional capital goods, and some was diverted through taxation to government operations.

It is these outgoing streams of income that make the wheels of business and of government revolve. As the money flows through these various channels it calls forth new productive activities, which in turn generate money income which passes again into the hands of the people at successive intervals of time. It will be noted, however, that owing to fluctuations in business activity the amount of aggregate income may vary materially from year to year. The dollar figures given on the three reservoirs indicate the changes in the magnitude of national income in the three years included.

The diagram on page 25 indicates in more concrete terms the allocation of income for major purposes and the way in which this is related to economic organization. The rectangle at the left side of the chart represents the reservoir of national money income. Much the largest portion of this money income is disbursed at retail stores, hotels and restaurants, automobile filling stations, railway and steamship agencies, educational institutions, theatres and other places of recre-

[3] See *The Formation of Capital*, by the author.

ation or pleasure. In the case of commodities, as distinguished from services, intermediary institutions are commonly found between the ultimate consumer and the producer. That is to say, in addition to the retail agencies, wholesalers or commission houses may act as middlemen between the manufacturer and the consumer. In either case the purchasing power expended through retail and service agencies constitutes the demand for consumers' goods, which calls forth a flow of goods and services from productive enterprise (indicated in the large rectangular area to the right) back through distributive channels to consumers.

A second portion of the money income is saved. Some of it flows from individuals directly to new business enterprises, but a much larger portion is handled by intermediary investment institutions, including savings banks, insurance companies, and investment banking institutions engaged in the marketing of securities. The savings assembled are transmitted to borrowers who desire to use funds for the expansion of productive capacity—indicated at the right of the diagram under the caption "New Private Capital."

A third portion is appropriated in the form of taxes with which to finance the operations of federal, state, and local governments. The larger part of it is disbursed for current operations though a substantial amount is used in the financing of new public capital of various types.

It will be observed that dotted lines have been drawn from the various sectors of economic activity indicating the onward flow of money income which is being generated. This process has already been indicated in the diagram on page 23.

In addition to the flow of money income directly from the hands of individuals, liquid capital may be derived from the commercial banking system through a process of credit expansion. Such credit is at times rendered available to governments as well as to private enterprise. Discussion of the phenomenon of bank credit must be reserved for elucidation in connection with chapters dealing with commercial banking.

CHAPTER IV

THE EVOLUTION OF THE MONETARY SYSTEM

In order that money might perform effectively its various functions, it was necessary to develop a system of regulations that would give precision to business transactions involving the use of money. In this chapter we shall consider the various problems that have arisen in connection with the regulation of the different forms of currency, and describe the evolution of the monetary system, culminating in the adoption of the gold standard by most of the nations of the world.

I. COINAGE PROBLEMS

The first problem that arose in connection with the use of money as a medium of exchange was that of coinage. If the pieces of metal used as money were not of uniform certified weight, it is evident that traders would be put to no end of inconvenience in weighing the currency tendered in the settlement of obligations. Because of the high value of gold and other precious metals a very slight variation in weight would involve considerable loss.

Bullion containing gold and silver varies widely in the amount of impurities contained therein; and it is accordingly necessary that it be assayed before it is coined. It is also easy to melt gold and silver coins and debase them by adding copper or other metal. In order to permit exchanges to be made with certainty, it is, therefore, imperative that the fineness as well as the weight of coins be attested.

Many centuries elapsed after the various forms of metal began to be struck into coins before a satisfactory coinage technique was developed. Indeed it was not until the eighteenth century that mechanical processes were sufficiently perfected to give us coins which were uniform either in weight and fineness or in appearance. Moreover, in earlier times there were numerous private mints issuing coins of varying weight and fineness. The economic consequences of the prevailing currency confusion have been vividly portrayed by Macaulay:[1]

The old, crude, hammered coins of Great Britain were of varying weight, slightly irregular shape, and with unmilled edges. As a result they were easily

[1] This and the following quotation are taken from *History of England*, II, pp. 544–545.

clipped and mutilated. . . . In the autumn of 1695 it could hardly be said that the country possessed, for practical purposes, any measure of value. It was a mere chance whether what was called a shilling was really tenpence, sixpence, or a groat. The results of some experiments that were tried at that time deserve to be mentioned. The officers of the exchequer weighed £57,200 of hammered money which had recently been paid in. The weight ought to have been 220,000 ounces. It proved to be under 114,000 ounces. Three eminent London goldsmiths were invited to send £100 each in current silver to be tried by the balance. The £300 ought to have weighed almost 1,200 ounces. The actual weight proved to be 624 ounces. The same test was applied in various parts of the kingdom with practically everywhere similar results.

It may well be doubted whether all the misery which had been inflicted on the English nation in a quarter of a century by bad kings, bad ministers, bad Parliaments, and bad judges was equal to the misery caused by bad crowns and bad shillings. Those events which furnish the best themes for pathetic or indignant eloquence are not always those which most affect the happiness of the great body of the people. The misgovernment of Charles and James, gross as it had been, had not prevented the common business of life from going steadily and prosperously on. While the honor and independence of the state were sold to a foreign power, while chartered rights were invaded, while fundamental laws were violated, hundreds of thousands of quiet, honest, and industrious families labored and traded, ate their meals, and lay down to rest, in comfort and security. But when the great instrument of exchange became thoroughly deranged, all trade, all industry, were smitten as with a palsy. The evil was felt daily and hourly in almost every place and by almost every class, in the dairy and on the threshing-floor, by the anvil and by the loom, on the billows of the ocean and in the depths of the mine. Nothing could be purchased without a dispute. Over every counter there . . . was wrangling from morning to night. The workman and his employer had a quarrel as regularly as the Saturday came around. On a fair day or a market day the clamors, the reproaches, the curses, were incessant; and it was well if no booth was overturned and no head broken. No merchant could contract to deliver goods without making some stipulation about the quality of the coin in which he was to be paid. Even men of business were often bewildered by the confusion into which all pecuniary transactions were thrown. The simple and the careless were pillaged without mercy by extortioners whose demands grew even more rapidly than the money shrank. The price of the necessaries of life, of shoes, of ale, of oatmeal, rose fast. The laborer found that the bit of metal which, when he received it, was called a shilling, would hardly, when he wanted to purchase a pot of beer or a loaf of bread, go as far as a sixpence.

Although the penalties against clipping and mutilating the currency were most severe, it was almost impossible to check the practice:

The severity of the punishment (clipping carried the penalty of death) gave encouragement to the crime. For the practice of clipping did not excite in the common mind a detestation resembling that with which men regard murder, arson, robbery, nay, even theft. The injury done by the whole body of clippers to society as a whole was indeed immense; but each particular act of clipping was a trifle. To pass a half-crown after paring a pennyworth of silver from it seemed a minute and almost imperceptible fault. Even while the nation was crying out most loudly under the distress which the state of the currency had produced, every individual who was capitally punished for contributing to bring the currency into that state had the general sympathy on his side. Constables were unwilling to arrest the offenders. Justices were unwilling to commit. Witnesses were unwilling to tell the whole truth. Juries were unwilling to pronounce the word guilty. There was a general conspiracy to prevent the law from taking its course . . . The offenders who were convicted looked on themselves as murdered men, and were firm in the belief that their sin, if sin it were, was as venial as that of a schoolboy who goes nutting in the wood of a neighbor.

An effective coinage system, uniform in character, was obviously indispensable if trade were to be efficiently and honestly conducted. Uniformity could be obtained only by means of monopoly, and naturally this meant *government* monopoly. Thanks to the perfecting of coinage methods, counterfeiting, sweating, or otherwise tampering with metallic currency no longer presents serious problems.

The several objects to be attained by a good system of coinage have been stated as follows: (1) to prevent counterfeiting; (2) to prevent the fraudulent removal of metal from the coin; (3) to reduce the loss by legitimate wear and tear; (4) to make the coin an artistic and historical monument of the state issuing it and the people using it.

The rules and regulations governing the coinage process at the present time in the United States illustrate the nature of the control of coinage by governments. To facilitate the conversion of bullion into coin, mints are maintained in Philadelphia, Denver, and San Francisco. Assay offices, which purchase bullion for the Government and serve the public by making assays of ores and bullion, are located at Seattle and New Orleans. The Government makes no charge for the service of coining, but there are certain mint charges to cover costs. These include the charges for assaying or testing the fineness of the metal, melting the bullion, removing the impurities and base metal, and adding the copper alloy. These charges of course vary somewhat with the amount and nature of the base metals contained in the bullion.

To make sure that new coins are of standard weight, the superintendent of each mint tests separately five coins out of every thousand. Four times a year the coins which have been tested are forwarded to the mint at Philadelphia where further tests of weight are made by a special Assay Commission. These tests are known as the "trial of the pyx" because the coins after the first test are placed in a pyx until they are sent to Philadelphia.

Gold coins were withdrawn from circulation in 1934[2] and additional silver dollars are not now required for circulation purposes. Hence the coinage is now confined to subsidiary silver, nickel, and copper coins. Only the silver coins are tested by the Assay Commission. The tolerance, or allowable error, is one and one-half grains per coin. Under the law a director of a mint which is found to have issued underweight coins must be relieved of his office. Only once during the past twenty-five years have any coins been found to be under the limits of tolerance.

II. GRESHAM'S LAW AND BIMETALLISM

A defective coinage system not only encouraged tampering with the currency, but it also resulted in the better coins' being replaced in circulation by the inferior coins. This tendency, which had long been observed, was finally stated by Sir Thomas Gresham, a royal agent of Queen Elizabeth, in the form of a monetary law, in substantially the following terms:

Whenever legal tender coins of the same face value, but of different weights or degrees of fineness, are in concurrent circulation the light-weight or base coins tend to drive the full-weight pure coins out of circulation.

The reason why the light-weight or base coins will drive the full-weight and pure coins out of circulation—wholly or in part—is not difficult to see. In making foreign payments money is accepted only by weight; hence the full-weight and pure coins are sent out of the country in payment of foreign balances, while the base or light-weight coins are retained for domestic circulation. Full-weight and pure coins may also be melted down and used as bullion. While the general public does not discriminate between coins unless there is a considerable variation in value, money changers, bullion dealers, and bankers are quick to derive a profit from such variations. History is replete with instances where light-weight and base coins have driven "good coins" entirely out of circulation.

After the technique of coinage had been perfected, Gresham's law appeared in a new guise, namely in connection with the bimetallic system. *Bimetallism*, under which both gold and silver are employed, not only as media of exchange but also as standard money, appears to have been adopted by all the leading European countries at the beginning of the modern era, without discussion—as a mere matter of course. Since both gold and silver were adapted to exchange purposes and since it was everywhere assumed that a large volume of currency was an

[2] For explanation, see pp. 45–49.

unmitigated blessing, both metals appear to have been by common consent adopted as the standard of value. It was not until late in the eighteenth century that any agitation for the elimination of bimetallism developed, and, save in England, it was not until the latter half of the nineteenth century that the double standard was abolished.

The operation of Gresham's law under bimetallism must be stated in a slightly different form from that given above, as follows:

When two metals of the same nominal value, but of different bullion value, are freely coinable at the mints and are of unrestricted legal tender power, the metal that is overvalued at the mint tends to drive the other from circulation.

The difficulty in this connection may best be illustrated by reference to some actual cases from our own bimetallic history. Our first coinage law, passed in 1792, fixed the coinage ratio of silver to gold at 15 of the former to 1 of the latter. At the time, the relative value of gold and silver bullion in the commercial markets was about 15.3 to 1. That is to say, it took 15.3 ounces of silver bullion to equal in value 1 ounce of gold; but in the form of coins it took only 15 ounces of silver to equal an ounce of gold. Accordingly, silver had a greater value at the mint than it had in the form of bullion. Since specie must always be used in making international payments, gold rather than silver was always sent whenever a foreign obligation had to be settled. Gold was quite as good as silver for this purpose; but, on the other hand, it did not pay to take gold to the United States mint to be coined, because it had a greater exchange power as bullion than it had as coin. Similarly, it did not pay to ship silver out of the country in settlement of foreign obligations, because silver brought a higher return as compared with gold when it was taken to the mint and converted into coins. Accordingly, gold was driven out of circulation and silver became the actual standard of value.

In 1834 Congress changed the coinage ratio from 15 to 1 to 16 to 1. At that time the market ratio of silver to gold was about 15.7 to 1. With the new ratio it required 16 ounces of silver to equal 1 ounce of gold in the form of coins, but only 15.7 ounces of silver to equal an ounce of gold in the form of bullion. Thus gold became relatively overvalued at the mint, and accordingly gold was sent to the mint for coinage, whence it shortly reappeared in the channels of circulation. Indeed, even before the act was finally passed, a shipment of gold was en route from England to the United States to take advantage of its overvaluation at the United States mint.

The reason why the controversy over bimetallism did not arise at a much earlier period was that until the coinage process had been perfected, the cause for a disappearance of metal from circulation seemed to lie simply in the disparity between light-weight or debased coins, and full-weight, pure coins. But after one problem was solved a new one appeared in its place: One or the other of the two *standard* metals was always disappearing.

Those who contended that the bimetallic standard could be made to work successfully, looked to a so-called "compensatory action" to prevent a variation of the market from the mint ratio. In brief, the argument runs as follows:

With the mint ratio at 16 to 1, if silver should be worth in the market, say, 16.1 to 1, silver would be overvalued at the mint and gold undervalued. Silver would accordingly be in increased demand at the mint and gold in decreased demand, with the result that the value of silver would be raised and the value of gold lowered, thus operating to restore the ratio to 16 to 1. And if perchance the market ratio should become 15.9 to 1, then gold would be overvalued at the mint and silver undervalued, whereupon an increased demand for gold and a decreased demand for silver would bring the ratio back to 16 to 1. Since this compensatory action would work immediately and automatically as soon as any variation between market and mint ratio appeared, the readjustment would be practically instantaneous, thus effectively preventing the operation of Gresham's law.

Scientific writers on the subject recognized that without an international bimetallic standard the system would break down. If France, for instance, had a ratio of 15 to 1, whereas the United States had a ratio of 16 to 1, it would pay the bullion dealers to ship silver from the United States to France, where a higher coinage value existed.

During the protracted struggle over bimetallism, a number of international conferences were held with a view to securing the adoption of an international bimetallic standard. These conferences, however, came to nothing. National jealousy was manifested in connection with the unit to be adopted—whether mark, franc, pound, or dollar should be chosen. In all these conferences, moreover, England was apathetic because she had for a great many years possessed a single gold standard and was on the whole well satisfied with the results attained under it; indeed, there was good reason for believing that England's commercial and financial supremacy was in no small degree due to the exceptional stability of her monetary system.

It remains to inquire whether, with international bimetallism, the compensatory action would, as many economists have contended, under all circumstances insure a practical equalization of mint and market ratios. The table on page 34 indicates that the production of these metals has fluctuated widely with changes in mining conditions.

PRODUCTION OF GOLD AND SILVER IN THE WORLD SINCE THE DISCOVERY OF AMERICA[a]

Period	Gold Annual Average for Period		Silver Annual Average for Period	
	Fine Ounces	Coinage Value	Fine Ounces	Coinage Value
1493–1520.............	186,470	$ 3,855,000	1,511,050	$ 2,085,249
1521–1544.............	230,194	4,759,000	2,899,930	4,001,903
1545–1560.............	273,596	5,656,000	10,017,940	13,824,757
1561–1580.............	219,906	4,546,000	9,628,925	13,287,916
1581–1600.............	237,267	4,905,000	13,467,635	18,585,336
1601–1620.............	273,918	5,662,000	13,596,235	18,762,804
1621–1640.............	266,845	5,516,000	12,654,240	17,462,851
1641–1660.............	281,955	5,828,000	11,776,545	16,251,632
1661–1680.............	297,709	6,154,000	10,834,550	14,951,679
1681–1700.............	346,095	7,154,000	10,992,085	15,169,077
1701–1720.............	412,163	8,520,000	11,432,540	15,533,392
1721–1740.............	613,422	12,681,000	13,863,080	18,988,261
1741–1760.............	791,211	16,356,000	17,140,612	24,032,852
1761–1780.............	665,066	13,761,000	20,985,591	29,465,868
1781–1800.............	571,948	11,823,000	28,261,779	38,712,985
1801–1810.............	571,563	11,815,000	28,746,922	38,070,986
1811–1820.............	367,957	7,606,000	17,385,755	23,204,768
1821–1830.............	457,044	9,448,000	14,807,004	19,373,780
1831–1840.............	652,291	13,484,000	19,175,867	25,160,656
1841–1850.............	1,760,502	36,393,000	25,090,342	32,755,444
1851–1855.............	6,410,324	132,513,000	28,488,597	38,191,813
1856–1860.............	6,486,262	134,083,000	29,095,428	39,296,285
1861–1865.............	5,949,582	122,989,000	35,401,972	47,488,205
1866–1870.............	6,270,086	129,614,000	43,051,583	57,224,164
1871–1875.............	5,591,014	115,577,000	63,317,014	81,887,894
1876–1880.............	5,543,110	114,586,000	78,775,602	91,198,514
1881–1885.............	4,794,755	99,116,000	92,003,944	102,161,180
1886–1890.............	5,461,282	112,895,000	108,911,431	106,624,291
1891–1895.............	7,882,565	162,947,000	157,581,331	123,811,652
1896–1900.............	12,446,939	257,301,100	165,693,304	102,448,170
1901–1905.............	15,606,730	322,619,800	167,995,408	95,942,178
1906–1910.............	20,971,575	433,520,960	197,251,516	114,496,790
1911–1915.............	22,411,608	463,290,898	202,474,938	114,901,606
1916–1920.............	18,890,644	390,505,582	184,646,538	171,200,469
1921–1925.............	17,326,512	357,771,548	222,361,844	157,873,198
1926.................	19,117,568	395,198,984	253,795,166	159,568,635
1927.................	19,058,736	393,979,954	253,981,085	144,947,005
1928.................	18,885,849	390,386,574	257,925,154	151,213,780
1929.................	19,207,452	397,153,303	260,970,029	139,960,836
1930.................	20,903,736	432,118,638	248,708,426	96,309,849
1931.................	22,284,290	460,650,527	195,919,987	56,842,265
1932.................	24,098,676	498,163,970	164,892,802	46,506,363
1933.................	25,400,295	525,070,547	169,159,054	59,200,666
1934.................	27,372,374	958,033,090[b]	190,398,156	91,929,942[b]
1935.................	29,999,245	1,049,973,580	220,704,231	142,535,205
1936.................	32,960,158	1,153,605,530	251,443,689	114,152,920

[a] From *Annual Report of Director of the Mint.*
[b] Figures for 1934 and thereafter are on the basis of $35 an ounce.

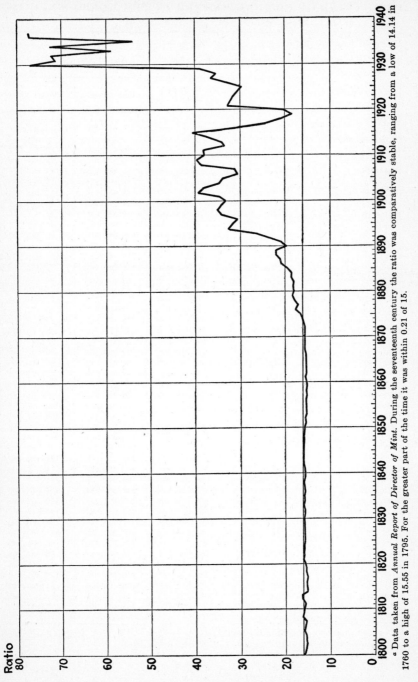

COMMERCIAL RATIO OF GOLD AND SILVER, 1800–1937[a]

[a] Data taken from *Annual Report of Director of Mint*. During the seventeenth century the ratio was comparatively stable, ranging from a low of 14.14 in 1760 to a high of 15.55 in 1795. For the greater part of the time it was within 0.21 of 15.

In the years following 1849, for example, there was a tremendous increase in the supply of gold because of the discovery of the rich gold fields of California and Australia. The effect upon the commercial ratio of the two metals is indicated in the chart on page 35.

If there were but minor variations in the supply of the two metals, it is possible that the compensatory action would operate to maintain the commercial ratio of gold and silver at a parity with the mint ratio. It is hardly probable, however, that the system would work under all circumstances. If the gold mines should be completely exhausted and if at the same time the output of silver should increase at a rate hitherto undreamed of, it is doubtful, to say the least, if the compensatory action could prevent a fall in the relative value of silver.

III. THE ADOPTION OF THE GOLD STANDARD

Notwithstanding the difficulties inherent in the bimetallic system, more than a century was required to secure the adoption of a single standard by the leading commercial nations. Such a narrowing of the monetary base was opposed by various groups: by the silver industry for obvious reasons; by the debtor class who feared that it would result in a fall in commodity prices inimical to their interests; and by others who confused money with wealth and accordingly believed that a reduction in the quantity of the circulating medium would mean a net reduction in the nation's wealth.

England was the first country to abandon bimetallism, the single gold standard having been adopted in the year 1816. Portugal was next in order, abolishing the free coinage of silver in 1854. Three years later, the states composing the German Zollverein and the empire of Austria entered into a monetary treaty and adopted the single silver standard. Shortly after the establishment of the empire in 1871, Germany, however, shifted to the single gold standard.

The states composing the Latin Monetary Union (France, Belgium, Switzerland, and Italy), which had been formed in 1865 in an endeavor to secure a uniform international double standard, one by one virtually[3] went over to the single gold standard in the decade of the seventies.

In 1873 the Scandinavian Monetary Union was formed by Norway, Sweden, and Denmark, and a single gold standard was adopted. In 1874 silver was entirely demonetized. Holland limited the coinage of silver in 1873 and two years later adopted a single gold standard. Spain began the restriction of silver money in 1876, and completed the process in 1878. In 1876 Russia suspended the coinage of silver, except

---

[3] One says *virtually* because silver was usually retained as a standard coin; it was thus a "limping" standard that was adopted.

as required for trade with China. In 1899 Russia adopted the single gold standard. Finland adopted the single gold standard in 1877, and in 1878 Austria-Hungary abolished the free coinage of silver. In 1893, after a protracted controversy, the mints of India were closed to the free coinage of silver. And in 1898 Japan definitely adopted the single gold standard. Practically all of the small states of the world also adopted either the single gold standard or the gold exchange standard, under which redemption is guaranteed in gold or its equivalent in some foreign country.

In the United States it appears to have been more or less an accident that gold rather than silver became the standard. After the coinage law of 1834, which fixed the mint ratio at 16 to 1, silver was undervalued at the mint and hence it was unprofitable to have it coined. For many years thereafter silver coins were out of circulation. When the coinage system was revised in 1873 the standard silver dollar was omitted from the list of coins that might be struck at the mints; and thus gold became the single legal standard. Had the silver dollar not been undervalued at the mint—owing merely to the legislation which fixed the mint ratio at an even 16 to 1 when the market ratio was only 15.7 to 1—it is altogether improbable that it would have been demonetized. If, on the other hand, rich silver mines, rather than gold mines, had been discovered in 1849, and the commercial ratio had in consequence changed to say, 17 to 1, it would have been unprofitable to coin gold. Under these circumstances a revision of the coinage laws might conceivably have resulted in the demonetization of gold.

As a matter of fact the so-called "crime of 1873" did not at the time attract any public attention, for the simple reason that it was not profitable to take silver to the mints. But with the great increase in the output of silver resulting from the discovery of the Comstock lode, the market ratio of silver to gold passed the 16 to 1 mark; and as soon as it was found that silver would not be purchased by the mints, it was charged that the act of 1873 was a crime. Under the influence of the silver mining interests and of those who desired a cheaper currency, the coinage of silver was partially restored by the Bland-Allison Act of 1878. Another law, known as the Sherman Silver Purchase Act of 1890, still further increased the quantity of silver that might be coined, although it did not go so far as to restore the bimetallic system.

The question of the restoration of bimetallism was the great issue in the presidential campaign of 1896. The Republican party, standing for the single gold standard for the United States until such time as the leading commercial nations of the world should agree to adopt "international" bimetallism, was successful at the polls by a narrow margin.

The Democrats, led by William Jennings Bryan, stood for national bimetallism at the ratio of 16 to 1. Four years later, on March 14, 1900, Congress enacted a law known as the "gold standard law," by which the United States definitely established gold as the pecuniary unit.

Reference to the statistics of gold production after 1896 and to the movement of prices (as depicted on page 16) will serve to reveal the main reason why the bimetallic controversy was not continued. If the cyanide process had not been developed, if the Klondike and South African fields had not been opened, and if prices had continued to fall after 1896 as they had fallen in the previous decade, it is not at all improbable that bimetallism would have been a recurrent issue in American politics. Indeed, it had a brief revival in 1920 when, as a result of a great demand for silver for monetary use in the Orient, the ratio temporarily passed the hallowed 16 to 1 mark. Again it became a public issue in the depression of 1929–1933, which was ascribed by many to a shortage of money. The improvement in the ratio of silver to gold (see chart) led, moreover, to a successful revival of demands for the government purchase of silver.[4]

IV. FORMS OF MONEY IN THE UNITED STATES

The metallic and paper currency of the United States is of varied forms and denominations, reflecting a checkered legislative currency history. It has included gold and silver coins, bullion, and bars, minor coins of other metals, government paper issues, and various forms of bank money. The relative importance of these types of currency has varied greatly at different times in our history.

With the establishment of the gold standard in 1900 all other forms of currency assumed a position of secondary importance. All the other types of money were, however, retained as a part of the circulating medium—though in some cases provision had been made for gradual retirement. The value of silver and minor coins and also of paper currency, including that issued both by the Government and by banking institutions, was maintained at a parity with gold by making them redeemable directly or indirectly in gold. The various forms and relative amounts of currency in the United States at selected periods are shown in the tables on pages 39 and 40.

Gold and gold certificates.—It will be observed from the table that no gold currency is now in circulation. In our early history it was extensively employed as a medium of exchange, particularly in the gold mining areas of the west; but eventually it was replaced

[4] For discussion see pp. 49–51.

STOCK OF MONEY AT THE END OF EACH FISCAL YEAR[a]
(000 omitted)

June 30—	Gold	Silver Bullion	Standard Silver Dollars	Subsidiary Silver	Minor Coin	United States Notes
1913.......	$ 1,870,762	....	$568,273	$175,196	$ 56,951	$346,681
1919.......	3,113,306	....	308,146	242,870	82,909	346,681
1924.......	4,488,391	....	503,755	277,614	102,445	346,681
1925.......	4,360,382	....	522,061	283,472	104,004	346,681
1926.......	4,447,397	....	533,491	288,923	108,891	346,681
1927.......	4,587,298	....	537,944	295,590	113,295	346,681
1928.......	4,109,163	....	539,962	299,010	116,689	346,681
1929.......	4,324,351	....	539,961	304,187	120,640	346,681
1930.......	4,534,866	....	539,960	310,978	126,001	346,681
1931.......	4,955,921	....	539,958	308,619	126,887	346,681
1932.......	3,918,596	....	540,008	304,883	126,493	346,681
1933.......	4,317,554	....	540,007	298,634	126,746	346,681
1934.......	7,856,181	$ 1,560	540,007	295,892	127,711	346,681
1935.......	9,115,643	313,309	545,642	312,416	133,040	346,681
1936.......	10,608,417	708,211	547,080	331,716	139,057	346,681
1937.......	12,318,271	835,196	547,080	358,899	150,954	346,681

June 30—	Federal Reserve Notes	Federal Reserve Bank Notes	National Bank Notes	Total[b]	Percentage Reserve of Federal Reserve Banks[c]	Percentage of Gold to Total Money
1913.......	....	....	$759,158	$ 3,777,021	....	49.53
1919.......	$2,687,557	$187,667	719,277	7,688,413	50.8	40.49
1924.......	2,339,048	10,596	778,012	8,846,542	83.7	50.74
1925.......	1,942,240	7,176	733,366	8,299,382	77.8	52.54
1926.......	1,995,206	5,713	702,669	8,428,971	76.6	52.76
1927.......	2,077,473	4,854	704,146	8,667,282	78.7	52.93
1928.......	2,002,811	4,155	699,621	8,118,091	70.1	50.62
1929.......	2,194,970	3,711	704,294	8,538,796	77.1	50.64
1930.......	1,746,501	3,260	698,317	8,306,564	84.7	54.59
1931.......	2,101,578	2,974	697,004	9,079,624	86.2	54.58
1932.......	3,028,397	2,772	736,674	9,004,505	60.2	43.52
1933.......	3,336,866	141,326	970,601	10,078,417	68.4	42.84
1934.......	3,350,988	160,666	954,695	13,634,381	69.5	57.62
1935.......	3,492,854	84,354	769,096	15,113,035	73.9	60.32
1936.......	4,296,310	53,300	371,722	17,402,493	78.7	60.96
1937.......	4,508,973	38,472	272,164	19,376,690	79.7	63.57

[a] Data taken from *Annual Report of the Secretary of the Treasury.*

[b] The totals involve a duplication to the extent that United States notes, Federal Reserve notes, Federal Reserve bank notes, and national bank notes, all included in full, are in part secured by gold, also included in full. Gold certificates, silver certificates, and Treasury notes of 1890 have been excluded, however, since they are complete duplications of the equal amounts of gold or silver held as security therefor and included in the totals.

[c] Ratio of total reserves to deposits and Federal Reserve note liabilities combined. From Federal Reserve bulletins. These figures are averages for the month of June.

FINANCIAL ORGANIZATION

MONEY IN CIRCULATION AT THE END OF EACH FISCAL YEAR[a]
(000 omitted)

June 30—	Gold Coin	Gold Certificates	Standard Silver Dollars	Silver Certificates	Treasury Notes of 1890	Subsidiary Silver
1913	$608,401	$1,003,998	$72,127	$ 469,129	$2,657	$154,458
1919	474,875	327,552	79,041	163,445	1,745	229,316
1924	393,330	801,381	54,015	364,414	1,423	252,995
1925	402,297	1,004,823	54,289	382,780	1,387	262,009
1926	391,703	1,057,371	51,577	377,741	1,356	270,072
1927	384,957	1,007,075	48,717	375,798	1,327	275,605
1928	377,028	1,019,149	46,222	384,577	1,304	278,175
1929	368,488	934,994	43,684	387,073	1,283	284,226
1930	357,236	994,841	38,629	386,915	1,260	281,231
1931	363,020	996,510	34,326	377,149	1,240	273,147
1932	452,763	715,683	30,115	352,605	1,222	256,220
1933	320,939	265,487	27,995	360,699	1,186	256,865
1934	....	149,740	30,913	401,456	1,189	280,400
1935	....	117,167	32,308	701,474	1,182	295,773
1936	....	100,771	35,029	954,592	1,177	316,476
1937	....	88,116	38,046	1,078,071	1,172	340,827

June 30—	Minor Coin	United States Notes	Federal Reserve Notes	Federal Reserve Bank Notes	National Bank Notes	Total
1913	$ 54,954	$337,215	....	....	$715,754	$3,418,692
1919	81,780	274,119	$2,450,278	$155,014	639,472	4,876,638
1924	96,952	297,790	1,843,106	10,066	733,835	4,849,307
1925	100,307	282,578	1,636,108	6,921	681,709	4,815,208
1926	104,194	294,916	1,679,407	5,453	651,477	4,885,266
1927	108,132	292,205	1,702,843	4,606	650,057	4,851,321
1928	111,061	298,438	1,626,433	4,029	650,212	4,796,626
1929	115,210	262,188	1,692,721	3,616	652,812	4,746,297
1930	117,436	288,389	1,402,066	3,206	650,779	4,521,988
1931	117,393	299,427	1,708,429	2,929	648,363	4,821,933
1932	113,619	289,076	2,780,229	2,746	700,894	5,695,171
1933	112,532	268,809	3,060,793	125,845	919,614	5,720,764
1934	119,142	279,608	3,068,404	141,645	901,872	5,373,470
1935	125,125	285,417	3,222,913	81,470	704,263	5,567,093
1936	134,691	278,190	4,002,216	51,954	366,105	6,241,200
1937	144,107	281,459	4,168,780	37,616	268,862	6,447,056

[a] Data taken from *Annual Report of the Secretary of the Treasury.*

by the more convenient gold certificates, which were redeemable dollar for dollar in gold. In 1933, an "executive order" of the President required the surrender to the Treasury of gold coin, gold bullion, and gold certificates. Accordingly all of the gold supply is now held in the Treasury and nearly all of the gold certificates are held either by the Treasury or by the Federal Reserve banks.[5]

[5] For an explanation of these changes see pp. 45–49.

Silver, silver certificates, and Treasury notes of 1890.—The silver dollar was once widely used as a medium of exchange, but, as the table indicates, the amount now in circulation is less than 40 million dollars. The use of silver certificates as claim checks to silver deposited in the Treasury, was authorized by the Bland-Allison Act of 1878. Silver was not popular as a circulating medium and the purpose of authorizing the issue of certificates was to encourage its circulation in substitute form.

The Treasury notes of 1890 owe their origin to the Sherman Silver Purchase Act of that year. This act, which was repealed in 1893, substantially increased the schedule of government silver purchases. This silver was paid for with the newly issued Treasury notes. The maximum amount outstanding, in 1893, was $153,931,002. The law read that these notes were redeemable in *coin*. In order to prevent their depreciation the Treasury decided that they must be redeemable in either gold or silver at the option of the holder. In due course, with a view to simplification of the currency, they were canceled as they were received by the Treasury and were replaced by silver dollars coined from the bullion originally purchased with the notes. In turn, silver certificates were issued for circulation purposes in place of the silver dollars. The Treasury notes have now almost entirely disappeared from circulation.

The table shows that the Treasury held silver bullion to the amount of $835,196,000. This represents purchases made under silver purchase legislation since 1933. (See pages 50 and 51.)

The subsidiary metallic currency of the United States consists of the silver dollar, half-dollar, quarter, dime, nickel, and one-cent piece. All of these coins now have a face value greater than their value in the form of bullion. Such coins are called *token* coins. The silver dollar is still officially called a *standard* coin, although it has been in a subsidiary position since 1873. It has never been directly redeemable in gold, its parity being maintained by making it acceptable by the Treasury as the equivalent of gold.

Fractional silver coins were originally of proportional weight with the silver dollar; but since 1853 they have contained about 7 per cent less silver. The nickel, or five-cent piece, is a combination of copper and nickel—three-fourths copper and one-fourth nickel. The cent is composed of 95 per cent copper and 5 per cent tin and zinc. Both fractional silver coins and minor coins are struck only as the needs of trade, evidenced by the demand for "change" at the banks, require. The Government purchases the bullion in the market; and the profit—called seigniorage—which arises from coining money with a face value greater than that of the bullion content, goes to the Government.

United States notes, or greenbacks, were issued during the Civil War to meet the expenses of the Government. Since 1900 they have been backed by a cash reserve of $150,000,000, held as a special fund in the Treasury. The amount of these notes outstanding has not changed since 1879, the law providing that any notes redeemed in cash at the Treasury shall be promptly reissued.

Since bank notes, Federal Reserve notes and Federal Reserve bank notes are issued by banking institutions, discussion of the principles and methods of regulation involved will be found in chapter XXIII.

In concluding this discussion, a word is necessary with respect to the principle of legal tender. If business is to be conducted with both dispatch and certainty, and if endless disputes over the kind and quality of the thing which is tendered in payment of debts are to be avoided, there must be some *lawful* means of payment. It has been necessary, therefore, to confer upon money, at least upon certain forms of money, the quality of *legal tender*.

It is to be noted, however, that the tender of money in payment of an obligation may be refused by the person to whom the money is proffered, without an automatic cancellation of the debt. The law holds that the tender must be made continuous. However, the payment of interest on the obligation automatically ceases with the tender of lawful money; and certain legal advantages are also lost to the creditor.

Prior to 1933 the various forms of currency in this country had widely varying provisions with respect to legal tender. Silver dollars might be specified against in the contract; minor coins were legal tender only in certain limited amounts; and there were no legal tender provisions for some forms of paper currency—though they were acceptable means of payment since they were convertible into gold. In 1933 all forms of currency in the United States were made legal tender for all debts, public and private, public charges, taxes, duties, and dues.[6]

V. AN INTERNATIONAL MONETARY SYSTEM

As has already been indicated, most of the leading countries of the world adopted the single gold standard during the course of the nineteenth century, the notable exceptions being China, India, and Mexico. The gold standard law of the United States, as already noted, was enacted in 1900. For many years thereafter, we had what amounted to an international monetary system, based on gold.

The essentials of a full gold standard for any country are as follows: (1) The monetary unit must be defined in terms of a fixed

[6] For discussion of the currency legislation of 1933 see chap. V.

amount of gold of a specified fineness. (2) The government must be willing to purchase for monetary use at the fixed mint price all of the gold presented to it for sale, and to coin as much as may be demanded for the purposes of circulation. (3) All other forms of currency must be redeemable in gold, or claims on gold, at the fixed ratio. (4) Gold imports and exports by any who wish to make them must be unrestricted.

When a large number of important countries operate their monetary systems in accordance with the foregoing principles, there exists, in effect, an international monetary system. This is brought about, not by the establishment of a single unified world currency in place of separate national systems, but simply through the co-ordination of national systems into an international complex. The fact that the national monetary units are defined in terms of fixed quantities of gold makes it possible to compare any two of them and to establish parity between them. The fact that under the gold standard there exists in each country adhering to it an unlimited market for gold at a fixed price, through coinage or purchase by the Treasury or the central bank, and that gold can, generally speaking, always be freely shipped from one country to another, assures that deviation from the gold parities will be confined within narrow limits. The basis of this international co-ordination is a common standard of value, operating through the mechanism of stable foreign exchange rates.

Discussion of the operation of the foreign exchanges, and the economic consequences of the recent breakdown of the international monetary system must, however, be reserved for chapter VI.

CHAPTER V

RECENT CHANGES IN THE AMERICAN MONETARY SYSTEM

The monetary discussions and experiences of the nineteenth century gradually led, as we have seen, to the almost universal adoption of the single gold standard as the basis of monetary systems. It came to be assumed, moreover, that monetary issues—at least those pertaining to the standard of value—had been permanently settled. But the financial dislocation produced by the World War quickly caused the belligerent nations and eventually most of the neutral countries to suspend gold payments and to withdraw gold from circulation. The gold standard system was re-established during the post-war years, but the economic disruptions of the world depression of 1929–33 resulted in a new abandonment of the gold standard by a large number of countries, and in a general breakdown of the international monetary and credit system. These developments as they relate to the international exchanges will be discussed in chapter VI. Here we shall be concerned only with the repercussions upon the American monetary system.

A series of legislative enactments and executive orders, beginning in 1933, profoundly modified the entire monetary system of the United States. The factors and considerations responsible for these developments may be briefly summarized.

As a result of widespread fear with respect to the stability of American finance, the hoarding of gold had assumed large proportions in 1931 and 1932. Moreover, withdrawals of short-term credits held by foreigners led at times to an enormous flow of gold abroad—amounting in September and October 1931 to $703,000,000; in May and June 1932 to $448,000,000; and in the winter of 1933 to $305,000,000. The extremely large accumulation of gold in the United States (see page 74) enabled this country to withstand the strain; but many people came to regard the problem of maintaining the gold standard as one of great difficulty. The banking panic of the winter of 1933, which finally led to the closing of practically all the banks of the country on the very eve of the inauguration of a new administration, served to intensify public concern over the stability, and the usefulness, of the existing currency and banking system.[1] Indeed, the erroneous view was widely held

[1] For discussion of the banking crisis, see chap. XXII.

that an insufficient quantity of gold was the primary cause of the depression and ensuing difficulties.

Meanwhile, however, plans had been virtually completed for the holding in London of a World Monetary and Economic Conference for the purpose of re-establishing international monetary stability and freer trade relations as a cornerstone of world economic reconstruction. Very thorough preparation for this conference had been made by an international commission of experts; and, as a basis for negotiation, the recommendations of this commission had been submitted to, and approved by, the principal governments of the world, including the United States. Before the London Conference was held, however, the United States had abandoned the gold standard and later, at the conference itself, declined to co-operate in the negotiations that were under way.

I. AMERICA'S DEPARTURE FROM THE GOLD STANDARD

The abandonment of the gold standard was accomplished in two stages. The first step grew out of the control of the monetary and credit situation during the banking crisis of March 1933. By an executive order on March 10 the President forbade all banks to pay out or export gold, except by permission of the Secretary of the Treasury. This measure, which constituted a formal suspension of the gold standard, was occasioned more by internal hoarding than by fear of further foreign withdrawals; hence there was reason for regarding it simply as a temporary defensive measure.

Meanwhile the dollar exchange remained fairly stable during the second half of March and the first half of April. Although other forms of United States currency were no longer redeemable in gold, and free (or unlimited) gold exports were forbidden, gold could still be obtained, under license, for international transactions. In fact, the exceptions granted permitted sufficient latitude to enable the continuance of normal international settlements.

The second step in the process of abandoning the gold standard was taken by an executive order issued on April 20, which made it clear that the Administration intended definitely to depreciate the dollar. This order made the partial embargo on gold exports an absolute one, and in effect served notice that no more gold would be released for export. On the same day, the so-called Thomas Amendment to the Agricultural Adjustment Act was introduced in Congress. The purpose of this enactment was to grant the President, along with other monetary powers (see next section), the authority to reduce the gold content of the dollar by not more than 50 per cent. This congressional

Act had been given express approval in advance by the Administration; indeed, it was an Administration measure. It became law on May 12.

It was apparent that this legislation would affect the so-called gold contracts. As a result of the greenback currency depreciation of the Civil War period it had become a common practice in this country to write into public and private bonds and other contracts (as a specific safeguard against changes in the monetary standard) a provision for payment "in gold coin of present degree of weight and fineness." Would demands for payment under such contracts, in gold coin or in additional sums in other forms of currency sufficient to offset the reduction in the weight of the gold dollar, be enforceable? On May 26 a joint congressional resolution was introduced, which became a law on June 5, declaring that gold clause contracts obstructed the power of Congress to regulate the value of money and were inconsistent with the declared policy of Congress. It was therefore provided that such contracts might be discharged in any form of legal tender currency, and that "no such provision shall be contained in or made with respect to any obligations hereinafter incurred." By the same resolution, the provision contained in the Thomas amendment by which all forms of currency were made full legal tender, was re-affirmed and made more specific.

The World Monetary and Economic Conference, participated in by representatives of 64 nations, met according to schedule in London early in June. Preliminary discussions were held with respect to the re-establishment of an international monetary system based on gold. But the uncertainty with respect to the policy of the United States, arising out of the recent legislative developments, cast a shadow over the conference from the beginning. Rumors led to fluctuating exchange rates, and, in turn, to unstable prices of securities and commodities. At this juncture President Roosevelt ordered American participation in the monetary discussions discontinued on the ground that the attempt to arrive at stabilization was premature. The Conference adjourned shortly thereafter.

The explanation of these changes in American monetary policy is to be found primarily in a growing belief that recovery could best be promoted by independent American policies. The principal requirement was believed to be a rapid advance in commodity prices. President Roosevelt and some of his advisers had become converted to the following views: That economic recovery was impossible without an antecedent rise in commodity prices; that while a number of different measures might be required to bring about such a price advance it could not be fully achieved without a reduction in the gold content of the dollar; and that prosperity in the future should be sought through a stabilization of domestic commodity prices on a pre-depression level.[2]

The depreciation of the dollar was considered desirable, also, because American foreign trade had been adversely affected by the depreciation of the currencies of foreign countries. Accordingly, in conferring upon President Roosevelt the power to devalue the dollar, Congress stated explicitly that the amount of reduction in the gold content should be such "as he [the President] finds necessary from his investigation to stabilize domestic prices or to protect the foreign commerce against the adverse effect of depreciated foreign currencies."

The view of the Administration was explicitly set forth in official statements presented to the World Economic and Monetary Conference:

> The sound internal economic system of a nation is a greater factor in its well-being than the price of its currency in changing terms of the currencies of other nations. It is for this reason that reduced cost of government, adequate government income, and ability to service government debts are all so important to ultimate stability. So, too, old fetishes of so-called international bankers are being replaced by efforts to plan national currencies with the objective of giving to those currencies a continuing purchasing power which does not greatly vary in terms of commodities.[3]

. . . .

> The revaluation of the dollar in terms of American commodities is an end from which the government and the people of the United States cannot be diverted. We wish to make this perfectly clear: We are interested in American commodity prices. What is to be the value of the dollar in terms of foreign currencies is not and cannot be our immediate concern.[4]

The next important step with respect to gold was taken at the end of October, when the so-called gold purchase plan was inaugurated. Under this scheme the Government began a program of "monetary management" based upon an attempt to regulate commodity prices by altering the dollar price of gold per ounce. For several weeks thereafter the appropriate governmental agencies steadily advanced the price at which they were prepared to buy all gold brought to them, and at which they were, in fact, purchasing substantial quantities of the metal abroad. However, the experiment in managed currency, based on the gold purchase plan, was abandoned—for reasons shortly to be noted—within a few weeks of its inauguration.

[2] See chart on p. 16 for an indication of the extent to which prices had declined.
[3] July 3, 1933
[4] July 5, 1933.

On January 30, 1934, Congress, at the request of the President, passed the Gold Reserve Act. This Act provided that the President's power to devalue the dollar should be fixed within the limits of 50 and 60 per cent of the old content. On January 31 the President formally devalued the dollar by fixing its gold content at 15$\frac{5}{21}$ grains of gold, nine-tenths fine, or 59.06 per cent of its former weight. The statutory price thus became fixed once more, but at $35 rather than at $20.67 per ounce.

The devaluation automatically increased the dollar value of the gold stocks that had been accumulated in the hands of the Government by the difference between $20.67 and $35 per ounce. The profit thus accruing to the Treasury amounted to about 2.8 billion dollars.[5]

The new act, which now governs the monetary system of the United States, provides for a permanent abolition of gold coinage and of gold circulation in any shape or form. The Treasury alone is empowered to hold the metal. All gold coming into private possession, either by new production or by importation, must be sold to the Treasury. Gold required for industrial uses, or for the settlement of international obligations, can be purchased only from the Treasury.

Against the gold held by it, the Treasury is authorized to issue gold certificates, dollar for dollar—that is, with a 100 per cent coverage in metal. These certificates are to be a special type of currency. They cannot be put into circulation; they can be used only by the Federal Reserve banks as a part of the basic reserves. The Act provides that the gold taken over from the Federal Reserve banks shall be paid for with such certificates, and introduces an appropriate modification into the note-issuing procedure of the Reserve banks.

On January 31, 1934, the Secretary of the Treasury issued new regulations regarding gold transactions. He announced that the Treasury would thenceforth be prepared to purchase, through the United States mints and assay offices, all gold offered at $35 per ounce of fine metal, less one-quarter of one per cent and "an amount equal to all mint charges." He also made it clear, however, that "this price may be changed by the Secretary of the Treasury without notice other than by notice of such change mailed or telegraphed to the mints." Under the terms of these regulations, acquisition, transportation, melting, treating, importation, exportation, and earmarking of gold remain prohibited, except under license issued by agencies designated by the Secretary of the Treasury and at his discretion.

These Treasury regulations also provided that "the Federal Reserve banks may from time to time acquire from the United States

[5] Out of this profit two billion dollars was segregated to constitute an exchange stabilization fund; 642 millions was used to retire national bank notes.

by redemption of gold certificates . . . such amounts of gold bullion as, in the judgment of the Secretary of the Treasury, are necessary to settle international balances." In a public interpretation of this provision, the Secretary of the Treasury announced that he would release gold for export whenever the foreign exchange value of the dollar in terms of foreign gold currencies should reach the theoretically computed gold export point. As long as the Secretary of the Treasury continues, as he has thus far, to interpret his discretional powers in this manner, the gold mechanism becomes once more operative in governing the foreign exchange relations between the United States and those countries which maintain a gold standard.

Until recently the gold bullion was all held in vaults in the mints and in the Treasury at Washington. For greater safety about five billions of gold is now stored in a depository in Fort Knox, Kentucky, and more than a billion dollars of silver is stored at West Point.

II. OTHER MONETARY LEGISLATION

The monetary program of the new Administration also involved a number of other significant changes. Several types of monetary reform were being urged by special groups as a means of increasing the quantity of money in circulation, promoting prosperity, and raising prices. In addition to the advocates of gold devaluation there were the Federal Reserve credit expansionists, the greenbackers, and the silverites, who wished at least a partial re-establishment of bimetallism.

The strategy of the Administration in the spring of 1933 was to place in the hands of the President the power to use whatever monetary or credit devices might prove to be necessary. It was felt that such a delegation of power would enable the President to delay, or to defeat, extreme monetary and credit measures, and at the same time give him the right to utilize, within limits, whatever monetary mechanisms the exigencies of the developing situation might require. Thus permissive powers with respect to Federal Reserve credit, United States notes, and silver were also incorporated in the amendment to the Agricultural Adjustment Act to which reference has already been made.

The President was authorized, at his discretion, to direct the Secretary of the Treasury to enter into an agreement with the appropriate authorities of the Federal Reserve system for an expansion of the volume of Federal Reserve currency and credit. This was to be accomplished, (1) through the purchase by Federal Reserve banks of government securities from commercial banks and private individuals, or (2) by the direct sale of Treasury bills and other government obligations to the Federal Reserve banks in an aggregate amount of not more than three billion dollars.

In the event that the Federal Reserve system should refuse to enter into the necessary agreements, or in the event that the President should decide that the creation of a still greater volume of currency was needed, he was authorized to avail himself of the Treasury note-issuing powers of the original "greenback" act of February 25, 1862. It was provided, however, that these notes should be issued only for the purpose of retiring government obligations, and the maximum was set at three billion dollars. Neither of these powers has been utilized.

The Administration's silver legislation was incorporated in a Silver Purchase Act, approved by the President on June 19, 1934.[6] Its primary purpose was to placate the silver mining interests and to appease those whose monetary philosophy still ran in terms of bimetallism. This act made it mandatory for the Treasury to increase its stocks of silver until they equaled in value one-third of the monetary stocks of gold held by it, or until the market price of silver should reach $1.29 per ounce—the old 16 to 1 ratio. This silver was to be procured from three sources: (1) the nationalization of all silver bullion held in the country, (2) the purchase of newly mined domestic production, and (3) the purchase of foreign silver. The act directed the issuance of silver certificates in a face amount not less than the cost of the silver purchased.

The total purchases to June 30, 1937, amounted to 1,280,677,719 fine ounces, representing a value at current coinage rates of $2,801,482,-510. The domestic silver has been purchased at varying prices, the highest, and prevailing, price being 77.57 cents per fine ounce.[7] The foreign silver was purchased at an average price of 64.3 cents in 1935, of 45.1 cents in 1936, and of 44.9 cents in 1937.[8] Over four-fifths of the entire purchases have consisted of foreign silver. These silver transactions yielded to June 30, 1937, seigniorage profits to the extent of $811,700,000.

The silver purchase program has been devoid of merit. It had been contended that it would stimulate trade with countries on the silver standard; but in fact it had the opposite effect, disorganizing our trade with China and Mexico, and forcing the former country off the silver standard. Although it failed to achieve the objective of restoring the nineteenth century price of silver, it nevertheless greatly stimulated

[6] The Thomas Amendment also authorized the President to accept silver in payments of accounts owed by foreign governments to the United States in an aggregate amount of not more than 200 million dollars and at a price of not more than 50 cents an ounce.

[7] In March, 1938, the price was, however, reduced to 64 cents.

[8] These prices are the so-called "New York official quotations."

the production of the white metal and gave enormous subsidies to the silver industry, both at home and abroad. While resulting in large seigniorage profits to the Treasury, it at the same time amassed great additional silver reserves which are wholly unnecessary from the point of view of the monetary requirements of the nation.

III. GOLD DEVALUATION AND THE PRICE LEVEL

It was contended by the advocates of the gold devaluation plan that the reduction in the weight of the dollar would lead to a proportional rise in the prices of commodities. This was supposed to follow automatically from the changed value relations between gold as a commodity and other commodities. Concretely, it was held that as the price of gold was increased from $20.67 an ounce to $35 an ounce, commodity prices would rise in exact proportion.

Before considering the trend of prices during the period in question it should be noted that the Government's price raising program was by no means confined to monetary policies. The Agricultural Adjustment Act was designed to raise the prices of agricultural products through restricting their output, and the National Industrial Recovery Act was intended to raise the prices of industrial products, both by restrictions upon output and through increases in wage rates. Moreover, the Administration's policy of promoting recovery by extensive outlays of public funds was designed to stimulate increased demand and increased prices.

Notwithstanding this many-faceted program of price stimulation, the level of commodity prices did not increase in proportion to the advance in the price of gold. The chart presented on the next page shows, from March 1933 to June 1938, the price of gold, the general level of wholesale prices, and the prices of a selected group of basic commodities which are very important in the export trade. While the price of gold rose between October 1933 and the end of January 1934 by approximately 60 per cent, the general level of wholesale prices rose less than 25 per cent in the entire period from April to January. In view of the fact that in the next four years the highest level shown by the index was 148 in April 1937, as compared with 100 in 1933, it is evident that the lack of adjustment cannot be explained simply in terms of a *lag*.[9]

It will be noted, however, that the prices of basic commodities which are important in the export trade advanced in close relationship to, though even more rapidly than, the price of gold. The explanation of this close correspondence is to be found in the fact that, with the

[9] For further discussion of gold in relation to prices, see chap. XXIX.

PRICE MOVEMENTS OF GOLD, ALL COMMODITIES, AND FOREIGN TRADE COMMODITIES, 1933–1938[a]

(February 1933 = 100)

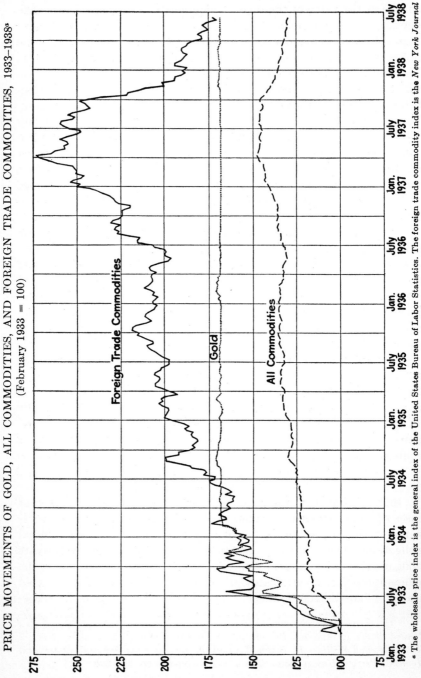

[a] The wholesale price index is the general index of the United States Bureau of Labor Statistics. The foreign trade commodity index is the *New York Journal of Commerce* daily index of 30 basic commodities, all of which are relatively important in foreign trade.

change in the value of the dollar, there needs to be a new "exchange quotation" for the dollar. When foreigners sell goods in the United States they will demand a larger number of dollars than before, and the prices of imports, as expressed in the new dollar, will therefore rise. The prices of exports are also stimulated. Since a franc, for example, will now exchange for more dollars and buy more American goods than before, demand for the now cheaper American goods will be stimulated. For example, it will be more economical for the time being to buy American wheat or cotton than Argentine wheat or Egyptian cotton. This increased demand will naturally stimulate exports and produce an advance in prices. Such a rise in price might be gradual in character were it not for the fact that speculators, foreseeing an inevitable rise, will at once buy such commodities, and thus cause a sharp advance in prices.

In the case of commodities purchased and sold in the domestic market, however, there is no corresponding stimulus to demand. Only in so far as the resulting higher costs of goods entering into international trade might indirectly affect the prices of other goods made from such higher-priced materials would there be a direct stimulus toward higher prices of domestic commodities. Thus anything like a generally uniform rise of prices resulting from a reduction in the weight of the dollar should not have been expected.

It was this failure of the general level of prices to follow the price of gold, together with a resumption of interest on the part of the Administration in international financial stabilization as a means of promoting a restoration of international trade, that was responsible for the abandonment of the gold management program in January 1934. During the ensuing years there has been no further change in the gold content of the dollar.

IV. THE "GOLD CLAUSE" CASES

In February 1935, the Supreme Court delivered opinions on four cases which questioned the validity of the Joint Resolution of Congress with respect to the abrogation of the "gold clauses" in contractual obligations. The first two cases dealt with the payment of private obligations containing gold clauses; the third was concerned with the redemption of gold certificates; while the fourth pertained to the gold clauses in government bonds.[10]

---

[10] The cases were *Norman C. Norman v. Baltimore and Ohio Railroad Co.; United States of America Reconstruction Finance Corporation et al. v. Bankers Trust Co.* and *William H. Bixby, Trustees; F. Eugene Nortz v. United States;* and *John M. Perry v. United States.* (See 294 *U.S. Reports*, pp. 240–316.)

The Joint Resolution provided that all such obligations "shall be discharged upon payment, dollar for dollar, in any coin or currency which at the time of payment is legal tender for public and private debts." The petitioners in each of these cases (all of which arose after the devaluation of the dollar) demanded payment in gold, or, since that was no longer possible, in the equivalent in present legal tender currency of gold of the former weight and fineness. That is, they demanded one dollar and sixty-nine cents in present currency for every dollar called for in the original agreement.

The Supreme Court rendered a decision in each case by a five to four majority, supporting the constitutionality of the Joint Resolution, and refusing to admit the claims for payment of more than the face value of the obligations. The various issues involved may best be shown by a brief résumé of the arguments put forth by the Court, including those of the dissenting justices.

1. The Majority Opinion

The private cases.—In the two private cases, which involved identical issues, the analysis in the majority opinion was, in brief, as follows:

Previous decisions of the Court with respect to gold clause obligations were briefly disposed of as irrelevant, since gold had not at that time been withdrawn from circulation by act of Congress.

These contracts were "not contracts for payment in gold as a commodity, or in bullion, but were contracts for the payment of *money.*" It was admitted, however, that they were intended to protect against a depreciation of the currency.

The Constitution granted to Congress the power "to coin money, regulate the value thereof, and of foreign coin," and this authorization was "designed to provide the same currency, having a uniform legal value in all the states." It also added the express power "to make all laws which shall be necessary and proper for carrying into execution" the other enumerated powers. In addition, mention was made of "a national government with sovereign powers." In previous decisions, these words were interpreted to include the power to forbid mutilation, melting, and exportation of gold and silver coin.

From these various statements it appears that any private contracts which interfere with the Government's policy of regulating the currency, as the gold clauses obviously do, hamper Congress in the exercise of its sovereign rights, and therefore cannot stand. It is an established principle that "contracts, however express, cannot fetter the constitutional authority of the Congress." For instance, private contracts which interfere with subsequent rulings of the Interstate Commerce Commission have never been upheld.

The principle established in the Fifth Amendment "forbidding the taking of private property for public use without just compensation or the deprivation of it without due process of law" is dismissed on the ground that this provision refers only to direct appropriations. "A new tariff, an embargo, or a war, might bring upon individuals great losses; might, indeed, render valuable property almost valueless,—might destroy the worth of contracts. But whoever supposes that, because of this, a tariff could not be changed or a non-intercourse act or embargo be enacted, or a war be declared?"

The Joint Resolution itself states that these contracts interfere with the regulatory policy of Congress, a point which was further stressed in the report of the committee which recommended its adoption. At the time of its adoption there were outstanding 75 billion dollars, or more, of such obligations, which if actually paid in gold would have interfered directly with the congressional policy. Therefore the obstructive character of the gold clauses is very clear.

The point is also made that since all economic activity is now being carried on with the devalued dollars, great economic dislocations would be produced if those in debt were required to "pay one dollar and sixty-nine cents in currency when they are receiving their taxes, rates, charges or prices on the basis of one dollar of that currency."

In summing up the Court said:

We are not concerned with consequences, in the sense that consequences, however serious, may excuse an invasion of constitutional right. We are concerned with the constitutional power of the Congress over the monetary system of the country and its attempted frustration. . . . Exercising that power, the Congress has undertaken to establish a uniform currency, and parity between kinds of currency, and to make that currency, dollar for dollar, legal tender for the payment of debts. In the light of abundant experience, the Congress was entitled to choose such a uniform monetary system, and to reject a dual system, with respect to all obligations within the range of the exercise of its constitutional authority. The contention that these gold clauses are valid contracts and cannot be struck down proceeds upon the assumption that private parties, and States and municipalities, may make and enforce contracts which may limit that authority. Dismissing that untenable assumption, the facts must be faced. We think that it is clearly shown that these clauses interfere with the exertion of the power granted to the Congress and certainly it is not established that the Congress arbitrarily or capriciously decided that such an interference existed.

The gold certificate case.—The plaintiff in this suit against the United States Government had owned $106,300 in gold certificates, which he surrendered to the Treasury under protest, in accordance with the executive order of January 15, 1934, and received therefor not the gold to which he considered himself entitled, but $106,300 in other currency which was not redeemable in gold. When the dollar was subsequently devalued, he maintained that he had been deprived of his property without due process of law and had been damaged in the sum of $64,334.07, for which amount, with interest, he brought suit against the Government.

After a brief discussion of the history of gold certificates and of the laws relating to them, the Court stated that these bills were currency, "not contracts for a certain quantity of gold as a commodity"; that "they called for dollars, not bullion"; that had the notes been redeemed in gold coin the plaintiff would have had to surrender it likewise, for the same amount as he did receive; that there was at the time no free market for gold nor could he legally possess it; and therefore that he had sustained no actual damages and hence could not bring suit.

The government bond case.—This case was concerned with the redemption of a $10,000 United States Liberty Loan bond. The Court stated the opinion that such a bond was a definite contract and enforceable as such, that the Government was as much bound by such an obligation as was any individual, and that it had no right to repudiate such an obligation.

There is a clear distinction between the power of the Congress to control or interdict the contracts of private parties when they interfere with the exercise of its constitutional authority, and the power of the Congress to alter or repudiate the substance of its own engagements. . . . By virtue of the power to borrow money "*on the credit of the United States*," the Congress is authorized to pledge that credit as an assurance of payment as stipulated,—as the highest assurance the Government can give, its plighted faith. To say that the Congress may withdraw or ignore that pledge is to assume that the Constitution contemplates a vain promise, a pledge having no other sanction than the pleasure and convenience of the pledgor. This Court has given no sanction to such a conception of the obligations of our Government.

The powers conferred upon the Congress are harmonious. The Constitution gives to the Congress the power to borrow money on the credit of the United States, an unqualified power, a power vital to the Government. . . . Having this power to authorize the issue of definite obligations for the payment of money borrowed, the Congress has not been vested with authority to alter or destroy those obligations.

We conclude that the Joint Resolution of June 5, 1933, in so far as it attempted to override the obligation created by the bond in suit, went beyond the congressional power.

This is, however, an action for breach of contract. The plaintiff seeks to make his case solely upon the theory that he is entitled to one dollar and sixty-nine cents in the present currency for every dollar promised by the bond, regardless of any actual loss he has suffered. The plaintiff can recover no more than the loss he has sustained. The change in the weight of the gold dollar did not necessarily cause loss to the plaintiff of the amount claimed. Since there is no free market for gold, and since gold coin, if he could legally possess it, would be worth no more than any other form of currency (inasmuch as all forms are now legal tender) he has sustained no actual loss and therefore has no claim for damages.

2. The Minority Opinion

The four dissenting justices presented their opinions on the four different cases as one. The argument may be summarized as follows:

Just men regard repudiation and spoliation of citizens by their sovereign with abhorrence; but we are asked to affirm that the Constitution has granted power to accomplish both.

Gold clause contracts are definite enforceable contracts, and have been interpreted as such not only by the Supreme Court in all previous decisions, but by the courts of other countries and the Permanent Court of International Justice as well.

They were intended to afford a definite standard or measure of value, and thus to protect against a depreciation of the currency and against the discharge of the obligation by payment of less than that prescribed. . . . The borrower agrees to repay in gold coin containing 25.8 grains to the dollar or the currency value of that number of grains. . . . Irrespective of any change in currency, the thing loaned or an equivalent will be returned. . . . The present currency consists of promises to pay dollars of 15$\frac{5}{21}$ grains. . . . The calculation to determine the damages for failure to pay in gold would not be difficult.

The oft repeated rule by which the validity of statutes must be tested is this—"Let the end be legitimate, let it be within the scope of the Constitution, and all means which are appropriate which are plainly adapted to that end which are not prohibited but consistent with the letter and spirit of the Constitution are constitutional."

The fundamental problem now presented is whether recent statutes passed by Congress in respect of money and credits, were designed to attain a legitimate end; or whether, under the guise of pursuing a monetary policy, Congress really has inaugurated a plan primarily designed to destroy private obligations, repudiate national debts and drive into the Treasury all gold within the country in exchange for inconvertible promises to pay, of much less value.

We do not deny the right of Congress to coin money and regulate the value thereof. The legal tender cases are irrelevant, since the purpose of the laws they dealt with "was to meet honorable obligations—not to repudiate them." The Court has heretofore ruled that a "power to regulate is not a power to destroy," and that the Fifth Amendment limits all governmental powers. "The authority of Congress to create legal tender obligations in times of peace is derived from the power to borrow money; this cannot be extended to embrace the destruction of all credits."

After commenting on the fact that the gold clauses in corporate bonds were approved by the Government when they were executed, the minority cites quotations from the speech of the Senator who presented the Joint Resolution, as evidence that its purpose was to cheapen the dollar in order to raise prices and bring about the depreciation of contractual obligations. This was the destruction of lawfully acquired rights. Moreover, it is interesting to note "that ready calculation of the exact loss suffered by the Philippine Government [as a result of this bill] moved Congress to satisfy it by appropriating, in June 1934, $23,862,750.78 to be paid out of the Treasury of the United States."

The Joint Resolution "was aimed directly at those contracts and had no definite relation to the power to issue bills or to coin or regulate the value of money. . . . This Resolution was not appropriate for carrying into effect any power entrusted to Congress. The gold clauses in no substantial way interfered with the power of coining money . . . or providing an uniform currency." If such a bill is allowable, if Congress has this right, then it can continue this process until the dollar contains only one grain of gold, and enough paper profits have been made to cancel the entire public debt.

This is not an indirect but a direct destruction of property, and therefore there must be just compensation. The majority argument that, since there was no market for gold and it was illegal to possess it, there was no damage, is not admissible, because it was Congress which brought about that condition. "Obligations cannot be legally avoided by prohibiting the creditor from receiving the thing promised."

A government is as much bound by its promises as is an individual, and the results that would follow a loss of faith in the word of the sovereign would be extremely serious.

If an individual should undertake to annul or lessen his obligation by secreting or manipulating his assets with the intent to place them beyond the reach of creditors, the attempt would be denounced as fraudulent. . . . Loss of reputation for honorable dealing will bring us unending humiliation; the impending legal and moral chaos is appalling.

Perhaps the most striking feature of these sharply divergent interpretations of the constitutional issues involved in this currency legislation is the apparent failure of the two sides to meet upon a common ground of legal argument. There seems to be little agreement as to the precise issues involved; seldom is there a straight meeting of minds. The differences in interpretation and conclusion are evidently to be explained almost entirely by fundamental differences in approach to the problem—as indicated by the prefatory statement of each group. The majority were interested mainly in determining the rights of Congress, in its sovereign capacity, to adjust the currency system in terms of what Congress conceived to be the greatest good of the greatest number. The minority, on the other hand, were preoccupied with the rights of individuals and the corresponding limitations on the congressional power, which had been imposed by the Constitution— also, of course, in the interests of the common weal. It is not difficult to see how opposing conclusions might be reached from these divergent premises. It is more difficult for the layman to understand why the justices should not have manifested a clearer conception of the nature of their own differences and thus have made their analysis more conclusive.

While no judgment is here expressed upon the legal issues connected with the gold clause cases, a few comments may be appropriate with respect to the economic considerations involved. The fact is clear that had the gold clauses been sustained enormous financial losses would have been suffered by certain groups of people. The payment of $1,690 to all holders of $1,000 gold clause bonds would have meant that the equity of stockholders in the corporations concerned would have been proportionally decreased. Had commodity prices risen in proportion to the advance in the price of gold, shareholders would have had compensating gains. But, as matters stood, a decision in favor of the bondholders would have meant a great advance in bond values and a corresponding decline in stock values.

Thus a sustaining decision would clearly have created more inequity than it cured. This is especially the case in view of the fact that wholesale commodity prices had risen only about 25 per cent and the cost of living index only eight per cent. Most of the bonds then outstanding, both government and private, had been purchased long before the depression and on a price basis substantially above that prevailing at the time the gold clause cases were tried. To be sure, it could be argued that the price adjustment was not yet complete—that prices would still rise in proportion to the change in the dollar. But such an ultimate outcome was at best debatable. Meanwhile a decision sustaining the gold clauses would have been certain to produce financial readjustments of far reaching significance, and might have disastrously affected the whole economic and financial situation. Complex difficulties of this type were not foreseen by those who favored the devaluation program. They serve nevertheless to reveal the difficulties involved in tampering with the monetary standard.[11]

V. A "PROVISIONAL" GOLD STANDARD

In concluding this discussion of recent changes in American monetary policy, we must inquire whether the gold standard any longer exists and how the value of currency is now regulated, if at all. In the light of the requirements, or conditions, essential to the operation of a full gold standard, it is clear that the present system is of a hybrid character.

While there is virtually no restriction on gold for export, gold cannot be obtained for purposes of domestic circulation, and it can be procured for non-currency uses only with special permission. Although there is no longer unlimited—or indeed any—coinage of gold, the Treasury is nevertheless under obligation to purchase, at a fixed price, all the gold brought to it. The dollar is moreover defined as a fixed quantity of gold of a specified fineness. The subsidiary forms of money are no longer freely redeemable in gold, but it is provided that "gold certificates owned by the Federal Reserve banks shall be redeemed at such times and in such amounts as, in the judgment of the Secretary of the Treasury, are necessary to maintain the equal purchasing power of every kind of currency in the United States."

Notwithstanding the fact that all forms of subsidiary currency are irredeemable, they have not depreciated in comparison with gold. All payments are, in fact, made in subsidiary forms of money, mainly in paper currency or in credit instruments, redeemable in paper money. The various forms of subsidiary currency are, however, exchangeable one for another.

In considering this redemption question a great contrast must be noted between the present situation and that existing at the time when

---

[11] The effect of currency devaluation upon international exchanges and international economic conditions will be discussed in chap. VI.

the original greenback currency of the Civil War period was made irredeemable. Then the Government possessed no gold reserve at all; and it was not until 1879 that a reserve fund of modest proportions was accumulated as a part of the general funds of the Treasury. Now the Treasury possesses extraordinarily large gold holdings, the ratio of gold coin and bullion to all forms of government currency amounting to over 60 per cent. Thus redeemability hinges not on ability to maintain gold payments but upon monetary policy.

CHAPTER VI
THE FOREIGN EXCHANGES

The monetary and credit system has developed more or less independently in the various countries of the world. Hence there is little uniformity in the value of the various monetary units and even less uniformity in nomenclature. Accordingly, in conducting trade and financial transactions across national frontiers it is necessary to effect an exchange of currencies whereby the person entitled to payment may receive the money current in his own country instead of having to accept foreign currency. This is the function of the foreign exchanges. The foreign exchange mechanism, moreover, makes it possible to settle the vast majority of international trade and financial obligations without requiring the movement of specie[1] across national boundaries. The range of transactions requiring settlement may be most clearly revealed by a statement of the principal sources of international payments that normally exist between the United States and Great Britain:

Transactions requiring payments to British citizens (tending to cause an outflow of funds from the United States):

1. American imports of British goods
2. Premiums on policies of British insurance companies
3. Freight bills payable to British ship-owners
4. Purchases abroad by American tourists
5. Interest and dividends on British investments in United States

Transactions requiring payments to American citizens (tending to cause an inflow of funds to the United States):

1. Exports of goods to Great Britain
2. Maturing insurance policies payable to Americans
3. Interest and dividends on American investments in Great Britain

In connection with numerous items, there are payments to be made both ways, as is indicated in the case of interest and dividend charges on investments. We have included, however, only the more important current trade and service items on each side of this statement of

[1] Ordinarily specie (or bullion) alone is acceptable in international monetary settlements, and it is acceptable by weight and fineness only.

international income and outgo. We have omitted lending and investment operations, since we are for the moment concerned only with those operations which require practically immediate settlement. It is necessary to say *practically* immediate, since much of the trade is conducted on a short-term credit basis.

I. THE EXCHANGE MECHANISM

International payments are effected largely without the shipment of specie by sending bills of exchange abroad in lieu of actual cash. In order to make the process clear, it will be necessary to point out, first, precisely what is meant by the parity of exchange, "gold points," and bills of exchange. The following discussion relates to the situation under an international gold standard system.

Before the disorganization of international currency relations which occurred during the world depression (see pages 75–80) exchange between the United States and England was said to be at par when a sterling bill was worth $4.866 in American currency. What does par or parity of exchange mean, and how is this quotation, 4.866 derived? Parity of exchange is nothing but a simple statement of the relative value of American and British coins. The British monetary unit, the pound sterling, contained 4.866 times as much gold as the American monetary unit, the dollar. The par exchange rate thus depends upon the gold content of the monetary units of the different countries.

The par of exchange between the United States and Germany was 23.8—which means that the value of the gold mark was 23.8 cents in United States money. The equation may also be expressed the other way round, as 4.2 marks to the dollar. The money of each of the various countries had its particular parity as compared with United States coins, and in turn the pound sterling, franc, etc., each had its parity with the coins of all the other countries. It is unnecessary for our present purpose to enter into a detailed discussion of all these quotations, for they all involve a common principle.

The use of bills of exchange reduces currency shipments. Their function in this connection may best be revealed by the use of some concrete illustrations. Let us assume that Mr. A in New York has sold £1,000 worth of goods to Mr. X in London, and that at the same time Mr. B in New York has purchased £1,000 worth of goods from Mr. Y in London. It is apparent that, if it could be arranged so that B could pay A and X could pay Y, it would not only save inconvenience for all concerned but would also render unnecessary the shipment of any currency to settle these obligations. If A were to draw an order (or bill of exchange) on X in London ordering X to pay Y £1,000 and could sell the bill to B, he would receive his money from B; then if B sent this bill over to Y and Y presented it to X, who paid it, both obligations would have been settled without the shipment of any currency.

But in practice there are usually two difficulties which prevent this simple solution of the problem. In the first place, A is not usually acquainted with B, and X is not as a rule acquainted with Y. Secondly, the amounts involved in the two transactions are not usually identical. Accordingly, dealers in foreign exchange (banks and brokers) are required as financial intermediaries. When A draws his bill of exchange for £1,000 on the London buyer of his goods, he takes it to a foreign exchange banker, who pays him, when exchange is at par, $4,866. The banker then sends the bill to London to a correspondent bank, which presents the bill to X for payment. The payment is next deposited with the London bank to the credit of the New York bank. Now when B wants to buy a bill of exchange he goes to the foreign exchange banker and the banker sells him a draft drawn against this London bank account—a draft for £1,000, or for whatever amount the buyer may desire. B then sends the draft to Y in London and Y presents it to the bank against which it is drawn and receives his payment. The New York banker thus acts as an intermediary between A and B, serving in effect to bring them together, and serving also to make "change," that is, to break up bills of exchange into whatever denominations are required.

Sometimes these bills are drawn directly by the exporters against foreign banks with which the foreign importer has made arrangements for the purpose. They are sometimes drawn payable at "sight," that is, when presented, and sometimes they run for thirty, sixty, or ninety days, etc. The drafts may have attached to them documents in the form of bills of lading and other shipping receipts, or they may be what are known as "clean bills," unaccompanied by any documentary evidence. There are many angles to the problem, giving rise to many different types of bills involving different methods of payment; but the foregoing simple illustration will suffice to reveal the essential principles in all cases. It should also be pointed out that bills of exchange are not always drawn by American banks or American exporters against foreign banks, and sold to American importers who have remittances to make. The process may be reversed, with American banks doing the financing—the method actually employed in any given case being a matter of agreement between the parties to the transaction.[2]

[2] For a more detailed discussion see chap. XVII, sec. IV.

The price of exchange is determined by the demand for and supply of bills. In the illustration above we assumed that exchange was at par. In fact, it is sometimes above and sometimes below par. The price of a bill of exchange is, like the price of wheat or any other commodity, a reflection of the relative demand for, and supply of, bills in the market at the moment. If at any given time £1,000,000 worth of sterling bills were offered for sale in New York and £1,000,000 worth were demanded, the price would be at par, that is, at 4.866. But if only £1,000,000 worth of bills were offered in the market for sale, and £1,200,000 worth were demanded, the price would be bid up above 4.866 by those who desired the bills as a means of meeting their obligations abroad. On the contrary, if only £800,000 were demanded, the sellers would have to make concessions in order to dispose of their bills.

The maximum extent to which the price of exchange can be bid up or forced down, as the case may be, is determined by the costs involved in shipping the actual specie. I should be willing to pay as much as $4,885 for a bill of exchange with which to settle a £1,000 obligation, because that would be cheaper than shipping the currency; but I should not be willing to pay more than that, because it would then be cheaper for me to ship the actual specie instead. On the other hand, I should be willing, if necessary, to sell a £1,000 bill of exchange for $4,845; but not for less, since it would then be cheaper for me to pay the expense of importing the actual currency. These points, 4.885 and 4.845, are known as gold-exporting and gold-importing points.

The supply of and demand for bills of exchange in the New York and London exchange market depend at any time not merely upon the relative volume of exports and imports. They depend upon all of the international operations outlined above (and also, as we shall see, upon loan and investment operations). Whatever the occasion for remittances of funds to Great Britain, bills of exchange are demanded in the market, and whatever the occasion for payments to the United States, bills of exchange are drawn and offered for sale. For instance, if an individual is contemplating a trip abroad, he places, say, $1,000 with his bank, with an express company, or with one of the tourist agencies, and asks for letters of credit or traveler's checks. It is then necessary for the bank where the funds have been deposited to transmit means of payment to Great Britain. This it does by buying a bill of exchange which, when sent to a correspondent bank abroad, is credited to the account of the American bank and, when properly signed by the authorized party, is made available for the payment of checks.

Roundabout operations minimize the flow of specie. Thus far we have been illustrating the principles involved in foreign exchange by reference to the relations that obtain between the United States and Great Britain. The mechanism of the exchanges also makes it possible for a roundabout settling of balances involving three or more countries. For instance, there has long been a triangular trade situation involving the United States, Great Britain, and Brazil. The United States imports from, more than she exports to, Brazil; Great Britain has an unfavorable balance with the United States; and Brazil's imports from, exceed her exports to, Great Britain. Thus Great Britain owes the United States, the United States owes Brazil, and Brazil owes Great Britain. The exchanges make it possible for the United States to pay for her imports from Brazil by bills of exchange drawn against London bank accounts, such bills being acceptable because they can be used in paying Brazilian obligations to Great Britain. In a similar way, since Canada has ordinarily had an adverse balance with the United States, but a favorable balance with England, it has usually been advantageous all around for Canadian importers from the United States to meet their obligations by means of bills of exchange drawn against London banks by Canadian exporters to Great Britain.

Arbitrage transactions also assist in this process of roundabout settlement. The skillful trader makes a careful study of the quotations in all the foreign exchange markets at any given time. By virtue of temporary variations in rates of different countries he may make a slight profit by buying exchange in one market and selling simultaneously in another. These arbitrage transactions often involve several markets, and they thus tend to stabilize all the exchanges and hold them at a common level, with movements of currency a last-resort measure.

The supply of bills in relation to the demand for such bills in any given market shows considerable fluctuation. In the United States, for example, there has normally been an excess supply of foreign bills in the autumn and early winter when American exports of cotton and wheat are largest, with a resulting tendency for the price of bills to be depressed to the gold-importing point. In the spring, heavy imports of British textiles and other manufactured goods not infrequently occasion a bidding-up of exchange rates to the gold-exporting point. Statistics of international gold movements are usually presented on an annual basis, the totals given representing merely the net difference between the various shipments in and the various shipments out.[3]

[3] For a description of the process by which payments between different sections of the United States are effected with practically no movements of specie, see discussion of the Federal Reserve clearing system, pp. 300–303.

II. THE SIGNIFICANCE OF CREDIT OPERATIONS

Thus far in this analysis of international exchange we have kept loan and investment operations out of the picture and considered only such current transactions as call for practically immediate payment. The earlier writers on the theory of foreign exchange gave no adequate consideration to the part that credit in its various forms plays in the exchange market and in connection with the movement of specie. The accepted theory, stated in its simplest form, was that an adverse balance from trade and service operations in country A results in an outflow of gold, which is soon followed by a decline of prices in that country and a rise of prices in country B to which the gold moves. The resulting shift in price levels makes country A a good market in which to buy but a poor market in which to sell, and vice versa. The result is a curtailment of imports into A and an expansion of exports therefrom, with a consequent shift in the supply of and demand for bills of exchange. In due course, gold will flow back to country A and tend to restore the equilibrium.

It has always been recognized that short-term bank credits, in the form of finance bills, frequently serve as a buffer against currency movements. If bankers possess at a given moment an inadequate supply of trade bills with which to meet the current demand, they may draw bills on their own account against foreign correspondents and thus increase the available supply of exchange. This they often do when they foresee that the balance is likely soon to shift the other way. Such an operation, it will be seen, amounts to a temporary loan from the foreign correspondent. And it tends to lessen the volume of international specie movements.

But this is only a small part of the significance of credit in connection with foreign exchange operations. International loan and investment transactions of various types, and of ever increasing amounts, are constantly taking place between countries. Bankers shift balances between countries in wholesale fashion in order to take advantage of variations in interest rates; individuals make extensive deposits in foreign banks—for considerations of safety as well as because of variations in interest rates; stocks and bonds of foreign corporations are purchased and sold in enormous quantities; and huge loans, both public and private, are floated in foreign countries. Moreover, investors in country A may be purchasing securities issued by corporations in country B at the very moment that investors in country B are purchasing securities in country A.

Loan and investment operations naturally affect the exchange market quite as directly as do current trade and service operations.

When this fact was noted by earlier writers on the theory of international finance, it was still assumed that the significance of credit operations was merely that they reduced the flow of specie at any given time—equilibrium still being maintained by specie movements and consequent price and trade readjustments.

The truth of the matter is that loan and credit operations, or "capital movements" as they are often called, profoundly affect the whole international equation. At the very time when there is a heavy adverse balance on account of current trade and service transactions, there may be a heavy inflow of specie as a result of "capital," or credit, operations. For example, in the early nineties Russia had a substantial deficiency of exports and was yet importing large quantities of gold annually. The explanation lay in Russia's policy of purchasing foreign gold with a view to the establishment of the gold standard. The gold was purchased abroad like any commodity and the fact that the supply of ordinary Russian export bills was inadequate did not prevent such purchases. Russia merely borrowed abroad in order to procure all the bills required to pay for commodity and gold imports combined. But obviously the gold movement was not a result of antecedent trade and credit operations. Rather, the policy of accumulating gold necessitated foreign borrowing.

The experience of the United States since the World War will serve to illustrate the many factors that enter into the balance of international payments and affect the movements of specie. The diagram on page 69 shows the balance each year from 1922 to 1936 inclusive. The various areas in each bar show the movements of merchandise; service items, interest and dividends; long-term and short-term capital movements; and the flow of specie. Since the data are not precise, a balancing area labeled "unknown" is included at the top of each pair of bars.

In every year from 1922 to 1935 inclusive exports exceeded imports, and the trade and service items combined showed a net balance in favor of the United States. But frequently instead of an inflow of specie there was a large outflow. The balance is accounted for by credit operations which showed large net extensions to foreigners, during the late twenties, but a net flow in the opposite direction during the depression. The reverse capital movement of recent years is largely the result of the repurchase and redemption of foreign securities previously sold in the United States and an extensive "flight" of liquid funds to what appeared a safer refuge in the United States. (For further discussion of the recent gold movements see pages 82 and 83.)

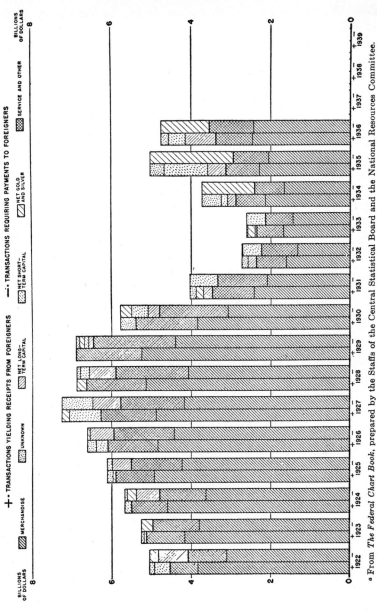

BALANCE OF INTERNATIONAL PAYMENTS OF THE UNITED STATES[a]

++ TRANSACTIONS YIELDING RECEIPTS FROM FOREIGNERS
—· TRANSACTIONS REQUIRING PAYMENTS TO FOREIGNERS

MERCHANDISE · UNKNOWN · NET LONG-TERM CAPITAL · NET SHORT-TERM CAPITAL · NET GOLD AND SILVER · SERVICE AND OTHER

[a] From *The Federal Chart Book*, prepared by the Staffs of the Central Statistical Board and the National Resources Committee.

It is evident from the diagram that trade readjustments did not follow the movements of gold and silver. Moreover, there is no correlation between the movements of specie and the movements of commodity prices. For example, in the latter part of 1919 and the early months of 1920 gold was flowing out of the United States at the rate of nearly $50,000,000 a month and yet prices were rising with extraordinary rapidity. After the collapse of the boom in 1920, gold flowed back in huge volume and yet prices declined precipitately. The trade readjustments were normal accompaniments of the business cycle and prices moved in directions opposite to that implied by the classical theory. The truth appears to be that with such possibilities for expanding and contracting credit currency as now exist, the movement of specie between countries is of little consequence in connection with ordinary price changes. (For discussion of the relation of gold to prices see chapter XXIX.)

III. WAR-TIME DISRUPTION OF EXCHANGES

At the outbreak of the World War the normal adjustments of international trade and financial relations were very quickly disrupted. In the autumn of 1914 there was a great rush on the part of European holders of American securities to sell them in American markets as a means of securing funds required for war purposes. At the same time the usual autumn movement of United States cotton and other products was checked both by a temporary decline in European demand for such goods and by the fear of German raiders. Insurance rates also increased tremendously, so that the gold-exporting point no longer remained at 4.885. So great was the demand for sterling bills as compared with the supply that sterling exchange rose at one time as high as $7.00, though it soon declined to $5.00, a figure still substantially above the previous maximum. Other exchanges fluctuated in similar fashion.

In the autumn of 1915, however, when the Allies began to buy great quantities of war supplies in the United States, the situation was sharply reversed: the supply of bills of exchange outran the demand, and exchange quickly fell to the gold-importing point. For a time, the European countries allowed gold to be exported; but such exports had to be checked before very long because of the disastrous effects upon European monetary systems. The balance of payments ran so heavily against European belligerents that the pound sterling, for example, soon declined to $4.48 and the franc from 19.3 to about 16.5 cents. It became necessary to resort to credit operations as a means of "pegging" the exchanges. By borrowing from the United States, the

European governments were enabled to go into the market and increase the demand for bills of exchange whenever the rate sagged. The pound sterling was "pegged" at a rate of about 4.765.

Shortly after the War, with a view to effecting a gradual restoration of the normal functioning of the international exchanges, the European governments abandoned artificial control of exchange rates. Because of the large adverse balance of payments, however, it was necessary to retain the embargoes on gold shipments, lest heavy outflows of gold completely wreck European monetary systems. The results of the international economic losses and maladjustments which the war had caused were quickly shown in a sharp fall in exchange rates in practically all European countries. The table which follows gives the average exchange rates of a number of European countries annually from 1918 to 1924.

EXCHANGE FLUCTUATIONS, 1918–1924
(Annual Averages)

Country	Unit	Par	1918	1919	1920	1921	1922	1923	1924
Great Britain	Pound	$4.867	$4.755	$4.426	$3.664	$3.849	$4.429	$4.575	$4.417
Germany[a]	Reichsmark	.238	.172	.067	.018	.012	.002	.00002	.230
France	Franc	.193	.178	.137	.070	.075	.082	.061	.052
Italy	Lira	.193	.131	.114	.050	.043	.048	.046	.044
Belgium	Franc	.193	.137	.128	.074	.074	.077	.052	.046
Netherlands	Florin	.402	.468	.394	.344	.337	.385	.391	.382
Sweden	Krone	.268	.328	.255	.205	.225	.262	.266	.265
Switzerland	Franc	.193	.229	.190	.169	.174	.191	.181	.182
Austria	Krone	.203	.104	.031	.005	.002	.0001	.00001	.00001
Hungary	Krone	.203	.083	.031	.004	.003	.0009	.00016	.00002
Poland[b]	Mark	.238	......	.038	.005	.0008	.00019	.00001	b

[a] The figure for 1923 is the average for the first nine months. The Rentenmark system was instituted in November 1923, and the German currency was practically stable thereafter.

[b] The figure given for 1919 is the average for July–December. There are no earlier data available. From January to April 1924, the average was 11.3 cents per million marks. On the latter date Polish currency was stabilized on the basis of the zloty as the unit.

The process of depreciation may be illustrated by the experience of France. The chart on page 72 shows the fluctuations of the French franc from 1914 to 1937. Our attention for the moment will be centered on the period preceding the stabilization of 1928. The depreciation during the early years of the war amounted to approximately 10 per cent. The cessation of "pegging" operations by the French government resulted in a precipitate decline in the value of the franc from over eighteen cents in March 1919 to a low point of less than six cents in April 1920. From the end of 1920 to the early part of 1922, however, the general trend was upward, from around six cents to more than nine cents. After 1922, it fell irregularly but persistently until 1926.

DOLLAR EXCHANGE VALUE OF THE FRANC, 1914–1937

Stabilization was finally effected in 1928 at a value of 3.92 cents, or about one-fifth the pre-war parity.

The numerous ups and downs shown in the chart were due in part to seasonal commercial movements, in part to psychological factors which have influenced speculation in the franc, at times to changes in money rates and bond prices, and at other times to credit operations, as in the case of the Morgan loan of 1924. However, the general downward movement of the franc reflects with fair accuracy the progressive deterioration in the financial position of the country.

IV. RESTORATION OF STABLE EXCHANGES, 1924–1929

In the light of the economic disturbances which accompanied the depreciation of foreign exchanges in the early post-war years, the conclusion was finally reached that world economic recovery could not be secured without a restoration of stable exchanges based on an international gold standard. Accordingly, in the years from 1922 to 1929, and particularly after 1924, the leading nations of the world cooperated in the re-establishment of a stable system of international exchanges. As the table below indicates, one after another of the principal European countries succeeded in establishing stable currencies at or below former parities. The United States contributed to the process by promising exchange stabilization credits and by adopting credit policies designed to promote the redistribution of the world gold supply.

EXCHANGE STABILIZATION, 1925–1929
(Annual Averages)

Country	Unit	Pre-war Par	1925	1926	1927	1928	1929
Great Britain	Pound	$4.867	$4.829	$4.858	$4.861	$4.866	$4.857
Germany	Reichsmark	.238	.238	.238	.238	.239	.238
France	Franc	.193	.048	.032	.039	.039	.039
Italy	Lira	.193	.040	.039	.052	.053	.052
Belgium[a]	Belga	.965	.048	.034	.139	.139	.139
Netherlands	Florin	.402	.402	.401	.401	.402	.402
Sweden	Krone	.268	.268	.268	.268	.268	.268
Switzerland	Franc	.193	.193	.193	.193	.193	.193
Austria[b]	Schilling	.141	.141	.141	.141	.141	.141
Hungary[c]	Pengö	.175	.00001	.176	.175	.174	.174
Poland[d]	Zloty	.193	.177	.112	.113	.112	.112

[a] The belga, which is equal to 5 francs, superseded the Belgian franc October 26, 1926.
[b] The schilling replaced the krone and stabilization was accomplished at the beginning of 1925.
[c] After stabilization on January 1, 1926 the pengö replaced the krone.
[d] A post-war currency.

DISTRIBUTION OF WORLD GOLD SUPPLY, 1913–1937[a]
(In Millions of Dollars of 1929 Gold Content)

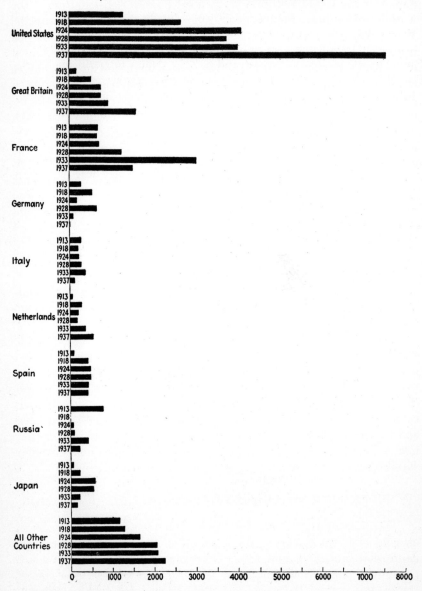

[a] Data compiled from Federal Reserve Bulletins.

[b] There is no figure available for Russia in 1918 or 1937. The figure for 1936 has therefore been used for 1937.

The disorganization of European trade and finance both during and after the World War resulted in a substantial redistribution of the world's gold supply. Before the entrance of the United States into the World War this country received great quantities of gold from Europe in payment for goods and services rendered. Again, after the removal of exchange restrictions in 1919 there was a large flow of currency to the United States to meet adverse international balances. Between 1925 and 1929 there was an outflow of gold. There was a slight increase in gold imports during the years of acute depression, 1929–1933, which was followed once more by an enormous increase in gold movements to this country. The diagram on page 74 shows the shift in the gold holdings of the principal countries by selected years from 1913 to 1937 inclusive. The figures include the gold holdings of governments and central banks. (The increase in the gold holdings of some of the European banks during the World War period resulted from drawing money out of the channels of circulation into the central banks.)

It will be seen from the chart that the proportion of the total gold supply held by the United States continued to expand for the first five years after the war, but that from 1924 to 1928 there was a considerable reduction. The export of gold from the United States was stimulated by means of cooperation between the Federal Reserve system and the European central banks.[4]

As a result of improved fiscal policies, somewhat better trade conditions, and very extensive foreign credits, all Europe succeeded between 1924 and 1929 in restoring either the gold standard or the variation thereof known as the "gold exchange" standard. In most cases, the process involved cooperation between the banks of different countries in granting credits for achieving the return to a gold basis and in standing ready to extend additional credits as and when they might be required for the maintenance of exchange and currency stability.

V. BREAKDOWN OF THE EXCHANGES DURING DEPRESSION

The program of re-establishing stable international exchanges based on gold had scarcely been completed when the coming of the world depression brought a new series of economic maladjustments which profoundly affected international financial relations. In due course, the greater part of the world either abandoned the gold standard or introduced exchange controls which restricted the free movement of gold in meeting international obligations.

[4] See discussion in chap. XXIV.

The breakdown of the international credit system and the disintegration of the gold standard began in Europe in 1931. These difficulties followed the financial collapse of Central Europe in May 1931 and were intensified by the enormous volume of short-term international credits then outstanding. The Hoover moratorium of June suspended reparation and war debt payments for a period of one year. The foreign short-term creditors of Germany and Austria agreed to "stand still" agreements with their debtors, under which withdrawals of foreign funds were either suspended or reduced to a minimum. Large new short-term credits were extended to Germany, Austria, and Hungary by the principal central banks, as well as by the Bank for International Settlements, which had been established as a means of facilitating reparation and other international debt payments. In addition, various means for controlling capital movements were introduced by some of the Central European countries themselves.

While these measures served to retard the process of financial disintegration in Central Europe, new strains soon developed elsewhere. The freezing of a huge volume of short-term funds in Central Europe inevitably led to apprehension over the safety of short-term funds in other quarters, and a mad scramble began for the repatriation of liquid funds while there was yet time. The most immediate, and by far the most serious, effect was the strain placed upon Great Britain, the second weak link in the short-term credit structure.

Great Britain was on the whole in a very strong creditor position. But her short-term obligations abroad exceeded her short-term claims against other countries. Her long-term investments could not quickly be converted into cash, and at the same time a large part of her short-term claims had become unrealizable because of the situation in Central Europe. Meanwhile, however, Britain's own short-term obligations to foreigners were payable on *demand*.

Within a short time the run on the relatively slender gold reserves of the Bank of England precipitated a foreign exchange and monetary crisis. In an attempt to meet the strain and prevent a collapse of the financial and monetary structure, the Bank and the British Treasury contracted loans in the United States and France during the late summer of 1931 to the amount of 650 million dollars. But even these resources were insufficient to meet the double drain occasioned by the simultaneous withdrawal of foreign funds and the flight of British capital which followed the revelation of a critical budget situation. On September 21 the British government took the momentous step of abandoning the gold standard.

In October the strain was transferred to the United States. As in the case of Great Britain, the long-term debts due the United States were of no immediate use and the short-term claims were largely frozen. Thanks to its enormous accumulations of gold, the United States was able to stand the strain.

Great Britain's abandonment of the gold standard resulted in a wholesale breakdown of the international monetary system. The British act of September 1931 was a signal for similar action on the part of a large number of other countries. As soon as the gold standard system began to crumble, governmental control of foreign exchange transactions also began to be widely introduced. Some countries used exchange control in conjunction with the abandonment of gold for the purpose of regulating fluctuations in foreign exchange rates; others employed it to prevent depreciation of their currencies, thus insuring a nominal maintenance of the gold standard. In either case, these artificial measures represented essentially an abandonment of the gold standard.

The rapidity with which the international gold standard system disintegrated is shown in the tabular exhibit on the following page. The varying degrees of exchange depreciation which occurred and the effects upon exchange ratios between leading countries are revealed in the diagram on page 79.

The disintegration of the gold standard exerted a profound influence upon trade and tariff policies. The struggle to maintain financial solvency, the collapse of international credit, and the sudden alteration in the terms of competition resulting from the depreciation of currencies, led to utter confusion in the field of commercial policy. The following enumeration of some of the methods adopted during this period gives a graphic picture of the trade war that followed the breakdown of the gold standard.

In the sixteen months after September 1, 1931, general tariff increases had been imposed in twenty-three countries, in three of them twice during the period—with only one case of a general tariff reduction. Customs duties had been increased on individual items or groups of commodities by fifty countries, in most cases by a succession of enactments which, in several countries, numbered over twenty tariff changes in the sixteen months. Import quotas, prohibitions, licensing systems and similar quantitative restrictions, with even more frequent changes in several important cases, had been imposed by thirty-two countries. Import monopolies, for the most part of grains, were in existence in twelve countries; milling or mixing regulations in sixteen others. Export premiums were being paid in nine, while export duties or prohibitions had been imposed in seventeen.

This bare list is utterly inadequate to portray the harassing complexity of the emergency restrictions that were superimposed upon an already fettered world trade after the period of exchange instability was inaugurated by the abandonment of the gold standard by the United Kingdom in September1931. By the middle of 1932, it was obvious that the international trading mechanism was in real danger of being smashed as completely as the international monetary system had been.[5]

DISINTEGRATION OF THE GOLD STANDARD SYSTEM
I. Countries Which Abandoned the Gold Standard

Prior to 1931	Jan.–Aug. 1931	Sept.–Dec. 1931	Jan.–June 1932	July–Dec. 1932	Year 1933
Argentine Australia	Mexico	Bolivia Canada Colombia Denmark Egypt Finland India Ireland Japan Malaya Norway Palestine Portugal Salvador Sweden United Kingdom	Chile Ecuador Greece Peru Siam	South Africa	Austria Estonia United States

II. Countries Which Introduced Exchange Control

Brazil Chile Germany Hungary Spain	Argentine Austria Bolivia Bulgaria Colombia Czechoslovakia Denmark Estonia Greece Latvia Nicaragua Uruguay Yugoslavia	Costa Rica Ecuador Rumania	Japan Paraguay	United States	

[5] League of Nations, *World Economic Survey*, 1932–1933, pp. 16–17.

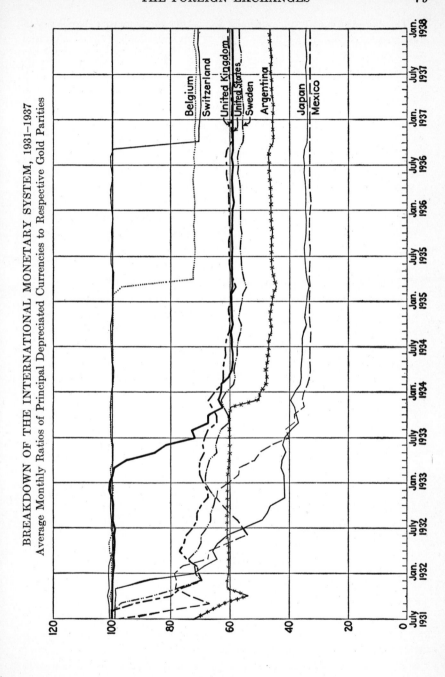

BREAKDOWN OF THE INTERNATIONAL MONETARY SYSTEM, 1931–1937
Average Monthly Ratios of Principal Depreciated Currencies to Respective Gold Parities

In due course many countries, especially those of South America, defaulted outright on international indebtedness, while others adopted novel devices for relieving the strain of foreign payments. Various countries declared "transfer moratoria," under the terms of which annual payments to foreign creditors were to be made in domestic currency to a designated institution within the country, but would not be subject to conversion into foreign currencies except under certain prescribed conditions. In many cases, even current payments on account of commercial transactions were "blocked" or suspended, and a considerable part of international trade thus came to represent merely forced loans by exporters in one country to importers in another.

Finally, out of all these difficulties grew the system of clearing arrangements, under the operation of which a substantial portion of international trade was reduced to barter terms. Since a clearing arrangement could be operated successfully only between two countries, the use of such arrangements naturally tended to bring about a direct trade balance between each pair of countries. The growth of this bilateral balancing process greatly reduced the scope of roundabout trading operations, diverted commerce from its accustomed channels of economic advantage, robbed the trade process of much of its necessary flexibility, and served to intensify the vicious interaction between trade shrinkage and financial and monetary disintegration.

The ultimate consequence of this series of national measures—the suspension of gold payments, exchange controls, increased tariffs, import quotas, monopolies, licensing systems, each of which was introduced with a view to maintaining the stability of a particular country—was to produce profound instability in the international economic system as a whole. However unavoidable or inescapable some of these policies may have been, once the breakdown of the international monetary system had begun, the net result was greatly to reduce production, increase unemployment, and impoverish the people of the world.

VI. RECENT TRENDS AND CURRENT PROBLEMS

The breakdown of the World Economic and Monetary Conference resulted in an interesting grouping of nations with respect to currency policies and relations. The British Empire, together with the Scandinavian countries, which had established a close relationship between their currencies following the abandonment of gold by Great Britain, strengthened the arrangement, and Japan adopted a policy of maintaining her currency in a condition of stability with respect to the pound sterling. This group of countries came to be known as the Sterlingarea, with all the countries of the group tying their currencies, so to speak, to the pound sterling. Six countries—France, Belgium, Italy, Holland, Switzerland, and Poland—constituted what was known as the Gold Bloc. The United States, Germany, and some other countries, including those of South America, followed more or less independent policies with respect to currency and exchange control.

1. *Exchange Stabilization.*—At the end of January 1934, as we have already seen, the United States established a fixed price for gold and removed virtually all restrictions on the export of gold. Two billion dollars of the profits derived from the devaluation of the dollar were set aside as an exchange stabilization fund with which the Treasury might buy or sell foreign exchange with a view to maintaining the stability of the dollar. While no information has been published with respect to the administration of the stabilization fund, it is apparent that the exigencies of the foreign exchange situation have not been such as to require its extensive use in stabilization operations.

Such a stabilization fund was already in existence in Great Britain, and a number of other countries subsequently established similar funds. As a result of these developments the period of violent exchange fluctuations was succeeded in the countries which abandoned the gold standard by a period of comparatively stable exchange relations.

The nations which maintained their former gold parities after the greater part of the world had undergone depreciation found themselves handicapped in international trade relations; and the pressure soon led to modification of their currency policies. Belgium abandoned gold payments and substantially reduced the weight of her currency unit. Two years later, however, Belgium re-established a full gold standard, on the basis of the smaller currency unit. Italy and Poland established systems of exchange control at the end of 1935. France abandoned the gold standard in September 1936, necessitating a similar action on the part of Holland and Switzerland. At the same time, Italy devalued her currency. The currencies of Italy, Poland, and Switzerland were controlled within narrow limits; those of France and Holland, were not "pegged," but were permitted to "float" in accordance with the variations in the supply of and demand for bills in the market— although their exchange values are regulated by means of stabilization funds similar to those of the United States and Great Britain. In April 1938, however, after a severe decline the franc was again devalued (see chart on page 72), with the approval and support of Great Britain and the United States.

In concluding this discussion a word must be said with respect to the prospect of future changes in the international exchange rate of the dollar. One of the purposes of the original devaluation was to improve the position of the United States in international trade competition. It is now abundantly clear that a further devaluation of the dollar could not bring even temporary gains in this direction—for the simple reason that a further change in the dollar would be immediately offset by corresponding changes in the value of the currencies of the Sterlingarea and no doubt of others as well. Conversely, changes in the currencies of other countries could be immediately matched by similar modifications of the dollar. In other words, it would no longer be possible for any country to gain from competitive devaluation. The destructive effects of competitive devaluation upon international trade as a whole are now generally recognized; and the treasuries of the world are prepared to prevent such disorganization in the future.

It is not to be inferred from the foregoing, however, that there is no possibility of further modifications in the exchange value of the dollar. It is by no means impossible that the dollar might decline as a result of large issues of irredeemable paper currency, the breakdown of the Government's fiscal system, or a serious derangement of general financial and economic conditions.

2. *The Future Distribution of Gold.*—In the years which have elapsed since 1933 the maldistribution of the world's gold supply has been greatly accentuated (see chart page 74). In percentage terms the proportion held by the United States has been enormously increased. A portion of the increase in gold dollars resulted automatically from the devaluation of the dollar unit; but there has also been an enormous inflow of gold to the United States in recent years—the net imports amounting to $4,441,106,000 in the three years 1935 to 1937. These extraordinary imports were largely attributable to a "flight of capital" occasioned by unsettled political and economic conditions in other countries. With the coming of a new American depression this movement ceased, at least temporarily.

Other countries showing notable increases in gold supply are Great Britain and Russia: the former because of relatively stable conditions, attractive to foreign funds; the latter on account of a marked increase in gold production. Countries showing significant reductions in gold holdings include Germany, France, Italy, Japan, and Australia. It has been estimated that some 10 billion dollars of the present gold holdings of the relatively stable countries represent international balances seeking investment or safety. To protect themselves against sudden shifts in international funds the Central Banks in these countries have impounded or "sterilized" a large part of this excess gold, by means of higher reserve requirements, stabilization funds, and "inactive gold funds," or through a failure to revalue gold reserves in proportion to the reduction in the currency unit. In the United States, for example, almost 6 billion dollars of gold in one form or another has been put aside to meet possible withdrawals of foreign funds, without disturbance to our credit structure, while Great Britain could lose 2.5 billions in gold without undermining her credit foundations.[6]

The distribution of the world supply of gold now bears little relation to the monetary requirements of the various countries. Some countries, as we have seen, have a vast excess—though the impounding process to which reference has just been made tends to nullify the possibility of so-called credit inflation. Were the international gold standard to be re-established, countries having a deficiency for reserve purposes would have to secure substantial loans from the countries having a surplus of gold. A return to a normal functioning of the international gold standard and the international exchanges is evidently beset with difficulties. It can be accomplished only by means of international agreements along the lines contemplated by the ill-fated World Economic and Monetary Conference of 1933.

[6] For discussion of the sterilization of gold in the United States see chap. XXIV, sec. IV, 3.

CHAPTER VII

GOVERNMENT FINANCE AND MONETARY STABILITY

In previous chapters attention has been called to currency instability arising from defective coinage and from the operation of the bimetallic system. The primary source of monetary disorganization, however, is found in the exigencies of government finance. The historic illustrations of extreme currency depreciation and price inflation have nearly always been associated with the breakdown of the fiscal system. When revenues from taxation or from loans have been insufficient to meet unavoidable obligations, governments have always resorted, in one way or another, to the creation or manufacture of currency with which to cover the deficiency.

I. METHODS OF "MANUFACTURING" MONEY

Various means of creating money have been utilized by distressed governments. In the Middle Ages, when currency consisted chiefly of metallic coins, it was a common practice for the king's treasurer to sweat or clip coins passing through his hands, thereby acquiring a profit, which was the equivalent of an increase in taxes. But since the resulting lack of uniformity in coins disorganized the currency system it was found advisable to recoin the entire volume of currency, replacing existing coins by new units of value containing a larger percentage of base metal. The difference, or seigniorage, was then coined and used in meeting government obligations.

After the development of paper money the process of diluting the currency became simpler, for it was necessary merely to print government promissory notes and pass them out in payment of current obligations. This method was employed, for example, by the Continental Congress of the American Revolution, by the Confederate States during the Civil War, and also to some extent by the United States Government during the same struggle. It will be seen that this process was not only less costly but also much quicker than that of tampering with the metallic money. However, it was for the same reason capable of much greater abuse.

With the evolution of banking and credit currency, more refined methods of procuring an increase in fiscal resources were devised.

84

Instead of issuing their own promissory notes in the direct payment of obligations, treasuries found it convenient to borrow the required funds from banks, with the latter assuming the role of issuing agents. The process involves giving the banks interest-bearing obligations of the government payable at future dates in exchange for non-interest-bearing bank notes payable on demand. These demand obligations may assume the form of either bank notes or checking accounts. Sometimes these government notes are sold on a straight business basis to private banking institutions and sometimes they are sold to government-controlled central banks. During the World War both of these alternatives were extensively employed.

It will be seen that when government obligations are sold in private financial markets, there is an independent check on the credit position of the government—though even here considerations of patriotism or public necessity may render such a check more nominal than real. On the other hand, when the government exercises its control over a central bank in order to borrow from it, there is no external judgment. To put the matter another way, the government is merely issuing its notes through a subsidiary agency. It has the practical advantage, however, that an appearance of independence is maintained.

It should not be inferred from the foregoing comment that there is never any valid excuse for the policy pursued by government treasuries. In the Middle Ages taxation machinery was not only inadequate, but there was no large supply of liquid funds available; hence debasing the currency was the only practical means of procuring money with which to "defend the realm from foreign invaders." In the case of the French and American revolutionary governments there was also justification for the resort to paper money. Taxation was slow and wholly insufficient; and well-established bond markets and investment banking institutions had not yet been developed. There was less excuse, it is true, during the Civil War, as far as the North was concerned. But it needs to be borne in mind that even at that time investment banking machinery was poorly organized, and it is easy to understand why, under the circumstances, there should have been a partial resort to the use of irredeemable paper currency.

II. THE LESSONS OF EXPERIENCE

The results of the extensive use of paper currency have always been disastrous. The historian Finlay tells us that the depreciation in the value of the circulating medium during the fifty years between the reign of Caracalla and the death of Gallienus annihilated a great part of the trading capital in the Roman Empire, and rendered it impossible to carry on commercial transactions not only with foreign countries but even with distant provinces.

A second illustration may be taken from the experience of France during the period of the French Revolution. Paper currency had been issued in great quantities in the hope of providing the liquid capital necessary for economic recovery from the ravages of war. Being irredeemable in specie, it fluctuated widely in value and eventually became utterly worthless.

What the bigotry of Louis XIV, and the shiftlessness of Louis XV, could not do in nearly a century was accomplished by this tampering with the currency in a few months. Everything that tariffs and custom-houses could do was done. Still the great manufactories of Normandy were closed; those of the rest of the kingdom speedily followed, and vast numbers of workmen in all parts of the country were thrown out of employment. . . . In the spring of 1791 no one knew whether a piece of paper money, representing 100 francs, would, a month later, have a purchasing power of 100 francs or 90 francs, or 80, or 60. The result was that capitalists declined to embark their means in business. Enterprise received a mortal blow. Demand for labor was still further diminished. The business of France dwindled into a mere living from hand to mouth. This state of things, too, while it bore heavily against the interests of the moneyed classes, was still more ruinous to those in more moderate, and most of all to those in straitened circumstances. With the masses of the people the purchase of every article of supply became a speculation—a speculation in which the professional speculator had an immense advantage over the buyer. Says the most brilliant apologist for French Revolutionary statesmanship, "Commerce was dead; betting took its place."[1]

The effects of the depreciated paper of the Revolutionary War period upon the debtor and creditor classes have been vividly described by a writer of the time, as follows:

The aged who had retired from the scenes of active business to enjoy the fruits of their industry found their substance melting away to a mere pittance, insufficient for their support. The widow who lived comfortably on the bequests of a deceased husband experienced a frustration of all his well-meant tenderness. The laws of the country interposed, and compelled her to receive a shilling where a pound was her due. The blooming virgin who had grown up with an unquestionable title to a liberal patrimony was legally stripped of everything but her personal charms and virtues. The hapless orphan, instead of receiving from the hands of an executor a competency to set out in business, was obliged to give a final discharge on the payment of 6d. in the pound.[2]

[1] Andrew D. White, *Paper Money Inflation in France* (1876).
[2] David Ramsey, *History of the American Revolution* (1789).

The impossibility of controlling the value of the currency, and the demoralizing influence of depreciation are indicated in the following summary of our experience with paper currency during the Revolutionary War.

Congress resolved [January 11, 1776] that "whoever should refuse to receive in payment Continental bills, etc., should be deemed and treated as an enemy of his country, and be precluded from all trade and intercourse with the inhabitants. . . . " This ruinous principle was continued in practice for five successive years, and appeared in all shapes and forms, i.e., in legal tender acts, in limitations of prices, in awful and threatening declarations, in penal laws with dreadful and ruinous punishments . . . and all executed with a relentless severity by the highest authorities then in being, viz., by Congress, by assemblies and conventions of the states, by committees of inspection, and even by military force; and though men of all descriptions stood trembling before this monster of force, without daring to lift a hand against it during all this period, yet its unrestrained energy ever proved ineffectual to its purposes . . . ; at best its utmost effect was like that of water sprinkled on a blacksmith's forge, which indeed deadens the flame for a moment, but never fails to increase the heat and force of the internal fire. . . .

It has polluted the equity of our laws; turned them into engines of oppression and wrong; corrupted the justice of our public administration; destroyed the fortunes of thousands who had most confidence in it; and has gone far to destroy the morality of our people.[3]

The Confederate currency issued by the South as a means of financing the Civil War became utterly worthless. Even the modest issue by the United States Government of 400 million dollars of "greenbacks" was accompanied by a depreciation of over 60 per cent, at the maximum; and it was not until fourteen years after the war was over that this currency became redeemable in gold and hence no longer a disturbing factor in the financial system. The extent of the depreciation is indicated in the price chart on page 16.

In the fifty-year period preceding the World War an effort was made to separate fiscal from monetary functions. In the United States, for example, a fund of 150 million dollars was established as an "inviolable" reserve against outstanding government paper obligations. Moreover, under the National Banking System, established in 1863, the issuing of bank currency was vested in privately organized institutions, divorced from the exigencies of government finance and political control. Students of money and banking generally were of the view that society had finally learned an extremely costly lesson, namely, that it is absolutely essential to keep the fiscal and monetary

[3] Pelatiah Webster, *Strictures on Tender Acts* (1780).

functions of government separate. Fiscal operations, it was held, constitute one problem, while the maintenance of a stable standard of value and the manufacture of currency for the requirements of trade constitute other and wholly separate problems. This latter function was delegated to banking institutions as a means of avoiding the disasters resulting from unbridled government finance.

Then came the World War of 1914 to 1918. Nearly every belligerent nation, under the tremendous pressure of the war's financial requirements, again fell from grace. As the *kings* of the fifteenth century had done when the enemy was at the gates, the *people* of the twentieth century likewise debased the currency in order to get the indispensable revenues required. The methods, however, showed a still further refinement; for now, in the main, instead of mutilations of the metallic currency or the issuance of government promises to pay, we have bank notes issued by the central banks. The process has already been described.

The United States did not resort to the issue of irredeemable paper currency during the war; but there is little doubt that, if the struggle had continued for two or three more years, this country could not have avoided currency depreciation. Indeed, as it was, a substantial portion of the funds required was procured from bank credit expansion. The process involved the sale of government securities directly to the banks and also to individuals, who were encouraged to borrow from the banks the greater part of the means of payment.

After the World War many European countries continued to issue currency as a means of covering budget deficits. In consequence of the demoralization of internal fiscal conditions, and in many cases because of huge reparation payments to foreign countries, it was quite impossible to procure the necessary revenues either from taxation or from bond issues. A resort to the banks through the sale of short-time promises to pay thus appeared the only practical alternative to insolvency. In the end, however, the inflation process also usually brought insolvency.

The table on page 89 shows the changes in the note circulation of the German Reichsbank during the war and postwar periods up to the date when the so-called Rentenmark stabilization occurred.

As in previous cases of extreme currency depreciation, the effects upon business were utterly demoralizing. As the mark continued to fall in value, it became the height of unwisdom for any class of society to deposit money in banks or to invest in securities. The national motto of Germany was said to have become: "Save and you are lost; spend freely, speculate, or buy foreign currency, and you win." No class could, under the conditions prevailing, make provision for old age or effect savings for a rainy day.

GERMAN CURRENCY INFLATION 1913–1923[a]

Date	Note Circulation (Marks)	Equivalent of Note Circulation in U.S. Dollars	Gold Holdings (Marks)
Dec., 1913.......	2,593,000,000	$ 617,240,000	1,266,187,000
Dec., 1918.......	22,188,000,000	2,682,500,000	2,262,167,000
Dec., 1919.......	35,698,000,000	749,700,000	1,089,499,000
Dec., 1920.......	68,805,000,000	942,600,000	1,091,636,000
Dec., 1921.......	113,639,000,000	602,300,000	995,392,000
Dec., 1922.......	1,280,095,000,000	128,000,000	1,004,843,000
Jan. 6, 1923....	1,336,500,000,000	153,697,500	1,005,000,000
Feb. 7, 1923....	2,253,963,000,000	61,983,980	1,005,000,000
Mar. 7, 1923....	3,871,256,000,000	187,755,910	1,005,000,000
Apr. 7, 1923....	5,624,110,000,000	267,145,225	1,005,000,000
May 7, 1923....	6,723,070,000,000	183,203,657	913,909,000
June 7, 1923....	9,309,532,000,000	121,023,916	756,914,000
July 7, 1923....	20,241,750,000,000	91,087,875	707,000,000
Aug. 7, 1923....	62,326,659,000,000	19,944,530	596,351,000
Aug. 15, 1923....	116,402,515,000,000	41,904,905	516,122,000
Aug. 23, 1923....	273,906,373,000,000	62,998,465	512,122,000
Aug. 31, 1923....	663,200,000,000,000	69,636,000	510,486,000
Sept. 7, 1923....	1,182,039,000,000,000	35,461,170	490,000,000
Sept. 15, 1923....	3,183,681,000,000,000	30,244,969	490,000,000
Sept. 22, 1923....	8,627,730,000,000,000	50,040,834	470,000,000
Sept. 29, 1923....	28,228,815,000,000,000	138,321,193	444,000,000
Oct. 6, 1923....	46,933,600,000,000,000	51,626,960	443,000,000
Oct. 15, 1923....	123,349,786,603,000,000	30,837,446	443,000,000
Oct. 22, 1923....	524,330,557,246,000,000	11,797,437	467,000,000
Oct. 31, 1923....	2,496,822,908,936,000,000	14,980,937	467,000,000
Nov. 7, 1923....	19,153,087,468,804,000,000	7,661,234	467,000,000
Nov. 15, 1923....	92,844,720,742,927,000,000	23,211,180	467,000,000
Nov. 23, 1923....	223,927,315,083,796,000,000	44,785,463	467,000,000
Nov. 30, 1923....	400,267,640,291,750,000,000	60,040,146	467,000,000

[a] Data compiled from official reports.

Business men, however, sought to find a way out by using the earnings of industry in hiring labor to build additions to plant and equipment, instead of building up reserve and surplus investments and maintaining adequate bank balances. The result of this was to increase materially the fixed capital of business and industrial concerns, but also to wipe out almost completely the working or liquid capital. In this connection, it will be borne in mind that not only were no *additions* made to liquid working capital, but the *accumulated* surplus funds invested in securities, together with bank deposits, were rendered practically valueless. The process thus left Germany with a tremendous dearth of working capital; and the German economy has not even yet completely recovered from the economic and financial consequences of the widespread financial ruin that was wrought.

The social consequences have been portrayed by a German observer in the following poignant phraseology:

The depreciation of the mark created a country divided into three classes: one that suffers silently and goes under in decency; another that profiteers cynically and spends recklessly; and a third that writhes in desperation and wishes to destroy in blind fury whatever is left of a government and society that permit such conditions.

GERMAN SMALL CHANGE IN 1923

III. RECENT TRENDS IN THE UNITED STATES

As already indicated, the United States succeeded in going through the World War without currency depreciation. In the ensuing decade the government debt was substantially reduced and by 1929 nothing seemed more remote than the possibility that the stability of the monetary system might again be menaced by government fiscal instability. However, the results of the great depression of 1929–1933 and the policies pursued in the succeeding years quickly altered the situation.

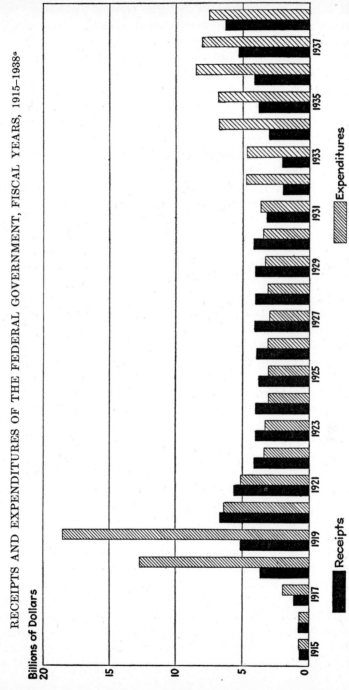

RECEIPTS AND EXPENDITURES OF THE FEDERAL GOVERNMENT, FISCAL YEARS, 1915–1938ᵃ

Billions of Dollars

Expenditures

Receipts

ᵃ Data from annual reports of the Secretary of the Treasury. The 1938 figures are preliminary. The receipts do not include profits from monetary deflation.

Two factors are responsible for the great deterioration in the Government's fiscal position in recent years. First, the contraction of revenues during the course of the depression, together with the added financial responsibilities imposed upon the Federal Government, naturally resulted in huge deficits. Second, some of the major recovery policies followed by the Roosevelt administration as a means of promoting recovery served to enlarge the deficits even in a time of business expansion. The theory underlying the Government's fiscal policy in relation to recovery was that an extensive outpouring of government money would facilitate the restoration of sound economic and financial conditions. It was believed, in a word, that after the so-called industrial pump was thoroughly primed the water would flow freely and adequately. A recovery of business activity would be generated and in due course the expansion in national income would readily permit a balancing of the budget—because, as the need for unemployment and other relief waned, government expenditures would automatically decline, and at the same time revenues from taxation would automatically increase. The pump-priming program would thus produce the means essential to the re-establishment of sound finance.

The outcome of this spending program from the fiscal point of view is revealed in the receipts and expenditures of the Federal Government and in the growth of the public debt. The diagram on page 91 shows the revenues derived from sources other than borrowing, and the expenditures for the fiscal years 1915 to 1938 inclusive. It will be seen that the deficits began in the fiscal year 1931 and that on the whole they have been larger in the recovery period than they were in the depression years 1930 to 1933.

The cumulative effects of these deficits upon the public debt are revealed in the diagram on page 93. In order to place recent history in perspective, we present the figures for the entire period since 1915, It will be observed that the public debt in 1938 was nearly two and a half times as great as it was in 1930, and approximately 50 per cent above the high point reached during the World War. Meanwhile the total national income, out of which taxes have to be paid, remains substantially below the level of pre-depression years. Meanwhile, also, state and local government tax requirements have greatly increased.

The government deficits have been covered by borrowing in the financial markets. The Government has not found it necessary to use the profits derived from the deflation of the currency to print paper money or to borrow directly from the Federal Reserve banks. The President was authorized by Congress to issue non-interest-bearing

Treasury notes (greenbacks)—though in an amount not to exceed three billion dollars.[4] It proved possible, however, to obtain all the money required, and at extraordinarily low rates of interest, by the ordinary process of selling bonds and short-term Treasury obligations.

AGGREGATE FEDERAL DEBT, FISCAL YEARS 1915–1938[a]

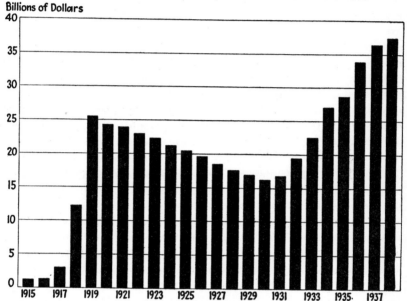

[a] Data from annual reports of the Secretary of the Treasury. The 1938 figure is preliminary.

Over half of these government issues have, however, been sold to commercial banking institutions rather than to individuals or savings institutions. Between December 31, 1930, when the deficits began to accumulate, and June 30, 1936, the member banks of the Reserve system absorbed 7,596 million dollars and the Federal Reserve banks 1,701 millions, out of a total of 16,270 million dollars.[5] When government obligations are sold to the commercial banks the Treasury receives a deposit account against which it draws for meeting its current obligations.

The low interest rates are attributable chiefly to two factors: the very large bank reserves resulting from the inflow of gold from abroad

[4] These notes could be issued only for the purpose of purchasing outstanding government securities or meeting maturities on government obligations.

[5] It is not possible to indicate with precision what proportion of the total purchases have been made from the money savings of individuals, what amount represented a shifting of assets, and how much originated in bank credit expansion.

(see pages 82, 83); and the dearth of ordinary investment outlets for the funds of individuals and financial institutions. This latter situation is in turn related to the effects of the government spending program on the capital and investment markets.

The monetary and fiscal policy of the Government may be compared to a two-edged sword. On the one side the outpouring of government funds undoubtedly served to stimulate business activity in the markets for consumers' goods. On the other side, the threat of financial instability, occasioned by monetary manipulation and the rapid growth of the public debt, militated against the making of long-term contracts and hence retarded the flotation of securities and the reconstruction of capital goods. In consequence, the recovery of business was incomplete and the restoration of the nation's productive capacity was seriously retarded. With relief expenditures continuing on a high plane and with national income remaining substantially below former levels, the budget continued to present a difficult problem.[6] Thus, after four years of recovery, the goal of an equilibrium between revenues and outlays, with a margin for debt reduction in preparation for a period of possible future strain, was still receding.

It was not until we were at the very threshold of a new depression in the summer of 1937 that the Government finally decided to make a vigorous effort to balance the budget, chiefly through the curtailment of unnecessary expenditures. Within a short time, however, it became apparent that the curtailment of revenues and the pressure for increased expenditures would make further progress toward fiscal equilibrium impossible—until such time as business might again recover. At the present time (mid-1938) the ultimate stability of government finance and in turn of the monetary system thus remains seriously in doubt. The deficit for the fiscal year 1938–1939 is officially estimated at about four billion dollars.

It should also be noted here that the fiscal position of nearly all the leading countries of the world has deteriorated in recent years. The financial burdens imposed upon governments in affording relief during the depression, in aiding recovery, or in carrying out new military programs have resulted in substantial increases in public indebtedness —without a like increase in the tax-paying capacity of the nation. The following table shows the growth of public debts in various countries from 1932 to 1937. Owing to the prevailing tendency among governments to conceal, or at least to delay showing, the full extent of the increase in public indebtedness, these figures in many cases

[6] For a fuller discussion, see *The Recovery Problem in the United States*, the Brookings Institution, 1937.

materially understate the extent to which government finance has deteriorated.

INTERNAL PUBLIC DEBTS, 1934–1938[a]

(In Millions of the Standard Monetary Units of the Respective Countries)

Country	1933	1934	1935	1936	1937	1938
United States....	22,539	27,053	28,701	33,545	36,427	37,604[b]
Japan...........	5,984	7,268	8,210	8,976	9,702	.....
Germany........	9,290	10,347	10,753[c]	12,761	14,684	16,274
France.........	303,537	324,014[c]	341,437	337,761	No	......
Italy...........	97,215	102,622	107,078[d]	107,078	......	......
Hungary........	327	357	432	477[c]	485	......
Poland.........	759	1,346	1,475	1,739	2,130	......
United Kingdom.	6,799	6,994	6,866	6,865[c]	6,877	7,114
Australia........	607	629	650	666	675	......
Sweden.........	2,359	2,349	2,487	2,387[c]	2,237	2,411[e]
Norway.........	827	810	837	841	872	......

[a] *Statistical Yearbook of the League of Nations*, 1937–1938. [b] Preliminary. [c] Revised. [d] September. [e] February.

IV. THE INFLATION ISSUE

The fiscal trends which we have been considering have led many observers to conclude that numerous countries, including the United States, are faced with an inevitable financial breakdown and ensuing inflation of prices. Without expressing a judgment as to the probable outcome of current trends, it may be possible to clarify the inflation issue by pointing out that discussions of this problem relate to three different types of price advances. That is to say, an inflation of prices may be rooted in different conditions or developments.

One type of inflation is that which arises directly from monetary policies, involving a reduction in the weight of the currency unit. A second type of inflation is that accompanying an expansion of bank credit, superinduced by an abundance of loanable funds offered at low rates of interest. The third type is that which we have been discussing in this chapter. It originates in the disintegration of government finance and leads to the issue of irredeemable paper money and depreciation of the foreign exchanges. Current discussions involve, and more or less confuse, all three types.

A further reduction in the weight of the dollar is possible, but does not appear probable—at least until there is a breakdown of government credit. There are two reasons which lead to this conclusion: first, such a policy would work at direct cross-purposes with the

Government's trade agreement program; and, second, it would not now be an effective means of raising American prices relatively to those of other countries. (See discussion on pages 77–80.)

Bank credit, or commercial inflation, is not likely to occur as an independent phenomenon because of other conditions affecting the business situation. Throughout the course of the recovery movement we have had a plethora of gold and bank credit resources, and interest rates have been unprecedentedly low; but credit inflation has not resulted. The explanation is that there has been a lack of convincing evidence that such funds could be put to profitable employment.[7]

Inflation resulting from the gradual disintegration of government finances is the type that is most likely to develop. This is, unhappily, the kind of inflation which once under way is the most difficult to control and the most devastating in its consequences. The restoration of fiscal equilibrium is thus a problem of paramount importance.

It should be pointed out in this connection, however, that the process of fiscal and financial disintegration may proceed slowly. For example, since 1931 the Japanese treasury has been covering huge deficits by borrowing directly from the Bank of Japan—the process which Germany followed to disaster in the war and early post-war years. Yet at the end of seven years the Japanese financial system had not disintegrated—though it is to be noted that commodity prices have risen sharply since 1937. Thanks to a fair degree of equilibrium in international trade and service operations, and more recently to exchange control, it was possible to maintain relatively stable exchange rates. It would thus appear that in the absence of exchange demoralization the inflationary process does not develop rapidly. It does not follow, however, that a disintegration of the financial system can ultimately be escaped.

To guard against the conclusion that fiscal inflation necessarily leads to irremediable disaster, it must be noted that sometimes governments have been able, by heroic measures, to halt a serious inflationary movement before it resulted in the disintegration of the entire economic system. For example, the French Government in 1926 checked a disastrous fall in the franc by a financial program which involved sharp increases in taxes, already extremely onerous, and the stabilization of the franc at a level some 25 per cent lower than the formerly prevailing rate. Even so the consequences to both taxpayers and owners of fixed income securities were serious; and there was left a legacy of

---

[7] For further discussion of the problem of credit inflation, see chap. XXIV, sec. III, 3; for discussion of the relation of money and credit to prices, see chap. XXIX.

economic distress and discontent which has remained to this day a potent source of social and political instability.

V. INTERRELATIONS IN THE FINANCIAL SYSTEM

The analyses in this and the two preceding chapters have revealed how closely the various parts of the complex financial system are interrelated. A disorganization, whether in currency and banking, the foreign exchanges, or public finance, may result in general financial and economic instability. Whenever a country reduces the weight of its monetary unit, issues irredeemable paper money, or fails to maintain convertibility of bank currency into the standard money, the ratio at which its money will be exchanged for that of other countries declines, and international trade relations are disorganized. A breakdown of government finance also serves to depreciate international exchange rates, because it results in, or threatens, the abandonment of the existing monetary standard, and thereby leads to a flight of capital. A disorganization of the exchanges in turn has its repercussions upon monetary values, trade relations, and fiscal stability. Exchange depreciation may be produced either by an unbalanced state of international trade and financial operations or by an unbalanced domestic budget. If a nation's supply of bills of exchange available from export and service operations is insufficient to cover payments for necessary imports and other foreign obligations, the exchange will tend to fall—although it may be supported for a time by credit operations.

Sometimes exchange depreciation is due primarily to the one factor, sometimes primarily to the other, and sometimes to a combination of the two. For example, during the period of rapid depreciation of the German mark there was a huge deficit alike in the international balance of payments and in the domestic budget. German paper money was accordingly issued for the purpose of meeting foreign obligations as well as domestic operating expenses. In connection with the decline of the franc, however, it is interesting to note that while there was continuously a large budget deficit, the foreign trade and service accounts usually showed a considerable surplus; but this was more than counterbalanced by the flight of capital. Some writers hold that the difficulties start with currency inflation, while others contend that it is the depreciation of the exchanges caused by an unfavorable balance of payments with which the troubles begin. The truth of the matter appears to be that all these various parts of the financial and economic mechanism are interacting in their operation.

Similarly, the analysis has disclosed the international character of the financial structure. A breakdown of the financial system of any important country has serious repercussions upon international trade and financial relations. Thus the German, Austrian, and Hungarian financial debacles of the early post-war years so paralyzed international trade as to render it imperative for other countries to co-operate in the extension of credits for the re-establishment of the shattered financial structures of these distressed nations. Because of the vast amount of liquid funds available for investment—and speculation—changing financial and economic conditions in the various countries lead to quick migration of capital from one country to another and back again—movements which are disturbing alike to the exchanges and to internal financial conditions in the countries concerned. Thus in 1925 and 1926 the difficult fiscal situation of France resulted in large exports of French funds; then with the restoration of confidence accompanying fiscal reforms under a unified government, there was a vast inflow of funds to France, consisting of returning French capital, and also foreign funds. The most striking evidence of the interrelations between the financial systems of the various countries is, of course, that afforded by the events of the world depression to which reference has been made.

In conclusion, a great shift in public opinion and in national policies during the course of recent years should be noted. Because of the economic disturbances produced by the breakdown of the international monetary and credit structure in 1931–1933, many people believed that *internationalism* was the source of difficulty, and that hence the remedy was to be found in a return to economic *nationalism.* The failure of nationalistic policies to bring full economic recovery to the world has, however, already set the tide moving again in the direction of cooperation in international financial organization.

CHAPTER VIII
THE NATURE AND FUNCTIONS OF CREDIT

With this chapter we pass from a study of the nature and functions of money to a consideration of the part that credit plays in the general economic organization. The great importance of the institution which we loosely call "credit" finds emphasis in such common expressions as: "modern industrial society is a credit society"; "credit is the heart and core of the industrial system"; and "credit is the life-blood of commerce and industry." What is the nature of this striking phenomenon? In what does its great service consist, and why, precisely, does it occupy so prominent a position in the economic system of today?

It is the purpose of the present chapter to consider the nature of credit operations, to study the numerous types or classes of credit that exist today, to indicate the significance of the institution of credit from the point of view of economic organization, and to reveal some of the types of credit institutions that have evolved to meet the needs of a capitalistic society.

I. THE NATURE OF CREDIT

In simple business parlance, credit involves merely getting something now and paying for it later. It is synonymous with borrowing, the essential element in credit operations always being the postponement of payment for something that has been received. It is important to bear in mind that the thing loaned (on credit) may be either commodities or funds. Goods sold on time involve credit; indeed, we usually say that they are sold "on credit." Such merchandise may be paid for by a return of goods in kind; though under modern conditions the obligation is usually settled by money payments. Loans of money by a bank or other financial institution, or by one individual to another, similarly involve a future payment, the credit consisting in allowing the individual to have the use of funds which he is to return at a later time.

Practically all credit operations are expressed in terms of the pecuniary unit. It may also be observed that it is in connection with credit, or borrowing operations, that the standard for deferred payments, discussed in chapter II, finds its function in industrial society.

99

While credit is thus closely associated with the monetary system, it should not be confused with money, and the reader should be especially careful to distinguish between credit and credit instruments, which will be discussed in chapter IX. Credit is a lending operation, involving a postponed payment; credit instruments, on the other hand, are the written evidences of antecedent credit operations, that is, of agreements to pay at some future date. As will be seen in the following chapter, it is the credit instruments, not credit, that serve as important media of exchange.

II. THE VARIOUS KINDS OF CREDIT

From the point of view of the institutions or individuals utilizing credit, the various types or kinds of credit operations that exist in the modern world have been classified as follows: public credit; capital credit; mercantile credit; individual or personal credit; and banking credit.

By *public* credit is meant the borrowing operations of governments, whether national, state, or local. In a broad way it is in contrast to *private* credit of all kinds. Public credit may be used either for long- or for short-term financial requirements.

By *capital* credit, or *industrial* credit, to employ another term, is meant the credit used by manufacturing and producing corporations in procuring the necessary permanent capital required for their operations. The corporation agrees to return to the purchaser of its bonds at some future date the equivalent of the funds borrowed, with interest. In a sense the purchaser of stocks also loans funds to the corporation with the understanding that he is to receive dividends in the future (if earned) and ultimately, if the business is liquidated, his share of the capital. It is the usual practice to exclude from capital credit the investments that are made by individuals in a business largely their own, such as a partnership.

Mercantile credit is the term applied to the borrowing operations of jobbers, wholesalers, commission merchants, and retailers, in connection with the movement of goods from first producer to ultimate consumer. Another term sometimes used synonymously with mercantile credit is commercial credit. The distinction between commercial and other forms of credit is made clear in the section which follows.

Individual or personal credit obviously takes its name from the fact that it is connected with individuals rather than with public or private corporations. Individuals borrow money from acquaintances and from financial institutions for a wide variety of purposes; and, more important, they purchase consumptive goods on time from retail stores. In cities the goods thus borrowed are usually paid for at the end of each month, except in cases where they are sold on the installment plan. But in the rural communities the settlements are commonly made at longer intervals, usually at crop-selling times.

Banking credit relates to the process by means of which banking institutions are enabled to attract the funds of depositors and to make loans and create obligations, payable on demand, which are not backed by a dollar-for-dollar cash reserve. This process will be discussed fully in subsequent chapters.

Credit may also be classified according to the nature of the use to which the funds borrowed are devoted. Here three distinct types of credit operations may be distinguished, namely, investment, commercial, and consumptive credit. The problem of repayment, as we shall see, is essentially different in the three classes.

Investment credit is that which is used in connection with the development of business enterprises, such as railroads, factories, workshops, stores, farms, mines, etc. The funds borrowed are used mainly for the creation of "fixed" or durable forms of capital goods; hence the term "fixed capital." In consequence of the productivity of capital goods, the borrower plans to pay the principal of the loan out of the accumulated earnings of the business over a period of years; and accordingly, the credit instruments employed usually call for payments a good many years later.

Commercial credit is that employed in financing the production, manufacture, and marketing of goods—in furnishing working capital. In contrast with the case of investment credit, the borrower is here usually in a position to repay his loan in a very short period of time. A concrete case will serve to illustrate the difference. Mr. X, a wholesaler, borrows, let us say, $10,000 from the bank and purchases a stock of goods with the money. In the course of two months he sells these goods for $12,000, or at a gross profit of 20 per cent, the goods themselves being the direct means of liquidating the loan. Similarly, the manufacturer, Mr. Y, borrows $20,000 with which to operate his plant and equipment. In the course of three months, say, he has produced and sold $25,000 worth of goods, thus being enabled to repay his loan directly from the uses to which the borrowed funds were put.

Consumptive credit involves the granting of loans or the selling of goods on time to individuals who use the money or the goods received for the purpose of satisfying consumptive wants. If the obligations thus created are met at maturity, it will not be because the funds, or property, borrowed were devoted to productive uses, but because the borrower has other sources of income. Such credit, therefore, usually involves somewhat greater risk of not being paid at maturity, than does either investment or commercial credit.[1]

III. THE BASIS OF CREDIT

There has been much discussion, participated in by both economists and practical credit men, concerning the essential basis of a credit or borrowing operation. Some writers on the subject have stoutly insisted that confidence is the basis of all grants of credits; that if one did not have confidence that the borrower would repay a loan one would never think of making the loan, save on grounds of friendship or philanthropy. Others have held that property, rather than confidence, is the basis of all genuine credit transactions. Some insist that character is the essential factor; while still other writers have indulged a propensity for alliteration by stating that the bases of credit are character, capital, and capacity; or the man and the means; or reliability and resources.

Without attempting to enter into a discussion of the reasons for these different statements of the basis of credit, we present a tabular exhibit of matters commonly investigated by competent credit men, which indicates that while confidence must exist before a loan will be granted, such confidence has its basis in a knowledge both of the borrower's financial standing and ability and of his personal integrity. Factors commonly investigated may be grouped in two general classes, as follows:

PERTAINING TO THE MAN	PERTAINING TO THE BUSINESS
a) Record for honest dealing	a) Ratio of quick assets to current liabilities
b) Personal attributes	b) Amount of capital invested and property owned
1. Gambling or drinking tendencies	c) Earnings of the business
2. Political and other "outside" activities	d) Character and turnover of stock
3. Style of living, including wife's ambitions	e) Location of business
c) Ability	f) Character of the business organization
1. Common sense and shrewdness	g) Insurance carried
2. Education and training	h) Nature and intensity of the competition
3. Age and general experience	
4. Success already attained	

This list of factors is by no means inclusive; it is designed merely to suggest the character of the investigation that must be made if credit is to be conservatively extended. It will be noted, also, that the points raised in the parallel columns are not entirely unrelated. A

[1] For further consideration of consumptive credit see chap. XIX.

man of excellent business ability, for instance, would be practically certain to have a proper ratio of quick assets to current liabilities, substantial earnings, etc.; and, on the other hand, if it were found that a business was poorly equipped and managed, there would be a definite reflection upon the manager's business capacity. Investigation, both of the man and of the business, usually serves, however, to furnish a more adequate basis for a sound judgment than investigation of either one alone.

One may conclude from this brief analysis that before deciding to extend credit one should have confidence, first, in the ability of the borrower to pay as promised, and, second, in his willingness and intention to pay. One is a matter of property and business ability; the other a question of honesty and business integrity. The basis of credit may be diagrammatically presented as follows:

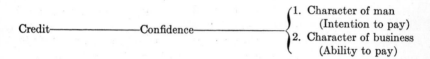

Credit————————Confidence———————— {
1. Character of man
  (Intention to pay)
2. Character of business
  (Ability to pay)

IV. ECONOMIC SIGNIFICANCE OF CREDIT

While the economic significance of the credit system cannot be adequately discussed in the present chapter, a few of the ways in which credit is of assistance in the conduct of modern affairs and some of its broader social aspects may, however, be suggested.

Credit enables governments to obtain possession of funds with which to meet pressing emergencies, when no other means are available. It also enables individuals to surmount temporary difficulties or embarrassments. For example, it makes possible the purchase of goods for consumptive requirements pending the receipt of income; it permits the purchase of a home before all of the purchase money is in hand; and it makes possible the acquisition of an education on borrowed funds.

Credit makes it possible for honest and capable men without capital to secure the funds required for the conduct of modern industry. Similarly, it enables people with funds in excess of their immediate needs to lend the surplus to capable men of affairs for utilization in productive activities. This process of lending funds tends to shift "capital" from the hands of those who do not have the desire or the ability to make use of it to those who are both willing and able to assume the risks of business enterprise. The result is a more effective utilization of the national resources.

The ability to borrow makes it possible for the business manager to adjust the volume of his capital to the varying requirements of business. When the demand for his products is very large at certain seasons and in certain years of extraordinary business activity, he may enlarge the volume of output by borrowing additional working capital, while in dull seasons and years he may reduce the volume of capital employed.

With reference to the broader aspects and relations of the credit system, it may be pointed out that its development has depended upon the growth of three things: first, a sense of business morality, or what may amount to the same thing, a recognition of the fact that honesty is the best policy; second, a relatively stable monetary standard for deferred payments; and third, a legal system designed to safeguard the rights of individuals and to enforce a prompt fulfillment of contracts. The evolution of these three supports of the credit system has been one of the most significant features of the transformation from medieval to modern industrial society. All of these developments have been very closely interrelated; moreover, each has contributed to, and each has been accelerated by, the growth of the credit system.

The institution of credit has made possible the growth of large-scale business enterprise and, in turn, the specialized industrial society of the present time; for the moment industry passed beyond the handicraft stage, each enterprise usually required a volume of capital greater than could be furnished by the proprietors. Accordingly, borrowing became an indispensable handmaiden of business. The growth of the capitalistic (profit-making) system of industry has been marked by an ever enlarging scale of business enterprise, instituted, under the competitive régime of the eighteenth and nineteenth centuries, in the expectation of obtaining greater profits through enlarged output and decreased costs of production.

The various stages in the transformation from the medieval non-profit-making household economy to the twentieth-century capitalistic industrial system are outlined in chapter X. It need merely be noted here that the steadily expanding scale of both industrial and commercial undertakings is dependent upon ever enlarging aggregations of capital, the assembling of which has been made possible only by a great extension of the credit system, whereby funds may be raised for a given enterprise from a veritable multitude of individual investors. Small accumulations of capital, which cannot be effectively utilized by their owners, are thus joined with other accumulations and placed under the control and management of individuals who are able to make the most effective use of capital resources.

Since nearly every business enterprise is nowadays in greater or lesser degree dependent on the use of borrowed funds, it is not difficult to understand why writers should stress the importance of credit in the extravagant terms noted in the introductory paragraph of this chapter. Credit is in truth a pervasive, fundamental institution—one that is indispensable to the conduct of a capitalistic industrial system.

CHAPTER IX

CREDIT INSTRUMENTS

The borrowing or credit operations of modern society are evidenced by written documents, drawn up in legal form, and known as credit instruments. As has already been noted, the term "credit" is often loosely employed in such a way as to give the impression that credit is a form of currency. It is not credit, however, that is used as currency; it is rather the instruments which are the written evidences of antecedent credit operations that serve as media of exchange. In the present chapter we shall consider the various types of credit instruments which are employed in modern credit operations and discuss the development of certain legal principles which have made possible the effective use of these instruments in transferring the ownership of wealth.

As is indicated in the diagram presented on page 133, the capital of modern corporations is usually divided into two classes, fixed and working. The financial instruments that are used in evidencing the loans made in the raising of fixed capital are usually called "investment credit instruments"; while those evidencing borrowed working capital are generally known as "commercial credit instruments." We shall consider separately the various types of instruments that fall within each class.

I. INVESTMENT CREDIT INSTRUMENTS

The two principal types of investment credit instruments utilized in raising capital for corporations are bonds and stock certificates, or shares. It is perhaps necessary to explain why a share of stock is designated as a credit instrument. A shareholder is legally not a creditor of the corporation but a joint owner in the enterprise; he receives income from his shares only in case earnings are sufficient to permit or warrant the payment of dividends. On the other hand, the bondholder, as a creditor of the corporation, is legally entitled to interest on his investment, regardless of the volume of earnings. Although the stockholder is legally not a lender of funds to the corporation, he is nevertheless for all practical purposes commonly an "outsider" lending his funds in anticipation of a return. The rank and file of investors in stocks are not, in fact, actively interested in the management. Indeed, it is a rare thing for any but a relatively small group of insiders to exercise voting prerogatives. The familiar expression, "Shall I invest in stocks or bonds?" indicates clearly enough that in a majority of instances the purchaser makes no differentiation between stock and bonds, save as to relative certainty of income and chance of enhancement in value.

The fact that a bond is usually secured by a mortgage on the property does not guarantee that there will be no loss. In the event that earnings are not sufficient to pay interest on bonds, the bondholders may foreclose under the terms of the mortgage and take possession of the property; but an enterprise with earnings insufficient to permit the payment of interest on its bonds cannot ordinarily be sold at a price which would equal the amount of the bondholder's investment—whatever may have been the evaluation originally placed upon the property. Nor is there any assurance that the bondholders can conduct such an enterprise at a profit; indeed, there is a certainty that they cannot do so when the mortgage is against only a portion of the corporation's property. In the event that interest on bonds is not paid, it is therefore usually wise to effect a financial re-organization, by means of which the amount of outstanding bonds is reduced by converting some of the bonds into stock. It is thus apparent that in the last analysis the safety of both bonds and stock depends upon the earning power of the corporation. It remains true, however, that bonds are usually the more conservative investment by virtue of their prior claim to earnings. It should be noted, moreover, that many corporations now have no bonded indebtedness; hence the stockholders are entitled to all the earnings.

1. *Bonds.*—The terminology employed in connection with the many different types of bonds that are in use nowadays is baffling to the layman. For instance, a certain bond may be described as follows: five per cent railroad collateral trust, refunding, registered, coupon bond. The whole matter may be greatly simplified by classifying bonds from certain points of view as follows:

1. According to the nature of the issuer
    a. Government bonds—national, state, territorial, county, city, township, school district, etc.
    b. Corporation bonds—transportation, public utility, industrial, reclamation, real estate, timber, etc.
2. According to security
    a. Secured bonds

    (1) By the original issuing corporation
       (*a*) Mortgage bonds, classified according to
          1—Claim against property
             a—Senior bonds
             b—Junior bonds
          2—Limitations on amount of future bonds
             a—Closed bonds
             b—Open bonds
             c—Open end bonds
          3—Extent of property protection
             a—Bonds with after-acquired clause
             b—Bonds without after-acquired clause
       (*b*) Collateral trust bonds
          1—Securities of independent companies
          2—Securities of allied companies
    (2) By a corporation other than the original issuer
       (*a*) Assumed bonds
       (*b*) Guaranteed bonds
       (*c*) Joint bonds
  b. Unsecured bonds
    (1) Debentures
    (2) Income bonds
    (3) Receivers' certificates
3. According to maturity
  a. Notes
  b. Short-term bonds
  c. Medium-term bonds
  d. Long-term bonds
  e. Perpetual bonds
4. According to termination
  a. Terminated by conversion
    (1) Convertible bonds
    (2) Inconvertible bonds
  b. Terminated by refunding
    (1) Refunding bonds
    (2) Non-refunding bonds
  c. Terminated by redemption
    (1) Redeemable bonds
    (2) Unredeemable bonds
  d. Terminated by sinking fund method
    (1) Bonds with sinking fund
    (2) Bonds without sinking fund
  e. Terminated by serial method
    (1) Serial bonds
    (2) Non-serial bonds

In the case of a first-mortgage bond the bondholders have a prior claim against property in case the principal or interest is not paid. Since it is obviously impossible to give each bondholder a piece of the mortgage, the mortgage is placed in trust, and in the event interest is not paid the bondholders as a group may foreclose under the terms of the agreement and take possession of the property. A second mortgage, as the name indicates, constitutes a secondary claim. Anything left after payments have been made to the owners of the first mortgage may be devoted to meeting the claims of the second-mortgage holders.

A collateral trust bond is one which is secured, not by real estate or other physical property owned by the corporation, but by stock or bonds of other companies owned by the issuing corporation. This type of security is mainly found in connection with railroad companies. The term "trust" indicates that these collateral securities are placed in trust with a trust company or other trustee. In the event that interest is not paid on such bonds, the holder may seize the collateral which is held in trust.

A debenture bond has no mortgage security, and merely constitutes a claim against the property and income of the corporation secondary to that of any outstanding mortgage bond. Its claim is, however, prior to that of preferred stock. The debenture is often regarded as identical with an "income" bond; but the distinguishing characteristic of the latter form of obligation is that in the event income is not earned it does not carry over as an obligation to be met subsequently.

The short-term note is frequently employed in raising fixed capital. The designation "short-term" is employed because the notes in question usually run from one to five years rather than for long periods, as is the case with bonds. These notes usually have a claim against only the income of the company. Accordingly it is customary for payments on the principal to be made serially; that is, a certain percentage of the total debt is paid back annually, thus gradually increasing the security back of the loan. Short-term notes are usually issued to meet temporary emergencies. In periods of tight money and high interest rates, or of general uncertainty over the industrial future, it is difficult to sell long-time bonds on favorable terms; hence it has been found expedient to sell short-term notes which can be refunded into long-term bonds at a more propitious time.

2. *Stocks.*—Shares of stock are divided into two main classes, preferred and common. As the term indicates, preferred stock has a prior claim on dividends and usually, in the event of liquidation, on the assets of the business. Because of the existence of common stock as a participant in the earnings of the corporation, it is obviously necessary to limit the extent to which preferred shares may receive dividends. A range of from four to eight per cent is found.

Preferred stock may be either cumulative or non-cumulative; participating or non-participating; convertible or non-convertible. With cumulative stock the dividends which cannot be paid in any year, because of low earnings, accumulate in subsequent years as an obligation prior to that on common stock. The owner of participating preferred stock is entitled to share in the earnings beyond the stated return on the preferred, the extent of the participation depending upon the specific terms governing the issue. Preferred stock may be *convertible* into common stock as a means of increasing its potential earning power.

Some modern preferred stocks are almost as stable as bonds. There may, for example, be no bonds outstanding; and it is sometimes provided that no bonded debt may be created without the consent of preferred stockholders owning, say, 75 per cent of such stock. Again there may be special provisions for creating a cumulative sinking fund for retiring the issue. Or it may be provided that no dividends may be paid on the common stock until a reserve has been set up out of earnings for the protection of preferred stockholders. When such provisions for protection against dilution of earnings or assets are in force the preferred-stock owner is in a position almost as secure as that of a bondholder. It remains true, however, that in case dividends are not paid, the individual shareholder ordinarily has no right to take possession of the property of the corporation, as has a bondholder under the terms of the usual mortgage. Preferred stock is also similar to a bond in that it bears a fixed rate of return; but it must be borne in mind that in the case of a bond the payment of the return is mandatory, while in the case of preferred stock, even cumulative stock, the payment is discretionary.

The common stock of the corporation merely represents claims to such earnings as may be available after the payment of dividends on bonds and preferred stock. Dividends on common stock will accordingly vary widely in amount. Moreover, since common stock is regarded as speculative and uncertain as to dividends, the majority of corporations do not hesitate to "pass" common-stock dividends as a measure of financial conservatism, even though the earnings might frequently be sufficient to pay a moderate return.

Common stock also may be classified from several points of view. Classified according to *authorization* common stock may be either issued or unissued. The former is outstanding in the hands of the public and a part of the capital structure, while the latter has not as yet become a part of the actual capital. According to *ownership* common stock may be owned either by the public or by the company itself. In the latter case it is called treasury stock, which differs from unissued stock in that it has once been sold to the public and then re-acquired by the corporation through gift or purchase, and not retired. According to *voting power* common stock may be voting or non-voting stock, the latter being frequently called Class A stock.

Finally common stock may be issued with or without a *par value.* Until comparatively recent years stock was always issued at a so-called par, or nominal, value. The most common par is $100, although stock is often issued at a par of $50, $25, $10, $5, $1; and in the case of highly speculative stock the par has sometimes been as low as 5 cents. Dividends are paid as a percentage of the assigned par value. When shares are issued on a no-par basis they are sold simply as equal portions of whatever values exist, as gauged by the financial markets. Dividends are paid as so many dollars per share. Stock without a par value is perhaps of advantage in that it is not so likely to mislead the innocent investor, who somehow will persist in believing that a stock whose par value is $100 will ultimately be worth $100, even though its temporary market price may be below that figure; hence he may pay for it more than its real worth.

Stockholders' *"rights"* are an interesting but little-known form of credit instrument. They have arisen out of the exigencies of corporate financing. For instance, when the existing stock of a corporation is selling at, say, 105, additional capital can easily be raised by offering for sale new shares at par, or slightly above. But if additional shares are to be offered for sale at a bargain, it is only equitable that the existing stockholders should be given the first chance to subscribe for the new issue, because the increased capitalization may well affect the value of outstanding shares. Accordingly, it is the usual practice to allow shareholders to subscribe for the new issue in proportion to the amount of their holdings; indeed, in many states stockholders have a legal right to subscribe for new stock at par. Such stockholders' privileges are known as "rights," and they are issued to shareholders in the form of transferable instruments. Upon the receipt of one of these instruments, the shareholder may either avail himself of the opportunity to purchase stock at par, or whatever the figure mentioned, or he may sell his right to another. These rights are in fact bought and sold on the stock exchanges in the same manner as bonds and shares.

II. COMMERCIAL CREDIT INSTRUMENTS

Commercial credit instruments—promissory notes and bills of exchange—are the written evidences of the commercial borrowing operations discussed in the preceding chapter. Because of the nature of the uses to which funds borrowed for working-capital purposes are devoted, these instruments run for short periods of time only. Especial importance is attached to them because of the prevalent use of certain forms of bills of exchange as substitutes for money, a phenomenon made possible, as we shall see, by the principle of negotiability, which was developed in the seventeenth and eighteenth centuries as an important feature of the "law merchant."

Book accounts.—Many credit operations are evidenced merely by entries in the account books of business men—"accounts receivable" in the books of the seller (or lender), and "accounts payable" in the books of the buyer (or borrower). While such informal credit extension is quite as significant as any other, it does not concern us here for the reason that it does not give rise to tangible legal instruments.

The promissory note.—A promissory note is an unconditional written promise by X, the maker, to pay at a definite future date a sum of money to Y, the payee. It may or may not designate the place at which payment is to be made. Promissory notes may be issued by banking and other institutions and by governments as well as by individuals, and as a result of non-commercial as well as of commercial obligations.

The draft or bill of exchange.—A bill of exchange, or draft, is an unconditional written order signed by X (the drawer) ordering Y (the drawee) to pay at a definite date a definite sum of money to F (the payee). The payee may be the same person as the drawer. Before a time draft is good, the drawee must indicate his willingness to honor it by signing his name below the word "accepted" written across the face of the bill.

Bills of exchange may be classified from several points of view. In the first place, we have (1) foreign and (2) domestic, or inland, bills. A foreign bill is legally defined as one, the drawer and drawee of which live in different countries or different states of the United States; while a domestic bill is one, both parties to which live within the same state. This classification is of importance from the legal point of view, but from the standpoint of commercial and banking practice the distinction is without significance.

We have thus far been using the terms "bill of exchange" and "draft" indiscriminately. The two terms are, in fact, commonly used interchangeably; for instance, we speak of drafts on London or bills of exchange on London, and we say New York exchange or drafts on New York. In order to give precision to our terminology it will be well for us to use the term "draft"—and this appears to be a growing custom—when speaking of domestic operations, whether or not they cross state lines; and the term "bill of exchange" when speaking of international credit instruments. A bank draft is an order drawn by one bank on another bank, although it is not necessary that the party to whom it is payable be a bank.

Again, bills may be classified in accordance with the nature of the operation giving rise to the draft. Hence we have bankers' or finance bills, trade or commercial bills, and accommodation bills. Bankers' bills are used merely as a means of making payments and transferring balances between banks. A trade draft, or a "trade acceptance," to use the more common term, is an order drawn by a seller of goods against the buyer of the goods and accepted by the latter. Accommodation drafts are drafts which do not arise out of any business transaction already concluded, and there may or may not be an intention to purchase goods with the funds procured; it is a "non-trade" draft. "Accommodation" is a term that has been handed down from English commercial practice and is not frequently employed in the United States at the present time.

Finally, bills of exchange are classified as demand and time bills. A demand bill is one payable "at sight," that is, immediately upon presentation, while a time bill is one payable at some definite date in the future.

Notes and drafts arise in connection with identical types of business operations. Mr. Jones, a wholesaler, sells goods on credit to Mr. Smith, a retailer. The transaction may of course be evidenced merely by "open accounts" from Smith in Jones' books, and "accounts payable" to Jones in Smith's books. But, passing by this informal method of evidencing the credit operation, the sale of goods by Jones to Smith may give rise either to a promissory note or to a trade draft, according to the commercial practice in vogue. In the case of a promissory note, Mr. Smith takes the initiative and writes the instrument evidencing his obligation to pay Jones. In the case of the trade draft, Jones takes the initiative, writes the order against Smith, and sends it to Smith, who honors the draft by writing "accepted" on its face. The result is the same in either case: Smith has signed a legal instrument obligating himself to pay Jones.

In case Jones wishes to borrow from a bank in anticipation of the payment of the obligation by Smith, he may do so by having a bank *discount* either Smith's note or Smith's acceptance. From the standpoint of the bank, the security is identical in both cases. With the note the bank has Smith's promise to pay at maturity and a secondary liability on the part of Jones, as indorser. With the draft the bank again has Smith's promise to pay, by virtue of his acceptance of the instrument, and it has Jones' secondary liability, as maker of the draft. Which form of instrument is employed at any time depends upon the custom of manufacturers and merchants. In Europe the draft is characteristically employed. In the United States both drafts and notes were in common use before the Civil War; but because of the risks of price changes during the period of greenback currency American commercial practice gradually took the form of selling on "open" or book account. Except in a few special lines credit instruments came to be employed only in cases where the creditor's standing was not first class, as when an account was not paid at maturity and a note was given in "settlement." After the passage of the Federal Reserve Banking Law in 1913 an effort was made to restore the extensive use of credit instruments in the form of trade and bank acceptances; but the movement has met with little success.

Checks, bank notes, and bank drafts are the forms of paper which circulate most widely as substitutes for money. While they have commonly been classed as "credit instruments," they are strictly not credit instruments at all, for they are not evidences of a *postponed* payment, the essential characteristic of a credit operation. A few words of explanation will serve to clarify this issue.

A check is a credit instrument in the sense that it must be honored by the bank before it is the equivalent of cash, just as credit is involved in a business operation when one receives goods a second or so before he passes the money over to the seller; there is a brief interval during which the seller is waiting to be paid. But no one really regards such a business transaction as a credit operation.

A cashier's check, a certified check, and even an uncertified check in the vast majority of instances, are in practice precisely as satisfactory means of payment as actual cash. Even though they are credit instruments in form—mere promises, direct or implied, to pay cash—this distinction has little practical significance. For the same reason the bank note, which is a promise by a bank to pay to the borrower on demand a certain specified sum of money, is not a credit instrument; it passes everywhere as an equivalent of money.

III. THE USE OF CREDIT INSTRUMENTS IN TRANSFERRING WEALTH

The law has greatly facilitated the use of credit instruments in transferring the ownership of wealth, by formulating principles relating to salability, transferability, and negotiability. The various forms of credit instruments—bonds, shares, notes, drafts, checks, certificates of deposit, etc.—possess these three attributes in varying degrees.

1. SALABILITY AND TRANSFERABILITY

Only a brief word of explanation is necessary with reference to the concept of salability. By means of a sale an individual may transfer to another person all of his ownership rights in a piece of property. The law of sales has been made applicable to all of these credit instruments; and an owner of one of them may therefore always transfer to another at least the same amount of ownership of the instrument, and thus of the property which the instrument represents, that he himself possesses.

While salability is an obvious prerequisite to the transferability of any of these instruments, it does not fully explain the latter. For instance, a credit instrument, unlike tangible personal property, may be automatically transferred by the mere process of indorsement, that is, by writing one's name on the back of an instrument that is made payable to him or to his order; or, in the case of an instrument made payable to bearer, it may be transferable merely by delivery, that is, by passing it on to another. Similarly, an instrument that has been indorsed in blank, that is, by the owner's writing his name on the back of it without designating any specific payee, is also transferable by mere delivery. The ease with which these instruments may be transferred renders their use as a means of exchanging the ownership of wealth much more general than would otherwise be the case.

But transferability may involve more than this. For even though he himself has no title at all, a possessor of an instrument that is payable to bearer may transfer to another a valid or unimpeachable title. A bearer instrument is thus for all practical purposes equivalent to money. But this borders on the principle of negotiability, to a consideration of which we may now turn.

2. THE PRINCIPLE OF NEGOTIABILITY

An instrument, to be negotiable, must, in the nature of the case, possess the attribute of salability, and be transferable from one person to another, either by indorsement or by delivery. But it must have other attributes as well. As usually defined, a negotiable instrument differs from a simple contract, or "chose in action," in that a "bona fide purchaser for value," innocent of any irregularity as between the original parties to the contract, obtains a title to the instrument that is free from all personal defenses and equities of prior parties. A purchaser of a non-negotiable instrument, however, takes the instrument subject to all its original defenses and is apparently supposed to protect himself by an investigation of the origin and history of the instrument. While there are some exceptions to this principle, while transferability with a better title is not an exclusive attribute of a negotiable instrument, it nevertheless possesses this attribute in a very high degree; and it is commonly said to be its distinctive characteristic.

In order to possess the quality of negotiability, an instrument must conform to certain requirements prescribed by the custom of merchants—now codified in the law of negotiable instruments. The instrument must be drawn up in a certain prescribed form, it must be sold in a specified manner, certain precise steps must be followed in presenting it for payment, and a definite procedure must be pursued in giving notice of its dishonor in case of non-payment.[1] These requirements originally related only to commercial credit instruments in the form of promissory notes and bills of exchange, and the history of the law of negotiability is associated with commercial, rather than with investment, credit instruments.

The law governing negotiable instruments had its inception in the customs of the mercantile world. The instruments themselves were born of the necessities and needs of *merchants*, as is indicated by the fact that the law relating to such instruments is usually known as "the law merchant." The custom of making such notes and bills of exchange payable to order or bearer arose in England early in the seventeenth century.[2] But until 1756, when Lord Mansfield, "the father of the law merchant," expressed and molded into the form of definite rules of law the numerous customs that had grown up among merchants in connection with these instruments, the law of bills and notes was in a more or less chaotic condition. Lord Mansfield made the law merchant an integral part of the great body of the English law, which was inherited by the American colonies, and, in due course, by the American commonwealths.

During the first century of American legal history, differing interpretations of the law merchant developed in the various states, with the result that commercial practice was seriously handicapped. About 1890, however, a movement was initiated to bring about a codification of the law merchant, with a view to securing uniformity in the various jurisdictions. A negotiable instruments bill was finally drafted in 1896

---

[1] For details see p. 119.

[2] Promissory notes and bills of exchange appear to have been used by various nations of antiquity. There are records of their use in Babylonia and Syria, in Athens and in Rome. It appears, indeed, that by the time of Justinian the fundamental principles of the bill of exchange and the promissory note were pretty well developed. After the Dark Ages we find them arising again with the trading operations of Italian cities; and by the middle of the thirteenth century the bill of exchange had apparently become a common document.

by a "committee on commercial law," and this has since become a law in nearly every state in the Union, in a few instances, however, with more or less important modifications.

The reason for developing the principle that an instrument in the hands of an innocent third party should be free from personal defenses and collateral claims existing between prior parties was to facilitate the use of such an instrument as a means of making payment. In the settlement of transactions between merchants at the great fairs and market places in early England there was plenty of occasion for irregularities. For instance, the maker of an instrument might have entered into the transaction without consideration, and if a third party were asked to accept an instrument subject to such defenses as an original maker might set up, he would usually refuse because of the risks involved. Accordingly, it was necessary to devise a means whereby the purchaser of such an instrument would be protected from irregularities of which he could have no cognizance without a careful investigation of the origin and history of the instrument in question.

To be negotiable, an instrument must be drawn up in a certain definite way in order to prevent misrepresentation or fraud. The conditions that must be met to make an instrument negotiable are as follows:

1. *It must be in writing.*—No oral contract could be negotiable. A written contract may be either in writing or in printing, and the writing may be executed with any substance, as ink or pencil.

2. *It must be properly signed.*—It is usual that the signature be made by writing in full the name of the signer; but a mark or any other character intended to be the signature will suffice. The signature is usually placed at the close of the instrument, although if it is clear that it is meant for a signature it may be placed on any part of the instrument.

3. *It must be negotiable in form, that is, payable to order or bearer.*—It must be clearly shown to be the intent of the party making the instrument to execute a negotiable paper; and to make this intent clear there must be some expressed words showing such a purpose.

4. *It must be payable in money only.*—The reason for this requirement is to insure that the amount be definite. By the term "money" is meant the legal tender of the country.

5. *The amount must be certain.*—The sum payable is considered fixed and certain if it is a definitely stated amount with interest, or in stated instalments, or with exchange (the bank's charges for collection), or with the cost of collection in case payment is not made at maturity.

6. *It must be payable to a designated payee.*—It is not necessary to name the specific party, but it must be payable to a person or persons who can be definitely ascertained at the time of the payment.

7. *It must be payable absolutely.*—If the instrument is so drawn that any condition might arise that would render it of no effect, it is not a negotiable paper. Consequently a promise to pay a certain sum out of a designated fund is not negotiable; this is the case even though the fund exists at the time and although the condition that would nullify the contract had not in fact arisen.

8. *It must be payable at a time that is certain.*—The date of payment must be definitely stated; though it may be payable on or *before* a certain definite date, or at a certain time *after* the happening of some future event. The contingent event must be certain to occur, however, or the promise will not be absolute.

Negotiability depends upon certain legal procedures as follows:[3]

1. *Indorsement.*—The indorsement must be on the instrument itself or on a paper attached to it. The indorsement must relate to the entire instrument; a part cannot be transferred by indorsement, or a part to one party and the remainder to another.

The obligation of an indorser to a transferee, like that of a drawer of a bill, is that the indorser shall pay the instrument, provided the maker does not, and also provided it is duly presented for payment and upon refusal is duly protested and notice of protest given the indorser. In domestic bills and notes the protest may be omitted and instead notice of non-payment may be given the indorser. It should be noted that the contract of the maker of a note or the acceptor of a bill is absolute; each is liable in any event. But the contract of the indorser and of the drawer of a bill is conditional upon the failure of the maker or acceptor to pay upon proper protest and notice to him.

If the indorser of a note wishes to avoid any personal liability, he may indorse "without recourse" and sign his name. He thus expressly stipulates that he will not be liable if the maker does not pay. There is an implied warrant, however, that the signatures of the maker and all prior indorsers are genuine, that is, that they are not forgeries. The intent and purpose of such indorsement is merely to pass title to the instrument.

2. *Presentment and demand.*—To fix the liability of the drawer or indorser it is necessary to present the instrument to the drawee and demand payment. Presentment consists in exhibiting the instrument to the payer or in handing it to him, while demand is a request either to accept or to pay it as the case may be. If the paper is payable at a bank,

[3] For the following material credit is given to Gano, *Commercial Law.*

the mere fact that at the time of maturity the paper is at the bank at which it is payable is sufficient presentment and demand, provided the drawer has knowledge of the fact. Presentment must be made on the day on which the instrument falls due, unless some "inevitable accident" or other legal obstacle prevents such presentment. The fact that both the holder and indorser know that the note will not be paid when due and that the maker is dead and the estate insolvent does not relieve the holder from his obligation to make presentment and give notice of dishonor.

3. *Notice of dishonor.*—After the payment has been refused and the instrument dishonored, notice of such dishonor must be given to the drawer of a bill of exchange and to each indorser. Any drawer or indorser to whom such notice is not given is discharged. If the parties reside in the same place, the notice must be given the following day. If they reside in different places and notice is sent by mail, it must be deposited in the post office so as to go the day following the dishonor; if given otherwise than through the mail, it must be done in time to be received as soon as mailed notice would have arrived. The notice may be given by the holder or his agent or by any party who may have to pay the debt and who is entitled to be reimbursed.

When there are several indorsers, the last indorser can look to the previous one, or, in fact, to anyone who has indorsed before him, as well as to the maker or acceptor. The notice of dishonor may be either oral or written, and may be either delivered personally or sent through the mail.

4. *Waiver.*—Notice may be waived, in which case the obligations will be assumed without the formal notification. The indorser may also add "protest waived," the effect being to waive presentment and notice of dishonor as well.

5. *Protest.*—Protest is a formal declaration in writing and under seal, of an officer called a notary public, certifying to the demand and dishonor. Protest of foreign bills of exchange is necessary, but it is not required in the case of notes, checks, and inland bills, although it is often employed in giving notice of their dishonor. The notary makes the presentment and demand; if the bill is not honored he issues a certificate, stating that presentment and demand have been made and judgment refused, and that notice has been sent to the maker and all indorsers of the note.

There are certain absolute defenses. It has been stated above that a negotiable instrument in the hands of an innocent purchaser for value is not subject to the defenses that might be interposed to it between original parties—the purpose being to make such instruments serviceable as media of exchange. But while the law was desirous of doing everything possible to facilitate commercial operations, it was necessary to protect the original maker of the instrument against abuse. The courts have therefore recognized certain absolute defenses, of which the following are illustrations:

1. *Non-delivery.*—If either the maker or acceptor of an instrument, or the agent of either, passes the instrument to a third party; or if it gets into the hands of a bona fide holder through negligence, the instrument is considered as having been delivered. But if the holder has been deprived of possession by fraud or theft, he cannot be compelled to pay to any subsequent holder. In the view of the law such an instrument was not delivered and no contract exists.

2. *Fraud in making the instrument.*—If in the making of the instrument there was fraud of a nature that would vitiate an ordinary contract, the law holds that no contract exists; and the maker or acceptor of such an instrument cannot, therefore, be held responsible for payment to innocent third parties.

3. *Alteration or forgery.*—Where there has been a material alteration, or forgery, the law holds that the minds of the parties have not met and there is thus no contract. An alteration of the terms of a negotiable instrument, either by a party to the instrument or one in lawful possession of it, destroys its validity. It is obvious that if the law made an individual responsible for the payment of an instrument on which his name had been forged, it would not only work a gross injustice upon the individual in question but would be a distinct encouragement to the practice of forgery.

4. *Want of capacity to contract.*—The contract represented by the instrument is not genuine if the parties to the contract do not have the capacity to contract, as in the case of an infant or a person who has been adjudged insane.

These absolute defenses which may be set up by the original maker of an instrument do not apply, however, to individuals who have indorsed the instrument as it passed through their hands. Every person who negotiates such an instrument warrants that it is genuine, that he has good title to it, and that all prior parties have capacity to contract. The indorser, therefore, unless the indorsement is without recourse, assumes liability for the payment of the instrument.

The law of negotiable instruments is extraordinarily complex and the exceptions to and qualifications of the general principles that have been categorically stated above are legion. In this very brief discussion of the transferability and negotiability of credit instruments, the purpose has been merely to indicate the evident purpose and intent of the law to render these instruments more serviceable in meeting the needs of commerce and industry.

It remains to note the extent to which the various forms of instruments possess the different attributes under consideration. All of them are salable; some of them are transferable without change of ownership rights; others show improved title in the hands of an innocent third party; some of them are transferable by indorsement only; others by delivery merely. In each case it appears that the law has been seeking, consciously or unconsciously, to facilitate the use of the instrument in the particular ways desired.

Some commercial credit instruments are used extensively as substitutes for money, while others are not. As we have seen above, the origin and development of the principle of negotiability and transfer by indorsement are ascribed to a desire to facilitate the use of notes and drafts as media of exchange. Moreover, it is probable that in early times promissory notes and bills of exchange frequently changed hands numerous times, thus performing an important exchange function. Nowadays, however, it is only checks, bank notes, and bank drafts that serve extensively as media of exchange. It is to be noted that this list includes only *demand* instruments; and it will be recalled that they are not, strictly speaking, credit instruments.

The reason that a bill of exchange drawn by A against B is seldom used by A as a means of paying a debt owed by A to C is, first, that two such obligations may not mature on identical dates, and, second, that they are not usually of equal amounts. If B's debt to A for $1,000 is due March 1, and A's debt to C for $1,200 is due March 5, B's accepted draft is obviously not a convenient instrument with which to pay C. The method nearly always employed nowadays is for A to deposit in a bank funds received from B and draw his check against his account in favor of C or to ask the banker for a cashier's check or a draft on another bank, made payable to C.

The law and procedure governing negotiable instruments arose in the mercantile or commercial credit field, and are therefore commonly associated with commercial credit instruments. With the development of corporate industry, however, these principles came to be applied, in greater or lesser degree, to investment credit instruments as well.

The transferable qualities of a bond vary. One drawn to order is on a par with the ordinary bill of exchange or promissory note drawn to order; it is transferable to the same extent and in the same manner, and the liability of the parties to it is fixed in the same way. A bond payable to bearer, that is, a non-registered bond, passes title by delivery just as does a bearer commercial instrument. A registered bond, however, is not transferable by indorsement, nor is it negotiable. Bond coupons are usually bearer-instruments, and are transferable by delivery, with all the legal consequences that follow from the transfer of any negotiable bearer-instrument.

Shares of stock are ordinarily transferable either by an order indorsement or by an indorsement in blank. The indorsement operates as a power of attorney to remove the name of the former owner and place the name of the new owner on the certificate. A mere possessor of a share of stock (or of a registered bond) has, however, no title at all, even though it is indorsed in blank; and he cannot pass title to a bona fide transferee. A certificate of stock is therefore not negotiable in the ordinary sense; there are no formal requisites; and there are no questions concerning the fixing of liabilities of the parties to the instrument, etc. Shares of stock are, however, readily transferable.[4]

[4] Bills of lading and warehouse receipts also possess in substantial degree the qualities of transferability and negotiability. While not credit instruments, bills of lading and warehouse receipts are evidences of ownership of wealth. For further discussion of these instruments see pp. 257–260.

CHAPTER X
THE EVOLUTION OF CREDIT INSTITUTIONS

The great growth of credit operations which followed the development of large-scale business enterprise, particularly that organized on the corporate basis, has been attended by the development of an extensive and interdependent financial structure, designed to facilitate the raising of the funds required for capitalistic industry. The varied types of financial instruments, agencies, and institutions that are utilized in connection with the borrowing operations of business enterprise, are outlined in the diagram on page 133. This diagram is designed to afford the reader a general view of the financial structure of society, with its complex interrelations, as a preliminary to the detailed study of the numerous particular institutions which will constitute the subject matter of succeeding chapters. Before discussing the diagram it is essential to consider certain features of the corporation, which are responsible for its evolution as the prevailing form of business organization today.

I. THE CORPORATION AS A DEVICE FOR RAISING CAPITAL

In discussions of the corporation as a form of organization for the conduct of business, its advantages over the partnership have usually been listed as follows: (1) greater ease of raising capital; (2) perpetual (or, at least, definite) existence; and (3) centralization of managerial responsibility and power. The really outstanding advantage of the corporation is its greater effectiveness in assembling the capital required for large-scale enterprise.

Partnerships may be—and some have been—given a perpetual life. Partnerships may delegate the management to a single individual or group of individuals and hold them responsible for results, quite after the fashion of the corporate organization. Indeed, some modern partnerships are thus organized; while the "silent partner" is, of course, a common phenomenon. Being without shares of stock and bonds and without the principle of limited liability, the partnership cannot possibly effect the accumulation of the large quantities of capital required by the great majority of modern businesses. Some modern partnership associations, it is true, have the equivalent of shares and some have been organized with a limited liability; but these features constitute the very essence of the corporate form of organization. To the extent that they have now been taken over by partnerships the latter may be said to have been "corporationized."

The corporation is for several reasons an effective agency for the raising of capital. In the first place, the division of the capital into small units in the form of shares of stock or bonds makes it possible to attract funds from people of very moderate means. Second, the division of the shares and bonds of corporations into small denominations also makes it possible for individuals to diversify their investments and thus reduce to a minimum the risks of loss. Even so small a fund as $10,000 may be invested in a hundred or more different companies.

Third, the division of corporate securities into bonds and shares serves to attract the investments of people of different temperaments and of different economic position. Bonds, constituting a first claim upon earnings, make their appeal to those who are by temperament conservative, or whose economic position is such as to make safety of investment the prime requisite. On the other hand, stock offers an opportunity for higher returns and thus appeals to people who are willing to take chances in the hope of large rewards, and to those whose economic position is such that they can afford to assume larger risks.

Similarly, the division of stock into preferred and common shares is calculated to appeal to investors of different degrees of conservatism. The preferred stock, while not so safe as bonds, is still relatively safe in well-established companies, and it yields a higher return than bonds. Common stock is subject to still greater risks, but affords the possibility of very large returns. Nowadays there is, moreover, a great variety of sub-classes of shares, notes, and bonds, all designed to facilitate the raising of funds through varied appeals.[1]

Fourth, the easy transferability of bonds and shares, made possible by the development of organized stock exchanges, enables an individual to withdraw his investment in a corporation at almost a moment's notice. The significance of this for our present purpose is that the ease with which one may get out of a corporation has an important bearing on one's willingness to get in. One is not necessarily committed to a given undertaking once and for all; with readily marketable securities the investor retains almost instantaneous command over capital.

Fifth, the large aggregations of capital made possible by virtue of these various advantages, together with the limited-liability principle discussed below, give to the corporation unusual competitive strength and stability, which in turn render securities the more attractive to the investing public.

[1] See pp. 107–108.

Sixth, the corporation now universally embodies the principle of limited liability, i.e., liability of each shareholder only to the amount (usually) of his individual stock. This is indispensable to the assembling of the vast amounts of capital required by modern business establishments, for it would be utterly impossible to induce an individual to purchase shares of stock in a corporation of large size if his individual liability to creditors were equal to the entire capital. Unlimited liability will be assumed only where the owners are few in number, where they are well known to one another, and where the amounts involved are relatively small.

It should be noted that the principle of limited liability applies only to stock, the bondholders being creditors of the corporation. It is apparent, finally, therefore, that even without the principle of limited liability the corporation would have advantages over the ordinary partnership in the assembling of capital, since the sale of bonds would in any event make it possible to draw funds from a large number of investors.

The growth of large-scale enterprise was dependent upon limited liability. Light will be thrown upon the importance of this principle from the point of view of facilitating the raising of capital by a brief review of its history. For a considerable period during English industrial history, joint-stock companies did not enjoy the principle of limited liability. Following a period of great speculation in the shares of unincorporated "companies,"[2] in which many people were financially ruined, the so-called Bubble Act of 1719 prohibited unincorporated companies from acting as corporate bodies or selling transferable stock. This prohibition interfered with the formation of genuine trading companies and "greatly hindered the employment of accumulated capital."[3] The strict enforcement of the act, however, was found to be impracticable and for many years it was allowed to remain a dead letter, many new unincorporated companies continuing to be formed.

The Bubble Act was repealed in 1825 and the Crown was empowered to grant charters of incorporation; but the individual owners of the corporation were made personally liable for the whole or any part of the debts of the corporation. During the next thirty years men of financial and social standing held aloof from concerns in which the smallest investment involved so great a risk. Of 4,049 companies registered provisionally from 1844 to 1855, 3,084 were abandoned before complete registration.

[2] See p. 127.
[3] S. E. Perry, "History of Companies' Legislation in England," *Journal of the Institute of Bankers*, Vol. XXIX.

The principle of limited liability was so important, however, for the raising of the capital required for the rapidly expanding size of industrial enterprises that Parliament finally passed an act in 1856 permitting the formation of corporations "with limited or unlimited liability, with all the benefits of incorporation." Banking and insurance companies were, however, still excluded. The complete acceptance of the limited liability principle, together with the adoption of a general incorporation law, paved the way for the great expansion in the size of business enterprise that marked the second half of the nineteenth century. In particular, there resulted a stimulus to investments in foreign countries where the risks incident to unlimited liability were especially heavy.

In the United States, it appears that the principle of limited liability was accepted from the very beginning. We find that "limited liability was recognized as an attribute of an incorporated company almost invariably without specific mention; indeed, it was a principal object of incorporation."[4] With scarcely an exception, early American corporations, in fact, enjoyed the advantages incident to limited liability.

II. STAGES OF CORPORATE DEVELOPMENT

A study of the changes in the organization of industry from the Middle Ages to the present time indicates that the development of the corporation was in truth very largely governed by capital-raising requirements. While the germ of the corporate idea is no doubt to be found in the guild associations of the early Middle Ages, the first corporations of significance, from the point of view of business enterprise, were the great trading companies of the sixteenth and seventeenth centuries. These companies were organized for the purpose of developing trade with foreign dominions and as colonizing agencies.[5]

The early corporation embodied numerous features; it was a bundle of special rights and privileges, and has been aptly called a collection of monopoly grants of power. While there was no single reason for the use of the corporate organization, in every case a primary factor was the necessity of procuring capital from a large number of individuals. Moreover, owing to the uncertainties both of ocean transportation and of trade, unusual risks were involved, and proved a serious deterrent to the advancement of large sums by any one individual. The corporation

---

[4] Davis, Joseph H., *Essays in Earlier History of American Corporations*, IV, 317–329.

[5] The joint stock principle was also used in the sixteenth and seventeenth centuries in mining companies, and in nearly every important monopoly. William E. Price, *English Patents of Monopoly*, p. 131.

made it possible for individuals to distribute their risks over a number of different undertakings.

Investment opportunities were few before the corporate era. These early corporations were necessary not alone for the raising of capital for overseas enterprises. They appear to have been quite as serviceable in the accommodation of would-be investors. Macaulay writes:

During the interval between the Restoration and the Revolution the riches of the nation had been rapidly increasing. Thousands of busy men found every Christmas that, after the expenses of the year's housekeeping had been defrayed out of the year's income, a surplus remained; and how that surplus was to be employed was a question of some difficulty. In our time, to invest such a surplus, at something more than three per cent on the best security that has ever been known in the world, is the work of a few minutes. But in the seventeenth century, a lawyer, a physician, a retired merchant, who had saved some thousands and who wished to place them safely and profitably, was often greatly embarrassed. Three generations earlier, a man who had accumulated wealth in a profession generally purchased real property, or lent his savings on mortgage. But the number of acres in the kingdom had remained the same; and the value of these acres, though it had greatly increased, had by no means increased so fast as the quantity of capital which was seeking for employment. Many, too, wished to put their money where they could find it at an hour's notice and looked about for some species of property which could be more readily transferred than a house or a field. A capitalist might lend on bottomry or on personal security but, if he did so, he ran a great risk of losing interest and principal. There were a few joint-stock companies, among which the East India Company held the foremost place; but the demand for the stock of such companies was far greater than the supply. Indeed, the cry for a new East India Company was chiefly raised by persons who had found difficulty in placing their savings at interest on good security. So great was that difficulty that the practice of hoarding was common. We are told that the father of Pope, the poet, who retired from business in the City about the time of the Revolution, carried to a retreat in the country a strong box containing near twenty thousand pounds, and took out from time to time what was required for household expense; and it is highly probable that this was not a solitary case. At present the quantity of coin which is hoarded by private persons is so small that it would, if brought forth, make no perceptible addition to the circulation. But in the earlier part of the reign of William the Third, all the greatest writers on currency were of opinion that a very considerable mass of gold and silver was hidden in secret drawers and behind wainscots.

The natural effect of this state of things was that a crowd of projectors, ingenious and absurd, honest and knavish, employed themselves in devising new schemes for the employment of redundant capital. It was about the year 1688 that the word stockjobber was first heard in London. In the short space of four years a crowd of companies, every one of which confidently

held out to subscribers the hope of immense gains, sprang into existence—
the Insurance Company, the Paper Company, the Lutestring Company,
the Pearl Fishery Company, the Glass Bottle Company, the Alum Company, the Blythe Coal Company, the Swordblade Company. There was a
Copper Company, which proposed to explore the mines of England, and
held out a hope that they would prove not less valuable than those of Potosi.
There was a Diving Company, which undertook to bring up precious effects
from shipwrecked vessels, and which announced that it had laid in a stock
of wonderful machines resembling complete suits of armour. In front of the
helmet was a huge glass eye like that of a Cyclops; and out of the crest went
a pipe through which the air was to be admitted. The whole process was
exhibited on the Thames. Fine gentleman and fine ladies were invited to the
show, were hospitably regaled, and were delighted by seeing the divers in
their panoply descend into the river and return laden with old iron and ship's
tackle. There was a Greenland Fishing Company, which could not fail to drive
the Dutch whalers and herring busses out of the Northern Ocean. There was a
Tanning Company, which promised to furnish leather superior to the best
that was brought from Turkey and Russia. There was a society which undertook the office of giving gentlemen a liberal education on low terms, and which
assumed the sounding name of the Royal Academies Company. In a pompous
advertisement it was announced that the directors of the Royal Academies
Company had engaged the best masters in every branch of knowledge, and
were about to issue twenty thousand tickets at twenty shillings each. There
was to be a lottery—two thousand prizes were to be drawn; and the fortunate
holders of the prizes were to be taught, at the charge of the Company, Latin,
Greek, Hebrew, French, Spanish, conic sections, trigonometry, heraldry,
japanning, fortification, bookkeeping, and the art of playing the theorbo.

The second stage in corporate development came during the
seventeenth and eighteenth centuries when the corporate principle was
extended to such enterprises as insurance, banking, and inland naviga-
tion. The importance and the supposed limitations of the joint stock
company during this period may be glimpsed by reference to the following quotation from Adam Smith:

The only trades which it seems possible for a joint stock company to
carry on successfully without an exclusive privilege are those of which all
the operations are capable of being reduced to what is called routine. . . .
Of this kind is, first, the banking trade; secondly, the trade of insurance in
fire and from sea risks and capture in time of war; thirdly, the trade of making
and maintaining a navigable cut or canal; and fourthly, the similar trade of
bringing water for the supply of a great city.

He adds that in order to render the use of the joint stock company
feasible, two other circumstances should concur: "first that the undertaking is of greater and more general utility than the greater part of

the common trades; and secondly, that it requires a greater capital than can easily be collected into a private copartnership." It appears that the corporation was not regarded as particularly well adapted to the efficient conduct of most lines of business, but that it was a very useful device in lines of activity where it was necessary to raise large sums of capital.

The third stage in corporate history may be designated the transportation period, beginning in England about 1780. Adam Smith, who wrote in 1776, had foreseen the use of the corporation in connection with canal building, although the great era of canal transportation came after his time—from 1780 to 1815. The corporation was almost universally used as a means of assembling the large capital required for canal construction. It is significant, from the point of view of the capital-raising function of corporations, to note that the canal companies did not conduct transportation; the canal barges were run by individual boatmen. The use of the corporation was here dictated solely by capital-raising requirements. This was also true of the turnpike companies.

With the development of railway transportation after 1830 the use of the corporation was greatly extended. While in the case of the railroads the corporation was early used both as a capital-raising and as an operating device, the capital-raising feature was of primary importance. It was manifestly impossible to raise the required funds by individual or partnership means. As with the old trading companies, not only was the volume of capital required very large, but the risks assumed were likewise exceptional.

The fourth stage is that of the extension of the corporate form of organization to producing, manufacturing, and mercantile enterprises. Although the corporation was used to some extent in ordinary business in both England and the United States before 1800, it was not until after the development of efficient and cheap transportation systems that it became the dominant form of organization in manufacturing and mercantile lines. During the earlier years of its history the factory system did not require very large aggregations of capital, for the simple reason that markets were narrowly circumscribed, owing to the inadequacy and the great cost of transportation, as also to the decentralization of wealth and population. The volume of output that could be sold by any single plant was thus definitely limited. Under these conditions only a few thousands of dollars of capital were required for the largest business establishment, and individuals and partnerships found no serious handicap in financing such enterprise. But while the early factories did not require large capital, their development gave rise to an insistent pressure for wider markets in order to make possible a larger and more profitable scale of industrial enterprise, thus undoubtedly hastening the development of efficient transportation.

The widening of markets that resulted from the development of modern transportation facilities gave in turn a tremendous impetus to the enlargement of the size of business undertakings. Given cheap transportation to the markets of the world, there was almost no limit to the profitable size of the business unit. By 1845 railroad transportation had definitely made a place for itself, both in England and in the United States; and before 1860 it had succeeded in linking the great Middle West with all the markets of the world.

There followed in the second half of the nineteenth century a gigantic effort on the part of industries to expand the scale of their productive operations to a point where they could take full advantage of the world markets that were available to them. Cheap transportation meant reduced costs of goods in distant markets. And the enlarged output made possible by widened markets still further reduced the cost per unit and made possible a competition over ever widening areas. This tremendous growth in the size of producing units, and in the magnitude of the commercial and distributing businesses concerned with the marketing process, made the use of the corporation as a capital-raising device quite as indispensable here as it was in foreign trading, finance, insurance, and transportation. Where, formerly, factories required a capital of perhaps a few thousand dollars, the large-scale business enterprises of the present necessitate capital accumulations of millions and even hundreds of millions of dollars.

Thus did the changing structure of industrial society, with the ever increasing size of business undertaking and ever enlarging capital requirements, gradually extend the scope of corporate industry, until today the corporation is the dominant form of business organization. Without minimizing the advantages of the corporation as an operating agency, it may be repeated that intrinsically and historically the corporation is a capital-raising device. The development of the corporation has, moreover, called into existence most of the financial institutions that function in the economic system of today.

III. PROBLEMS ARISING FROM CORPORATE ORGANIZATION

The very effectiveness of the corporation as a device for raising capital has given rise to difficult problems with respect to management, trusteeship, and the control of business enterprise. Indeed, so far-reaching are the implications of some of these problems that many observers believe that social policy calls for very strict governmental control of corporations, if not for a reversal of the trends that characterized the nineteenth and early twentieth centuries. The shortcomings of the corporation to which attention has been directed are of various types.

The facility with which the corporation permits the assembling of large aggregations of liquid funds has resulted in the growth of business organizations of giant proportions, the operations of which cover wide geographic areas and embrace varied types of business activity. The degree to which business has become concentrated in very large corporations is indicated by the fact that in 1933 some 46 per cent of the assets of corporations engaged in manufacturing and about 35 per cent of the resources of those engaged in mining and quarrying, were held by corporations having assets of 50 million dollars or more.[6]

In the view of many it is easily possible for corporations to become so large as to militate against efficiency—though in the nature of the case one cannot generalize as to the precise point at which decreasing efficiency begins. It is also frequently urged that the large corporation is opposed to the best interests of democracy in that it affords smaller opportunity for individuals to develop their talents and rise to positions of independence and leadership. As far as *independence* is concerned the point is obviously well made; but there is no evidence in support of the other contentions.

Another problem arises out of the tendency toward divorcing ownership from management. The fact that most stockholders are unable, or unwilling, to devote any attention to the affairs of the corporations in which they have investments, means that the managers often have wide latitude in the administration of a business in which their own individual shares may not be large. They are also in a position to take advantage of "inside information" not available to the rank and file of stockholders. However, it should be noted that it is sometimes possible for "absentee owners" who know little about the business to interfere with the management to the detriment of other stockholders. Whatever the merits of these various contentions it is obvious that the corporate form of organization lacks the close-knit unity and the personal touch which characterize the individual and partnership type of business enterprise.

A more serious problem arises out of the concentration of control which the corporation makes possible. A bare majority of the stock

[6] U.S. Treasury Department, *Statistics of Income for 1933*, pp. 173–174.

ownership can always determine the policy of the corporation. Moreover, various devices have been developed which in practice may enable a comparatively small group of stockholders or a small amount of stock to control enormous capital assets. The use of *proxies*, the issuance of *non-voting stock*, and the transference of voting power to *voting trusts* are all conducive to this end. It should be observed, however, that such devices are often indispensable to the conduct of corporate enterprise; without them it would frequently be impossible to procure a sufficient number of votes at a stockholders' meeting to permit the transaction of business.

The most difficult problem which has arisen pertains to intercorporate control. This may take the form simply of one corporation's purchasing the stock of other enterprises for the purpose of eliminating or controlling competition. Moreover, through the medium of "holding companies" a small unit of capital may obtain control over a vast field of enterprise. Major control of a whole group of operating companies in a given field, or even in different fields, may thus be obtained by a single financial corporation; and, in turn, a series of holding companies may be controlled by a *super*-holding company at the top of the corporate pyramid. It is in connection with developments of this sort that the charges of inefficiency and undemocratic organization are most commonly made and are most difficult to meet.

IV. THE MODERN FINANCIAL STRUCTURE

In the diagram on page 133 the arrows pointing downward from fixed capital indicate the movement of the securities that are issued by corporations through the financial institutions that assist in marketing them to the ultimate purchasers, who in the last analysis furnish the funds to the corporation. In some cases the securities do not find lodgment with individual investors but are purchased by financial institutions, as is indicated by the arrows which point to savings banks, insurance companies, etc. In these cases, however, the funds are still furnished by individual savers, namely, the shareholders, depositors, etc. These financial institutions thus serve as intermediaries in the process of rendering individual savings available for the uses of corporate industry.

The stock exchange has been placed at one side of the diagram in order to indicate that it is seldom a direct intermediary in the marketing of securities Rather it is a great central market place of which use is made by nearly all of the various types of financial institutions in connection with their operations, as well as by the ultimate investors in securities. These various relations will be made clear in the

INSTITUTIONS UTILIZED IN FINANCING CORPORATE ENTERPRISE

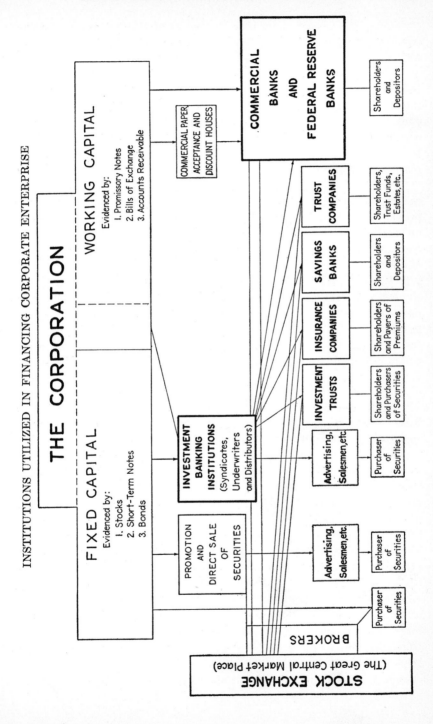

chapter on the stock exchanges. The lines connecting the stock exchange with the different institutions are designed to indicate in a general way the interrelations that exist.

Finally, it will be seen that the commercial banks are directly concerned with the raising of working capital, and indirectly associated with investment banking institutions in the raising of fixed capital. Note the transverse line connecting commercial and investment banks. A line might also be drawn from the commercial banks to the fixed capital side of the corporation; for to a considerable extent they purchase securities directly and make loans to corporations for fixed capital purposes.[7]

To safeguard against misconception it is necessary to state that the diagram could not be made to reveal all phases of the modern financial structure without complicating the picture to the point of obscurity. It will be well, therefore, to point out here certain things which are not indicated.

First, although a line is drawn from the corporation directly to the ultimate purchaser of securities, the chart fails to convey an adequate idea of the vast amount of capital that is raised without the assistance of financial intermediaries. A very great number of our corporations have raised their capital by direct subscription; indeed, it may perhaps safely be said that a large percentage of our present-day corporations secured their start by converting individual firms or partnerships into corporations and issuing shares of stock to the owners. There are many "close" corporations—those which have never raised any funds from general subscription. Among some of the more important of such corporations are: most of the great New England cotton mills; several of the larger chemical companies; the Du Pont Company; many of the great department stores in all the large cities of the country; the large corporations in the aluminum, brass, zinc, asbestos, and sulphur industries; and the great majority of investment houses. Perhaps the most conspicuous example of the close corporation in the United States at the present time is the Ford Motor Company. Mr. Ford and his son are now said to be the sole proprietors of the largest privately owned business in the country.

Second, the chart does not reveal the raising of capital by the common process of creating a surplus through setting aside a portion of the earnings for expansion of the business. A very large amount of capital is thus raised, especially by corporations. It will be noted that this method involves merely a decision of the directors of the corporation with reference to the disposition of earnings.

[7] For discussion of this development see chaps. XVII and XXI.

Third, the chart reveals only those credit operations which involve the borrowing of funds, as distinguished from actual goods. Working capital in part takes the form of materials bought on credit. A retailer, for instance, may do most of his borrowing by buying goods from wholesalers on time. But since the wholesalers, who sell these goods on credit to the retailer, usually borrow from the commercial banks during the interval while awaiting payment, it comes to much the same thing in the end—working capital is largely borrowed from the commercial banks. The chart does indicate, however, that a portion of the working capital is usually derived from the sale of securities. Indeed, if a business is to have a good credit standing with its bank, it must, in fact, provide a considerable part of its working capital by stock subscriptions.

Fourth, one might conclude from the diagram that savings banks are associated only with the problem of raising fixed capital. As a matter of fact, savings institutions also often make loans for working capital purposes (see chapter XIII).

Fifth, the position of the trust company in the financial structure of society is not adequately revealed. As the chart is drawn it would appear to be related only to the raising of fixed capital and to be in a position parallel with savings banks and insurance companies. In fact, as we shall later see (chapter XIV), the trust company performs so wide a variety of functions that it is impossible in the present diagram to indicate its relationship to the entire financial structure. Its commercial banking department would go with the commercial banks, the bond department with the investment banking institutions, the savings department with the savings banks, the insurance department with the insurance companies. But, in addition, the trust company performs a great variety of services for the holders of corporate securities in connection with the safekeeping of valuables, the holding of mortgages in trust, the transfer of ownership of stocks and bonds, and the financial re-organization of companies.

Finally, the diagram tends to give a false impression of specialization by financial institutions. The truth is that there is often conducted under one roof and by a single administrative organization a great variety of financial activities. Just as the trust company has many departments, the commercial bank nowadays usually has associated with it savings and bond departments, and, in recent years, trust departments as well. The designations given on the diagram must, therefore, be considered as representing types of financial functions rather than (in every case) distinct and specialized financial institutions.[8]

[8] See discussion in chap. XXII.

The remaining chapters of the volume will be devoted to a discussion of the services and functions that are performed by the numerous parts of this financial organization, the problems of regulation that have arisen in connection with the various types of financial institutions, and the interrelations of this intricate financial mechanism with the larger economic organization of which it forms so important and integral a part.

CHAPTER XI

CAPITAL REQUIREMENTS AND SOURCES OF CAPITAL

The sketch of the evolution of the modern capitalistic organization presented in the preceding chapter centered attention upon the way in which the growing magnitude of capital requirements stimulated the development of a series of interrelated financial agencies. Before discussing the particular functions of these various institutions it is desirable that some attention be given to the problem of raising capital, as it presents itself to borrowers. What is the nature of their capital needs, and what are the sources from which funds may be obtained? Inasmuch as governments as well as business enterprises have occasion to raise funds in the financial markets, we shall consider both private and public credit operations.

I. RAISING CAPITAL FOR PRIVATE BUSINESS

As the chart on page 133 indicates, business enterprises employ both fixed and working capital. The primary distinction that has always been made between these types of capital is that the former is embodied chiefly in fixed properties—plant and equipment—while the latter consists of materials directly utilized in the producing process. When attention is shifted from these tangible properties to the funds which make their acquisition possible, it is said that a company raises fixed capital for the purpose of acquiring or building plant and equipment, and working capital in order to procure raw materials, supplies, pay-roll money, etc., for use in the producing process. In line with these purposes, fixed capital would be borrowed for long periods of time and working capital for shorter periods.

There is, however, a third classification of capital which should be noted here. In addition to fixed properties of long life and materials in process of manufacture, etc., many business organizations require large amounts of equipment having a life of from one to five years. This is commonly referred to as intermediate capital and the borrowing operations involved, as "intermediate credit." Traditionally, such capital has been raised either through long-term borrowing, or by the indefinite renewal of short-term loans; and much of it is still raised in these ways. But in recent years there have been developed financial agencies which

137

specialize in intermediate credit operations, especially in the field of agriculture.[1]

While these forms of capital, and the attendant borrowing operations, are functionally different, it is important to bear in mind that in actual practice these distinctions are usually not so clean cut. Indeed, the overlapping is so great, and the lines between are so blurred, that it is often difficult to segregate the various types of capital, except by reference to their physical aspects. Funds borrowed on a short-term basis may be applied to investment purposes, while funds obtained from the sale of bonds and stock may be used for working capital. In fact, it is regarded as essential that such working capital as represents the permanent minimum required should be raised from the sale of securities. In like manner, intermediate capital may be procured on the basis of long-term, short-term, or intermediate credit instruments. It remains true, nevertheless, that the raising of fixed capital usually involves the sale of securities, either directly to investors or through investment banking institutions, while the raising of working capital more often involves borrowing from commercial banking institutions.

The traditional definition of working capital does not, however, adequately cover the term as it is currently employed in corporate accounting. It emphasizes assets in the form of inventories, cash, etc., but ignores certain offsetting liabilities. Corporate practice employs the term *net working capital* to express the difference between the *current assets* and the *current liabilities*. The net figure thus represents the amount of working capital that is owned by the corporation— that is, by the stockholders and bondholders combined.

To give a realistic picture of this whole problem it is necessary to scan the various capital and income items as they appear in the financial accounts of a corporation. The condensed statement on page 139 shows the principal items on the balance sheet and the income account of a typical large industrial corporation. It should be observed that of a total capitalization of 143 million dollars, about 42 million dollars represent working capital, while the balance is invested in fixed forms of capital. Since the surplus is only 33 million dollars, it is apparent that some of the working capital must have been derived from the sale of securities.

In discussing the problems involved in raising business capital it is necessary to differentiate between the raising of capital for new enterprises, and the procurement of additional capital for established and more or less seasoned companies. The former involves direct

[1] See chap. XXVI.

solicitation of funds from potential participants in the enterprise. The latter may be procured either from internal sources—that is, from earnings, and from individuals already connected with or interested in the company—or from external sources. The process of raising capital outside of the company includes (1) the direct sale of securities to

SIGNIFICANT ITEMS IN A CORPORATE FINANCIAL STATEMENT

I. Fixed Capital:

Bonds	$ 47,900,000
Short-term notes	5,000,000
Preferred stock, 5 per cent	10,000,000
Common stock (no par)	47,312,000
Surplus	33,152,000
Total capitalization	**143,364,000**

II. Working Capital:

Cash	17,163,000
U.S. Government Securities	780,000
Inventories	28,867,000
Net receivables	5,517,000
Total current assets	**52,327,000**
Bank loans	1,000,000
Accounts payable	2,686,000
Reserve for taxes	3,550,000
Other	2,820,000
Total current liabilities	**10,056,000**
Net working capital (current assets less liabilities)	**42,271,000**

III. Income and Its Distribution:

Gross income from sales	**110,744,000**
Operating expenses	87,443,000
Depreciation charges	5,215,000
Taxes	3,508,000
Net income	14,578,000
Interest charges	1,913,000
Available for dividends	12,665,000
Dividends paid	7,682,000
Addition to surplus	4,983,000

individuals; (2) the public offering or flotation of securities through the medium of investment banking institutions; and (3) borrowing from commercial banks on the basis of commercial credit instruments. The two latter types of operation will be considered in subsequent chapters, security flotations through investment banks in chapter XII, and commercial bank loans in chapter XVII. At this point we shall discuss only the direct means of raising capital.

1. Security Sales Through Promoters

In former times businesses obtained their capital directly from interested parties—individual owners, or a small group of persons who organize the enterprise. Moreover, a large percentage of present-day corporations secured their start by converting individual firms or partnerships into corporations and issuing shares of stock to the owners. Even today many new businesses, particularly those in speculative lines, are financed in the early stages by direct subscriptions on the part of a limited number of interested persons. Such individuals are usually in a financial position to assume the risks involved; if all goes well they realize large profits, while if the enterprise proves unsuccessful, they pocket their losses. However, many corporations have procured all, or a substantial part, of the funds required from the sale of securities through professional promoters and dealers.

A promoter has been defined as "the person who brings about the incorporation and organization of a corporation. He brings together the persons who become interested in the enterprise, aids in procuring subscriptions, and sets in motion the machinery which leads to the formation of the corporation itself."[2]

The enterprise may be either a new venture or a combination of a number of existing companies. The promoter first obtains options on the properties needed, and then endeavors to interest parties who may be willing to supply the necessary funds. At times the promoter may himself supply the initial funds, and later obtain reimbursement by the sale of stock to the general public. These promoters are of various classes and include the professional promoter, who devotes his entire time to the task of discovering business opportunities and raising funds, and the so-called side-line promoter, who engages in such activities only intermittently.

The promoter of a new issue of securities has at his disposal various means for reaching the investing public. As the diagram on page 133 indicates, one of these means is newspaper advertising, a method that has been followed every extensively in recent years. It is particularly efficacious in boom periods when the general public is both prosperous and credulous. A second method is the sending of circulars through the mails to a list of selected names. This method is perhaps the cheapest of all. Its effectiveness depends largely upon the care and judgment with which the list of names has been chosen. The telephone is also extensively utilized. Another method involves the employment of

---

[2] Cook, W. W., *A Treatise on the Law of Corporations Having Capital Stock*, (8th ed., 1923), Vol. III, pp. 2435–2436.

salesmen who interview potential investors and attempt to convince them of the exceptional nature of the opportunity offered. While more costly than newspaper or circular advertising, this method possesses the advantage that goes with personal contact. The plausible salesman, who can look a hesitating and stammering investor in the eye, is in a much more strategic position to silence doubts than is the cold page of a newspaper or circular letter, or the mere voice over the telephone. It is not to be considered that the foregoing methods are necessarily mutually exclusive. All, indeed, may be resorted to simultaneously.

The following case illustrates the nature of the high pressure advertising that has sometimes been used in connection with the sale of fraudulent securities. A St. Louis business organization checked up on the mailings which a Texas oil firm (so-called) sent to one person. There was a total of 91 mailings, and the report summarizing the facts says: The material itself weighed approximately 11 pounds; 125 envelopes were used; 79 multigraphed pages were sent, represented by 13 one-page letters, 20 two-page letters, 6 three-page letters, and 2 four-page letters; 52 fake newspapers of four or more pages were mailed; 39 pieces of highly lurid prospectus material were utilized; 34 return post cards were furnished; and 72 subscription blanks were inclosed.[3]

It is in connection with the flotation of stocks in new companies that the gravest abuses and the most difficult problems in the control of corporate finance have been found. Since the companies involved are new and untested, and moreover often operate in essentially speculative lines of enterprise, the risks to investors are necessarily great. Moreover, there has been a large amount of fraudulent promotion of fake enterprises. Vast sums have been taken annually from ignorant investors by the sale of utterly worthless securities. The mail frauds alone that have been discovered and stopped by the Federal Government in a single year have amounted to as much as 129 million dollars. There is, of course, no way of estimating the volume of undetected fraud; and there are numerous cases lying within the twilight zone between fraud and legitimacy for which the laws afford no redress.

There are well-known "earmarks" of a swindle. From an analysis of a large number of promotions that proved to be swindles, the following earmarks of a stock-offering of doubtful or fraudulent character have been compiled. It will be evident, however, that honest promotion schemes usually possess some of these "earmarks":

1. The argument that the investor should buy immediately because the price of stock will be advanced within a short time. It is obvious

---

[3] Taken from a publication of Stromberg, Allen and Co., Chicago.

that the arbitrary advancing of the price by a promoter does not increase the true value of the security.

2. The argument that the investor should send a remittance by return mail, or, better still, by wire because there are only a few shares left for distribution. Such golden opportunity, however, usually knocks a second time.

3. The argument that "prominent citizens" are associated with the company and that accordingly the merit of the stock as an investment is virtually guaranteed.

4. The argument that other companies engaged in the same or a similar line of business have made millions from an original investment of little or nothing.

5. The argument that the company desires to place its stock in the hands of very small investors, so that control may not become vested in a "coterie of capitalists." A similar argument is that the company desires to permit only a limited number of persons in each state or in each city to buy the stock. Democratic organization and control as a means of preventing the capitalistic octopus from reaping the rewards of the wonderful idea to which the company has the exclusive right is regarded as a very effective selling device. Companies of this sort always delight in the opportunity to enrich people who find themselves in moderate circumstances.

6. The argument that the company has orders and contracts already in sight, or under consideration, or about to be under consideration, which will insure large earnings on the stock issued.

7. The argument that the company has assets greatly in excess of its stock issue. Mention is seldom made of offsetting liabilities.

Among the physical earmarks of swindling promotion literature, the following have been listed:

1. A picture of the president of the corporation. He is usually a clean-cut, aggressive type of individual, "distinctively American" in appearance.

2. A picture of a factory or of an oil field or of a mine shaft, in some part of which is displayed a sign showing that the photograph is *genuine.*

3. The adoption of a name that is similar to that of a well-known firm or corporation.

4. The absence of reputable financial or banking support.

5. Testimonials of character by unknown persons with imposing business titles.

6. Permitting purchases in installments. The installment plan is to be distinguished, however, from the partial-payment plan used by

many reputable brokers for well-seasoned listed stocks. Installment sales do not usually permit the investor to require a return of the money invested, even in case of fraud. On a partial-payment contract with a reputable broker, however, the investor may order the sale of his stock at the market price and the immediate remittance of his balance.

The career of a promoter is often a vivid one. There have been many cases of actually fraudulent promoters who have carried on their operations for many years. The following biography of a crooked promoter is not untypical.

Death stepped in yesterday and cut short the kaleidoscopic financial career of George Underhill, past master in the art of extracting the mites from the pockets of the middle class in exchange for brilliantly colored stock certificates.

Underhill's most recent stock-selling venture was the Spring Nut Lock Company, said to be capitalized for $4,000,000, the stock of which was peddled in small lots, chiefly by appeals sent through the mails and advertising in magazines circulating in the small towns and rural communities.

Another venture of recent date was the organization of a syndicate to promote what was called the Ford machine gun.

He embarked in the promotion business in 1904, when he attempted to float the Tennessee Development Company. This concern, which was one of his own creations, was capitalized at $500,000, and Underhill endeavored to exchange stock certificates for gold by extensive advertising.

He painted rosy pictures of the money-making possibilities of this stock, playing up the idea of a "triple profit." The plan was to buy Tennessee lands from which the timber would be cut, making one profit; then sheep were to be turned loose to graze upon the land, thus making a second profit; and finally, coal could be mined from beneath it, thus reaping a third profit.

But Underhill waxed even more eloquent in his advertising literature, holding out as inducements to possible investors, in addition to the triple profit, an added "probable oil find" and "other products from the land, such as fruit and farm produce, the bottling and sale of mineral water, the sale of pipe clay, the raising and sale of poultry, hogs, cattle, mules and horses, the breeding of Angora goats for fanciers, etc."

He intimated that as much as 60 per cent in annual profits might be realized from this venture, but according to persons who investigated the proposition the whole scheme revolved around a hundred-acre farm in Tennessee, owned by Underhill's father.

In March, 1905, he was president and treasurer of the George Underhill Company, advertising agents, which was forced into bankruptcy. Liabilities of the company aggregated $39,396, and creditors received practically nothing.

In 1906 Underhill launched into the promotion business again, and became fiscal agent for the Hoosac Tunnel Mining Company. He sold $200,000 worth of stock during that year, but the company proved a failure.

During the same year he sold stock in the Trinity Mining Company. Some of it was sold as low as 35 cents a share. Later he sold stock in the Copper Gold Mines Leasing Company and was also active in a concern known as the Continental Securities Company.

In 1915 Underhill sold stock in the Eagle Macomber Motor Company of Sandusky, Ohio. On May 13, 1915, he was arrested by the federal authorities on orders from Cleveland, Ohio, where he had been indicted on a charge of using the mails to defraud. This was in connection with the sale of 2,000 shares of stock in the Buick Oil Company to a woman in Youngstown, Ohio.[4]

The evils and abuses involved in the direct selling of securities eventually led to the passing of restrictive legislation, first by the various states and finally by the Federal Government. The character of these regulatory measures will be discussed in chapter XVI. It should be noted, however, that many fraudulent securities continue to be issued.

2. Expanding Capital from Earnings

Funds required to expand established enterprises are often procured without resort to the general investment market. The method most universally employed is that of utilizing a portion of the annual earnings. In our earlier history a large part of our capital investment came from such "plowing back" of earnings. In the case of the individual firm or partnership this simply meant restricting withdrawals for living expenses, the balance all going for expansion. With corporations the process is more formal, involving a decision of the management with respect to dividend policy. It is regarded, generally speaking, as sound business policy not to pay out all of current earnings as dividends, but to strengthen and stabilize the financial position of the company by means of annual accretions in the form of surplus. Moreover, regulated industries, notably commercial banking institutions, are sometimes required to accumulate a surplus. In American industry as a whole in the period of the 1920's the surplus was usually increased annually by more than two billion dollars. In the ensuing years of depression surpluses were heavily drawn upon in meeting interest requirements and operating expenses. In recent years the accumulation of surplus has been restricted both by meager income and by a federal tax on undistributed earnings.[5]

It should also be pointed out here that much capital has been accumulated by means of generous depreciation charges and generous

---

[4] From the *Chicago Tribune*, April 5, 1918.

[5] For discussion of the effects of this tax see F. Slade Kendrick, *The Undistributed Profits Tax*, The Brookings Institution, 1937.

reserves for possible contingencies. If a company's plant or equipment has a life of 25 years and if depreciation is charged at the rate of six per cent, it is evident that provision is being made for more than mere replacement. While the tax laws regulate the amount of depreciation and reserve charges that are allowable before computing the net income, there is no doubt that over the years depreciation and reserve accounts have constituted an important source of internal capital accumulation. It is important to recognize, also, that ordinary depreciation provides a means of *replacing* worn-out capital, without which funds for replacement would have to be procured in the money market.

Similarly, capital is often created through the process of charging improvements in plant and equipment to operating expenses. The productive efficiency of the capital of a company may also be increased through the replacement of obsolete equipment by new equipment of an improved type. The dollar investment may remain the same while the capital capacity is greatly enlarged. In passing it should be observed that a large part of the capital accumulations on farms has been the result of a direct process of clearing and improving the land, constructing roads, fences, buildings, etc.

In concluding this discussion it should be noted that there are many large corporations which have never raised much, if any, fixed capital through public stock subscription. These are usually family enterprises or so-called "close" corporations, the bulk of the stock of which is held by a very small group of persons. Among some of the more important of such corporations are: most of the New England cotton mills; several of the larger chemical companies; many of the great department stores in all the large cities of the country; the large corporations in the aluminum, brass, zinc, asbestos, and sulphur industries; and the majority of investment banking houses. The most conspicuous example of the family corporation in the United States is the Ford Motor Company. Mr. Ford and his son are now said to be the sole proprietors of the largest privately owned business in the country. Some of these companies procure extensive short-term loans for working capital purposes, while others shun all borrowing operations.

3. Raising Capital from Individuals Affiliated with the Company

Business enterprises often raise funds from officers, stockholders, or employees, and at times, also, from purchasers of the companies' products. The borrowing of funds from officers is usually for emergency purposes and is evidenced by either a note or an open account. The raising of capital from employees and customers usually involves subscriptions to stock.

The existing stockholders of a corporation may supply capital by means of privileged subscriptions, or rights, giving them the opportunity to subscribe to additional stock under advantageous terms. This method of raising capital is generally utilized in a period when stock market prices are rising. In addition, capital is sometimes raised from shareholders by means of special assessments for needed improvements, especially in connection with re-organizations.

At times many corporations have followed the policy of raising funds by the sale of securities to their own customers. This method presents certain advantages in that it may serve to widen the market for products, and, if the stock should rise in value, to increase public goodwill. This process is particularly adapted to the use of public utility companies. The average public utility experiences steady growth and hence has a continuous need for additional capital. The sale of securities in small amounts to customers takes care of the ordinary needs for extensions, while the sale of securities to the general public provides for improvements of an extraordinary character. Since the utility is a monopoly and under government control, its revenues tend to be comparatively stable; hence its securities make an appeal to the investor who has little knowledge of finance but wishes safety for his principal. The hazards to which this industry has been subjected in recent years have of course materially changed this situation.

The sale of stock to employees, like that to customers, has a double objective—to obtain additional capital and to improve industrial relations. As a rule, stock has been sold to employees under terms more favorable than those offered to the investing public. Moreover, it is usually offered on a deferred payment plan, whereby the employee pays a certain amount out of his weekly wage. A limit has usually been placed on the amount sold to a single employee. At times corporations have agreed to repurchase the stock in the event of a sharp fall in price, rather than see their objectives nullified by losses which employees could ill afford. In general, the sale of stock to employees as a method of raising capital has not proved very successful. It worked well in periods of advancing prices, but in times of depression it involved heavy losses to the companies and at the same time entailed perhaps more ill will than good as far as industrial relations were concerned.

In concluding this discussion of the various ways in which corporations may procure funds without resort to the capital market it may be noted that the choice between the use of internal and external sources of funds depends upon a number of factors. If the corporation shows a steady and satisfactory rate of return, it can very well raise its capital from within. On the other hand, if the earnings are meager or irregular, external sources of capital must be tapped. In general, funds raised from internal sources are used for fixed capital, while working capital should be obtained from external sources, either through the sale of securities or by borrowing from commercial banks.

The company that is able to raise its capital from within—either by restricting dividends or by the sale of stock to affiliated groups— possesses undoubted advantages. As a rule the cost of such financing is considerably less than when funds are borrowed in the market. Again, a company that is independent of the money market is un- affected by variations in money rates or by credit stringencies. More- over, it is less affected by the depression phase of the business cycle, when business in general encounters difficulty in obtaining new capital to continue its operations. On the other hand, an enterprise which finances itself solely by this method cannot take full advantage of the prosperity phase of the business cycle.

4. DEMAND FOR CAPITAL BY CLASSES OF BUSINESS

Marked differences exist in the methods of raising capital employed by business corporations. Attention has already been called to the extent to which some types of business have met their fixed-capital requirements with little, if any, resort to the money market. We shall now note the varying practices of major classes of private business— railroads, public utilities, and industrial enterprises—particularly in respect to the relative use of stocks and bonds.

The American railroads throughout their entire history have followed a policy of raising capital through the sale of securities, particularly bonds. Their short-term bank loans have been of negligible importance and the bonded indebtedness has nearly always exceeded the stock outstanding. The figures for selected years since 1921 are shown in the following table, which also gives the comparative figures for public-utility and industrial corporations. The burden of railway debt proved an unbearable one for many roads during the depression which began in 1929.

The electric-light and power companies, which constitute the most important type of public utilities, have followed a safer policy with reference to the raising of capital. As in the case of the railroads, very little capital has been obtained through short-term borrowing. How- ever, they have procured a much larger portion from the sale of stocks than have the railroads, which has been helpful in enabling them to escape the pressures to which railroads have been subjected in time of depression.

Industrial corporations, including mining, manufacturing and trading companies, have in recent years completely changed their policy of raising capital. Before the World War, most American industrial enter-

SECURITY ISSUES BY TYPES OF BUSINESS
(In Millions)
(Figures Represent New Issues in the Specified Years)

Class	1921		1925		1929		1933		1937	
	Number	Per cent	Number	Per cent	Number	Per cent	Number	Per cent	Number	Per cent
Railroads:										
Bonds......	352.7	100.0	364.1	95.7	413.2	75.6	12.0	100.0	200.1	100.0
Stocks......	.....	0.0	16.2	4.3	133.3	24.4	.....	0.0	.....	0.0
Public utility:										
Bonds......	374.9	76.2	972.3	65.7	702.8	36.4	27.2	79.5	144.3	61.4
Stocks......	117.1	23.8	508.7	34.3	1,229.1	63.6	7.0	20.5	5.8	38.6
Industrial:										
Bonds......	825.9	84.4	1,552.9	69.3	1,434.7	23.3	1.1	1.0	411.2	50.9
Stocks......	152.4	15.6	686.5	30.7	4,726.3	76.7	113.4	99.0	397.1	49.1

prises, including even large corporations, obtained most of their working capital through short-term borrowing from banking institutions. During the war period this practice was intensified because the investment market was largely restricted to government issues. As a result of rising prices and an expanding volume of business due to the war boom the current debt of a large group of industrial corporations increased from 8,544 million dollars in 1913 to 16,750 million dollars in 1920. In the depression following 1920, this large unfunded debt proved a serious menace to many industrial corporations; but fortunately this depression was short-lived. Throughout the remainder of the twenties the industrial corporations obtained less and less capital from commercial banking channels and more and more through investment financing, and as a result there was a complete change in the relation between their current debt in the form of notes and accounts payable and their fixed debt in the form of bonds and mortgages. Whereas in 1921 short-term debts accounted for approximately 80 per cent of the total, by 1932 they amounted to only about 50 per cent.

Industrial corporations have always made a much larger use of stock issues than have either the railroad or public-utility groups. This fact is in part attributable to the larger element of risk ordinarily involved in industrial enterprises, but it is also a reflection of general policy. As the table on page 148 shows, the proportion of industrial capital raised through stock sales increased rapidly during the twenties at a time when the stability of industrial enterprise was increasing.

METHODS OF RAISING LONG-TERM CAPITAL 1919–1937[a]

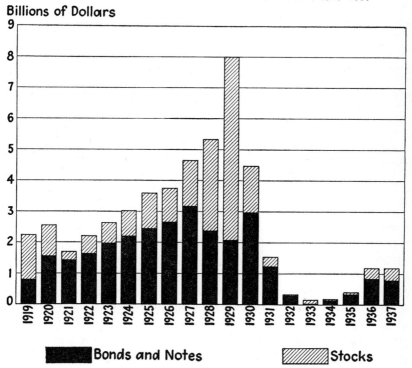

a Data from *Commercial and Financial Chronicle.*

The great argument in favor of stock issues is that greater flexibility is permitted in adjusting disbursements of income in the light of changing business conditions.

The accompanying chart shows the aggregate amount of new financing by all types of corporations through the use of bonds and short-term notes and stock from 1922 to 1936. It will be seen that the proportion of stocks increased very rapidly during the twenties, but has since declined.

II. RAISING PUBLIC CAPITAL

In recent decades the role of government in connection with economic activities has been constantly expanding. This has been true in all countries and is characteristic of state, provincial, and local, as well as of national governments. Whereas in the nineteenth century government operations in connection with capital enterprise were confined to a relatively few fields, particularly to military works and transportation, they now cover a wide range of activities. Accordingly, an analysis of capital requirements in modern society would not be complete without a brief account of the purposes for which and the ways in which governments raise funds. This problem has already been touched upon in chapter VII, but since attention was there focused on the relations of federal government finance to monetary stability, some further discussion is necessary at this place.

The financial requirements of governments are normally met largely from taxation revenues. However, even when the annual tax receipts are adequate to meet current expenditures it is usually necessary to borrow for the purpose of meeting outlays which are temporarily in excess of revenues. The Federal Government finances these "working capital" requirements by the sale of Treasury notes or certificates of indebtedness, chiefly to commercial banks. Local government agencies have typically used for this purpose an instrument known as the "tax anticipation warrant." These short-term government obligations when issued by stable governments are a highly satisfactory form of short-term investment for banks, since they combine safety with assurance of prompt payment at maturity. They are usually purchased on a discount basis, and the yield is as a rule very low.

The more important financial requirements of governments are those arising out of war needs and in connection with the development of public enterprises involving large outlays which can be liquidated only over a period of years. The former require the raising of large sums by bond issues; and it is expected that they will be paid off in due course out of ordinary tax receipts. Outlays for public enterprises may be liquidated either from ordinary sources of revenue or from the earnings of the enterprises themselves. When the latter is the case they are of course directly analogous to private capital enterprise. It should be noted here, however, that a considerable amount of public capital development in the United States has at times been financed directly out of tax revenues. This is particularly true with respect to river and harbor improvements, military properties, and government buildings.

Federal government expenditures for purposes which may be described as public capital construction have increased greatly in recent years. For example, an aggregate of $381,644,000 for such purposes in 1930 had increased by 1934 to $947,800,000, which is close to the level of succeeding years. The detailed classification of such expendi-

tures for 1930 and 1934 is shown in the following table. Inasmuch as
few of these enterprises yield income to the Government, they have to
be paid for out of ordinary tax receipts.[6]

FEDERAL GOVERNMENT EXPENDITURES FOR CAPITAL
CONSTRUCTION

Item	1930	1934
Government buildings..........................	$ 44,921,000	$ 78,706,000
Military capital..............................	112,338,000	124,109,000
Public roads.................................	86,239,000	267,882,000
Waterways and harbors......................	69,195,000	79,115,000
Flood control...............................	26,690,000	40,984,000
Public Works Administration loans (capital construction).................................	....	149,335,000
Reconstruction Finance Corporation loans (capital construction)...........................	....	67,434,000
Miscellaneous other.........................	42,261,000	140,235,000
Total...................................	$381,644,000	$947,800,000

State and local governments also raise large amounts of capital
for the purpose of developing enterprises deemed socially important.
These include schools and school buildings, roads and streets, rapid
transit, waterfront and harbor improvements, sewerage facilities, etc.
The outlays for education, highways, and welfare purposes, particularly, have for many years shown a tendency to increase. Outlays for
these purposes are covered in part from general taxes and in part from
special taxes levied in connection with the enterprises themselves.
In 1932, for example, state and local government receipts from public
enterprises amounted to 2,494 million dollars, as compared with
6,358 millions in tax revenues.

The growth of the net indebtedness of all local governments from
1912 to 1932, the last year for which detailed data are available, is
shown in the following table:

NET DEBT OF ALL LOCAL GOVERNMENTS, 1912–1932
(In Millions of Dollars)

Class	1912	1922	1932
Counties................................	371.6	1,273.2	2,390.8
Cities, towns, villages, and boroughs........	2,871.6	4,679.3	8,842.1
School districts..........................	118.9	1,052.9	2,039.8
Other civil divisions.....................	35.7	625.6	1,599.1
Total................................	$3,475.9	$7,753.9	$15,215.6

[6] For credit operations of the Government, see chap. XXVIII.

A brief statement only is necessary with reference to the methods by which long-term government borrowing operations are carried out. The Federal Government uses the Federal Reserve banks as fiscal agents in the marketing of its securities, both long, intermediate, and short-term. The Federal Reserve banks sell the securities to banking institutions, insurance companies, and individuals.[7] Mention should also be made of the fact that there are two or three security houses which specialize in government securities, both domestic and foreign, providing a ready market for the sale or acquisition of government issues. State and local government bonds are typically handled through the investment banking houses which are discussed in the next chapter. Some of these houses specialize in providing a continuous market for the purchase and sale of municipal securities.

[7] For further discussion see chap. XXIII, sec. V.

CHAPTER XII

MARKETING SECURITIES THROUGH INVESTMENT HOUSES

The growth of corporate enterprise has necessitated the development of investment banking institutions as intermediaries in the process of assembling the vast accumulations of liquid capital required. The securities that are marketed by these financial houses include the issues of railroad, public utility, industrial, and other corporations, and of federal, state, city, county, township, and other local government bodies. Real estate securities are usually not marketed through these investment channels.[1] Until comparatively recent times *stock* issues were not handled by investment banks, which were commonly referred to as *bond houses*, but nowadays these institutions handle all types of securities. Some houses, however, specialize in the marketing of bonds; some are mainly concerned with issues of high-grade stock, common as well as preferred; while others handle both bonds and stock.

I. HISTORY OF INVESTMENT BANKING

Investment banking institutions are of comparatively recent development, their history running parallel with that of the corporate form of industry, outlined in chapter X. Investment financiers, however, have existed for many centuries. In medieval times kings and governments received their revenues, as now, largely from taxes. Since the need for funds was practically continuous, while the taxes were received only intermittently, there developed the practice of securing "advances" from powerful financiers, to whom the collecting of taxes was "farmed out" as security for loans. The financial needs of the various European rulers were at times so great that the financiers to whom they looked for aid came practically to dominate the political as well as the financial life of Europe. Where the "tax security" was insufficient, valuable property was sometimes mortgaged to the financiers. For instance, in 1487 Jacob Fugger, having grown tremendously wealthy through operations in trading, mining, and banking, received the rich mines of the Tyrol as a guaranty for the payment of

---

[1] For a discussion of the marketing of urban real estate bonds and mortgages see chap. XXVII.

a loan to Duke Sigismund. This was followed by large loans to Sigismund's successor, Maximilian, and to Pope Julius II; while after the death of Maximilian, Charles V succeeded in becoming Roman emperor "by the purchase of electors on funds borrowed from the Fuggers." By 1524 the Fuggers had assumed control of a large part of the Spanish land taxes and mines; they had establishments in Poland, Hungary, Antwerp, and Naples; and their operations and power extended from Belgium to India.

These early private bankers conducted their operations mainly with their own funds or by means of capital raised from a small group of persons closely associated with them. The investment banker in the modern sense—as the intermediary who mobilizes the funds of a large number of individuals by selling them securities—did not appear until the end of the eighteenth and the beginning of the nineteenth centuries.

During the period of the Napoleonic wars certain of the belligerent governments, particularly Great Britain, floated public securities through private investment bankers, notably the Rothschilds. This firm was first established in Frankfurt, but later opened branches in London, Paris, Vienna and Naples. It was not until well toward the middle of the nineteenth century that investment bankers began to float private corporate securities, chiefly those of the railroads which were then being built on the Continent.

The private unincorporated houses of Europe remained supreme in the field of investment banking until the end of the nineteenth century, though on the Continent, particularly in Germany, the large incorporated banks, which conducted both investment and commercial operations, gradually assumed an important role. After the World War however, these private investment houses were severely shaken by the disturbed conditions and in most countries lost their importance.

In the United States there was little investment banking prior to 1860. The small-scale private enterprises conducted on an individual or partnership basis procured their capital directly from those immediately interested. The financing of public works and railroads was effected partly through loans from banking institutions—often directly affiliated with the enterprise—and partly by the issue and sale of securities to the investing public. The funds were generally obtained for these early corporations from local investors, principally of the merchant class, "ranging from the small country storekeeper to the wealthy metropolitan merchant importer; there were others, however, as well: retired farmers or merchants; widows of substance; children who had inherited well; landed proprietors who had picked up public securities; successful speculators in stocks; and a considerable body of small savers in town and country. In numerous cases funds were also secured from outside the locality—principally in financial centers such as New York, Boston, and Philadelphia,"[2] From the beginning some capital was also drawn from abroad. In the Colonial period a considerable volume of funds was annually brought in by immigrants, and there were some loans to this country by European capitalists.

The Revolutionary War was financed mainly by the issue of paper currency. Although the funds required to wage the War of 1812 were procured in part from the sale of securities, most of the issues were placed, not among the general public, but with a few individual capitalists, such as John Jacob Astor. Until the outbreak of the Civil War, the Federal Government entered the general capital market only at rare intervals, as in financing the Mexican War. The state governments, however, were heavy borrowers. In the 1820's New York floated a bond issue to finance the Erie Canal, and the success of this venture led other states to issue securities for the construction of public works. As municipalities increased in size they also began to borrow for the purpose of public improvements. The funds required for these local government enterprises were procured in part from local capitalists and in part from foreign lenders. By 1828 some 14 million dollars of the federal debt was held by British and five millions by continental investors.[3] Foreign investors also held the larger part of the state debts; but only a small part of the municipal indebtedness was held abroad.

The few existing private bankers, such as George Peabody, whose house was later to become J. P. Morgan and Company, engaged in a variety of banking operations, not only in the sale of American securities to foreign investors, but also in foreign exchange and in stock brokerage. The more important private foreign banking houses of Europe such as the Rothschilds and Barings, conducted agencies in this country.

Investment banking, as we know it today, arose from the financial requirements of the Civil War. In order to raise the necessary funds, the Federal Government resorted to the flotation of securities to the public at large. This task was intrusted to Jay Cooke who is known as the father of modern investment banking in this country. Cooke employed the device of distributing the federal securities by means of salesmen throughout the United States and even in Europe.

[2] Davis, *Essays in Early History of American Corporation*, IV, pp. 279–302.
[3] Chatters, Carl H., *Municipal Debt Defaults*, 1933, p. 10.

The last quarter of the nineteenth century witnessed the growth of a number of private investment banking houses, notably the firms of J. P. Morgan and Company in New York and N. W. Harris and Company in Chicago. These houses undertook to finance not only the needs of federal, state, and municipal governments, but also those of the railroads and the new industrial combinations of the late nineteenth and early twentieth centuries. At this time American investment houses also began to float occasional issues of foreign securities. In 1915 and 1916 American houses marketed large loans for the allied governments, while in the twenties they floated a great volume of securities not only for European but also for South American governments.[4]

II. FUNCTIONS OF INVESTMENT BANKING INSTITUTIONS

The terminology that is commonly employed in speaking of the work of investment banking institutions is somewhat confusing. Some

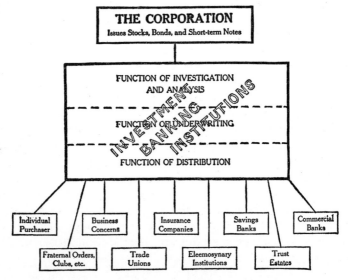

writers speak of houses of first purchase, of underwriters, and of distributing bond houses in a way that would lead one to believe that they are distinct and specialized institutions, each performing a particular task and that only. If a clear view of the work of investment banks is to be gained, it will be necessary to make a classification that runs in terms of functions rather than in terms of institutions. The

[4] For detailed discussion of foreign investments in the United States, see Lewis, Cleona, *America's Stake in Foreign Investments*, The Brookings Institution, 1938.

diagram on page 156 attempts to set forth the several functions that are performed by investment banks.

In brief, the function of investigation and analysis is to determine whether a proposed bond issue has sufficient merit to be offered to a conservative investing public. It is the function of underwriting to assume the risks that inhere in the raising of the funds required and to insure the corporation that it shall have its funds on a specified date, whether or not the securities have been sold to the investing public. It is the function of distribution to sell an issue of securities to investors. All of these functions may be, and usually are, performed by a single institution, although there is some degree of specialization by investment bankers. Such concerns as Morgan, Stanley and Company are interested solely in original investigation and underwriting, while, on the other hand, there are many small security houses whose activities are mainly confined to retail distribution.

III. INVESTIGATION AND ANALYSIS

The original investigation and analysis of an issue of securities may be undertaken by any investment bank, large or small. There are a great many relatively small issues of securities put out by medium-sized concerns that are handled by small and inconspicuous investment houses. In the case of very large issues, however, a few great financial houses have dominated the field.

The problem of investigation and analysis arises whenever a corporation approaches an investment banker with a request for assistance in the marketing of an issue of securities. The task of the investigation is, first, to ascertain whether the proposed issue is sound, and second, to name a selling price that will be satisfactory to the corporation and will at the same time enable the banker to make a profit on the transaction. It must be clearly understood that the investment banking institutions which we are now considering are concerned not with speculative issues but with securities which are conservative in character. In making an analysis:

The investment banker avails himself of all possible information—that furnished by the engineer, the accountant, the banker and the successful business leader—and reduces it all in the crucible of his experience and training. The security which passes the acid test of this process may be regarded as possessing the merits to which the reputable investment banker certifies.[5]

The fixing of a price by the investment banker is sometimes easy and sometimes difficult. In the case of a corporation that has outstand-

[5] From an article published by A. H. Bickmore & Co.

ing issues enjoying a broad and active market, the naming of a satisfactory purchase price is under ordinary circumstances not difficult.
The existing market for an issue of this character is carefully studied,
as is also the general bond market situation at the time. A bid is then
made at a figure sufficiently under current quotations for such securities to insure a reasonable profit to the investment banker. The fixing
of a price on a new and untried issue, however, requires the most
careful judgment. The best that can be done is to make comparisons
with the current prices of issues of a similar character. Since the investment market is often capricious, many losses are sustained by the
investment banker.

The task of investigating and analyzing the numerous factors
which govern the value of investment securities varies considerably
with the different types of issuing bodies. In the case of government
issues, safety depends primarily upon the adequacy of the taxation
revenues of the issuing government; but there is also involved a
consideration of the legality of the issue. The analysis of public-utility
securities involves the question of franchise rights and of regulation by
public-utility commissions, as well as the potential earning power of
the company in question. Similarly, in the case of railroad issues there
must be considered the earning possibilities of the road, together with
the regulations imposed both by the Federal Government and the various states through whose territory the railroad runs. With industrial
securities, the analysis is largely concerned with the ascertainment of
earnings, although in the case of monopolies the problem of governmental regulation is also a factor. With all classes of securities, the
character and ability of the management are, of course, matters of
paramount importance.

The diagram on page 161 is designed to show the factors that enter
into a determination of bond values. While some writers would doubtless arrange the items somewhat differently, it is believed that this
broad classification into legal, technical, psychological, and economic
factors will assist the reader in understanding the nature of the
analysis required.

The following analysis[6] of bond values indicates the variety of
technical and economic factors that must be weighed in the balance.

To the task of investment analysis should be brought an equipment that
consists not merely of a knowledge of accounts; that is useful chiefly to open
the gates of knowledge. As much information as possible should be gathered
with respect to the nature of the business, its methods and possibilities of
operation, and the relation of the enterprise to the remainder of the industrial

---

[6] From an article in *Chicago Banker*, January 18, 1913, by H. S. Mott.

or commercial community. It has been said that the newspaper man should be a Jack-of-all-trades. It might well be said that the dealer in securities should be a master of all trades. Through all the investment analysis should be applied the horse sense of a sound business experience, for financial miracles ceased with Aladdin and his lamp.

Investment analysis is concerned primarily with just three things, as follows: (a) profits; (b) the relation of assets to liabilities; and (c) physical property. Secondary factors are (a) the nature of the specific security offered; and (b) the conditions at present existing and likely to exist in the investment market. Under these five headings can be taken into account all the facts that make or unmake security investments. And out of the answers obtained by subjecting questions to facts and figures is constructed that projection of opinion—that prophetic vision—which constitutes the only real investment judgment.

I confess to an uncontrollable prejudice for a scrutiny of the income account as the first method of approach to the problem of bond values. When an enterprise makes real money for its shareholders, it also makes values in use for the physical property it owns. . . . Physical values out of use, even temporarily, shrink to distressingly small proportions, as the records of the bankruptcy courts disclose.

Preliminary investigation should subordinate the other elements of safety to the question of earnings. Current earnings and expenses should be compared with similar items at least for the preceding year, but preferably with those of a number of years preceding. Gross earnings or gross sales of merchandise should be expected to show more or less steady increases, for the business, like the individual, that merely stands still goes backward.

If one company manufactures harvesting machines, another a standard, moderate-priced automobile, and another conducts a large mail-order business in the rural districts, will the demand for their goods be affected by large or small crops—the prosperity or the adversity of the farmers? If a network of trolleys is built in the territory of a railroad, will the road's passenger traffic be curtailed? If natural gas is discovered near a large city and shortly will be delivered to consumers at thirty cents a thousand feet, how will the company manufacturing gas for ninety cents a thousand feet to the consumer be affected? To what extent is the market for a company's product dependent upon tariff duties? Do the records of other similar cases guide opinion? Or is experience of little service? In any event before we make an investment, wisdom dictates that we form some solidly based opinion on these or other matters that may be pertinent. It is the future status of our securities that interests us.

But suppose, as is frequently the case, we find that the demand for a commodity is fairly stable or, better still, shows a well-marked tendency from year to year to expand, with a likelihood that the tendency will continue. It is not, after all, gross earnings that are applicable to dividends on stocks, or, for that matter, to interest on bonds; it is net income. If expenses increase as rapidly as gross earnings, the values of the securities involved stand still or, in the comparative appraisals of the market, decline. What do the expense accounts show? Does the cost of conducting the business increase more rapidly than do gross earnings or by a larger percentage? If so, in what items and why? When these questions shall be adequately answered, we shall be in a position reasonably to determine whether the increase in expenses, if there be an increase, is due to avoidable or unavoidable causes, whether the increase is a fluctuation or discloses a tendency, and whether part or all of the increase in expenses, such as outlay for betterment and reconstruction, is likely to yield larger profits in the future.

The creation of reserve funds for depreciation, insurance, etc., and periodical charges to net earnings for their continuation and expansion according to the probable needs of the business, greatly enhance the investment values of securities. Property in use derives a large part of its value as a going concern and, therefore, for security holders by having worn-out parts constantly replaced and by being protected against unusual hazards. If, then, net earnings increase by a percentage as large as, or larger than, gross earnings, and if good judgment dictates that the conditions surrounding the volume of business done, the prices obtainable, and the expenses, are unlikely to change for the worse, the securities of such a corporation, other things being equal, should be desirable investments.

Assets and liabilities.—The financial status of an enterprise at the close of business on a particular day makes an exhibit with which bankers as lenders of money are familiar. As an exhibit of a company's ability to repay loans in a short time, it is of more service than the income account. For the purpose of investment analysis it is subordinate only to the income account. It is presumed to be an exact statement of all assets and all liabilities. Actually, in many cases, it is nothing of the sort. The property accounts among the assets sometimes contain items of intangible, as well as items of tangible, property. Good-will, franchises, patents, etc., when they are rated high as assets, produce water in securities purer than that to be brought to New York by the new Catskill aqueduct. Capital stock theoretically is fully paid and in a balance sheet is treated as money owed to stockholders. But actually it is often not fully paid, and, except as required through dissolution and liquidation, the amount it represents is never legally owed to anybody. The surplus of current assets over current liabilities, or, as surplus is called, "net quick assets," constitute the working capital of a concern. Its proportions in relation to the need for working capital are of the utmost importance. Many a soundly based enterprise has passed into control of the courts because its promoters failed to supply it with the sinews of war or its management paid out all profits in dividends.

In the balance sheet also should appear the accumulations of the various reserve funds which, to the extent that they are profits reserved against remote contingencies, may be considered as part of the surplus account. A profit and loss account, or even surplus itself, may mean much or little, according to the nature of the equities in assets that it represents. A profit and loss deficit never should appear except in the construction stages of an enterprise.

DETERMINATION OF BOND VALUES

LEGAL FACTORS

Legality of the issue
Nature of the security
Taxation provisions
Responsibility of trustee
Powers of regulating commissions

TECHNICAL FACTORS

Engineering
Building, equipment, etc.
Organization of factory, etc.
Character of output

Accounting
Income
Sinking fund or amortization
Reserves and depreciation
Net worth
Net working capital

Financial Details
Maturity
Dates of interest payment
Interest rates
Coupons and registration

BOND VALUES

ECONOMIC FACTORS

Peculiar to this Concern
Nature of business
Character and skill of
  managers
Location of plant
Condition of market
Labor conditions
Insurance

General Economic Conditions
Money market conditions,
  present and prospective
Volume of other issues
Stage of the business cycle
Industrial unrest
Political stability

PSYCHOLOGICAL FACTORS

Public familiarity with the enterprise
Good-will enjoyed
Speculative sentiment
Name given to bond
Reputation of banking house

Among assets almost invariably the largest account is "cost of property." This account includes all fixed, or more or less permanent, assets needed in the conduct of the business, such as real estate, plants, machinery, equipment, etc. As it is against part or all of the physical property included in this account that mortgage bonds usually are issued, the make-up of the account obviously is important. In it might be included the original cost of a branch railroad that long had ceased to yield profits or to be kept in good repair, and of which the value in use of the physical property would be hard to discover. Or it might be found that a plant was adapted to profitable production only under circumstances of manufacture or of competition that have passed. Or worse than all, good-will may become the basis for the issuance of "mortgage" securities through the purchase of another going concern. The methods of arriving at "cost of property" through betterments, additions, depreciation, and reserve deserve careful consideration. These all have to do with the future status of the mortgaged fixed property. We should make some reasonable determination that its value in use in the future shall be as much as, if not actually more than, at present.

The success of investment bankers will obviously vary with the degree of their mastery of the legal, technical, psychological, and general economic factors which enter into the determination of investment values.

IV. UNDERWRITING

The ability of a corporation to construct new plant and equipment or to extend the scope of its operations in any direction is dependent upon an available supply of funds. Since an issue of bonds or stock is subject to the conditions of a capricious market, the securities can sometimes be quickly sold to the investing public at a favorable price while at other times months or even years may be required for their absorption at almost any price. The function of underwriting has arisen as a means of protecting the borrowing corporation from the vagaries of the investment market—of insuring the possession of the funds required at the precise time that they are needed.

It is difficult to make a precise statement about the function of underwriting for the reason that the term is often loosely used, having different meanings for different people. It will make for clearness of understanding, however, if we always keep in mind the fact that whoever participates in underwriting agrees, if a slang expression may be pardoned, to "hold the bag" in case the securities are not sold to ultimate investors. Sometimes a single institution may underwrite an entire issue; but in more cases a considerable number of houses unite for the purpose.

In the diagram on page 156, underwriting is placed in an intermediate position between investigation and analysis, and distribution. There is good reason for this, because in point of time the underwriting follows the investigation and analysis and precedes the distribution of securities.

A joint-account arrangement, or an underwriting syndicate, is formed whenever a house has in charge an issue that is larger than it can handle conveniently with its own resources. There are a number of investment banks in the larger cities of the country which are able to handle with their own resources an issue of securities of two or three millions of dollars. The number of houses which can handle without assistance issues in excess of five million dollars is, however, limited. Issues as large as fifty million dollars are not at all uncommon; but they are handled by a syndicate of underwriting houses.

The nature of the entire process of underwriting and marketing securities may best be revealed by some concrete illustrations involving the joint-account arrangement and the underwriting syndicate.

Under a joint-account arrangement several investment bankers "participate" in the underwriting. Suppose, for instance, that company A has in charge an issue of securities which it cannot handle satisfactorily alone. It seeks the assistance of companies B, C, and D. Let us assume that the amount of the issue is ten million dollars and that company A takes four millions and the B, C, and D companies two millions each. Under this arrangement each banking house agrees to advance to the corporation on a stipulated date a sum of money proportionate to the extent of its participation. To be concrete, let us suppose that the A company had decided that the bonds could be marketed at $98 per share and that in view of the expenses incident to the marketing process, the corporation should receive $95 per share. The corporation would therefore receive $9,500,000, four-tenths of which would be underwritten by A and two-tenths by B, C, and D, respectively. If the bonds were sold at $98, the gross profit to the four concerns for bringing out the issue and underwriting and distributing it would be $300,000, from which, of course, would have to be deducted the expenses incident to the business.

Let us suppose that the issue had been underwritten on January 1 and that the date fixed for payment of the funds to the corporation was February 1. If investors look upon the issue with favor at the price of $98, it may be that it can all be sold during the interval; but if the investors are not favorably disposed it may be that only a small portion can be sold before February. In this event, the participating investment bankers must pay for the securities out of their own resources or with funds borrowed from commercial banks. Since their own resources are usually small in proportion to the volume of securities which they are handling, it is generally necessary to borrow heavily, on the basis of promissory notes backed by the securities that are being underwritten as collateral.

If the bond market continues to be apathetic with reference to this particular issue, the participants will either have to "carry the securities" on borrowed funds for a considerable period, sometimes many months, or offer them at a lower price to the public. The former alternative involves tying up funds for an indefinite time, with a loss of interest during the interval; the latter involves accepting a loss through selling at a price that will not cover the expenses that have been incurred.

Under this joint-account arrangement the houses concerned act both as underwriters and distributors. They divide the profits, or losses, in direct proportion to the participation, regardless of the number of shares each house may be able to sell. The joint-account is a species of partnership. It usually calls for an undivided, or unlimited, liability of the participants, though sometimes the agreement provides for a division of the liability. The securities are also handled as a "lump," under the management of some member of the group of associated houses; even the borrowing from the banks is a joint affair.

The underwriting "syndicate" assumes the risks of marketing. In the case of large issues, and often in the case of small ones handled by a banking house or houses of limited resources, a selling syndicate is formed for the purpose both of distributing the risks more widely and of facilitating the sale of the securities. Such a syndicate may be formed by an individual house, or by a group of houses handling an issue of securities on joint-account, as described above.

To make the illustration as concrete as possible, let us assume that X company has investigated a proposition for an issue of 50 million dollars of four per cent bonds. Since the issue is larger than could be handled successfully by a single house, or even by a group of houses operating on joint-account, the X company proceeds to organize a syndicate to underwrite the issue. The X company alone deals with the borrowing corporation, acting as an intermediary between the houses which participate in the underwriting and the corporation whose securities are being issued. As we shall see, this house gets a special return as a reward for bringing out the issue and for organizing and managing the syndicate.

In the case under consideration, suppose that X company has agreed to pay to the corporation a price of 95, and that it has been decided to offer the issue to the investing public at 98. Assume, also, that a commission of one per cent must be paid to those who assist in the selling of the securities. This leaves a possible two-point difference for profits to the managers of the issue. If no underwriting syndicate were formed, this would all go to the X company; but since this house has not sufficient resources to assume conveniently the risks involved in so large a venture, it foregoes the chance of securing all the profits—and of standing all the losses—and distributes the opportunity and the risk among a number of houses.

Let us now assume that the underwriters in the case cited agree to buy at 95¼ any bonds that are not taken by the public at 98, before the date set for advancing the funds to the corporation. X company is thus assured of a profit of $2.50 per $1000 bond, less expenses for its services in connection with the original analysis and investigation and the organization and management of the underwriting syndicate. By virtue of their agreement with the underwriters they have contracted themselves out of any risk of loss, except as they also may participate in the underwriting process, as noted below.

It is often good business policy for a large house to organize an underwriting syndicate, even though it could assume the entire risks alone. By calling in a number of houses to participate in the underwriting it conserves some of its own resources and thereby is enabled to take on additional issues as opportunity offers—additional issues on which it will receive a return for its work as original investigator and as organizer and manager of a new syndicate.

If the sale is a success, the underwriters who have agreed to buy at 95¼ the bonds which are sold at 98 receive 1¾ per cent for the risk they have assumed—the distributors getting the other one point as noted above. If the sale is not a success, the underwriters must accept the bonds at 95¼, and then either tie up capital indefinitely by holding the securities for a more favorable market, or accept a heavy loss by selling at a figure below their purchase price. If they elect to "carry" the securities it will be necessary for them to borrow most of the requisite funds from the commercial banks.

Many banking houses may participate in the underwriting. In the case of an underwriting syndicate of the sort just described, the house of first purchase may also participate in the underwriting, thus acting in a double capacity. Similarly, the participating underwriting houses may perform a double function—soliciting subscriptions for the sale of bonds and assuming the risks of underwriting. In the example above, an investment banker would receive one dollar per bond as a distributing agency, and two dollars as an underwriter. It is important to bear in mind, however, that the actual amounts received for any of the functions connected with the marketing of securities vary with different issues and at different periods of time.

One of the things to be guarded against by the underwriting syndicate is the passing of an issue of securities into the hands of speculators before the expiration of the underwriting agreement. If purchased by speculators who have misjudged the potential demand, securities will often be thrown on the market. Such precipitate selling may serve greatly to depress the price, with resulting losses to the underwriters.

Syndicates are always temporary organizations, being dissolved as soon as a particular transaction is completed. They are being formed continuously, however, and a given house may at one time be a member of several syndicates. It is usually good business policy to form an underwriting syndicate, apart from the reason noted on page 165, for syndicate operations enable a wider distribution of risks. Invitations to participate in syndicate operations are usually reciprocal; and the risks are obviously more widely distributed if a house has underwritten a million dollars' worth of securities issued by five different companies than when it has underwritten a million of a single issue.

V. DISTRIBUTION

The volume of corporate securities has attained such enormous proportions in modern times that the distribution function has required the development of elaborate selling organizations. Besides the large houses, which exercise at once the functions of investigation and analysis, underwriting, and distribution, there are many small dealers and brokers who assist in the retailing of securities.

The larger houses maintain offices in the leading financial centers, such as New York, Boston, and Chicago, and also in London. The American offices are all connected by private wires and it is not unusual for a single concern to dispose of five million dollars' worth of bonds in a day. In order to accomplish such a feat it is necessary for the banking house to be in close communication with institutions, brokers, and groups of individuals, who can act quickly and buy in large quantities. A considerable percentage of such sales would be to the smaller dealers and brokers, and much of the remainder to savings banks, and insurance and trust companies.

As already indicated, *distribution* relates to the selling end of the bond business—to the placing of securities in the hands of ultimate investors. To guard against confusion of thought it may again be stated that distribution is not a function which is specialized in exclusively by certain houses. Under the American system as it has evolved all of the investment banks perform this as well as the other functions. For instance, when a single house brings out an issue and underwrites it without assistance, it also markets the issue. Similarly, when a group of houses together underwrite an issue, they also unite in the selling process. And when a syndicate has been organized, the various houses participate both in the underwriting and in the distribution of the issue; indeed, the participating houses are often spoken of as a "selling syndicate." In general it may be said, however, that the tendency is for only one house, or a small group of houses, to bring out an issue and organize the syndicate; for a considerable number of houses to participate in the underwriting; and for a very much larger number to take part in the selling campaign.

It should be noted, also, that a member of the syndicate is not necessarily obliged to sell the same amount of securities that it has underwritten. For instance, a house may agree to underwrite $100,000 of bonds; but it may undertake to sell only $50,000. If the entire issue is successfully marketed, the house in question receives its underwriting profit on $100,000 and its distributing commission on $50,000. If the issue is not all sold, it must buy in its share of the unsold portion and assume the risks of marketing it at a loss. It would still receive its selling commission, however, on whatever amount it had individually succeeded in marketing.

The distributors assume some of the risks. In a sense the outside distributors, that is, those not members of the underwriting syndicate, also perform an underwriting function; for they are not permitted to return any securities for which they have subscribed. Since distributors buy at a fixed price, say one point less than the price to the public, they are taking a chance of not being able to market the securities at a profit. If the issue does not go well, they will have either to sell at a price below what they have paid for the securities, or to hold them for a rise. It will be noted, however, that while these small houses and brokerage offices thus assume some of the risks involved, their risks as distributors are only in proportion to their purchases; they do not guarantee that the entire issue will be bought, as does the original underwriting syndicate. Another way of stating the matter is that the original underwriters assume the risks first, and then pass them on, in whole or in part as the case may be, to the distributing houses. Even though not members of the syndicate, these retail dealers are debarred, by written agreement, from selling below the syndicate price before the termination of the syndicate underwriting agreement—as is the case with the participants in the syndicate.

Since each subscription is made in ignorance of the amount that is being subscribed for by other houses, an issue may be over or undersubscribed. In the case of an oversubscription, allotments of bonds for distribution are made in such proportion as the total number of bonds to be issued bears to the total amount subscribed for. For instance, if an issue has been oversubscribed by 25 per cent, the number of bonds available would be to the number of bonds subscribed for as 100 to 125, or 4 to 5; hence if a house has subscribed for $100,000 of bonds it would be allotted $80,000 and the distributor's commission would be paid on only $80,000. If, on the other hand, the issue is undersubscribed, the subscribing house receives its commission on the amount actually subscribed for.

At the beginning of this functional analysis of investment banking operations in the United States, attention was called to the fact that a given banking house commonly participates in two or more functions. The combination of underwriting and distributing functions in a single house has given rise to some of the most serious abuses in the field of investment banking. The difficulty is that the effort to make profits from both underwriting and distribution leads to a conflict of objectives. The primary obligation of the underwriter is to the borrowing corporation, and his service should be rendered on a strictly professional basis. When an underwriting house engages in distribution it builds up an extensive sales organization, and in order to keep this organization at work it may appear necessary to take offerings which do not measure up to the best standards—meanwhile putting pressure on the distribution force to sell them at a price which may offset underwriting mistakes and losses. Similarly, when a distributor engages in underwriting he assumes a financial burden which in some measure disqualifies him from serving his clients in a spirit of detachment. In the view of many close students of the problem a complete separation of underwriting from distribution is essential to the successful operation of the investment banking system.

VI. SUNDRY SERVICES OF INVESTMENT BANKS

One of the chief problems of any security dealer is that of building up a clientele—a task which usually requires many years of activity in the cultivation of cordial relations based on service. The investment banker often becomes an adviser to his customers and assists them in selecting the best types of securities for their particular requirements. He also furnishes a great deal of general information on all matters pertaining to the investment business, and frequently offers a general investor's service, as distinguished from the special service rendered when a particular security is sold. Investment houses furnish reports to customers on any securities, municipal or corporate, which are of public record; and they answer questions about securities on the basis of information which they have accumulated and which they believe to be reliable. Tabloid investment lessons are often printed in the columns of newspapers and periodicals, in pamphlets and monographs; some houses even put out a daily news sheet containing items of interest to investors and suggestive discussions of investment problems; and even the radio is employed.

Investment houses assist in giving marketability to securities. One of the most interesting developments in connection with the maintenance of the good will of customers is the practice of buying back securities from those to whom they have been sold, thus giving to such securities a ready marketability. The investment banker also endeavors to supply his client with any security that he may desire to purchase. If the stock or bond required is one of which the house has been a distributor, it will endeavor to repurchase from customer B the securities required by customer A. If the securities sought by the customer have never been handled by this house, it is necessary for the banker to "pick them up" in the market. In order to repurchase securities once sold and to furnish its customers at any time with the securities required it is necessary for the banking house to have funds available for the purpose and to maintain a "trading position" in the investment market. Whenever a house wishes to buy or sell a few shares or bonds of a given issue it gets in touch with other houses which may have such securities on hand or may be able to get them from some of their customers.

The investment bank serves as financial adviser to corporations. It not only finances a corporation in its initial stages, at the time of its original organization; but it may also aid the company continuously in connection with refunding and expansion operations. The banker becomes a financial adviser to his client. Additional securities need to be issued from time to time and the banker is in a position to recommend favorable periods for putting out such issues and also to advise as to the best type of security to issue under the existing circumstances. It is not to be understood from this, however, that the larger corporations depend entirely upon any one investment banker. There is competition among the bankers for business; and the wide-awake house studies carefully the financial needs of the various corporations, with a view to acquiring the business of those which have maturing obligations to be refunded or new issues to be sold for the provision of additional funds.

VII. CAPITAL REQUIREMENTS AND PROFITS OF INVESTMENT BANKS

As compared with manufacturing or producing establishments the capital requirements of investment houses are relatively small; they are small even as compared with those of the ordinary commercial or savings bank. Since the investment banker deals merely in credit instruments rather than in concrete material goods, a large plant is obviously unnecessary; and since the investing public is reached chiefly by salesmen and correspondence, the building and equipment are small as compared with those of commercial or savings institutions whose customers must frequent the bank. All that is needed is office space for those who are engaged in the legal, engineering, accounting, and economic analysis that is required and in the preparation of advertising literature.

As the foregoing description of the investment business has indicated, investment houses are, however, often required to invest their own funds in the securities which they are handling, particularly in connection with the function of underwriting. But the amount of their own capital that is required is not so great as might be expected, for the reason that they are in a position to borrow heavily from the commercial banks, using securities as collateral for the loans. For instance, the underwriter may borrow from 50 to 90 per cent of the value of the securities in his possession, the percentage depending upon the marketability of the securities, and at times upon government regulations.

There has been much discussion of the profits made by investment bankers and it has often been asserted that the returns in this field of enterprise are exorbitant. This view is in part attributable to a failure to appreciate that the "spread" between the price paid to the corporation and the price at which the securities are marketed represents gross rather than net profits; and in part it is due to the common practice of generalizing on the basis of a particular instance of handsome profits—forgetting the cases where profits were low and even where losses were actually sustained. The truth is that the risks and expenses involved vary widely with different securities and at different times, depending upon the character of the security and the state of the investment market. Accordingly, the gross profit, represented by the margin between buying and selling prices, will vary markedly with different issues.

In the post-war period, until 1929, the profits of the investment bankers on new securities, particularly those of foreign governments and domestic holding companies, were often very large. However, the highly competitive condition of the investment banking business tended in some degree to restrict profits even in years when the volume of issues was large. The security crisis of 1929 brought heavy losses to many investment banking houses; and in the ensuing period their profits, owing to the meager volume of new securities, were small. As a result, most investment banking houses were unable to replenish the capital losses suffered in the crisis of 1929. Their business was further curtailed by the growing corporate practice of dispensing with the service of investment banking houses altogether and placing securities directly with large institutional investors such as insurance companies and investment trusts. As a result of the comparative stagnation of the capital markets in recent years not only have profits been meager, but the number of houses and the amount of capital involved have decreased.

VIII. INVESTMENT BANKS AND THE GENERAL ECONOMIC ORGANIZATION

We have thus far been discussing the nature of the operations engaged in and the services performed by investment banks, with only incidental reference to the social importance of such institutions. It remains to indicate the larger significance of investment banking in relation to the functioning of the economic system as a whole. Its service is manifested in connection with the cost of producing commodities and with the allocation or distribution of industrial energy.

The investment banker relieves the borrowing corporation of a very difficult and expensive task—that of raising the funds required for its operations. It is conceivable that a corporation, however large, might take care of its own financing—that is, issue its own securities, send out advertising literature and salesmen, and await the inflow of funds from ultimate investors before beginning its business activities. Most corporations are, however, poorly equipped for the marketing of securities, and the costs involved would be much greater to them than to a regularly organized investment house.

The advantages possessed by an institution that specializes in the raising of capital are obvious enough. First, it has acquired experience and skill in advertising and salesmanship. In the nature of things the acquisition of such skill is out of the question for a corporation, which has the task of raising capital only periodically, perhaps two or three times in a generation. It should be observed that, under these circumstances, it would not be feasible for a corporation to have a specialized "capital-raising department" as a permanent part of its organization. It must accordingly either use relatively untrained officials for the task of raising capital or employ (at high cost) specialists whenever the necessity arises. Second, a security house can do much of its advertising of any particular issue along with other issues, thus dividing the expense involved. Moreover, the corporation usually finds that the task of organizing the business and making preparation for an effective utilization of the funds to be raised requires its full energy.

In the third place, the investment bankers make it possible for a corporation to enter into contracts and to proceed with the development of its business in the light of definite knowledge, both as to the amount of the funds that will be received and as to the time at which they will be available. The investment market is capricious; securities may be sold quickly—possibly sooner than is necessary for the purposes of the corporation—and at a favorable rate; or it may be that months will be required for their final absorption by investors, and that the price at which they can be sold will be much below what the corporation had estimated. But the underwriters, as we have seen, guarantee to the corporation a definite amount of funds at a definite time. If a corporation did not know in advance what the total quantity of funds would be, it could not be certain, when making contracts incident to the development of the enterprise, that such contracts could be carried out. And if it did not know *when* its financial resources—whatever the total amount—would be available, it would have no assurance that its contracts could be fulfilled promptly or that production could be carried out according to schedule. Indeed, the risks involved here would be so great that many an enterprise partly launched would need either to curtail its operations or else completely wind up its affairs, owing, not to any fundamental weakness on the part of the enterprise, but only to the exigencies of the investment market. Such failures carry in their train a great waste of industrial resources.

This analysis of the services which investment banks render corporations amounts merely to saying that the underwriting and distributing functions serve to reduce substantially the cost of raising capital required by modern large-scale enterprise. This reduction in the cost of capital-raising makes it possible for enterprises to produce and to sell more cheaply than would otherwise be the case.

Investment bankers also perform an important service in directing the distribution of industrial energy. In the first place, they play a dominant role in directing the flow of capital and labor between different industries and between different establishments in any given industry. As the economic system is now organized, business managers reach a tentative judgment that the development of a new industry or the construction of an additional plant within an existing industry will prove profitable. The proposal for an issue of securities as a means of raising the necessary capital is then submitted to the investment banker for approval. Since the banker will suffer financial loss as well as a lessening of his reputation for sound and conservative judgment if his estimate of the proposition proves in error, it is essential that he bring to bear in his investigation and analysis all the technical, legal, and accounting knowledge and economic prescience that can be mustered.[7]

Every year a great many hopeful enterprises are denied funds by those who hold the purse strings. And while mistakes are often made, there is little question that the veto power resting in the hands of the investment bankers has prevented much dissipation of capital in fruitless ventures. While it is sometimes possible, in the event a given application is denied by conservative banking houses, to sell the securities directly, it is nevertheless true that the strategic position of investment banks in the capital markets makes them a dominant factor in the distribution of productive energy. It will be noted that a banking house may deny an enterprise funds because the men who are back of it are lacking in integrity or business ability, as well as because the enterprise does not promise well from a business standpoint. The investment banking houses thus tend to insure both that the management of industries shall be in the hands of honest and able men, and that social energy shall be directed into the most profitable channels. Under the conditions imposed by the gigantic scale on which industry is now conducted, control of the distribution of capital is a task of paramount importance. Because of the great quantity of fixed capital required, the waste of social energy entailed is enormous whenever an industry proves unprofitable or a large enterprise in any given industry goes on the financial rocks.

The wisdom with which investment banks perform this important function depends upon two factors or conditions: first, the intellectual capacity of the investment analysts; and second, the disinterestedness with which the service is performed. Unfortunately, those engaged in investment banking activities in the United States have not always occupied a position of professional detachment. As has already been pointed out, distributors carrying small risks and under financial

---

[7] It is possible that the importance of the investment banker may show a decline in the future; for commercial banks are now authorized to make loans for as long as ten years. See discussion chap. XXI, sec. III.

temptation or pressure to push the sale of whatever securities may be available, often give inadequate consideration to the safety of the issues they handle. Moreover they are often obliged to participate in the selling of mediocre issues through fear that failure to do their part here will mean loss of the opportunity to share in the distribution of select issues.

Again investment bankers have often had divided or conflicting interests. By becoming directly interested in particular companies they have sometimes disqualified themselves from exercising a true judgment with respect to such companies or their competitors. Moreover, when they become more interested, as they have at times, in gains from manipulating the market than in earnings from the underwriting and distribution service, they impede rather than promote the proper distribution of the productive energy of society. It is of the utmost importance that the business of investment banking be maintained on a genuinely professional basis.

CHAPTER XIII

INTERMEDIARY INVESTMENT INSTITUTIONS

In the preceding chapter our interest was centered on the services which investment banking institutions render in bridging the gap between borrowing corporations and the sources of investment funds. Reference to the diagram on page 133 indicates that the sources of funds tapped by the investment banker include not only individual investors but also a series of intermediary financial institutions— investment trusts, saving banks, insurance companies, and trust companies. Whereas the investment bank has its relations chiefly with corporations, the institutions now to be considered are primarily interested in aiding the investing public. They assemble funds from large numbers of individuals for whom, in effect, they purchase securities—the individuals being given claims for their shares in such holdings. In the case of the savings bank the claim is in the form of a deposit account; the insurance company issues a policy; the trust company gives either a deposit or a receipt; and the investment trust issues securities to those who furnish it funds. In this chapter we shall consider the work of investment trusts, savings banks, and insurance companies. Because of the varied services rendered by trust companies a separate chapter is reserved for the analysis of their operations.

In the chart on page 133 these institutions are indicated merely as financial intermediaries in raising capital for business enterprises. It should be understood, however, that they also assist in raising funds required by governments—federal, state, and local; in furnishing capital for agricultural purposes; and in financing urban real estate operations.

I. THE INVESTMENT TRUST

During recent years, the investment trust, a new type of financial institution as far as the United States is concerned, has come to play an important role in connection with the marketing of securities. An investment trust may be described as an agency for the co-operative buying and selling of securities for a group of associated investment beneficiaries. It assembles funds by the sale of its own securities, which may be in the form either of stocks or of bonds, and then invests these

175

funds through the purchase of the securities of other corporations or governments, either domestic or foreign. The investment trust has long existed in certain European countries, where it was organized as a means of facilitating the marketing of foreign securities. It was expected that this institution would play a similar role in the United States, but the trend has in fact been otherwise. As a background for the discussion of the present status of the investment trust in this country, it is desirable to present a brief description of this institution as it developed in other countries and in the United States.

The origin of the investment trust can be traced to the formation of the Société Générale de Belgique in the first quarter of the nineteenth century. This institution was formed by the royal family of Holland before the separation of Belgium and Holland. After the separation of these two countries, the stock of the company fell into private hands and in the course of time the institution acquired securities in a wide range of corporations. Since the institution purchased these securities not only for investment but also for control, it was not a pure investing trust. The investment trust made considerable progress in Switzerland, but had little success in France, Germany, or the rest of the Continent. Its greatest development occurred in England, where in the third quarter of the century a number of these institutions were formed.

The early British investment trusts followed highly speculative policies and suffered heavy losses in the panic of 1890, which seriously depressed securities on the various stock exchanges of the world. However, the British trusts profited by these unfortunate experiences, and as a result, until the World War, followed conservative policies by investing in high-grade securities and accumulating large surpluses to meet contingent losses. The capitalization of English trusts generally consists of preferred stock which carries with it a prior claim on dividends, usually fixed at about 4½ or 5 per cent. There is also priority as to assets upon liquidation. The second class of stock is the ordinary, or what we call common, stock which generally receives additional earnings on the trust after the dividends on the preferred stock have been paid. The former type of stock therefore gives a limited yield and greater security, while the latter offers a higher yield with increased risks. In 1933 the total capital of the British investment trusts was estimated at a billion dollars.[1]

The evolution of the investment trust in the United States has passed through three stages. The period of early growth, when the emphasis was on foreign issues, covered the early post-war years.

[1] *Stock Exchange Practices*, p. 334.

There were only 17 registered companies in 1924, and the total estimated assets amounted to less than 15 million dollars. The second stage, from 1925 to 1929, was a period of mushroom growth, during which the estimated market value of the assets rose to a maximum of about six billion dollars. Operations were confined chiefly to American securities. The third stage, covering the years from 1930 to 1935, is known as the consolidation period. As a result of shrinkage in security values the assets dropped to 1.5 billion dollars in 1932, subsequently rising to approximately 2.4 billions, as of December 31, 1935. The number of companies at the end of 1936, was 1,077.

The enormous expansion in the investment trust field in the years 1925 to 1929 was a part of a general development in the field of finance resulting from a superabundance of investment money and the speculative spirit of that period. Other manifestations were found in the vast extension of foreign loans, in the development of holding companies, in the flotation of fraudulent and speculative securities, and in speculation in the stock market. The investment trust ideal was so perverted in practice that the institution itself came near to being destroyed. Banking houses formed investment trusts into which they unloaded unsalable securities, or by which they controlled other companies without investing substantial amounts of their own money. Stock exchange houses organized their own trusts in order to obtain the resulting commission business. Almost every financial group was interested in some sort of investment trust, and mismanagement was widespread. In the ensuing depression, losses to stockholders in many investment trusts were staggering; in cases where the trusts had borrowed money, the entire equity of the stockholder was often wiped out. By 1932, the term "investment trust" was anathema to the average investor. In that year the shares of some well-managed trusts were selling at only half the value at which their holdings could be sold in the market. However, the re-organizations of ensuing years along lines suggested by the successful experience of a few well-managed trusts have again placed this institution in a position to render a useful service.

1. *Types of investment trusts.*—Three major kinds of investment trusts have been found in British and American experience. The first, and most common, is the general management, or discretionary, trust; the second is the specialized management trust; and the third is the fixed, or non-discretionary, trust. It should be remembered that trusts issue securities of their own— and that it is these issues which furnish the medium through which the public participates in the operations of the trust. Sometimes the issues include bonds, preferred stock, and

common stock, though the last is not always offered for sale to the public, being retained by the managers of the trusts.

The *general management* trust is the original British type and its discretion extends to the purchase of all classes of securities. The principle underlying this type of trust is that the holder of its shares, however small his investment may be, is enabled to become a part owner in a large number of representative and marketable securities and at the same time obtain the advantages of expert management, which extends not only to the initial choice of securities, but to the shifting of them from time to time in the light of changing conditions.

The specialized management investment trust restricts its operations to some particular field of investment. It operates on the assumption that certain lines of financial and business activity offer greater investment opportunities than do others, particularly where the management of the investments is intrusted to men expert in such fields. The special knowledge of these officials enables them not only to select the most desirable securities but also to shift investments from one to another as conditions of the moment may dictate. Such specialized trusts have been confined chiefly to the banking, insurance, mining, and aviation industries. It is the view of some that such specialized trusts have an opportunity of real importance in connection with the financing of new industries.

The fixed, or non-discretionary, investment trust differs from the discretionary institution in that investments are confined to a fixed list of representative and diversified securities, on the theory that a permanent investment in certain definite shares will prove remunerative in the long run, regardless of industrial and financial changes. The fixed investment trust had its great development during the early part of the 1929–1933 depression and was designed to protect the investor against the evils that had been disclosed in the management trusts. While trusts of the fixed type proved popular for a time, they subsequently lost favor because of the relatively high "overloading charges" (costs of distribution and trustees' fees) and the obvious elimination in this type of trust of the possibility of a constant supervision and adjustment of the portfolio.

A distinction should be drawn between an investment trust and a holding company. These two financial institutions are similar in nature in that they are devices for the purchasing of the securities of other corporations. They differ, however, in an essential respect. The aim of a holding company is to attain control of the management of the corporation whose securities it has purchased. On the other hand, the primary purpose of an investment trust in buying the securities of other corporations is to derive a satisfactory income yield, or even a gain from the rise in the price of these securities.

2. *Lessons of experience.*—In the case of the general management trust it is obvious that success is totally dependent upon the honesty, impartiality, and skill with which the portfolio is selected and supervised by the management. As has already been indicated, the promoters of industrial trusts in the late twenties were primarily interested in objectives of their own. Instead of devoting primary attention to the investment interests of their clients, they often purchased large blocks of common shares, or warrants to buy such blocks, for a negligible consideration. By and large, trusts which issued bonds and cumulative preferred stocks, as well as common shares, fared badly. However, in spite of the poor record of perhaps the majority of investment trusts during the depression period, it became evident that certain trusts had made an enviable showing. Some of these were connected with security houses; others were directed by "investment counsel"[2] firms; while still others were managed by independent organizations.

It should be pointed out here that there is an important distinction between investment trusts of the so-called self-liquidating type and those which are straight stock companies. In the case of the former, the holders of shares may at any time obtain the approximate liquidating value of their holdings from the trust itself. The trust merely sells certain of its assets and pays the holder of its shares. The straight stock company, on the other hand, simply sells its stock to the public and is not thereafter concerned with the value of these shares, which is determined in the markets. Since the stocks of many investment trusts of this type sold at less than half their liquidating values during the depression, it is apparent that from the standpoint of the average investor the self-liquidating type of trust represents the more attractive investment medium.

In the Revenue Act of 1936 the so-called mutual type of investment trust was accorded definite tax advantages in the form of exemption of its earnings, providing they were distributed to shareholders. To qualify as a mutual investment trust the company must among other things (1) be self-liquidating; (2) invest not more than 5 per cent of its assets in one security; and (3) distribute in dividends at least 90 per cent of its earnings, including profits on security transactions.

3. *Requirements for sound and efficient service.*—Notwithstanding our unsatisfactory experience, the investment trust may be so organized as to constitute a very useful intermediary institution. To attain

[2] See p. 181.

this end it must, however, meet certain definite tests. The following seem to be the essential principles and requirements for successful operation:

1. The management of the trust should consist of honest, intelligent, experienced individuals, and the trusts should be managed solely in the interests of the investing clientele.

2. The fee for management should be clearly set forth and it should be in the form of a fractional percentage of the capital value of the portfolio.

3. The overloading charges in the form of the cost of distributing shares, trustees' fees, etc. should be strictly controlled.

4. The clearly stated policy of the trust should be to own a widely diversified list of representative and marketable securities.

5. The trust should publish frequently clear and inclusive statements of its portfolio, showing the percentages of bonds, preferred stocks, and common stocks held, as well as their distribution by companies, and by types of industries. The balance sheet of the trust and a detailed statement of income and expenses should also be available at frequent intervals.

6. The capital structure of the trust should be conservative, and senior securities in the form of bonds and even preferred stock should constitute a very small percentage of the total capital structure. Indeed, there is much to be said for limiting the trust to the issue of common stocks.

7. Any changes in management or policies should be currently reported to stockholders.

Under the present tax ruling, companies of the mutual type have distinct advantages, and it would therefore appear that companies should be organized in this form. However, since this law requires that profits from security transactions be included in dividend disbursements it is open to some question.

The British practice has been to include in the income of the trust only interest and dividends received on securities held—with the profits from the purchase and sale of securities entered into a reserve account against possible future depreciation in security values. It is only after a period of years that these profits may be passed on to shareholders. Such a conservative practice is, of course, akin to the provision of our banking laws which requires the accumulation of a surplus for the protection of depositors, and to the practice of most business concerns in setting up ample reserve funds.

In view of the magnitude of the financial resources commanded by investment trusts, and the consequent control or influence which they may exert over finance and industry, the desirability of legislation defining their powers and functions, prescribing uniform methods of accounting and reporting, and supervising in a general way their operating activities is apparent.

In connection with this discussion of investment trusts, attention should be called to a kindred agency which has been developed in recent years—the *investment counsel*. As the name suggests the primary function of such agencies is to advise individual and institutional investors about the selection and management of security portfolios. They operate on varying principles. Sometimes they assume responsibility for the complete management of an account; more often they merely advise with reference to purchases and sales of securities; and in some cases they offer participating shares in an investment trust of their own. They charge a commission for their services, varied according to the character of the service and the value of the portfolio.

The service is intended to be of a two-fold character: first, to select a sound and well-balanced list of securities adapted to the circumstances and needs of each client; and second, to shift their security holdings, from time to time, from bonds to stocks, and vice versa, with a view to taking advantage of major market trends. Their greatest service has been in restricting the portfolios of their clients to representative and marketable securities. A potential weakness arises from the fact that the volume of business has become so large that the simultaneous recommendations, by several of the larger firms, to buy or sell may have a pronounced effect upon the security market.

II. SAVINGS INSTITUTIONS

There are several different types of savings institutions, as follows: (1) mutual, or trustee; (2) stock; (3) savings departments of commercial banks; (4) postal; and (5) co-operative. Co-operative savings banks are institutions organized mainly for the purpose of promoting thrift, through co-operative action, among special groups of individuals. They include building and loan associations, fraternal societies, credit unions, etc., the consideration of which will be reserved for other chapters.

1. *Mutual savings banks.*—The mutual institutions are located chiefly in the manufacturing centers and towns of the New England and eastern states. The mutual, or trustee, savings bank does not possess any capital stock, the funds being derived solely from deposits. The depositors are thus the mutual owners of the bank. They do not receive interest on deposits; but the net earnings of the company are divided among them in the form of interest and profits. The mutual

institutions are not managed by a board of directors elected by the stockholders, but by a body of non-depositing trustees, who usually hold office perpetually and who are actuated mainly by the desire to render a public service through the faithful discharge of a responsible trust.

The "guaranty savings bank" is a mongrel type. The state of New Hampshire has what is known as the "guaranty savings bank," a combination of the mutual and stock institution. The guaranty savings bank accepts both regular and "special" deposits. The latter are in effect its capital stock. The mutual or regular depositors are paid a certain stipulated rate of interest, and any excess of earnings above this is available for dividends on the "special deposits." It is in this agreement to pay a stipulated rate of interest to mutual depositors that the guaranty savings bank differs essentially from the mutual institution. The term "guaranty" is derived from the fact that the special deposits comprise, like capital stock and surplus in a stock savings bank, a sort of guaranty fund for the general depositors, the earnings derived from the use of the special deposits being available for payment of interest to mutual depositors.

There were 564 mutual savings banks in operation in 1937, having aggregate assets of 11,644 million dollars. The assets were about equally divided between securities, of which 40 per cent were government issues, and loans and discounts. A considerable portion of the latter doubtless represented working capital. Real estate holdings constituted only about seven per cent of the earning assets.

2. *Stock savings banks.*—These institutions differ from mutual savings banks in that they are organized as private profit corporations, which raise capital from shareholders and hope to pay dividends from earnings. These institutions are organized under state laws and are located mainly in the Middle West. They are typically of very small size, having a capital of from 10 to 15 thousand dollars. Their number has, moreover, declined steadily for many years, until now there are left only about 300. Their combined assets aggregated in 1935 only a little over 900 million dollars. They have come to accept both time and demand deposits, and to make short-term loans as well as to invest in securities and other fixed properties. Hence they are now scarcely distinguishable from the ordinary commercial bank. Indeed, the Comptroller of the Currency decided in 1936 to cease publishing their returns separately and to include them with state commercial banks.

3. *Savings departments of commercial banks.*—The commercial banks of the country maintain savings departments which in recent

times have come to play a very important role in the raising of funds. Most state commercial banks, particularly in the South and West, have always received savings accounts to a greater or less degree; in many cases, indeed, it has been found that so-called commercial banks conduct mainly a savings business. Trust companies, moreover, almost universally have savings departments.

The development of savings departments in national banks is a matter of the last twenty-five years; for until an important decision was rendered by the Comptroller of the Currency in 1903, there were only a few national banks that had savings departments, the majority of them believing that it was illegal to accept savings accounts. In answer to a question from a western banker as to whether a national bank could operate a savings department, the Comptroller ruled:

There does not appear to be anything in the National Bank Act which authorizes or prohibits the operation of a savings department by a national bank. . . . The expediency of the National Bank Association, organized for the purpose of doing the business of discount and deposit, engaging in the business of a savings bank is one for the determination of the Board of Directors.

Because of the strong competition for deposits among the different types of banks, the national institutions rapidly availed themselves of the privilege granted under this decision and established savings departments. By 1912 about 45 per cent of all national banks had taken action in this direction. The movement was further facilitated when the Federal Reserve Act of 1913 provided that a reserve of only three per cent need be kept against "time deposits" in national banks. The McFadden Act of 1927 went the whole way by definitely conferring upon national banks the right to maintain savings departments.

The aggregate volume of savings deposits in national banks has increased from 820 million dollars in 1913 to 7,103 millions in 1937. The savings deposits of trust companies and state commercial banks, which include the deposits of stock savings banks, amounted in 1937 to 6,260 million dollars.

The successful management of a savings bank or savings bank department depends upon the recognition of two main principles: first, that the loans and investments must be of a conservative type and widely distributed, both geographically and by industries; second, that a sufficient reserve in cash must be maintained to enable the bank to pay current bills and to meet the withdrawal requirements of those who have placed funds on deposit with the bank.

With a view to insuring the conservative management of savings institutions, legislation has been developed which prescribes the character of the loans and investments that may be made and lays down provisions regarding the maintenance of reserves. These laws, however, vary widely in different states; and in some, mainly in the South and West, there is no legislation at all. The New York law, applying to mutual savings banks, has served as a model for many other states, and a summary of its provisions will therefore indicate the most approved form of savings bank legislation at the present time. The following are the types of investment that may be made:

1. In the bonds of the United States and New York state.
2. In the bonds of other states which have not defaulted within ten years.
3. In the municipal bonds of New York state municipalities.
4. In the bonds of any city in a state admitted to statehood prior to 1896, which has not defaulted on any of its bonds since 1861. The debt of such a city, however, must not exceed 7 per cent of its assessed valuation.
5. In the first mortgages on real estate in New York state. Such mortgages must not exceed 60 per cent of the value of improved property or 40 per cent of the value of unimproved property.
6. In the first mortgage bonds of strong railroads which have paid for at least five years dividends at the rate of 4 per cent on their stock; but the stock must be at least equal in amount to one-third the debt of the road.
7. In the first mortgage bonds of railroads in New York on the same conditions. Not more than 25 per cent of the deposits shall be invested in railroad bonds and not more than 10 per cent in the bonds of any one road.

The provisions of this law do not permit, much less insure, a wide distribution of risks; emphasis is rather placed upon the necessity of "patronizing home industry." The distribution by industries is also somewhat restricted, owing to the emphasis that has been placed upon bonds enjoying a conservative reputation at that time.

The successful operation of a bank requires the maintenance of a satisfactory reserve which may be defined as the ratio of cash resources to deposit liabilities. We find that, as a rule, mutual savings banks are not required by law to hold any minimum cash reserve; but interestingly enough a maximum reserve is usually fixed, on the theory that unnecessary reserves constitute idle money and that the trustees need to be discouraged from allowing funds to accumulate. The New York law, for example, provides that any mutual savings bank may keep on hand, or on deposit with any national bank, New York state bank, or trust company an available fund not exceeding 20 per cent of its deposits. Stock savings banks, on the other hand, are in many states required to maintain a minimum reserve in specie, commonly from 5 to 10 per cent.

Legally, savings banks have the right to require from depositors a notice of withdrawal; and it is commonly said that savings banks do not need, therefore, to keep their resources in a form where they can be readily converted into cash. But in practice this right to demand a notice is nowadays seldom exercised. As an accommodation to the depositors, the savings banks early developed the practice of paying depositors on demand, whenever it was convenient for them to do so. The result was that the depositors soon came to consider that the savings bank informally agreed to return their funds whenever they were needed, notwithstanding the formal requirement that notice of withdrawal be given. The keen competition for deposits among savings banks gradually led to an all but universal abandonment of the practice of requiring notice of withdrawal, even though at times it was not convenient for the savings banks to meet depositors' demands. The competition of commercial banks, which have never required notice of withdrawal, also aided in nullifying the withdrawal provision; for the typical depositor regards a bank as a bank and does not carefully distinguish between savings and commercial institutions.

4. *Postal savings banks.*—Agitation for a postal savings bank system in the United States began as early as 1871, when the first postal savings bill was introduced into Congress. In the ensuing years about eighty bills for the establishment of a postal savings system were advanced, and the system was strongly advocated by eight different postmasters-general of the United States. It was not until 1910, however, that postal savings banks were finally established in this country.

The chief argument for the postal savings system was that it would stimulate saving among people in moderate circumstances, particularly the immigrant class, who either distrusted the regular savings institutions or found their facilities inconvenient or inadequate. The panic of 1907, which made it impossible for many of the savings banks to pay deposits on demand, greatly augmented the dissatisfaction with private savings banks and accelerated the movement for public institutions. The savings facilities of the country were not, in fact, evenly distributed, a large percentage of the savings banks being concentrated in a few states of the Union. In the South and West, particularly, opportunities for depositing money in savings banks were said to be wholly inadequate, although those who made this statement usually overlooked the fact that state and national commercial banks, particularly the former, furnished facilities for savings. Nevertheless, it was widely believed that if the Post-Office Department should open offices in cities, towns, and villages not provided with adequate savings facilities, economy and thrift would be greatly promoted and funds which would otherwise be hoarded or sent abroad by immigrants for deposit in European postal savings banks would be made available for investment purposes in this country.

The main objection to the postal savings system was raised by a special interest, namely, the existing savings and commercial banks of the United States. These banks urged that the existing facilities were fairly adequate and that for the Government to invade the field of banking was an unwarranted interference with private initiative. As we shall see, the fear on the part of bankers that postal savings would lessen the volume of their deposits has been rendered groundless by certain provisions of the act designed to protect the regular savings institutions.

The following are the important provisions of the postal savings law:

An account may be opened and deposits made by any person of the age of ten years or more, in his or her own name, and by a married woman in her own name, and free from any control or interference by her husband; but no person may at the same time have more than one postal savings account.

Deposits will be accepted only from individuals and no account will be opened in the name of any corporation, association, society, firm, etc., or in the names of two or more persons jointly. No account will be made in trust for another person (as is the case in many foreign countries).

No person may ordinarily have a deposit account in excess of $2,500, exclusive of accumulated interest, except by special authorization of a board of trustees (an official board for the supervision of the system, composed of the Postmaster General, Secretary of the Treasury, and the Attorney General of the United States). With such authorization additional deposits may be accepted "not to exceed in the aggregate $1,000 for each depositor, but upon which no interest shall be paid."

No account may be opened for less than one dollar, nor will fractions of one dollar be accepted for deposit at any time.

The interest rate shall be 2 per cent on deposits which have remained for at least one year, and will be computed only from the first of the month following the day on which the deposit was made.

Postal savings deposits will be evidenced by certificates of deposit issued in the name of the depositor. These will be non-transferable and non-negotiable.

To enable any person to accumulate and deposit amounts less than one dollar, depository offices furnish free of charge postal savings cards to which ten-cent postal savings stamps may be affixed. Ten stamps will be accepted as a deposit of one dollar.

Any depositor may withdraw the whole or part of his funds by surrendering at the depository office the savings certificates properly indorsed. The postal savings funds shall be deposited by the postmasters in certain designated depository banks, which may be either national or state, savings or commercial banks. If no local bank has qualified in a particular town or locality, then the funds shall be deposited in a qualified bank which is most convenient to such locality.

Five per cent of the funds received by any depository bank shall be turned over to the board of trustees and be kept with the Treasurer of the United States as a lawful money reserve against postal savings deposits.

Before any bank is qualified to receive postal savings deposits, it must turn over to the board of trustees of the postal savings system public bonds or other securities approved by the board of trustees and deemed sufficient and necessary to insure the safety and prompt payment of such deposits on demand.

If at any time the postal savings deposits in any city exceed the amount which the qualified banks therein are willing to receive under the terms of this act, the board of trustees may invest all or any part of such amount in bonds and other securities of the United States. And if, in the judgment of the President of the United States, the general welfare and interest of the United States require it, the board of trustees may invest all or any part of the postal savings funds, except the reserve fund of 5 per cent, in bonds and other securities of the United States.

Any profits received by the Post-Office Department shall be covered into the Treasury of the United States as a part of the postal revenue.

The limiting of the account of any one depositor to $2,500 does not measure the full possibility for further utilizing the postal savings banks, for the law provides a means whereby individuals may purchase United States postal savings bonds paying 2½ per cent interest.

Any depositor may surrender his deposit or any part thereof in sums of twenty dollars, forty dollars, sixty dollars, eighty dollars, one hundred dollars, and multiples of one hundred dollars and five hundred dollars, and receive in lieu of such surrendered deposits, under such regulations as may be established by the board of trustees, the amount of the surrendered deposits in United States coupon or registered bonds of the denominations of twenty dollars, forty dollars, sixty dollars, eighty dollars, one hundred dollars, and five hundred dollars, which bonds shall bear interest at the rate of 2½ per centum per annum, payable semiannually, and be redeemable at the pleasure of the United States after one year from the date of their issue and payable twenty years from such date.

The growth of the postal savings system was much less rapid than had been anticipated. There was a growth in the early years, but this was followed by a decline after the World War. In 1916 as many as 60 per cent of the depositors were immigrants. Owing to the restriction of immigration the per cent of deposits made by foreign-born residents has of course decreased in recent years. The number of depositors, however, has increased steadily—from 416,584 in 1929 to 2,791,371 in 1937. During the same period the deposits increased from 154 million dollars to 1,267 million dollars. The postal savings system has thus developed into an important agency for promoting savings among those whose incomes are too restricted to make other forms of saving readily feasible. It should be noted, however, that the banks are now voicing opposition to the system because the rates are so much above prevailing rates in the general money market. Moreover, the number of bank depositories decreased during the three years 1934 to 1937 from about 5,400 to a little over 3,200.

With a view to promoting thrift among school children a system of School Savings Banks was established in 1919. The number of schools participating increased steadily until 1931 when a peak of 14,628 was reached. As a result of the depression, the number has since declined to 9,034. By 1937 the total volume of savings was down to approximately 14 million dollars. Much more important as savings media are the "baby bonds" now being offered to the public on a discount basis.

III. INSURANCE COMPANIES AS SAVINGS INSTITUTIONS

Discussion of the work of insurance companies is ordinarily approached from the standpoint of their primary function of affording protection to life and property. It is nevertheless commonly recognized that the savings aspect of life insurance is very important. The insurance company, moreover, assists in the raising of capital, even when the individual payers of premiums do not have in mind the savings feature of insurance. Whatever the reason for taking out insurance, if the company is to make effective use of the premiums paid in, it is necessary to invest the funds so received. These investments always mean a transfer of funds from the individuals who furnish them to the corporations whose securities are purchased.

The insurance company is sometimes the only intermediary between the borrower and the saver of funds; and sometimes it is a secondary intermediary between the saver and the investment banks. Besides making investments in securities, insurance companies make a great many short-time "policy loans" to the individuals whom they have insured, and thus play an important part in the extension of funds for temporary consumptive or productive needs.

The table at the top of page 189, giving the assets of American life insurance companies for certain recent years, shows the nature of their loans and investments. The assets of fire insurance companies are not available for a similar exhibit; but the total assets are much smaller

ASSETS OF AMERICAN LIFE INSURANCE COMPANIES
(In Thousands of Dollars)

	1914[a]	1923[a]	1936[b]
Real estate.........................	$ 171,173	$ 143,058	$ 1,889,202
Real estate mortgages..............	1,706,365	3,661,910	4,703,069
Bonds.............................	1,981,751	3,815,846	11,373,270
Stocks............................	82,552	24,449	521,641
Collateral loans...................	20,351	23,506	4,585
Loans and premium notes...........	735,348	1,198,108	3,056,613
Cash..............................	95,160	119,961	785,608
Deferred premiums.................	68,832	195,861	
All other assets...................	73,716	171,919	554,494
Total admitted assets.............	$4,935,252	$9,454,620	$22,888,482

[a] *Insurance Yearbook*, 1929.

[b] Compiled from *Proceedings of the Thirty-First Annual Convention of the Association of Life Insurance Presidents*, p. 73.

than those of the life insurance companies, and they usually have from 40 to 50 per cent of their investments in the form of stock.

The table which follows shows the distribution of mortgage investments as between farm and other mortgages and also the geographic

MORTGAGE HOLDINGS OF LIFE INSURANCE COMPANIES[a]
DECEMBER 31, 1936
(In Thousands of Dollars)

Division	Farm mortgages	Other mortgages	Total mortgages
New England........................	$ 17	$ 129,041	$ 129,058
Middle Atlantic.....................	242	1,634,405	1,634,647
East North Central..................	179,856	845,822	1,025,678
West North Central.................	474,868	218,483	693,351
South Atlantic......................	23,633	336,091	359,734
East South Central..................	40,478	121,002	161,480
West South Central.................	98,332	142,128	240,460
Mountain..........................	12,839	33,884	46,723
Pacific.............................	28,677	309,722	338,399
Territories and Possessions...........	22	776	798
Total.............................	$858,964	$3,771,354	$4,630,318

[a] Compiled from *Proceedings of the Thirty-First Annual Convention of the Association of Life Insurance Presidents*, pp. 75–76.

distribution of the mortgage investments of 52 life insurance companies which together hold 91.6 per cent of the assets of United States legal reserve companies. It will be seen that the amount loaned on farm mortgages in the eastern states and also on the Pacific Coast, is small as compared with the amount loaned on other mortgages. In the Middle West, on the other hand, farm mortgages are of much greater relative importance. It should also be mentioned that the percentage of farm mortgages to the total of mortgages has been decreasing during the last five years.

The cash reserves of insurance companies may ordinarily be very small for the reason that they have no deposits subject to withdrawal on demand. Payments are made whenever losses are sustained or whenever policies mature; and in the case of a large company these payments run in fairly uniform amounts and can be met out of current receipts. In the case of unusual losses, larger payments, of course, have to be made; but some time necessarily elapses while the company is making an investigation of the claim, and in the interval there is usually sufficient opportunity for the company to dispose of some of its investments. It is obviously necessary, however, to keep a fair proportion of the assets in readily marketable securities.

The growing practice of making loans to policyholders has given rise to a new reserve problem. Policy loans are made in accordance with an agreement to lend a certain percentage of the surrender value of the policy at a fixed rate of interest at any time the insured desires such a loan. The growth of this practice has raised the question: In view of the agreement to make loans on demand, should not insurance companies, like the banks, be required to maintain a substantial cash reserve and to invest a portion of their assets in short-time commercial paper and acceptances? The dearth of such paper in recent years has precluded much expansion in this direction; but the insurance companies have become very large holders of short-term government issues.

The practice of making loans on demand caused serious difficulties for the insurance companies in the depression after 1929. A large proportion of their policyholders made requests for such loans and as a result the companies were forced to sell large volumes of securities at a time when their values were severely depressed. The insurance companies suffered such heavy losses that policy loans were curtailed by official action.

IV. THE ECONOMIC SIGNIFICANCE OF SAVINGS INSTITUTIONS

In the foregoing pages we have described the different types of savings institutions in present-day society and considered the chief problems arising in connection with their practical operation. We may now consider the character of the services that savings institutions perform in the modern economic system.

We have already seen that in the large the function of savings institutions is to assist in the raising of capital for modern business enterprise—to bridge the gap between the individual saver and the borrowing corporation or other enterprise. It will be pertinent to inquire now whether savings institutions are necessary middlemen; whether the function ascribed to them could not more efficiently be carried out without such financial intermediaries. It may be asked, Why should not the individual savers buy their securities directly, and thus receive four or five per cent instead of two or three, as is the case when they deposit their funds in savings institutions and allow the savings banks to do the investing? We shall find that there are several reasons why it is better for many people to make savings deposits rather than to invest in securities directly.

Savings institutions facilitate the making of investments in numerous ways. First, there are a great many people whose knowledge of investment values is so negligible that direct investment in securities involves the assumption of very great risks.

Second, the savings of a very large percentage of the public are too small to make direct investments in securities practicable. One should ordinarily have as much as one thousand dollars before attempting to invest in securities. Savings institutions, however, do reach the smallest accumulations; they gather in even the penny savings of society and make them available in larger aggregations for the purposes of business.

Third, unless one has a considerable volume of savings, the problem of safe-keeping is a deterrent to investments in bonds. A safety-deposit box costs from three to five dollars a year; and if one has only a hundred-dollar bond, the interest is largely absorbed in paying for the safety box. The savings bank deposit, however, is taken care of by the bank.

Fourth, the savings bank method of effecting savings is generally more convenient than making direct investments in bonds. Savings institutions are usually located conveniently for the investor of small means and are kept open for business at hours which facilitate the making of deposits. Moreover, the making of a deposit is simplicity itself—merely handing the funds through a window and receiving an entry in a deposit book. The postal savings banks, as we have seen, offer still greater conveniences in this connection.

Fifth, a deposit in a savings bank can usually be more easily recalled in case of need than can an investment in bonds. While this is not so true in the case of large investments, where the investors maintain close relations with bond houses and select their securities with a view to ready marketability, it is practically always true of small investments in securities. As we have seen, a savings bank deposit is ordinarily payable on demand and payable in full. A bond of small denomination very frequently cannot be quickly disposed of; and even bonds of large denomination may be marketed at a given time only at a loss.

More important than any of the foregoing services that are performed by savings institutions is the fact that they enable one to lessen the risks of investment. No matter how excellent one's knowledge of the value of securities may be, there is always some risk of loss with any given security. And, in accordance with the theory of probability, the percentage of loss is always less, the wider the distribution of investments. This is simply an application of the old adage, "Don't carry all your eggs in one basket." By virtue of its very large investments, the savings bank can always distribute its risks widely; while an individual can do so only if he is comparatively wealthy.

The mutual savings institutions are, in reality, nothing but a device for pooling the investments and the losses of the depositors, thereby lessening the risks assumed by each. The stock savings bank accomplishes the same result by a more roundabout process. Individuals turn their funds over to the bank and receive the promise of the bank to repay them in full; and the bank diversifies its investments as much as possible in order to reduce the chances of loss. The resources contributed by the shareholders of the bank may also be drawn upon to prevent loss to depositors. The risks of loss to the individual are thus very greatly lessened.

The large insurance companies perhaps present the best examples of widely diversified risks. By virtue of their very great size, these companies are able to invest in bonds and securities of any number of corporations and in real estate mortgages on farms throughout the length and breadth of the United States, not to mention foreign countries. It is thus impossible for a large company to suffer a total loss, except in the event of a complete destruction of the existing economic order. Every depositor in a large savings institution, and every person insured in a large insurance company, is in effect a part-owner of all the corporations, farms, etc., whose securities and mortgages have been purchased by the bank or insurance company, and his potential losses are thereby reduced to a negligible minimum.

A further word is in point with reference to the savings that are effected through life insurance companies. When one takes out life insurance, he places a premium, albeit a negative premium, upon making additional savings; for if one does not meet his payments as they mature, he stands to lose a part of the savings previously made. Since many people are so constituted that they cannot resist the impulse to spend unless they have a heavy penalty hanging over their heads, the insurance system is a most useful device for inducing provision for the rainy day.

In the light of these considerations it is clear that the savings banks do perform important services as middlemen in the process of bringing borrowers and lenders together. The stock savings banks and the insurance companies are accordingly entitled to the difference between the interest which they pay on deposits and the interest which they receive from their loans and investments in securities. The various conveniences of savings institutions, and the reduction of risks afforded by virtue of the wide distribution of loans and investments, compensate the individual saver for the lower rate of return which he receives when he invests in savings institutions instead of investing directly in securities. It may be observed, moreover, that no one is compelled to make investments through savings institutions; if one prefers he can secure the higher rate of interest by investing directly in securities.

Finally, the savings institutions, like the bond houses, assist to some extent in directing the flow of industrial energy. This is particularly true of the stock savings banks of the South and West, where investments are not circumscribed by state legislation, as is the case with the mutual institutions of the East. Such savings institutions, as we have seen, invest directly in the securities of local and other enterprises and they make short-time loans to corporations and businesses, both at home and in other centers. In making these direct investments the savings bank officials must pass judgment upon the honesty and integrity of the management and upon the ability of the borrowing enterprise to pay the loans at maturity. Like the investment bank analysts, they hold a veto power over the expenditures of funds for any given purpose; and in proportion as the judgment of savings bank managers is superior to that of the rank and file of savings depositors, the distribution of industrial energy is thus more efficiently directed.

CHAPTER XIV

TRUST COMPANIES AND THE MODERN FINANCIAL SYSTEM

In many respects the most interesting financial institution of the present day is the trust company. The growth of this institution, called into being to meet the diverse requirements of a capitalistic economic system, was nothing short of phenomenal during the era of financial consolidation which began with the turn of the century. Popularly confused with the type of business organization that was declared illegal under the Sherman Anti-trust Law, the trust company is, in truth, only a special type of financial institution that developed to fill the gaps in an incomplete financial structure. In the course of its evolution, however, it has not only rounded out the financial system; it has invaded the field of most of the other financial institutions as well. The trust company has been described as "the department-store of finance," and "the omnibus of financial institutions."

The first trust companies in the United States, organized early in the last century, combined the business of insurance with that of trusteeship for individuals and estates. However, all forms of insurance except fidelity and suretyship have been taken over by the regular insurance companies; and even these two are more and more being surrendered to specialized fidelity institutions. Although the rapid increase in the number and size of private fortunes and estates in the second half of the nineteenth century greatly expanded the volume of trustee business for individuals, it was the phenomenal growth of the corporation which gave the trust company its largest and most distinctive field of enterprise. The great variety of ways in which the trust company is of service to the corporate system of finance is set forth in summary form in the section which follows.

I. THE SCOPE OF TRUST COMPANY OPERATIONS

The nature and variety of financial operations engaged in by trust companies may be seen from a summary of the powers conferred upon such institutions by the law of the state of New York:

1. *Banking:* A trust company may
a) Receive deposits of money.

b) Lend money on real or personal securities.

c) Accept for payment at a future date drafts drawn upon it by its customers.

d) Buy and sell exchange, coin, and bullion.

e) Discount and negotiate drafts, promissory notes, bills of exchange, and other evidences of indebtedness.

f) Issue letters of credit authorizing the holders thereof to draw drafts upon it or its correspondents at sight, or upon time not exceeding one year.

g) Give its bonds or obligations when moneys, or securities for money, are borrowed or received on deposit, or for investment.

2. *Investment:* A trust company may

Purchase, invest in, or sell stocks, bonds, mortgages, and other securities.

3. *Agency:* A trust company may act as

a) Fiscal agent, transfer agent, registrar of the United States, any state, municipality, body politic, or corporation, and in such capacities may receive and disburse money, transfer, register, and countersign certificates of stock, bonds, and other evidences of indebtedness.

b) Attorney in fact for any lawful purpose, for any person or corporation (foreign or domestic).

c) Agent.

d) Agent for married women with respect to their separate property.

4. *Fiduciary:* A trust company may

Take, accept, execute any and all such legal trusts, duties, powers of whatever description, not prohibited by law, as may be granted to, confided in, conferred upon, intrusted to, transferred to, vested in it by court of competent jurisdiction or surrogate, and may act under the order or appointment of such court, as

a) Guardian, receiver, trustee of the estate of any minor.

b) Depositary of moneys paid into court whether for the benefit of any minor, person, corporation, or party.

c) Trustee, guardian, receiver, committee of the estate of any lunatic, idiot, person of unsound mind, habitual drunkard.

d) Receiver, committee of the property or estate of any person in insolvency or bankruptcy proceedings.

e) Executor of or trustee under the last will and testament, or administrator with or without the will annexed, of the estate of a deceased person.

f) In any other fiduciary capacity.

For person, persons, municipality, body politic, corporation (foreign or domestic), or authority by will, grant, assignment, transfer, or otherwise, it may act as

a) Executor or trustee under will or deed.

b) Trustee for married women with respect to their separate property.

c) Trustee under marriage settlements.

d) Trustee under separation agreements.

e) Depositary under stipulations between persons engaged in litigation.

f) Depositary in escrow of cash, securities, agreements.

g) Depositary under lease contracts.

h) Depositary under syndicate and reorganization agreements.

i) Depositary or agent of voting trustees under voting trusts.

j) Trustee under mortgages issued by corporations (foreign or domestic), municipalities, or bodies politic.

k) Trustee under equipment trusts.

And according to the terms of, and being accountable to all persons in interest for, the faithful discharge of every such trust, duty, or power which it may accept, it may receive, take, manage, hold, dispose of, sell any property, real or personal, wherever located, and the rents and profits thereof.

5. *Safe-keeping:* A trust company may

Let out receptacles for the safe deposit of personal property.

Receive for safe-keeping bonds, mortgages, jewelry, plate, stocks, securities, valuables, upon such terms and conditions as it may prescribe.

The first two types of operation engaged in by trust companies, namely, banking and investment, are in this treatise discussed elsewhere—banking in the chapters on savings and commercial banking, respectively, and investment in connection with the marketing of securities. In this chapter, therefore, we shall consider only the operations listed above under the functions of agency, fiduciary, and safe-keeping. It should be noted in passing that a large number of national and state banks have been given trust powers in recent years, and that most of these institutions operate separate trust departments. A discussion of the influence of the trust company in broadening the scope of other types of financial institutions will be found in chapter XXII.

II. SERVICES TO INDIVIDUALS AND ESTATES

The trust company performs its services for individuals, for estates, and for corporations. The principal services to individuals and estates are: (1) execution and administration of wills; (2) management of living trusts; (3) holding of *escrows* as depositaries; and (4) acting as custodians of property or securities. Some of the services which are rendered chiefly to corporations are also extended to individuals as occasion may require. Since the custodial service is of equal interest to corporations and to individuals it will be discussed under a separate section—IV.

For estates the following services may be enumerated: (1) administrator, executor, guardian, and conservator; (2) trustee under wills; (3) receiver and assignee; (4) depositary for money and property of estates under order of the probate Court; (5) depositary for alien property custodian. The advantages of the trust company over an individual in acting as trustee of estates are stated by one trust company as follows:

It is a fiduciary organization manned by trained officers, experienced in the technique of modern trust and agency duties. It is the trustee for many estates the property of which requires manifold skill and composite knowledge to produce the maximum income therefrom. It is a trustee with continuous existence and therefore not subject to the limitations of an individual and the frailties of human life; it is able to give uninterrupted service from generation to generation. It is a trustee that has no family prejudices to bias its judgment. It is a trustee that has the financial ability to carry on an estate without embarrassment to the beneficiaries, while property matters are in an unsettled condition. It is a trustee that has at its command a great many sources of counsel and knowledge in regard to investments. It is a trustee that does not need to give bond (for which an estate or trust must pay), because of its own ample capital and surplus.

It is now a common practice for a trust company to tender the services of its officers for the drawing of wills and to act as their custodian until the death of the testator. Such service is usually performed without charge, in case the company is appointed executor of the estate.

Trust companies sometimes manage insurance funds. This service involves the use of a "trust agreement." The policies are made payable to, or are assigned to, the trust company as trustee, and at the death of the insured the company collects the proceeds of the policy, of which it has meantime been the custodian, and applies such proceeds according to the terms of the trust agreement. Since many insurance companies do not write policies allowing stated payments to be made to beneficiaries, this plan furnishes an opportunity for the insured to have his insurance paid in any manner desired. Trust agreements are sometimes made so that the beneficiary may be paid stated annuities out of the proceeds of life insurance. This arrangement is especially valuable where a man is not able to carry an amount of insurance such that the income alone will support his family.

The so-called *living trust* may be created for any purpose which might appear to serve the needs of a property owner. The principal types are (1) trusts to be administered for the benefit of the owner during his life and of other designated persons after his death; (2) trusts for the benefit of other persons; (3) trusts for philanthropic or public purposes; and (4) trusts in lieu of a will. Such trusts enable an individual to escape as much of the routine business of managing his property as he may wish, to obtain counsel with respect to investment policy, and to plan and prepare the way for the effective administration of the estate upon his decease.

The service that may be performed under the living trust is highly flexible and is adapted to the needs and desires of the individual. One of the most common purposes of the living trust is to provide an assured income to the individual and his family—as protection against the vicissitudes of fortune. In this respect it resembles the life insurance annuity.

An *escrow* was originally defined as "a deed placed by the grantor in the hands of a third party to be delivered to the grantee upon the fulfillment by the latter of certain specified conditions." The need for an escrow grows out of the fact that contingencies or altering circumstances may arise between the making of an agreement and its final consummation. A common illustration is that of a real estate transaction in which the purchaser wishes to bind the deal but at the same time to be protected if a search of the title should disclose a flaw.

The use of the escrow has been greatly extended in modern times. Mortgages and notes as well as deeds may be placed in escrow; and trust companies are often made depositaries of various articles of value which are to be held for delivery under conditions similar to those under an escrow arrangement. While not escrows in the strictly legal sense, they amount to practically the same thing and are sometimes called "informal" escrows. It is the duty of the holder of an escrow to deliver the instrument to the grantee upon his performance of his part of the contract, or to withhold the instrument in case the contract is not fulfilled.

III. SERVICES PERFORMED FOR CORPORATIONS

The services rendered by trust companies to corporations are of an indispensable character; indeed, without them the system of corporate enterprise would be impossible. The corporation is dependent upon the trust company in connection with the raising of fixed capital, with the managing of certain of its financial affairs as a going concern, and with safe-guarding the interests of both creditors and shareholders in the event of insolvency and financial reorganization. Moreover, investors in corporate securities are largely dependent upon the performance of certain trust company operations.

The principal ways in which the trust company is of service in connection with corporate financing are as follows: (1) as trustee under mortgages and indentures, securing bond and note issues; (2) as trustee under equipment trust agreements; (3) as transfer agent; (4) as registrar of securities; (5) as depositary under reorganization agreements; and (6) as fiscal agent.

1. *Trustee under mortgages.*—Under the system of corporate finance, bonds of small denomination are sold, as we have seen, to the general investing public on the security of a mortgage, which recites the conditions under which foreclosure proceedings may be started and states what property is to be turned over to the bondholders in case of insolvency. The appointment of a reliable trustee for the protection of the mortgage is accordingly indispensable to the successful operation of the system of issuing securities.

Before a trust company accepts a mortgage trust, great care is taken to ascertain the correctness of the statements that are made and the legality of the mortgage. It is customary to require from a counsel of the corporation issuing the mortgage an opinion that the document has been drawn up in proper form and that it fulfills the requirements of the state in which the property to be mortgaged is situated. When the preliminary arrangements have been completed, the mortgage is executed in duplicate and acknowledgment of the acceptance of the trust is made by the trust company.

A closely related service is in connection with the engraving and issuing of the bonds. Bonds are usually engraved by responsible engraving companies from plates especially prepared for the purpose. Precautions are taken by the trustee to prevent any impressions' being lost or stolen; and sometimes the engravers are required to give security against loss resulting from negligence on their part. After the bonds have been printed, they are sealed with the corporate seal, attested by the officers of the issuing corporation, and then sent to the trust company, which certifies and delivers them as provided in the mortgage. Before certification, however, each bond is examined to insure its being in proper form.

Where the mortgage provides for a sinking fund for a gradual retirement of the bonds or for their payment at maturity, it is the duty of the trust company to see that such sinking-fund provisions are complied with. It thus acts as a sort of enforcing agent for the bondholders.

In the case of "collateral trust" bonds,[1] the collateral is held by the trust company for the protection of the bondholders. Sometimes the terms of the mortgage provide that the issuing corporation may make a substitution of collateral, in which case it is the duty of the trustee to make sure that the substituted securities are fully equal in value to the original ones.

2. *Trustee of equipment trusts.*—Equipment trusts arise from a special type of financial borrowing—that by railroad companies for the purpose of acquiring new rolling stock. As a means of making securities attractive to buyers, an arrangement is effected with the builder of railway cars whereby the railroad company may make a partial payment upon the delivery of the cars and give notes for the remainder. These notes, which usually mature serially over a period of years, are sold to investors. The title to the cars is vested in a trust company as trustee, and the railroad company leases the cars from this trustee. The rental received by the trustee from the railroad is sufficient in amount to meet the annual interest on the notes and to retire a certain number of them each year. In this way the railroad is enabled to borrow the funds with which to purchase equipment at relatively low rates of interest and to pay off the obligation during the life of the rolling stock.

3. *Transfer agent.*—Trust companies are usually chosen to act as agents for transferring the ownership of corporate securities. This function may involve merely the transfer of existing shares from one holder to another; the substitution of a new issue for an old; or an issue of bonds in place of an issue of stock. As an instance of the latter, if a railroad company should decide to call in some of its outstanding securities and replace them by an issue of a different type, a trust company would be chosen to receive the old bonds from their holders, issue receipts for them, and later issue the new securities to the owners of these receipts. If money is to be paid on either side, it is distributed by the trust company, which thus acts as custodian of the interests of both the public and the corporation.

The services of a transfer agent have been described as follows:

The duty of the transfer agent is to act for the issuing corporation in the matter of making transfers of the ownership of its stock from one holder to another. This involves the passing upon the regularity and legality of the assignment of title; the noting of the transaction upon the transfer books of the corporation; the cancellation of the old certificates and the execution and

[1] See p. 108.

delivery of new certificates. Incidentally it involves the furnishing to the corporation of a certified list of the stockholders whenever the books are closed for the payment of dividends, and at other times as demanded.

The performance of these duties requires that the transfer agent be the custodian of the stock books and the seal of the issuing corporation and of a supply of blank certificates. The certificates, bound in book form so that each certificate and its stub form one page, and numbered consecutively, are before delivery to the transfer agent signed by the proper officers of the corporation. The face of the certificate usually contains the provision that it is not valid unless countersigned by the transfer agent. On its back is usually printed an assignment of the stock and an irrevocable power of attorney. . . .

Before making delivery of a certificate, the transfer agent dates it, fills in the name of the new holder and the number of shares represented, affixes the seal of the issuing corporation, and attaches the proper signature to the transfer agent's certificate.

The practical work of transferring stock requires a high degree of intelligence and care and a thorough knowledge of the law governing such transfers. The risks involved, aside from possible clerical mistakes, errors in bookkeeping, dishonesty or gross carelessness on the part of the employees who actually do the work, include mistakes of law or of fact in making transfers on forged indorsements, or on insufficient authority, or in violation of law, especially in cases of certificates held by persons as trustees for others. Certificates indorsed in blank are often presented for transfer by persons other than the holders of record. The transfer agent must know the signatures of stockholders or otherwise identify them beyond question. Where stock is held in fiduciary capacities, the agent must know the terms and powers under which it is held. When a certificate is presented for transfer, the transfer clerk should know that the certificate itself and the power of attorney accompanying it are genuine; that the transferrer is legally competent to make the transfer; that no notice has been given the company of any outstanding claims against the stock; that, in the absence of direct notice, there is no implied notice of claims, such as the certificate itself may give when standing in the name of a trustee.

On the subject of the exact liabilities assumed by the transfer agent in agreeing to perform these services, there is a considerable difference of opinion, which is readily accounted for by the fact that there is no statute law covering the case, and very little law in the shape of court decisions. While the office is sometimes undertaken under special contract which details the liabilities to the issuing corporation, the more common method of appointment is by a mere resolution of the directors of the issuing corporation appointing the Blank Trust Company as the transfer agent of its stock, and the acceptance of the appointment by the latter. This method assumes that the duties and liabilities of the position are so well known as to require no definition; an assumption which is justified so far as routine duties are concerned, but which as to liabilities seems inconsistent with the divergent opinions held by officers of banks and trust companies which act as transfer agents. The difference of opinion does not concern what the trust company accepting an appointment expects and intends to undertake, but has reference to possible implied and incidental obligations which it does not intend to assume, but for which, in the opinion of some writers, the courts may hold it responsible. It is well understood in banking and trust circles that the transfer agent undertakes to say to the purchaser of the stock which it has countersigned no more nor less than that such stock is a genuine portion of the capital stock of the issuing company, that the said company has been duly authorized to do business by the secretary of the state in which the company is incorporated, and that the signatures of the officers to the certificates of stock are genuine.[2]

4. *Registrar of securities.*—The purpose of having an independent registrar of stock, or of registered bonds, may best be disclosed by reference to the origin of the practice. In 1863 occurred the notorious Schuyler frauds, in which Robert Schuyler, who was president and also transfer agent of the New York and New Haven Railroad Company, apparently over-issued the stock of his company. Since such practices, if unchecked, would soon bring the entire securities' business into disrepute, the New York Stock Exchange, in order to prevent a recurrence of such frauds, adopted a rule in January, 1869, which required all active stocks to be registered by an agency approved by it. The duties of a registrar are stated by Herrick as follows:

The duty of the registrar of stock is to register, or record the issue of, certificates of stock after they have been issued by the transfer agent, for the purpose of preventing an over-issue of such stock. Before assuming its duties the registrar must be furnished with authentic information as to the total amount of stock authorized to be issued, if none has been issued; or as to the total amount of stock authorized to be issued and the amount outstanding, if part or all has been issued. After the total amount of shares authorized to be issued has been registered, new certificates are not registered except upon the cancellation of outstanding certificates for the same number of shares.

In practice the registrar keeps a registry list, and as stock is transferred by the company or its transfer agent it receives in each case the old certificate as surrendered and the new certificate as prepared to take its place, it compares the two, it notes upon its registry list the surrender and cancellation of the old and the issue of the new in substitution, and it thereupon identifies the new certificate by its signature upon its face as a part of a stated authorized issue.

The liabilities involved are at the present purely a matter of opinion, as there is practically no law on the subject.[3]

It is almost a universal practice for a corporation to select as registrar a different trust company from the one which serves as transfer agent. The function of the registrar is to operate as a check

[2] Herrick, Clay, *Trust Companies*, pp. 413–416.
[3] Herrick, Clay, *Trust Companies*, pp. 425–426.

upon any error or irregularity; and with a single institution acting both as registrar and as transfer agent there is obviously a greater possibility that an over-issue of securities will not be detected. Where registrar and transfer agent are separate institutions, collusion would be necessary to permit an over-issue; the separate agents in a sense act as checks upon each other.

5. *Depositary under re-organization agreements.*—In case of the default of interest on bonds, a committee is usually formed to represent the bondholders. This committee formulates a plan of financial re-organization; and, pending the re-organization, the committee calls for the deposit of the bonds, the interest on which has been defaulted, with some trust company, which is designated as depositary. In exchange for these securities the trust company gives temporary receipts, good for a limited number of days only. Since the process of re-organization usually requires several months—if not years—these temporary receipts are later exchanged for engraved certificates of deposit which are in transferable form and available for trading on the stock exchange like regular bonds and shares. These certificates specify the kind and value of the security deposited and the terms under which the certificate is issued, and state that the trust company holds the securities on terms agreed to by the owners thereof.

Financial re-organization is also necessary whenever a consolidation of several corporations into a single company is effected. The trust company is here also called upon to act as depositary during the process of financial re-organization.

The trust company may also act as assignee and receiver when a firm or corporation becomes insolvent. The appointment of a trustee as assignee may be made either at the request of the owners of the business, who wish to protect their property, or at the instance of creditors, who wish to safeguard their interests. The property may be turned over to the trust company by an assignment, in which case the assignee's duties usually consist of collecting the debts and requiring creditors to prove their claims.

The trust company acts as receiver under appointment by a court, and the object is generally to tide an embarrassed enterprise over a period of difficulty. Since the receiver is merely an officer of the court, it has no powers other than those conferred upon it by the court. The court authorizes the issue of receiver certificates to provide funds for the purchase of equipment, the maintenance of the property, and the conduct of the business. Such certificates may be made a first lien on all assets, even taking precedence over mortgages and other secured obligations. In this way the receiver is enabled to secure the necessary capital with which to place the company upon a satisfactory financial footing.

6. *Fiscal agency.*—As fiscal agent for a corporation, the company takes either general or special charge of the finances of the corporation, according to the terms of the agreement. It may assume the role of treasurer, having charge of all receipts and disbursements; or it may act merely as agent for the payment of coupons, interest, and dividends, either under the terms of a mortgage or independently of any trusteeship.

A certain trust company states that as fiscal agent it will assume custody of securities, give notice of maturities, and collect coupons as they come due; take custody of title deeds, insurance policies, and other documents, keeping all necessary records incident thereto; examine periodically the condition of corporations whose securities are held and advise with the proper officers of the organization with respect to the replacement of securities that are becoming less valuable; examine periodically real estate when under lease, especially where the lease requires the payment of taxes and observance of obligations by tenants in the matter of repairs and replacements; keep separate general books under such accounts as the corporation may direct.

One trust company suggests:

The management of business corporations may well consider the advantage of having general salary accounts, dividend, interest, investment, bills payable, profit and loss, and other general and controlling accounts kept separate from the accounts of the operating office and from the observation of employees therein.

In many cases the volume of such general office business, even inclusive of records of directors' and stockholders' meetings, would not warrant the considerable expense of a suitable separate corporate office. In such cases the fiscal agency service of this company gives all the benefits of such an office at a nominal cost.

As agent for the payment of interest, dividends, etc., the trust company receives from the corporation, in advance of the date when interest or dividends are due, a sum of money equal to the total amount to be paid. In the case of coupon bonds the interest is held subject to the call of the owner, while in the case of dividends on stock and interest on registered bonds checks are sent to the owners whose names appear on the register held by the registrar.

Although coupons are made payable to bearer, a record is made of the names of the persons who present them for payment at the counter of the trust company, or of the names of the banks presenting them on behalf of their customers. The trust company keeps a record of the numbers of the bonds from which the coupons are cut. When paid the coupons are cancelled by the punching of holes in them; and they are then filed away by bond numbers, to be returned at intervals, usually monthly, to the issuing corporation.

Trust companies also act as fiscal agents for educational and charitable institutions, clubs, lodges, etc. The nature and significance of such service are stated by one trust company in the following language:

The functions of educational, charitable, and similar institutions continue uninterruptedly from generation to generation. Executive officers, serving for the most part without compensation, change frequently, involving a transfer of records and securities, always with the danger of loss of records and of inadequate attention to the changing values of securities. It is therefore highly desirable to secure continuity of service, permanent housing of important records, and prompt and efficient handling of the routine work of the organization.

The Trust Company will provide such secretarial and stenographic service as may be required for giving necessary notices of meetings; will transcribe minutes and resolutions accurately and uniformly into the permanent records; will give notice of all dues and other obligations payable to the organization; will receive and acknowledge all payments made for the organization's account, and deposit the same, reporting at regular and special meetings the collections made and the items in default; will draw checks for authorized amounts covering all items payable, including annuities, interest, salaries, and current accounts, and will mail the same.

Oftentimes the secretary and the treasurer of an organization are persons who are absorbed in the duties of their own calling or are frequently absent from home. It is highly desirable that the responsibilities of these offices be in hands where routine will be promptly and efficiently handled.

In many cases the treasurer is allowed a fund for clerical assistance. Such a fund, applied to secure fiscal agency service, will relieve the treasurer of responsibility of oversight and will guarantee the accuracy and integrity of the records.

It is certainly an advantage and a matter of prestige to be able to obtain in the handling of the securities, accounts, properties, and investments of any organization the degree of accuracy, the absolute responsibility, and the safeguards of state supervision which are to be found in a trust company alone. Whatever the high character or ability of an individual, it is out of the question that he can bring to bear on such duties all of the highly specialized forces of a large banking institution.

Trust companies perform many services for "correspondent banks" and brokerage houses. In connection with out-of-town banks and brokerage houses, both in the United States and abroad, correspondent banking houses which deposit securities for safe-keeping in New York are given practically all the facilities of a branch office. A trust company in New York provides a place where all matters pertaining to the purchase and sale of securities may be cared for, thereby obviating (1) delay in making settlement, (2) delay in shipping securities to and from New York, (3) expense of postage, expressage, and insurance. The trust company also collects interest coupons and credits the amount to the correspondent banks, thus saving delay and expense in making collections. (This service is of importance for the reason that most large corporations maintain an agency for the payment of their coupons in New York City.) The trust company also prepares income-tax certificates for out-of-town banks; it looks after the collection of dividends, in many cases; and it provides facilities for effecting transfers of ownership of securities. Nearly all of the great corporations of the country maintain offices or agencies in New York where their securities may be transferred and registered. A representative of the trust company is thus in a position by personal interview "to discuss difficult questions with the various offices or agencies and to ascertain the proper papers to effect transfers, thus obviating the delay which usually occurs when the matter is handled by letter."

Foreign correspondent banks which deal in American securities find it of very great service to have an agency in New York. This is especially true when securities issued stand in the name of decedents, executors, administrators, trustees, or guardians; for in cases of this sort, the trust company relieves the correspondent banks from the necessity of familiarizing themselves with the diverse requirements of the different corporations and of the particular laws of the several states.

IV. THE TRUST COMPANY AS A CUSTODIAN

While trust companies are not the only financial institutions that maintain safety-deposit vaults and boxes for the safe-keeping of valuables and securities, they have from the beginning made a specialty of such business. Some of the larger companies have gone much further than merely to maintain safety-deposit boxes. The growth of large fortunes, which under modern conditions are invested mainly in corporate securities, has opened up a new field of work for the trust company— that of custodian of the securities and papers deposited with them by individuals. The amount of detail that must be looked after if the owner of a large volume of securities is to avoid losses and make the most of opportunities is so great that a responsible financial secretary and adviser is practically indispensable. In this capacity trust companies render a variety of important services, outlined by a large New York trust company as follows:

A. Availability

When securities are locked up in a safe deposit box, they are *not available* to the owner in case of sickness or absence from home. From this cause serious embarrassment often results, for, while a person may be entirely solvent, his securities may not be available in time of need, merely because for some reason he is unable to go to his safe deposit box in person.

On the other hand, when securities are held in safe-keeping, they are *available* to the depositor at any time. By letter, telegraph, or cable, he may direct their delivery or sale, and may withdraw them at any time to be used as collateral to loans. No matter where the depositor may be, his securities *are always subject to his control and direction.*

In order that our clients readily may direct the sale or delivery of stocks or registered bonds, the securities should be endorsed in blank with the signatures properly witnessed or guaranteed.

Where prolonged absence is contemplated, it is especially desirable to have the stocks or registered bonds stand in the name of a nominee of the trust company. . . . This makes it possible to sell a portion of the stock represented by a certificate and still have the remainder in negotiable form. For instance, if a depositor has a certificate for 100 shares of stock registered in his name and endorsed in blank, and while absent from the city desires to sell only 50 shares, the 100-share certificate must be split into two 50-share certificates, one of which may be registered in the name of the pending purchaser; but the other would stand in the name of the depositor and would necessarily not be endorsed and therefore would not be negotiable. The remaining 50 shares, therefore, would not be available for sale until endorsed by the depositor for that purpose. If, however, the certificate stood in the name of a nominee, the new certificate upon its receipt from transfer would be immediately endorsed by the nominee in blank, and would be ready for immediate sale upon proper instructions from the depositor.

The Trust Company is at all times responsible for the acts of its nominees, and requires them to file written instruments with the Company, declaring that the nominee has no ownership in the certificates standing in his name for that purpose, thus insuring that no claim of ownership may be made by the executors or personal representatives of a deceased nominee.

The Company makes no charges to its depositors for purchasing, selling, or delivering securities for their account. Depositors, if they desire, may direct purchases or sales through their own brokerage houses, requesting their brokers to receive or deliver the securities at this office. At the same time instructions should be given to this Company to receive and pay for the securities purchased, or to deliver and receive payment for the securities sold, and to charge or credit the depositor's account.

Orders may also be placed directly with the Company, which will effect the purchase or sale of securities through brokers.

Whether the order is placed directly through the broker or through the medium of the Trust Company, the broker's commission is (of course) added to the purchase price or deducted from the proceeds of the sale, but the Trust Company makes no charge for its services. In order to insure the genuineness of all orders and to protect our depositors against fraud, their signatures are filed with the Trust Company, and are compared with all written instructions.

It is advisable for our depositors to arrange secret code signatures known only to the depositors and the officers of this Company, which will identify all instructions sent by cable or telegraph. If desired, secret code words may be agreed upon to cover any specific transaction concerning which the depositors may desire to give instructions, thus saving the expense of long messages.

Persons traveling will find it very economical to make use of the public codes, such as Lieber's code and the Western Union code, which are especially adapted for general communications, and Hartfield's New Wall Street code which is expressly designed to cover all transactions in securities. One or the other of these codes may be found at the offices of all our correspondents and very generally in any telegraph office or large banking house.

B. Routine Care

1. Collection of principal and income:

a) Collection of principal of maturing bonds: The principal of bonds as they mature is collected and the proceeds either remitted to the depositor or credited to his account, under advice. Notice of principal of bonds becoming due and payable is given a month in advance in order to allow the depositor to arrange for reinvestment without the loss of interest.

b) Collection of bond interest: Coupons upon bonds are detached and deposited for collection when due, the proceeds being either remitted to the depositor or credited to his account, under advice.

c) Collection of dividends: Where the stock stands in the name of a depositor, in order that the Trust Company may receive the dividends as they are paid, the depositor must sign a "dividend order." Where stocks are held in our care, it is recommended that the dividends be made payable to this Company, for account of the customer, in order that it may be assured that the dividends are received. Failure to receive a dividend when due, leads to an immediate investigation; and the depositor is notified in case the dividend is either increased or reduced.

2. Preparation of certificates required under the Federal Income Tax Law preliminary to the collection of coupons, registered interest, or dividends: The Federal Income Tax Law surrounds the collection of income with considerable detail more or less vexing to the investment holder. This detail the Trust Company is prepared to assume under an agency appointment, and thereafter such information as may be required by the Federal Income Tax Law incident to the collection of the income of its depositors is prepared and submitted by the Trust Company without further action of its depositors.

3. Statements:

Depositors receive periodically, at such times as they may request, statements of securities which they have deposited in safe keeping, showing

a) The amount of each security

b) Its description

c) Its due date

d) Dates on which interest or dividends are paid and the income return.

C. Supervision of Deposited Securities

The average individual is kept informed concerning his holdings only through his own efforts. Unless he personally keeps constantly in touch with the information published from time to time relative to his securities, he may lose many opportunities either to act to his advantage or to save himself from possible loss. For instance:

1. His bonds may be called for payment, either at the option of the issuing company or through the operation of some sinking fund. After the date on which a bond is called for payment, interest ceases. If the holder's attention is not called to this he loses the interest which he would have received had his money been invested immediately.

2. His bonds may have the valuable right of being converted into stock on or before a certain date, upon the expiration of which the privilege is lost.

3. He may have the right to subscribe to new issues of stocks or bonds. Generally, this privilege is evidenced by a certificate, which is commonly known as "a right," which entitles the holder to subscribe to stocks or bonds upon paying a certain sum not later than a certain date, after which the privilege ceases.

4. In time of business depression, committees are often formed for the protection of securities and may require their immediate deposit. Committees usually fix a certain date on which securities must be deposited; after this date a penalty attaches. Further, committees sometimes protect only the securities deposited with them, and the non-co-operating security holder, especially in the case of stocks, may not receive substantial advantages which might be gained by acting with the committee.

5. Receivers may be appointed for property in which he is interested. This may make it advisable to dispose of the holdings immediately, before greater loss is incurred.

6. Notice of opportunity to sell bonds to sinking funds. We endeavor to keep our depositors in touch with these opportunities, as they often afford the best opportunity of disposing of securities which have a narrow market.

In addition to the above services, which are rendered automatically but only at the express request of our depositors, periodical examinations of their holdings are made by investment experts with a view to determine whether it seems advisable to recommend either a change in their securities because of new conditions which have arisen, or in order to secure a more balanced and conservative investment.

D. Additional Services Rendered to Depositors

The services already enumerated are those directly connected with the care and supervision of securities, but there are many other matters which we are pleased to attend to when requested, such as

1. *Payment of:*

Taxes on real estate and personal property
Interest on bonds, mortgages, and bank loans
Premiums on life and fire insurance policies
Rent of houses or apartments
Storage charges
Allowances to children, relatives, or dependents

In other words, the service is not confined within formal limits, but responds to the needs of our depositors.

2. *Transfer of securities.*—We are pleased to undertake to effect the transfer of stock certificates and registered bonds which our clients desire to have transferred either to their own names or to the names of beneficiaries under wills or deeds of trust.

3. *Care of securities for executors, administrators, guardians, and committees.*—Individuals acting in the capacity of executors, administrators, guardians, trustees, or as committee for incompetent persons having securities in their charge, instead of placing the securities in safe deposit, may be relieved of the routine care and trouble in handling securities by depositing them in the custody of the Company.

The custodial services that have been outlined above are performed for individuals. Trust companies also act as custodians of the securities of firms and corporations. Modern enterprises often invest surplus funds, reserves, etc., in securities, and the deposit of such securities with a trust company eliminates the expense of providing secure and costly vaults and renders it unnecessary to require the giving of bonds by employees for the faithful discharge of their responsibilities.

V. THE ECONOMIC SIGNIFICANCE OF TRUST COMPANIES

The foregoing survey of the broad scope of trust company operations is sufficient to disclose the very important role played by these institutions in the modern economic system. In a very real sense it may be said that the development of a financial institution of this type was indispensable to the growth of the large-scale corporate form of capitalistic enterprise which involves so many details of financial management and so difficult a task of safeguarding the equities both of the corporate enterprise itself and of the owners of its securities. Similarly, the great accumulations of wealth during the last few generations have rendered it practically impossible for individuals to serve efficiently as trustees of estates, or even to handle effectively their own financial affairs.

The economic importance of the trust company may be indicated in a general way through comparison with other financial institutions. The diagrams on pages 333 and 335 show the growth of trust companies as compared with state and national banks from 1865 to 1935, in terms both of numbers and of capital employed. It will be seen that while the number of trust companies is relatively small the *average* capital is very much larger than that of either national or state banks. It should be remembered, however, that the capital of trust companies includes that of the banking departments as well as that used in connection with the trust business proper.

The economic significance of the *trust* services which these companies render has been expressed in the following terms:[4] (1) conservator of private property; (2) clearing house of equities; (3) stabilizer of investment; and (4) stabilizer of enterprise. The trust company conserves property through serving as guardian of the property of infants and incompetents; by means of real estate trusts and escrows; by acting as transfer agent and registrar of stock; and as receiver and reorganizer of embarrassed or bankrupt companies. It serves as a clearing house of equities when it administers a will or a bankrupt estate and distributes the proceeds among the various claimants. It stabilizes investments through the conservative handling of estates or trust funds committed to its administration and by means of investment advice to clients. Finally, it stabilizes business enterprise by virtue of the varied services performed as conservator, clearing house for equities, and investment expert.

[4] See Smith, James G., *The Development of Trust Companies in the United States*, chap. IX.

CHAPTER XV

THE STOCK EXCHANGE AND CAPITAL RAISING

In the chart on page 133 showing the financial institutions associated with the raising of capital under modern conditions, the stock exchange was placed at one side and designated a central market place. The reason for this arrangement, as already indicated, is that the exchange is not usually a direct intermediary between the borrowing corporation and the lender of funds, its services being rather of an indirect nature. We shall find, however, that the stock exchange is of vital importance to practically all of the institutions that make up the financial structure of society.

In considering the importance of the stock exchange from the point of view of capital raising, it will not be necessary to enter into a detailed technical discussion of manipulation, "wash sales," the system of "puts and calls," etc. The purpose here is merely to reveal the way in which the stock exchange is organized and the role that the mechanism thus provided plays in connection with the process of raising capital for business enterprise.

I. HISTORY OF STOCK EXCHANGES

The rise of stock exchanges is directly associated with the development of the corporation as a capital-raising device. From the moment shares of stock were issued by corporations, both investors and speculators began trading in them. "No sooner were there bits of paper to deal in than jobbers or brokers sprang up to handle them, and by natural gregarious processes these dealers gathered in one spot." The extreme character of some of the earliest stock speculation in England is described in the quotation from Macaulay given on pages 127–128. Twenty years later there developed a great speculative mania, which culminated in the South Sea Bubble of 1717.

These early speculations were conducted on the rotunda of the Bank of England and at the Royal Exchange, which had been established for the purpose of exchanging abraded and clipped coins, both foreign and domestic. Later, as the business expanded, neighboring streets and coffee houses were utilized, and Exchange Alley, Old Jonathan's Coffee House, Corn Hill, Lombard Street, and Sweeting's Alley became the centers of activity. When old Jonathan's burned down in

212

1748, New Jonathan's, located in Threadneedle Street, succeeded it. In 1773 by common consent of the brokers who traded there, New Jonathan's was converted into "The Stock Exchange," which was "wrote over the door." By 1843 the value of the securities listed on the London Stock Exchange was over a billion pounds; by 1875, about 4.5 billion pounds; and by 1933, more than 18.5 billion pounds. The Paris Bourse developed more slowly and it was not until the third quarter of the nineteenth century that it became an important part of the financial system of France. Even more tardy was the growth of the Berlin Stock Exchange, which did not attain importance until the end of the nineteenth century.

The New York Stock Exchange, as at present organized, is the result of more than a century of evolution. The first organization of stock brokers in the metropolis dates from 1792, though it was not until 1817 that the organization assumed a definite form. The rules and regulations governing operations have been modified and extended from time to time to meet the changing requirements of a rapidly expanding industrial and financial system. The New York exchange is a voluntary non-profit-making association, limited to 1,250 members, of whom about half are usually active.

Memberships on the Exchange have a market value, which varies with fluctuations in the volume of trading. In 1869 they sold for $3,000, while between 1920 and 1925 the average was around $100,000. In the boom period, 1925 to 1929, they increased in price by approximately $100,000 each year, reaching a peak of $625,000 in February 1929. In the ensuing decade they reached a low of $51,000—in 1938. The Exchange as such does no business; it merely provides facilities to members and regulates their operations. The governing body is an elective committee of 40 members.

The average annual volume of stock sales on the New York Stock Exchange in the decade 1899–1909 was 196,500,000, at prices which involved an annual average turnover of 15.5 billion dollars. During this same decade bond transactions averaged about 800 million dollars a year. In the boom market of 1928–1929, five million share days were not infrequent, and at the time of the great collapse in October 1929 a record of 16,410,030 shares in one day was reached. The total volume of trading for the year 1928 was 920 million shares; while the bond sales amounted to 2,940 million dollars. As a result of the great depression and the accompanying damper on speculation, the volume of trading has been reduced to a mere fraction of the former amount.

The New York Curb, or "outside" market, really antedates the New York Stock Exchange, the latter, indeed, having been an outgrowth of street trading in the eighteenth century. Long before the organization of the Stock Exchange in 1817 a group of brokers congregated daily around a tree in the old-time financial district of New York and there executed orders for customers. The incorporation of these brokers into a formal organization did away for a time with outside trading; but under varying conditions curb trading was continued throughout the nineteenth century. It was not, however, until the great development in stock operations, brought about by the era of corporate development and financial consolidation beginning about 1898, that the Curb market became of real importance. Thereafter it afforded a public market place where persons could buy and sell securities not listed on any organized exchange.

Until after the World War, the Curb market was held in the open air and occupied a section of Broad Street, where an inclosure was made in the center of the street by means of a rope, within which the traders were supposed to confine themselves, leaving space on each side for traffic. During the period of active trading, however, the crowd often extended from curb to curb. In 1920 there were about 200 subscribers, of whom 150 appeared on the Curb each day. So great eventually became the scope of the Curb market that it was necessary to organize and house it. In 1921 it was moved into a magnificent building, constructed for the purpose, and organized as a full-fledged exchange, with ticker service and listing rules, and with floor trading restricted to members only.

The Curb constitutes an important part of our machinery for trading in securities. Although listing requirements have been adopted, they are not always rigidly enforced, and many securities are traded in which are excluded from the larger exchange. The Curb also offers an "unlisted trading privilege" which maintains a market for "rights" and for many securities which have not been officially listed.

The services performed by the Curb market have been well summarized as follows:[1]

First, it is the market place for the issues of many of the industrial, mining, and miscellaneous enterprises that are constantly being created.

Second, it provides a ready market for the securities of small concerns whose capitalization may be of relatively moderate size. With par values ranging from ten cents to twenty-five dollars, a satisfactory market for these securities would be impossible but for the existence of the Curb market, notwithstanding that these securities possess a merit in many cases as great as do those listed on the regular exchange.

[1] From a pamphlet by Edward E. Epps & Co., Curb Securities Dealers, New York.

Third, it affords facilities for holders of securities that are not listed on any exchange to get accurate quotations thereon and to market their holdings quickly when so desired.

In contrast with the organized security exchanges there are also unorganized "over-the-counter" markets. The Stock Exchange and the over-the-counter market differ in a number of respects. The former provides a public center where the forces of supply and demand for securities come together, while the over-the-counter market provides no direct meeting place. On the Stock Exchange the bid on each security transaction is known to everyone, since a public record of the final quotation of the transaction is made; but in the over-the-counter market the bid is known only to the parties directly involved in the transaction, and no public record of the quotation aside from sporadic newspaper quotations is entered. The distinctive feature of the Stock Exchange, therefore, is its public character, while the over-the-counter market is essentially a private financial agency.

There are special reasons why a given security may be bought or sold in the over-the-counter market rather than on the Stock Exchange. The issuing corporation may have only a small capitalization, and it may therefore not be worth while to list its securities on the Stock Exchange. The stock may have a high price, and therefore not be attractive to the average investor. Or a stock may be closely held and hence may offer little speculative interest to the trader. Again, a corporation, for reasons of its own, may be unwilling to make public the information which the Stock Exchange requires before listing corporate securities. Banks prefer to have their stock traded through the over-the-counter market rather than listed on an organized exchange, because they feel that the wide fluctuations in the price of the stock when listed, and the extensive publicity which follows, might influence the prestige and standing of the bank and possibly, in case of a declining market, cause depositors to lose confidence. Finally, municipal securities must of necessity be traded in over-the-counter, because they are usually payable serially over a period of years.

In most of the European countries the stock exchanges of the great financial centers eventually attained almost a complete monopoly over the machinery for the buying and selling of securities. Until about 1850 the exchanges of Manchester and Leeds actively competed against London, particularly for the listing of railroad securities. However, after the middle of the century the London market grew in strength, and today it handles the vast majority of securities bought and sold in England. In France some of the provincial exchanges, such as Lyons and Bordeaux, were also for a time important, but by the end of the century the Paris market accounted for most of the listed securities. Similarly, Frankfort and Hamburg long operated security markets competing against Berlin, but before 1914 Berlin had obtained complete domination.

This trend toward concentration of security trading in one market has not developed in the United States to the extent that it has abroad. In Chicago, Boston, Philadelphia, and San Francisco, New York faces vigorous competition. In 1935 New York accounted for 24,453 million dollars of bonds out of 31,475 million dollars, and for only 1,483 million shares out of 2,213 million shares listed on all the registered exchanges of the country.

II. THE ORGANIZATION OF THE STOCK EXCHANGE

The purchase and sale of securities on the Stock Exchange are participated in by the members of the Exchange and their agents. While for many years the members acted only in the capacity of brokers, at the present time many of them are principals as well as agents, trading on their own account as well as for their customers. From the functional viewpoint the members of the Stock Exchange may be grouped as follows:

1. *Commission brokers.*—These members constitute the most important class of operators. They receive orders for the purchase and sale of securities from the public, serving both individuals and financial institutions such as insurance companies and banks. They handle transactions either on a cash basis or on a margin account.

2. *"Two dollar" brokers.*—These brokers obtained their name because of the fact that originally their commission on an order of 100 shares of stock was a flat rate of two dollars, rather than a percentage. Today, however, the commission varies—either above or below this price. These brokers have dealings only with commission houses.

3. *Specialists.*—Nearly every important stock has a specialist, and in the case of active stocks there may be several. They act as brokers for the account of others; at the same time they may also trade in the stock for their own account. While the direct purpose of such private transactions is to derive a profit from the difference between purchase and sale price, it is contended that such dealings also serve the public interest by maintaining an orderly market and narrowing the range of fluctuations in stock prices. This practice has, however, been severely criticized on the ground that the specialist has a decided advantage over the general public, since by his knowledge of future orders to sell or future orders to buy the particular stock in which he is specializing,

he is able to judge in advance the probable trend of the market and to act accordingly.

4. *Odd-lot dealers.*—These operators handle transactions in less than the trading unit, which is 100 shares, and so facilitate the security operations of small traders and investors. The odd-lot dealer purchases securities in round lots, that is in trading units, for his own account and then sells whatever number of shares a purchaser may desire. He acts therefore not as a broker charging a commission but as an intermediary making a profit. The odd-lot dealer conducts his business with the commission brokers and not with the general public. While the commission brokers are numerous, the odd-lot dealers are very few in number.

5. *Floor traders.*—These members are free-lance traders who are not limited to any particular securities but operate in any issue. They act on their own account and complete their own orders. Thus they are jobbers or dealers and not brokers. The floor trader has a decided advantage over the outside trader in that he saves the cost of commissions on all transactions and furthermore is frequently able to obtain advance information on the technical position of the market. It is claimed by some that the floor traders perform an important public function by assisting in the maintenance of a continuous and orderly market for securities; others contend that they merely follow the trend upward or downward and so really accentuate rather than limit fluctuations in security prices.

6. *Inactive members.*—Numerous prominent capitalists, both in New York and elsewhere, who are large purchasers or sellers of securities on their own account, hold memberships in order to save commissions and to realize miscellaneous advantages which close association with the Exchange affords. They differ from the floor traders in that they rarely appear personally on the floor of the Exchange.

The "listing" of securities is a safeguard against fraud and irregularities. Before securities can be traded in on the Exchange they must be listed by a committee of the Stock Exchange which passes on applications. The Hughes Committee on Speculation states the importance of listing in the following words:[2]

While the Exchange does not guarantee the character of any securities, or affirm that the statements filed by the promoters are true, it certifies that due diligence and caution have been used by experienced men in examining them. Admission to the list therefore establishes a presumption in favor of the sound-

[2] *Report of Hughes Committee on Speculation in Securities and Commodities,* 1909, p. 2190.

ness of the securities so admitted. Any securities authorized to be bought and sold on the Exchange which have not been subjected to such scrutiny are said to be in the unlisted department, and traders who deal in them do so at their own risk.

The Committee on Stock Lists lays down detailed requirements with reference to the engraving and printing of bonds and shares, the form in which these securities shall be made out, and the specific information that must be cited on the securities, the purpose being to prevent counterfeiting. The application for listing must be accompanied in the case of stocks by such papers as the following: copies of the charter of incorporations; by-laws; leases and special agreements; copy of resolutions of stockholders authorizing an issue; certificate of proper public authority for an issue; opinion of independent counsel as to legality of (a) organization, (b) authorization, (c) issue, (d) validity of the securities; details of distribution of securities; certificate of registrar showing amount of securities registered; report of a qualified engineer covering actual physical condition of property; map of property; contemplated expansion; specimens of all securities to be listed. The requirements with reference to bonds are even more detailed, owing to the many different kinds of mortgage liens and the rights of bondholders thereunder. The cost of listing is $50 for each million dollars, or fraction thereof, computed on the par value. With securities of no par value, it is $50 for each ten thousand shares.

A corporation whose shares are listed on the Exchange must agree to publish and submit an annual report to its stockholders at least fifteen days before its annual meeting, showing an income account and balance sheet for itself and constituent and subsidiary companies which it owns or controls. The report must also contain a statement of the physical condition of the corporate properties at the time.

A large part of the stock bought and sold in the Wall Street offices of brokerage firms is of course for the account of operators who live in New York. In addition the large brokerage concerns have a remarkably extensive telegraph system whereby orders are gathered from far-distant points. The "wire map" of any one of a half-dozen or so of the large houses looks like a complete railroad guide of the United States. One particular firm reaches by privately leased duplex wire from its main Wall Street office to such cities as Baltimore, Washington, Charlotte, Charleston, Atlanta, Savannah, Augusta, Jacksonville, New Orleans, Memphis, Chicago, Cleveland, Cincinnati, Omaha, Colorado Springs, Denver, Salt Lake City, Butte, Spokane, San Francisco, Pasadena, Los Angeles, Coronado Beach, and San Diego. It also has wire connections to Boston, Portland, Montreal, Toronto,

Detroit, Gary, Indianapolis, Louisville, Kansas City, Milwaukee, St. Paul, and Winnipeg. These wires may connect with branch offices or merely with correspondent firms.

Through weekly market letters and special reports brokers undertake to supply their customers with information about inactive and unlisted securities, such as the history of the issuing corporations and general trends in the industries with which they are connected. Many of them have also been tempted to forecast market changes in the light of general economic conditions. Unfortunately much of this service has been of a superficial character. Moreover, the opportunity for fraud has been quite as great here as in the direct selling of securities, discussed in chapter XI. The advertising material formerly sent out by "fly-by-night" brokerage houses makes quite as interesting reading as that of the promoter of speculative and fraudulent companies; and the losses of the victims of such alluring literature have been perhaps as great as those resulting from promotion swindles. Such operations have of course always been fought by the Stock Exchange and by the legitimate brokerage houses. The regulatory machinery set up by the Securities and Exchange Commission to prevent such abuses is discussed in the next chapter.

The methods by which stock exchange operations are carried out have been summarized as follows:[3]

1. *Purchasing outright.*—There are two methods of buying or selling stocks through members of the New York Stock Exchange, viz., buying or selling outright for cash, and buying or selling on margin.

When purchasing stock outright, or what is commonly termed "for cash," a person pays the entire cost of the stock plus commission. It is customary to have the stock transferred to the name of the buyer, especially if the stock is one upon which dividends are paid, the same being paid to the party in whose name the certificate is made out. At times, however, the purchaser desires to leave the stock with the broker in order to facilitate its sale when desired, and the certificate is placed in an envelope marked as property of the owner to be delivered when called for. In this case the stock is often left in the broker's name and the customer is credited with the dividend when payable, or a check for that amount is forwarded to him. Thus the buyer receives the dividend but does not have the trouble of endorsing the certificate and sending it to the broker when he desires to sell. Non-dividend paying stocks when purchased outright are also often left in the original "street name," as a certificate endorsed by a stock exchange house is a good delivery at any time one may wish to sell, and one has no trouble about endorsing, witnessing, etc.

2. *Purchasing on margin.*—When purchasing on margin, the broker buys the stock, paying for same in full, but loans the customer a certain amount,

[3] Adapted from a statement of a New York brokerage house.

holding the certificates as collateral and charging interest on this debit balance. The difference between the amount loaned and the purchase price is deposited by the customer, being what is commonly termed "margin." The percentage of the purchase price of the stock which may be loaned by the broker is determined by the Federal Reserve Board and is subject to change. As of June 1, 1938 the amount which the broker might loan was fixed at 60 per cent of the purchase price. It is customary for the broker, using the stock as collateral, to borrow from a bank the amount which he lends the customer. The rate of interest which the broker pays the bank is usually somewhat lower than the rate at which he lends to the customer, thus giving the broker a slight profit on the debit balance.

The customer may at any time pay off his loan, together with any interest which may have accrued since the purchase, and take up the stock. If after the purchase of a stock on margin the market price declines enough to reduce the margin substantially, the customer is requested to put up additional margin. If he fails to do so, the broker will sell the stock, reimburse himself for the amount borrowed upon it, and return to the customer the remainder of the margin. A customer is, of course, always given opportunity to deposit additional margin. There is no limit to the length of time stocks may be carried on margin as long as the amount of margin is sufficient to protect the broker.

3. *Selling outright.*—In selling stock held outright in a customer's name, the customer must endorse the certificate, spelling the name exactly as it is spelled on the face and have same witnessed, but should fill in none of the other blank spaces on the back of the certificate. The commission for selling is the same as for buying, and in addition the seller pays the taxes levied by the state of New York and the Federal Government.

4. *Selling margin stock.*—When selling stock held on margin, the customer simply gives the order to the broker, who sells the stock, delivers the certificate, and credits the customer's account with the proceeds, less commission and state and federal taxes.

In selling stock short, the broker sells the stock, borrows it, and delivers same on regular delivery day. The margin required is a protection against a rise in the market instead of a decline. If the market reacts, the customer may repurchase the stock at a lower figure, his profits being the difference between the sale price and the purchase price, and if the market advances and he buys in, or "covers," at a higher figure, his loss is also the difference between the sale price and the purchase price. This is simply the reverse of purchasing stock and then selling, the sale being made first and the purchase later. When the stock is covered, the broker returns same to the party from whom he originally borrowed it. No interest is charged a customer on the transaction, except when the stock is borrowed at a premium because of a great scarcity. This, however, is a very rare occurrence. The margin required is usually the same as on stock purchases.

5. *Stop loss orders.*—Stop loss orders are used by a great many traders to limit the amount of possible loss on any transaction, and often they save one from losing his entire margin. A stop loss order for the purchase or sale of a

stock means that the purchase or sale, as the case may be, is to be made "at the market" when a certain price is reached. For instance, if United States Steel is selling at 70, and an order is placed to sell 100 shares at 68 stop, it means that when a sale of 100 shares or more is made on the Stock Exchange at 68 or less, 100 shares are to be sold "at the market," that is, at the best price obtainable. At times, however, it might close above 68 one day and open below 68 the next morning, or even during the day might break from a price above to below 68 without a sale at that figure, in which case the stop loss order would be executed as soon as a sale was made under 68. Conversely, if an order is given to buy 100 shares at, say 72 stop, it means that 100 shares are to be purchased "at the market" when a sale of 100 shares or more is made at 72 or higher.

III. ECONOMIC FUNCTIONS OF THE STOCK EXCHANGE

In analyzing the character and significance of the functions rendered by the Stock Exchange in a financially organized society we shall begin with a statement of those services about which there is little disagreement and end with a brief discussion of those which are of a controversial nature. Finally, some consideration will be given to the changing importance of the exchanges.

In the first place, the Stock Exchange makes possible investments for short periods of time. Many individuals, business firms, and corporations have on hand funds that are temporarily not required, because of either seasonal variations in the volume of business or a general dullness of trade. By virtue of an organized market these funds may be invested in securities, with assurance that they can at any time be reconverted into cash at the market price then current. In the absence of the stock market such funds would either remain in idleness or be deposited in commercial or savings banks, where the interest return would be substantially lower.

Second, the activities of speculators result in price quotations which reflect with a fair degree of accuracy the relative values of corporate properties. Specialized financial experts devote their energies unceasingly to a scrutiny of values; "bulls and bears, bankers and brokers, speculators and investors, all over the world bid and offer against each other by cable and telegraph and record the epitomized result of their bidding in the prices current on the stock exchange." While personal gain is the motive of these speculators, the net result of their activities is none the less to determine and reveal the relative investment values of the various issues. It is to be noted that the larger the number of operations and the greater the number of securities traded in on the various exchanges, the more accurate becomes the stock exchange index of values.

The effect of this world-wide trading is also to stabilize the prices of securities in different markets. This result is most clearly revealed in connection with international securities, such as the bonds of the principal governments and of large corporations, like the Pennsylvania Railroad and the General Electric Company of Germany. For bonds of this class

the telegraph keeps prices at almost exactly the same level in all the stock exchanges of the world. If the price of one of them rises in New York or in Paris, in London or in Berlin, the mere news of the rise tends to cause a rise in other markets; and if for any other reason the rise is delayed, that particular class of bonds is likely soon to be offered for sale in the high-priced market under telegraphic orders from the other market, while dealers in the first market will be making telegraphic purchases in other markets. These sales on the one hand, and purchases on the other hand, strengthen the tendency which the price has to seek the same level everywhere; and unless some of the markets are in an abnormal condition, the tendency soon becomes irresistible.[4]

This stabilization process promotes the development of a world financial organization, the concrete evidence of which is best shown by reference to the list of over 1,100 securities, representing industries in all parts of the world, which are traded in on the London Stock Exchange.

In the third place, the stock market facilitates the process of distributing capital among different industries, among different plants in a given industry, and among different countries and regions of the world. In chapter I we discussed the role of the pecuniary unit in this connection. It may now be noted that the distribution is worked out through the purchase and sale of shares of stocks and bonds which are quoted on the organized exchanges, in terms of the pecuniary unit. The fluctuations in prices of different securities, being reflections of fundamental underlying conditions, indicate in general in what directions capital can find its most profitable investment.

Finally, one of the greatest functions of the security markets is to facilitate the "carrying" of new securities during their seasoning period. In the event that a new issue of securities does not go well and remains unsold at the expiration of the underwriting agreement, it becomes necessary for the underwriters either to carry these securities on borrowed funds, in the hope of a favorable turn in the market, or to sell them at a convenient opportunity and pocket their losses. The market places provide the means for either holding or disposing of the securities. If the underwriters decide to carry the securities for a time, they must, as indicated in chapter XII, borrow heavily from the com-

4 Marshall, Alfred, *Principles of Economics* (4th ed., 1898) Vol. I, p. 403.

mercial banks. This they are enabled to do only because the stocks and bonds in which they are dealing are a satisfactory collateral security for bank loans, in consequence of their ready marketability.

These unmarketed, or "undigested," securities may remain subject to speculative activity for considerable periods of time, not infrequently for several years, depending upon the state of the investment market and the character of the security in question.[5] This speculation, conducted with money borrowed from commercial banks on amply margined collateral security, makes it possible for a corporation to procure the funds required for developing its business, even though its securities do not as yet commend themselves to ultimate investors. Meanwhile the subjecting of its securities to the test of speculation gradually serves to indicate their actual value and thus to induce individuals to "pick them up" for investment purposes.

It should be observed that the analysis at this point ties back with that in chapter XI on the direct marketing of unseasoned or speculative securities. Here is clearly one way of raising capital for untried enterprises that does not place the risks upon the investing public. It is, moreover, a method of very great importance; for many highgrade stocks now held by investors have passed through a probationary period as purely speculative issues. It has been estimated, indeed, that stock speculation served as a means of furnishing, in the first instance, probably the greater part of the fixed capital that was used in the great period of industrial expansion following 1898. The volume of stocks and bonds annually being issued by new corporations far outran the absorbing power of the investment market, and securities aggregating hundreds of millions of dollars could not be sold to ultimate investors. The National City Bank of New York has estimated that in 1900 over 60 per cent of the stock of our largest corporations whose securities were listed on the New York Stock Exchange was held in the names of stock brokerage houses and represented speculative accounts. Indeed, the history of the capitalization of our leading corporations shows that new stock issues almost invariably run through a period in which they are held by the speculative public in brokers' names (on funds borrowed from the commercial banks), the proportion so held gradually diminishing over a number of years as they find their way into investment portfolios.

Stock markets, investment banks, commercial banks, speculators, and investors are thus intimately related to the process of marketing

[5] For actual data concerning the relative holdings of certain stocks by brokers and individuals over a period of years, see J. E. Meeker, *The Work of the Stock Exchange*, pp. 593–594.

corporate securities; and the entire mechanism would break down if any of its interdependent parts should cease to function. In the absence of a securities market, both borrowing corporations and the investing public, including savings banks and insurance companies, would be without an indispensable index of relative values. Without the stock market and the commercial banking system, underwriters and distributors of securities would find it impossible to conduct their operations. The stock market could not perform its function in "carrying and testing" unseasoned securities in the absence of commercial bank loans to speculators; and the commercial banks, in turn, could not make loans to speculators if it were not for the Stock Exchange, which at once indicates the value of the collateral offered as security for the loans and makes possible its ready sale in case of need. The full significance of the part that the commercial banks play in the process cannot, however, be made clear until we have studied the commercial banking mechanism in some detail.

The features of the stock exchange which have given rise to most controversy are those of margin trading and short selling. Such operations involve the extensive use of credit, and it is believed by many observers that they promote wide market fluctuations and carry no compensating advantages. It should be made clear that buying stock on margin differs essentially from the purchase of goods on an installment basis. The latter are bought for use and are in due course to be paid for in full; the former are usually purchased simply with a view to resale when the price has risen "sufficiently." Since the margin trader usually does not expect to buy the stock in full he is not restrained in the scope of his credit operations as is the purchaser of goods on installment. If his credit standing is good—and it usually is as long as stock prices are advancing—he can greatly pyramid his holdings. The result—when general conditions are propitious—may be an enhancement of stock prices quite out of line with underlying values. The traditional view that margin trading tends to promote market stability does not therefore appear well founded and is certainly not supported by any statistical evidence.

On the other hand, margin trading does seem to provide a more adequate market than would otherwise exist. Various studies of the stock market seem to demonstrate that issues in which there is active speculation generally have a more continuous market than do those in which speculation is inactive or entirely absent. Thus the general public finds a broader and more active market in which to buy or sell for investment purposes. This appears to be the only important service of margin trading.

Short selling differs from margin buying in that the gain is sought in falling rather than in rising prices. The fact that short selling involves the sale of property not actually owned has given rise to widespread criticism. "Bear raiding," or organized short selling, is therefore frequently charged with bringing about unduly low prices for particular stocks, or with unsettling the entire security market. On the other hand, short selling is defended on the ground that it operates as a brake upon a stock market rise unjustified by the earning power of a particular stock or by general economic conditions. The truth seems to be that short selling, like margin buying, may, under certain conditions, promote excessive swings of the market, out of line with realities. However, it undoubtedly serves to provide a check upon undue optimism and to restrain advances; and margin buying may serve in turn to counteract the effects of heavy short sales. If one of these practices is permitted the other should therefore be allowed. The real question is whether the use of credit in either of these directions is a stabilizing factor.

The sharp statement of this issue brings us to a consideration of certain changes in the nature of stock market speculation in modern times which have an important bearing upon the economic effects of speculation. The traditional view as to the significance of stock market speculation was based on the assumption that those who engage in such trading operations are interested only in the relative movements of particular securities. It seemed obvious that the careful scrutiny of each issue by professional speculators, operating on both sides of the market, would aid in bringing into alignment all issues, in terms of relative values, and also in stabilizing values as a whole. But as the market became more perfectly organized, and as the emphasis in financial operations in general shifted from stable income on investment to the realization of profits through forecasting general business trends and riding the market up or down, the economic effects of stock speculation also changed. The wide fluctuations that have characterized the market in recent times have undoubtedly been amplified by speculative activities, participated in by the public as well as by professional operators. Income is regarded as a secondary consideration; the real objective is the enhancement of principal. In this "education," brokers, investment trusts, and investment counsellors play an important role.

While we have long had occasional periods of "wild speculation," the conception of the security market to which we are here referring is a comparatively recent phenomenon. Moreover, it is especially characteristic of the United States, where it is doubtless chiefly

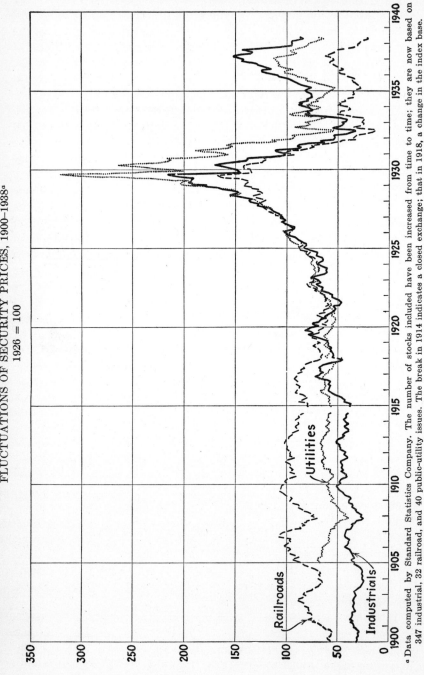

FLUCTUATIONS OF SECURITY PRICES, 1900–1938[a]
1926 = 100

[a] Data computed by Standard Statistics Company. The number of stocks included have been increased from time to time; they are now based on 347 industrial, 32 railroad, and 40 public-utility issues. The break in 1914 indicates a closed exchange; that in 1918, a change in the index base.

attributable to the growing volume of liquid funds that have become available as national wealth and income have expanded, and as the supply of available credit has become more abundant. The correcting or minimizing of the evils growing out of credit operations lies not in the abolition of speculation but in more effective control. The remedy for the speculative spirit lies in education—and experience.

By way of concluding this discussion of changing conditions, attention should also be called to certain developments which have been tending to reduce the relative importance of the stock exchange in the financial system. Even in the pre-war period the growth of huge integrated banking institutions, particularly in Germany, led to a policy of settling many of the purchases and sales of securities made by a bank's customers "within the bank"—without resort to the exchange. Today even in the United States there is a large amount of direct security-trading which is not conducted through the organized markets. Government issues which have come to occupy so important a place in the financial markets are not traded through the exchanges. Finally, the vast liquidation of security values in recent years, the stagnation in private capital enterprise, and the accompanying government regulation, have together brought a vast shrinkage in the volume of stock exchange business as well as a diminution of interest in stock market operations. This trend may, however, prove only a temporary movement; for a period of economic expansion would necessitate the flotation of a large volume of new issues and a resurgence of stock market activity.

CHAPTER XVI

THE REGULATION OF THE INVESTMENT
CREDIT SYSTEM

The four preceding chapters have been devoted to a discussion of
the various types of financial agencies and operations which taken
together comprise what may be called the investment credit system.
We have covered the capital requirements of both government and
private enterprise; the machinery for marketing securities, directly,
and through investment houses; the role of intermediate investment
institutions; the varied services of the trust companies; and the
function of the stock exchange in providing a continuous market for
the purchase and sale of the investment credit instruments which
evidence the ownership of corporate properties. In this final chapter
of the section we shall discuss the development of public regulation in
relation to the various institutions which make up the investment
credit system.

I. REGULATIONS APPLIED TO CORPORATIONS

The regulation of the corporation itself has arisen out of conflicts
of interest between corporate owners and managers and between the
corporation and the public. Through the sale of its securities to the
investing public the corporation has brought about widely diffused
ownership of business properties. It has been estimated that in 1928
as many as 18 million names were recorded as stockholders on the
books of corporations in the United States.[1] Inasmuch as a given
individual may own stock in several corporations this figure of course
exaggerates the number of individuals who own stock; but it is estimated that the actual number of individual stockholders ranged from
4 to 7 millions in 1929.[2] While these figures clearly reveal the trend
toward the democratization of ownership of American corporations,
they also indicate that actual management is substantially detached
from ownership. The interests of the two groups are not necessarily
identical.

[1] Means, Gardiner C., "The Diffusion of Stock Ownership in the United
States," *Quarterly Journal of Economics*, 1930, pp. 561–600.
[2] Berle, Adolph A. and Means, Gardiner C., *The Modern Corporation and
Private Property*, 1933, p. 91.

The possible conflict of interests between the corporation and the public arises chiefly in connection with the issuing of securities in excess of the true value of the assets, in the expectation that the prices or rates charged will, in due course, permit the payment of interest and dividends on the excess capitalization.

To safeguard the interests of the public, both federal and state governments have extended their regulation over the various classes of corporations, particularly the utilities and railroads. In general the financing of industrial corporations has not been regulated. Until after the close of the nineteenth century there was virtually no public control over public utilities. The lead in regulating such companies was taken by New York state in 1905 through the formation of a commission which was granted the power to regulate the securities issued by the utility companies in the state. Other states followed and by 1917 every state, except Delaware, had such a commission. While the first purpose of most of these statutes was to regulate the rates charged by public utilities, in recent years most state commissions have been given power to regulate capitalization and to determine the proportion between stocks and bonds, and even the prices at which they may be sold by the corporation.

In the post-war period this state regulation of public utilities was seriously checked by the development of holding companies which in time obtained control of most of the operating companies. The holding company was generally beyond the reach of the state commissions. In certain cases these holding companies performed important services by enabling the local operating company to borrow more economically, and they also conveyed advantages in the form of centralized purchases, improved technical and engineering advice, etc. However, the holding companies often engaged in various unsound financial policies such as purchasing operating companies at inflated values, and then using these values as a basis for floating their own overcapitalized issues. The holding companies also pyramided capital by creating holding company on top of holding company, thereby enabling a small investment to control an enormous amount of operating company assets. With the coming of the depression these holding companies found the rowing hard, and the operating companies were often forced to grant them "upstream loans"—the sound credit of the latter being utilized to support the unsound credit of the former.

These evils could not be corrected by state legislation, and as a result Congress passed in 1935 the Federal Public Utility Act. This Act sought particularly to regulate the financial practices of holding companies in the field of gas and electric utilities. Holding companies must now register with the Securities and Exchange Commission, and are not permitted to issue or sell securities without the consent of that agency. Furthermore, the law compelled holding companies to simplify their capital structures and rearrange them on a sounder basis. Under the Act each holding company is required "to confine itself to a single integrated public utility system and to such other businesses as are reasonably incidental, economically necessary, or appropriate thereto." The Commission is also given control over all intercorporate relations between a holding company and its subsidiaries.

The railroads have been under the jurisdiction of the Interstate Commerce Commission ever since 1887, but it was not until 1920 that this body was given power to regulate the finances of the carriers. All new securities issued by the railroads, with certain minor exceptions such as those with a maturity of less than two years and with a par value of less than five per cent of a company's capitalization, must have the approval of the Commission. The Commission was also given the power to regulate the minimum price at which a railroad might sell a new issue of securities to an investment banking house. Moreover, the law endeavored to force the investment houses to compete for railroad issues.

Corporate financing has also come under government regulation in recent years through the revision of the bankruptcy laws. During the nineteenth century the Federal Government enacted numerous bankruptcy statutes, particularly in periods of acute financial depression. Such statutes were not, however, well adapted to meet the financial emergencies arising in connection with the wholesale distress of large corporate enterprises. The enormous difficulties accompanying the depression of 1929 finally resulted in a drastic revision of the federal bankruptcy laws, particularly through the addition of what is conveniently referred to as Section 77B, which makes it possible for a corporation to re-organize its capital structure without being legally adjudged a bankrupt. Moreover, the new law enables individual owners of stocks or bonds to form protective committees to safeguard their interests, whereas formerly such protective committees were mainly controlled by the investment banking houses which had sold the securities. In the past a dissenting minority was frequently able to block even a sound plan for corporate reorganization. The new statute was framed to overcome the obstructing tactics of dissenting minorities and to expedite the re-organization of corporations which possess earning power and hence have the possibility of early financial rehabilitation.

II. LIMITATIONS ON GOVERNMENT FINANCIAL ISSUES

Chapter XI showed that capital, both fixed and working, is raised not only by corporations but also by municipal, state, and federal governments. There is, of course, practically no effective control over the financing of the Federal Government, but state, and particularly municipal, financing has been placed under regulation. In the first half of the nineteenth century the states, in financing their public works, expanded their debts too rapidly, and as a result a number of them defaulted on their obligations. In order to prevent a recurrence most states shortly adopted constitutional amendments specifically limiting the amount of debt which they might contract. These limitations related to the purpose, the amount, and the security of the debt. It was usually specified that the debt should be contracted only for a public purpose; that it have a definite maturity date, which should synchronize with the life of the public undertaking which was being financed; and that the debt must not exceed a maximum percentage of the assessed valuation of the property within the jurisdiction of the state.[3]

As a result of flagrant defaults in the period after the Civil War, similar restrictions were placed upon the debt-creating power of municipalities. From the end of the nineteenth century until the nineteen-thirties, notwithstanding unsound tendencies in municipal finance, no serious defaults occurred, the general prosperity and increasing tax-paying capacity offsetting the weight of mounting indebtedness. However, the great depression which began in 1929 resulted in widespread municipal defaults, involving more than 2,000 local governments.[4]

In 1933 Congress passed the National Municipal Bankruptcy Act to meet these conditions, but the Supreme Court declared the Act unconstitutional. The task of regulating municipal credit was, therefore, placed upon the states themselves. State statutes enacted for this purpose are of two types. One group, such as the New Jersey law, gives a state commission temporary supervision over municipal finance whenever a locality is in default on its obligations. The state commission then makes every effort to place the finances of the locality on a sound basis; upon attaining this end its task is over. On the other

---

[3] Secrist, Horace, *An Economic Analysis of the Constitutional Restrictions upon Public Indebtedness in the United States* (University of Wisconsin Bulletin, Madison, 1914) p. 54.

[4] Chatters, Carl E., *Municipal Debt Defaults*, Public Administrative Publication No. 33, 1933, p. 11.

hand, other states, such as North Carolina, have instituted a system of continuous supervision over the finances of local governments. A municipality must apply to the state commission whenever it wishes to place a new issue of securities, and the commission will grant its approval only if sound principles of public finance are observed. This commission may also require the installation of uniform municipal accounting systems and may regulate the investment of the sinking funds of the local governments.

Not only has there been an extension of government regulation of domestic financing but the flotation of foreign securities in American markets has also come under the jurisdiction of the Federal Government. It was not until 1922 that the Federal Government undertook to supervise foreign loans; and during the twenties they were regulated not by act of Congress but merely by informal rulings. An American banking house, about to float a foreign loan, either public or private, was required to inform the State Department of the details of the issue, in order that it might determine whether the proposed loan harmonized with the diplomatic interests of the United States. The State Department, in co-operation with other government departments, investigated the issue and expressed informally its approval or disapproval—making it clear, however, that it was not concerned with the soundness of the loan.

As a result of disastrous experiences with foreign issues, in the early thirties Congress passed the Johnson Act, which prohibits any foreign government from borrowing in the American capital market if such foreign government has previously defaulted on its obligations to the United States Government or its citizens. Most major European countries, because of their default on war debts owed the American Government, are thus prohibited from further borrowing here under the terms of the Act. Foreign countries which do not fall under the ban imposed by the Act, must, if they wish to float securities in this country, comply with the provisions of the Securities Act of 1933, which will be discussed in section IV.

III. CONTROLLING INVESTMENTS OF INTERMEDIARY INSTITUTIONS

The various institutions included in this category are controlled by the laws of the states in which they operate, the only exception being the investment trust, which remains unregulated. The regulations extend to provisions with respect to capital stock, the accumulation of surplus, the maintenance of reserves, and so forth, as well as to the character of investments, but it is the last with which we are here chiefly concerned.

Insurance companies, mutual savings banks, and to a varying extent other types of savings institutions, must confine their investments to classes of securities approved by state regulations. In the case of insurance companies such regulations afford wide latitude for managerial discretion. Even life insurance companies, which are more carefully supervised than other types of companies, are permitted to invest funds in a broad range of securities. Formerly such investments were restricted to bonds and mortgages, but eventually the leading states also permitted investments in preferred stocks. Fire insurance and casualty insurance companies have large holdings of common stock.

In contrast, the investments of the mutual savings banks are rigidly restricted. These institutions may place their funds only in bonds and mortgages, and, in some states, in limited forms of commercial paper. Moreover, the bond investments are restricted largely to railroad, utility, and government obligations which in turn must meet certain specific tests. This system of legal tests has been subject to criticism on various grounds. It has been claimed that it represents the investment sentiment of a past generation; that placing an issue on the legal list creates an artificial market for the bonds, so that the yield does not reflect the true credit position; and that the mere fact that a bond is on the legal list frequently induces an investor to purchase it without sufficient investigation. However, the mutual savings banks have shown an exceptional record of stability during recurring periods of depression.

In certain states, such as Massachusetts, stock savings banks are required to segregate savings or time deposits and invest the funds received in legally prescribed bonds. In most states, however, the investment of such savings funds is not regulated by law.

Until very recently national banks were permitted to invest in bonds with practically no restriction. The Banking Act of 1935 gave the Comptroller of the Currency the right to restrict the security purchases of national banks, and in accordance with this provision the Comptroller prohibited the purchase of "speculative issues." The eligibility of securities is determined in accordance with their ratings in the leading investment manuals. However, since these investment services themselves often find it difficult to distinguish between investment and speculative securities, there is room for considerable improvement in the Comptroller's ruling.

IV. REGULATION OF TRUST FUNCTIONS

Trust companies have never been subjected to much government control, except in connection with their banking departments. Even here the regulations were usually much less stringent than were those pertaining to regular banks, and as we shall see in chapter XXII, which discusses the process of integration in the field of finance, the liberality shown to trust companies gradually forced a relaxation of restrictions upon, and permitted a broadening of the powers of, commercial banking institutions.

As far as the trust functions were concerned, the state laws conferred upon trust companies very broad grants of power, which enabled them to develop along flexible, experimental lines. It should be borne in mind, however, that their operations have been subject to the laws pertaining to trust and agency business in general. There appears to be little doubt that these laws have, on the whole, insured the faithful performance of the manifold services which the trust conpanies assume.

However, the closer scrutiny to which all types of financial operations have been subjected since the great depression has led to a demand for the supervision of trust functions by the Federal Government. The first step in this direction was the establishment, by the Banking Act of 1933, of a system of trust company examinations under federal government supervision. This Act required all corporations, associations, or business trusts which receive deposits, to submit to periodic examinations by the Comptroller of the Currency or by the Federal Reserve bank of the district in which they are located, and to make and publish periodic reports showing in detail their financial condition. Failure to comply with these provisions is subject to the same penalties as were already provided by law in connection with national banks.[5] Since such companies are not incorporated under federal law and are therefore not subject to the supervision of the Federal Reserve banks or of the Comptroller of the Currency, decision as to whether they fulfill the general requirements of the law must be made by the Department of Justice.

A second proposed step is to place *trust indentures* under the supervision of the Federal Securities and Exchange Commission.[6] These instruments embody the terms, agreements, obligations, etc. covering each issue of securities. The primary purpose of the suggested regula-

[5] For similar regulations pertaining to national and state banks see chap. XXII.

[6] See Barkley Bill (1937), S. 2344.

tion is to safeguard investors by ensuring the disinterestedness of trustees, by prescribing their duties and obligations more definitely, and by making them liable for losses chargeable to their negligence. Such regulation presents great complications and involves the danger of so increasing the obligations and risks incurred by the trustee that no institution or individual could afford to assume the responsibility of trusteeship.

V. SUPERVISION OF THE MARKETING OF SECURITIES

The investment banking business developed under private auspices and was long subject only to such legal control as applied to any corporation, partnership, or business owned by an individual. However, in endeavoring to protect the investor from fraudulent promotion schemes, and to furnish prospective purchasers of speculative securities with adequate information on which to base an intelligent judgment, nearly all the states, beginning with Kansas in 1911, have passed what is known as blue-sky legislation. This expression was adapted from the wording of a court decision which referred to "speculative schemes that have no more basis than so many feet of blue sky."[7]

The state laws regulating the issue of securities are of two principal kinds. The first type seeks to regulate the sale of all securities (except certain exempted issues such as those of governmental bodies) by requiring investment bankers to obtain state permission for the sale of a new issue. The second type, such as the Martin Act in New York State, is concerned merely with bringing criminal action against issuers of and dealers in fraudulent securities. State legislation did not, however, prove very effective. The greatest difficulty lay in the fact that the wide variations in the laws of different states have afforded many loopholes for the sale of fraudulent securities. Stock issued by a corporation in one state may be sold in another state, even though similar issues of corporations organized under the laws of this state could not be sold within its boundaries.

Because of the failure of blue-sky legislation to protect investors from loss in connection with fraudulent and highly speculative issues—and also, it should be added, to prevent abuses in connection with securities issued by large and well-established corporations through "reputable" investment banking institutions—it was finally deemed necessary for the Federal Government to assume supervision over this division of the financial system, and in 1933 Congress passed the Securities Act.

[7] *Hale* v. *Geiger-Jones*, 242 U.S. 339.

This statute was based on the "disclosure principle" embodied in the British Companies Act which had been in operation for almost a century. The Federal Securities Act sought "to provide full and fair disclosure of the character of securities sold in interstate and foreign commerce and through the mails and to prevent frauds in the sale thereof." Like the state blue-sky laws the Securities Act does not apply to securities issued by or guaranteed by the federal, state, or municipal governments; to the issues of national or state banks; those of non-profit making organizations, and common carriers; to certificates of receivers; or to short-term commercial paper. Issues of less than $100,-000 or having a maturity of less than a year were excluded. The Act also exempted certain operations such as private offerings of securities, brokerage transactions undertaken on unsolicited customers' orders, and the exchange of securities in corporate re-organizations without the payment of commissions. The Act does apply to all other stocks, bonds, debentures, or notes. As was the case with state blue-sky laws, the Federal Securities Act requires the registration of all such securities sold in interstate commerce, and imposes liabilities for false registration statements and for the omission or misstatement of a material fact.

The Act is based on the assumption that the investing public is protected if it receives adequate and truthful information regarding securities which it is asked to purchase. It is still possible to float low-grade securities, for the statute prohibits only fraudulent issues, and makes no attempt to regulate the quality of an offering. It would seem, however, that the financing of promotional ventures is difficult under the new statute. Of all promotional issues made without investment banking support, less than 20 per cent of the amount registered was sold within the year following the effective date on the registration statement; in 40 per cent of the cases not one share of stock or a single bond was sold.[8]

Through the efforts of the Securities and Exchange Commission a large volume of low-grade securities has undoubtedly been withheld from the market. For a three-year period, until the middle of 1936, as a result of its stop orders, refusal orders, and withdrawal orders, the Commission had vetoed proposed issues amounting to over 408 million dollars,[9] the greater part of which was accounted for by the investment trust, the electric light and power, the manufacturing, and the precious metal mining groups. The most serious difficulties were encountered in the fields of investment trusts and the precious metals. Notwithstanding the low repute of such issues even in the twenties, these two groups

[8] *Law and Contemporary Problems*, Duke University, p. 53.
[9] *Law and Contemporary Problems*, op. cit., p. 32.

continued to account for most of the low-grade securities. In the case of the investment trusts the promoters frequently were men whose lack of integrity had been established.

The operations of investment banking have naturally been greatly affected by the Securities Act and in many respects the machinery has had to be adjusted to meet the new conditions. For example, where formerly the originating of an issue was commonly undertaken by one banking house, a number of houses now perform this function. The main reason for this change is that provision in the Securities Act which imposes a heavy liability on the underwriting house, thereby making it unwilling to assume liability for the entire issue. The regulations, particularly in the act as first passed, were so detailed and often so impracticable as to make compliance virtually impossible. While amendments or modifications of rulings have served greatly to clarify and simplify the problem, the time required and the costs involved remain as impediments to security flotations, except those of the most conservative character. As a result there is a strong tendency to obtain needed capital by other means than public flotations—from earnings, from the direct placement of securities with large investors, and from intermediate-term loans from commercial banks.[10] In the case of many small enterprises, moreover, there is an increasing tendency to look to the Government as a source of capital.

Whether a satisfactory balance can be achieved between reasonable safety to investors, on the one hand, and the maintenance, on the other hand, of a healthy flow of investment money to the channels of productive enterprise, remains to be seen.

VI. CONTROL OF THE STOCK EXCHANGE

The stock market boom of the late twenties, the excessive use of commercial bank credit in financing market activities, the striking decline in values that followed 1929, and the huge losses to both investing institutions and individuals, naturally suggested the need of regulating the operations of the security exchanges as well as the original issuing and sale of securities. In 1934 Congress extended the scope of its control over security transactions by means of the Securities Exchange Act. By an amendment of June 25, 1938, the regulatory power of the Commission was extended to include over-the-counter brokers and dealers operating in interstate or foreign commerce.

Under the terms of this statute all security exchanges in the country are required to register with the Securities and Exchange Commission and to comply with such rules of practice as the latter may pro-

[10] For discussion of the last see p. 323.

mulgate. The alternative is the denial of the privileges of interstate commerce and the use of the mails. The exchanges and all individuals having dealings thereon are subject to examination by the Commission and must keep such records and make such reports as the Commission may prescribe. In addition the Commission is given power to fix and regulate the duties and activities of dealers, brokers, specialists, floor traders, and odd-lot dealers, and to control "over-the-counter" operations. The Commission has the task of preventing security price manipulation by means of wash sales, speculative pools, etc., violation of its rules in this connection being made a criminal offense.

Control over the volume of commercial bank credit available for the securities markets has been provided in two ways: first, by giving the Board of Governors of the Federal Reserve system the power to prescribe margin requirements; and second, by prohibiting brokers and dealers from borrowing except from member banks of the Federal Reserve system or from such non-member banks as agree to comply with the regulations of the Securities and Exchange Commission. The Board of Governors of the Federal Reserve system has also been given power to suspend from the privileges of the system any member bank which after due warning continues to extend credit for speculative purposes. Margin requirements have been greatly increased, with a view to restraining speculative tendencies.

It had been hoped that the regulation of the Stock Exchange and the security markets would not only eliminate evils connected with security issues and security trading, but would also prevent wide market fluctuations and especially such debacles as that of 1929. While regulatory measures may possibly have served to restrain in some measure the strong stock market advance of 1936 they obviously did not prevent the catastrophic decline of 1937. The fact is that the break in prices in the autumn of 1937 was quite as sharp as that of the autumn of 1929. Whether this was due to the lack of the usual volume of short selling, as some observers hold; to the acute business decline; or, as others believe, to deep-seated distrust and fear of the political and economic future, cannot be established from available evidence. In any case stable security markets are still far from realization.

CHAPTER XVII

THE PRACTICAL OPERATIONS OF THE COMMERCIAL BANK

In this chapter we pass from consideration of investment credit operations to the process of raising working, or operating, capital. By reference to the chart, page 133, it will be seen that business enterprises borrow working capital from commercial banks, using promissory notes and bills of exchange as evidences of the credit obligations involved. The chart also indicates that to some extent this borrowing from commercial banks is done through commercial paper houses and commercial credit or discount companies, which act as intermediaries in the process. The remaining chapters of the volume will be largely devoted to a discussion of the functions of the financial institutions that are associated with the raising of working capital.

As has been suggested at various points in the preceding chapters, however, commercial banks also play an important role in connection with the raising of fixed capital. Indeed, the chart on page 133 is designed to indicate that the commercial banks, including the Federal Reserve system, occupy a position of paramount importance in the entire financial structure. In studying the commercial banking system, therefore, it will be our purpose to reveal the manifold relations of commercial banking with the other parts of the financial system; this chapter is designed to lay the basis for an analysis of the significance of commercial banking by outlining the practical organization and operations of an individual bank.

Before considering the nature of commercial banking operations, it should be pointed out that commercial banks are classified into national, state, and private institutions. A national bank, as the name indicates, receives its charter from the Federal Government; while a state bank receives its charter from the particular state in which it is located. It may be recalled that trust companies, chartered under state laws, usually operate commercial banking departments. Private banks, as the name implies, are unchartered institutions, conducting their operations without specific grant of authority. They were long subject only to those legal regulations which surround other private business,

239

but in recent years state laws have come to require that private banks submit to the same provisions as do incorporated institutions.

I. INCIDENTAL SERVICES OF COMMERCIAL BANKS

Commercial banks perform a great variety of services, some of them being in the nature of incidental conveniences to individuals and businesses, and others of fundamental importance from the standpoint of the general economic system. The less significant ones may conveniently be disposed of once and for all at this place.

First, commercial banks serve as places of security for the keeping of funds that are temporarily not needed by their owners. As they have well-equipped vaults, and are managed (with rare exceptions) by men of integrity, the risk of loss to the owner from fire, theft, or other contingencies is very slight.

Second, commercial banks serve as money changers. In accommodating each individual customer with the kinds and denominations of money desired, they supply the community as a whole with the forms of currency best adapted to its commercial needs. They perform this function in part through the issue of their own notes, and in part by acting as agencies of the Government for its issues of paper currency, subsidiary silver, and minor coins.

Third, through the system of checks, or deposit currency, the commercial banks make possible the use of a form of currency which is a particularly convenient means of payment. A check may be written for odd amounts, as well as for even figures. This is a great economy of time, for it is a very simple matter to write a check for $27,965.29, whereas to count that amount of money, even if large denominations are used, requires no little time; and the risk of error in counting is at the same time of course eliminated. Both checks and bank notes are also inexpensive media of exchange.

Fourth, the use of checks greatly reduces the risks of monetary transactions. Unless indorsed in blank, checks are good only in the hands of the person to whose order they are drawn; and accordingly the risks from possible loss or theft are virtually negligible.

Fifth, the check system greatly facilitates the keeping of accounts by individuals. Indeed, the banker practically takes over the individual's bookkeeping; for when a person deposits with his bank all the money he receives in a year and makes all his payments by check, he always has an accurate record of his financial status. The statement rendered at the end of each month presents a record of all funds received and all funds paid out, and shows the balance on hand. The canceled checks, moreover, serve as valid receipts for the payment of obligations.

Sixth, the commercial banks perform important services for individuals in transmitting money from one part of the country to another. Upon receipt of the necessary funds, the bank draws a draft upon a correspondent bank in the city where the payment is to be made, asking it to pay the designated party a specified amount of money. Settlements between the two banks may be made only periodically; and by virtue of the machinery for canceling obligations that has been developed, cash seldom moves in the transmission of such funds. The risk of loss or theft is thus reduced to a minimum. Banks perform a similar service for individuals in cashing checks which are drawn on banks in other localities. The work of banks in effecting international exchanges should be recalled in this connection.

Seventh, bankers act for their customers as collection agents for promissory notes, drafts, coupons, etc. The individual turns his credit instrument or claim over to the bank for collection at or before maturity. Upon receiving the funds, through its messenger service or by way of correspondent banks, the bank credits the individual's account with the amount received. If the obligation is not paid, the individual is notified and the bank officials are in a position to serve as witnesses to the fact that the claim has been duly presented.

Eighth, the loan officials of a commercial bank undoubtedly aid in promoting financial integrity and business ability. In the protection of their own interests bankers always pay close attention to the moral character and the ability of the parties with whom they deal. They inquire whether they are honest or tricky, industrious or idle, able or efficient, prudent or speculative, thrifty or prodigal. Since the banker is used as a reference as to a man's "respectability" and honesty and punctuality in meeting pecuniary engagements, it is necessary for individuals always to have regard for such considerations and to qualify as well as may be for the good opinion of the banking fraternity.

These various services are only the simpler ones performed by the commercial banks. Their functions in connection with the issue of bank notes and the creation of bank credit or deposit currency remain for later consideration. It need merely be stated here that it is these functions, in modern times particularly the latter, which constitute the distinguishing characteristics of commercial banking; they give it its paramount importance in the general economic organization of the modern world.

II. ANALYSIS OF COMMERCIAL BANKING OPERATIONS

The nature of commercial bank operations may best be revealed through an analysis of a balance sheet or "financial statement of condition." Indeed, only by employing the technical terms used in commercial banking and by showing concretely how practical banking operations are reflected on a balance sheet, can one gain an accurate understanding of commercial banking. A balance sheet of a large national bank is shown on page 246.

The purpose of a balance sheet is to show at a glance the financial condition of the institution. All of the debts, or obligations, of the bank are arrayed under the heading "liabilities," and all of the property of the bank together with the debts and obligations owing to it, are grouped under "resources" or "assets." The liabilities of a bank are of two classes: those to the stockholders, and those to the creditors, or customers, of the institution. The stockholders' liabilities are classified under three headings: capital, surplus, and undivided profits. These items, taken together, represent the difference between the total amount of resources and the liabilities to the creditors; they thus represent the net worth of the business—what is owned by the proprietors. Many accountants refer to these items as "proprietorship items," and do not list them among the liabilities; but since the financial statements of banks always include them as liabilities, we shall here follow the latter practice. The reason for classifying them as shareholders' liabilities may be understood, if one conceives of the banking corporation as a business entity to which the stockholders have intrusted their funds in the capacity of investors. Capital, surplus, etc., are thus owned, not by the bank, but by the individuals who have bought its certificates of stock. The stockholders have the shares as evidence of the obligation of the bank to them; and in turn the bank must enter on its books a statement of the amount of capital it owes to shareholders.

As a means of revealing the nature of the commercial banking business, we may begin with a newly organized bank and carry through a series of practical operations. Let us assume that there are issued 10,000 shares of stock, having a par value of $100, which sell at $110 per share. After an expenditure of $100,000 for a building and necessary furniture and fixtures, the preliminary statement of the bank would stand as follows:

Resources		Liabilities	
Cash	$1,000,000	Capital stock	$1,000,000
Banking house, furniture, and fixtures	100,000	Surplus	100,000

Let us assume next that when this bank opens its doors for business it does not solicit deposits of cash, but merely states in its preliminary announcement that it is in a position to make loans to manufacturers, merchants, etc. A number of business men then come to the bank for loans with which to conduct their business operations. Mr. A is given a loan of $100,000 for three months, the interest at four per cent being deducted in advance. What changes, immediately speaking, would this cause on the bank's balance sheet? On the assets side an entry of $100,000 would be made, under the heading "Loans and discounts." Mr. A is entitled to withdraw from the bank $99,000, the other $1,000 being the amount of the interest, deducted in advance. Mr. A may withdraw the $99,000 in actual cash if he desires; but it is usually more convenient to have the bank enter it to his credit as a deposit account against which he may write checks. The balance sheet would, for the moment, then stand as follows:

Resources		Liabilities	
Loans and discounts......	$ 100,000	Capital stock.............	$1,000,000
Banking house, furniture, and fixtures...........	100,000	Surplus.................	100,000
Cash...................	1,000,000	Deposits................	99,000
		Undivided profits........	1,000
Total..............	$1,200,000	Total..............	$1,200,000

It is thus apparent that this commercial bank has created a deposit account without the receipt of any actual cash—merely as a result of a loan operation. But suppose now that Mr. A. writes a check for $99,000 in favor of Mr. X, another business man in this community. Suppose, also, that Mr. X desires to be a customer of this bank. Upon receipt of the check, Mr. X presents it at the bank and asks that an account be opened in his name, with the $99,000 credited to the account. The result of this operation, as far as deposits are concerned, would be merely to deduct $99,000 from Mr. A's account and add $99,000 to Mr. X's account. The total deposits in the bank would be unchanged. While X's deposit account came over the counter in the form of a check presented to the bank, it is obvious that it is still *indirectly* the result of the loan that was made to A. No cash has as yet been brought to the bank; nor has any been paid out.

Mr. X, however, now has the right to withdraw $99,000 in cash from the bank, if he so desires; but since it is more convenient in the great majority of instances to meet his obligations by means of checks, he will probably have occasion to withdraw little, if any, cash. Let us assume that Mr. X writes four checks of $24,750 each to M, N, O, and P, respectively. M, N, O, and P, desiring to do business with this bank, in turn present the checks for deposit. The net result is to leave the total of deposits unchanged; though instead of being credited to X, the deposits are now credited to the accounts of M, N, O, and P— $24,750 to each. In their turn, M, N, O, and P may write checks against their deposit accounts, for varying amounts and to the order of various people. If all the people receiving such checks in turn present them to this bank for credit to their accounts, it is obvious that, while there will be an ever changing personnel of depositors, the total of deposits will remain at $99,000.

Now in practice not every business man would desire to bank with this particular institution. Suppose, for instance, that one of these checks comes into the hands of Z, who is a depositor in another bank in the same city. Z will take the check to the other bank and there deposit it to his credit. But if bank No. 2 gives Mr. Z a deposit account of, say, $10,000 upon the presentation of a check on bank No. 1 for that amount, it is obvious that bank No. 2 must collect that amount from bank No. 1. Nevertheless, in the banking system as a whole, there remains an increase of $100,000 in total bank deposits. This is substantially true even though some of the original deposit is withdrawn in cash—for this cash will, in turn, be deposited in some bank.[1]

Commercial banks also receive deposits of cash and of claims to cash. For example, a customer in opening a checking account with a bank may present through the paying teller's window such items as the following: (1) $1,000 in cash; (2) $1,000 in checks on other banks which are members of the Clearing House Association; (3) $2,000 in checks on other banks in this town, not members of the Clearing House Association; (4) $2,000 in checks on banks in other cities; (5) $3,000 in certified checks on this bank; (6) $3,000 in cashier's checks on this bank; and (7) $4,000 in drafts on correspondent banks. The depositor will have entered to his credit as a deposit the sum of these items, or $16,000. On the assets side, the cash would be increased by $1,000 and the remaining items would find reflection on the balance sheet under such headings as: exchanges for the clearing house; checks on other banks in this city; checks on out-of-town banks; and due from banks and bankers. On the liabilities side, deposits would of course be increased by $10,000; but the cashier's checks outstanding would be decreased by $3,000, and the certified checks by a like amount.

Investments in securities are analogous to loans. Let us suppose now that the bank invests $50,000 in government bonds and $20,000 in

---

[1] A more complete explanation of the process of creating deposits here suggested and the general significance of this phenomenon must be reserved for subsequent discussion (see pp. 303–308).

other bonds. These items on the assets side of the balance sheet would of course be increased by the amounts indicated; and the individual, government, or corporation from which these bonds were purchased could either ask for payment in actual specie or take a deposit account with the bank, against which checks might be written at will. The process here is identical with that discussed above in the case of loans.

Another type of banking operation is that of note issue. The process of issuing bank notes is analogous to that of creating deposits through the making of loans. An individual who secures a loan from the bank may be paid by an issue of bank notes as well as by the taking of a deposit account. The issue of bank notes was once the chief method by which commercial banks made loans; and in the nations of Continental Europe it is still the most important means of extending credit. But in England and the United States the issuing of bank notes has steadily declined in importance, and it is now an obsolete function in this country. The extent of the decline in recent years is shown in the table on page 39.

The banking operations which we have discussed reveal the origin of many of the items shown on the summarized balance sheet of any commercial bank. There is presented on page 246 an actual balance sheet of a very large national bank. A few words of explanation will suffice to indicate the character of the items which have not been covered in the preceding discussion.

"Overdrafts" indicate the extent to which checks have been drawn in excess of the sums on deposit. Banks are not supposed to honor overdrafts, but there are usually a few cases in which checks slightly in excess of the deposits are paid—the depositor being notified immediately that he must cover the amount.

The assets item, "Customer's liability on account of acceptances executed," and the corresponding item on the liability side, "Acceptances executed by this bank," etc., arise out of the making of bank acceptances. When a bank accepts a draft or bill of exchange (see discussion on page 112) it becomes liable for its payment. At the same time, however, the maker or drawer of the draft assumes an obligation to provide the bank, before the maturity of the acceptance, with funds sufficient in amount to cover it. Thus, when the bank accepts such an instrument, the amount of the obligation thus incurred is entered on the liability side and a corresponding item is set up on the assets side. Item 21 on the liability side means that other banks have accepted drafts for this bank and that this bank has agreed to make reimbursement before the date of maturity.

BALANCE SHEET OF A NATIONAL BANK[a]

Assets

1. Loans and discounts...............................	$ 193,225,241.73
2. Overdrafts.......................................	3,342.28
3. United States Government obligations................	523,505,758.00
4. Other bonds, stocks, and securities..................	59,963,783.91
5. Customers' liability on account of acceptances executed..	725,327.80
6. Banking house, $13,150,000.00. Furniture and fixtures, none...	13,150,000.00
7. Real estate owned other than banking house...........	3,654,918.29
8. Reserve with Federal Reserve Bank...................	230,907,298.88
9. Cash, balances with other banks, and cash items in process of collection......................................	70,099,832.92
10. Cash items not in process of collection................	104,790.81
11. Acceptances of other banks and bills of exchange or drafts sold with endorsement of this bank..................	137,038.10
13. Other assets......................................	11,221,191.14
Total Assets...................................	$1,106,698,523.86

Liabilities

14. Demand deposits of individuals, partnerships, and corporations.......................................	$ 415,642,609.65
15. Time deposits of individuals, partnerships, and corporations...	145,235,054.81
16. State, county, and municipal deposits................	81,264,789.53
17. United States Government and postal savings deposits..	69,181,614.71
18. Deposits of other banks, including certified and cashier's checks outstanding...............................	277,405,391.26
19. Acceptances of other banks and bills of exchange or drafts sold with endorsement of this bank..................	137,038.10
20. Acceptances executed by this bank for customers and to furnish dollar exchange...........................	768,443.49
21. Acceptances executed by other banks for account of this bank..	27,512.15
22. Interest, taxes, and other expenses accrued and unpaid..	5,630,953.47
23. Dividends declared but not yet payable and amounts set aside for dividends not declared....................	62,500.00
24. Other liabilities..................................	444,832.58
25. Capital account:	
Class A preferred stock.............. 25,000,000.00	
Common stock.................... 50,000,000.00	
Surplus........................... 17,500,000.00	
Undivided profits—net.............. 4,690,641.98	
Reserves for contingencies.......... 13,707,142.13	
Total Capital Account.........................	110,897,784.11
Total Liabilities..............................	$1,106,698,523.86

[a] Continental Illinois Merchants Loan and Trust Company, Chicago.

Items 11 and 19 also require discussion together, for it will be observed that they are identical in amount. What has happened is that this bank has sold some bank acceptances which it had previously bought, and as a result of indorsing these acceptances has become liable for their payment. At the same time the banks which were the original acceptors can be looked to by this bank for payment. Thus these transactions have given rise in effect to contingent liabilities and to contingent assets.

This bank has both preferred and common stock. Ordinarily commercial banks have not had preferred stock, but during the banking crisis and re-organizations of 1933 many banks received from the Federal Government financial aid for which preferred stock was given the Government.

It should be noted that the "surplus," "undivided profits," and "reserves for contingencies," are together equal to nearly 50 per cent of the preferred and common stock.

III. VARIOUS TYPES OF COMMERCIAL BANK LOANS

Since the profits of a commercial bank are derived mainly from loans and investments, the test of efficient bank management is to be found in the wisdom with which such extensions of credit are made. The character of loans and investments by commercial banks is a matter of exceptional importance, by virtue of the fact that these institutions are by their very nature committed to paying depositors upon demand. If a bank has on hand insufficient funds with which to meet demands for cash, and if it is unable to secure them from any source, it must close its doors and announce insolvency, notwithstanding the fact that ultimately its assets may prove ample to meet the claims of depositors in full. Since the entire modern business structure is dependent upon the smooth functioning of financial institutions, commercial banks are in a position of exceptional responsibility. They are the final repositories of the cash resources of the nation, and upon the efficiency of their operation depends the safety of the whole complex credit structure. Bank suspensions, resulting from inadequate cash reserves or unsatisfactory assets, always produce serious losses to depositors, and attending disruption of business. Accordingly, the development of a satisfactory "loan policy" is the most vital problem of bank management.

In the making of bank loans there are two main problems. First, there must be assurance that the borrowers are in sound financial position. Second, the maturities of loans must be arranged so as to facilitate the meeting of the varying demands for cash at different times and at different seasons. We shall presently see that the problem of maintaining adequate cash resources with which to meet these varying needs largely depends, in a highly developed banking structure, upon interbank relations. But since the individual bank is the unit of the system, we may best begin our study by a consideration of the various types of lending operations that are engaged in by the typical commercial banking institution.

There are numerous types of bank loans. The ordinary commercial bank has the option of lending funds (extending credit) in the following ways: (1) on single-name promissory notes of individuals and corporations; (2) on two-name paper, *i.e.*, indorsed notes or accepted drafts (trade acceptances); (3) on the security of real estate mortgages; (4) on promissory notes secured by other notes as collateral; (5) on promissory notes secured by stocks and bonds; (6) on drafts secured by bills of lading; (7) on promissory notes and drafts secured by warehouse receipts; (8) by investments in stocks, bonds, short-term notes, mortgages, etc.

Loans may also be classified according to whether they are time loans (thirty, sixty, ninety days, or more) or demand loans. Demand loans are of two types: (1) the so-named "call" loans, where the loan is of indefinite duration but terminable at a moment's notice at the option of either the bank or borrower; such loans are made chiefly in New York City, and are used in connection with stock market speculation; (2) demand loans, where it is understood that the bank will allow the loan to run indefinitely, in the absence of any untoward development which might imperil its ultimate safety. Such a loan is in effect ordinarily terminable only at the option of the borrower.

1. *Single-name borrowing.*—Borrowing on the single-name promissory notes of individuals or corporations has come to be the most common means of obtaining bank loans in the United States. Such loans are made directly to business borrowers—usually, though not always, for working capital purposes. Since the safety of such loans depends upon the general condition of the borrower's business and also upon the responsibility of the management, it is incumbent upon the bank to make a careful investigation of all information pertaining to the borrower's integrity, ability, and financial resources.

In its analysis of the character and integrity of the borrower, the credit department of a bank has recourse to various sources of information. It sends out letters to references given by the credit applicant and to others whose opinions might be of value; and it secures reports from the commercial agencies, and from other banks with which this borrower has had relations. A personal interview is usually requested in order that a first-hand impression may be gained; and considerable collateral information is often "picked up" from trade reports, newspaper comments, etc., as well as from the general "gossip" of the business community.

By far the most important source of credit information nowadays is the financial statement, with supplementary information that is furnished directly by the borrower. The use of the financial statement as a basis for loans dates back only to the nineties and its great development has occurred mainly during the last twenty-four years. Before the advent of the financial statement the banker relied only upon his general knowledge of the borrower's honesty and business ability. And as long as industry was conducted on a relatively small scale and business relations were of a highly personal sort, by direct observation and by the current gossip of the community with which he was in intimate touch the banker could obtain a fairly accurate line on credit risks. But with the great growth in the size of business undertakings in the last generation, together with the inherent impersonality of urban life, the bankers of the financial centers have found it absolutely necessary to supplement personal impression and gossip by investigation based upon the financial records of the borrowing corporation or business. The development of systematic accounting methods necessitated by the great size and complexity of business was of course an indispensable handmaiden to the change in the methods of credit extension.

Different banks use somewhat different forms of financial statements. A typical form for corporations is shown on page 250. It will be observed that it contains an income or profit-and-loss account, as well as a statement of resources and liabilities. Besides the balance sheet and profit-and-loss account, collateral information is usually requested as follows: (1) contingent liabilities; (2) fire insurance on merchandise, on buildings, and on machinery and tools; (3) life insurance on officers' lives; (4) average amount of goods on hand; (5) at what time of the year liabilities are heaviest and at what time lightest; (6) total sales for last fiscal year; (7) average terms of sales and average terms of purchases; (8) regular time of taking inventory; (9) suits pending against the corporation; (10) authorized capital, subscribed and paid in; (11) annual dividends. The names and addresses of the officers and directors are also called for, with a statement of the number of shares of stock held by each. There are also blanks for trade and bank references.

There is no occasion here for making a detailed analysis of a financial statement. Suffice it to say that from the standpoint of bank management the most significant items on the balance sheet are the

BORROWER'S STATEMENT—Corporation

Name (Corporate style under charter)_____

Business_____

Address_____

To the UNION TRUST COMPANY.

The following is a true statement of the financial condition of this corporation on the_____day of_____19____, made to the UNION TRUST COMPANY, for the purpose of obtaining credit. We agree to notify said Bank promptly of any material change in our condition.

FILL ALL BLANKS WRITING "NO" OR "NONE" WHERE NECESSARY

ASSETS				LIABILITIES		
Cash on hand............................	....	....	..	Notes Payable for Merchandise............	....	....	..
Cash in.................bank.............	....	....	..	Notes Payable to own banks for borrowed			
Notes Receivable, all good, owing				money...................................	....	....	..
by customers.................$.......				Notes Payable to other banks or for paper sold	....	....	..
Less Notes Receivable, discounted				Other Notes Payable......................	....	....	..
and sold.....................$.......				Open Accounts not due....................	....	....	..
Balance Notes Rec. on hand............	....	....	..	Open Accounts past due...................	....	....	..
Accounts Receivable, all good, owing by				Due to Foreign Banks on account of credit...	....	....	..
customers.............................	....	....	..	Accounts due Directors and Stockholders.....	....	....	..
Notes or Accounts Receivable, owing by				Bonded Debt........(when due........)...	....	....	..
Directors, Stockholders and Agents......	....	....	..	Interest on Bonded Debt....................	....	....	..
Accounts over 60 days past due...........	....	....	..	Chattel Mortgages........................	....	....	..
Merchandise finished, at actual present cash				Deposits of money with us.................	....	....	..
value................................	....	....	..	Other Indebtedness and of what composed...	....	....	..
Merchandise unfinished, at actual present							
cash value............................	....	....	..				
Raw Material............................	....	....	..				
Real Estate							
Market Value.................$.......							
Less Mortgages...............$.......							
Equity.............................	....	....	..				
Machinery and Tools......................	....	....	..				
Stocks, Bonds and Investments...........	....	....	..				
Other Assets and of what composed........	....	....	..	Capital....................................	....	....	..
				Surplus, including undivided profits..........	....	....	..
TOTAL				TOTAL			

Dr. PROFIT AND LOSS ACCOUNT, FISCAL YEAR ENDING_____191____ Cr.						
Actual expense of conducting business......	....	....	..	GROSS PROFITS			
Bad debts charged off.....................	....	....	..	From Merchandise........................	....	....	..
Charged off for depreciation...............	....	....	..	From Interest and Discount................	....	....	..
Dividends Paid..........................	....	....	..	From Investments........................	....	....	..
Net Profits.............................	....	....	..	From other sources.......................	....	....	..
TOTAL				TOTAL			

liquid assets and liabilities, or, as the phrase usually goes, the quick assets and current liabilities. The quick assets are: cash on hand and in banks, notes and accounts receivable, merchandise, and raw materials. The current liabilities are: notes and accounts payable, and any other debts that are payable within a few months. All of the items on the liabilities side except capital, surplus, and bonded debt may usually be regarded as current.

Suppose now that a borrower who desires a loan of $100,000 presents a financial statement to the bank which shows quick assets totaling $800,000 and current liabilities amounting to only $200,000. Can the loan safely be granted, assuming that the management of the concern is in honest and capable hands? The banker sees that within the next few months the company will have to meet $200,000 of obligations, besides the $100,000 which would be owing to the bank in case the loan were made. By reference to the quick assets he discovers that the company either has on hand as cash, or will have as cash income during the same period, $800,000, to which may be added the $100,000 borrowed from the bank, which we may assume is to be used in buying additional raw materials. This is $600,000 more than the current liabilities. The company could thus suffer substantial losses through the failure of its debtors to pay notes and accounts in full and through depreciation of merchandise and raw materials before its ability to meet all current liabilities would be imperiled. Indeed, the quick assets would have to diminish more than two-thirds before the business would be unable to meet its current obligations in full.

The excess of quick assets over current liabilities constitutes the margin of safety for the banker. There is a general credit rule to the effect that the quick assets should be at least double the current liabilities. The margin required for safety, however, varies widely in different lines of business, at different times, and even in different localities. One must accordingly regard this rule as only a very rough approximation.

Fixed assets and long-time liabilities, the profit-and-loss account, and the information contained in the answers to the appended questions are used as collateral information and as checks on the accuracy of the financial statement. Concretely, if the ratio of quick assets to current liabilities were in a given case a scant two to one, and if the account in general looked very doubtful, the information presented in the statement of fixed assets and liabilities, in the profit-and-loss account, and in the answers to the appended questions might nevertheless indicate that the loan could safely be granted. On the other hand, an apparently satisfactory statement, as far as quick assets and current liabilities are concerned, sometimes appears very different in the light of these collateral data.

Funds borrowed on single-name paper are sometimes devoted to fixed-capital purposes. In the illustration above we assumed that the loan of $100,000 was used for the purchase of additional raw material, thereby increasing the quick assets by $100,000. If the funds were used, however, to build additional warehouses, or to buy additional equipment, there would be an increase in the fixed and not in the quick assets. In this case the ratio of quick assets to current liabilities, after the loan had been made, would be $800,000 to $300,000 rather than $900,000 to $300,000. The use of these funds for fixed-capital purposes would not, however, necessarily make the loan unsafe or much less likely to be paid at maturity; the inflow of funds to the business within the life of the loan might still be more than sufficient to permit the payment of the loan at maturity.

While funds borrowed from the commercial banks are thus frequently employed for fixed-capital purposes, it nevertheless remains true that most of the credit extended in this form by commercial banks is devoted to the purchase of raw materials or stocks of goods to be used in the operation of the factory, store, or other business establishment.

2. *Double-name borrowing.*—There are three ways in which the names of two persons may appear on a piece of paper given in connection with a bank loan. First, an individual desiring to borrow may strengthen his credit by inducing someone else to put his name on the note as indorser. However, such accommodation indorsements do not bulk large in the total of bank loans.

The most common form of two-name paper in the United States is that which arises out of the discounting of customers' notes. Mr. A sells goods to Mr. B and requires Mr. B to give a promissory note as evidence of the transaction. Now A may discount this note with the bank, indorsing it in the process. Many people feel that in numbers there is strength and that since the bank here has two persons to whom it may look for payment, the note is doubly secure. The truth of the matter is, however, that as a rule the bank looks for payment only to the party who presented the note to the bank, namely, to the indorser —the reason for this being that the original drawer of the note is generally unknown to the bank, whereas the indorser is usually a regular customer. The safety of the bank loan, therefore, depends primarily upon the standing of the individual upon whom the bank relies for payment.

A second type of two-name paper is that which grows out of the so-called trade acceptance which involves the drawing of a draft by a seller of goods against the buyer, who formally *accepts* the draft and agrees to pay it. Such paper is widely used in other countries and was extensively employed in the United States prior to the Civil War. An unsuccessful effort to revive the practice was made shortly after the establishment of the Federal Reserve system in 1914. The fact is that the security back of the two-name trade acceptance is typically not so great as that back of the single-name promissory note.

Two-name paper in the form of trade acceptances or discounted customers' notes is less adequately secured than the single-name promissory note for the reason that it ignores the ratio of quick assets to current liabilities. With such paper the attention is focused simply on a particular consignment of goods; whereas in the case of loans based upon promissory notes the condition of the business as a whole is taken into account.

3. *Loans secured by real estate mortgages.*—Whether commercial banks should be allowed to make real estate loans has long been a controversial question. From the organization of the national banking system in 1863 until 1913 national banks were, in fact, forbidden to make any loans on real estate security; but under the Federal Reserve Act of 1913 and various amendments thereto, national banks are permitted to make realty loans to a limited degree. On the other hand, the laws of the various states have always permitted the making of loans on real estate security. We are not for the moment concerned with the advisability of the practice of making loans on the security of real estate mortgages; we are here interested only in the fact.[2]

4. *Loans secured by promissory notes as collateral.*—In cases where the borrower's security is not regarded as adequate he may be required to deposit as additional security the notes of others which he holds. In case the borrower does not pay his note, the bank may take possession of the collateral notes and collect the amount due from the makers thereof. The volume of such loans is, however, relatively small.

5. *Loans secured by stocks and bonds.*—The great growth of the corporation in modern times and the enormous issue of securities that this has entailed have given rise to a very extensive practice of making loans on the security of stocks and bonds as collateral. The individual gives the bank a promissory note, as in the case of an unsecured loan; but, in addition, he *hypothecates* with the bank stocks and bonds, which may be sold by the bank in the event that the loan is not paid.

Collateral loans must be protected by a margin of value. In order to make sure that the bank will not suffer loss when selling the collateral that has been placed for a loan, the banker insists upon a margin.

[2] For further discussion see pp. 313–315.

That is to say, if a loan of $100,000 is secured by high-grade, readily marketable bonds, the bank would require the deposit of bonds having at the time a market value of, say, $110,000. In the case of stocks the margin required must of course be considerably greater; moreover, the amount of margin that is required with any particular class of bonds or stock will vary widely, depending upon the relative fluctuations in value of the different securities. It may be observed that a highly important factor to consider is the quickness with which such securities can be sold. This depends upon the number of units that are daily bought and sold on the exchanges.

The integrity of the borrower is important even when collateral is given. Although the bank has security to fall back upon in case the loans are not paid at maturity, it nevertheless cannot ignore the integrity and honesty of the borrower. Many cases have arisen where a dishonest borrower has pledged securities to which he had no title, or an imperfect one; and there are many other ways in which, even with collateral loans, a dishonest or unscrupulous individual may cause the bank much trouble and inconvenience, if not actual loss. Accordingly, bankers feel it necessary to make a careful analysis of the borrower's general moral and financial standing before making collateral loans.

There is a difference, however, between a non-collateral and a collateral loan in that, in the case of the latter, the bank has an exclusive claim to assets which have been deposited with it, while in the case of the former it is merely one of several creditors; although it must be remembered that where the ratio of quick assets to current liabilities is large the chance of loss to the bank is very slight indeed. In the case of a collateral loan, nevertheless, the stocks and bonds, if well selected, can be very quickly disposed of; whereas in case a non-collateral loan is not paid, considerable time must ordinarily elapse before the bank can hope to come into possession of funds.

Many collateral loans are made for commercial purposes. Loans on collateral owe their origin to various circumstances. Sometimes collateral is required by the bank because there is doubt as to the individual's ability to pay the loan promptly at maturity from the proceeds of his ordinary business operations. For instance, if the borrower's ratio of quick assets to current liabilities is scant and general conditions are not particularly favorable, the bank might refuse to make an unsecured loan. But if the individual had collateral to offer, the bank might make the loan with safety. In a case such as this the funds borrowed would doubtless be used for commercial purposes.

Frequently such loans are made to individuals who are not engaged in the producing, manufacturing, or marketing of goods. In the case of a consumptive loan, the bank knows that the employment of the funds will not directly result in creating the means of repaying the loan. The collateral deposited at the bank is accordingly looked to as the main security. If the individual is able to pay the loan out of income received, well and good; if not, the collateral may be sold by the bank in settlement of the obligation.

Loans secured by stocks and bonds are often used directly or indirectly for fixed-capital or investment purposes. Commercial banks make extensive investment loans to investment bankers to assist them in connection with the underwriting and distributing of securities; to individual investors who find it necessary to borrow temporarily a portion of the funds required in the making of an attractive investment; and to business men who wish to use the funds for fixed-capital requirements. In all these cases, if the loans are not paid at maturity, the bank is protected, since it can obtain cash by the sale of the collateral in the securities markets.

Finally, collateral loans are extensively used in speculative operations. Speculative loans are of two main sorts, those made to real estate and similar dealers, and those made to traders on the stock exchange. With both types, collateral security is practically always required. In the case of real estate and similar loans it may perhaps be asked, Why should collateral be required, in view of the fact that the funds borrowed are used for working-capital purposes, that is, in the purchase of real estate or other commodities that are shortly to be sold at a profit? Are such operations not as truly commercial in their nature as are the purchase and sale of ordinary merchandise? The reason for denoting such loans as speculative in their nature is that the time at which the sale will be made is much less certain than in the case of ordinary merchandising; and there is also greater likelihood of a loss in connection with the transaction. Accordingly, the bankers commonly insist upon collateral security in the form of stocks and bonds.

A discussion of the process of lending to stock exchange speculators requires first a description of the call loan system. While a "call" loan is one that is terminable at a moment's notice at the will of either the borrower or the bank, in practice such loans always run at least one day, payment on demand meaning that they are subject to call on the day following. There is also a rule that loans cannot be called by the bank or paid by the borrower after 1:00 P.M., unless notice has been given before that hour.

The reason for the development of the call loan system lies in the nature of stock market speculation.   An individual who buys securities with borrowed funds does not know at the time of the borrowing just when he will be able to repay the loan, for that depends upon the trend of the market. If he were to contract a loan for thirty days, and at the end of four days should have sold his stock, he would find it necessary to pay interest for an extra twenty-six days. The cost of speculation is accordingly very greatly reduced if one is enabled to repay the loan at any time desired. The call loan system also has its advantages from the viewpoint of the banker. By virtue of the fact that a metropolitan bank can demand immediate payment of a call loan, it does not need to carry so large a cash reserve as would otherwise be the case. It can keep its funds more fully utilized and thereby increase its earning power. In times of financial crisis, however, the call loan system may be a source of serious difficulty.

The interest rates on call loans are subject to very wide fluctuations. They have ordinarily been lower than any other rates; but on several occasions they have gone beyond 100 per cent. For instance, the call loan rate rose to 127 per cent on October 29, 1896; to 186 per cent on December 16, 1899; and to 125 per cent on December 28, 1905. These high rates occur at times when there is a great dearth of loanable funds and a heavy demand for both commercial and speculative purposes, a stock market boom often giving rise to a very great temporary demand for funds. The reason why call rates average lower than unsecured and collateral time loans is that the call loan funds are what may be designated as residuary funds. The bank's first business is to take care of commercial borrowers and others who secure time loans on collateral. Funds not required for these purposes are available for market operations.

The making of loans for stock market speculation is associated with margin trading, discussed in chapter XV. We there saw that the individual who bought securities on margin paid, say, 10 per cent down, and borrowed the rest from the broker. But the broker is not a banker and has no funds of his own to lend. His ability to permit the speculator to buy on a margin is contingent upon his own ability to borrow the funds from his bank. Typically speaking, a broker is required to keep a balance with the bank equal to 10 or 15 per cent of the amount of his borrowings.

Loans to stockbrokers are temporarily unsecured. The broker cannot buy the stock until he has secured a loan, and he cannot obtain a loan except on the security of the identical collateral which is to be purchased with the borrowed funds. The method adopted to extricate him from his dilemma is for the bank to certify a check for $1,000,000 drawn by the broker against his account of $200,000—a process known as "overcertification." With this check the broker buys the stock and then deposits it as security for the loan. It is apparent, therefore, that in certifying the broker's check the bank has in effect given him temporarily an unsecured loan. Such a practice ordinarily involves very little risk, since a good credit standing is absolutely indispensable to the broker—a primary requisite for success.

The practice of overcertification was long indulged in by both national and state banks. But since it is akin to an ordinary overdraft the procedure was eventually frowned upon by the Comptroller of the Currency and the national banks have gradually abandoned the practice, substituting therefor so-called "morning" loans to brokers for whatever amount appears to be necessary for their daily business. These loans are based on the single-name paper of the broker, that is, on his unindorsed individual note. The only difference between this and overcertification is that with the morning loan the bank has the broker's written promise to pay, while in the case of the overcertification it has not; both are temporarily unsecured loans.

6. *Loans secured by bills of lading.*—Among the forms of collateral available as security for bank loans none is more interesting or more important than the bill of lading. This instrument, which is issued by a transportation company, is of a threefold character, that is, it performs at once three different services: First, it is a receipt for designated goods, accepted for shipment by the carrier; second, it is the written evidence of a contract to transport and deliver the designated goods to a designated person upon terms specified in the instrument; and, third, it is a document of title to the goods. The importance of these instruments in connection with banking operations may be readily indicated.

A dealer in cotton, grain, or merchandise purchases goods for sale in another market. Some little time must necessarily elapse between the date of shipment and the receipt of funds from the buyer—the length of time, of course, varying with the distance and with the terms of payment. The seller, however, usually needs the funds immediately, in order to pay for the produce which he has just shipped, or to buy more, in case the present consignment has already been paid for. Accordingly, he draws a draft upon the purchaser of the goods and discounts this with the local bank, turning over to the bank at the same time the bill of lading that has been received from the railroad company. The bank thus has in its possession a draft—not yet accepted —and also an instrument which bears on its face evidence that there has been an actual shipment of goods and which at the same time conveys the title of these goods to the banker—for only the holder of the bill of lading has the right to demand the goods from the railway company.

The bank sends the bill of lading, attached to the draft, to a correspondent bank in the city where the buyer lives. The draft is presented to the purchaser of the goods for payment, in case it is a demand draft, and for acceptance in case it is a time draft. If the goods are to be paid for immediately, the bill of lading will of course be surrendered forthwith to the buyer of the goods, who can then secure their release from the railroad company. In the case of a time instrument, it is still necessary for the buyer to get possession of the goods if he is to use them in his business. The bank therefore directs that the goods shall be delivered to the purchaser, but on conditions which protect its own interests. This process ordinarily involves the use of what is called a "trust receipt." Both sellers and buyers of goods thus borrow with bills of lading as collateral security: the sellers during the period while the goods are in transit; and the buyers for such additional time as may be necessary.

There are two kinds of bills of lading, as classified from the point of view of ease of transfer—the straight bill, which states that the goods are consigned or destined to a specified person, and the order bill, which is made payable to the order of some person. In the nature of the case, a straight bill cannot be transferred by indorsement, while an order bill is always thus "negotiable" under the federal Bill of Lading Act, unless it is specifically made "non-negotiable" by the shipper. It should be observed that the transfer of order bills of lading by indorsement does not render them available as substitutes for currency; they do not possess all the requisites of a fully negotiable instrument in that they do not call for the payment of a specific sum of money. The purpose of giving them a ready transferability by indorsement is to permit the title to the designated goods to be easily passed from one party to another, and thus to facilitate the use of these instruments as collateral for loans. For the purpose of eliminating irregularities and frauds in the use of bills of lading there was finally evolved a federal Bill of Lading Act, which became effective January 1, 1917.

Bills of lading are used in connection with two main classes of goods, as follows: first, general merchandise and groceries; second, commodities, such as live stock, grain, cotton, and perishable produce. It appears that a very large percentage of the business of the wholesale grocers in the large financial centers, the bulk of the business in poultry and game, and about 75 per cent of the business in the butter-and-egg trade are handled on order bills of lading.

7. *Loans on warehouse receipts.*—Another form of borrowing is that on the promissory note of an individual secured by a warehouse

receipt as collateral. As in the case of ordinary single-name borrowing, the underlying security is goods, but there is a difference in that the warehouse receipt is issued against specific goods held in storage; whereas the ordinary single-name commercial loan is based upon the general assets of the borrower, a loan protected by a warehouse receipt is based upon the specific assets. Moreover, the holder of a warehouse receipt, like the possessor of a bill of lading, has control of the disposition of the goods in question.

Wherever it is convenient to do so, the warehouse receipt is employed as a basis of credit. We have already seen that it is impossible for a manufacturer to give such an instrument in connection with materials that are in process of manufacture, and that, similarly, it is usually impossible for a merchant to use his merchandise as collateral for a loan for the reason that it must be on display. But certain kinds of goods, notably whiskey and other beverages, grain, cotton, hides, sugar, canned goods, etc., are commonly held for considerable periods of time in warehouses; and receipts against such goods are well adapted to serve as collateral for loans. The warehousing business has developed very rapidly in recent years, and accordingly loans on warehouse receipts as collateral have been rapidly expanding in volume.

Improving legislation is, moreover, rapidly placing the warehousing business upon a secure basis. In recent years various states have passed warehousing laws and installed systems of licensing and inspection, so that warehouse receipts are now among our most reliable forms of commercial instruments. A United States Warehouse Act was passed on August 11, 1916. This Act permits the issuance of licenses by the Secretary of Agriculture for the operation of warehouses for the storage of agricultural products. The license brings the operation of the warehouse under an inspection service of the Department of Agriculture and makes it incumbent upon the owner of the warehouse to give bonds for the faithful discharge of his obligations to the owners of commodities placed in his custody. The inspection service includes an examination of the warehouse before the license is issued, and from time to time thereafter, together with an examination of the competency of the warehouseman in classifying, weighing, and certifying the produce received.

Every warehouse receipt issued under this law shall state the following things: (1) location of warehouse; (2) date of issue; (3) consecutive number; (4) to whom deliverable; (5) rate of storage charges; (6) description of products; (7) grade or other class; (8) that it is issued under the United States Warehouse Act; (9) the interest of warehouseman, if any; (10) advances and liabilities for which warehouseman claims a lien.

Warehouse receipts, like bills of lading, are documents of title to the goods in storage. They are sometimes negotiable and sometimes not, depending upon the conditions under which they are issued. Like bills of lading they are not substitutes for currency and do not embody all the requisites of a full-fledged negotiable instrument; they do not call for payment in money, for example, but only for the delivery of certain specified goods.

With bills of lading and warehouse receipts as security, as in the case of stocks and bonds, the bank usually requires a margin of safety. That is to say, on a bill of lading or warehouse receipt of high standing and against a commodity which is not subject to wide fluctuations in value, such as grain and cotton, the bank may lend as much as 90 or 95 per cent of the market value of the produce against which the receipt is issued.

It may also be pointed out that the giving of collateral in the form of a bill of lading or warehouse receipt is not required by the bank on the ground that the loan would otherwise be unsafe. Indeed the business out of which warehouse receipts and bills of lading grow is essentially commercial in its nature. The use of warehouse receipts and bills of lading as collateral for loans is mainly attributable to their convenience for the purpose, and to the fact that through their hypothecation as collateral security the borrower is enabled to obtain somewhat larger advances than would otherwise be the case. In fact produce dealers are commonly granted large loans on their single-name notes, and it is only when loans in excess of this amount are desired that the collateral is required.

8. *Investments in stocks, bonds, short-term notes, mortgages, etc.*— While investments in securities are not usually classed as loans they differ only in the length of time for which the credit is extended. In general, it may be said that the investments of commercial banks in stocks are negligible in amount. Because of the wide fluctuations to which stock values are subject, it is regarded as bad banking practice to hold shares, save temporarily as a means of salvaging bad debts. But most commercial banks have long followed the practice of investing a considerable portion of their assets in high-grade bonds, and a smaller amount in mortgages, warrants, etc. The extent and the growing importance of such investments will be discussed in chapter XXI.

The foregoing discussion of the various types of commercial banking transactions has related to the financing of domestic business requirements—the unsecured loan operations being associated mainly with the manufacture and distribution of industrial products and the collateral loans and investments with the financial markets. The role of commercial banks in connection with agriculture will be discussed in chapter XXVI. A brief reference was made in chapter VI to the part that banks play in the foreign exchange markets, but some further discussion of the way in which commercial banks participate in the financing of foreign trade is here necessary.

IV. COMMERCIAL BANKS AND FOREIGN TRADE

While there is little essential difference between the principles governing the financing of domestic and the financing of foreign trade, the two fields differ materially in the technical methods employed. We shall consider in turn the use of bills of exchange and commercial letters of credit, which originate respectively with exporters and importers.

When a bill of exchange is drawn by an exporter on the importer to whom the goods have been sold, it is generally secured by shipping documents, including a bill of lading, an insurance policy, and a commercial invoice. In cases of doubtful credit a "trust receipt" may also be required, under which the seller retains ownership of the goods pending their sale. The exporter gives the bill, together with the shipping documents, to his own bank, which in turn forwards it for collection to its correspondent in the country of the importer. This foreign correspondent bank then presents the bill to the importer. If the terms of sale call for cash, the bill of exchange is paid immediately and the importer receives the documents and obtains possession of the goods. On the other hand, if the sale is on a credit basis the documents are surrendered to the importer upon his *acceptance* of the draft, which constitutes a promise to pay at maturity. Thus the cost of financing the transaction is carried by the importer, when the terms are for cash, and by the exporter when the terms are for credit.

The exporter may, however, shift the credit burden by having his bank discount the draft. The bank then forwards the bill of exchange and the shipping documents to its correspondent and in due course obtains reimbursement from the importer for the full amount of the draft. The burden of financing the transaction may also be divided between the exporter and his bank. In this case the bank does not discount the draft but advances a certain percentage of the amount of the draft and the exporter then finances the remaining amount. The percentage of this advance will depend upon various conditions, such as the character of the product being marketed, the credit standing of the parties, and the stability of the currency of the country against which the bill of exchange is drawn.

The greater part of foreign trade transactions is now financed by the importer's bank through an instrument known as a letter of credit. This is a document addressed by one party, the issuer, usually the importer's bank, to another party, known as the beneficiary and generally an exporter, whereby the latter is authorized to draw a draft on the issuing bank, which undertakes to honor, that is accept or pay, the draft when it is presented. The purpose of this arrangement is to place the credit of a well-known bank back of its client, the importer, thereby enabling the exporter in a distant country to ship goods on credit with increased confidence.

The successive steps in the operation of the letter of credit are as follows. First, the importer requests his bank to open the credit and in consideration agrees to reimburse the bank for this service. The bank then issues its letter of credit to the exporter. The latter then ships his goods, and presents the commercial documents, together with the draft and the letter of credit, to his own local bank. This institution makes a careful comparison between the terms of the letter of credit and the documents and draft. If the latter fulfill all the terms, the draft is purchased, and the exporter thus gets his money. This negotiating bank then forwards the draft to a correspondent located in the same city as the bank which issued the letter of credit. The correspondent presents the draft to the issuing bank. This institution notes whether the documents fully comply with the terms of the letter of credit which it has issued, and, if all the provisions have been observed, it then honors the draft.

Because of the numerous types of foreign trade transactions, various classes of letters of credit have been developed. From the standpoint of security they may be either *clean* or *documentary*, the former providing for payment of the draft without the necessity of presenting any documents, and the latter requiring the presentation of documents as a condition precedent. From the standpoint of time, letters of credit may be either *cash* or *acceptance*, depending upon whether they call for the honoring of the draft immediately upon presentation (at sight) or only for acceptance, with payment to be made at a specified later date. Again, drafts drawn on a letter of credit may be payable either in dollars or in foreign currency. The most important distinction is whether or not the letter of credit may be canceled—that is, whether it is revocable or irrevocable. A revocable letter of credit implies a promise to honor the draft, with the qualification that this promise may be rescinded at any time, while an irrevocable letter of credit is an unconditional promise to pay by the issuing bank and is therefore more advantageous from the standpoint of the exporter.

Over the years the letter of credit has been the subject of considerable litigation among parties engaged in the financing of foreign trade. The cases involved have been particularly serious in periods of depression when commodity prices have declined and buyers have been loathe to accept goods which they have been forced to sell at prices below cost. The controversy deals particularly with the extent of and the limitations upon the liabilities of the issuing bank.

As a result of the losses and risks involved, a concerted campaign to eliminate abuses was finally undertaken, which eventually resulted in the formulation of a series of legal principles governing the responsibilities of the parties involved. It is now universally recognized that a bank cannot cancel an irrevocable letter of credit before its date of maturity. On the other hand it is generally recognized that a bank cannot be held responsible for the validity of shipping documents accompanying a draft which it has honored, or for the genuineness of the consignment of goods. As a result of these developments the conduct of international trade has in recent years been placed upon a safer and more satisfactory basis for all concerned.

CHAPTER XVIII

SUPPLEMENTARY COMMERCIAL CREDIT INSTITUTIONS

In this chapter we shall discuss the functions of a number of credit agencies which serve to supplement the work of commercial banks in financing the production and marketing of industrial products. The discussion will include the operations of commercial paper houses, the discounting of accounts receivable and of acceptances, the so-called "factoring" in the textile industry, and the financing of installment sales by commercial credit or finance companies. The various financial agencies to be considered have evolved to meet certain types of credit needs which, because of the specialized character of the business or the unusual risks involved, were not being adequately provided for by the commercial banks. Some of them are now of waning and others of growing importance. Since some of these financial agencies engage in more than one type of credit operation the discussion will be developed on the basis of functions rather than institutions.

I. THE MARKETING OF "COMMERCIAL PAPER"

"Commercial paper" is a term that has been employed somewhat indiscriminately in the description of varying types of operations. Sometimes it is used as a general designation of paper that arises out of commercial as distinguished from investment transactions; sometimes it is restricted to paper which conforms strictly to the legal definition of "commercial" or "self-liquidating" obligations; and again it is employed to include all forms of short-term instruments whether originating with banks, discount companies, or special commercial paper houses. At this place we are concerned only with the last named type, which involves the sale of the promissory notes of business enterprises in the general financial market.

The commercial paper house which has handled the marketing of promissory notes in modern times is an outgrowth of the "note-shaving," or brokerage, business that existed in this country in the early years of the nineteenth century. Note brokerage arose in response to a very definite economic need. It was found by the business men of a given locality that it was at times impossible for them to secure from local banks all the funds which they required; and at certain seasons it was accordingly necessary to seek banking accommodation in other centers. And since it was not always possible, or at least convenient, for the borrower personally to arrange for loans at a distance, certain individuals seized the opportunity of obtaining commissions by acting as brokers in effecting the sale of notes and bills of exchange owned by merchants and traders. The note broker did not advance the funds to the borrower, but merely undertook to sell the customer's paper in return for a commission. In case no sale was made the paper was returned to the borrower. In order to effect a sale the broker of course usually undertook to convince the lending banker that the borrower was a man of character and ability, but he did not guarantee the paper. His service was merely that of intermediary between borrower and lender.

With the rapid development of the country following the Civil War and the increasing volume of intersectional borrowing that attended the ever-widening scale of our economic and financial activities, the note brokerage business was gradually superseded by the work of the commercial paper house—an institution that has aptly been called a "quasi-banking establishment." The commercial paper house is a "middleman," searching out the *demand* for commercial credit, wherever it exists, and also finding the *supply*, regardless of territorial limits.

The commercial paper house acts as a broker in that it brings buyer and seller—that is, lending bank and borrowing customer—together, and receives a commission, regularly one-quarter of one per cent of the face value of the note; but it is more than a broker in that it advances the funds to the borrower and runs the risk of having to hold the paper until maturity. Where the note broker merely said to the borrower, "I shall sell your note to a bank if I can and charge you a commission for the service," the commercial paper house says, "We will advance you the funds on your note and then dispose of the note to a buyer if we can; but if we cannot dispose of the paper we will carry the loan until maturity." It should be understood that the commercial paper house never desires to hold the paper to maturity; that it seeks to make its profits out of the commissions which it receives as middleman. And since its chance of large profits lies in obtaining commissions on a very large volume of sales, it will be seen that carrying paper serves to reduce the possible gains that can be made.

The capital of commercial paper houses is relatively small in comparison with the volume of business handled. This is because they are in a position to borrow heavily from the commercial banks; for in case a house has on hand paper that the market will not absorb, it can borrow the funds necessary to hold the paper until maturity, by using the notes of its customers as collateral for loans. While commercial paper houses analyze the credit standing of borrowers before purchasing their paper, it is important to note that they do not guarantee the paper—they merely warrant that it is legally executed and that it is the genuine promise to pay of an actual person or corporation. The banker buys the paper, not on the strength of the indorsement by the commercial paper house, but on the strength of the borrower's own financial standing. Indeed, the commercial paper house does not indorse the paper which it handles. A note is made out "pay to the order of ourselves," rather than to the order of the commercial paper house; and is then indorsed in blank by the makers. It is accordingly unnecessary for the commercial paper house to attach its name to the document, for the title is transferable by mere delivery. The notes are usually of from four to six months' duration, ranging in amount from $2500 to $10,000. They may be sold either locally or in other communities.

The heyday of the commercial paper business was during the period from 1915 to 1920. Prior to that time the sale of notes was resorted to chiefly to meet seasonal needs or to take advantage of temporarily lower rates in other markets. Such paper constituted an important source of income not only to the banks of the smaller cities but also to the large metropolitan institutions at seasons when their own resources were greatly augmented by the deposits of country bank correspondents. Being highly liquid, commercial paper was regarded as an excellent "secondary reserve."

During the war period the expansion of business, together with a marked rise in the level of prices and costs, necessitated a great increase of borrowing for normal working capital purposes. When the "line of credit" established for a company by its local bank was fully utilized—the amount being determined not only by the concern's credit standing but also by considerations of risk distribution on the part of the bank—the additional funds required were sought in the general market, through the medium of the commercial paper house. Flexibility was thus provided for both banks and borrowers; and the total volume of banking accommodations was enlarged. The business reached its peak in 1920, when 26 houses reported outstanding paper aggregating 1.3 billion dollars. Since the notes ordinarily run for six months the annual volume of business may be taken as roughly twice the amount outstanding on any given date. Since 1925 the business has steadily declined in importance. The table which follows shows the average amount of commercial paper and bank acceptances, outstanding annually from 1925 to 1937. The bank acceptance business will be discussed presently.

OPEN MARKET COMMERCIAL PAPER AND BANK ACCEPTANCES
OUTSTANDING, 1925–1937[a]
(In Millions of Dollars)

Year	Commercial Paper	Bank Acceptances	Total
1925	744	696	1440
1926	629	691	1320
1927	585	848	1433
1928	494	1073	1567
1929	322	1298	1620
1930	489	1471	1960
1931	264	1253	1517
1932	105	784	889
1933	95	712	807
1934	156	597	753
1935	174	394	568
1936	188	342	530
1937	297	367	664

[a] Average for year.
From *Annual Reports of the Board of Governors of the Federal Reserve System.*

Many commercial paper houses have gone out of business in recent years or have diverted all or the bulk of their resources to the handling of securities. Moreover, the character of the business has undergone something of a reversion, the larger corporations ceasing to sell any considerable volume of paper, the bulk of what remains being that of smaller enterprises of lesser credit standing. In the light of this trend the risks involved in advancing funds pending the sale of the paper often appeared prohibitive: hence many dealers have again become mere brokers of paper, not unlike those of the nineteenth century.

The factors primarily responsible for the general decline of the commercial paper business are the equalization of interest rates in different parts of the country, which the Federal Reserve system has promoted; the increase in the working capital of the larger corporations; the greater ease of procuring capital through security flotations; the decline in the level of prices; and the enormous expansion in the lending power of the commercial banks, especially since 1933.

However, there has been a new development in this field in recent years, which is of very great interest. The amendment to the banking laws, prohibiting the payment of interest on demand deposits, has forced many large industrial corporations, life insurance companies, and other reservoirs of liquid funds, including universities and charitable foundations, to find some method of investing short-term funds on at least a moderately remunerative basis. Hence they have become large purchasers of a select type of commercial paper—the unsecured promissory notes of the large discount finance companies. These companies sell their paper directly, instead of through commercial paper houses, to banks, industrial corporations, and institutional investors. Back of such finance company paper is the self-liquidating portfolio of installment receivables. The Board of Governors of the Federal Reserve system has made such finance company paper eligible for rediscount, although even before that event the paper of the largest companies enjoyed the lowest commercial rates. Finance company paper ordinarily has maturities of from six to nine months and is sold in units of from $5,000 to one million dollars.

Reference should be made at this place to the discount of trade and bank acceptances. With the organization of the Federal Reserve system in 1913, a vigorous effort was made to develop an American discount market, on the theory that such a market would facilitate the raising of additional working capital by business enterprises and at the same time give increased liquidity and added flexibility to the commercial banking structure.[1]

The acceptance business and the discount market have not, however, developed in this country as had been anticipated. Notwithstanding the fact that the Federal Reserve banks gave continuous aid by establishing preferential rates and making liberal purchase of bank acceptances, the total volume of such credits outstanding reached a peak in 1930 of less than 1.5 billion dollars, of which about 60 per cent was connected with foreign trade operations. At the present time there are only three discount houses and the volume of paper outstanding has declined to less than 400 million dollars. (See table, page 267.)

Three factors are mainly responsible for the waning use of the bank acceptance. The first is the decline in export trade, to which this instrument was best adapted. The second is the essential superiority, in terms of underlying security, of the single-name promissory note of a business corporation.[2] The third is the declining need for outside banking accommodations that has resulted from the general business and price trends of the last fifteen years—to which reference has been made above.

---

[1] For discussion of the problem of bank liquidity see pp. 316–321.

[2] For the explanation of this apparent phenomenon see discussion on pp. 248–252.

II. THE DISCOUNT OF ACCOUNTS RECEIVABLE

The selling, assigning, or discounting, of accounts receivable enables a company to supplement its working capital. Unable to borrow on its own promissory note, and having neither customer's notes nor trade acceptances available for discount at a commercial bank, a business enterprise still has in its accounts receivable a resource which may be used to procure cash. The sale of accounts receivable by a financially distressed concern, without its customers' being informed, is naturally open to serious criticism. However the discount of receivables by well-rated enterprises which are in a position to make, at least temporarily, an effective use of more money than they can secure through regular banking channels is in a very different category. A company may have all the elements necessary for success, such as a good product, good territory, high character, salesmanship, etc., but lack sufficient capital to meet the terms customary in the trade. Under these circumstances it is entitled to credit.

Such accounts are sold to discount companies, which provide the funds in part out of their own resources and in part from the proceeds of bank loans. When a receivable has been sold a notation is made on the ledger to the effect that the collection on such account belongs to the discount company which has purchased the receivable. As the company receives payments on such receivables the cash is deposited in a special bank account to the credit of the company which has purchased the account. Ordinarily the seller is under contract to repurchase any uncollected account.

The sale of accounts receivable for the purpose of securing additional working capital is analogous to the sale of notes through commercial paper houses. The growth of this practice accompanied the development of discount or financing companies whose primary function is the financing of installment sales. Whereas the regular commercial banks would not have engaged in the business of purchasing accounts receivable, some of the finance companies have found here an important field of enterprise. If such credit extension is based upon a careful investigation of the credit standing of the seller of the accounts and his customers, there is no prohibitive risk involved. In fact, there is no evidence to show that losses resulting from this form of credit extension have been exceptionally large.

Analogous to the sale of accounts receivable is the so-called "factoring" process. In the textile, paper, and certain other manufacturing industries producing staple products which move rapidly into fabrication and distribution channels, it has long been the custom for a manufacturer to limit his working capital to an amount sufficient to finance his raw materials and work in process, and sell his accounts for cash when his merchandise is shipped, openly notifying and directing the buyer to pay the invoice to a third party—the factor. The manufacturer who factors his sales is paid for his product whether the invoice is collected or not. The manufacturer is not contingently liable to the factor for credit losses, but he guarantees his merchandise and adjusts with his customers disputes as to quantity specifications.

The two essentials of factoring are: first, the complete assumption of the credit risk by the factor; and, second, the *notification* of the debtor (that is, the buyer of the merchandise). It is these elements which distinguish this division of credit operation from the accounts receivable business discussed under the preceding heading.

Factoring orginated as an extension of the activities of the commission merchant who provides manufacturing specifications and also disposes of the product—a customary practice in the textile industry. The commission merchant was in an excellent position to appraise the credits of his customers and his assumption of the credit risk was a natural development. In effect, the factor acts as the credit department for the manufacturer. Some factoring operations are still carried on by textile commission houses, but to a considerable extent in recent years the factoring operation has been taken over by companies that specialize, in their knowledge of credits, in the mercantile fields which they serve. Such factoring firms employ substantial capital and borrow on favorable terms both from the banks and in the open market, *i.e.*, on their own unsecured commercial paper, which has been eligible for rediscount by the Federal Reserve banks since the central banking system was created. The relationship between the factor and his client, the textile manufacturer, is necessarily very intimate and in practice results in a close community of interest.

III. FINANCING INSTALLMENT SALES

During the past thirty years there has grown up a very interesting system of financing the distribution of numerous products which, because of their substantial value and durable quality, are frequently sold on the installment basis. The institutions engaged in this financing are variously known as finance companies, commercial credit companies, and discount houses. It is in the automobile business that this method of financing has had its most important development, but it has also been extensively utilized, especially in recent years, in connection with a wide range of commodities sold on the installment plan.

It is of interest first to note how the opportunity for the discount companies to develop the field of automobile finance came about. The automobile was long regarded by the commercial banker as in a different class from staple products, involving larger risks because of its specialized character and the extensive stocking required. Moreover, automobile dealers, as distinguished from manufacturers, usually had relatively small resources, buying cars largely on credit, and in turn selling them largely on credit. Indeed, because of the character of their business it would have been uneconomical for them to employ the necessary capital. Thus the automobile discount company found an opportunity for profit while performing a function of great importance in enabling the automobile industry to grow as rapidly as the demand for its products justified.

Automobile financing operations are of two types, connected respectively with 'the purchase of cars from the manufacturers and the sale of cars by the dealers to customers. The former is commonly called *wholesale*, or *floor*, financing, while the latter is known as *retail* financing. Some discount or commercial credit companies engage in both these types of operation. Moreover, some houses also purchase accounts receivable as described in section II above. The process as a whole can be made clear only by discussing the wholesale and retail operations separately.

1. *The wholesale operation.*—It should be noted at the beginning that the automobile manufacturers, instead of selling cars to dealers on open accounts, maintain a policy of requiring cash at the time of delivery. This practice is attributable to the fact that the rank and file of automobile dealers have traditionally lacked large financial resources. An opportunity was thus presented to the finance company to assist the dealer in one of two ways: by a loan with which to buy cars, or by purchasing the cars directly, with the dealer still functioning as merchandiser of the automobiles. The latter alternative was chosen as involving the minimum of risk. In some cases the manufacturers have organized finance companies as subsidiaries, thus indirectly financing the marketing of their own cars.

The instrument most commonly employed in the arrangement between the finance company and the dealer is the *trust receipt*. This receipt, signed by the dealer, acknowledges that the vehicle is the property of the finance company, held in trust by the dealer, and promises that it will not be removed or used except upon written authorization from the finance company. Under this plan the finance company must depend primarily upon the honesty of the dealer, because if the car so pledged is sold it cannot be recovered from an innocent purchaser. When the car is sold the dealer is of course in a position to pay the finance company the wholesale price of the car, plus charges.

2. *The retail operation.*—Since only four out of every ten cars are sold to retail purchasers on a full cash basis, the financing of installment sales requires large capital and credits to carry the purchasers. It is here that the finance companies have found their greatest opportunity. The process involves requiring the buyer of a car to make a substantial initial, or "down," payment, and to liquidate the balance in monthly installments. Standards governing the amount of the down payment and the duration of the installment period have been so carefully developed that losses are very small, only a little over one per cent even in a time of acute depression. The amount of the down payments on new automobiles usually ranges from 25 to 40 per cent, being adjusted in the light of changing business conditions. The terms run as high as two years, but eighteen months is normally regarded as a sound limit. The average life of all the paper held by a company at any given time is something like six to eight months. The duration of the paper is related to the amount of the down payment; the smaller the buyer's equity the more important it is to require short maturities.

In financing the retail purchase of cars the finance companies operate under one or the other of two major plans, with certain variations, namely, "with recourse" and "without recourse." The "with recourse" plan may involve the dealer's absolute endorsement of the note, his contingent endorsement, or merely his agreement to repurchase the car in the event of default by the purchaser and the inability of the finance company to collect—the repurchase being contingent upon the return of the car to the dealer in good condition.

The "without recourse" plan simply means freeing the dealer from any liability. This system has come to be widely used, particularly by the smaller companies. It has been objected to on the ground that inasmuch as it relieves the dealer of making careful credit investigations it tends to promote increased sales and to stimulate overproduction of cars.

There are two major groups of finance companies: First, there are a few whose operations cover the entire country; and, second, there are those which serve only regional or local areas. One of the national companies is owned by and the others are more or less closely affiliated with automobile manufacturing companies. Many of the local companies operate in exactly the same way as the national companies. In some sections competition is very keen, while in other places, usually in the sparsely settled districts, the national companies have no competition at all.

The funds employed by the discount companies are procured from several sources. All of them, large and small, must of course have their own capital as a basis for their operations. The larger companies issue their unsecured debentures for sale in the capital markets, while the smaller companies, because their credit position is not so well established, find it necessary to use collateral trust notes instead of debentures. The larger companies also sell their commercial paper in the open market (see page 267), and maintain lines of credit at the commercial banks.

The charges made by finance companies are included in a net addition to the unpaid balance (after deducting the down payment) which also covers insurance. The amount of the charge varies with the extent of the "unpaid balance" and the duration of the loan. The earnings of finance companies generally have been at about the same level as in other comparable lines of business.

The scope of installment selling has been materially extended in recent years. The finance companies buy installment receivables from dealers handling household appliances such as refrigerators, musical instruments, furniture, and other durable commodities, and also advance funds for machinery used in manufacturing, construction work, and property improvements. This type of financing, which is sometimes referred to as "industrial business," is handled in two different ways. Under the first method the finance company collects directly from the maker of the installment contract. In this case the paper is usually purchased with full recourse to the dealer or manufacturer. The second, or indirect collection method, is employed with small purchases ranging typically from $50 to $100. Since it would be uneconomical for the finance company to collect directly such small sums, the contract is made between the finance company and the dealer, who undertakes to make his payments on schedule, taking care of his own collections. Such loans to dealers are, of course, similar to ordinary bank loans and require careful appraisal of the credit standing of the borrower. As in other cases, however, the finance company is a financial intermediary between the bank and the user of the credit.

At this place mention must be made of the fact that there is a vast amount of installment credit business which is handled on a different basis from that which we have been here discussing. Such business includes store sales on the installment plan, as well as personal loans on automobiles and other goods as collateral. Such operations will be discussed in the ensuing chapter. It will, however, be of interest here to indicate the extent of the installment credit business as a whole.

The magnitude of the installment credit business may best be revealed through comparison with total retail sales and open account credit sales. For 1929 the total of installment sales to consumers is estimated at 6.5 billion dollars, or 13 per cent of all retail sales; while sales on open or charge accounts aggregated 10.3 billions, or 21 per cent of the total. For 1937 installment sales are estimated at 4.75 billion dollars, or 12 per cent of all sales, while open account sales amounted to about 8.2 billions—again about 21 per cent of all retail operations. There was a rapid expansion in the installment business during the twenties, but in recent years the percentage of retail operations conducted on the installment plan has remained fairly constant—decreasing slightly in periods of depression and rising somewhat in times of active business.

IV. SIGNIFICANCE OF INSTALLMENT CREDIT INSTITUTIONS

The economic significance of installment credit has long been a subject of vigorous discussion and controversy. On the one side it is charged with encouraging habits of extravagance, leading people to make purchases which they cannot afford, and forcing subsequent curtailment of necessary outlays. In its larger implications it is held to be a factor of major importance in producing oscillations of business, stimulating overexpansion in good times and then necessitating sharp curtailments in periods of recession.

The proponents of installment selling, on the other hand, point to its great importance in enabling consumers to enjoy the use of costly durable goods considerably sooner than would otherwise be the case, the process meanwhile stimulating business activity and employment. Moreover, it is contended that the installment credit system, as conducted by well-managed institutions, has placed retail credit on a much sounder basis than formerly prevailed and has thus safeguarded the interests and welfare of all concerned.

In the case of the well-organized conservative commercial credit institutions, there is no doubt that installment sales perform an important function and do not contribute, at least materially, to business instability. The remarkable stability of such companies in periods of depression attests to the soundness of their methods in general. It is of course true that it is necessary to restrict new purchases in order to liquidate installment obligations; but for that matter it is necessary to restrict purchases in order to accumulate cash with which to make a payment in full. While installment credit makes it possible to expand total purchases during any given period, it does not differ in this respect from any other form of credit. The degree of alternating expansion and contraction is in fact much greater in other types of credit than it is in the installment field. On the whole the case for well-managed credit institutions specializing in the marketing of durable consumers goods rests on solid grounds.

The discount companies have filled a breach in the financial structure. They have devised methods which at once minimize their own risks and insure the earnings of profits, while at the same time they make it possible for the commercial banking institutions and the investing public indirectly to furnish the bulk of the funds required. Without the growth of these institutions, the development of the automobile and kindred industries would probably have been seriously impeded.

In concluding this discussion a few words must be said about the relation of government to the business of installment financing. In recent years two states have enacted laws regulating automobile financing, and numerous others have passed statutes directed at specific abuses. Numerous bills have been introduced into Congress for the regulation of installment financing, and the Department of Justice is concerned with the question whether credit companies directly associated with manufacturers may not be operating in restraint of trade. Finally the Government has been exerting pressure on automobile finance companies to reduce the time period for which credit is extended.

In other directions, however, direct encouragement has been given to installment purchases. For example, the Federal Government has set up an insurance plan in connection with housing and home-modernization operations, involving exceptionally liberal terms, both as to initial payments and maturity dates. It has, moreover, organized and completely financed the Electric Home and Farm Authority, for the purpose of stimulating the consumption of electricity.[3]

The financial agencies discussed in this chapter have been referred to in the title as "supplementary commercial credit institutions." This is because their origin and development, like those of the commercial banks, have been associated with the financing of business enterprises engaged in the production and marketing of commodities. It will have been noted, however, that the institutions which are engaged in the financing of installment sales indirectly assist in the financing of consumers. In fact such agencies are commonly classed as consumer credit institutions. However, because of the methods of operation of the

---

[3] For further discussion of the former see chap. XXVII, and of the latter, chap. XXVI.

larger discount companies and their affiliation, direct and indirect, with business enterprise, it has seemed preferable to separate the discussion of discount companies from that of financial agencies making direct loans to consumers, which will be considered in the following chapter. It should be borne in mind, however, that some of the smaller discount companies participate directly as well as indirectly in consumer financing, and likewise that some of the consumer lending agencies engage in financing installment credit operations. There has been a general trend in recent years away from the specialization that formerly characterized this field of financial enterprise.

CHAPTER XIX

CONSUMPTIVE CREDIT AGENCIES

From the point of view of the uses to which borrowed funds are devoted, credit was classified in chapter VIII under the headings investment, commercial, and consumptive credit. Loans made for consumptive purposes are distinguished from investment and commercial loans in that the use to which the borrowed funds are devoted does not provide the means for repaying the loans, within either a short or a long period of time; they are not self-liquidating, but must be paid out of other resources. The phase of consumptive credit discussed in the preceding chapter did not involve the loan of *money* to consumers, but rather to middlemen, who are thus enabled to sell consumptive goods on a *time payment* basis. In this chapter we shall consider chiefly the making of money loans directly to individual consumers.

Consumer loans are made for a variety of purposes, including provision for dire necessities, the purchase of luxuries, the payment of medical or legal fees, the meeting of funeral expenses, the consolidation or payment of pressing debts, the making of home improvements, the meeting of assessments, the paying of educational fees, etc. Loans for such purposes are typically small but in the aggregate they constitute a significant part of the national credit structure. Such credit is provided by a variety of financial agencies, ranging from the disreputable loan shark office, at one extreme, to the dignified personal loan department of the large commercial bank, at the other.

A striking feature of the modern financial system has been the almost complete absence—until recent times—of "legitimate" financial agencies organized for the purpose of extending credit for consumptive purposes. Historically speaking, the lending of money in small sums for consumptive purposes has in the main been left to private interests which, acting without public grant of power, and indeed usually outside the pale of the law, ruthlessly exploited precisely those classes of society which could least afford exploitation.

The explanation of the tardy development of legitimate consumptive credit institutions is apparently the age-old prejudice against the charging of high interest rates to persons in distressed circumstances. Since consumptive loans are not devoted to uses

277

which directly provide the means of repaying the loan, and since the borrower for consumptive purposes is commonly in moderate circumstances, if not actually in distress, such loans necessarily bear a much higher rate of interest than do those made for industrial, commercial, or agricultural purposes. Hence lending for consumptive purposes was not a popular vocation. It will be recalled, moreover, that the Bible condemns all interest as usury, and therefore unjust. The Biblical law came in time to be incorporated into the civil codes of Western European nations and it was not until the beginning of the modern era that any interest charge was legal. The philosophy underlying this prohibition of all interest is ascribable either to a sympathetic regard for the poor or to a recognition of the economic impossibility of their paying interest. In ancient times funds were borrowed almost exclusively for consumptive purposes—virtually to prevent starvation—and such loans were in consequence regarded as in the nature of almsgiving. To exact interest from a poverty-stricken class seemed to violate every principle of common humanity.

But with the development of capitalistic industry and the attendant borrowing of funds for productive purposes, the charging of interest appeared in a very different light. When a borrower devoted the funds procured to productive enterprise, it was readily seen that he was making a gainful use of the loan and was therefore able to pay back the principal with a bonus, and also that the lender was foregoing a like profitable employment of the capital, and was therefore entitled to a recompense. Gradually the charging of interest on such loans was universally legalized; but even to the present day we find survivals of the old prejudice in the usury laws of the various states, which prohibit exorbitant interest rates, that is, rates above a certain prescribed maximum—slightly above the normal going rates.

The existence of usury laws has made it necessary for any financial agency desirous of making loans for consumptive purposes to charge unlawful rates of interest, with the result that the risks of fine and imprisonment involved have contributed to still higher charges than would otherwise have prevailed. Various types of financial institutions have been developed through private initiative for the extension of consumptive credit to individuals in need of financial assistance. Some of these institutions have a long history and have operated in defiance of usury laws. Others are of recent development and conduct their business under legal sanction. Among those which have long been in existence are the pawnbrokers and the loan sharks. The more recently developed agencies include licensed personal finance companies, credit unions and axias, industrial banks, remedial-loan societies, and personal loan departments of banks. It should also be noted that a large volume of consumer credit is extended by financial institutions whose primary function is the making of business loans. For example, commercial banks, savings banks, and insurance companies, particularly the last, make loans to depositors and policy holders for consumptive requirements.

Related to these types of institutions are the building and loan associations, which we shall discuss in chapter XXVII, and labor banks, which combine the lending of funds to labor groups with general banking operations. Such banks had a vigorous growth in the early post-war period, but have suffered reverses in recent years. Since they engage in general banking operations they are properly classed as commercial banks and are in fact regulated as such.

I. THE MAGNITUDE OF CONSUMER CREDIT

Before discussing the operations of the various types of consumer credit agencies, it is desirable to obtain a general view of their relative importance, and also to note the magnitude of consumer credit operations as a whole. Exclusive of retail open or charge accounts and instalment sales, which belong in a somewhat different category, the estimated amount of consumer credit extended by consumer credit institutions in 1936 is shown in the following table.

CONSUMER CREDIT BY TYPES OF LENDING AGENCIES 1936[a]

	Loans Made During Year	Loans Outstanding in December 31
Illegal lenders	$ 160,000,000	$119,000,000
Pawnbrokers	165,000,000	110,000,000
Personal finance companies	423,000,000	285,000,000
Industrial banks	350,000,000	234,000,000
Personal loan departments of banks	195,000,000	129,000,000
Credit unions	80,000,000	55,000,000
Remedial-loan societies	54,000,000	34,000,000
Total loans	$1,427,000,000	$966,000,000

[a] From Margaret Grobben, "Volume and Classification of Consumer Loans," *The Annals of the American Academy of Political and Social Science*, March, 1938 p. 74.

The foregoing figures do not measure the full extent of consumer borrowing. Among other forms of consumer credit are advances by relatives and friends, philanthropic and other special loan funds, life insurance policy loans, loans to veterans on adjusted compensation certificates, and loans by building and loan associations to members.

A considerable amount of the credit extended by commercial and savings banks also is used for consumptive purposes. The amount of these various forms of credit fluctuates widely with varying economic conditions. During the depression, life insurance policy loans were very large, the amount outstanding at the end of 1935 being estimated at 2,300 million dollars. Veterans' borrowings were also exceptionally large in that year, owing to the "bonus" legislation, the amount being estimated at 1,666 millions. It was estimated that advances by relatives and friends reached a maximum of one billion dollars.

II. ILLEGAL LENDERS

The so-called loan shark has long found a profitable field of enterprise in the United States; and notwithstanding the vigorous efforts that have been made in recent years to eliminate such business, it still flourishes in many states. These illegal money-lenders, who now usually operate under corporate form, maintain a permanent loan capital which is employed solely for the purpose of making small loans to individuals in distress. They extend credit in three principal ways: (a) on promissory notes of the borrower, unsecured or with a co-maker, (b) on notes secured by chattel mortgages, and (c) by assignment of wages or salaries.

Loan-shark contracts customarily run for from three to four months, to be repaid in weekly or monthly installments. The amount of the usury is concealed in the note, the principal of which is usually the sum of the interest and the amount paid the borrower. The note is an imposing "iron-clad" contract in which the borrower usually confesses judgment, waives notice, rights, etc., appoints the lender his attorney in fact, and in general guarantees the loan shark against all contingencies. The short repayment schedule commonly leads to renewals attended by excessive costs. In most of these transactions if a borrower does not repay his loan within six months, the amount of interest paid exceeds the principal received. Rates are apparently never less than 120 per cent per year, the most usual rate is 240 per cent, and in some states from 360 per cent to 480 per cent a year is common.

The loan sharks engage in practically every type of small-loan operation. They are found in the pawnbroking field where jewelry, clothing, etc., are pledged as security. The greatest volume of operations and the most vicious practices are found in connection with loans to wage and salary earners, where the assignment operates as a real club over the heads of borrowers, since many employers discharge workers whose wages are garnisheed. Loans secured by chattel mortgages formerly were confined largely to household furnishings but are now commonly used also in connection with automobiles. The auto loan shark, who takes care of "refinancing," assesses extremely high charges by means of bonuses, discounts, insurance fees, recording fees, etc.; and if the borrower is delinquent, he is subject to "seizure" or "constable" fees and storage charges.

The gravity of the loan-shark evil even a decade ago is indicated by the following statement:

Auto loans are disguised as purchases in an elaborate legal setting. Stocks and insurance are sold on a commission basis, and money loaned for these purchases. Interest charges on real estate loans are concealed as "brokerage." Wage assignments are taken for jewelry sales, and loans are made on the jewelry immediately. The loan shark of today maintains a lobby to resist regulatory law, cultivates political protection, retains prominent legislators as counsel, and hides his iniquity in a corporate form. His counsel has brought forth many ingenious schemes of evading or avoiding the patchwork of our state usury laws.[1]

There has also developed in recent years a loan agency business akin to that of loan sharks and pawnbrokers, involving loans on personal property, especially automobiles. The operations of such irresponsible agencies rise and fall with the changing tempo of business activity and the changing psychology of buyers. In the period 1935–1936 for example, many installment credit agencies were organized where one might either borrow money or finance credit operations. "In California, a night club has closed and its plant and staff have been converted into a money-lending organization. In Texas, half of the real-estate loan companies have turned part or all of their assets into consumer credit contracts. Throughout the whole West, every garage and every second filling station is a depot for automobile loans either as principal or agent."[2] Such loans have been felicitously described as "pawnshop operations with perambulating collateral."

There has also been a great extension of store sales on the installment plan. Such sales include so-called "soft" goods and other nondurable commodities, often of the luxury variety. With much of this type of business the credit analysis is of a superficial sort and because of the risks involved the charges are necessarily high. The down payments and the terms vary with the commodity and also with individual

[1] Leon Henderson, *Usury in Necessitous Loans*, issued by the Russell Sage Foundation.

[2] From address by Rolf Nugent, Russell Sage Foundation, delivered at the convention of the American Association of Personal Finance Companies, September 21, 1937.

stores or dealers. The typical down payment is 10 per cent for most classes of goods. The maximum time within which payment must be made shows a wide range—from six months to "unlimited," with twelve to twenty-four months the most common period.

III. THE BUSINESS OF PAWNBROKING

One of the chief resources of individuals in need of funds has always been the pawnbroker. Indeed, pawnbroking appears to be the oldest form of banking operation, if such it may be called; for from earliest times and among all peoples the pledging of personal effects as security for advances of money has existed in one form or another. At the present time pawnbroking plays an important role in furnishing consumptive credit in most, if not in all, the leading cities of the world. Since the business of pawnbroking requires a dense urban population, its greatest development in the United States has been during the last fifty years.

A pawnbroker is defined by the laws of the District of Columbia as "any person, corporation, member or members of a corporation or firm who loan money on deposits or pledge of personal property or other valuable things other than securities or printed evidence of indebtedness or who deal in the purchasing of personal property or other valuable things on condition of selling the same back again at a stipulated price." The second part of this definition, relating to the purchase of property to be resold at a stipulated price, is especially important, because it renders it impossible for individuals to resort to this means of avoiding laws which are directed only at the lending of *funds.*

The pawnshop makes its profits by lending its own capital. It does not, as a rule, borrow from banks. The earnings are derived either from an interest charge on the money loaned, or from a "special charge" of so many per cent a month, or from a combination of the two methods. In the absence of restrictive legislation, added profits are also often derived from the sale of unredeemed property that has been pledged.

The regulation of pawnbroking in the United States is anything but satisfactory, and varies widely in different states. Nearly all the states and territories have a general law requiring the payment of an annual license fee or occupation tax, or authorizing municipalities to license and tax the business. In about half the states pawnbrokers are subject to the additional requirement of giving bond for the proper conduct of their business. Fifteen states have no provision governing so vitally important a matter as the rate of interest which pawnbrokers may charge. Moreover, the states which do fix interest rates show wide variation. The most common charge permitted by the law is 3 per cent a month, and the highest is 10 per cent a month, on loans under $25. A sliding rate of interest based upon the amount of the loan is provided in many states. About half the states make no provision with reference to extra charges, such as for storage, preservation, or insurance of the pledge.

Most states restrict the pawnbroker's right to sell the collateral, regulating both the manner of sale and the length of time for which the pledge must be held. Where the method of sale is prescribed, the usual requirement is a public auction after notice has been given to the borrower. In only a few states is there any provision made for the loss of a pawn ticket, and in only three states are pawnbrokers required to carry insurance on pledges for the benefit of the owner. A majority of states have in recent years made the Uniform Small Loan Law (see page 284) apply to pawnbrokers. While legislation on the subject of pawnbroking has been extended and while the plane of the business has been substantially raised in recent years, there is still room for improvement.

IV. PERSONAL FINANCE COMPANIES AND REMEDIAL-LOAN SOCIETIES

While the personal finance or small-loan companies and the remedial-loan societies have a common purpose, the former are privately organized and conducted for profit, whereas the latter are conceived as community enterprises and are operated for service rather than for gain. Since the remedial-loan societies are now of declining importance, they may be dismissed with a very brief statement.

The first remedial-loan society was organized in 1859, but the principal development was from 1905 to 1915. These societies were promoted for the purpose of competing with both loan sharks and pawnbrokers, and to demonstrate what rates were feasible for this type of business. While they are not concerned with earning profits, they do pay limited dividends. In some states they operate under special charters or special legislation, and in other states they are licensed under the small-loan acts which are discussed below. The security required is sometimes chattels, sometimes jewelry, and sometimes co-maker promissory notes. The average loan is less than one hundred dollars. The charges range from 10 to 36 per cent per annum for loans on jewelry and from 12 to 34 per cent on chattels. The outstanding society, which handles well over half the total remedial-loan business, charges at the rate of 12 per cent per annum. The maximum number of such societies was 40 in 1915. None has been organized since 1918, the total number at present being about 20, and the participants numbering slightly over a million. The decline is attributable to the development of personal finance companies, which minister more directly to the needs of the poorer classes.

The development of the private small-loan companies has been promoted by the Russell Sage Foundation, which has drafted a Uniform Small Loan Law; this law has been enacted in more than half the states, and with variations, in three-fourths of them. It requires the licensing of all lenders making small loans ($300 or less) at a rate above that permitted by the general usury law. An applicant must satisfy the State Commissioner that he has liquid assets of at least $25,000, give a bond of $1000 as security, and pay an annual license fee. The license may be revoked on ten days' notice. Chattel mortgages and wage assignments may be taken as security, but not more than 10 per cent of each wage payment may be collected from the employer. The act permits an interest rate not exceeding $3\frac{1}{2}$ per cent a month on actual unpaid balances. No other fees may be collected unless paid by the lender to a public official for the recording or releasing of the security.

The rates charged run from 36 to 42 per cent annually, as compared with rates of from 6 to 8 per cent permitted under the general usury laws. This provision of the act has provoked no little criticism. The maximum rate was determined upon, however, only after very careful investigation into the cost of conducting the small-loan business; and experience has demonstrated that when lower rates are prescribed capital is not attracted to this field of enterprise. Factors which necessitate a high rate are: (a) the fact that the company receives no compensating deposits in any form, as does a commercial bank; and, (b) the fact that the average loan is small, probably less than $150, with a consequent high unit cost of investigation and collection. While the losses have been small, they have been averted only by means of an expensive collection system. The best evidence of the essential soundness of the Uniform Small Loan Law is the steady increase in the number of companies operating under its provisions and in the volume of business which they conduct.

A study of the character of the small-loan business among 260,000 families in New York in 1936 revealed as many as twenty different purposes for which loans were procured. The consolidation of bills accounted for 21 per cent of the total; medical-dental-hospital expenses, 14 per cent; clothing, 11 per cent; automobile financing, 6 per cent; business needs, 6 per cent; and travel expense, fuel, taxes, and home furnishing, 5 per cent each. Among other uses we find that assisting relatives accounted for 3.3 per cent, food and rent for 2.5 per cent, and education for 1.4 per cent.

There are now several thousand finance companies or offices doing business under the Uniform Small Loan Law, which supply credit to approximately two million families. About two-thirds of these companies operate as chains, the largest of which has one or more offices in nearly 100 cities. The proportion operating as chains is, moreover, increasing because of the advantages inherent in large-scale enterprise.

V. CO-OPERATIVE CREDIT UNIONS AND AXIAS

The co-operative credit union not only makes loans but also acts as an agency for the promotion of thrift and business responsibility among its members. It is, moreover, concerned with furnishing productive as well as consumptive credit to its members. Unlike most of the institutions discussed in this chapter, the credit union was first developed in other countries.

Originating in Germany about the middle of the last century, credit unionism has, in the course of its development, assumed two different forms, known after their respective founders as the Raiffeisen and Schulze-Delitzsch systems. One or the other of these systems—the difference between them need not here concern us—has been adopted with modifications in most of the leading countries of the world. The connecting link between these systems and the United States was the Caisse Populaire in Canada. The first of these institutions, which are found only in the Province of Quebec, was established in 1900. Unlike the European co-operative unions, which made loans primarily for productive purposes to small merchants, artisans, manufacturers, and farmers, the Canadian institutions adapted the technique exclusively to consumptive loans. The first credit unions in the United States, formed in New Hampshire and Massachusetts in 1909, were modeled after the Canadian institutions. In North Carolina alone were they modeled directly after the co-operative (Raiffeisen) banks of Germany.

The advantage of the credit union has been set forth by some of its leading proponents as follows:

In order to be thrifty many a man requires something more than agencies to receive his deposits and return them to him, when needed, intact with interest: he requires an agency which will make its hours of business conform to his convenience, which is conveniently located, which does not require him to stand in line for a long time awaiting his turn at the expense of his lunch hour and possibly of some of his employer's time; he requires an agency to which he is not ashamed to bring a dollar, fifty cents, or even a quarter; an agency which will constantly remind him of his resolution to save and which will reward his thrift by extending credit to him upon easy terms of repayment secured solely by his character and personal worth—credit which will enable him to effect economies in purchasing and embarking in productive enterprises, and will protect him from the usurer. By its proximity and convenience it persuades the man who has not been reached by the savings bank to become thrifty, and this without interfering with the growth of ordinary banking institutions; instead, it actually increases the field of the banks. It makes the accumulated capital available to the person who assisted in its accumulation. It does not become a substitute for the building and loan association or the remedial loan society; instead, it becomes a complement of these agencies, for the basis of the security for its loans is not collateral but character.[3]

The credit union, as it was originally introduced in the United States, had as one of its principal functions the supplying of credit to farmers. Farm credit unions, however, failed to develop to any considerable extent, although at one time there were as many as thirty operating in North Carolina, with a few scattered through the Middle West.

Some very interesting credit unions have been organized for making short-time loans to Jewish farmers. The Jewish Agricultural and Industrial Aid Society had, in 1913, seventeen credit unions, all located in eastern states. The principle underlying these co-operative associations is the extension of credit by the association as a whole to any member who is in need of funds. These unions are quasi-philanthropic enterprises, and the loans are made at an exceptionally low rate of interest.

Most credit unions in this country are now organized among groups of employees in industrial plants or commercial establishments. In New York and Boston there are numerous credit unions among small merchants, and there are also several large unions which have been fostered by Catholic parishes. From the year 1909 when the Massachusetts Credit Union Law was enacted, until well after the World War, the development of credit union legislation was slow; but it has increased rapidly in recent years owing chiefly to the efforts of the Credit Union National Extension Bureau. Over forty states have passed credit union acts. In 1934 Congress authorized the establishment of the federal credit union system, which will be discussed in the chapter on agricultural finance.[4] Plans have been suggested for the establishment of a central credit union bank by means of which credit unions having uninvested funds might lend to other credit unions having loan de-

[3] Arthur H. Ham and Leonard G. Robinson, *A Credit Union Primer.*
[4] Chap. XXVI.

mands greater than they could meet. In 1915 there were but 48 credit unions in operation and in 1925 only 257. By the end of 1935, however, there were more than 2,400 operating under state laws, having a membership of more than 500,000. Up to June 30, 1937, 2,356 federal credit unions had been chartered.

The capital of the credit union is furnished by the members, membership being procured (in New York) by the purchase of one or more shares of stock. The maximum par value of the shares is $25, but in practice the value is usually $10 or less, and in some cases as low as $1.00. The shares may be purchased on the installment plan and are transferable. Each purchaser of stock must also pay an entrance fee which is used for defraying organization expenses. The management is vested in a board of directors, a credit committee, and a supervisory committee elected periodically by the general membership and serving without compensation. Loans are made only to members. The maximum rate of interest in New York is one per cent a month, simple interest. Loans of $50 or less may be obtained on promissory notes without indorsement. Beyond that a co-maker is usually required; and in the case of larger loans, a real estate or chattel mortgage may be required in addition. The maximum loan in New York is $2,000. In the case of all loans, the shares held by the borrowing members have to be pledged as collateral. For the country as a whole the rates range from seven to eighteen per cent.

Credit unions succeed best in closely-knit groups, such as employees of one business firm or government department, members of a labor union, or of a club or lodge. As a rule, there must be at least fifty members in order to provide sufficient capital; but four-fifths of the employers in the United States do not employ so many as fifty persons. There are also neighborhood unions; but the chances of success decrease as a union spreads out and the management loses close touch with the affairs of the members. Credit unions therefore are not available to everybody. Moreover, the building and loan associations have proved serious competitors.

Another credit agency developed in recent years is known as the *axia*. It is organized among racial groups and operates entirely without charter or license. It combines savings and loan functions, and, in general, operates on lines similar to those of the credit unions. The amount of loans which these agencies had outstanding at the end of 1935 has been estimated at six million dollars.

The history of the co-operative credit unions has shown conclusively the desirability of basing these institutions on the principle of self-help rather than on philanthropy in any form. Experience has also shown that the organization to be successful must spring from a genuine co-operative desire among the group of organizers and that it must depend upon management by its own members. While these institutions have originated in other countries, they are in tune with the American principle of self-reliance, and their recent growth in urban communities indicates that they have come to stay and that they will play a role of steadily increasing importance.

VI. INDUSTRIAL BANKS

One of the most interesting institutions developed in recent years for extending credit in small sums for consumptive requirements is the so-called industrial bank, which makes loans to individuals on mere personal responsibility. This type of financing was inaugurated by Arthur J. Morris in 1910 at Norfolk, Virginia, and was known as the Morris Plan Bank. This plan has been adopted with modifications in many states, and we have now several types in addition to the Morris Plan, among which may be mentioned the Wimsett System, the Citizens' System, the Trustees' System, the Hood System, and the Morgan Plan. The misleading term "industrial" is justified on the ground that the loans are usually made to the industrial classes.

The bulk of this business is carried on by units of large chains or systems. As a rule, the parent company owns only a minority stock of the local bank, the stock being given as consideration for the installation of the system or plan. The real control is vested in the local bank. Some states have adopted industrial bank acts. In others these banks operate under laws which were not specifically intended to regulate this type of business, while in still other states they operate without any enabling act. In 1933 an amendment to the National Banking Act permitted these institutions, many of which are often associated with commercial banks through holding companies, to join the Federal Reserve system. Loans are made as a rule either on paper signed by two individuals (co-maker paper) or on paper bearing one or more indorsements. The methods employed vary somewhat in different systems, and in any particular system the methods are adapted to the legal requirements set by the states in which the banks operate; hence, it is impossible to generalize with precision. As a rule, in addition to the borrower, there must be two co-makers of the note who are jointly and severally liable with the maker for the payment of the loan. The applicant furnishes references as to his character and information as to his money income, and the co-makers must do the same. It is required that payments on the loan be made weekly, semi-monthly, or monthly, as the borrower may prefer. Since the interest is deducted in advance and the loan is paid in installments, it will be seen that the actual cost to the borrower is very much greater than the nominal rate would indicate. In fact a six per cent loan amortized weekly over 50 weeks means an effective rate of over 17 per cent. Instead of amortizing the loan the borrower is sometimes required to make regular payments into a savings account, which will in due course permit the liquidation of the obligation. Interest is not, however, paid on the accumulating deposits. It is estimated that the real annual costs to borrowers range from 12 to 34 per cent, with 17 to 18 per cent common figures.

In addition to loaning money, many industrial banks have developed a life insurance business, chiefly through the Morris Plan Insurance Society, created in 1937. While borrowers are not ordinarily compelled to take out insurance with the company, the advantages in so doing are always stressed. Such insurance protects the borrower, the indorser, and the bank, besides providing an important supplementary income to the bank.

The character of the business of the industrial banks has been steadily broadening in recent years. They now make extensive loans on collateral covering a wide range of activities. Moreover, they no longer engage merely in small-scale operations, for loans as high as $75,000 have been made. The average, however, still remains low—the Morris Plan banks showing an average in 1936 of only $250. A classification of Morris Plan loans in 1936 showed that only 50 per cent were made on the co-maker basis; and that 15 per cent were automobile discounts and 15 per cent Federal Housing loans. About 40 of these institutions have become members of the Federal Deposit Insurance Corporation, but few have joined the Federal Reserve system.

VII. PERSONAL LOAN DEPARTMENTS OF BANKS

Commercial banking institutions traditionally looked askance at consumer loans, as carrying prohibitive risks and perhaps involving a disservice to society. It was not until the successful development of the specialized industrial banks that the commercial institutions came to see in consumptive loans a legitimate and possibly lucrative field of enterprise. The first personal loan department of a commercial bank was established in 1918, and by 1928 the number had increased to 22. As a rule the loans made during this period were not profitable to the banks, though this fact was not discovered until cost-accounting systems were inaugurated in the late twenties.

The great depression and the restriction of commercial bank opportunities in other directions, however, led to a renewal of interest in consumer loans. The movement was, moreover, greatly stimulated by the Federal Housing Commission's plan of insuring loans for the modernization of homes, with repayments on the installment plan. As a result a large number of banks have now established separately organized personal loan departments operating on principles similar to those of the industrial banks. In 1938 several hundred banks were operating personal loan departments, and the loans outstanding aggregated something like 200 million dollars.

Loans are made both on endorsed, or co-maker, paper, and on collateral. As an indication of their relative importance one may cite the experience of a large New York bank which entered this field in 1935. During the first two years it made about 30,000 co-maker loans amounting to nearly $10,000,000, averaging a little over $300; and 5,000 single-name loans amounting to $1,500,000, averaging $270. During the same period this bank also made 15,000 house moderniza- tion loans totaling $13,000,000, averaging $810.[5]

These bank loans are made for practically the same purposes as those extended by the personal finance companies, with debt payments, medical and dental services, home furnishing and repairs making up a large part of the total. Loans for "business requirements" are, how- ever, naturally much larger, accounting for 20 per cent of the total in the case of one large institution. Loans made by personal loan depart- ments, like those made by the industrial banks, are discounted; hence the actual rates are much higher than the nominal charges. They range from 7 to 23 per cent. The cost of credit is usually less than with the industrial banks because interest is allowed on deposits which are being accumulated to meet the loan at maturity.

It is interesting to note that very few of the personal loan depart- ment loans are made to the laboring classes—nearly all the borrowers belonging to the professional, clerical, and tradesmen groups. They thus apparently serve to supplement the work of other consumptive credit institutions.

VIII. THE SIGNIFICANCE OF CONSUMER CREDIT

In the light of the developments that we have been discussing it is evident that consumer credit is no longer a neglected field of enterprise. Great progress has been made in most parts of the country in elim- inating extortionate money lenders operating in defiance of law; and funds for legitimate needs can as a rule now be readily procured at rates, which, if still high as compared with those on business loans, are nevertheless usually moderate in relation to the costs and risks

[5] John B. Paddi, "Personal Loan Department of a Large Commercial Bank," *Annals of the American Academy of Political and Social Science*, March 1938, p. 136.

involved. The danger, in the view of many observers, is no longer a dearth of consumer credit, but a superfluity, which encourages commitments for other than essential requirements, thus complicating rather than ameliorating the borrower's situation. However this may be, it is evident that the growth of private consumer credit institutions and the development of government lending agencies and the social security system have profoundly altered the credit position of those in the lower income strata of society.

In concluding this discussion a word should be said about the great emphasis that has been placed in recent years upon the importance of consumption in relation to the operation of the economic system as a whole. Numerous observers, noting that an expanding consumptive demand is essential to the expansion of production, have jumped to the conclusion that an enhancement of purchasing power through consumer credit inflation is essential to the successful operation of the economic system. Some would have this accomplished directly by means of expansion of bank credit for the financing of consumer purchases, while others would have the Government act as an intermediary in continuously distributing purchasing power to the masses by means of funds obtained from bank credit expansion. The latter method has been extensively employed in recent years—though it has thus far been conceived only as an emergency measure—as a means of stimulating recovery from depressed conditions.

Whatever merit an expansion of credit to consumers may have as a pump priming device, the suggestion of continuously enhancing consumer buying power by means of credit inflation is economically unsound. It fails to note that the extension of credit under private auspices requires demonstration—at least periodically—of a capacity to meet the debt obligations; and that if such credits are permanently extended through government channels, without thought of liquidation, the very foundations of the credit system will in due course be undermined, not to mention the effects upon the spirit and character of the recipients of the credit bounty. Moreover, the whole conception confuses money income with real purchasing power. As a long run matter the ability of consumers to buy is governed by the relation between their money wages and other incomes and the prices at which consumptive goods are sold in the markets; and this ratio can be progressively improved only by means of progressive increases in productive efficiency. The system of consumer credit is significant only in so far as it lessens the cost of essential consumer purchases, promotes more stable business conditions, and stimulates an increase of productivity.

CHAPTER XX

THE COMMERCIAL BANKING SYSTEM

In chapter XVII we studied the practical operations of a commercial bank, treating it virtually as an isolated institution operating independently of other banks. The truth is, however, that commercial banks are closely interrelated, each individual institution being in the ordinary course of its business brought into contact with other banks—with those in the same city or community, with those in other cities, and even with the institutions of other countries. Taken as a whole, the commercial banks constitute what may be called a "commercial banking system." In the present chapter we shall consider first the nature of these interrelations and the steps by which a large number of separately owned and operated institutions have gradually been welded into an integrated banking organization; and then we shall show how this commercial banking system has been able to multiply many times the volume of circulating media. It is this function of manufacturing credit currency that distinguishes commercial banks from other types of financial institutions and accounts for their dominant position in the financial organization as a whole.

I. CLEARING-HOUSE ASSOCIATIONS

The banks of all the important financial centers of the country have worked out certain of their relations through clearing-house associations. A clearing-house association may be defined as an organization of banks designed to promote in every possible way the mutual interests of the members. The most common of these mutual services and the one that has excited by far the greatest popular interest is that of *clearing* checks. The practical operation of the clearing house in this capacity may be readily described.

Let us assume that in a given city there are twenty banks which are members of the clearing-house association. Each day bank No. 1 receives from its depositors a considerable number of checks which have been drawn against each of the other nineteen banks; and, in turn, each of the other banks receives checks drawn on all the rest. Bank No. 1 credits to the deposit accounts of its customers the checks from the banks against which they have been drawn. Before the hour set for exchanging the checks at the clearing house the clerks in bank No. 1 assemble them in bundles, so that all of those that are payable by each bank will be together. The total amount of the checks to be presented to each bank is also added up on a sheet of paper. At the hour of clearing, messengers from the several banks appear at the clearing house and exchange the checks with one another. The actual time required to make the exchanges varies from about two to ten minutes; and scarcely a half hour elapses from the opening of the clearing house until the entire morning's work of debiting and crediting the proper accounts has been completed.

To relieve the congestion of work in the banks in the larger financial centers a considerable percentage of the checks that are cleared are not actually sent through the clearing house, although their totals are included in the sums which appear upon the clearing-house records. The reason for this procedure is as follows: The clearing usually occurs at 10:30 A.M.; and after that hour the bank continues to receive checks from its customers, so that by the end of the day it has assembled a large number of checks payable by other banks. Again after the opening of the bank the following morning a large number of checks is soon received. Now, if bank No. 1, for instance, did not present any of the checks to the other banks until, say, eleven o'clock, the end of the clearing period, there would then be an enormous rush in assorting them and crediting them to the proper accounts. The process is greatly facilitated if the checks accumulated after the clearing hour are sent, in the afternoon of that day, to the banks upon which they are drawn, and if, say, the first hour's collection in the morning is sent over in advance of the 10:30 A.M. clearing hour. Bank No. 1 therefore sends its accumulated checks drawn on banks Nos. 2, 3, etc., to these banks and trades them for a "batch" of checks drawn against itself, which the other banks have received from their depositors. Each bank can thereupon begin at once the work of debiting the checks to the proper accounts. By having the receipt of the checks spread over the entire day, it is much easier to take care of the enormous amount of routine clerical and accounting work that is necessarily thrust upon the larger institutions.

Some banks will of course not have presented so large a total of checks as are presented against them and will therefore owe cash to the clearing house, while other banks will have cash due. In the aggregate, however, the debts and credits must exactly balance. The significant fact is that the greater part of the interbank obligations are thus canceled. There are numerous ways of paying the balances. The most common method in the larger financial centers, prior to the adoption of the Federal Reserve system, was through the use of clearing-house certificates. Under this method each member of the clearing-house association deposited a portion of its cash resources with the clearing house and was given in exchange clearing-house certificates. These certificates were commonly of large denominations—one, five, and ten thousand dollars. If bank No. 1 owed to the clearing house $200,000, it would turn over to the clearing-house manager $200,000 in clearing-house certificates. If bank No. 2 had a balance of $100,000 due from the clearing house, the clearing-house manager would pay to bank No. 2 $100,000 of the clearing-house certificates which he had received. In a word, the clearing-house manager merely acted as intermediary in the transfer of these clearing-house certificates from the banks which had unfavorable balances to the banks which had favorable balances. It will be seen that the use of these clearing-house certificates greatly lessened the risk of transferring funds, for if a messenger carrying them were robbed, no loss would be sustained by the banks, since the clearing-house certificates were acceptable only in the paying of balances between banks.

Since the establishment of the Federal Reserve system, and the affiliation with that system of all the important state banks and trust companies in the larger financial centers, the process of settling clearing-house balances has been still further simplified. In Chicago, for instance, each bank belonging to the clearing-house association has funds on deposit with the Federal Reserve Bank of Chicago. Accordingly, when the clearing has been completed, the manager of the clearing house notifies the Federal Reserve Bank that the deposit account of bank No. 1 should be decreased by $200,000; the account of bank No. 2 increased by $100,000; the account of bank No. 3 increased by $50,000; the account of bank No. 4 decreased by $40,000, etc. Thus by means of simple bookkeeping entries on the books of the Federal Reserve Bank, each bank in the clearing-house association has added to or subtracted from its funds the amounts necessary to settle its account.

Moreover, this system extends to all the banks of each Federal Reserve district. For example, all the banks belonging to the Milwaukee clearing house are affiliated with the Federal Reserve Bank of Chicago. As soon as the clearings have been completed in Milwaukee, the manager of the Milwaukee clearing house telegraphs to the Federal Reserve Bank of Chicago the amounts which should be debited and credited to the accounts of the different Milwaukee banks.

Clearing-house associations have also been the means of eliminating certain competitive banking practices, thereby increasing the stability and soundness of the commercial banking system as a whole. James G.

Cannon,[1] the authority on clearing-house practices, says: "The tendency has been to include within the legitimate field of clearing houses all questions affecting the mutual welfare of the banks and the community as a whole." The most important of the special functions designed to raise the plane of banking operations are as follows: (1) fixing uniform rates of interest on deposits; (2) fixing uniform rates of exchange and charges on collections; (3) conducting clearing-house bank examinations; (4) effecting mutual co-operation among banks in time of acute financial strain.

1. *Fixing uniform rates of interest on deposits.*—Like the savings banks, commercial banks have sought to expand the volume of their resources available for lending purposes by attracting deposits through the offer of interest on commercial accounts. The necessity of paying deposits on demand was of course recognized; but where an average balance above a certain minimum was kept by an individual, it was recognized that interest could be paid on such portion of the funds as was left more or less continuously with the bank. As a means of attracting as large a volume of deposits as possible, some banks offered rates of interest that were higher than normal, thereby endangering their solvency.

It is of course possible that a bank might be able to pay higher than the going rate of interest if by this means it secured a substantial increase in its volume of business. But where competition is keen the raising of interest rates by one bank usually forces the others to follow suit; and when all banks pay higher interest rates on deposits, they merely lessen the margin of banking profits that can be obtained and imperil in no small degree their own financial security.

It gradually became apparent that in the interest of sound banking the raising of rates on deposits as a means of attracting business was detrimental to the banks as a whole and thus to business in general. The clearing-house associations provided a means of regulating such competitive practices. Rates of interest were agreed upon as early as 1881 in Buffalo; and other associations have gradually fallen into line. While the agreements differed somewhat in different cities, two per cent per annum was for many years the usual rate on deposit balances above a certain minimum, commonly $1,000. This rate applied both to bankers' balances and to the deposits of individuals. Owing to large reserves and consequent low money rates, in recent years no interest is now paid on deposits.

The fixing of interest rates on loans has also been considered by many clearing-house associations. In most instances, however, the

[1] *Clearing Houses*, p. 150.

suggestion has for two reasons not met with favor: First, the individual banks look upon the lending of money as their most distinctive prerogative and would regard agreements upon the rates at which money should be loaned as a virtual elimination of all individual initiative in bank management; and second, such agreements—whatever the rates determined upon—would doubtless smack of monopoly control and invite restrictive legislation.

It is an interesting observation that there is much more likely to be agreement on interest rates in country towns and villages than in large financial centers. There appear to have been many cases of informal agreements between banks in small towns that interest rates should not be less than four, six, or eight per cent, as the case may be. In the larger cities, however, there is undoubted independence in this matter, although in the nature of things there is seldom any wide disparty in rates, owing to the very close competition that exists.

2. *Fixing uniform rates of exchange and collection charges.*—Everyone dislikes to pay exchange and collection charges. One of the best devices for attracting additional business, therefore, has been the elimination, or the reduction, of such charges. Any particular bank might easily more than make good the losses sustained by furnishing drafts to customers and collecting items free of charge, out of the enlarged volume of business obtained as a result of such a policy. But when all the banks of a given community, under the impetus of competition, engage in rate cutting, it is obvious that the collection costs to the banks as a whole cannot be counter-balanced by an increased volume of business for the banks as a whole. The clearing-house associations again provided the mechanism for agreements on uniform exchange and collection charges; and again it was in Buffalo, in 1881, that the first agreement was made. A scale of charges was adopted and put into successful operation. The rates were not high, and were arranged as nearly as possible to cover the costs incurred by the banks in performing the services in question.

While many difficulties have been encountered in some places in controlling this phase of banking competition, the practice of agreeing upon uniform charges has been gradually extended throughout the country. The adoption of the Federal Reserve Act, however, and the development of a new collection system, now accomplish the same results by other means.[2]

3. *Conducting clearing-house bank examinations.*—Clearing-house bank examinations are of still more recent development, the first one having been organized in Chicago on June 1, 1906. The examination

[2] See pp. 300–303.

of banks by an agent of the clearing-house association constitutes an attempt by the banks themselves to control and safeguard the interests of the credit structure as a whole through a system of supervision which greatly reduces the chances of bad banking practice and consequent banking failures. A statement of the origin of the system of clearing-house bank examinations in Chicago will best serve to reveal the reasons for this significant development.

In the autumn of 1905 it was discovered by the federal bank examiner that a large national bank in Chicago, of which a prominent financier was president, was insolvent. The president of this bank was also in control of two state banking institutions and it was evident that the three institutions were involved in mutual difficulties. The status of affairs was discovered on a Saturday morning; but owing to the fact that the money market was in a somewhat strained condition at the time, it was deemed inexpedient to make an immediate public announcement, lest a "run" on these banks might so shatter general confidence that a financial panic of serious proportions might be precipitated. Accordingly, the announcement was postponed until Monday; and during the interval a committee of leading bankers and business men met with the federal examiner to consider ways and means of meeting the situation. Fearing a general loss of confidence in Chicago banks, these men actually advanced several millions of dollars in order to prevent a "run" upon the insolvent institutions. The president of the banks paid the personal penalty of imprisonment, but only a small part of the millions advanced to prevent a general disruption of credit was ever paid.

It was from no altruistic motive that the financiers of Chicago thus underwrote the losses of an erring member; it was rather enlightened self-interest which dictated their policy. In the light of this experience, however, it was decided that some means should be developed, if possible, to prevent a recurrence of such a disaster. Many bankers and business men had for some time been aware of the fact that the banks in question were in an unsound condition, the funds of these institutions having been used for railroad and other enterprises in which the president was interested. It was known that these enterprises were in financial difficulties and that the good funds of depositors were being steadily diverted from the financing of ordinary conservative business to the rescuing of the bad funds already invested elsewhere. Upon the occasion of his previous examination, six months earlier, the federal bank examiner had not fully perceived the gravity of the situation—doubtless because there was juggling of accounts between the state and national institutions. It was believed, therefore, that the only remedy for this condition was to develop a means whereby other banks could bring pressure to bear to correct an obviously dangerous situation, before it could get so bad as to imperil public confidence in banking institutions generally. Accordingly, the clearing-house association devised a system of examinations as a means of eliminating bad banking practices on the part of any of its members. The examiner's report on a bank is always made available to its president for consideration by the board of directors. The system thus inaugurated in Chicago was in due course copied in a large number of the leading cities of the country.

In periods of acute financial strain clearing-house associations have also frequently attempted to give relief through equalizing reserves and issuing clearing-house *loan* certificates. The equalization of reserves involves what amounts to a pooling of the cash resources of the members of the clearing-house association. Some banks, of course, have larger reserves than others and some links in the chain are accordingly weaker than others. An equalization of reserves is thus designed to strengthen the position of the weaker banks. A clearing-house *loan certificate* differs from the clearing-house *certificate* discussed above in that, instead of being a claim check to cash that is on deposit in clearing-house vaults, it is in the nature of a loan from the clearing house, on the security of collateral deposited with a clearing-house committee.

II. RELATIONS BETWEEN BANKS IN DIFFERENT CITIES

In the evolution of the commercial banking system it has been found necessary for banks in different cities to develop what are known as "correspondent" relations. The principal services rendered to one another by correspondent banks may be listed as follows: (1) acting as collecting agencies; (2) giving one another advice and information pertaining to financial and business affairs in their respective localities; (3) holding deposits of excess funds; (4) borrowing from one another, as occasion requires.

1. *Acting as collecting agencies.*—Every important bank receives from its customers in the daily course of business many checks drawn on banks in other towns and cities. Such checks are customarily at once credited to the account of the depositor who presents them; and it is accordingly necessary for the bank to collect the amounts involved from the banks upon which they are drawn. Before the establishment of the Federal Reserve collection system, checks and drafts upon a bank in another city were sent by mail either directly to that bank or to some other bank which would act as an agent in the process. Each bank endeavored to collect its checks in the easiest and cheapest way possible. Sometimes this involved sending the check directly to the

bank upon which it was drawn; sometimes it meant sending it to a correspondent bank located in the same city as the drawee bank; and sometimes it was necessary to send it to a correspondent bank in another city, whence it would be "relayed" to the city where the drawee bank was located, being sent either directly to the bank in question or to a correspondent bank, whichever way was most convenient and least costly.

Having developed gradually without any concerted effort at systematization, this collection process was on the whole cumbersome, time-consuming, and costly. During the entire period that a check was in transit, the bank which had cashed it was counting the uncollected item as a part of its available reserve. The "float," or volume of checks in transit in this roundabout process of collection, was characteristically very large, and it amounted to a substantial reduction of the actually available reserves of the banking system. The method, moreover, often proved an annoyance and a financial burden to the customers for whom the checks were collected. Collection charges were typically very diverse and often appeared to be arbitrarily discriminatory. For want of any standards—aside from those agreed upon in some of the clearing-house associations—many banks undoubtedly charged excessive rates, while others did not even cover the costs entailed. This method was eventually supplanted by the Federal Reserve collection and clearing system. (See pages 300–303.)

Besides collecting checks and bank drafts for one another, correspondent banks also render a great deal of mutual service in collecting business notes and bills of exchange. For instance, a customer of a bank in Grand Rapids, Michigan, may have a promissory note due from an individual in Chicago. The process of collection is greatly facilitated if he turns this note over to his bank for collection. The bank sends the note to its correspondent in Chicago, which then either details a messenger to collect the note at maturity or notifies the maker that it is due and payable at the bank on a stipulated date, the procedure depending upon the terms of the agreement in each individual case.

Another form of collection involving the use of correspondent banks is found in connection with the payment of principal and interest on bonds and mortgages. For instance, an individual in Bloomington, Indiana, may own bonds the interest and principal of which are payable at the National City Bank of New York. As the coupons, and ultimately the principal, fall due, they are presented to the local bank in Bloomington, which sends them to its correspondent in New York, where they are presented to the National City Bank for collection.

2. *Exchanging advice and information on financial and business affairs.*—Correspondent banks render a great deal of indirect service to one another. The banks in the larger cities publish monthly analyses of business conditions, digests of important legislation, and special reports on various subjects, which are sent free to all correspondents, thus helping to keep the country bankers posted on general economic conditions. The city banker also advises the country banker with reference to investment opportunities. The country banker, on his part, supplies the city correspondent with information on business conditions in his locality and on the character and standing of business men in his community with whom the city banker may have dealings, either directly or indirectly.

3. *Holding deposits of excess funds.*—In order to secure a certain amount of financial concentration, or centralization, our national banking laws formerly permitted the banks of the smaller cities to deposit a portion of their reserves in the banks of the larger cities.[3] The general practice was for the city banks to pay two per cent interest on these reserve deposits, the banks being able to do this by virtue of the possibilities of a remunerative employment of the funds thus received in stock exchange and other financial operations. The outlying banks also loaned additional funds to their city correspondents during periods of slack business in the country; and this practice has not been affected by the newer banking legislation. Funds that would otherwise be idle are thereby given employment, at a low rate of interest, the while remaining subject to call for more remunerative investment as soon as occasion offers.[4] New York was of course the primary center to which such funds were attracted.

4. *Borrowing from one another.*—The borrowing relations between correspondent banks were developed as a means of securing additional cash as occasion demanded. Instead of relying merely upon maturing loans to provide ready funds when needed, the banks found it simpler in practice to borrow from one another the funds required to replenish depleted reserves. Such borrowing was accomplished by numerous devices, of which the most common were the rediscount of customers' notes, the sale of bonds, and the sale of open market commercial paper.

III. CLEARINGS AND COLLECTIONS UNDER THE FEDERAL RESERVE SYSTEM

The Federal Reserve system has effected some noteworthy changes in our clearing and collection system, which should be explained at this

---

[3] For details see p. 307.

[4] We shall later see that this practice has serious weaknesses in times of financial stress (p. 308).

place. As finally evolved, there are two parts to this Federal Reserve collection system: (1) intra-district clearings, and (2) inter-district clearings. The former relates to the collection and clearing of checks between banks in the same Federal Reserve district; the latter to that between banks in different Federal Reserve districts. We may consider each in turn.

1. *Intra-district clearings.*—Under a ruling of the Federal Reserve officials each of the twelve Federal Reserve banks is required to exercise the functions of a clearing-house for its members and for certain qualified non-member banks, known as "clearing member banks." Under this system each Federal Reserve bank is to receive at par, that is, without collection charges, "checks drawn on all member and clearing member banks, and on all other non-member banks which agree to remit at par through the Federal Reserve bank of their district." The extension of the "privilege" to non-member banks is of course designed to universalize the process.

Under this plan a member bank in Milwaukee, which receives a check drawn on a bank in Springfield, Illinois, sends it to the Federal Reserve Bank of Chicago, which in turn sends it directly to the member bank in Springfield for collection at par. Since all banks within a given district have deposit accounts with the Federal Reserve banks, the accounting may be taken care of merely by debiting and crediting the accounts of member banks at the Federal Reserve bank. It should be noted, however, that the proceeds of the check are not made available for withdrawal by the Milwaukee bank or counted as a part of its reserve until sufficient time has elapsed to permit it to be actually collected and the funds returned to the Federal Reserve bank. The amount of time that must elapse before it can be counted as reserve varies with the distance of the bank upon which the check is drawn from the Federal Reserve bank which is collecting it.

2. *Inter-district clearings.*—The system of inter-district clearings is a necessary complement to the intra-district clearings. Under the plan every Federal Reserve bank receives at par checks drawn upon any bank within its district (whose checks can be collected at par), when presented by banks outside the district. That is to say, if a check drawn on a Chicago bank is cashed by a bank in San Francisco it will be sent to the Federal Reserve Bank of Chicago where it will be received at par and be collected from the bank upon which it is drawn. The San Francisco bank, however, does not itself send the check to the Chicago bank; for since it is in a different reserve district it has no direct relations with the Chicago reserve institution. It therefore sends the check to the Federal Reserve Bank of San Francisco, which acts as agent in the process of collection. Nor does the Federal Reserve Bank of San Francisco

send each check individually for collection to the Federal Reserve Bank of Chicago. As in other clearing operations, counterclaims largely offset one another.

Clearings between Federal Reserve banks are effected by means of a "clearance fund in Washington." The Federal Reserve law has required each Federal Reserve bank to forward to the United States Treasury, for credit to the account of the clearance, or settlement fund, under the administration of the Federal Reserve officials, $1,000,-000 in cash, plus an additional amount equal to its indebtedness at the moment to other Federal Reserve banks. At 10:00 A.M., eastern time, each bank sends a telegram to the Federal Reserve governors stating the amount it has credited to other Federal Reserve banks during the preceding day. Just as the Federal Reserve Bank of Chicago now effects the settlement of the daily balances of Chicago clearing-house banks by increasing or decreasing the deposit accounts of each bank, as determined by the record of the daily clearings, so the Board of Governors adds to or subtracts from the account of each Federal Reserve bank in the settlement fund. In case the balance of any Federal Reserve bank falls below $1,000,000, it must be immediately replenished by sending additional cash to the Treasury. It should be added that the balance thus maintained by each Federal Reserve bank is counted as a part of its legal reserve. The establishment of this clearance fund has rendered the volume of money that needs to be shipped from one section of the country to another almost negligible in quantity. The system of intra- and inter-district clearings has, moreover, practically eliminated the "float." This result is regarded by many as the greatest achievement of the collection system.

The cost of collecting checks was originally borne by the banks which were receiving the benefit. Each Federal Reserve bank kept a record of the cost of performing the service and charged the amount to the bank for which the service was rendered, the usual charge being one and one-half cents per item. But in 1918, in order to popularize the system with the banks, all service charges were abolished. This move proved successful in bringing the national banks into the "par collection" system.

As a means of extending this collection system to include state institutions, the Federal Reserve banks undertook—at the time the compulsory feature for member banks was introduced—to collect for member banks, and for such state banks as had voluntarily joined the clearing system, checks drawn on any state bank which would agree to remit its items at par. This many state banks agreed to do. All banks, whether member or non-member, which remitted checks for collection at par were henceforth known as "par" banks and in order to facilitate the collection of checks, the Federal Reserve officials issued a monthly supplement to the *Federal Reserve Bulletin*, their official publication, giving a list—with map—of the par institutions. This effort to universalize the par collection system has, however, never been completely successful. Many state banks, especially in the west and south, fearing the loss of fees, have remained outside the system.

IV. THE COMMERCIAL BANKING SYSTEM AND THE MANUFACTURE OF CREDIT CURRENCY

Thus far in this chapter we have been describing certain mechanical features of the banking system whereby the conduct of business has been facilitated and expedited. We are now prepared to consider the fundamentally significant function of the commercial banking system, namely, the creation of credit or deposit currency. To make the process clear it will be necessary simply to extend the analysis of individual commercial banking operations begun in chapter XVII to the banking system as a whole.

We have already seen that in commercial banking the granting of a loan commonly gives rise to a deposit account, and that a commercial bank requires a cash reserve against deposits, of only moderate proportions. If there were only one bank in a given community and if every customer of this bank used a checking account as a means of payment, a bank which possessed at the beginning of its lending operations a cash reserve of $100,000 could gradually extend its loans and create deposit accounts to many times the amount of its reserve. Indeed if no one ever asked for cash no reserve whatever would be required. In practice, however, not everyone does refrain from drawing cash. A bank may safely count on having to redeem a certain percentage of its claims in actual cash. But since this percentage is ordinarily small, it is unnecessary for the bank to carry a dollar in cash for every dollar of claims.

The primary problem is to determine what percentage of outstanding deposits at any one time is likely to be called for in the form of actual cash. Let us assume that experience shows that not more than 10 per cent is ever demanded in cash. Under these circumstances it would be possible for the bank to make loans and create new deposit accounts not only up to the full amount of the $100,000, but even to ten times that amount. It is apparent that to the extent that checks are presented for cash, the reserve will be depleted. But this reserve of cash will also be periodically replenished by the repayment of loans falling due—or by actual deposits of cash made by new customers.

There will be a more or less continuous outflow of cash from the bank and also a more or less continuous inflow.

When we complicate the system still further by assuming that there are a large number of banks in a given community and that each is daily making loans and creating deposit accounts against which checks are drawn and deposited in this or other banks, we approach the actual situation that exists in large financial centers. And, as we have seen in our study of clearing-house associations, in settling the counterclaims of the associated banks only as much cash moves as is necessary to pay the net balances between each bank and all the other members.

The situation may now be complicated yet another degree by articulating the activities of this community, which we have thus far assumed to be self-contained, with the business and financial activities of other communities in which commercial banks have also been developed. Some of the checks drawn against deposit accounts in the community in question will be sent to individuals in other communities and these checks will be deposited in banks outside the community in which they originate. Will it not now be necessary, when these checks are presented for payment, for the second community to draw funds away from the first? The answer once more is that thanks to the collection and clearance system already described cash will move only to settle net balances which cannot be offset by counterclaims. Just as balances between banks which are members of a clearing-house association are settled without the movement of specie, so also, by virtue of the correspondent relations that obtain between banks in different centers, together with the Federal Reserve clearance system, cash moves in the settlement of balances between banks in different centers only as a last resort. The commercial banking system, indeed, is international in its scope; for, as we have seen in chapter VI, the foreign exchanges operate so as to minimize the flow of specie between nations.

The assumptions that we have been making in the preceding paragraphs are directly applicable to the facts of the modern financial system. The use of checks in making payments, while of gradual development, is now almost universal in the larger cities for all except the smallest transactions. Hence the ratio of cash to deposits—the reserve that must be kept—has been a steadily declining one. Under a system where the use of checks as a means of making payments is practically universal, where individual depositors seldom present checks for payment in cash, and where banks—whether in the same or in different cities—largely cancel their payments to one another, it has been possible for the commercial banking system ordinarily to maintain convertibility of deposits into cash with a very small ratio of reserve money to outstanding deposit liabilities.

It should be emphasized in connection with this analysis of deposit currency, that the creation of bank credit has not been accomplished overnight by a single, individual bank. It has been only gradually developed through the operation of the commercial banking system as a whole. A newly established bank cannot forthwith make loans to several times the amount of its cash resources, nor could a bank receiving a deposit of gold promptly multiply its loans. The demands for cash to meet checks, presented mainly through the clearing house, would quickly exhaust the reserve and compel a contraction of loans, or force insolvency. It is nevertheless true that in the course of its evolution the commercial banking system has been able to expand enormously the ratio of deposit currency to cash reserves.

In all the foregoing discussion we have been referring to a normal situation in which the commercial banking credit system and the exchanges are functioning smoothly. At times a particular bank may be subjected to a very heavy pressure for funds; and, if its cash is insufficient to meet the demands and if it cannot sell some of its assets or borrow from other banks, it will have to close its doors. Similarly, the banks of a whole community or of the whole nation may, as a result of a loss of confidence on the part of depositors, be subjected to demands for funds beyond their capacity to meet. In case of a panic of this kind all the banks naturally have to suspend cash payments, and the commercial credit structure and the international exchange system break down.

Because of these risks banks are required by law to keep substantially larger reserves than are dictated by "till money" needs. In the interest of protecting bank depositors from loss, the law requires the keeping of what may be termed an "ultimate" or liquidation reserve. By virtue of this requirement the depositors are certain to receive a considerable cash payment in case the bank becomes insolvent.

The growth of the credit structure relative to cash reserves from 1864 to 1937 is shown in the chart on the next page. We have included under "Credit Currency" national bank notes as well as deposits—because national bank notes, like deposits, arise out of loan transactions. In order to indicate the interrelations of loans and investments on the asset side and deposits and notes on the liability side, we are also superimposing on the chart the growth of loans and investments. These items indicate the volume of credit that was being extended by

the national banks in one form or another for business requirements
in each successive year.

Attention should first be directed to the striking parallelism in the
growth of loans and investments on the one hand and deposits and
note circulation on the other. Sometimes loans and investments exceed
deposits and notes, and sometimes the opposite is true; but the lines

GROWTH OF THE CREDIT STRUCTURE OF NATIONAL BANKS,
1864–1937

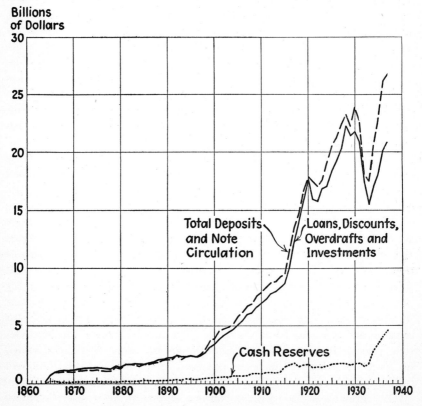

always run closely together. Note next the widening gap between the
line for cash reserves and that for deposits and note circulation. At the
beginning of the period the ratio was about one to four; in the eighties
it ran about one to six or seven; from 1900 to 1914 it was about one to
eight or nine; from 1920 to 1932 it ranged around one to twelve or
thirteen. In the last few years it has moved the other way because of a
simultaneous increase in reserves and slack demand for bank loans.
The gradual widening of the spread between cash reserves and deposits

and notes in circulation as the banking system evolved was not attributable to any reduction in reserve requirements. That is to say, we did not keep modifying our laws so as to permit demand obligations to be backed with progressively smaller reserves of cash; there was in fact no change in reserve requirements until 1913. The decreasing ratio was rather the result of a more complete development of the credit system on a national scale.

In the earlier years it was necessary for each bank to hold much larger reserves in its own vaults than was the case after the system became more highly integrated. The organization of clearing houses enabled each bank to get on with smaller reserves than before. Similarly, the development of correspondence relations between the banks of the financial centers and outlying institutions made it possible, ordinarily, for the banks of the smaller cities to borrow funds, in case of need, from the larger banks. The development of security exchanges where stock collateral and bond investments could be quickly converted into cash also served gradually to lessen the amount of cash that each bank had to hold in its own vaults.

The system of redepositing reserves, whereby the same money counted as reserves in two places at once, was also gradually developed during this period. The law provided for varying reserve requirements for the banks in the largest cities, in cities of intermediate size, and in the smaller cities and towns. These banks were classified respectively as central reserve city banks, reserve city banks, and country banks. The reserve requirements were 25 per cent, 25 per cent, and 15 per cent respectively; but the reserve city banks were permitted to keep half of their reserves on deposit in central reserve banks, while the country banks might keep three-fifths of theirs on deposit in reserve city or central reserve city banks. Hence they needed to keep only 12.5 per cent and 6 per cent respectively in their own vaults. These reserves, which were deposited with the central reserve and reserve city banks, also counted as a part of their own legal reserves. Thus the same cash might serve simultaneously as reserve in two or three different places. With duplications eliminated the net reserves—the ratio of cash to deposits in the banking system as a whole—came to be less than 10 per cent.[5]

[5] Under the Federal Reserve system the reserve requirements for national banks were reduced to 13, 10 and 7 per cent respectively, for the various classes of banks. It then became possible for the banking system as a whole to conduct its operations on the basis of only 4 or 5 per cent reserve. For a good discussion of this subject, see H. L. Reed, "Credit Expansion under the Federal Reserve System," *American Economic Review*, VIII (1918), 270–282. For recent changes in reserve requirements see chap. XXIV, sec. IV.

In time of financial strain, this system of redeposited reserves served to intensify the difficulties. In order to meet the demands of depositors the country and reserve city banks respectively withdrew their reserve balances from the financial centers, thus intensifying the difficulties of the latter. The system which appeared satisfactory when economic and financial conditions were stable or improving, was found to be worse than useless at the very moment when it should have helped to withstand the shock of financial crisis. The revelation of the weakness of this system was, as we shall see, in large measure responsible for the establishment of the Federal Reserve system.

Our interest at this place, however, is not in the shortcomings of the commercial credit system as revealed in times of crisis. We are concerned merely with indicating how the commercial banking system as a whole has in effect manufactured a vast quantity of deposit currency which is equivalent, under ordinary circumstances, to money. This credit currency was gradually created through the process of making loans, which in turn gave rise to deposits in the banking system as a whole. In the absence of this phenomenon, deposits would have been limited to the metallic and government paper money actually placed with the banks; and such deposits would have been but a fraction of those arising out of our credit mechanism.

One of the most vital and controversial questions in economic literature is the effect of this increase in our currency supply upon the efficiency of wealth production and upon the level of prices. Has the evolution of this commercial banking currency been attended merely by a rise in the level of prices, with no increase in production, or has the multiplication of the volume of loanable currency that has been effected tended to stimulate production and to increase the wealth of nations? Two schools of thought have been developed, the one contending that the quantity of money is a matter of entire indifference and that the net result of the creation of deposit currency is merely to change the price-level; the other holding that under certain circumstances an increase in the supply of deposit currency facilitates productive operations—indeed that it is indispensable to the process of economic growth. Discussion of the relation of credit to prices must, however, be reserved to the last chapter.

V. THE CENTRAL POSITION OF COMMERCIAL BANKING IN THE ECONOMIC SYSTEM

The diagram of the financial system, presented on page 133, and the discussion of the various purposes for which commercial banks extend credit, outlined in chapter XVII, indicate the dominant position that the commercial banking system occupies in the entire financial structure. Our financial fabric as a whole is so constructed and operated as to concentrate a very large, and a steadily increasing, percentage of our "lawful money" in the vaults of commercial banks rather than in those of other financial agencies. The investment banks require relatively little actual money. Their business is largely that of intermediaries, and their transactions are nearly always effected on the part of both their customers and themselves by checks on commercial banks. Similarly, the insurance companies require specie or legal tender in almost negligible quantities. Such "funds on hand" as they are required to hold may be kept in the form of a checking account with a commercial bank. The savings banks likewise hold very small cash reserves, and look to the commercial institutions for accommodation in case of need. Accordingly, all these institutions are most intimately related to and dependent upon the successful functioning of the commercial banking system. An inadequacy of commercial banking funds may mean a direct lessening of the underwriting activities and other operations of investment bankers, and an impairment of the ability of savings institutions and insurance companies to meet their financial engagements and obligations. And whenever there is a breakdown of this complicated commercial banking machinery the entire financial mechanism is thrown completely out of gear.

Not only does the commercial banking system constitute the center of the entire financial structure, but it lies as well at the basis of all modern business operations. It is, indeed, the foundation of the whole complex economic organization of modern society. Every business concern is ordinarily dependent, directly or indirectly, upon the commercial banks for a continuous supply of borrowed capital. Let it once more be emphasized and let it again be visualized by reference to the chart on page 133 that the operations of the commercial banks are not confined merely to making loans for working capital; through the loans which they make to other financial institutions and through direct loans to corporations for fixed-capital purposes, and especially through the purchase of corporate securities, real estate mortgages, etc., and through loans on collateral, they are also vitally related to the raising of fixed capital and to the entire investment market. It follows that whenever there is a collapse of the superstructure of commercial banking credit the entire economic organization is paralyzed. Efforts that have been made to safeguard the commercial banking mechanism will be considered in later chapters.

CHAPTER XXI

THE CHANGING CHARACTER OF COMMERCIAL BANKING

The character of commercial banking operations has been undergoing continuous change, the so-called commercial bank of today bearing little resemblance to its eighteenth century prototype. Commercial banking originated in England not only before the period of large-scale corporate enterprise, but also before the factory and wage systems were developed. Production was still conducted chiefly on a handicraft basis, and the only business enterprises that required substantial liquid capital were those engaged in trade or commerce. While the overseas trading and development companies were usually given financial assistance by the government, those engaged in domestic commerce depended on individual or partnership capital, supplemented by temporary borrowings. It was here that banking institutions, which had first been organized as offices for the safe-keeping and exchanging of money, found a fruitful field for loan operations. Deposits, payable on demand, could be loaned out on a short-term basis in financing the seasonal or other exceptional requirements of business men who were concerned with commercial activities involving the distribution of commodities between producers and consumers. Hence the term "commercial" bank.

Economic observers who were concerned with analyzing and interpreting the economic institutions of their time naturally described and discussed the commercial bank in terms of the conditions under which it then operated. In the words of Adam Smith:[1]

. . . A bank cannot consistently with its own interest, advance to a trader the whole or even the greater part of the circulating capital with which he trades; because, though that capital is continually returning to him in the shape of money, and going from him in the same shape, yet the whole of the returns is too distant from the whole of the outgoings, and the sum of his repayment could not equal the sum of its advances within such moderate periods of time as suit the conveniency of a bank. Still less could a bank afford to advance him any considerable part of his fixed capital; of the capital which the undertaker of an iron forge, for example, employs in erecting his forge and smelting-house, his workhouses and warehouses, the dwelling-houses of his

[1] Adam Smith, *Wealth of Nations*, p. 234.

workmen, etc.; of the capital which the undertaker of a mine employs in sinking his shafts, in erecting engines for drawing out the water, in making roads and wagon-ways, etc.; of the capital which the person who undertakes to improve land employs in clearing, draining, manuring, and ploughing waste and uncultivated fields, in building farmhouses, with all their necessary appendages of stables, granaries, etc. The returns of the fixed capital are in almost all cases much slower than those of the circulating capital; and such expenses, even when laid out with the greatest prudence and judgment, very seldom return to the undertaker till after a period of many years, a period by far too distant to suit the conveniency of a bank. . . .

The commercial bank thus came to be regarded as an institution which not only was, but should be, concerned merely with the furnishing of short-time funds for financing the purchase of commodities, the sale of which would make possible the liquidation of the loans. It was emphasized by succeeding writers that such loans usually were, and always should be, backed by specific consignments of commodities, evidenced by bills of exchange drawn by the seller upon the purchaser.

Once this description of commercial bank operations had been incorporated in economic literature in the form of a statement of principles, the conception of the "true nature" of the commercial bank remained fixed for more than a century. This view of the proper functions of banking, moreover, found incorporation in the banking legislation of many countries, including the United States. It was the theory underlying our national banking law of 1863, and it was given added emphasis in connection with the Federal Reserve Act of 1913. Indeed, a large portion of the discussion leading up to the adoption of the Federal Reserve system stressed the importance of keeping bank assets liquid by confining the use of bank funds to short-time loans to business men engaged in the producing and marketing of goods—loans which would be "automatically self-liquidating" in two or three months through the sale of goods bought with the very funds that had been borrowed. Loans, the proceeds of which were used for the creation of fixed capital, plant, and equipment, were to be viewed with suspicion and kept to the smallest possible minimum. The act itself drew a sharp line between investment and commercial uses of funds and sought to confine the activities of commercial banks mainly to the financing of commodities in the hands of manufacturers, wholesalers, and retailers respectively.

Economists, moreover, continued to state the principles of banking in terms of the old conception. Thus J. Laurence Laughlin, who played an important role in the development of the Federal Reserve system, wrote:

The business of the bank consists of dealing in the commercial paper which grows out of current transactions. When a man desires funds for a long period, he should get them, not from the bank, but from those who have spare capital to invest for some considerable period of time. The bulk of banking business. . . . consists of instruments evidencing claims upon individuals, stated in terms of money, and resulting from operations requiring a comparatively short period for their consummation.[2]

When practical bankers were asked to discuss commercial banking they usually ignored the evidence found on the banks' financial statements and quoted instead the principles expounded in economic and banking treatises. While the conception of "commercial" was gradually being broadened to include loans to manufacturers as well as to middlemen, emphasis continued to be placed upon self-liquidation in a short period of time through the sale of goods purchased with the borrowed money. It was recognized that commercial banks did sometimes extend loans for investment purposes but this was regarded, in the nature of the case, as unsound banking practice.

The statement presented on page 246, showing the financial condition of a large national bank, and the accompanying discussion of the nature of commercial bank operations, have already made it clear that commercial banks do not now restrict themselves to short-term loans of a commercial character. The fact is that with the evolution of large-scale corporate enterprise in the field of production as well as of distribution, and with the development of security markets and a highly complex economic and financial system, the range of credit operations engaged in by the commercial banks has undergone profound transformation. The term industrial would now be fully as accurate as commercial; and they are engaged in long-term quite as much as in short-term credit operations. Moreover, their operations are as intimately related to government as to private business enterprise.

I. THE GROWTH OF INVESTMENT OPERATIONS

The truth is that commercial banks in the United States have never confined themselves wholly to the field of commercial credit. Throughout the nineteenth century they engaged in a wide range of activities which were related to long-term capital requirements as well as to genuinely commercial transactions. In the period before the Civil War these fixed-capital operations were primarily connected with agriculture, but in the latter half of the nineteenth century they became quite as extensive in the field of industrial enterprise. The reports of both national and state banks for any date one may care to choose reveal

[2] *Banking Reform*, p. 76.

large holdings of bonds. For example, in 1870 the national banks had investments of 402 million dollars in government bonds and of 32 millions in other bonds as compared with aggregate loans of 972 millions. A thorough analysis of the situation in 1916 revealed that approximately 50 per cent of all the loans made by national and state banks and trust companies were devoted to intermediate or long-term investment purposes even though nominally extended on a short-term basis. With investments in securities included, approximately two-thirds of the credit extended by the commercial banking system went for fixed rather than for working capital purposes.[3]

In other countries the trend has been similar. It has long been recognized that such was the case in Germany and Japan, where commercial banking support of industrial enterprise was notorious; but it was assumed that in England at least, the commercial banks had continued to hew to the line, avoiding the temptation to tie up their funds in enterprises which were not of a short-term liquid character. However, the facts clearly indicate that the trend in Great Britain was also steadily in the direction of a larger participation in long-term investment enterprise. Since well before 1900 they have been large holders of investment securities.[4]

Trends in the United States since 1900—as far as the national banks are concerned—are shown in the diagrams on page 314. Strictly comparable data are not available for state commercial banks and trust companies, but the fact is that these institutions have been even more closely affiliated with investment operations than have the national banks.

The first diagram, which shows total loans as compared with total investments, reveals in a broad way the growing relative importance of long-term, as compared with short-term, operations. It should be borne in mind that a substantial amount of the obligations which nominally appeared as short-term, really represent intermediate or long-term credits. From 1900 to 1915 the aggregate investments were not quite one-third the aggregate loans; during the war and post-war years the percentage gradually increased; and after 1929 it increased so rapidly that by 1937 aggregate investments were nearly fifty per cent greater than the total volume of loans.

The second diagram compares unsecured loans with those secured by real estate and by stocks and bonds as collateral. Again it should be borne in mind that the former classification does not represent *com-*

---

[3] See article by the author, *Journal of Political Economy*, 1918, pp. 638–663.
[4] For further discussion of foreign banking trends see chap. XXV. See also, Waldo F. Mitchell, *The Uses of Bank Funds*, 1925.

LOANS AND INVESTMENTS OF NATIONAL BANKS, 1900–1937[a]
(In Billions of Dollars)

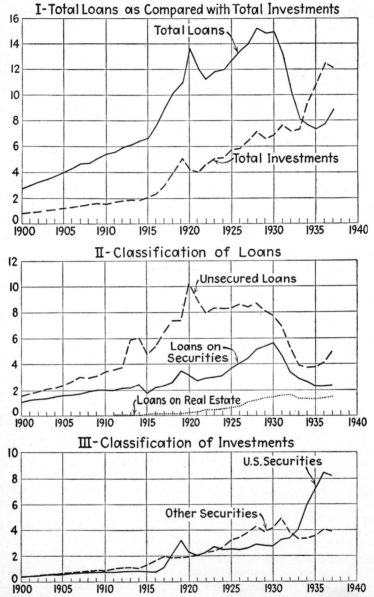

I-Total Loans as Compared with Total Investments

Total Loans

Total Investments

II- Classification of Loans

Unsecured Loans

Loans on Securities

Loans on Real Estate

III- Classification of Investments

U.S. Securities

Other Securities

[a] Compiled from data in the *Annual Report of the Comptroller of the Currency*, 1915, 1927–1937. Unsecured loans includes one- and two-name paper, acceptances, and, after 1914, loans on personal securities (chattels). Real estate loans were not permitted prior to 1911. Loans on securities includes loans on personal chattels prior to 1915.

mercial paper exclusively. Real estate loans are not shown separately before 1911. They appear of negligible importance until 1927, in which year the law relating to the conditions under which real estate loans might be made was modified.[5] However, a large volume of bank credit, particularly in agricultural communities, has always been extended on the basis of real estate, though such loans were nominally evidenced by short-term promissory notes which were indefinitely renewable.[6] The ratio between collateral loans and unsecured loans has fluctuated widely—varying with changes in the volume of commercial business and of stock exchange operations respectively.

The third diagram shows the relative increase in the holdings of government as compared with other securities during the past twenty years. Prior to the World War government bonds were used almost exclusively as reserve against bank note issues. The proportion of "governments" increased sharply during the World War period, declined during the twenties, and then increased very rapidly again after 1932.

INVESTMENTS OF NATIONAL BANKS JUNE 30, 1937[a]

U.S. Government securities, direct obligations	6,902,521
Securities guaranteed by U.S. Government as to interest and principal	1,316,674
Obligations of federal agencies:	
Federal Land banks	125,494
Federal Intermediate Credit banks	73,545
Joint stock land banks	14,124
Territorial and insular possessions of the United States	13,589
State, county, and municipal securities[b]	1,451,629
Bonds, notes and debentures of private corporations:	
Railroads	673,942
Public utilities	638,563
Real estate corporations	30,172
Other domestic corporations	466,023
Stock of other domestic corporations:	
Real estate corporations	32,307
Banks and banking corporations	26,765
Other domestic corporations	113,294
Stock of Federal Reserve banks	79,680
Foreign securities:	
Obligations of foreign central governments	92,365
Obligations of foreign provincial, state, and municipal governments	39,533
Other foreign securities	32,067
Total bonds and securities of all classes	12,122,287

[a] From the *Annual Report of the Comptroller of the Currency*, 1937.

[b] Including school, irrigation, drainage, and reclamation districts, and instrumentalities of one or more states.

[5] See p. 331.

[6] For further discussion see chap. XXVI, sec. I.

It should be noted here that the investments in other securities include large holdings of state and local governments and their subdivisions. The funds procured from the sale of government bonds, both federal and state, have been used in part for meeting current operating expenses and in part for the development of public capital enterprises. This is particularly true of state and municipal issues. The table on page 315 shows the classification of investments of national banks as of June 30, 1937.

The changing character of commercial banking operations is also indicated by the changing proportions of time and demand deposits. Theoretically, time deposits can safely be used as a basis for long-term loans—though, as we have seen in our analysis of savings bank operations, time depositors normally expect to be able to draw out their money on demand, or at least on very short notice. In any case the growth in investment operations has been accompanied by a more or less corresponding increase in time deposits. The following table shows the relative proportions of demand and time deposits in the national banking system by ten-year intervals from 1910 to 1937.

DEMAND AND TIME DEPOSITS OF NATIONAL BANKS[a]

Year Ending June 30	Total Amount	Demand Deposits		Time Deposits[b]	
		Amount	Percentage of Total	Amount	Percentage of Total
1910	5,070.5	4,636.9	91.5	433.6	8.5
1920	13,671.8	10,186.3	74.5	3,485.5	25.5
1930	19,475.0	10,926.2	56.1	8,548.8	43.9
1937	22,192.1	14,403.8	64.9	7,788.3	35.1

[a] Compiled from *Annual Report of the Comptroller of the Currency.*
[b] Includes postal savings.

II. THE PROBLEM OF LIQUIDITY

The fact that commercial banks have become increasingly involved in intermediate and long-term investment operations does not, of course, prove that such a trend is not beset with dangers. The issue turns on the problem of maintaining that liquidity of assets which is essential to the payment of deposits on demand. In analyzing this problem it will be necessary to consider the situation both in ordinary times and in periods of acute financial strain. The statement which follows is summarized from an analysis made by the author in 1918, which related to the so-called independent banking system which

preceded the establishment of central credit reservoirs under the
Federal Reserve system.[7]

1. Liquidity in Normal Times

To what extent, first, are commercial loans to customers to be
relied upon as the source of a steady inflow of funds to a bank? Theoretically, a short-time commercial loan, whether based on a specific
transaction or on the excess of inflow over outflow of funds within the
period of the loan, is almost certain to be paid at maturity, because
the use of the funds during the life of the loan automatically creates the
means of repayment. In practice, however, we find that commercial
loans made to a bank's own depositors are by no means universally
liquidated at maturity. In the country banks it is not an uncommon
practice to grant repeated renewals—a loan often being extended for
many years. Such loans make possible the purchase of equipment and
live stock, and often they have helped to finance the purchase of the
land itself. Even in commercial centers renewals of commercial loans
are very common, if not indeed the rule. Well-informed bankers have
estimated that from forty to fifty per cent of the unsecured loans in
the large cities are renewed at maturity. In fact, banks usually grant
their customers renewals whenever they ask for an extension—as long
as there are no disquieting developments in connection with the borrower's business.

The reason for renewing short-term loans with such regularity is
in part the stress of competition between rival banks and in part the
continuous nature of loan requirements. Rather than being distinctly
seasonal in character, the volume of output of many staple products
remains comparatively uniform throughout the year.

The theory is that a commercial loan based upon consumable products
liquidates itself. But until the world stops eating and drinking, or wearing
clothes, or consuming fuel, there is a new note right behind the one liquidated
by the consumable commodities. Across the continent there is a line of sheep
and a commercial note on the tail of each sheep in endless procession. There is
no fluctuation possible with commercial notes based on consumable commodities unless prices are changed, or the capital of the merchant, or middleman,
is expanded.[8]

While this is no doubt pressing a good point too far, it is nevertheless
true that to pay a maturing loan usually means borrowing again
immediately, since the business does not have sufficient working capital
of its own to finance its operations. It has been found more convenient

[7] *Journal of Political Economy*, 1918, pp. 705–731.

[8] C. W. Barron, *Federal Reserve Act*, pp. 70–71.

to grant each customer a "line of credit," to "rate" a borrower as a $10,000 or a $100,000 safe risk, and to force no payments as long as he keeps within the limit that has been set.

The view formerly prevailed that all borrowers should be expected to liquidate at least once a year. In periods of business expansion, however, this proved impossible. If they succeeded in liquidating completely with one bank, it was only by means of loans procured at other banks. In the aggregate the banks as a whole provided business as a whole with permanent working capital.

In the light of these conditions, the banks found it impossible to rely upon commercial loans to customers to provide an inflow of funds as needed. Accordingly, they looked to other types of assets to provide a "secondary" reserve quickly convertible into cash. Among these were the following: (1) Open market commercial paper, which they were not under obligation to renew at maturity; (2) call loans, which were payable on demand; and (3) bonds, which could be quickly sold in the securities market. Many banks also relied upon loans from their correspondents. Time collateral loans were little more dependable than commercial loans for here also the relations with customers tended to be of a continuing nature.

In ordinary times, then, liquidity was provided not so much by maturing loans, properly scheduled, as by the disposition of assets in the financial markets. It was found that the way to get on with a minimum of cash reserves was not by relying upon maturities, but by maintaining a considerable quantity of assets that could be shifted to other banks or individual purchasers at any time as necessity might require. *Liquidity* is, in fact, tantamount to *shiftability*.

2. LIQUIDITY IN TIME OF CRISIS

In periods of acute financial strain, when liquidity is of primary importance, the problem is materially different. In the first place, almost none of the maturing loans can be depended on to yield cash, for when a crisis has reached an acute stage borrowers are always hard pressed, and renewals are certain to be almost universally demanded. Indeed, it is a very first principle that the bank's customers must be "carried" in time of stress.

Banks have long recognized the complete unreliability of commercial loans to customers as a secondary reserve for crises, and have in various ways attempted to substitute other assets for commercial paper as the "secondary" reserve, notably open market commercial paper and call loans. Open market paper, however, proved little better than any other commercial paper; for if a borrower was obliged to pay such notes it was necessary for him to seek additional accommodation at his regular bank. While a particular bank might thus obtain some relief the position of the banking system as a whole was not improved.

It was only after much distressing experience that the banks came to realize that call loans possess no considerable convertibility into cash in time of crisis. As viewed by the individual bank, call loans appeared to possess ideal liquidity, being terminable at the will of the bank and safeguarded by an ample margin of readily marketable securities. But in time of crisis it is impossible to obtain much relief from this source. Usually the borrower on call cannot pay, and the banks therefore must attempt to sell the collateral. But when all banks are endeavoring to sell collateral and none wish to buy, the market for securities is demoralized.

Investment in bonds as a secondary reserve for crises has also had its period of popularity in banking circles. Such investments are more satisfactory than stock collateral because they are more stable in value and have a broader market. However, as the experience of 1932-33 demonstrated, when all banks wish to liquidate bonds simultaneously, bond prices also may be demoralized. On the whole, however, bonds have constituted the most satisfactory secondary reserve; for they can usually be quickly sold for cash, at some price.

Our own banking experience, as well as that of all other countries, has taught with the greatest possible conclusiveness that ability to pass through a crisis without suspension of specie payments and widespread credit disruption does not rest upon the payment of maturing loans. It depends rather upon the maintenance of central reserve reservoirs from which distressed banks may obtain the funds required to meet the demands and needs of customers.

In summary, the theory of liquidity as first developed related to a situation in which each bank was an independent entity, depending wholly upon maturing loans to provide a return flow of cash. It had no correspondent banks to which it could turn for help and there were no organized exchanges in which securities could be liquidated. With the evolution of an interrelated banking system and extensive security markets, the problem of maintaining liquidity assumed an entirely new form. It became chiefly a matter of disposing of certain assets in the market or of borrowing from affiliated financial institutions.

Since the establishment of the Federal Reserve system the problem of obtaining cash for seasonal or emergency requirements has been simplified by making it possible for the member banks to shift assets to or borrow from the Federal Reserve banks. The types of assets that are now liquid from the standpoint of the individual banks are simply those which are legally shiftable to Federal Reserve banks. Liquidity has thus become a matter of legal definition. The central reservoir of credit provided by the Federal Reserve system makes it possible for banks to carry distressed customers and to expand the total volume of credit—as long as the member banks have acceptable assets on which to borrow from the Federal Reserve banks.[9]

3. Depreciable Assets in Relation to Failures

To guard against any possible misunderstanding it must now be emphasized that this analysis of the nature of the problem of liquidity does not indicate that the character of loans and investments may be ignored. On the contrary, the quality of a bank's portfolio remains of fundamental importance. Bank failures are in fact usually attributable to unsound rather than to unliquid assets. Moreover, the really significant ratio is not that of cash and secondary reserves to deposit obligations but the ratio of deposits to depreciable assets—that is, to loans and investments which under adverse conditions may suffer sharp declines in value. A bank may have a very satisfactory reserve ratio and yet have to close its doors because its portfolio has so depreciated that its credit standing is undermined. This ratio is also more important than that of capital to deposits; capital may be relatively large but if the assets are heavily depreciable the position of the bank may still be unsound.

In concluding this phase of the discussion specific reference must be made to the experience during the banking crisis of 1932–33. Numerous students have pointed out that the banks which suffered the greatest distress were typically those which were heavily involved in security operations, particularly in connection with real estate enterprises. Not only did real estate loans not prove liquid but in many cases the shrinkage of values was so great as to wipe out the security back of the loans. Similarly, many low grade railroad, public utility and industrial bonds proved so unstable that they could be converted into cash only at ruinous prices. The collateral back of time loans also depreciated so heavily as to bring large losses to the banks. While short-term commercial loans did not in the main prove liquid, the losses involved were nevertheless relatively small. The conclusion usually drawn from this experience is that the old theory that credit could be safely expanded only for short-term, self-liquidating paper was once more amply demonstrated.

[9] For discussion of the Federal Reserve system see chaps. XXIII and XXIV.

Before accepting this conclusion it should be recalled that in the crisis of 1920–1921 the experience was exactly the reverse of that of 1932–1933. On the former occasion practically all the difficulties arose in connection with commercial loans. Bond holdings were not only marketable, but as a rule they were stable in value. On the other hand, the decline in the value of commodities was so catastrophic (see diagram, page 16) that even though the loans may have been made with what appeared like an ample ratio of quick assets to current liabilities, the margin of safety was quickly destroyed. The weakest assets in the portfolios of the banks were those which fulfilled most accurately the description of automatic self-liquidating loans, namely, the trade acceptances evidencing a specific sale of commodities. Even when such goods were warehoused and secured by negotiable warehouse receipts, the banks were obliged to take enormous losses. When they attempted to protect themselves by taking over the title to specific commodities their position was not improved; indeed, they found themselves confronted with the problem of trying to sell commodities in a market from which the bottom had disappeared. The situation was similar to that in 1907, although rendered more acute by virtue of the extraordinary decline in commodity prices and the accompanying wholesale cancellation of orders. Under the conditions existing, the banks could only wait until a revival of business enabled them gradually to liquidate, usually at a heavy sacrifice, the commercial loans which had been contracted during the preceding boom period.

The explanation of this sharp contrast between the two periods under consideration is to be found in the fact that in the boom period preceding the collapse of 1920 speculative activities and price advances centered largely in the commodity markets, whereas in 1929 they centered almost entirely in the security markets and in the field of urban real estate. Accordingly, in the one case the depreciable assets were chiefly the commercial loans, whereas in the other they were mainly securities. In both cases it was bad management to make continuous extensions of bank credit on the security of highly inflated assets.[10]

III. COMMERCIAL BANKING TRENDS IN RECENT YEARS

The diagrams on page 314 show enormous fluctuations in the volume of bank loans since 1913. In the case of the unsecured loans there was: (1) an extraordinary expansion during the years 1915 to 1920 —from four to more than ten billion dollars; (2) comparative stability

[10] The failure of agricultural banks not only after 1929 but throughout the twenties is discussed on pp. 353–354.

in the twenties at a level a little above eight billion dollars—notwith-standing a rapid increase in the total volume of national production; (3) a sharp decline during the depression years following 1929, with comparatively little expansion during the recovery period 1933–37. Loans on securities showed a rapid increase throughout the twenties, but since 1929 there has been a decline similar to that in the case of unsecured loans.

The war-time rise in the volume of unsecured loans was attributable to three factors: a rapid increase in the volume of business; an extra-ordinary rise in the level of prices, and hence in costs of conducting business; and the restriction of the investment market to public capital issues. The decline in the twenties was due in some degree to the fall in the level of prices but more largely to the ability of business enter-prises to finance expansion either from earnings or by the flotation of securities in the investment market. The great expansion of security loans during the twenties is largely explained by the rapid growth of stock market speculation, while the decline in both types of loans during the depression is a manifestation of the severe deflation which occurred. The failure of bank loans to expand materially during the recovery period following 1933 is attributable to several factors includ-ing the lower prevailing level of prices, the restricted volume of business activity, the lack of a satisfactory credit position on the part of many potential borrowers, and government regulations applicable to certain types of credit operations.

The declining importance of commercial bank loans in recent years suggests that the heyday of commercial bank enterprise may possibly be past. It should be borne in mind, however, that certain develop-ments might quickly alter the outlook. If, for example, we should have a period of great industrial expansion accompanied by rapidly rising prices, the demand for commercial bank loans would again increase greatly. Moreover, a resumption of security flotations on a large scale would inevitably mean a substantial expansion of security loans to underwriters and professional speculators.

Reference has been made to a restriction of commercial bank loans in consequence of the unsatisfactory credit position of many would-be borrowers. The great depression affected the commercial system in a double way. On the one hand, the epidemic of bank failures emphasized the importance of conservative lending policies and led to a tightening up of banking regulations and examinations in the interests of affording depositors more adequate protection. On the other hand, the long continued depression led to a serious deterioration in the financial position of large numbers of business enterprises, particularly those of medium and small size. Thus at the very time when commercial banks were being required to exercise unusual caution, the recovery and expansion of business appeared to necessitate more than ordinarily liberal extensions of credit. In the main these financial requirements appear to have been for permanent working capital and for the replacement of equipment.

Since the Securities Act, as well as the inherent risks involved, made it difficult for such companies to float securities, something of an impasse developed. A way out of the difficulty was finally sought in the form of commercial bank loans maturing serially over a period of years. During the last two or three years this new type of loan has had a vigorous growth, particularly in the larger financial centers. Such loans may be either secured or unsecured. While there is no set formula, the typical loan runs for five years or less, with regular serial payments. The borrower must have a record of earnings, even in depression years, sufficient to enable him to cover the annual interest plus serial payments. Since no financing charges need be incurred in connection with such loans, it is both cheaper and more convenient to borrow in this way than through the registration and flotation of securities.

In this connection it is interesting to note that such loans range from 100 thousand dollars or even less, to as high as 30 or 40 millions. Several banks have usually participated in making the larger loans; and in cases where the borrower wishes the serial payments to be extended for more than five years arrangements are sometimes made with insurance companies to take the longer maturities, leaving the banks the shorter ones. It is not impossible that loans of this type will become increasingly important in bank portfolios.

The problem here discussed has also found reflection in recent modifications of government policy with respect to credit extensions. On the one side, the Comptroller of the Currency and the Directors of the Federal Deposit Insurance Corporation, approaching the problem mainly from the point of view of safeguarding deposits, have in recent years scrutinized bank loan policies more carefully than ever before. On the other side, the Board of Governors of the Federal Reserve system, desiring to stimulate business recovery through credit expansion, have sought a liberalization of credit policies. The Board of Governors no longer adhere to the former theory of commercial bank liquidity, emphasizing rather the character of the loan, and disregarding whether it is made for a longer or a shorter period of time.

Following discussions among the various governmental groups involved, an agreement was finally reached whereby loans up to ten years may be made by commercial banks under certain conditions.

It has been agreed that the banks may buy investment securities for which a public flotation is not feasible "provided the issuing commercial or industrial enterprises can demonstrate their ability to service such securities"—that is, cover interest and amortization charges. The amortization requirement calls for no curtail the first year and for only 75 per cent of the principal to be extinguished by the maturity date.[11]

In the light of the changes which have been outlined in this chapter it is evident that commercial banks have become hybrid financial institutions, even as far as their commercial bank departments are concerned. Their investment operations are quite as important as their commercial business. They also participate extensively in trust services and have at times engaged extensively in underwriting and distributing security issues. Although the commercial banks are now forbidden to participate in underwriting, they still bear little resemblance to the specialized institutions which originated in the eighteenth century. The forces responsible for the integration of the banking business will be discussed in the following chapter.

[11] Agreement published June 27, 1938.

CHAPTER XXII

THE EVOLUTION OF AMERICAN BANKING REGULATION

Commercial banking was one of the earliest forms of business to be subjected to government regulation. Because of the almost universal demand for the accommodation which banking affords, and because of the tremendous power that is inherent in the control of loanable funds, the banking business has long been regarded as quasi-public in its nature. Indeed, many people have asserted that banking operations are of such importance to the public that they should be actually conducted by the government itself; that to permit private interests to control the supply of bank currency and make profits from the use of people's money is to foster one of the most vicious of monopolies. This extreme view has, however, never gained general acceptance; nor until recently have we, in fact, subjected all banks in the United States to some form of governmental control. Indeed, in a few states it is still possible for individuals to engage in a general banking business subject to virtually no regulation.[1]

It is the purpose of the present chapter to discuss in summary fashion the evolution of the present complicated system of banking regulation in the United States. It will be necessary to consider both state and national institutions, and to indicate the ways in which the growing complexity of the economic and financial system and the changing character of commercial banking, as outlined in the preceding chapter, brought modifications in the system of regulation. The history of American banking divides itself into three stages: from 1790 to the Civil War; from the Civil War to the inauguration of the Federal Reserve system in 1914; and from 1914 to the present time.

I. BANKING BEFORE THE CIVIL WAR

In the period before the Civil War banking operations in the United States were mainly conducted either by private bankers or by institutions chartered under state laws. The only national banks were the First Bank of the United States (1791–1811) and the Second Bank

[1] In 1937 there were 85 private banks in the United States, having total assets of $107,071,000.

of the United States (1816–1836). These government institutions made comparatively few loans to individuals. Private business requirements were provided for by private loan agencies and by various types of chartered state banking institutions.

1. The First and Second United States Banks

Only a brief statement is necessary with reference to the work of these federal institutions. They were organized for three major purposes: (1) to act as fiscal agent for the United States Government in the collection and disbursement of federal revenue; (2) to assist the Treasury in times of financial emergency, through the purchase of government bonds; and (3) to promote a sounder and more stable bank-note currency and to exercise an influence in stabilizing business and financial conditions generally.

The First Bank of the United States performed a genuinely important service during the first twenty years of our national history. It acted as fiscal agent in the collection and disbursement of government funds at a time when the problems involved were particularly difficult because of inadequate private financial facilities. The First Bank also loaned several million dollars to the Government during a period when federal revenue was both uncertain in amount and intermittently received. The bank did not, however, exert any appreciable influence on the general financial conditions. The charter expired in 1811 and failed of renewal by a single vote in the Senate.

The Second Bank of the United States had a checkered career. It was very badly managed during the first few years of its history; it extended credit with abandon and failed to maintain adequate specie reserves. It exerted no restraining influence upon the activities of the state banks, and on the whole it exercised an unfavorable, rather than a favorable, influence during the boom period and crisis of 1817–1819. In the decade of the twenties, however, the Second Bank appears to have been competently managed and of genuine assistance in conducting the fiscal operations of the Government. Moreover, in the critical year 1826 the bank apparently exerted some influence in stabilizing business conditions. It never accomplished much, however, in the way of securing a more stable bank-note currency.

With the accession to power of President Jackson, in 1829, the Second Bank, owing to a combination of circumstances, became a political issue. From this time on, the management of the institution deteriorated, and its usefulness was seriously impaired; and when in 1833 President Jackson ordered the withdrawal of federal deposits from the bank, its fate was virtually sealed. The later unfortunate

EVOLUTION OF BANKING REGULATION 327

history of the Second Bank is attributable, not to any inherent defect in the bank itself, but rather to the exigencies of an era during which the doctrine that the centralization of political and financial power was essentially undemocratic was in the ascendancy. The charter was not renewed in 1836; and from that date until 1863 the United States was without any national banking institution.

2. State Banking Systems

Throughout this period the banking laws of the various states were extremely diverse and with a few exceptions extraordinarily lax. In consequence the management of the state banks was usually no better than that of the private institutions which flourished at the time. While improvements were being made in the latter part of the period, banking organization remained, on the whole, in a deplorable condition until after the Civil War. There were a few noteworthy exceptions. The so-called Suffolk Bank system of New England developed a method of note redemption analogous to the check collection system of the Federal Reserve banks today. The prompt redemptions required made it necessary for these banks to keep in a comparatively liquid condition. The New York Free Banking system permitted any group of individuals to engage in banking as long as they conformed to the requirements of a general law; and it required that notes be secured by the deposit of bonds and mortgages. This system served as a model for the national banking system. The Indiana State Bank was a successful branch banking system, in which a central board of control formulated and enforced rules with respect to the kinds of loans that the various branches might make.

In the thirties branch banking became nearly universal throughout the Middle West and South. However, the wholesale failures that occurred in the panic of 1837 brought the branch banking system into such disrepute that it was generally abandoned shortly thereafter. Rhode Island in 1837 and New York in 1844 passed laws expressly prohibiting the organization of branches, while in numerous other states the banking commissioners interpreted the existing laws as failing to permit the establishment of branches.

II. NATIONAL AND STATE BANKING SYSTEMS, 1863–1913

The National Bank Act, passed in 1863, marked the beginning of a new era in American banking. The purpose of this law was to establish a uniform system of banking under the auspices of the Federal Government. At this stage the most important banking function was the issuance of bank notes rather than the creation of deposit currency, and the framers of the law believed that state banking could be eliminated through the levying of a tax on state bank note issues. A tax of 10 per cent imposed in 1866 did succeed in abolishing the note issues of state institutions; but it did not prevent the further growth of state banking.

The national banking system was conceived as an independent, or unit, bank system. It was believed that democratic principles involved the assumption by each bank of complete responsibility for the management of its affairs and the maintenance of sound financial conditions. Branches were not authorized. We have already seen that state branch banking came into disrepute as a result of the financial crisis of 1837, and it is interesting to note that no serious argument in favor of branch banking was advanced in the debates preceding the passage of the National Bank Act. State banks which joined the national banking system were permitted to retain existing branches; but those of the Middle West came into the national system as unit banks and the branch banking systems of the southern states were largely destroyed by the Civil War and its aftermath. Thus, for many years following the establishment of the national banking system branch banking was of virtually no significance in the United States.

1. The Regulation of National Banks

Framers of the National Banking Act profited much from previous state banking experience and several useful principles for the safeguarding of banking were incorporated in the federal law. The regulations laid down for the national banking system related to (1) the supervision of the original organization, (2) the prohibition of certain types of loans, (3) the maintenance of adequate specie reserves, and (4) bank examinations and reports.

Supervision of original organization.—In the early history of this country, to establish a bank required a special act of the legislature. The principle underlying special incorporation is that it permits each application for a bank charter to be considered by the legislature strictly on its merits. It worked out in practice, however, that the granting of charters to engage in banking commonly became a part of the system of political spoils. "Charters were granted by Whig and Democratic legislatures only to their own partisans . . . . and shares in banks, or the rights to subscribe to them, were parcelled out by 'bosses' in the several counties." The reaction from this system eventually led to the establishment in 1838 in the state of New York of a general incorporation, or "free banking," law to which reference has already been made. This system of incorporation was very generally followed by the western states during the decade immediately preceding the Civil War; and in the National Bank Act of 1863 it was adopted as an essential part of the national banking system. It has since been gradually copied by all of the state governments, the time involved in making legislative investigations as a prerequisite to the granting of a charter having proved quite as important a factor in the drift toward general incorporation as have the political evils of the special-charter system.

The national law provided for the establishment of a separate bureau in the Treasury Department, under the direction of a Comptroller of the Currency. It is the duty of the Comptroller not only to see that a new bank conforms with all the requirements of the incorporation law, but also to make sure that there is a reasonable need for the organization of an additional bank in the community in question. One of the most potent causes of bank failures has been the multiplication of banking facilities beyond the needs of business.

The National Bank Act, as amended, lays down the following regulations with reference to the minimum capital requirements for national banks: in cities of more than fifty thousand population, a capital of not less than $200,000; in cities of from six to fifty thousand inhabitants, a minimum capital of $100,000; in cities of from three to six thousand inhabitants, a capital of at least $50,000; and in towns of three thousand population or less, a minimum capital of $25,000. The purpose of these capital requirements is to prevent the organization of a large number of very small banks, which in the nature of things would usually be less efficiently managed, and would be certain to have a less extensive distribution of risks than would banks of larger size.

Another provision of the Act is that half of the capital shall be paid in before business is started. The explanation of this provision is found in state banking experience before the Civil War. The early state banking laws permitted banks to commence operations as soon as a small portion of the capital stock had been actually subscribed in cash, the rest of the capital usually being represented by promissory notes of the stockholders. It was made to appear to depositors that the capital was really paid in and represented genuine resources of the bank; but when failures occurred, the true situation was of course immediately disclosed.

The accumulation of a surplus is also required. The law provides that before the declaration of a (semi-annual) dividend each bank shall "carry one-tenth part of its net profits of the preceding half-year to its surplus fund until the same shall amount to 20 per centum of its capital stock." The purpose of this provision is to make sure that national banks shall gradually increase in size; for it is believed that the larger are a bank's resources, the greater is the security for its creditors.

With a view to safeguarding depositors, the law imposed a double liability upon shareholders. That is to say, in the event of a bank failure each shareholder was obligated to pay not only the par value of his stock but, if necessary, twice that amount. However, in the crisis of 1933 it often proved impossible to enforce this provision without virtually ruining shareholders, many of whom were individuals in moderate circumstances; and in consequence the provision proved more or less a dead letter. It was abolished when the Federal Deposit Insurance Corporation, which insures bank deposits, was established in 1934.

Regulation of loans.—Since the chief source of bank losses, aside from defalcations, lies in the failure of bank borrowers to meet their obligations, it has been found expedient to place certain restrictions upon the lending operations of the banks. The provisions of the national banking law governing loan operations are the result of previous banking experience which showed that certain types of loans were fraught with special danger. The loan provisions of the National Bank Act are as follows:

a) It shall be lawful for any such [banking] association to purchase, hold, and convey real estate as follows:

First. Such as shall be necessary for its immediate accommodation in the transaction of its business.

Second. Such as shall be mortgaged to it in good faith by way of security for debts previously contracted.

Third. Such as shall be conveyed to it in satisfaction of debts previously contracted in the course of its dealings.

Fourth. Such as it shall purchase at sales under judgments, decrees, or mortgages held by such association, or shall purchase to secure debts due to said association.

Such associations shall not hold the possession of any real estate under mortgage, or hold the title and possession of any real estate purchased to secure any debts due to it for a longer period than five years.

b) To one person or corporation: The total liabilities to any association, of any person, or of any company, corporation, or firm for money borrowed, including, in the liabilities of a company or firm, the liabilities of the several members thereof, shall at no time exceed one-tenth part of the amount of the capital stock of such association actually paid in and unimpaired and one-tenth part of the unimpaired surplus fund, provided that the total of such liabilities shall in no event exceed thirty per centum of the capital stock of the association. But the discount of bills of exchange drawn in good faith against actually existing values, and the discount of commercial or business paper actually owned by the person negotiating the same, shall not be considered as money borrowed.

c) On security of own stock: No association shall make any loan or discount on the security of the shares of its own capital stock, nor be the purchaser or holder of any such shares, unless such security or purchase shall be necessary to prevent loss upon a debt previously contracted in good faith; and stock so purchased or acquired shall, within six months from the time of its purchase, be sold or disposed of at public or private sale; or, in default thereof, a receiver may be appointed to close up the business.

Real estate loans were prohibited because they did not conform with the requirements for liquidity, as then interpreted. However, successive amendments to the law, beginning with the Federal Reserve Act of 1913, have made it possible for national banks to participate extensively in real estate financing. In 1927, the McFadden Banking Act authorized national banks to make real estate loans up to 50 per cent of the value of property offered as security, in aggregate amounts not to exceed 25 per cent of their unimpaired capital and surplus or one-half of their savings deposits. This provision was further liberalized in the Banking Act of 1935.[2]

The purpose of limiting the amount of credit that may be extended to any one person or corporation is to insure a relatively wide distribution of risks. The exception to the limitation stated in the last sentence under (*b*) above is attributable to the belief that two-name paper arising out of the purchase and sale of goods is always practically certain to be paid. In the light of the discussion of the relative merits of single- and two-name paper as given in chapter XVII, however, it would appear that there is very little merit to this particular exception.

The restriction against making loans on the security of a bank's own stock is mainly the result of some rather disastrous experiences in state banking practice before the Civil War. We have already seen that early state banking laws permitted banks to begin operations as soon as a relatively small portion of the capital stock had been paid in. The shares of stock already received by shareholders were often used as security for loans from the bank. In making the loan the bank issued notes; and these notes, which passed current as money, were then used by the shareholders as a means of purchasing additional capital stock. Thus it came about that a large amount of the bank's capital would be borrowed from the bank itself. In other words, the resources received by a bank from the sale of stock consisted in large

[2] See page 358.

measure only of its own liabilities, in the form of its outstanding notes. In the event of failure the true situation was of course quickly revealed.

The regulation of reserves.—The purpose of requiring banks to hold minimum reserves of cash is to restrain certain bankers, who, because of inadequate knowledge of banking principles or because of a disposition to take long chances with depositors' money in the hope of immediate gain for themselves, might allow the reserves to be depleted to a point which would endanger the solvency of the institutions. It is of interest to note in this connection that the United States is the only important country that has established minimum reserve requirements. Whatever may be the case in other countries, however, our own banking experience has definitely shown the wisdom of such requirements. In the early days of banking many institutions kept practically no reserves whatever, with the result that their outstanding notes depreciated in value and wrought havoc with the monetary system.

Banking examinations and reports. As a means of enforcing the provisions of the National Bank Act, there has been established in the Treasury Department a separate bureau under the direction of the Comptroller of the Currency. The Comptroller appoints examiners whose duty is to examine each bank in the federal system at least twice each calendar year, and oftener than that if it is considered necessary. In case these examinations reveal malpractices, inefficient banking methods, or a failure to conform fully with the requirements of the law, action is taken to correct the weaknesses disclosed; and if they are not shortly corrected, the bank's charter is forfeited.

Every national bank is also required to make three reports each year to the Comptroller of the Currency, exhibiting in detail the resources and liabilities of the institution at the close of business on any past date specified by the Comptroller. The Comptroller may also call for special reports from any particular bank whenever it is deemed necessary.

The national bank examiners also render assistance to the Comptroller of the Currency in helping him to form a judgment as to the advisability of granting an application for a national bank charter.

Regulation of bank notes.—In the period before the Civil War there were as many different kinds of bank notes as there were types of banks; and as a consequence of inadequate regulations and unsound practices the bank note currency of the country was a demoralizing factor in the monetary system as a whole. The primary purpose of the National Banking Act was to establish a satisfactory system of bank note currency. Such a system would involve (1) convertibility into

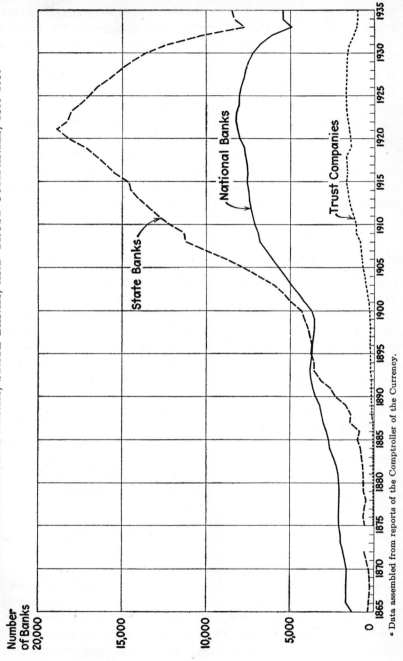

NUMBER OF NATIONAL BANKS, STATE BANKS, AND TRUST COMPANIES, 1865–1935[a]

ᵃ Data assembled from reports of the Comptroller of the Currency.

standard money; (2) ample security; and (3) elasticity, that is, responsiveness to the various requirements of trade. The first two of these requirements were provided for by the National Banking Act, but the third was overlooked.

Convertibility into standard money was secured by requiring the issuing bank to stand ready at all times to redeem its own notes whenever presented, and by requiring each bank to establish a five per cent cash reserve fund in the Treasury of the United States for redemption of such notes as might be presented there. The underlying security was provided for by requiring government bonds to be set aside as specific security for the notes issued. Originally notes could be issued only to 90 per cent of the par value of the bonds deposited; but this percentage was eventually raised to 100.[3]

2. State Banks and Trust Companies

It was in the period immediately following the Civil War that the great advantages of bank checks as compared with bank notes became manifest. Accordingly, state banks, even without bank note issues, were able to survive. Indeed, they increased very rapidly after 1885 and soon greatly outnumbered the national banks. Trust companies organized under state laws and conducting banking departments, also showed a rapid growth after 1890. The charts on pages 333 and 335 show the number of national banks, state banks, and trust companies, and the comparative size, as measured by capital resources, annually from 1865 to 1935.

It will be seen from these diagrams that the period of most rapid growth in the number of banking institutions was between 1900 and 1920. Indeed in the decade of the twenties there was a considerable reduction in the number of both national and state banks, a decline which continued during and was accentuated by the ensuing depression which culminated in the banking panic of 1933. National and state banks are found both in large cities and in small towns, with the state banks much more numerous in the smaller communities. The trust companies, because of the composite nature of their business, are located chiefly in large metropolitan centers. It is this fact which explains the much larger average size of the trust companies. The number of state banks has usually been several times the number of national banks. The number of state and national banking institutions in the country reached a peak of 30,812 in 1921. On June 30, 1937 the number was only 14,931 of which 5,299 were national and 9,632

---

[3] The problem of providing an elastic bank note currency will be discussed in chap. XXIII.

AVERAGE CAPITAL, INCLUDING SURPLUS AND UNDIVIDED PROFITS, OF NATIONAL BANKS, STATE BANKS, AND TRUST COMPANIES, 1865–1935

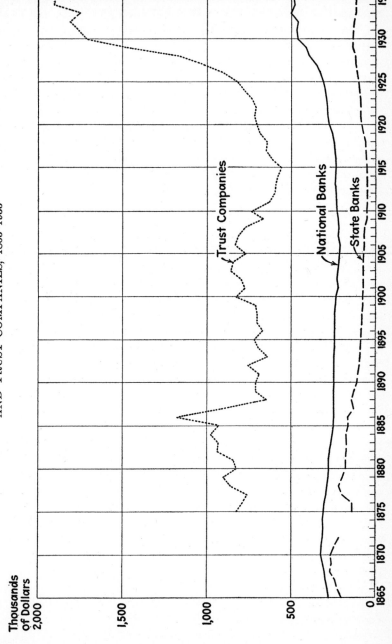

state institutions. Including mutual savings and private banks the total number of institutions in 1937 was 15,580.

The regulations pertaining to state banks were as a rule considerably more lenient than those governing the national institutions. The amount of capital required was usually smaller, and in many states there was no requirement for the accumulation of surplus. The loan provisions were more liberal, loans on real estate, for example, being universally permitted. Finally, reserve requirements were typically much smaller, and in some states the maintaining of a reserve was entirely at the discretion of the bank. Trust company legislation was, at first, even more lenient than that pertaining to commercial banks, although eventually it was brought into fairly close conformity with state bank legislation.

3. The Process of Financial Integration

From the analysis in preceding chapters it has become clear that there is now comparatively little specialization by financial institutions. We have seen, for instance, that savings banks do a considerable volume of commercial banking business; indeed, the stock savings banks are difficult to distinguish from commercial banks since they handle both commercial and savings accounts and make loans as freely for commercial as for investment purposes. We have seen that the commercial bank has become a hybrid institution, extending credit for fixed as well as for working capital purposes, making loans for consumption as well as for production, and maintaining savings, trust, insurance, and bond departments; and, until recent legislation prevented, some of the larger commercial banks engaged in underwriting activities. Commercial banks have also been affiliated with investment houses, with cattle loan companies, with discount corporations, and even with industrial banks making consumer loans. Commercial paper houses have at times included underwriting and bond distribution within the scope of their operations, while the larger discount companies have affiliations in the fields of insurance, commercial paper distribution, and the making of direct loans to consumers. Finally, we have seen that trust companies engage in a wide variety of financial operations including trusteeship, agency, suretyship, and both investment and commercial banking.

In a general way, it is therefore already clear that there is in fact no such clean-cut specialization among financial institutions as has been commonly supposed. But if we are fully to appreciate the extent to which integration has been carried out in the financial world, and the reasons for this trend, it will be necessary to study the development of the trust company as a type of financial institution and to indicate the effects of this development upon the operations of commercial banks.

While the laws of most states did not in the early days give to trust companies specific power to engage in commercial banking operations, the opportunity to increase their profits by accepting demand deposits and making short-time loans was so enticing that these institutions gradually assumed the functions of discount and deposit. They were thus brought into direct competition with national and state commercial banks, which were denied the power to engage in trust company business; and for a generation the commercial banks vigorously opposed this "unwarranted" invasion of their special field of enterprise. It was contended, moreover, that this broadening of the scope of trust company operations was as dangerous as it was illegitimate. Numerous cases came before the courts, and at first the decisions supported the contention that commercial banking was not a legitimate field for trust company operation. But as the trust companies of various states continued to extend the commercial side of their business, the state courts gradually came to accept the movement as inevitable.

The extraordinary growth of the trust companies is largely attributable to the inherent competitive advantages of the non-specialized type of financial institution. The fact that several types of financial operation are conducted in one building, and under one management, makes possible a most efficient utilization of the financial resources of the institution, for by virtue of the variety of services that are rendered, the officials of such an institution can be more closely in touch with all phases of financial and business problems than can those of a specialized institution. The analysis of the interrelations of financial operations and of the interdependence of finance and business that has been made in preceding chapters should make it apparent that an institution which by the nature of its work must keep in touch with every aspect of the economic and financial system would naturally be more far-seeing and hence more efficient in its management than would one which from the nature of its operations was brought into contact with only certain phases of the system.

The department-store type of financial institution also has had certain direct advantages in attracting business. One class of service naturally calls the attention of customers to the other classes of service; each department reinforces the others.

If the trustee needs to deposit money, the banking department is at hand: if the investor wishes to buy or sell, be it real estate, or stocks or bonds, the corporation is ready; if the agent finds a purchaser or a renter, that person is attracted toward the company; if the depositor wishes any of the services of the company, he is made to realize the helpfulness of his banker; if a new company is to be opened up through promotion of the enterprises incident thereto, then, there is a distinct drawing of the general patronage in the direction of the company; if the individual has any of the needs which are supplied by the company in active life and business, he is drawn to the company when he has a special trust to be performed whether during his life or after death . . . and so it is one interest attracts another.[4]

Aside from these administrative advantages the trust companies also have possessed certain special advantages over commercial banks because of less rigid legal requirements governing loans, reserves, etc. While there were undoubtedly certain dangers attending such lax regulation, particularly in view of the diversity of operations conducted, trust companies were nevertheless able to earn very satisfactory profits. And, on the whole, trust company failures were not more frequent than those of state and national banks of similar size.

Commercial banks ultimately found it expedient to engage in trust company operations. When they found it impossible to prevent the development of this "dangerous and illegitimate" type of financial institution known as the trust company, with interesting inconsistency they promptly sought to extend the scope of their own operations to include the whole range of trust business. This development in turn incurred the enmity of the trust companies, which henceforth inconsistently exerted all possible influence to confine the activities of commercial banks to their "legitimate" field of financial enterprise.

But the drift toward financial integration could not be checked; and by 1910 fifteen states had, in fact, granted to commercial banks the power to accept and execute trusts. While national banks were not successful in securing permission to engage in trust company business until the passage of the Federal Reserve law, they had, however, by devious methods succeeded in engaging trust company business long before 1913. The method most commonly employed was for the managers of a national bank or a state bank, in states where commercial banks were not permitted to conduct trust company business, to organize an affiliated trust company, which would be conducted in a "community of interest" with the commercial bank. According to the Secretary of the Treasury, there were in the year 1911 some three hundred cases of this sort. A second method was also frequently practiced—that of selling a majority of the stock of a national bank to a trust company, thereby effecting in practice a virtual consolidation of the two institutions.

[4] *Bankers' Magazine*, April, 1909, p. 637.

The facts as to the inevitable trend of financial development were eventually faced, and the Federal Reserve Act empowered the Federal Reserve officials to grant by special permit to national banks applying therefor, "when not in contravention of state or local law, the right to act as trustee, executor, administrator, registrar of stock and bonds, under such rules and regulations as the said board may prescribe."

The threatened loss of the special advantages, so long enjoyed by trust companies, led them to charge that the Federal Reserve authorization was unconstitutional, and two test cases were shortly brought before the state courts, in Illinois and Michigan. Both decisions, handed down in December, 1915, and September, 1916, respectively, held that the granting of trust powers to national banks was unconstitutional. But upon appeal to the Supreme Court of the United States, the decisions were reversed and congressional authority to grant trust powers to national banks was conclusively established, the issue being decided on the principle of implied powers laid down in the famous case of *McCulloch* v. *Maryland*.

The development of the trust business of national banks increased with great rapidity. At the end of 1936, as many as 1,923 national banks, having combined assets representing 87.5 per cent of total national bank assets, were authorized to exercise trust powers, while 1,573 banks had active trust departments. It is interesting to note that several hundred national banks now use the words "trust company" in their titles.

One further step was required to make department-store banking a universal phenomenon in the United States; for there were still many states that had not granted trust powers to commercial banks. Unable longer to withstand the tide, the New York legislature, on July 9, 1919, amended the state banking law and gave to the Superintendent of Banking the power to grant to banks applying therefor the right to "act as trustee, executor, administrator, registrar of stocks and bonds, guardian of estates, trustee and receiver of estates of lunatics, or in any other fiduciary capacity in which trust companies are permitted to act." The development of trust departments of state banks was thereafter rapid. The character of the operations of state banks and trust companies is now so similar that the Comptroller's reports ceased to classify them separately after 1935.

There has also been a similar integration in the field of savings banking. The commercial banks, both federal and state, as we have seen, operate savings bank departments, and at the same time the savings banks have in recent years invaded the field of commercial banking. This integrating movement in the field of savings banking has passed through practically the same stages as has the trust company development. Just as the commercial banks resorted to the courts to prevent the encroachment of trust companies upon their "legitimate" field of enterprise, so the savings banks appealed to the courts for protection when the commercial banks first began to invade their financial preserves; and precisely as the commercial banks, when they could not prevent the usurpation of commercial banking functions by trust companies, retaliated by entering the field of trust enterprise, so in like manner the savings banks—unable to check the invasion of their traditional field by the commercial banks (and likewise by the trust companies)—broadened the scope of their operations by taking over commercial banking functions. They desire, moreover, to assume trust functions as well.

It has been urged by some that department-store financial institutions contain elements of serious weakness and that great care must be taken if we are to avoid a substantial deterioration in banking methods. There are two grounds for this contention. First, it is urged that such an institution becomes a Jack-of-all-trades and master of none—that "only by specialization can the highest efficiency be obtained." A sufficient answer to this contention, at least as far as large institutions are concerned, appears to lie in the fact that there may be just as efficient management of the specialized departments of a single business as of specialized distinct businesses. Of more significance is the possibility that such an institution might fail to keep the accounts of the different departments separate, and to conduct each department on the principles demanded by the nature of its particular function. Mindful of this possibility, the Federal Reserve officials require of national banks exercising trust company powers that

the funds, securities, and investments held in each trust shall be held separate and distinct from the general funds and securities of the bank, and separate and distinct one from another. The ledger and other books kept for the trust department shall be entirely separate and apart from the other books and records of the bank.

A still greater danger resides in the possibility that the policies that should be pursued with respect to the administration of the business of various departments may at times conflict to such a degree that the true interests of clients may be neglected. It is chiefly because of the dangers inherent in this situation that recent banking legislation has divorced commercial banks from investment affiliates and from underwriting activities.[5]

[5] See page 357.

III. THE BROADENED SCOPE OF REGULATION IN 1913

The conception underlying the regulations of the national and state banking systems was that if a uniform and safe bank note currency were provided and the other operations of each individual bank were properly safeguarded, the banking system could be depended upon to perform its proper function in the economic life of the country. It was believed, moreover, that regulation of this sort would prevent the recurrence of financial crises such as those of 1837 and 1857. Experience soon showed, however, that the new banking legislation did not solve our currency problems. Bond-secured bank notes did not have the elasticity necessary to meet the seasonal fluctuations in the volume of business; and the system did not, moreover, eliminate banking panics. There was a disastrous breakdown of the credit system and a prolonged depression during the seventies, and another, somewhat less severe, followed in 1883. Again in the early nineties there was a severe and protracted breakdown of the credit and business system. Inasmuch as each of these crises was accompanied by an acute banking panic involving the suspension of specie payments, the ensuing depressions were naturally attributed primarily to defects in the banking system. At that time there was little appreciation of the manifold factors involved in what has come to be known as the business cycle. The frequency and the character of business fluctuations over the whole period from 1877 to the present time are shown in the chart on page 342. It will be seen that in addition to major fluctuations there is a more or less continuous series of minor oscillations.

1. THE MOVEMENT FOR BANKING REFORM

Although it early became apparent that the national banking system was defective, reform of our banking laws was slow in coming. The delay was in part due to the emphasis that was also being placed upon monetary issues. It will be recalled that the great crisis of the seventies was popularly attributed to the "crime of 1873" with respect to silver, and to the curtailment of the supply of greenback currency. Similarly, the depressions of the eighties and nineties were commonly regarded as evidence simply of an insufficient supply of money in the hands of the people. However, the acute tension in the money markets and the inability of the clearing-house associations to cope with the banking crises which periodically developed, had made it abundantly evident to close observers that the independent banking system was seriously defective.

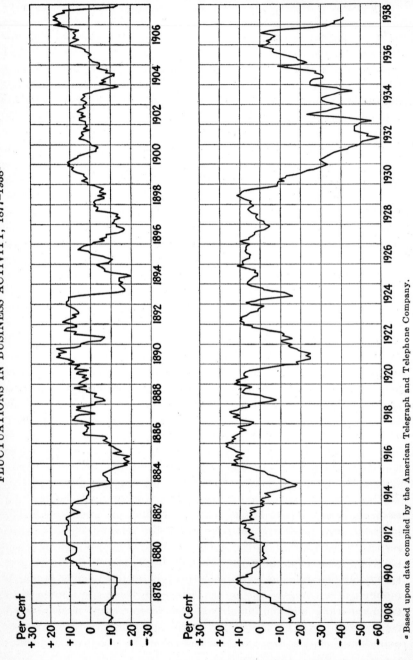

FLUCTUATIONS IN BUSINESS ACTIVITY, 1877–1938[a]

[a] Based upon data compiled by the American Telegraph and Telephone Company.

The panic of 1893 precipitated a genuine agitation for the improvement of our banking system, but before any legislation on the subject could be passed, there occurred the political campaign of 1896, the issue of which was once more the silver question. The success of the Republicans in this campaign was followed by the appointment of a monetary commission, composed of representatives of boards of trade, chambers of commerce, and other similar bodies, which met in Indianapolis in 1897 for the purpose of "making a thorough investigation of the monetary affairs and needs of the country in all relations and aspects, and submitting proper suggestions as to the evils found to exist and the remedies therefor." The findings of the commission were given publication, and a bill embodying the conclusions reached was presented in Congress in 1898. The Currency Act of March 14, 1900, carried some of these recommendations into effect. In the main, however, this act was concerned primarily with the money question. On the banking side all that was attempted was a stimulation of the growth of national, as compared with state, banks by decreasing the capital requirements and by permitting the issue of notes up to the full value of the government bonds held as security.

With the return of great business prosperity the need of reforming the banking system appeared less pressing to our legislators, who at best perceived none too clearly the fundamental weaknesses inherent in the system. The return of the Republicans to power, coupled with the establishment of a gold standard, undoubtedly satisfied most congressmen that henceforth financial difficulties would be unknown. Agitation for banking reform continued, however, among scientific students of the question, and there were also some congressmen, notably Charles N. Fowler, at that time chairman of the Banking and Currency Committee of the House, who persistently endeavored to secure the passage of remedial legislation, designed primarily to insure an elastic bank note currency based on commercial assets.

The financial panic of 1907 raised anew the agitation for banking reform, both in and out of Congress. It was observed that whereas other countries were equally subject to periodic fluctuations of commerce and trade, the United States appeared to be the only nation in which the banking machinery was incapable of alleviating the conditions that developed in time of crisis. Strong pressure, partly political, was brought on Congress to pass some emergency legislation; and after a very brief study of the problem there was passed the Aldrich-Vreeland Act of 1908, which made possible the issuance—under the control of currency associations organized around the clearing-house associations as nuclei—of bank notes secured by state and municipal bonds or by commercial paper. This act was frankly passed as an *interim* measure, to expire at the end of five years; and during this interval it was hoped that a genuine re-organization of the banking system might be effected.

To this end the act provided for the establishment of a National Monetary Commission, composed of eighteen congressmen, which was instructed to make a thoroughgoing investigation of banking and currency reform and to frame a bill for the creation of a new and panic-proof banking system. Under the chairmanship of Senator Aldrich, this commission conducted a very extensive investigation, drawing upon the experience of the entire world. Public hearings were held in the leading financial centers of Europe; numerous experts were drafted to make special investigations on various aspects of the problem, both in the United States and abroad; and a number of books and monographs on special banking problems were reprinted and published as part of the commission's findings.[6]

Meanwhile other students of the question were also at work on plans for the re-organization of our banking system, and numerous proposals were advanced by independent students—bankers and economists—and many measures were introduced into Congress. The Aldrich bill, resulting from the investigations of the monetary commission, was presented to Congress in January, 1911. In brief, this bill provided for a new banking organization modeled rather closely after the central banking systems of Europe; but because of American opposition to centralization of power, particularly financial power, and because of the unfortunate experience in our early history in connection with the Second Bank of the United States, it was felt that a bill proposing the establishment of a central bank would have no chance of becoming a law. Accordingly, resort was had to camouflage and it was proposed to establish a national reserve association, with headquarters in Washington and with branches in various leading financial centers throughout the land. The Aldrich bill met with extremely vigorous opposition, however, and there was at no time much chance of its enactment into law. While embodying many excellent features, it also had certain important defects; moreover, it looked suspiciously like "un-American centralization of power." With the return of the Democratic party to power in 1912 it was obvious that a new approach was essential. Eventually the Federal Reserve system, providing for democratic organization and decentralized control, was evolved.

[6] About forty-five volumes of material were published.

2. The Character of Federal Reserve Regulation

Discussion of the organization and functioning of the Federal Reserve system is reserved for the following chapter. Our interest for the moment is merely in revealing the changing conception of the nature of the problem involved in regulating banking and credit operations. The Federal Reserve Act had two major objectives: The first was to provide an elastic bank note currency that would expand and contract with the varying requirements of business, in both seasonal and cyclical periods. This end was sought by providing for the issue of a new form of bank note currency known as Federal Reserve notes. The second objective was to provide for a better organization and control of the commercial credit system; indeed, an adequate control of credit was regarded as the primary need. Whereas 60 years earlier attention was centered entirely on bank note issues, the emphasis was now on deposit currency. It had become clear that in times of seasonal strain trade was sometimes halted for want of an elastic deposit currency, that in years of great industrial activity there were no effective means of restraining inflationary tendencies, and that when a crisis was reached there was little chance of escaping a banking panic for the reason that the credit structure was rigid and inelastic.

The new law sought to regulate and control the credit system in three principal ways. The first was by reemphasizing the importance of short-term commercial loans as the legitimate field of commercial bank enterprise. This end was to be accomplished by furthering the development of a general discount market, by featuring the use of bank and trade acceptances,[7] and by making it possible for member banks to borrow from the Federal Reserve banks only on the basis of commercial paper. Acceptances were given preferential rates; while "ineligibility" provisions pertaining to rediscounts placed non-commercial loans in a distinctly secondary position.

The second control expedient was the "mobilization" of reserves. By transferring a part of the reserves of individual banks to central reservoirs it was possible greatly to reduce the reserve requirements of the individual banks and at the same time to build up adequate central reserves which could be utilized as a basis for credit expansion in time of crisis. The third device was the use of interest rates as a means of controlling credit conditions. It was believed that by raising the rate at which member banks could borrow from reserve banks in periods of

[7] See discussion on page 268.

great business activity, the expansion would be restrained, and that similarly in periods of dull business a reduction in the rate of discount would serve to stimulate recovery. As we shall see in the ensuing chapter, emphasis upon the control of credit has been greatly increased in the post-war period, and refinements in the method of control have been attempted.

3. The Effort to Unify the Banking System

It was hoped also that the credit organization might be strengthened by articulating state commercial banks and trust companies with the Federal Reserve system. Indeed, it was felt that unless the banking system as a whole could be unified, the effort to control credit might break down. How could a system, half organized and half unorganized, effect any substantial control over the business cycle or prevent financial crises and panics? In a word, how could a financial house divided against itself stand?

A vigorous early effort was made to induce the state banks to join the system. The great advantages of membership were pointed out; and veiled threats were made to the effect that in case the state banks did not join, in time of crisis they would be unable to secure any assistance in meeting the strain to which they would be subjected. For a time, however, the state banks expressed strong opposition to the system—because of its double examinations, double reports, conflicting laws, unusual expenses, and possible curtailment of privileges.

Foreseeing the impossibility of inducing state institutions to enter the system if the broad powers that had been conferred upon them under state laws were curtailed, the Federal Reserve officials felt that the conditions of membership should not preclude state institutions from exercising their statutory rights under state laws as before. For example, they were permitted to continue making loans on real estate security without regard to the restrictions imposed upon the making of such loans by national banks; although the Board reserved the right to refuse entrance into the system to a state bank which had so large a percentage of its loans invested in real estate as to impair, in the view of the Board, its liquid condition. The state banks were also given permission to withdraw from the system on a year's (later changed to six months') notice if after a fair trial they did not find membership advantageous.

Shortly after the entrance of the United States into the World War a new drive for securing the membership of the state banks was undertaken. Mobilization was the task of the time, mobilization of the army and navy, mobilization of man power and woman power, mobilization of labor, mobilization of industrial resources. Why not, therefore—most important of all—mobilization of the nation's financial resources? President Wilson seized the psychological opportunity and issued a stirring appeal to state bankers to join the Federal Reserve system and thereby to effect a complete mobilization of the banking resources of the United States. He urged that "cooperation on the part of the banks is a patriotic duty at this time and membership in the Federal Reserve system is a distinct and significant evidence of patriotism."

While this appeal doubtless had no little effect, the credit strain to which the individual banks were already subjected was probably a more potent influence in inducing the state banks to affiliate with the Federal Reserve system. The expanding volume of business and the rising prices and costs necessitated access on the part of the state banks to the central repositories of reserve money. The apathy that had previously prevailed with reference to the rediscount privilege was thus changed as if by magic to the liveliest interest. It had become highly profitable to affiliate with the Federal Reserve system. The number of state bank and trust company members increased from 37 at the end of 1916 to 930 at the end of 1918. However, the goal of universal membership in the system was never even closely approximated. State bank membership continued to increase for a time after the close of the war, and reached its peak in 1922, when 1,639 state institutions belonged to the Federal Reserve system. During the next three years, the number of state bank members in the system declined to 1,513, and on October 4, 1929, the number was down to 1,148. The decrease in membership was due in part to failures of banks in the agricultural districts, to consolidations, and to the conversion of state into national banks; but in large part it was the result of withdrawals from the system. However, most of the large state institutions, including trust companies, were members. In 1937 the number of state banks and trust companies belonging to the Federal Reserve system was 1,058, or 11 per cent of all state banks; approximately 66 per cent of the total resources of state banking institutions were incorporated in the system.

Instead of a growing unification of the banking system under federal law, we find the national banking system declining in relative importance during the twenties. The withdrawal of state banks from the Federal Reserve system was paralleled by the surrender of national charters by many national banks and the taking out of new charters under state law. During the same period, comparatively few new banks were organized under national law. Whereas for many years the aggregate resources of the national banks had greatly exceeded the aggregate resources of state institutions, by 1924 the resources of the national banks were only 43 per cent of the total and by 1929 only 38 per cent. The relative numbers of national and state banks are shown in the chart on page 333. At the present time, however, the resources of the national banks comprise 44 per cent of the total assets of national and state institutions.

The threatened extinction of the national banks led to the passage of the so-called McFadden Banking Act of 1927, which amended the national banking laws for the purpose of enabling more effective competition with state banks. This act, as has already been noted, made it possible for national banks to make loans on real estate. Equally important was the permission granted to national banks to establish branches, which will be discussed in the following section.

4. Branches, Chains, and Consolidations

The outstanding feature of banking development in the latter part of the nineteenth century was, as we have seen, the development of varied types of financial operations under a single departmentalized institution. In the following period, particularly after 1920, the striking development was the great increase in the size of banking institutions and the extension of the geographic area in which they operated. In the decade of the twenties there was in fact a substantial abandonment of the principle of independent banking.

Branch banking.—In most countries of the world banking operations have long been conducted by a relatively few very large parent institutions with many branch offices. We have already noted that branch banking was the prevailing form of organization in the early history of the United States, but came into disrepute as a result of the wholesale failures accompanying the crisis of 1837; that the national banking system did not authorize the establishment of branches; and that by 1890 branch banking, though permitted under some state laws, was virtually non-existent in this country. After 1900 branch banking under state auspices began to show a substantial increase, particularly within urban communities. In 1910 there were 329 branches; in 1920 there were 1,052; and in 1928 there were 3,230, less than one-third of which were operated outside the home city of the parent institution. Eighteen states had no branches in operation, and only eleven states permitted state-wide branch banking. About 57 per cent of the branch banks of the country were reported by three states—California, New York, and Michigan—and about 46 per cent were in four cities—San Francisco, Los Angeles, New York, and Detroit. The greatest development was in California, where nearly two-thirds of the banking establishments in the state were branches of larger institutions.

The first step in the development of branch banking under federal law related to foreign banks. Some private banks had established foreign branches and the laws of a few states permitted the establishment of branches abroad. However, American banking continued to be provincial; by 1913 there were all told only 32 branches and offices located abroad. The Federal Reserve Act authorized, as we have seen in chapter XVII, the establishment of foreign branches and subsidiary banking corporations with a view to promoting foreign trade. However, as a result of fluctuating conditions in the field of international trade, the development of foreign branch banking has been much less extensive than had been anticipated. In 1936 there were only nine banks which operated foreign branches and the total number of offices abroad was only about two hundred.

The McFadden Banking Act of 1927 authorized the national banks to engage in branch banking on a limited scale, the provisions of the law being as follows:

If a State bank is hereafter converted into or consolidated with a national banking association, or if two or more national banking associations are consolidated, such converted or consolidated association may, with respect to any of such banks, retain and operate any of their branches which may have been in lawful operation by any bank at the date of the approval of the Act.

A national banking association may, after the date of the approval of this Act, establish and operate new branches within the limits of the city, town, or village in which said association is situated if such establishment and operation are at the time permitted to State banks by the law of the State in question.

No branch shall be established after the date of the approval of this Act within the limits of any city, town, or village of which the population by the last decennial census was less than twenty-five thousand. No more than one such branch may be thus established where the population, so determined, of such municipal unit does not exceed fifty thousand; and not more than two such branches where the population does not exceed one hundred thousand. In any such municipal unit where the population exceeds one hundred thousand the determination of the number of branches shall be within the discretion of the Comptroller of the Currency.

This act, it will be seen, was intended to permit the national banks to compete on even terms with the state banks with respect to the conduct of branch banking operations within a given city. It did not, however, authorize general branch banking, and hence it did not enable national banks to compete effectively with the state banks in those states where the law authorized a system of state-wide branch banking. While the competitive position of the individual banks was strengthened by the act, it did not accomplish the purpose of strengthening the general position of the national banking system as a whole.[8]

Chain or group banking systems.—The growth of group banking was a part of the chain movement which has played so large a part in American economic organization in recent years. It was also a part of the financial merger or consolidation movement of the twenties, and as such its objective was gains from security dealings rather than from banking operations. Three distinct types of chains have been differentiated: First, there was a group in which the dominant element was a particular bank exercising direct or indirect, but none the less definite, control over a number of other banks. Second, there were those in which a non-banking holding company, not subsidiary to any particular bank, was the dominant element. Third, there was a group in which the dominant control was exercised by a person or by a group of individuals operating independently of any bank. In terms of numbers of chains and banks involved, the third group was the most important; but in terms of resources the first was much the largest.

The peak of the movement was reached in 1929 when chain or group banks existed in all but nine states of the Union. The total number of chains was 272, involving 1,784 banks. In many cases operations were not confined to a single state or to national or state banks alone. The general magnitude of the chain banking movement is indicated by the fact that the total resources of the chain groups in 1929 comprised roughly one-sixth of the total banking resources of the country. As a result of the banking readjustments of recent years, however, the chain banking movement has been virtually killed.

The chain banking form of organization is inherently inferior to the branch banking system. It is extremely difficult to maintain adequate supervision over a chain of banks. State banking officials are powerless to prevent the buying-up of stocks for the purpose of forming a chain; and after the chain is in operation and recognized as such, it is often impossible for state bank examiners to ascertain the true condition of the chain as a whole. If the examination is to be of value, all the participants in the chain must be examined simultaneously. This is difficult enough when the members of the chain are all in a given state, or are all members of the national banking system; but when the units are under the jurisdiction of different states or when some of them are state banks and others national banks, adequate supervision becomes

[8] For the extent of branch banking in 1935 see page 359.

virtually impossible. The possibilities of evasion through the shifting of assets are greater than under the unit banking system. And, most important of all, the depositor in a unit of the chain banking system is not protected by the assets of the system as a whole.

The chain banking movement would probably not have developed had the McFadden Banking Act authorized the establishment of state and nation-wide branch banking systems. With the general trend of the times toward the linking-up of geographically separated companies into single units, and with the system of individual unit banks breaking down as a result of protracted economic difficulties in the agricultural sections of the country, some form of associated banking was apparently inevitable.

Banking consolidation.—Since the beginning of the present century the consolidation movement in the field of finance has more or less paralleled the similar trend in manufacturing, transportation, and commerce. The concentration of financial resources was effected to some extent by the organization, *de novo,* of banking institutions of very large size, but even more through a process of affiliation and consolidation of existing institutions. The period of most rapid evolution in this direction coincided with the era of industrial combination, namely, the fifteen years from 1897 to 1912. The total number of banks in New York decreased from 130 to 120 during the ten years from 1901 to 1911. In 1896 the largest bank in New York City had less than $30,000,000 of deposits; by 1911 there were six New York institutions with more than $100,000,000 each; while in the five years from 1907 to 1912, one New York trust company increased its deposits from $20,000,000 to $166,000,000. In the year 1911 there were ten banks in the United States with deposits in excess of $75,000,000 each, seven of them located in New York and two in Chicago.

A factor of no little importance in furthering the movement toward financial concentration, particularly in the years after 1907, was the desire to strengthen the financial structure and to render less abortive the efforts of the banks to co-operate in future emergencies for the control of financial crises.

The bank suspensions, in New York particularly, during the panic of 1907, emphasized the dangers created for the community at large by weak or ill-managed institutions in a central money market. Finally, the incidents of that panic—including the temporary breakdown of credit facilities, the distrust by banks of one another, the lack of quick and effective co-operation to relieve the crisis—taught the supreme necessity for a banking power strong enough to meet the worst emergency. Concentration of the banking resources at the country's money center is, in the absence of a central institution such as the

Bank of England, the only means of controlling, promptly and effectively, a crisis of that kind.[9]

It was shown by the Pujo investigation of 1912 that eighteen selected financial institutions were affiliated through a system of interlocking directorates with banks, trust companies, transportation systems, public-utility companies, and trading corporations, involving some 746 directorships in 134 corporations possessing aggregate resources of approximately 25 billion dollars.[10]

Interlocking financial directorates were made illegal by the Clayton Act of 1914. The practical outcome of the money-trust investigation was the passing of an act designed to break up the system of interlocking directorates, by providing that

no person shall at the same time be a director or other officer or employee of more than one bank, banking association, or trust company organized or operating under the laws of the United States, either of which has deposits, capital, surplus, and undivided profits aggregating more than $5,000,000; and no private banker or person who is a director in any bank or trust company, organized or operating under the laws of any state, having deposits, capital, surplus, and undivided profits aggregating more than $5,000,000, shall be eligible to be a director in any bank or banking association organized or operating under the laws of the United States.

While the Clayton Act was complied with through more or less complete readjustments of directorates among the institutions concerned, it did not defeat the financial consolidation movement any more than the Sherman Act prevented consolidations in other fields. Indeed, outright consolidation was not opposed; on the contrary it was favored by the Government in the well-founded belief that the tendency had been to establish too many small banks. In 1918 there was passed the Consolidation Act which made it possible for two or more national banks to consolidate directly, without first going through the process of liquidation. The McFadden Act of 1927 permitted national banks to consolidate with state institutions. This legislation served greatly to accelerate the consolidation movement. The result was a considerable decrease in the total number of banks, the elimination of many weak institutions, and the evolution of a number of metropolitan institutions of literally staggering size. The consolidations which were consummated during the thirties have been mainly for the purpose of preventing the collapse of distressed banks.

[9] Alexander D. Noyes, *Atlantic Monthly*, CXI (1913), 653.
[10] Report of the Committee appointed to investigate the concentration and control of money and credit, 62d Congress, 3d Sess.

This consolidation movement is in part attributable to the necessity of maintaining banks of a size commensurate with the huge business requirements of the modern age. The more striking cases are, however, in some measure the result of rivalry for prestige among a few outstanding institutions in each financial metropolis. A similar consolidation of financial institutions has occurred in other countries, notably in Germany, Great Britain and Japan.[11]

5. BANK FAILURES IN THE TWENTIES

In the period from 1900 to the World War bank failures were few in number, notwithstanding the defects of the banking system. In the fifty-year period from 1864 to 1913 the average annual number of national bank failures was 11. In 1913 there were four national bank suspensions, while 40 state and private banks closed their doors. In view of the safeguards instituted by the Federal Reserve system it seemed little short of incredible that we should suffer in the decade of the twenties a veritable holocaust of bank suspensions—the number of failures finding no parallel since the collapse of "wild cat" banking schemes in the thirties and forties of the past century. During the nine-year period from July 1, 1920, to June 30, 1929, inclusive, 4,925 banks, or more than 20 per cent of the total number, closed their doors, tying up deposits of approximately 1.5 billion dollars.[12] Of these institutions, 4,228 were state and private banks and 697 were national banks.

Except for 1920–1921 this decade was not a period of depression but one of great prosperity. The failures were more numerous in the later years than they were immediately after the financial collapse of 1920; in fact, over four-fifths of the suspensions occurred after 1923. The number of failures in the six fiscal years, 1924 to 1929 inclusive, aggregated 4,279, of which 550 were national institutions. In the main these failures were confined to small country banks, approximately 60 per cent of the suspended institutions having a capital of $25,000 or less, and only about 10 per cent having a capital in excess of $100,000. The distribution of failures from June 30, 1921, to June 30, 1929, is shown in the table on page 354. In seven states over 40 per cent of the banks in existence in 1920 failed in the ensuing nine years, and in six other states between 25 and 40 per cent closed their doors.

This epidemic of bank failures cannot be attributed solely to the system of unit banking, for we also had this system in the period when

[11] See chap. XXV.
[12] These figures do not include about 500 banks which were reopened after re-organization.

failures were few. Although the organization of a vast number of very small independent banks, located in small towns, managed by inexperienced personnel, and having little opportunity to diversify loans and investments, made for inherent weakness in the banking system, persistently adverse economic conditions were nevertheless necessary to bring disaster to hundreds of banks annually for a decade. Two

	State and Private	National
New England states...................	23	3
Eastern states........................	41	16
Southern states.......................	1,170	122
Middle Western states................	1,241	188
Western states.......................	1,572	305
Pacific states........................	180	63
Hawaii...............................	1	

developments were primarily responsible for the persistent deterioration of country banking.

The first was the agricultural situation. The farm boom of the War and early post-war years was accompanied by a great expansion of bank loans made on the basis of highly inflated land values. In the face of falling agricultural prices more or less throughout the twenties, borrowers were unable to liquidate their loans with expected regularity, and in many cases there was difficulty in meeting the interest. This situation was exactly the reverse of that which prevailed from the late nineties to 1920 when the prices of agricultural products were rising.

The second factor was the extension of automobile transportation throughout the country. With the speed of travel thus increased it was no longer necessary to have a bank in every hamlet; indeed it was unnecessary to have so many small towns, which had been laid out to meet the needs of horse and wagon travel. The chain stores which banked in the larger centers contributed to the transformation. It was thus desirable that a large number of banks in this country should be eliminated; and it was inevitable that a reduction would come sooner or later.

IV. BANKING DEVELOPMENTS SINCE 1930

The great depression which began in 1929 culminated in the winter of 1933 in as severe a banking crisis as the United States had ever known—the banks of the entire country finally suspending operations. The panic of 1933, however, differed in one fundamental respect from any preceding one in that, instead of coming at the beginning of and ushering in a business decline, it did not occur until the very end of the depression. The collapse of the banking structure in 1933 was a result rather than a cause of the depression.

It does not follow from this fact, however, that unsound banking practices before 1929 were not a contributory factor in bringing about the depression and particularly in intensifying the strain, once a business recession was under way. There is no doubt that the liberal extensions of credit for stock exchange speculation, and especially for urban real estate operations on the basis of inflated values and with inadequate margins, contributed greatly to the difficulties. Moreover, the collapse of suburban banks and branches in 1932 affords conclusive evidence as to the vulnerability of institutions whose assets are invested in quickly depreciable properties. Attention has elsewhere been called to the chain of economic events that finally led to the great collapse of bond values.[13]

Our interest here, however, is not in tracing the detailed steps in the banking debacle, but in indicating the ways in which the crisis as a whole reacted upon banking organization and regulation. We shall consider in turn the bank mortality rate, the re-organization of the banking structure during the crisis, significant legislation pertaining to the operation of individual banks, the renewed stimulus to branch banking, and the establishment of a deposit insurance system. Changes affecting the organization and operation of the Federal Reserve system will be considered in the next chapter.

1. BANK SUSPENSIONS AND RE-ORGANIZATIONS

In each succeeding year of the depression the number of bank suspensions increased, the culmination being reached in March 1933. The table on page 356 shows number of failures, the capital, and the deposits involved, during the fiscal years 1930 to 1937 inclusive, with a subdivision for the crisis year ending June 30, 1933. The failures since 1934 are in most cases merely belated deaths of institutions which had been nursed along since 1933.

The general suspension of bank operations—euphemistically designated a bank holiday—lasted nearly a fortnight, at the end of which all those which were clearly in sound condition were reopened. The number that were definitely labeled insolvent in the three days March 14–16, exceeded the total number of suspensions in the 48 years from 1864 to 1912. The assets of these banks and other doubtful institutions were administered by "conservators" appointed by the Government. In many cases the conservators were chosen from the

[13] See pp. 76–77.

banks' former officers, in order to have the benefit of their intimate acquaintance with the affairs of their institutions. Moreover, since banks which had been placed under conservators were not necessarily insolvent, it was desirable to keep intact as far as possible the existing organization.

Many of the distressed banks were regarded as generally sound, needing only a replenishment of capital. In order to provide this addi-

BANK SUSPENSIONS, 1930–1937

Year ended June 30—	Number			Capital (in millions of dollars)			Deposits (in millions of dollars)		
	All Banks	National	State and Private	All Banks	National	State and Private	All Banks	National	State and Private
1930............	766	73	693	42	6	35	314	45	269
1931............	1,542	210	1,332	145	26	119	1,039	188	851
1932............	2,397	432	1,965	218	56	162	1,680	405	1,275
1933 (to March 4, 1933)........	1,083	171	912	67	21	46	426	138	287
1933 (March 13, 14, and 15)......	2,630	290	2,340	241	23	218	1,855	151	1,704
Subtotal.......	8,418	1,176	7,242	713	132	580	5,314	927	4,386
1933 (March 16 to June 30).....	75	1	74	7.1	.1	7.0	81	.5	80.5
1934............	143	2	141	9.4	.1	9.3	85.1	.2	84.9
1935............	29	3	26	.8	.1	.7	5.0	1.0	4.0
1936............	45	2	43	2.0	.3	1.7	11.0	5.0	6.0
1937............	44	2	42	1.9	.2	1.7	14.0	2.0	12.0
Subtotal.......	336	10	226	21.2	.8	20.4	196.1	8.7	187.4
Grand Total......	8,754	1,186	7,468	733.2	132.8	600.4	5,510.1	935.7	4,573.4

tional capital Congress authorized national banks to issue preferred stock for sale either to local investors or to the Reconstruction Finance Corporation. Several states gave similar authorizations to state banking institutions. Banks which were not thus authorized to issue preferred stock received loans from the Reconstruction Finance Corporation, evidenced by "capital notes" or debentures. This process undoubtedly gave much needed aid to many banks with inadequate capital and frozen assets. Moreover, until such time as these loans were liquidated, the Government was in a position to exercise direct control over the operations of these banks. The aggregate amount of such capital advances was $1,059,235,103, of which $593,943,250 had not been repaid on June 30, 1937. (For loans to all banks and trust companies, see table on page 477.)

On the whole the process of conserving the assets of insolvent banks and of rehabilitating those which were in distress was well conceived and efficiently carried out.[14] By the end of 1934, of the 1,417 national banks which had not been permitted to reopen immediately after the banking holiday, 1,088 had been re-organized or absorbed by other national banks; 30 had been voluntarily liquidated, paying depositors in full; and 294 had been placed in receivership. A number of these have subsequently been reopened.

2. New Regulation of Individual Banks, 1933 and 1935

The breakdown of the credit structure resulted in the enactment of two laws embodying extensive revisions of the national banking system—the Banking Act of 1933 and the Banking Act of 1935. These laws were concerned rather more with strengthening the organization and effectiveness of the Federal Reserve system than with regulating the activities of member banks. There were, however, a number of provisions relating to member banks which should be noted at this place.

The Banking Act of 1933 contained a series of provisions designed to restrain commercial banks from participation in investment and speculative activities. It proscribed direct participation in underwriting. It forbade member banks to continue affiliations with institutions engaged principally in the underwriting and marketing of investment securities; and prohibited officers, directors, or employees connected with an investment banking institution from serving in similar capacity in any member bank, except with special permission of the Federal Reserve officials. Similarly, private banking houses, such as J. P. Morgan and Company, were compelled to choose between commercial banking and investment banking. The Act also provided that no member bank might serve as an agent for other business enterprises in making security loans to brokers or dealers in investment securities—a practice which had grown to enormous proportions in the stock market boom of 1926–1929. Finally, the Federal Reserve authorities were authorized to fix from time to time for the member banks of each Federal Reserve district the ratio of security loans to the capital and surplus of the banks.

This act also sought to control the specially organized holding companies by means of which many of the chains or "group" banks had been effectuated. It denied to such holding companies the right to vote the shares of stock in a member bank which they own without

[14] See Cyril B. Upham and Edwin Lamke, *Closed and Distressed Banks*, The Brookings Institution, 1934.

permission from the Federal Reserve authorities. Finally it provided for branch banking and for deposit insurance, which will be considered in the following sections.

The Banking Act of 1935, apart from its relations to the Federal Reserve organization and the deposit insurance system, is important chiefly because it liberalizes the provisions with respect to member bank loans on real estate. Whereas the banking legislation of 1933, which was strongly influenced by Senator Glass, tried to force banks into purely commercial banking operations, the Act of 1935, which reflects the views of Federal Reserve officials, stresses the importance of permitting national banks to participate in real estate financing. Governor Eccles has stated that "member banks hold about ten billion dollars of the peoples' savings, and it is therefore proper and necessary that they invest a part of their funds in long-term undertakings." It was urged that such loans were essential to the preservation of the banks, which were suffering from the competition of many government loan agencies. The law gave discretionary power to the Federal Reserve officials to permit banks to make loans on real estate on even more liberal terms than those authorized by the McFadden Act of 1927.

3. Renewed Impetus to Branch Banking

The trend toward branch banking was accelerated by the depression and by the accompanying bank failures. Though it has no bearing on the merits of the issue, it is interesting to note that the great crisis in the 1830's was attributed to the weaknesses of the branch banking system and led to the establishment of the unit banking system, while a hundred years later the failures of unit banks in a period of crisis stimulated renewed interest in branch banking. The Banking Act of 1933 permitted national banks to establish and operate branches on the same general conditions as those prescribed for state banks and trust companies in the states permitting branch banking. The only significant variation in the regulations is that national banks desiring to establish branches outside the home city must have a larger capital than is prescribed in the legislation of some states. The geographical range over which branches may be established is co-terminous with that provided for under the legislation of the various states: where state banks are granted the right to establish state-wide branches, national banks are accorded that right; but in states where branch banking is confined to city limits, the national banks must also operate branches only within the home city.

Thus the movement for branch banking has made some progress. In 1935 the number of national and state banks which operated branches was 3,930, or 21.5 per cent of the total. Of these 1,499 were national banks. In the case of both national and state banks, however, branch banking is, as a rule, confined to urban areas. It is obvious, therefore, that the United States does not as yet have anything approaching a genuine branch banking system.

A primary objection that has always been raised to branch banking is that the managers of the parent institutions inevitably possess inadequate knowledge of conditions in the local communities served by the branches and that credit extension comes to be determined by inflexible rules rather than by intimate knowledge of local needs and potentialities. That this contention has some measure of truth is scarcely to be denied; but there is also much to be said on the other side. First, the management of existing local banking institutions is commonly none too well acquainted with the principles of sound banking; and the introduction of approved credit methods properly adapted to rural and small-town conditions, would perhaps result in a reduction of losses. Second, the "intimate knowledge" and "close acquaintance" of the local banker are often too intimate and close, and thus make for the undoing of bank and customer alike. It is sometimes difficult for the banker to resist the boom psychology of his community, and for that matter to prevent his sympathies for an individual in distress from mastering his judgment. On the whole, credit has probably been extended too fully under our system of independent banking.

If the formation of branch banking systems is made subject to the approval of national and state banking authorities, and if each system is then subject to adequate supervision, the result should be to strengthen our general banking fabric. This would be particularly the case if the branches were not confined to the home community of the parent bank and were thus enabled to reap the advantages that come from geographic diversification of loans and investments. The balance of advantage clearly lies in permitting branch banking without regard either to state or to Federal Reserve district lines. Only thus can we complete the unification of our banking and credit system which is required in the interests of general business and financial stability.

4. INSURANCE OF BANK DEPOSITS

A movement in the direction of the insurance or guaranty of bank deposits had been under way in this country ever since the panic of 1907. Oklahoma, Nebraska, Kansas, Texas, Mississippi, Washington and the Dakotas had enacted systems of somewhat varying character, none of which had proved able to cope with the multitude of bank failures which occurred during the decade of the twenties. The breakdown of the entire credit structure during the great depression resulted in the evolution of a Federal Deposit Insurance system, which was authorized in the Banking Act of 1933 and perfected by the Act of 1935.

This law provided for the establishment of a Federal Deposit Insurance Corporation, the stock being contributed jointly by the United States Government and the Federal Reserve banks. The stock is non-voting and does not pay dividends. The Board of Directors consists of the Comptroller of the Currency and two appointed directors, one of whom acts as chairman and chief executive officer. The income of the Corporation is derived from two sources: (a) the interest on investments of about $300,000,000 in United States Government bonds; and (b) assessments levied on insured banks, amounting to one-twelfth of one per cent annually on their total deposits. The Corporation may prohibit the payment of interest on demand deposits and regulate the rate to be paid on time deposits and savings accounts.

The participants in the insurance plan include all member banks of the Federal Reserve system, and approved non-member state banks. The insurance for any one individual depositor is limited to $5,000. When an insured bank is closed the Corporation is required to pay the depositors as soon as possible. It automatically acts as receiver for closed national banks under the supervision of the Comptroller of the Currency, and may act as receiver for closed state banks if appointed by the proper state authority; in most cases this appointment is given. The number of suspensions of insured banks to June 30, 1937 was 98, and the aggregate deposits amounted to $21,617,000.

The Corporation was also authorized, until July 1, 1938, to make loans to banks in distress or to purchase their assets in order to facilitate a merger with another bank and thus avoid the necessity of liquidation. The Corporation may also purchase assets from insured banks and guarantee one insured bank against loss resulting from the assumption of the liabilities of another insured bank. These powers have been used to bring about absorptions and mergers with a view to increasing the strength of the banking structure and thus reducing the possible insurance risks.

Thus far the system has worked satisfactorily; but it remains to be seen whether it could withstand a strain comparable with that of the early thirties or even of the decade of the twenties. Fortunately the elimination of some fifteen thousand weak banks since 1921 has enormously lessened the dangers inherent in a mutual insurance system.

V. THE LESSON OF EXPERIENCE

The outstanding lesson taught by this long history of banking organization and regulation in the United States is the inherent weakness of the dual system under which banks are chartered both by the Federal Government and by the various state governments. The defects of the organization of banks on the basis of independent units might have been in substantial measure overcome through their affiliation with and control by the Federal Reserve institutions. But as long as banks were permitted to operate under widely varying laws, a sound system of regulation could never be assured. When two systems of banking are operating simultaneously in a country the bad system will tend to eliminate the good system, even as bad currency tends to drive good currency out of circulation. That is to say, instead of bringing state bank legislation up to the level of national banking regulations, competition served always to reduce the latter to the leve, of the former. The most serious developments were, on the one handl the multiplication of the number of national banks with small capital resources, inferior management, and restricted opportunities; and, on the other hand, the inability to induce the rank and file of the state banks to become members of the Federal Reserve system. Without a complete unification of the banking system it is impossible to develop a genuinely effective system of regulation. At every step in the evolution of both federal and state bank regulations it has been necessary to give quite as much heed to the competitive aspects as to the effects upon the soundness of the banking structure.

The control situation has, however, been somewhat improved by the extensive participation of state banks in the deposit insurance system. It would be still further improved if all state banks were compelled to become members of the Federal Reserve system, which would subject them at least to indirect forms of control. Counsel for the Federal Reserve system in 1932 expressed the view that there is no constitutional obstacle to legislation which would force all the banks of the country into a national system. The same end might be secured by a tax upon the checks of state banks, even as the law of 1866 taxed state bank note issues out of circulation. The real barrier to the unification of the banking system appears to be political in character.

CHAPTER XXIII

THE FEDERAL RESERVE SYSTEM

The establishment of the Federal Reserve system by an act of December 23, 1913 marked the beginning of a new era in American banking development. The significance of the Federal Reserve law, as was pointed out in the preceding chapter, lay not in regulations pertaining to the operation of individual banks, but in the machinery provided for transforming a decentralized banking system into one of centralized control—for co-ordinating the activities of a multitude of individual banks in such a way as to give flexibility to bank note and credit currency and at the same time safeguard the whole credit and business structure.

It has already become abundantly clear that the Federal Reserve system did not give us a unified banking system, prevent bank failures, or eliminate economic and financial crises. The fact that it proved unable to surmount the weaknesses inherent in the dual banking system, and to bring stability to a highly complex business system operating in the midst of world economic disorganization, does not of course prove that the system was ill-conceived or badly administered. On the whole, the Federal Reserve system has rendered a great service, the significance of which can be appreciated only by reflecting upon the conditions which might have prevailed had we continued to operate on the basis of the old decentralized banking system.

The Federal Reserve system has undergone many changes since it began operations in November 1914. In fact, scarcely any session of Congress has closed without the addition of some amendments to the Federal Reserve Act. It was not until the 1930's, however, that sweeping changes in the structure and control mechanism of the reserve system were made. These changes apply not only to rediscount and open market operations, reserve requirements, and other technical problems relating to credit control, but also to the administrative framework of the system. In order to simplify the discussion, we shall concentrate on a description of the existing organization and operation of the Federal Reserve system, referring to the earlier organization only in so far as is necessary to clarify the major problems involved.

362

I. ADMINISTRATIVE FRAMEWORK OF THE SYSTEM

The organization of the Federal Reserve system as a whole is shown by the diagram on page 365. It will be noted that the supervisory organization consists of a Board of Governors, flanked by an Open Market Committee, and a Federal Advisory Council, and that there are twelve Federal Reserve banks located in financially strategic centers. Each of the Federal Reserve banks is managed by a separate Board of Directors. We may conveniently begin with a brief statement about the Federal Reserve banks themselves, and then consider the organization of the system as a whole.

1. *The Federal Reserve banks.*—The Federal Reserve Act divided the United States into twelve districts, chosen in the light of financial and commercial conditions as well as with a view to geographic distribution. The map on page 366 shows the boundaries of the twelve districts and the cities in which are located the Federal Reserve banks which constitute the units of the system. Several of the Federal Reserve banks have branches which operate in different parts of the districts, each branch usually having a portion of the district assigned to it. At present twenty-three branches and one domestic agency are in operation. In addition, two agencies have been established in Cuba, one by the Federal Reserve Bank of Atlanta and one by the Federal Reserve Bank of Boston.

The capital of the Federal Reserve banks was subscribed by the member banks of each district, each bank subscribing a sum equal to six per cent of its own paid-up capital stock and surplus. One-half of the subscription, or three per cent, has actually been paid in by the member banks, the remaining three per cent being subject to call. In view of the present large resources, it is doubtful whether the member banks will ever be called upon to pay the remainder of their subscriptions. Capital contributions were compulsory for the national banks that joined the system, but it was optional with each bank whether or not it should join. Only in one sense was there any compulsion: a national bank had to join the system if it remained a national bank; but it could surrender its charter as a national institution if it so desired and either take out a state charter or suspend operations.

The number of banks in each Federal Reserve district and the paid-in capital and surplus of each Federal Reserve bank on December 31, 1937 are shown in the table on page 364.

The Federal Reserve banks are managed by boards of directors, democratically chosen, and representing various group interests. The law provides that one-third of the board of nine members shall be known as Class A, one-third as Class B, and one-third as Class C directors. The Class A directors are chosen by and are representative of the stockholding member banks. The Class B directors must consist of individuals who at the time of their election are actively engaged in their district in some commercial, agricultural, or industrial pursuit. The Class C directors are selected by the Board of Governors of the Federal Reserve system, which is in effect the representative of the

District	Number of Member Banks	Capital of Reserve Banks (000 omitted)	Surplus of Reserve Banks (000 omitted)
Boston.............	357	$ 9,386	$ 12,774
New York..........	776	51,058	59,687
Philadelphia........	655	12,258	17,877
Cleveland..........	622	13,036	15,330
Richmond..........	405	4,896	8,373
Atlanta............	324	4,401	6,356
Chicago............	769	12,920	23,816
St. Louis...........	392	3,868	5,212
Minneapolis........	469	2,893	4,154
Kansas City........	733	4,091	4,755
Dallas.............	547	3,891	5,162
San Francisco.......	292	10,046	11,926
Total............	6,341	$132,744	$175,422

United States Government, and hence of all of the people. One of the Class C directors is called the Federal Reserve Agent and is the personal representative of the Board of Governors. It is his function to represent the Board of Governors in the management of the Reserve bank. Although the directors are thus chosen from special groups, as directors they must act as a unit and in the interests of the general financial welfare, as they see it. Two of the members of the Board of Directors belonging to Class C, act, however, in a dual capacity. The Federal Reserve Agent and the deputy Federal Reserve Agent are also representatives of the Board of Governors and have certain special duties to perform in this capacity.[1]

In still another way the act endeavored to secure a democratic organization and control. To insure against the domination of the board of directors by the larger and more powerful banks, the law provides that the banks shall be divided into three general groups, each group to contain roughly one-third of the aggregate number of member banks. Group number 1 would consist of banks of the largest capitalization; group number 3 would include the smallest banks of the district; and group number 2 the banks of intermediate size. Each of these groups of banks nominates and elects one Class A and one Class B

[1] See pp. 371 and 375.

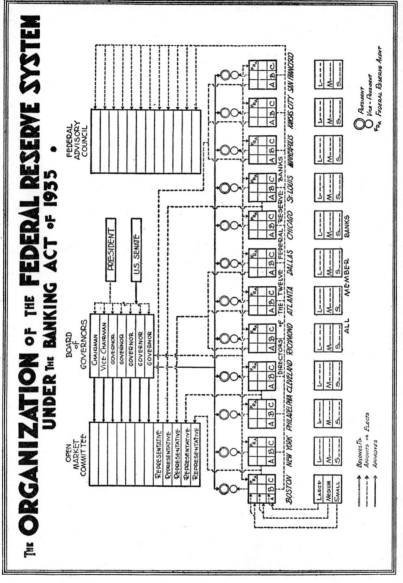

The ORGANIZATION of THE FEDERAL RESERVE SYSTEM UNDER THE BANKING ACT of 1935

(Prepared by American Bankers Association.)

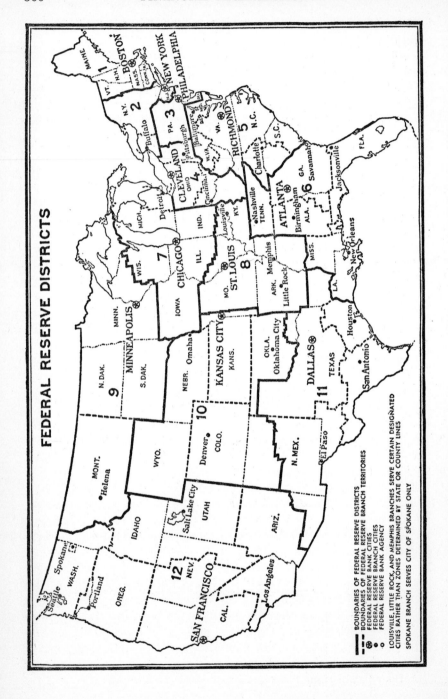

director. The directors thus represent not only the stockholding banks, but also the different classes of banks.

The original Federal Reserve Act made no provision for the chief executive officer of a Federal Reserve bank. In the course of time, it became the practice for the board of directors to select such an officer. He was known as the Governor of the bank, and was not a member of the board of directors. In a number of the Federal Reserve banks there was formed an Executive Committee, consisting of several members of the board of directors and the governor. In most Federal Reserve banks, the governor exercised more power than did the Federal Reserve Agent who acted as chairman of the board of directors. The position of chief officer was given legal recognition in the Banking Act of 1935, receiving the title of President. This officer is appointed for a term of five years by the board of directors of a Federal Reserve bank, the choice being subject to the approval of the Board of Governors of the Federal Reserve system (see chart, page 365). At the end of five years, the Board of Governors may again pass on the reappointment of the president of the bank. Similarly the first vice-president of the Federal Reserve bank must receive the approval of the Board of Governors; his term of office is also five years. The other vice-presidents and officers are appointed without the approval of the Board of Governors.

2. *The Board of Governors.*—The co-ordinating and controlling agency of the system as a whole is the Board of Governors. This board consists of seven members appointed by the President of the United States, with the approval of the Senate. Each member serves for a single term of fourteen years and may not serve for a second term. The principal officer is designated Governor and is appointed "to serve as such until the further order of the President." Under the Banking Act of 1935, both the Secretary of the Treasury and the Comptroller of the Currency, hitherto ex officio members of the Board, were removed. The removal of the former was urged on the ground that, in the past, he had exercised undue influence in the formulation of Reserve policy, favoring the interests of the Treasury rather than the credit needs of the country as a whole.

In successive amendments to the original Federal Reserve Act, the qualifications of the members of the Board had from time to time been changed. The Banking Act of 1935 restored the original qualification that the President in selecting members for the Board of Governors shall have "due regard to a fair representation of the financial, agricultural, industrial and commercial interests and geographical divisions of the country." It is further required that not more than one member of the Board shall come from any one Federal Reserve district.

The powers and duties of the Board of Governors are, in brief, as follows: It may suspend or remove any officer or director of a Federal Reserve or a member bank; it may suspend a Federal Reserve bank and take charge of it for the purpose of re-organization or liquidation; it may readjust or abolish altogether the classification of central reserve and reserve cities. It also has power to give preference to certain types of financial operations, and in various ways to modify and influence financial conditions. For the moment, however, we are not concerned with the details of the operations of the Board, the present purpose being merely to show its general relation to the system and to note that it is a co-ordinating and controlling agency.

3. *The Federal Advisory Council.*—As the name suggests it is the function of this council to assist the Board of Governors in its deliberations. The Council consists of one representative from each Federal Reserve district, chosen by the Board of Directors of the Federal Reserve bank of that district. This Council meets quarterly in Washington and at such other times and places as it may choose. Its function is purely consultative, the theory being that the intimate contact of its members with business and financial conditions in various parts of the country enables such a group to assist the Board of Governors to a better understanding of the economic and credit situation as a whole.

4. *The Open Market Committee.*—While it was intended that the primary business of the Federal Reserve banks be with their constituent member institutions, they have always had some connections with the general money market. The latter are known as "open market operations," and relate principally to the purchase and sale of bonds and acceptances. As we shall later see, these open market operations in due course came to be regarded as a very important means of controlling the volume of credit.

Although the original Federal Reserve Act provided that such open market operations were subject to the "rules and regulations prescribed by the Federal Reserve Board," in actual practice Federal Reserve banks themselves, particularly the Federal Reserve Bank of New York, assumed the direction of these policies. The Federal Reserve Board made serious efforts over the years to regain its authority, and finally, in the Banking Act of 1935, an Open Market Committee was provided for, consisting of the seven members of the Board of Governors and five representatives of the Federal Reserve banks. The latter are elected annually.

II. CREATING AN ELASTIC BANK NOTE CURRENCY

Among the defects to be remedied by the new banking system was the inelasticity of the bond-secured bank note currency. The Federal

Reserve Act met this problem, not by a complete elimination of the bond-secured notes, but by the creation of an additional form of note currency—one secured by commercial paper, or "assets." Indeed, as a result of this law there were three types of bank notes in the United States: (1) national bank notes (secured by government bonds, as before); (2) Federal Reserve bank notes (secured by government bonds); (3) Federal Reserve notes (secured by commercial paper). The third was a distinctly new form of currency, designed to give elasticity to the bank note system.

1. *National bank notes.*—During the period when the Federal Reserve bill was before Congress it was suggested that the national bank notes be entirely eliminated. It was found difficult to accomplish this, however, without involving heavy losses for the banks which had outstanding bond-secured currency. The two per cent government bonds, which were used chiefly as security for the national bank notes, had a market value substantially equal to the par value only by virtue of the fact that they carried the circulation privilege. Taking away from the bonds this privilege would have meant a fall in their value of approximately one-third; and for the national banks as a whole this would have involved a loss of over 200 million dollars. The opposition of the banks to the proposal to withdraw the circulation privilege from the two per cent government bonds was so vigorous that it was deemed expedient to adopt some other means of securing the ends desired.

A plan was finally worked out whereby a gradual retirement of the national bank notes could be effected. It was provided that any member bank which desired to retire any or all of its circulating notes might, through the intermediation of the United States Treasury, sell to a Federal Reserve bank at par the bonds which were serving as security. Under this plan the Federal Reserve bank which purchased the bonds pays the Treasury, and the Treasury agrees to use this money to redeem the outstanding national bank notes that had been secured in the past by these bonds. However, the banks were unwilling to retire their notes, and as late as 1932 the total volume outstanding was still about 700 million dollars or a reduction of only 14 millions from the amount outstanding when the Federal Reserve Act was passed. In 1935 the government took definite steps to retire all national bank currency by the simple expedient of calling for redemption the remaining issues of United States government bonds which carried the circulating privilege. 642 million dollars of the profits derived from gold devaluation were used for this purpose.[2]

[2] The Glass-Borah law of 1932, passed as a rider to the Home Loan Bank Act, in the hope of checking deflation had extended the circulation privilege to all United

2. *Federal Reserve bank notes.*—These notes owed their origin to the effort to provide for the retirement of the national bank notes. The plan merely involved transferring the bond-secured notes from the individual banks to the Federal Reserve banks. Each reserve bank was also authorized to issue additional notes up to the amount of its capital stock, but at the same time the gradual retirement of these notes was provided for by permitting the two per cent bonds, carrying the note issue privilege, to be exchanged for Treasury notes bearing a higher rate of interest, but without the circulating privilege. These notes have never been an important part of our banking and currency system and are being gradually retired. The amount outstanding in April 1938 was only 31 million dollars.[3]

3. *Federal Reserve notes.*—The process by which the Federal Reserve notes, which were designed to provide the elastic element in our bank note system, were issued may now be considered. Although the elasticity feature, as we shall presently see, was abandoned in 1932, it is essential that we analyze the various steps in the evolution and transformation of this new form of bank currency. The method of issue and retirement provided in the original law can best be made clear by a concrete illustration.

Let us assume that there is a heavy demand for additional bank note currency with which to market the crops, and that some of this demand is manifested at the First National Bank of Ottumwa, Iowa. How can this bank expand the volume of Federal Reserve note issues? The Federal Reserve law provides that a bank desiring to issue reserve notes may do so upon the security of commercial paper rediscounted with the Federal Reserve bank of its district. Accordingly, the Ottumwa bank indorses over to the Federal Reserve Bank of Chicago, say, a $10,000 promissory note of one of its customers, Mr. Jones, to whom a commercial loan has been made. The reserve bank of Chicago will give the Ottumwa bank Federal Reserve notes equal to the face value of Jones's note less the interest for the time which it has yet to run. The term "rediscounting" is used in this connection to indicate that a note which was originally discounted by a member bank is now discounted a second time. In a word, the Federal

---

States government bonds bearing interest at less than 3⅜ per cent. While 119 million dollars of additional notes were issued, they merely replaced other currency in circulation; and deflation continued.

[3] The Glass-Borah law of 1932 (see footnote 2) authorized the issue of these notes, on either government bonds or commercial paper as collateral. Over 200 million dollars of these notes were issued in the ensuing year; but they are now being replaced by Federal Reserve notes.

Reserve bank thus does for the member bank precisely what the member bank does for its customers—advances the face value of the note, less interest until maturity.

Before the notes can be issued by the Federal Reserve bank, however, the promissory note that has been received (or other notes of like quality and amount) must be placed in the custody of the Federal Reserve Agent of the Chicago Federal Reserve bank, who, it will be recalled, is the representative of the Federal Government on the directorate of the Federal Reserve bank. This agent has in his possession Federal Reserve notes that have been printed in advance; and upon receipt of the commercial paper he turns over to the Federal Reserve bank the quantity of notes demanded. The Federal Reserve bank then sends these notes to the Ottumwa bank, which is thereupon in a position to lend them to the individuals who are in need of seasonal funds.

It will make for clearness if we consider precisely how this operation will affect the balance sheet of the Ottumwa bank and of the Federal Reserve Bank of Chicago respectively. When the Ottumwa bank sends its customer's note to Chicago, its "Loans and discounts" are lessened by the amount of the note. The "Federal Reserve notes" received in exchange for the customer's note are carried as assets of the Ottumwa bank until such time as they are loaned to a customer, when "Federal Reserve notes" are decreased and "Loans and discounts" are increased by a like amount. As for the Federal Reserve bank, the rediscount has given it possession of a customer's note, which is carried as an asset under "Rediscounts." The "Federal Reserve notes" issued against the security of this commercial paper of course become liabilities of the Federal Reserve bank.

Thus we have secured an expansion of bank notes. It may be noted, moreover, that the new loan which the Ottumwa bank now makes gives rise to a new customer's note, which, if it has resulted from an ordinary commercial operation, is also available for rediscount with the Federal Reserve Bank of Chicago, and thus may likewise be used as a basis for still further issues of Federal Reserve notes. Thus as long as there continue to be commercial transactions which require the use of borrowed funds, the promissory notes arising out of these transactions will provide the basis for the additional currency required in financing them. Here is the same sort of expansibility that we have elsewhere found to characterize deposit currency.

It remains to consider the process by means of which Federal Reserve notes, thus issued, are reduced in volume when the need for them is past. For the purpose of illustration, let us consider the specific

$10,000 of Federal Reserve notes that were put into circulation by the Ottumwa bank. The individual who borrowed these notes uses them in meeting his obligations, and the individuals who receive them either deposit them directly in banks or use them in the payment of debts to traders and others, who in turn send them to their banks for deposit. They are now out of the channels of circulation; but they have not been returned to the Federal Reserve Bank of Chicago. What insures their return to their source?

We have seen that the Ottumwa bank secured funds from the Federal Reserve Bank of Chicago by the rediscount of a promissory note of Mr. Jones, one of its customers. At the maturity of this note, it will be sent to Mr. Jones for payment, by way of the First National Bank of Ottumwa. Jones will pay the necessary funds over to the Ottumwa bank in whatever way is most convenient for him. And, similarly, the Ottumwa bank will pay the Federal Reserve bank in whatever way is most convenient. Now the most convenient and least costly way for the Ottumwa bank to remit, is, in fact, by sending in any paper money, including Federal Reserve notes, which it has on hand. From this paper money, and other paper money sent in by other banks, the Chicago Reserve bank can sort out and retire the Federal Reserve notes. The Federal Reserve bank is, in fact, constantly receiving and paying out paper money, and the process of selecting notes to be retired is a simple matter. Since the national banks are not permitted by law to keep any of their legal reserve in their own vaults, they will always send their cash, above that needed for till money, to the Reserve bank of their district.

Suppose, now, that some of the notes issued through the Ottumwa bank should find their way into a national bank in Oskaloosa, Iowa. Will they then be returned to the Chicago bank for collection? The answer is that they will, for the reason that whenever it has occasion to make payments to the Federal Reserve Bank of Chicago (and such occasions are constantly arising) the Oskaloosa, like the Ottumwa, bank will use paper money, including Federal Reserve notes, for the purpose. It does not matter, therefore, what bank in the district receives the notes; they will always be sent in payment of obligations to the bank which issued them.

It is possible, however, that some of the notes that have been put into circulation in Ottumwa, Iowa, might find their way into banks in other than the Seventh Federal Reserve District. Concretely, let us suppose that some of them are sent in payment of obligations to the First National Bank of Akron, Ohio. Will they now be returned to the Federal Reserve Bank of Chicago for redemption? They will not, in fact, be sent directly to Chicago, for the Akron bank has no direct relations with the Chicago reserve institution. The Akron bank will, however, send these notes to the Federal Reserve Bank of Cleveland, whenever it has payments to make there. When these notes arrive at the Cleveland Federal Reserve Bank, they may be listed as assets of that bank; for they are liabilities only of the particular reserve bank which issued them. What, now, is to prevent the Federal Reserve Bank of Cleveland from again putting these notes into circulation and thereby preventing their redemption at the source of issue?

Incorporated in the law is a simple provision which insures their being sent to the Federal Reserve bank which issued them. It is provided that any Federal Reserve bank which pays out notes of other reserve banks shall be subject to a tax of 10 per cent of the value of the notes thus paid out. Since this tax destroys the profit that might be obtained from lending these notes, it insures their presentation to the Reserve bank which issued them, in payment of obligations due or in exchange for specie.

In the effort to give Federal Reserve notes an elastic quality the question of safety was not overlooked. In the illustration above Mr. Jones had given his promissory note to the Ottumwa bank. Now the Ottumwa bank had extended the credit to Jones on the strength of his business integrity and ability and his general financial standing. There is thus, first, a property security, presumably sufficient to insure the payment of the loan by Jones. In the second place, there is additional security in that the Ottumwa bank, when rediscounting Jones's note, indorses it and thus becomes secondarily liable for its payment. In the third place, the Federal Reserve notes are the liability of the Federal Reserve bank which issues them; and as such they have a prior lien upon all of the bank's assets. Moreover, the law requires that for every $100 of Federal Reserve notes issued, the Federal Reserve bank must hold a reserve of at least $40 in gold. Finally, these notes are the direct obligation of the United States Government. It is said that this provision was incorporated to please the still powerful political leader, William Jennings Bryan, who insisted that the Federal Reserve currency must be equivalent to government currency. In any event, all the taxable resources of the nation have been placed back of the Federal Reserve notes.

In the foregoing illustration of the elasticity of Federal Reserve notes we have been giving the impression that these notes are secured exclusively by commercial paper. Such, however, is not strictly the case, although the theory of the law was undoubtedly to make such paper the fundamental basis of the elastic note currency. The provi-

sions governing paper that is eligible as security for note issues have in
the main been identical with those governing paper that is eligible for
rediscount in general. These provisions have been continually broadened as the years have passed. Rediscounts may now be made on the
basis of "any sound assets." Other changes affecting the reserve notes
will be considered in the following section.

III. THE CONTROL OF CREDIT

A fundamental weakness of our national banking system, as we
have seen, was the lack of any adequate machinery for the control of
credit, or deposit currency, and hence for the control of business in
general. In times of seasonal strain trade was sometimes halted for
want of an elastic deposit currency; in years of great industrial activity
there were no effective means of restraining business commitments and
preventing thereby the development of conditions of acute crisis; and
when the crisis arrived, there was little chance of escaping a panic for
the reason that the credit structure was rigid and inelastic. The problem
of credit control, therefore, divides itself into three parts: (1) providing
the requisite amount of funds for seasonal business requirements; (2)
checking expansion of currency during the upward swing of the business cycle, at the beginning of a critical business situation; and (3)
expanding loans in time of acute crisis in order to tide the business
world over the period of tension. The Federal Reserve Act has attempted to provide the means for meeting all of these requirements.

1. THE MOBILIZATION OF RESERVES

The control of credit under the Federal Reserve system has been
made possible largely by means of what is commonly termed "the
mobilization of the reserves" of the banking system. This mobilization
of reserves has been effected in a variety of ways. It was of course
necessary, first, to divert a considerable portion of our monetary supply
from individual banks to Federal Reserve institutions. This shifting
was accomplished in part by requiring each member bank to subscribe
to the capital stock of the Federal Reserve bank of its district; in part
by requiring the member banks to keep their lawful reserves with
the Federal Reserve institutions;[4] and in part by exchanging Federal
Reserve notes for gold and gold certificates. Some government deposits
were also made with the Federal Reserve banks.

The exchange of Federal Reserve notes for gold and gold certificates
requires a word of explanation. It should be understood that Federal

---

[4] The original law required only part of the reserve to be so kept, but it was
amended later to include the entire minimum reserve

Reserve notes, once issued on the basis of commercial paper, were not necessarily retired when the underlying commercial paper matured; the notes could be kept in circulation provided the Federal Reserve bank turned over to the Federal Reserve Agent a like volume of gold or gold certificates. During the war period, in an endeavor to concentrate the gold supplies of the country in the central reservoirs provided by the Federal Reserve banks, the Reserve officials adopted a deliberate policy of exchanging Federal Reserve notes for gold and gold certificates, these notes thereby finding a wide use in the channels of circulation in place of the gold and gold certificates.

The issue of Federal Reserve notes in exchange for gold and gold certificates gave to the Federal Reserve banks a greatly increased capacity for note and credit expansion. On the basis of the gold secured by this process, a Federal Reserve bank could issue notes to two and one-half times the volume of gold on hand (the reserve required against notes being 40 per cent), and nearly three times the volume of deposit currency (the reserve required against deposits being 35 per cent). It should be understood, in this connection, that the gold and gold certificates exchanged for Federal Reserve notes, and held by the Federal Reserve Agent, still counted as reserves against outstanding notes.

This policy of concentrating the gold supply of the country in the Federal Reserve banks in order to make it available for a larger superstructure of credit than would be possible if it remained widely scattered in the vaults of individual banks, in the cash tills of a multitude of business enterprises, and in the pockets of innumerable individuals, was dictated by the enormous financial requirements of the war. With our gold resources thus effectively mobilized, it was believed, not without good reason, that we should be able to meet almost any financial demands that might be imposed upon us. In fact, this concentration of reserves, and the provision for their effective use which we are presently to consider, made possible an enormous expansion in the total quantity of both notes and deposit currency. The effect of these developments upon the reserves of the Federal Reserve banks is reflected in the chart on page 398.[5]

The final means of expanding the potential superstructure of credit was by reducing the reserve requirements of member banks. The

[5] After 1921, however, the gold reserves of the Federal Reserve banks were much larger than the business situation required. As a means of reducing the "menace" of excessive reserves, the Federal Reserve notes were retired and gold certificates were issued to take their place in the channels of circulation, thus again reducing the credit expanding capacity of the Reserve banks.

original act permitted a reduction from 25 to 18 per cent in the central reserve cities, from 25 to 15 per cent in the reserve cities, and from 15 to 12 per cent in the country banks. But after the great concentration of reserves that was brought about by the substitution of Federal Reserve notes for gold and gold certificates, these requirements were still further reduced—to 13, 10, and 7 per cent against demand deposits in banks in central reserve cities, reserve cities, and country towns, respectively; in each class of banks three per cent was required against time deposits. It should be observed, however, that since it was required that these minimum reserves should be kept entirely in the vaults of the Federal Reserve institutions, cash for till money purposes constituted an addition to these minimum reserve requirements.

Since no interest was paid on these reserve balances it was for years the practice of the member banks to carry actual reserves with the Federal Reserve bank but little in excess of the legal requirements. As late as 1932 the excess reserves, or the difference between the actual reserves and the legal reserves, amounted to only 35 million dollars. In recent years, however, because of the great importation of gold from abroad and the slack demand for funds, these reserves have become so excessive as to necessitate a modification of reserve policies. These changes will be considered on pages 411–416.

Under the former system the reserves of central reserve city banks constituted the central reservoirs of credit for use in times of emergency. As we have noted elsewhere, these reserves seldom proved adequate to meet acute tension in the money market; at best they were little in excess of the legal minimum requirements, and often they fell below. With the mobilization of reserves under the Federal Reserve system, not only could the minimum reserve requirements of the member banks be much lower, but those of the Federal Reserve banks could be much higher—40 per cent instead of 25 per cent. Under the Federal Reserve system, moreover, reserves have never fallen to the minimum requirements, though there was a near approach to the minimum in 1920. (See page 395.) Throughout most of the history of the Federal Reserve system the reserves of the Federal Reserve banks have been very much above the 40 per cent level, as is indicated by the chart on page 398.

Whether or not this economizing of reserves constitutes a real gain, depends of course upon the way in which these reserves are used in controlling the credit system along the lines suggested above. We must now, therefore, consider the machinery of credit control that was provided in the original law.

2. Providing Credit Currency for Seasonal Requirements

We found in the preceding chapter that in times of great seasonal activity the volume of bank reserves is not always sufficient to permit an expansion of bank loans and thus of deposit currency. Under the Federal Reserve system, however, it is always possible for an individual bank in need of funds to secure them from the Federal Reserve bank of its district by the rediscount of commercial paper, or the sale of acceptances in the market. We have already seen that such rediscounts may be made the basis for an issue of Federal Reserve notes; but in the present case, instead of taking notes, which are not available as reserve, the member bank receives a deposit account with the Federal Reserve bank which counts as cash in hand, and thus serves as a basis on which additional loans may be made. As long, therefore, as member banks have paper eligible for rediscount and as long as the Federal Reserve banks maintain adequate lending power through keeping large reserves, there can never be any possibility that the supply of deposit currency will prove inadequate for seasonal needs. The weak links in the banking chain are thus immeasurably strengthened and the supply of credit is made responsive to seasonal requirements.

Moreover, as soon as the seasonal strain is passed, such deposit currency automatically contracts; for when the loans which were procured in order to finance the seasonal requirements are paid, checks are drawn against deposit accounts in favor first of the member banks and then of the Federal Reserve institutions, thereby reducing the volume of outstanding deposit accounts. Such deposits will, moreover, not reappear until there is a fresh demand for funds to be used in connection with new business transactions.

3. Controlling Business Expansion

Checking an expansion of currency at the beginning of a critical business situation involved a somewhat different mechanism. When the first signs of business stress and financial strain appear, when it becomes clear that further expansion will carry in its train an inevitable credit collapse, it was believed that the brakes might be applied to industry in such a way as to cause a gradual rather than a precipitate readjustment of business conditions.

It was believed that there were two instrumentalities by means of which the business cycle might be effectively controlled. The first was the interest rate or, more precisely, the rate at which the Federal

Reserve banks rediscount the paper of member banks. As long as we had an independent banking system, with each bank acting largely on its own initiative, it was impossible to secure any concerted action in the control of the discount rate, that is, in raising the rate as a means of checking business expansion, for the reason that it did not appear to many banks to be necessary to restrict loans, and thus forego profits. Moreover, an agreement, if adopted, would probably raise the charge that the bankers were attempting to profiteer at the expense of business generally. Under the Federal Reserve system, however, a quick raising of interest rates may be effected through the action of the Board of Governors which cannot fairly be criticized as attempting to serve profit-making ends of its own.

The means by which the Board of Governors may secure a general increase in the interest rates are very simple. The Board is given the power of fixing the rates at which the Federal Reserve institutions may make loans to member banks, as also the rates which they shall pay when lending funds in the general market through the purchase of acceptances, etc. At a time when all member banks are finding it necessary to borrow from Federal Reserve banks the funds required to meet the demands of customers, a raising of the rates at which they borrow promptly results in the raising of discount rates by member banks to their clients.

The purpose of this raising of interest rates is to make the conduct of business more costly, to narrow the margins of profit, and hence to apply the brakes to further industrial expansion and bring about a gradual readjustment. In a word, it was believed that the Board of Governors, acting on an understanding of the phenomena of the business cycle, could through the instrumentality thus placed in its hands exercise an effective control over business conditions. If successful, such a policy would mean that the last stage in the upward swing of the business cycle would be eliminated—and with it, of course, the abundant employment and large profits which are enjoyed at such a period. But, on the other hand, it would prevent an economic collapse such as occurred in the past when business was allowed to continue its rapid expansion to the breaking-point, that is, to the point of complete exhaustion of the bank reserves; and it would bring about a business readjustment more gradual in its nature and hence involving less serious results to both capital and labor than would be the case if the upward swing were allowed to continue for a longer period.

The second means that was provided for the control of credit was known as open market operations. Under the original law every Federal Reserve bank was specifically empowered:

a) To deal in gold coin and bullion at home or abroad, to make loans thereon, to exchange Federal Reserve notes for gold, gold coin, or gold certificates, and to contract for loans of gold coin or bullion, giving therefor, when necessary, acceptable security, including the hypothecation of United States bonds or other securities which Federal Reserve banks are authorized to hold.

b) To buy and sell, at home or abroad, bonds and notes of the United States, and bills, notes, revenue bonds, and warrants with a maturity from date of purchase of not exceeding six months, issued in anticipation of the collection of taxes or in anticipation of the receipt of assured revenues by any state, county, district, political subdivision, or municipality in the continental United States.

c) To purchase from member banks and to sell, with or without their indorsement, bills of exchange arising out of commercial transactions.

d) To purchase and sell in the open market at home or abroad either from or to domestic or foreign banks, firms, corporations, and individuals, cable transfers and bankers' acceptances, and bills of exchange of the kinds and maturities by this act made eligible for rediscount with or without the indorsement of a member bank.

This power to deal in gold coin and bullion at home and abroad made it possible for the Federal Reserve banks to bid for gold at the weekly auction of gold in London or elsewhere, and thus to strengthen our own gold position in case of necessity. This gold may be paid for either by the sale of securities held by the Federal Reserve banks or by means of the purchase of foreign bills of exchange. The borrowing of gold on acceptable security is also designed to give the Federal Reserve banks a greater control over the nation's gold supply, by preventing an outflow of specie at critical periods. If this gold is borrowed abroad it will give rise to an increased supply of bills of exchange, thus tending to prevent the rate of exchange from rising to the gold-exporting point. If borrowed in the United States, it will result in a shifting of gold supply from the member banks to the Federal Reserve banks, thereby tending to raise the general discount rate in the United States and thus to discourage the export of specie. Further influence upon exchange rates may be exerted by virtue of the power of the Federal Reserve banks to buy and sell foreign bills of exchange in the open market in Europe.

The provision authorizing the Federal Reserve banks to purchase and sell bills of exchange, etc., as listed under (*d*) above, is intended to give the reserve banks a needed source of income, and also: (1) to enable them to purchase the acceptances of banks which are not members of the Federal Reserve system and which are hence not in a position to secure needed funds through the process of rediscounting, thereby materially strengthening the general credit structure; and (2) to enable them to exercise a direct influence upon interest rates at times when, owing to the lack of applications for rediscounts, they would be unable to influence interest rates through the ordinary process.

The practicability of these methods of controlling business expansion, as tested by experience, will be considered in the following chapter. We are for the moment concerned only with the theory of credit control.

4. Expanding Loans in Time of Acute Crisis

In the event that the attempt to control business expansion and to bring about a gradual readjustment by raising discount rates proved ineffective and business continued to expand until the stage of acute crisis was reached, it was still within the power of the Federal Reserve system to avoid the fourth stage of the business cycle, namely, the suspension of specie payments and the collapse of the entire credit structure, accompanied by financial panic. We have seen in the preceding chapter that in time of acute crisis the outstanding need is for an increase in bank reserves and an expansion of loans. The Federal Reserve system was designed to meet this need.

Under the terms of the law it was provided, as we have already seen, that the member banks should contribute to the capital stock of the Federal Reserve institutions; and they must also keep their reserves on deposit with the Reserve banks. These banks thus became central reservoirs of cash, the final repositories of the commercial banking system, and upon them was placed responsibility for maintaining reserves adequate for all emergencies. While, as we have already seen, the law prescribed relatively large minima, it was deemed necessary as a matter of policy for the Federal Reserve banks to maintain in ordinary times reserves greatly in excess of these figures in order that in case of emergency there would be available a practically "unlimited amount" of lending power. It should be recalled that before the establishment of the Federal Reserve system, our decentralized system of banking led each individual bank to expand its loans in periods of active business practically to the reserve limits; there could be no concerted action whereby funds might be set aside for emergency use only. A policy of providing funds for emergencies was, however, the very essence of the Federal Reserve system.

To understand clearly the amount of emergency expansion that was made possible, it will be necessary again to consider some actual transactions. Suppose in time of crisis the First National Bank of Chicago has a demand from its customers for additional loans. While its reserve is down to the minimum, it may make the additional loans by first taking, say, $100,000 of its customers' notes to the Federal Reserve Bank of Chicago for rediscount—thus lessening the loans of the First National Bank by $100,000 and increasing its cash reserve— in the form of a deposit account in the Federal Reserve bank—by a like amount. On the basis of this new reserve the First National Bank can now make additional loans to the extent of over $700,000.

It will be clear at once that so great an expansion of lending power as here suggested would be adequate to meet any except the most extraordinary credit demands. But in case of still further demands for funds, the First National Bank could take the $700,000 of new promissory notes that have come into its possession as a result of its additional loans, and rediscount them with the Federal Reserve Bank of Chicago, thereby acquiring additional deposits in the Federal Reserve bank, which are available as a reserve basis for still further loans. As long as there is eligible paper for rediscount and as long as the Federal Reserve banks have reserves above the minima prescribed by law, there is no limit to credit expansion.

The system of rediscounting strengthens the weak links in the banking chain. Indeed, it appeared that under this system the essentially weak links might be eliminated. Any bank within the First Federal Reserve District, for instance, could secure loans with which to meet the demands of its constituency regardless of its own condition as long as there was money in the central reservoir at the Federal Reserve bank. Rather than a scramble for reserves and a working at cross-purposes, such as existed before 1914, machinery was now provided which made possible co-operative action in meeting credit strains wherever they might appear. Not only may the banks of District No. 1 continue to secure accommodation from the Federal Reserve bank of that district as long as its reserve is not exhausted, but the Federal Reserve bank of District No. 2 may extend loans to the Federal Reserve bank of District No. 1. Thus a process of credit expansion can continue and relief can be given to individual banks, and through them to business concerns, until the average reserve of all the Federal Reserve banks has been drawn down to the minimum. Not only is there no weak link within a district but there is no weak district within the Federal Reserve system as a whole; each is as strong as any other.

Finally, the reserve requirements were not irreducible minima. The law made it possible, in case of acute emergency, to cut below the 35 and 40 per cent reserve requirements against deposits and Federal Reserve notes, respectively. The Board may also suspend for a period not exceeding thirty days, and from time to time may renew such suspension for a period not exceeding fifteen days, these reserve requirements, provided it establishes a graduated tax upon the amounts by which the reserves of the banks fall below the 35 and 40 per cent requirements. The rate of progression of the tax for the deficiency of the reserves against *notes* is provided by the act, though there is no such provision for *deposits*. The tax upon a deficiency in the reserve against notes is not more than 1 per cent per annum until the reserve falls to $32\frac{1}{2}$ per cent, and $1\frac{1}{2}$ per cent per annum upon each additional $2\frac{1}{2}$ per cent of deficiency or fraction thereof. Thus if the reserve against note issues should fall to 30 per cent there would be a tax of $2\frac{1}{2}$ per cent; if it fell to 29 per cent the tax would be 4 per cent; and if it fell below $27\frac{1}{2}$ per cent the tax would be $5\frac{1}{2}$ per cent. The tax schedule for deposits is left to the discretion of the Board.

The control of the interest rate was also looked upon as a useful aid in the event an acute crisis should develop: First, the raising of the rate would serve a negative function in discouraging all loans that could be done without. While it is highly important in time of crisis that every borrower who is in a sound financial condition be "carried" through the difficult period caused by the disruption of the credit structure and the consequent impairment of mutual credit operations, it was thought to be the part of wisdom to raise the discount rate to a very high figure as a means of deterring all borrowing that is not indispensable.

Second, the raising of the interest rate would perform a positive function in attracting additional funds to the United States from countries where rates were lower. European central banks had repeatedly attracted foreign funds in time of emergency by the use of this method. However, if a strain were felt simultaneously in all the leading commercial nations, and if all central banks should simultaneously raise interest, merely a stalemate would result. The United States would in any case be in a position to prevent an outflow of funds at a time when her bank reserves were low.

IV. THE SHIFTING CHARACTER OF RESERVE BANK ASSETS

In chapter XXI attention was called to the changing character of the operations of individual commercial banks, resulting from the evolution of the complex business and financial structure of the modern world. In particular, emphasis was placed upon the increasing relative importance of long-term credit operations represented by loans on securities as collateral and by direct investments in bonds. Although the original Federal Reserve Act reemphasized commercial operations and restricted rediscounts to genuine commercial paper, successive amendments have served to broaden the scope of Reserve bank operations, in line with the changing character of member bank business. Not only are they permitted to make loans to member banks on "any sound assets," regardless of maturities or the nature of the security, but they also engage very extensively in the purchase of securities.

At the time the Federal Reserve Act was passed, there were almost no government bonds available in the general market, the bulk of them being used as security for note issues. As a result of the World War, however, a great volume of government bonds became available for purchase by banking institutions as well as by individuals. Under the original Federal Reserve Act, the reserve banks were permitted to purchase only direct obligations of the Federal Government. The Act of 1935 authorized the purchase of government guaranteed obligations of the Home Owners' Loan Corporation, the Federal Land banks, etc. This act, however, specified that purchases of either direct or guaranteed obligations must be made only "in the open market and not directly from the Treasury." The purpose of this change was to lessen the possibility of dictation of open market policy by the Treasury.

The changing character of the business of the Federal Reserve banks since 1915 is indicated in the following table:

CHANGING CHARACTER OF FEDERAL RESERVE OPERATIONS, 1915–1937

Year	Bills Discounted		Open Market Purchases	
	Secured by Government Obligations	Other Bills	Government Obligations	Bills Purchased
1915	....	32,368	15,856	23,723
1920	1,141,036	1,053,842	287,029	260,406
1925	382,151	260,842	374,568	374,356
1930	89,437	161,961	729,467	363,844
1933	27,229	70,361	2,437,490	133,425
1937	9,340	3,507	2,564,000	2,827

It will be seen that in the early years the discount of commercial bills was very important, but that in recent years discounts, whether secured or unsecured, have declined to negligible proportions. The business of the Federal Reserve banks is now largely confined to open market purchases, with government bonds constituting the overwhelming proportion of the Federal Reserve portfolios. The explana-

ASSETS AND LIABILITIES OF THE FEDERAL RESERVE BANKS, DECEMBER 31, 1937

(In thousands of dollars)

Assets

Gold certificates on hand and due from U.S. Treasury	$ 9,119,891
Redemption Fund—Federal Reserve notes	9,436
Other cash	351,688
Total reserves	$ 9,481,015
Bills discounted:	
Secured by U.S. government obligations, direct or fully guaranteed	6,481
Other bills discounted	3,385
Total bills discounted	$ 9,866
Bills bought in open markets	540
Industrial advances	18,049
U.S. government securities:	
Bonds	751,539
Treasury notes	1,154,997
Treasury bills	657,479
Total U.S. government securities	$ 2,564,015
Total bills and securities	2,592,470
Due from foreign banks	$ 179
F. R. notes of other Federal Reserve banks	30,211
Uncollected items	693,487
Bank premises	45,027
All other assets	37,335
Total assets	$12,879,724

Liabilities

Federal Reserve notes in actual circulation	$ 4,283,611
Deposits:	
Member bank—reserve account	$ 7,026,809
U.S. Treasurer—general account	142,390
Foreign bank	171,750
Other deposits	235,743
Total deposits	$ 7,576,692
Deferred availability items	674,000
Capital paid in	132,744
Surplus (sec. 7)	147,739
Surplus (sec. 13b)	27,683
Reserve for contingencies	33,052
All other liabilities	4,203
Total liabilities	$12,879,724
Commitments to make industrial advances	12,928

tion of the growing change in the ratio of commercial to investment operations, and of bills discounted to open market purchases, is of course to be found in the fundamental trends of the times, which have been discussed elsewhere. A general balance sheet showing the resources and liabilities of the twelve Federal Reserve banks is presented on page 384.

Attention must now be given to the effect of these trends upon the Federal Reserve notes. The continuous decline in the volume of commercial bills in the portfolios of the Federal Reserve banks necessarily meant that the Federal Reserve notes came increasingly to be backed by gold instead of by commercial paper. In 1932 the amount of Federal Reserve notes outstanding was approximately 2,900 million dollars, of which about two billions was secured by gold and 900 millions by eligible paper. The Glass-Borah law of 1932 authorized the Reserve system to substitute in place of gold as backing for Federal Reserve notes its holdings of government securities, to the extent of 740 million dollars. Thus 740 million dollars of gold was released and made available for open market operations, which were intended to check the deflation. As we shall later see, this operation was not successful in staying the course of the depression. It did, however, mark the end of the attempt to maintain an elastic bank note currency based on commercial paper assets. In view of the preponderant use of the deposit currency system, this outcome is a matter of no great moment.

V. FEDERAL RESERVE BANKS AS GOVERNMENT DEPOSITARIES

From the beginning of our history, it has been necessary to consider the relation of Treasury funds to the money market. The Treasury Department normally receives funds largely from taxes. Some of the sources of taxation provide a fairly regular flow of income, but others a very irregular one. Similarly, some of the disbursements of the Government constitute a fairly regular outflow, while others are intermittent. Accordingly, there are times when the supply of funds in the Treasury is large, and there are times when it is small. There have been occasions, also, when, owing to the lack of a government budget, the total receipts have been considerably in excess of total disbursements. In consequence, the disposition of government funds has always been a problem of no little importance.

There follows a brief summary of the historical relations between the United States Treasury and the banks of the country.

1. From 1789 to 1791 the federal funds were mainly left in the hands of the collecting and disbursing officers, for the reason that there was no specific place for the custody of public money.

2. Between 1791 and 1811 public funds were kept chiefly in the First Bank of the United States, which was the fiscal agent of the United States Government.

3. Between 1811 and 1816, when the Second Bank of the United States was chartered, Treasury funds were kept mainly in state banks.

4. Between 1816 and 1833 the Second Bank of the United States was employed, although the state banks were still used to some extent.

5. Between 1833 and 1846 state banks were exclusively used. Charges of favoritism in the selection of state banks, and the growing opposition to close relations between the banks and the Treasury, led to the adoption of a new policy in 1846.

6. In 1846 an act was passed which established the so-called Independent Treasury, with nine sub-treasuries located in the large financial centers of the country. The term "independent" meant, of course, independent of the banks, public and private finance becoming completely separated, with the Government acting as its own banker. Private banks were used neither as fiscal agencies in the marketing of securities nor as depositors of public funds. This system continued without change until the Civil War and, with modifications, until 1920.

7. Difficulties in handling the financial requirements of the war led to some departure from the Independent Treasury system in 1861. With the establishment of the national banking system in 1863 the Secretary of the Treasury was authorized to deposit a part of the Treasury funds in certain national banks designated as depositary institutions for public money. For a time these banks were required to keep a special reserve against Treasury funds, although this practice was finally abandoned. The amount of public money deposited with the banks steadily increased in volume until at times there was only a very small working balance in the Treasury. The purpose of this system was to make excess Treasury funds widely available for the requirements of business. At times also the Treasury gave additional aid to banks in meeting seasonal strains upon their reserves. For example, in 1913 and 1914 arrangements were made for depositing Treasury funds on the basis of collateral security in banks in the agricultural regions.

The weakness of this system was that it placed upon the Treasury the great responsibility of deciding which sections of the country were most in need of government deposits and which of the many banking institutions would make the wisest use of such funds. It has been said of the Independent Treasury system that "it had the advantages of safety and of inspiring public confidence which the early banks had lost. On the other hand, it was not capable of keeping pace with the growth of business in the United States and had far outlived its usefulness at the time the Federal Reserve system was inaugurated."[6]

8. With the establishment of the Federal Reserve system a great improvement in the co-operative relations between the Treasury and the banking system was made possible. The Federal Reserve banks were appointed as fiscal agents in 1916; and in 1920 the sub-treasuries · were abolished. Under the present system the Treasury formulates the regulations governing the deposits of public money, the payment of agents, etc.; but the co-ordination of public and private finance is effected through the Federal Reserve system. Under this arrangement government deposits have been widely distributed throughout the entire banking community, in accordance with local requirements and the ability of individual banks to qualify as depositaries. The abundance of bank reserves in recent years has, however, alleviated the necessity of using Treasury funds for the easing of money market tension. The present depositary organization consists of the Treasury of the United States, twelve Federal Reserve banks and their branches, and three classes of depositaries—general, limited, and special.

General depositaries are member banks of the Federal Reserve system which have been authorized to accept deposits by the Treasury, for credit to the Treasurer's *general account*, which includes general, special, and trust fund receipts. The amount they are authorized to hold on deposit is fixed by the Treasury in accordance with the local need for funds, and any sums which they may receive in excess of their authorized balance must be forwarded immediately to the Federal Reserve bank of their district. Depleted balances may be replenished by a request to the Treasurer of the United States, who directs the proper Federal Reserve bank to credit the depositary's account. Before a bank is eligible to receive deposits, it must pledge authorized securities as collateral and deposit them with the Treasurer of the United States.

Limited depositaries are member banks authorized to accept deposits up to specified limits for credit to the *official checking accounts* of government disbursing officers and other government agencies. These depositaries are not permitted to accept deposits for credit to the Treasurer's general account. Like general depositaries, however, they must pledge authorized securities as collateral.

Special depositaries are private banking institutions other than those just mentioned (not necessarily members of the Federal Reserve system) which are authorized to keep a government loan account for deposits resulting from the sale of public debt obligations of the

[6] *Annual Report of the Secretary of the Treasury, 1926, p. 113.*

United States Treasury. Any incorporated bank or trust company may qualify as a special depositary by applying for such designation to the Federal Reserve bank of its district and pledging authorized securities with that bank as protection for the government deposits.

In addition to depositaries in continental United States, designated branches of American banking institutions serve as depositaries (usually of the class known as "limited depositaries") in the following foreign countries: Belgium, China, England, France, Italy, Japan and Panama.[7] Other institutions, including the Treasury of the Philippine Islands, are designated as depositaries of government funds to serve territories and island possessions of the United States.

The number of government depositaries and the amount of their deposits on June 30, 1937 are shown in the following table:

NUMBER OF DEPOSITARIES OF EACH CLASS, AND AMOUNT OF DEPOSITS HELD JUNE 30, 1937[a]

Depositaries	Number	Amount
Federal Reserve banks..............................	12	92,808,302
Member bank depositaries:		
General:		
To credit of Treasurer of U.S...................	376	9,714,610
To credit of other government officers...........		10,192,331
Limited...	890	20,436,307
Insular and territorial:		
General:		
To credit of Treasurer of U.S...................	13	5,151,791
To credit of other government officers...........		1,551,515
Limited...	.....	....
Foreign:		
General:		
To credit of Treasurer of U.S...................	2	1,202,100
To credit of other government officers...........		1,640,693
Limited...	10	293,840
Special depositaries................................	2,583	649,459,773
	3,886	792,451,263

[a] *Annual Report of the Secretary of the Treasury*, 1937, p. 105, supplemented by information from the Division of Deposits, office of Commissioner of Accounts and Deposits, Treasury Department.

The table indicates that 80 per cent of the government deposits are now placed with the special depositaries, which accept no deposits from either government officers or the public. This phenomenon is explained by the way in which government securities are marketed.

[7] List of depositaries issued by the Treasury Department, Division of Deposits, Oct. 1, 1937. Both of the depositaries in Panama are general depositaries.

After subscriptions to new offerings of public debt issues have closed, the Treasury notifies the Federal Reserve banks of the basis on which to allot securities to bank subscribers. A bank which has been designated as a "special depositary" may purchase the securities offered through the use of a "government loan account" at the Federal Reserve bank of its district. The effect of this arrangement is to permit these banks to participate in government issues at the subscription price and to pay for them gradually as the Government draws upon its balances at the Federal Reserve bank. This system was inaugurated during the World War to assist the Government in its extensive wartime financing operations; it has been retained because of its value in providing wide marketability for government securities.

CHAPTER XXIV

THE RESERVE SYSTEM IN OPERATION

During the first two years of its operation the Federal Reserve system was little used. The reduction of reserve requirements of the member banks by the Federal Reserve Act, coupled with an inflow of gold from Europe, resulted in a very great increase in the lending power of the individual banks. Accordingly, the rediscount facilities of the Federal Reserve banks did not appear to be necessary, and there developed the view among many of the bankers of the country that the importance of the Federal Reserve system had been greatly exaggerated. The entrance of the United States into the World War, however, quickly disillusioned the bankers as to the adequacy of their own resources. Moreover, the financial requirements of the war proved so enormous that the credit expanding power of the Federal Reserve system was quickly put to the test.

I. FINANCING THE WORLD WAR

At the time of the entrance of the United States into the World War, the volume of lending power possessed by the Federal Reserve banks was very large. The capital contributions of the stock-holding member banks, plus the transfer of reserves, gave substantial cash resources to the Federal Reserve banks at the very commencement of their operations. Later, the amendment to the Federal Reserve law which made it necessary for each member bank to keep all, rather than merely a portion, of its required reserve in the Federal Reserve bank of its district; the concentration of gold reserves through exchanging Federal Reserve notes for gold, as described above; and finally, the accession of the larger state banks to membership in the Reserve system, very greatly increased the volume of reserve money in the central reservoirs. In 1916 the ratio of cash to notes and deposits combined in the twelve Federal Reserve banks was about 87 per cent; and although for more than a year we had had one foot in the conflict, the net reserve was about 77 per cent at the time we formally entered the war in 1917. Our financial structure was, therefore, in an extraordinarily strong position for meeting the financial strain of a great war.

Expanding business and rising prices required a great increase of currency. As business expanded between 1915 and 1918, the volume of bank borrowings also necessarily expanded. And as the price level rose the volume of funds required in the financing of a given volume of business was also increased. Concretely, by 1918, when the price level was substantially double what it had been in 1914, there were required to conduct a given amount of business about two dollars to every one dollar that had been necessary before the war. That is to say, every business man found that he must have approximately twice the amount of money with which to meet pay-roll requirements, buy raw materials, etc., that had formerly been needed. The bulk of this additional working capital had to be borrowed from the commercial banking institutions.

After their excess reserves were exhausted, the member banks resorted to rediscounting at the Federal Reserve banks as a means of procuring the funds required for business uses. The result was to increase the discounts of the Federal Reserve banks on the assets side and to increase the liabilities in the form of either Federal Reserve notes or deposit liabilities. It should be kept in mind in this connection that the process did not occasion a withdrawal of cash from the Federal Reserve institution. On the contrary, cash resources were steadily increasing during the war period, owing to the policy of mobilizing the gold reserves. The significant fact is that the liabilities in the form of Federal Reserve notes and deposits increased much more rapidly than the cash, with the result that the reserve ratio necessarily fell.

Government financing also led to an enormous expansion of Federal Reserve notes and deposits. The size of government bond issues was so great that they were not subscribed in full by individuals out of their own savings. Liberty bonds were often purchased by individuals with funds borrowed from the bank on the security of previously purchased Liberty bonds as collateral. But more important was the purchase of Liberty bonds by the banks themselves. In each Liberty Loan campaign the banks helped "put the quota over" by purchasing in the closing hours of the campaign large quantities of the bonds on their own account. Since the lending resources of the individual banks were used up early in the war, they had to procure the funds with which to purchase Liberty bonds through rediscounting operations at the Federal Reserve banks. They could borrow the money with which to buy Liberty bonds from the Federal Reserve banks either on commercial paper or on government bonds as collateral—the latter alternative having been made possible by an amendment to the act, passed in 1916. Accordingly, as long as the Federal Reserve institutions possessed unused lending power, there was never the slightest danger that a government bond issue would not be subscribed in full, by the banks, if not by the public. The banks borrowed much more on the security of government obligations than through rediscounts of commercial paper.

That the Federal Reserve system enabled the financing of the war to be carried through with a minimum of difficulty is not to be denied. The most that can be said against the system is that it made the financing of the war too easy, encouraging the use of bonds for that purpose, thereby causing an inequitable distribution of the burden of war costs. Responsibility for the large use of bonds as a means of financing the war cannot, however, be placed primarily at the doors of the Federal Reserve system, the Treasury rather than the Federal Reserve officials being responsible for the methods of war finance.

The real issues of Federal Reserve policy and the adequacy of the system to do what it was designed to do, in connection with the prevention of banking crises and the control of credit and business conditions, are best tested by the experience of post-war years.

II. THE CRISIS OF 1920

As a result of factors which need not here be considered, the depression immediately following the Armistice was not of long duration. In April, 1919, there began a new upward swing of the business cycle, which brought to bear upon the Federal Reserve banks renewed pressure for funds. As is always the case in a period of very active business, the pressure on commercial banks for loans did not come merely from the manufacturing and mercantile interests; it came, to a very considerable extent, from stock exchange speculation, and from the flotation of new issues of corporate securities. Both speculation and investment, save in government securities, had been largely held in abeyance during the war period by restrictive legislation and by the activities of the Capital Issues Committee, which, in the latter part of the war, effectively prevented the sale of securities of concerns that were not deemed essential to the winning of the struggle. Hence when the post-war boom period developed, an extraordinary number of new loans were issued.

Another factor in the rapid depletion of our reserves after the Armistice was the outflow of specie from the United States to South America and the Orient to meet adverse trade balances. This amounted, between June 1, 1919, and January 1, 1920, to approximately 300 million dollars. It should be recalled in this connection that since in our financial system as a whole the cash reserves need be only about five per cent of the total outstanding claims against cash, every dollar of specie that is exported means a curtailment of credit possibilities to the extent of about twenty dollars.

The result of these various strains upon the financial system was shortly to reduce the reserve ratios in the Federal Reserve banks from around 50 per cent to a point dangerously near the minimum reserve requirements laid down in the Federal Reserve Act (see chart, page 398). By the end of 1919 the ratio of cash to Reserve notes and deposit liabilities combined, in the twelve Federal Reserve banks, was below 45 per cent. The question whether the Federal Reserve system might fail to control the expansion of credit and to prevent the recurrence of financial panics, such as had occurred in the old days of unorganized banking, therefore became of more than academic interest. It was frankly feared by many that if the central reserves should continue to fall until they reached the legal minima, we should not be in a very much better position to meet the conditions of an acute crisis than would have been the case under the old banking system.

The Federal Reserve officials have been criticized for their credit policy in connection with the crisis of 1920. In brief, it has been contended that the Board should have raised the rates of discount in the early summer of 1919 instead of waiting until the winter of 1920. The issues involved cannot be fully discussed here. It must suffice to point out that the advance in prices following the Armistice began at a time when government financial requirements were still at their height. The Victory Loan of 4.5 billion dollars had yet to be floated and a large volume of borrowing through the issue of Treasury certificates of indebtedness was still necessary. The Treasury Department was naturally desirous of placing these loans at as low an interest rate as possible. Whether the Board should have strenuously objected to this, on the ground that high rates of interest were necessary to check a dangerous business boom, is highly debatable. Until the early autumn of 1919 it was not apparent how severe the financial strain was to be. It was at that time deemed very important that every effort be made to promote a revival of business activity in order to facilitate the early rehabilitation of the depleted economic resources of the world; and it was feared that a sharp rise in discount rates early in 1919 would be a deterrent. After the details of the Victory Loan had been agreed upon, it was moreover impossible for the Federal Reserve officials to raise rates during the period of the Victory Loan financing, which ran to the end of the year 1919, without breaking faith with the bankers of the country, who had formulated policies and made loans on the understanding that this loan was to be put through at a low interest rate.

In the early summer of 1919, however, the Federal Reserve authorities issued an official warning, urging the necessity of curtailing loans for speculative purposes in the interests of "legitimate" commercial needs. This warning, which passed virtually unheeded by either the bankers or the speculative community, was not reiterated until the middle of October, by which time the credit situation had become very grave. On this occasion the banks of New York co-operated with the Federal Reserve officials, sharply raising rates on call money and actually restricting the volume of credit that brokers might obtain, with a resulting abrupt collapse of stock market values and the dissolution of the bull market that had prevailed—with an August intermission—since the early spring.

A curtailment of stock exchange speculation did not, however, and could not in the nature of things, suffice to relieve the monetary strain. What was needed was a thoroughgoing readjustment of prices to a lower basis—deflation, to use a common expression—even though it might be accompanied by a halting of business activity. Not until January, 1920, apparently, did the Reserve officials fully appreciate the gravity of the reserve situation and seek to effect a readjustment of conditions. After a conference with leading bankers it was then decided that the necessities of the credit situation demanded a real advance in discount rates. The first increase was not very great, however, for a cautious feeling of the way seemed advisable; and, moreover, it was still the belief of many that an elimination of loans for speculative purposes—commodity speculation as well as stock exchange speculation—would release a sufficient quantity of funds to take care of essential business requirements without necessitating any drastic readjustment of business. It was hoped that a moderate increase of discount rates, together with a sharp discrimination by bankers against speculative loans, would accomplish the desired results.

During the early months of 1920, however, the advance in interest rates appeared to have little effect upon business activity. In most lines of industry, the profits that might be derived from the use of borrowed funds were so great that interest rates were for the time a matter of only secondary importance. The volume of loans therefore continued to be large, business continued to be active, and prices continued to rise; and until March there was little *surface* indication that price and business readjustments were in store.

Despite subsequent further increases in the discount rates at the Federal Reserve banks, and at the member institutions as an immediate consequence, the credit strain became increasingly acute until late in May, when the Board again called a conference of bankers to consider how the volume of loans might be reduced and the reserves

replenished sufficiently to accommodate the autumn seasonal requirements without danger of a financial collapse. It was agreed at this
conference that before autumn it would be necessary to curtail loans
by about 10 per cent, if the banks were to be placed in a position to
meet, without serious difficulty, the demands that were certain to be
placed upon them during the crop-moving period.

Before considering subsequent events it will be well to refer briefly
to other changes in economic conditions which were conspiring to bring
about a readjustment of business and prices in the spring of 1920.
First, there was the breakdown of the transportation system, owing to
a combination of factors which need not be considered here. The
inability of the railroads to move commodities at the customary rate
slowed up the entire productive and distributive process and made it
necessary for business men everywhere to secure extensions of credit
for a longer period and for larger amounts than would otherwise have
been required. A new expression, "frozen credit," was coined to
describe this condition. The result of this inability of traffic to move
was to augment the pressure on the banks for loans and thereby to
reduce still further the ratio of cash to deposit and note liabilities,
which in May reached a low point of about 42.5 per cent in the twelve
Federal Reserve banks combined. In some banks the ratio fell even
below the 40 per cent minimum.

Another major factor that was contributing to a readjustment of
business conditions was the high cost of living. The steady rise in
commodity prices during 1919 and the first months of 1920, accompanied as it now was by substantial increases in rents, had finally
reached a point where it was forcing a curtailment of consumptive
demand. Whatever may have been the case earlier, it had by this time
certainly become true that the net annual wages of labor, generally
speaking, as well as the income of the salaried classes, were failing to
keep pace with advancing prices, with the result that the real purchasing power of the rank and file of the people declined. The "peak" of
prices was reached in the spring of 1920, among other reasons because
consumptive demand was not sufficient to absorb the existing volume
of production at the prices for which goods were then being offered.
Popular hostility to the continuous marking up of prices is also believed
by many to have finally led to a voluntary reduction of purchases. In
any event the result of the curtailed consumptive demand was manifested in the month of May in retail price concessions in silks, textiles,
leather goods, and a few other commodities.

Another change that undoubtedly contributed somewhat to the
unsettling of American business was the decline in our trade balance,
which became pronounced in the spring of 1920. It should be noted in

this connection that in several lines the prices of raw materials had begun to decline months earlier, particularly in those subject to world-wide market influences. The fact is that in 1920 readjustment was a world-wide phenomenon and occurred in countries that had not raised interest rates as well as in those that had. It appears to have had its definite beginning in the financial crisis in the Orient, which occurred in February, 1920, and was directly associated with the post-war collapse of the silk trade.

The several increases in interest rates that were made during the autumn and winter of 1919–1920 apparently had little, if any, effect in restraining business activity. Before an outright curtailment of loans was undertaken, the other factors to which reference has been made— transportation difficulties, rising living costs, a restriction of consumption, and falling prices of raw material, etc.—were operating to bring about a price and business readjustment.

The Federal Reserve system, however, undoubtedly prevented a panic in 1920. Beginning about the middle of May, the credit tension became of the acute variety that had in the past characterized the weeks immediately preceding a financial collapse. Just as soon as the decline in prices, with the concurrent slackening of industry and backing up of the speculative water, began, great numbers of business men were panic striken much as would have been the case in former times. The cancellation of business orders, the failure of creditors to meet their obligations promptly, the recurring slumps in inventory values, and the uncertainty as to the whole future trend of events developed a veritable business crisis—accompanied by the usual insistent pressure upon the banks for loans with which to tide over the interval of readjustment. There was one noteworthy difference, however, between this and similar occasions in the past. Widespread confidence in the Federal Reserve system proved a powerful sedative. There was no panic and no suspension of specie payments.

III. EXPERIENCE IN THE TWENTIES

The abnormal business and credit situation from 1915 to 1920 was followed by a decade of comparatively stable conditions. Hence the operations of the Federal Reserve system during this period may be studied in truer perspective. During this period some of the advantages as well as the limitations of the system became more clearly revealed.

In the first place, the Federal Reserve system unquestionably provided seasonal elasticity with respect to both note issues and deposit currency. Thanks to the more adequate reserves and the greater flexibility provided by the system, there was no longer periodic tension in the money markets resulting from purely seasonal changes in the volume of business. Moreover, seasonal fluctuations in interest rates were greatly reduced.

The period from 1922 to 1929 was marked by numerous business fluctuations of a cyclical character. The noteworthy movements (see chart on page 342) were as follows: Business expanded from late 1921 to early 1924, and then declined sharply for about six months. A new upward movement beginning in the autumn of 1924, continued at a high level until the recession of 1927, which was again succeeded by a strong advance culminating in the crisis of October, 1929. Both Federal Reserve notes and deposits proved responsive to the expanding and contracting requirements of business for credit accommodation. The only question at issue is whether the Federal Reserve system was other than a passive factor—whether it was promotive of stable economic progress, or whether it was in large measure responsible for the fluctuations which occurred—particularly, for the disastrous collapse of 1929.

1. The Evolution of Federal Reserve Policy

At the time the Federal Reserve law was passed it had been assumed that the primary guide to credit policy was the reserve position of those banks which held the reservoirs of cash. As long as there was an abundance of bank reserves it was believed that credit expansion could continue without danger to the financial and business structure; only when the reserve limits were being approached was it deemed necessary to take steps to safeguard the situation. However, after the drastic financial liquidation of 1920–1921, and a huge inflow of gold from abroad during the same years, the reserve ratio, that is, the proportion of cash reserves to notes and deposit liabilities combined, came to be, and remained, far in excess of the reserve requirements. The magnitude of the change is revealed in the chart shown on page 398. In the light of this situation it was obvious that if no credit restraint were imposed until the excess reserves were near exhaustion, an inflationary boom might prove of protracted duration and ultimately bring disastrous consequences.

Hence a better guide to discount policy was sought. It was felt that the Reserve system should have not merely a passive function but should contribute in a positive way to the promotion and maintenance of a sound and stable economy. However, the doctrine advanced by exponents of the quantity theory, that commodity price fluctuations could be controlled by a rigid control of the quantity of deposit currency, was not accepted.

It is the view of the Federal Reserve officials that the price situation and the credit situation, while sometimes closely related, are nevertheless not related to one another as simple cause and effect; they are rather both to be regarded as the outcome of common causes that work in the economic and business situation. The same conditions which predispose to a rise of prices also predispose to an increased demand for credit. The demand for credit is conditioned upon the business outlook. Credit is created in increasing volume only as the community wishes to use more credit—when the opportunity for the employment of credit appears more profitable. Sometimes borrowers want

RESERVE POSITION OF FEDERAL RESERVE BANKS, 1915–1937
(Chart Based on Averages for Each Year)

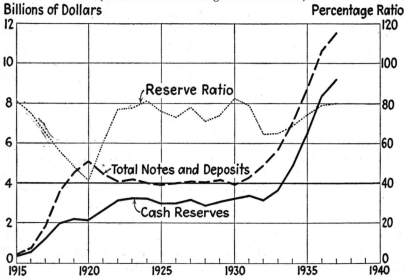

to borrow more and sometimes they are content with less. Sometimes lenders are ready to lend more and at other times less. Why this should be so depends on all those multifarious conditions and circumstances that affect the temper of the business community. For the most part these conditions lie beyond the radius of action of the Federal Reserve banks. When the business outlook is inviting business men are apt to adventure and new business commitments are made in increasing volume. But only later will these commitments be reflected in the possible rise of prices and an increase in the volume of credit provided by the commercial banks of the country. The Federal Reserve banks will not to any considerable extent feel the impact of the increased demand for credit until the whole train of antecedent circumstances which has occasioned it is well advanced on its course; that is, until a forward movement of business, no matter from what impulse it is proceeding, has gained momentum.[1]

[1] *Tenth Annual Report of the Federal Reserve Board*, pp. 31–32.

The general guides to credit policy which were evolved have been succinctly summarized as follows:[2]

First, though the ratio of notes and deposits to gold reserves is the banking index which enjoys the greatest prestige in the tradition of most countries, and especially in the tradition of the United States, it is not a serviceable working guide in the absence of an effective international gold standard. Since the international flow of gold does not exert a restrictive influence on credit in the countries from which the gold goes out, it would not be safe to allow it to work automatically in expanding credit in the countries into which the gold goes. The use of the reserve ratio as a test of credit policy rests on the automatic working of the gold standard, which cannot be effective for one country alone.

Second, the Federal Reserve Act clearly contemplates the exclusion of all Federal Reserve bank credit from speculative and investment uses and its limitation to productive uses; that is, agricultural, industrial, or commercial employment. The problem of credit control, therefore, involves both a qualitative and a quantitative determination. There will, however, be little danger that the credit created and contributed by the Federal Reserve banks will be in excessive volume if it is restricted to productive uses.

Third, the volume of credit will seldom be at variance with the credit needs as reflected in the demands of productive industry so long as the volume of trade, production, and employment on the one hand, and the volume of consumption on the other hand, are in equilibrium. When credit is provided to finance the movement of goods through the productive process or to promote the flow of goods from producer to consumer, the use is productive. When the effect of credit is to impede or delay the forward movement of goods from producer to consumer, credit is not productively used. Administratively, therefore, the way to keep the volume of credit issuing from the Federal Reserve banks from becoming very excessive or deficient is to keep it in proper relation to the credit needs which arise from the operating requirements of agriculture, industry, and trade, and to prevent the use of Federal Reserve credit for other purposes.

Fourth, an effective credit policy must be based on the wide variety of economic data which throw light on the changes taking place in the business situation and their relation to current banking

[2] Charles O. Hardy, *Credit Policies of the Federal Reserve System*, pp. 75–77. The Brookings Institution.

and credit needs. The factual basis of banking administration consists of statistical information relative to the rate at which goods are being produced and marketed.

Fifth, the Board and the Federal Reserve banks are collecting basic economic data bearing on the volume of production, trade, and employment, and the movement of prices, and a limited amount of information concerning stocks held by producers and distributors. These data are made available, not only to the Board and the banks, but to the business community. The cooperation of the public, based upon an understanding of the broad outlines of Federal Reserve credit policy, and upon the use of current statistical data, is of the greatest advantage to a good functioning of the Federal Reserve system.

These principles, which were enunciated in 1923, became the basis of Federal Reserve policy during the ensuing years. Inasmuch as chief reliance came to be placed upon open market operations as the means for controlling credit, we shall discuss this feature of Federal Reserve policy before considering the effectiveness of the discount rate as a regulator of business activity.

2. Open Market Operations as a Control Device

Prior to 1923 the Federal Reserve banks had bought government securities primarily as a means of earning operating expenses; but in that year the principle was enunciated that the purchase and sale of government securities should henceforth be undertaken only as a means of assisting in the regulation of general credit and business conditions. The theory was advanced that, in a time of depression, the Federal Reserve banks might increase the amount of money in circulation by purchasing government securities and in a time of active business they might decrease the circulation by selling such securities.

The first test of this theory came in 1922, when, from January to May, securities to the extent of 400 million dollars were purchased. Although these securities were bought for the purpose of increasing the earnings of the Federal Reserve banks rather than for the purpose of controlling credit, this fact does not, of course, alter the effect of the purchases upon the credit situation. In the first half of 1923 securities were sold in corresponding volume with a view to taking money out of circulation and restraining a too active business situation. In 1924 the process was reversed, and securities were bought in large quantities—as much as 500 million dollars between January and August. In 1925 and 1926 transactions were of smaller volume; but in 1927, with business declining, heavy purchases of securities were again made.

These security transactions did not, however, automatically control the quantity of credit in the channels of circulation. When securities were purchased Federal Reserve money did, of course, find its way into the money markets and thus into deposits of member banks, but since business was declining these funds were not used by the banks as a basis for expanding credit; rather they were employed to liquidate rediscounts at the Federal Reserve banks. Similarly, the heavy sales of securities in 1923 withdrew large sums from the deposits of member banks; but instead of contracting credit the member banks replenished their reserves by borrowing heavily from Federal Reserve banks through the rediscount method. The purchases of securities in 1924 and 1927 were again accompanied by a decline in rediscounts of like proportions; while in 1928, as securities were sold, rediscounts registered a more or less parallel advance. Thus the open market operations in the main merely shifted the character of bank assets from securities to discounts, or the reverse, without having an appreciable effect upon the total reserves and lending power of the member banks.

During this period it was vigorously contended by various theorists in the field of money that by means of open market operations the Federal Reserve banks could "pump money into the channels of circulation" and thereby automatically raise the level of commodity prices. It should, however, be clear from the experience cited above that the purchase of bonds in the open market does not put money into the ultimate channels of circulation—that is, into the pockets of the people. Most of these securities are purchased from the banks and the only result is that money is transferred from Federal Reserve banks to private member banks in exchange for bonds. Even when the purchases are made from individuals there is no assurance that more money will consequently be spent in the commodity markets. As a rule, the individuals who sell securities to the Government doubtless invest the proceeds in other securities rather than use the money to buy commodities.

If security purchases in the open market are to have any effect upon business and prices, it must be through their influence upon the reserves of member banks, and hence upon the volume of loans to business borrowers. If carried out on an extensive scale, open market operations may have a great influence upon the volume of member bank reserves. The Federal Reserve officials have long recognized that the value of open market operations lies not in their effect upon the money in circulation but upon the reserves of member banks, and thus upon interest rates. Their real function therefore is to supplement the interest rate method of control. Indeed, at times when member banks have no rediscounts at the Federal Reserve banks, or when they are not in need of securing accommodation there, the only means of affecting interest rates is by the indirect process of expanding or contracting member bank reserves through open market operations.

3. The Discount Rate as a Means of Control

Many economists and bankers had long held the view that the volume of credit expansion, and hence business conditions, could be readily controlled by means of adjustments of the rate at which business men might borrow. It was argued that recovery from a depression normally occurs as a result of expanding bank credit induced by low interest rates, and that hence recovery might be expedited by means of central bank policy. This theory was derived from a general principle of value, namely, that if the price of any commodity is lowered, *other things being equal*, the demand for that commodity will be increased. Since bank credit may be regarded as a commodity it would follow that, other things being equal, if its price falls, the demand for credit will expand; hence more credit will enter the channels of circulation, prices will rise, and business activity will be stimulated.

It will be observed that the underlying assumption in this theory is that other things do remain equal when interest rates decline. The fact is, however, that when interest rates decline in a period of depression, other things do not remain the same; indeed, it is because other things have changed that interest rates are declining. The explanation of declining interest rates in a period of deflation is the contraction of bank loans concurrently with the decline in the volume of business and the fall in the level of prices. As the volume of business shrinks, many loans are paid off and are not replaced by new ones of equal amount, because credit requirements are less. As loans are reduced the amount of unutilized reserves expands and interest rates decline. It is thus the changing business situation that is responsible for the decline in interest rates.

In any case it may still be argued that low interest rates will stimulate recovery. If money can be obtained at two or three per cent instead of the usual four or five, it would seem obvious that the opportunity for profit would be greatly increased. What has been so commonly overlooked, however, is the fact that interest is only one element in the cost of production, and in the majority of cases by no means the most important one. Indeed, in time of depression many businesses have sufficient funds of their own to finance a considerable expansion without resort to borrowing. The reason why such idle money is not put to work immediately is that the business man must appraise the balance of factors in the business situation as a whole, including wage and raw material costs and the prospect for sales in the existing state of the markets.

The truth is that low interest rates on bank loans have little power to stimulate recovery. Throughout the course of the recent depression we have tried more or less continuously to promote expansion by means of credit policies. The Federal Reserve banks have engaged in open market operations on a vast scale and interest rates have been reduced to the lowest levels ever known. When these attempts did not bring results, cooperating credit committees of business men and bankers were organized to help put currency into the channels of circulation. But all efforts were in vain as long as the economic situation as a whole remained unfavorable; money, like labor, remained unemployed. It was not until a combination of various factors started the recovery process that demands for increased banking accommodations began to appear. In fact, a phenomenon of the entire expansion period from 1933 to 1937 was the negligible increase in bank loans, even though interest rates remained at the lowest levels ever known.

The failure of low interest rates to bring revival is not merely a current phenomenon, to be explained by abnormal economic and political conditions. There does not appear to be any historical evidence to support the view that the situation was different in former times. In the long depression of the 1870's, for example, interest rates soon fell and for years were at an unprecedentedly low level. In England in 1875 and 1876 the Bank of England rate was for month after month as low as one per cent and at times the market rate fell to one-half of one per cent. An expansion of loans did not follow; instead, numerous banks were forced to go out of existence because of a lack of borrowers. The same situation prevailed in the nineties, both in the United States and in other countries.

The use of the interest rate as a means of controlling expansion is perhaps somewhat more effective. In periods of active business the need for loans is nearly universal, and hence the cost at which funds can be procured is obviously a factor to be considered. However, the rate of profit depends upon a combination of factors, among which the rate of interest is usually of minor significance. When the volume of business is expanding and prices are rising, the net profits may increase greatly even though the cost of borrowed money is rapidly advancing. An increasing interest rate is of some importance, not for its direct bearing upon the cost of production, but because it serves as an index of changing conditions and suggests the need of caution, thus indirectly affecting the tempo of business. In times of depression, however, there do not appear to be any comparable indirect results.

4. INTERNATIONAL COOPERATION

At this place mention should be made of the Federal Reserve policies which were directed toward international monetary rehabilitation. As has been pointed out in chapter VI, the gold standard was reestablished in the greater part of the world during the period 1924–1929. Since the United States, as a result of war and early post-war developments, had accumulated an undue proportion of the world gold supply,[3] it was deemed essential that this country should furnish aid in the stabilization of European currencies by promoting a redistribution of the supply of gold. Loans were made by the Reserve banks to Poland and Czechoslovakia; and the currency stabilization programs of Great Britain, Belgium, Italy, Rumania, and Poland were underwritten, so to speak, by the Federal Reserve system through an agreement to extend credit on demand. The arrangement with the Bank of England, which involved much the largest amount, was as follows: The Federal Reserve Bank of New York agreed to sell gold to the Bank of England at any time within two years, up to a limit of 200 million dollars, taking in exchange an equivalent deposit credit in sterling in the Bank of England. For this "credit" the Bank of England was to pay interest. No part of it was, however, actually used.

On several occasions the Federal Reserve banks bought acceptances payable in foreign currencies for the avowed purpose of aiding foreign central banks in maintaining the value of their currencies. The amounts involved in the twenties were, however, small, aggregating only about 60 billion dollars. During the crisis of 1931 they became more extensive. For example, on June 24 the Reserve banks agreed to purchase commercial bills from the German government to the amount of about 25 million dollars—the Bank of England, the Bank of France, and the Bank for International Settlements cooperating in providing a total of 100 million dollars. This agreement was several times renewed. During the British crisis in August, 1931 the Reserve banks agreed to purchase approximately 125 millions of British bills, with France undertaking to purchase a similar amount.

While these aids were helpful in relieving tension and alleviating fear, they did not succeed in materially modifying the international distribution of species. During these years there was also considerable discussion of the possibility of making use of the discount rate as a means of promoting the redistribution of the gold supply. Concretely,

[3] See chart, p. 74.

relatively low rates in the United States would induce the transfer of short-term credits from American to foreign markets, thus modifying the balance of payments. However, because of the importance assigned to the adjustment of discount rates with a view to controlling domestic business, little use was made of the discount rate as a means of aiding international trade and financial relations.

5. FEDERAL RESERVE POLICY AND THE STOCK MARKET BOOM

In concluding this discussion of Federal Reserve policy during the twenties, attention must be given to the attempt to check stock market speculation. The Federal Reserve authorities were subjected to some criticism during the period from 1924 to 1927 on the ground that the comparatively easy money policy being pursued was encouraging excessive stock speculation. In the light of the criteria which had been adopted as a guide to Reserve policy, it did not seem to the Reserve officials at the time that stock speculation was having a deleterious effect upon business—for if such were the case the statistics of business should have revealed the fact. As one of the officials stated: "The operations of the stock market are not the concern of the Federal Reserve system, except when the stock market is absorbing credit that is needed in general business, as was the case in the fall of 1919, or when the activity of the market and the rapid advance of many stocks threatens to breed a speculative fever which is liable to spread to commodities."[4]

By 1928, however, the Reserve officials began to express genuine concern over the stock market boom. In the first half of the year pressure was exerted toward restraining speculation by open market sales and advancing rediscount rates. At the same time, the credit situation was tightened as a result of a large outflow of gold. Call loan rates advanced from an average of 4.24 per cent in January, 1928 to 6.05 per cent in July. There was, however, no appreciable effect upon speculative sentiment. Moreover, business prosperity and speculation continued to advance together. In the second half of 1928 the repressive policy was slightly relaxed.

In February, 1929, the Reserve officials conceived a new method of exercising control over the stock market. Instead of merely increasing the cost of credit, hoping thereby to curtail its use, they devised a policy of "direct pressure." This involved a refusal of the rediscount privilege to banks having a volume of speculative security loans in

[4] George W. Norris, quoted by George E. Roberts, "Federal Reserve Control of the Money Market," *American Bankers Association Journal*, December 1925, Vol. XVIII, No. 6, p. 448.

excess of an amount deemed reasonable by the Reserve banks. During the ensuing months, however, there was a vigorous controversy between the Reserve officials and those of the Federal Reserve Bank of New York. The bank held that direct pressure was impractical and that the only effective means of control was to "put the brakes on" by raising discount rates, the first effect of which would be to restrict loans of a speculative character. The Reserve officials felt, however, that "advances would have to be so sharp—far beyond six per cent—that other lines of business would be severely affected and that a crisis might in consequence ensue. The Federal Advisory Council supported the position of the Reserve officials. However, the New York Reserve bank refused to cooperate, and in June the policy of direct pressure was abandoned. It was not until August 8 that the rediscount rate in New York was raised to six per cent.

At that time many students of the problem felt that the stock market collapse of 1929, and the ensuing economic depression, might have been prevented had the Federal Reserve officials utilized their powers earlier instead of waiting until the speculative mania had spread beyond control. Such a conclusion, however, is based upon an inadequate conception of the range of factors which contributed toward bringing on the great depression of 1929. While a restriction of the flow of credit for stock market operations was clearly desirable, it could not have prevented the ensuing depression. While we cannot here enter into a discussion of the causes of the world depression, it will perhaps be helpful to call attention to the various sources of maladjustment that existed in 1929. The following statement is taken from the author's analysis in *The Recovery Problem in the United States*.[5]

International trade and financial relations were fundamentally unbalanced, being supported for the time being by a continuous stream of funds from creditor to debtor nations.

The stabilized international exchanges were in many instances dependent solely upon the continuance of credits, particularly those of short duration.

The reconstruction of plant and equipment in the old industrial countries of Europe and the fostering of manufacturing development in the new nations established at the end of the war were intensifying international competition and further stimulating the growth of trade barriers.

The recovery and expansion of world agricultural production had depressed the prices of basic farm products everywhere, and at the same time unsold stocks were steadily accumulating.

[5] Pp. 24–26.

The governments of many countries were burdened with domestic indebtedness, and in few cases were budgets safely in balance.

The expansion of private credit, for both productive and consumptive purposes, had proceeded at a pace which could not be indefinitely maintained and which was storing up troubles for the future in meeting interest obligations.

In the United States the prolonged boom in the construction industry had served to replace deficiencies by surpluses, while the output of automobiles had reached a level difficult to maintain.

The distribution of income in the United States was becoming increasingly concentrated, and the flow of funds into consumptive channels was persistently inadequate to purchase at prevailing prices the full potential output of our productive establishments.

The flow of savings and of bank credit into investment channels was excessive, producing an inflation of security prices and consequent financial instability.

The depression was thus the outgrowth not of some one single disturbing element but of a number of factors. Inasmuch as the world economic system was vulnerable in several important respects, it was only a question of time until a break would occur somewhere —the precise moment and place being perhaps more or less a matter of accidental circumstance. Moreover, once a serious break occurred at any place in the complex mechanism the effects would spread throughout the entire system.

In view of these varied sources of maladjustment and the world ramifications of the problem, it was too much to expect that the Federal Reserve system, operating alone or even in conjunction with the Central Banks of other countries, could have maintained stability through monetary policies. As has been previously pointed out, the banking crises that had so commonly ushered in economic depressions in former times had given the impression that the causes of cyclical fluctuations must be primarily financial in character, and hence capable of control by monetary and credit policies. One of the great lessons of the world depression is that the control of the business cycle presents a vastly more complicated problem than had hitherto been assumed.

IV. THE RESERVE SYSTEM SINCE 1929

In the years since 1929 the Federal Reserve system has undergone a considerable transformation, designed to strengthen the control of the central Reserve officials over the banking system. Before considering the organizational changes in the banking legislation of 1933 and

1935, which were designed to achieve this goal, it is necessary to present a brief account of Federal Reserve policies during the course of the depression itself.

1. RESERVE POLICY, 1929–1933

Almost immediately after the collapse of the stock market boom in October, 1929, the Federal Reserve authorities adopted a policy of easy money as a means of preventing a severe business recession. Rediscount rates were rapidly reduced from 5 and 6 per cent at the various banks in October, 1929, to from 2 to 3.5 per cent in January, 1931. By June, 1931, the New York rate was down to 1.5 per cent. During this period, also, the Reserve banks made very large purchases of government securities as a means of increasing the reserves and the lending power of the member banks. However, the result was that the member banks merely used the proceeds to reduce their rediscounts at the Federal Reserve banks. Business loans were not in demand, even at cheaper rates; hence the sensible thing for the banks to do was to liquidate obligations.[6] When in the late summer and autumn of 1931 the international crisis led to heavy withdrawals of American gold, and hoarding began to develop on an extensive scale, a sharp reversal of discount policy became necessary. The resulting decline in the reserve ratio at the Federal Reserve banks—from 78.8 per cent at the end of August to 65.1 per cent at the end of November—created concern as to the safety of our reserve position. Accordingly, rediscount rates were sharply advanced, the New York rate being increased to 3.5 per cent in October; it remained at this level until February.

Federal Reserve policies during these years were not, however, able to stem the tide of the depression or to prevent the emergence of a banking crisis in the winter of 1933. The drastic decline in the prices of both commodities and securities, and the enormous contraction in the volume of production, threatened in due course the breakdown of the entire financial structure. The earnings of business enterprises generally were reduced to so low a level that the safety of the entire debt structure was imperilled. The collapse of bond values, which was accentuated by the efforts of banks and individuals alike to liquidate assets while some value yet remained, threatened the insolvency of financial institutions generally.

Government financial assistance had to be extended not only for the relief of debt-burdened farmers, but also to aid corporate debtors, including railroads, public utilities, industrial enterprises, and even

---

[6] The effort to inflate the currency by the issue of additional bond-secured notes should also be recalled (see p. 369).

financial institutions which had no corporate indebtedness. Moreover, the shrinkage of values was so great that regulations with respect to the valuation of the assets of insurance companies and banking institutions had to be relaxed lest wholesale insolvencies result. In effect, something approaching a general moratorium had become necessary. Attention has already been called, in chapter XXI, to the general unsoundness of a considerable part of the banking structure. The epidemic of failures in late 1932 and early 1933 in some of the larger cities disclosed a well-nigh hopeless situation, complicated in some cases by illegal, or at least highly irregular, uses of bank funds.

There is no doubt that the resources of the Federal Reserve banks were adequate to tide all of the member banks over the critical situation in which they found themselves. Certainly the banking *panic*, and the closing of all the banks of the country, could have been avoided had the Federal Reserve banks and the Reconstruction Finance Corporation been willing to overlook the shrinkage of bank assets and the evils that had been disclosed, and to combine in a joint effort to prevent closing the banks, whatever the cost. The situation at the time was greatly complicated by the fact that the crisis came in the interval between the election and the inauguration of a new administration. Whether all the interested parties should have joined forces to prevent the collapse will long be a subject of debate. Looking backward, however, it seems probable that the banking holiday and the wholesale re-organizations which followed gave us a sounder banking foundation on which to build than we should otherwise have had.

2. Improving the Mechanism of Control

The inability of the Federal Reserve system to check the stock market speculation of 1928 and 1929 and to stem the tide of the business recession was attributed in considerable part to the lack of concentration of power in the Federal Reserve authorities in Washington. The original organization, in the interests of democratic control, had vested large powers in the Reserve banks themselves. For example, the twelve banks were authorized to engage in open market operations and to change discount rates on their own volition. Under this system the power—and indeed the prestige—of the Governor of the Federal Reserve Bank of New York became much greater than that of the members of the Board of Governors. The truth is that the Federal Reserve Bank of New York tended to dominate the policies of the system. The Governor of the New York bank not only virtually controlled open market activities, but it was he rather than the Washington officials who conducted negotiations and worked out cooperative plans with the central banks of other countries. The conflict between the New York bank and the Board in relation to stock market speculation in 1929 has been noted in a preceding section.

The banking legislation of 1933 and 1935 sought to remove conflicting authority and to establish the dominance of the Federal Reserve officials in the management of the whole system. First, the prestige of the Washington officials was emphasized by specifying that the Board of Governors should have definite jurisdiction over all dealings and relationships between Federal Reserve banks and foreign banking institutions or their representatives. Second, the Reserve banks were forbidden to engage in open market operations except under regulations prescribed by the Board. Moreover, the principle was laid down that open market operations were to be engaged in solely with a view to stabilizing the general credit situation. At the same time a Federal Open Market Committee was created (see page 368) to supervise, conduct, and control open market transactions.

A third step designed to increase the control of the Federal Reserve authorities related to the fixing of discount rules. While each Federal Reserve bank nominally retains the right to establish its own rates of discount, such rates must be established or reaffirmed every fourteen days, or even more frequently if ordered by the Board of Governors. In reality, therefore, effective control has been transferred to the central authorities. A fourth step in the same direction was the conferring of power upon the Board of Governors to withhold supplies of Federal Reserve notes from a Reserve bank, and to refuse accommodations to member banks when the Board thinks such restrictions necessary to the maintenance of sound credit conditions.

Finally, the Act of 1935 gave the Board of Governors power to modify—within limits—the reserve requirements of member banks. This provision was a reflection of the fundamental change that had occurred in the general money market situation since 1930. A combination of factors had given the member banks an unprecedented increase in bank reserves, of which the most important were the reduced volume of normal credit demands, and the vast inflow of gold from abroad.

In the light of this development, it appeared that the member banks would not, for an indefinite period, be in need of any accommodations from the Federal Reserve banks—and consequently the Federal Reserve banks could exercise no effective control through the medium of advancing discount rates. The fear was also expressed that the unrestricted expansion of loans by member banks would sooner or later lead to a very dangerous credit inflation. In any case, it seemed a wise policy to safeguard the situation by giving the Federal Reserve banks the power to change the reserve requirements. The Act empowered the Board to modify the percentage ratios that had been established for the different classes of banks; the extent to which the ratios might be increased was limited to twice the existing percentages.

3. THE CRISIS OF 1937

Business and financial trends since the reorganization of the Reserve system have afforded opportunity to test the new process of control through a period of expansion culminating in a new depression. The policies pursued by the Board of Governors during these years are summarized below largely in the Board's own words.[7]

During 1936 the Federal Reserve system, as reconstituted, continued to pursue the policy of monetary ease which had been in

RESERVE POSITION OF MEMBER BANKS, 1930–1938[a]

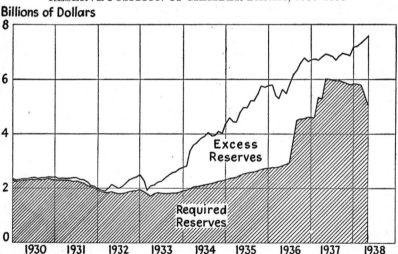

Billions of Dollars

a Data compiled from reports of the Board of Governors of the Federal Reserve system.

effect since the beginning of the depression, and money was available in abundance at the lowest rates of interest the country has known.

Reserves of member banks continued to increase rapidly throughout the year. They had been built up in recent years largely by the acquisitions of gold which followed revaluation of the dollar in January, 1934. Notwithstanding an increase in required reserves

[7] From *Annual Reports of Board of Governors of the Federal Reserve System*, 1936 and 1937.

resulting from a rapid rise in deposits, excess reserves by the summer of 1936 amounted to over three billion dollars. On the basis of these excess reserves and the legal reserve ratios then in effect, bank credit could have been expanded to twice the volume in use at the peak of business activity in 1929; and the gold inflow was still in progress.

In July, 1936 and again in January, 1937 the Board of Governors took action to increase reserve requirements and thereby to eliminate a large part of the excess reserves that had accumulated. The combined effect of these two actions of the Board was to double the reserve requirements of member banks. Thus the power conferred upon the Board by the Banking Act of 1935 to increase reserve requirements for the purpose of preventing injurious credit expansion was fully utilized.

The effects of these changes upon the reserve position of the member banks are shown graphically in the chart on page 411. The subsequent reductions in the requirements will be noted presently.

The Treasury cooperated in this program of controlling potential inflation by means of a new gold policy, designed to prevent further acquisitions of gold from increasing, and sales of gold from reducing, member bank reserves. This policy is commonly described as the "gold sterilization" process. The procedure is described as follows:

"Under this practice, as under the old, the Treasury pays for gold by drawing upon its balance with the Federal Reserve banks, thus transferring funds from Treasury account to member bank account at the Federal Reserve banks. The Treasury's balance is reduced by the operation and member bank reserves are correspondingly increased. At this point the change of practice is introduced. Before the adoption of the new gold policy it was the practice of the Treasury to replenish its balance with the Federal Reserve banks by utilizing the newly purchased gold to give the Federal Reserve banks equivalent credits in the gold-certificate account. Replenishment of its balance in this manner had no effect upon member bank reserves, which therefore retained the increase that had occurred when the gold was sold to the Treasury. Under the new policy effective December 24, however, the Treasury has followed the practice of setting aside its current gold purchases in an inactive account and replenishing its balance with the Federal Reserve banks by drawing funds from the market either through the use of existing balances or through borrowing. Thus funds are transferred back from member bank reserves to the Treasury account at the Federal Reserve banks, cancelling the increase in member bank reserves that occurred at the time the Treasury purchased the gold. While the net result of these operations is to leave unchanged the total volume of member bank reserves, they may have altered the distribution of these reserves among member banks.

The new Treasury policy has been applied not only to gold imports, but also to purchases of domestically mined gold. The factor which has been chiefly responsible for the growth of member bank reserves in recent years has thus been eliminated as a current influence in this direction. The excess reserves that had accumulated, however, were unaffected by the Treasury's action."

The Treasury and Federal Reserve measures taken together largely eliminated the basis of *potential* credit expansion.

However, the great volume of accumulated cash resources held by individuals and business concerns, which was well in excess of present needs, was not reduced by the action taken to diminish excess reserves of member banks. They continued to have a substantial amount of excess reserves on which to expand credit and could obtain additional reserves by recourse to Federal Reserve banks. But the necessity of calling Federal Reserve credit into use would once again make the banking system more directly responsive to Federal Reserve policy. The existing volume of bank deposits, moreover, was not reduced by the increase in reserve requirements, and these deposits, if more actively utilized, would be sufficient to finance a volume of business far greater than was transacted in 1936.

Federal Reserve policy, therefore, continued to be directed toward monetary ease. During 1936 business borrowing from banks and in the capital market showed a marked increase. Since both banks and other investors had unused cash resources, the financing of new capital needs, as well as an unusually large amount of refunding, was effected at exceptionally low interest rates. The large volume of idle funds still in the hands of investors should assure business of ample funds at moderate rates to finance further recovery, even without expansion of bank credit. The pressure of these investment funds in the security markets was supplemented by foreign investments in American securities amounting on balance since March, 1935 to about one billion dollars.

The rise in stock prices after March, 1935 had been rapid and nearly continuous, and from the autumn of 1935 to the spring of 1936 it was accompanied by an increase in credit extended for margin trading in securities, as well as by greater stock market activity. Under these circumstances it was considered advisable to restrict further buying on the basis of borrowed funds—buying that would be encouraged both by the speculative opportunities that existed in the stock market and by the extremely low rates at which loans on securities were available by reason of the accumulation of excess bank reserves. The Board, therefore, in January and March, 1936 took action to increase the margin requirements applicable to security loans made by brokers and dealers in securities, and in March also made these requirements, as increased, applicable to loans made by banks on stocks for the purpose of purchasing or carrying stocks registered on national securities exchanges. By these measures the Board undertook to check the growing use of borrowed funds for speculation in securities, without limiting the supply or raising the cost of credit available for commercial, industrial, or agricultural purposes. Extensions of credit by brokers and banks to finance margin trading declined somewhat after the Board's action but in the latter part of the year showed a small increase, which continued during the early months of 1937.

In the spring of 1937 an unexpected development occurred, namely, an incipient crisis in the bond market. Prices of government and high-grade corporate bonds had reached an extraordinarily high level in the latter half of 1936. Banks in New York City which had expanded their government security holdings at a rapid rate in the early part of 1936 had begun to sell in the latter part of that year, and continued to sell in the early months of 1937. As a result of these sales, the average yield on long-term government bonds rose from a little over $2\frac{1}{4}$ per cent in February to $2\frac{3}{4}$ per cent early in April.

In order to stabilize conditions in the money market the Federal Open Market Committee engaged in a series of open-market operations. Between March 10 and March 31, 1937 it increased the Federal Reserve system's holdings of Treasury securities by 104 million dollars, and at the same time reduced its holdings of short-term Treasury notes by 85 million dollars and its holdings of Treasury bills by 19 million dollars, so that the total of its portfolio of government securities remained unchanged. Between April 4 and April 28 the Reserve banks bought 96 million dollars of Treasury bonds. Government and other high-grade bond prices stopped declining in the early part of April. For the remainder of the year government issues moved gradually higher, interrupted by a reaction in the latter part of the summer. Prices of corporate bonds of the highest grade also rose; by July the recovery amounted to about half of the spring decline and thereafter prices of these obligations were generally maintained. Intervention by the Federal Reserve system in the bond market during March and April, therefore, helped stabilize that market.

A mid-summer 1937 review of the banking situation showed that the volume of funds for purposes of lending and investment was adequate in all classes of banks; that there was a continued increase in the banks' lending for business purposes; and that liquidation by banks of their government securities had practically ceased.

In order to bring Reserve bank discount rates into closer relationship with rates in the money market, in anticipation of possible seasonal demands for credit and currency in the autumn, the Federal Reserve banks in August and September reduced these rates. After these changes were made, the rate at the Federal Reserve Bank of New York stood at 1 per cent, the lowest central bank rate in history, and at the other Federal Reserve banks at 1½ per cent. By this action the Federal Reserve system made it easier for individual member banks to meet seasonal or exceptional demands by borrowing from the Federal Reserve banks, rather than by liquidating any of their assets.

Early in August, total excess reserves of member banks were in the neighborhood of 700 million dollars, but, owing to substantial withdrawals of balances by country banks, excess reserves at New York City banks had declined to below 50 millions as compared with 200 millions in May. It appeared, therefore, that the New York banks might experience some pressure in meeting the autumn demands for currency and for credit. To avoid the development of such pressure, easing action in the money market was undertaken.

The Board of Governors in September requested the Secretary of the Treasury to release 300 million dollars from the inactive, or sterilized gold account, and at the same time the Reserve system announced that it would stand ready to buy additional government securities in order to meet the expected seasonal demands on the banks for currency and credit. The Board stated that the purpose of this action was to maintain at member banks an aggregate volume of excess reserves adequate for the continuation of the system's policy of monetary ease for the furtherance of economic recovery. The procedure was in conformity with the usual policy of the system to facilitate the financing of orderly marketing of crops and of autumn trade. Together with the reduction of discount rates at several Federal Reserve banks, this action placed the member banks in a position to meet readily any increased seasonal demands for credit and currency and contributed to the continuation of easy credit conditions.

As a consequence of the release of gold in September, excess reserves of member banks increased to one billion dollars and continued around that level for the rest of the year. At New York City banks, where the effect of the gold was immediately felt, excess reserves rose to more than 400 millions and were thereafter maintained near that level. In November the Federal Reserve system purchased an additional 38 million dollars of government securities. In the latter part of the year there was another slight easing of money rates, and yields on long-term Treasury bonds declined to 2½ per cent.

Margin requirements on security loans, both by banks and by brokers, had been 55 per cent since early in 1936. This high level had been established at a time when security prices were advancing rapidly and security loans were increasing. High margin requirements earlier in the year had the effect of diminishing the amount of forced liquidation that a decline in stock prices might otherwise have caused. When security prices declined in the autumn and the volume of security loans diminished, the Board of Governors took action, effective November 1, to reduce the margin requirements on security loans, both by banks and by brokers, from 55 to 40 per cent.

In the spring of 1938 it was deemed wise to ease the reserve position again in the hope of promoting a new credit expansion. Hence, on April 14, 1938, reserve requirements were reduced to 12, 17½, and 22¾ per cent respectively for the three classes of member banks.

That these policies did not prove effective in controlling the general business situation is all too evident. Since the spring of 1937 we have had a stock market collapse and an acute business depression. As may be observed by referring again to the movement of stock prices in the chart on page 226, and to the general trend of business as shown in the chart on page 342, the current fluctuations have been quite as sharp as those of former times. The inability of the Board of Governors of the Federal Reserve system to control the business situation is simply evidence that many of the forces, which account for business fluctuations, lie beyond the control of monetary policy.

In concluding this discussion of the Federal Reserve system attention should be called to a point of view embodied in the new legislation, which marks a profound departure from the conception that had prevailed during the long period from the Civil War to 1933. As a result of the experience of the early nineteenth century in connection with the First and Second national banks and in the light of banking history in other countries, the opinion had crystallized that an efficient monetary and banking system, responsive to the requirements of business, necessitated detachment from political control. This conviction was responsible for the Independent Treasury system; for the segregation of the monetary from the fiscal functions of the Government in the

Currency Act of 1900; for vesting in the National Banking system the power to issue notes; and for the democratic organization of the Federal Reserve system and the independent political position accorded the members of the governing board. While the Secretary of the Treasury was ex officio a member of the Board, the view prevailed that the Treasury should not be permitted to dominate Reserve policies in the interests of government fiscal requirements.

Under the new organization, as we have seen, the powers of the Board of Governors have been greatly expanded, thereby circumscribing the independence of action of the member banks; and at the same time the Board of Governors has been placed more definitely under political control. This is accomplished through that provision of the law which makes the governor of the Board removable at the will of the President.

This shift is a reflection of the philosophy that not only is it a proper function of the Government to assume control over the entire credit system, but that only the Government can be depended upon to exercise such control in the interest of the public welfare as a whole. This conception appears to be the result of two factors—the failure of the former system of control to prevent financial crises, and the greatly increased importance of government fiscal and financial operations in the larger scheme of things. Whether the new alignment will be able to avoid the weaknesses disclosed in former periods of political control, time will demonstrate. As will be noted in the following chapter a similar trend is strongly in evidence in other countries.

CHAPTER XXV

THE BANKING AND CREDIT SYSTEMS OF OTHER COUNTRIES

Thus far in this treatise we have been surveying the evolution of the investment and commercial credit system in terms of American experience only. In order to provide a broader perspective in which to view the problem of financial organization in the modern world, and particularly in which to gauge the significance of current trends, we shall now present a brief account of the evolution and present status of the financial systems of other countries. In order to keep the discussion within bounds it will be necessary to confine attention to commercial and investment banking—ignoring the operation of such institutions as the stock exchange and the various forms of agricultural and consumer credit agencies. Even with this limitation, it will be necessary to be content with a mere summary of the principal features of the banking and credit systems of the more important countries. The first section of the chapter will outline the financial set-up in selected countries; the second will discuss certain phases of central banking experience and development; and the third will call attention to the international aspects of financial organization.

I. FOREIGN CREDIT SYSTEMS

In order to disclose the varying lines along which credit institutions have evolved we have selected for discussion the systems of Great Britain, France, Germany, and Japan, each of which has its distinguishing characteristics. A summary statement will also be made with respect to special features of the credit systems of other countries, with particular reference to developments during recent years.

1. GREAT BRITAIN

The British credit system consists chiefly of the following institutions: the joint stock commercial banks; the Bank of England; discount houses and bill brokers; and investment and savings institutions. The outstanding characteristic of British banking, historically speaking, was the functional specialization of the various types of institutions. However, as we shall see, in recent years there has been a strong tendency towards integration. Commercial banking expanded rapidly at the end of the eighteenth and the beginning of the nineteenth century. Commercial banks at first supplied credit simply to commercial interests which were engaged in the movement of goods through the channels of distribution.[1] Later they helped finance the manufacturers who were applying the technical improvements of the industrial revolution to productive processes. Commercial bank credit was originally extended exclusively in the form of circulating notes, and it was not until well into the nineteenth century that deposit currency became important.

At first these banks were mainly private enterprises, but in the course of time a growing number were operated as joint stock companies, and were located not only in London but also throughout the provinces. In the last quarter of the nineteenth century there took place an extensive merger movement which resulted in a comparatively small number of major banks. Indeed by the outbreak of the World War a very few banks controlled most of the commercial credit resources of England. At the present time the Big Five, comprising the Midland Bank, Lloyd's Bank, Barclay's Bank, Westminster Bank, and the National Provincial Bank, operate branches throughout all of England.

These institutions have generally been regarded as excellent examples of pure commercial banks, that is, banks which receive only demand deposits and grant only short-term loans and discounts. In reality, even before 1900 British banks were experiencing a development similar to, though less pronounced than, that of American commercial banks, and were placing a growing proportion of their assets in securities. In the post-war period this trend was intensified, and as a result the proportion of total securities to total assets rose from 15 per cent in 1925 to 27 per cent in 1934. In this period there was also an increase in the proportion of time deposits to demand deposits.

The condensed balance sheet of a typical joint stock bank is presented below; the figures are in thousands of pounds.

Liabilities		Assets	
Capital subscribed and paid up	15,858	Cash on hand and at Bank of England	70,783
Reserve funds	10,750	Cash at call	27,069
Acceptances and endorsements	8,532	British government securities	95,033
Deposit and current accounts	434,646	Bonds, stocks, and other investments	14,359
		Discounts and advances	246,628
		Premises and sundries including cover for acceptances	15,914
	£469,786		£469,786

[1] See quotation from Adam Smith, p. 310.

The keystone of the British financial system has been the Bank of England. This institution, which was founded in 1690, has been the dominant factor in governing the British money market. The affairs of the Bank are administered by a court of 24 directors, a governor, and a deputy governor. Over the years it became the unwritten rule that the directors must not at the same time be connected with any of the large joint stock banks, discount houses, or brokerage concerns, but must rather be drawn from the private investment banking houses or from the great business enterprises of the city. For many years the Bank was also completely independent of the Government. Eventually, however, it became the practice to include on the Board persons who had formerly been in the Treasury Department of the Government. Owing to emergency conditions during the war and postwar period, the relation between the Bank of England and the Government inevitably became much closer.

The Bank of England functions through two departments, known respectively as the Issue Department and the Banking Department. The primary function is the issuance of bank notes—a virtual monopoly privilege of issuing notes having been conferred in 1844 for the purpose of establishing a uniform bank currency throughout the country. The Bank of England is essentially a bankers' bank, having comparatively few dealings with the general public. The Banking Department receives its deposits from the Government and from the large joint stock banks. Unlike continental central banks, the Bank of England operates only a small number of branches, located in London and other principal cities.

The third important element in the British financial structure is the discount market for the buying and selling of acceptances. Two types of institution operate in this field, the discount houses and the so-called bill brokers. The discount houses, which are institutions of substantial size, operate on the basis of their own capital, supplemented by funds deposited with them, and by loans from the commercial banks, and at times from the Bank of England. They purchase acceptances with a view to holding them for some time, if not until maturity. In recent times they have also made large purchases of long-term securities. The bill brokers are individuals or firms having limited resources and specializing in the business of purchasing bills for the purpose of presently selling them to banks at a rate of discount slightly below that at which they were purchased. Since they operate, not on a commission basis but for profit, they are dealers rather than brokers in the ordinary sense. They borrow extensively from the commercial banks and, in emergencies, from the Bank of England.

The London discount market has for a century been international in scope. Owing to the momentum of an early start and to the stability of British currency following the establishment of the single gold standard in 1816, British banking houses came to finance a substantial part of all international trade. Thus operations in foreign exchange and foreign acceptances constituted a very important part of the business of bill brokers, acceptance houses, and commercial banks. The enormous volume of short-term credit instruments, which were readily salable in the discount market, gave a high degree of liquidity to the British commercial credit system.

In the field of investment banking, private houses, such as Rothschilds, Baring Brothers, and Ricardos, were established in the eighteenth century. These institutions, which came to be of enormous importance in the nineteenth century, confined their operations mainly to the flotation of foreign government loans, taking little or no part in the issuing of domestic securities. In fact, this policy has been continued even to the present time. In consequence, the close connection between large investment houses and industry which has characterized the United States, and more especially Germany and Japan, has never existed in Great Britain.

British banks have been severely criticized for what is frequently considered their failure to provide sufficient long-term credit for British domestic needs. Even the MacMillan Committee, which included bankers among its membership, in commenting on this matter in 1931, concluded that:

In the last few exceedingly difficult years, it would have been of high value if the leaders, for instance, of the steel or ship-building or other industries, had been working in the closest cooperation with powerful financial and banking institutions in the city with a view to their reconstruction on a profitable basis.

It should be noted here, however, that private investment houses have participated extensively in the acceptance market.

Operating in the field of investment banking also are a large number of private mortgage companies and investment trusts. As was pointed out in chapter XIII, the investment trust developed as a means of minimizing risks, and thus facilitating investment in foreign countries. Foreign trade and colonial development have also been promoted by the organization of British overseas banks, such as the Hong Kong and the Shanghai banking corporations. These institutions have their main offices in London, and operate branches in certain foreign areas such as the Far East and South Africa. They play an important role in financing the movement of goods not only from England to foreign countries, but also between foreign countries.

2. France

Banking developed more slowly in France than in England and it was not until the second half of the nineteenth century that a sound banking system was established. In the course of time there developed two types of private banking institution: the first, known as banques de depots, were essentially commercial institutions, of which the Crédit Lyonnaise, the Comptoir National d'Escompte, the Société Générale, and the Crédit Industriel et Commercial are conspicuous examples. The second, called banques d'affaires, are investment banks, of which the Banque de Paris et des Pays-Bas and the Banque de l'Union Parisienne are outstanding illustrations.

At first the former group confined their operations mainly to the receiving of deposits from the general public and to granting loans, while the latter were really underwriting syndicates formed either by a small group of private bankers or by large industrial corporations. In recent years, however, the distinction between these two types of bank has been largely eliminated. The deposit banks now also engage extensively in investment operations, while the investment banks solicit deposits from the general public. In general the banques d'affaires have a higher proportion of time to total deposits than have the deposit banks. Some of the latter developed extensive chains of branches throughout France. However, the provincial banks have nevertheless continued to hold their position.

The Bank of France, founded by Napoleon in 1800, has played a role of enormous importance in the life of France. Unlike the Bank of England, the Bank of France has developed an extensive business with the public. Moreover, it has performed investment as well as commercial banking services. Therefore, it has been necessary for it to operate branches throughout the country.

The administration of the Bank of France is vested in a Board of Regents which for many years was elected by the 200 largest holders of the stock of the institution. As a result, leading bankers and industrialists came to exercise an extensive control over the affairs of the institution. In fact, certain families possessed almost hereditary membership on the Board of Regents. In recent years, however, this close relationship between the Bank of France and the large banking and financial interests has been bitterly attacked by the radical parties, the feeling against the Bank being intensified by its unwillingness to accede to the heavy demands for loans when the Government came into the hands of the radical parties. As a result, in 1936, when the Government was controlled by a Socialist bloc, the organization of the Bank of France was drastically changed, provision being made for the election of a Board of Regents by all the stockholders, voting on the principle of one vote for each share holder.

The relation between the Central Bank and the Treasury has been much closer in France than in Great Britain. The Bank of France granted extensive credits to the Government during the Franco-Prussian War and its aftermath; during the World War it purchased a substantial part of the government security flotations; and in the early post-war period it indirectly financed much of the extensive program of physical rehabilitation in the devastated areas. Moreover, the Bank has for many years provided the funds required in financing Treasury deficits.   The process has involved exchanging Bank of France note issues for Treasury obligations. Although the Treasury has not at any time been able to liquidate these advances from budget surpluses, the indebtedness of the Treasury to the Bank has nevertheless been periodically reduced as a result of the successive devaluations of the franc.[2] By means of bookkeeping operations, the profits derived from devaluation have been used to liquidate Treasury obligations to the Bank.

On the investment banking side, France has evolved an effective mortgage banking system, co-ordinated through the medium of a central mortgage bank known as the Crédit Foncier. This institution serves most of the local mortgage companies and it extends credit both for agricultural development and for public works carried out under the auspices of local governments and the major "departments" into which France is divided. The funds are derived chiefly from the sale of Crédit Foncier bonds to institutional and individual investors. Since its loans have in the main been carefully made, the bonds of the Crédit Foncier have proved to be excellent for investment purposes. This investment mortgage system has served as a model for many other countries. Great private banking houses, such as the Rothschilds, also played an important role in French finance.

3. Germany

The development of the financial system of Germany came relatively late, for it was not until the second half of the nineteenth century that Germany passed through the industrial revolution. However, private banking, chiefly of an investment character, had long been developed in Germany, particularly in such financial centers as Frank-

[2] See chart and discussion, pp. 71–73.

fort, Cologne, and to a lesser extent Hamburg. It was not, however, until after 1850 that German banking underwent a rapid development. The third quarter of the century witnessed the founding of the Dresdner Bank, the Darmstädter Bank, and the Disconto-Gesellschaft. Later the organization of the Deutsche Bank completed a quartet of great incorporated banking institutions which gradually eclipsed the old-time private banking houses.

These institutions played a very important role in promoting the rapid industrial expansion of Germany during the 40 years preceding the World War, performing not only commercial but also important investment banking functions. They engaged not only in the receiving of deposits and the granting of commercial loans, but also formed syndicates and floated issues of stocks and bonds. The German banks were in fact intimately associated with German industry, the connection being effected by an exchange of directors between the banks and the industries. However, the industrialists had little voice in the affairs of the banks, while the banks had a decisive control over the industries.

Since the World War the position of the German banks has been seriously weakened by economic and political forces. The inflation debacle of the early post-war years so greatly impaired their capital that they were unable to withstand the strain of the depression, and the whole banking structure collapsed in 1931. After this general breakdown the Darmstädter and Dresdner banks were merged and the Disconto-Gesellschaft was combined with the Deutsche Bank. The position and influence of the banks have been further weakened by the policies of the National Socialist party.

The Reichsbank, the central bank of Germany, was established in 1875, shortly after the formation of the German Empire. Organized on lines similar to those of the Bank of England, this institution has played an active part in the economic life of the nation. It not only extends commercial credit but also engages extensively in investment operations, particularly through the medium of loans on securities. The relations of the Reichsbank to the Government have always been closer than has been the case in England and France. During the World War the Government relied upon the bank almost entirely for providing the funds required in financing the war. The process involved the purchase by the bank of short-term government obligations in exchange for the demand obligations of the Reichsbank, which could be used as currency, a method which was continued for some years after the war. With the rehabilitation of the Reichsbank under the Dawes plan, in 1924, control was largely removed from the hands of the Government. However, since the coming to power of the National Socialist régime, the control of the Government over the Reichsbank has been restored. At the present time the Reichsbank is again the source of the credit required for the meeting of government deficits.

4. JAPAN

It was not until the last quarter of the nineteenth century that Japan began the process of transformation from a feudal to an industrial state. Japan modeled her financial institutions, on a selective basis, after those of other countries, and developed every type of credit agency which a study of foreign experience had indicated as possibly serviceable in the process of economic expansion. As a result, the Island Empire has evolved an elaborate financial organization. There are four main types of institution: (1) those which are primarily concerned with short-term credit; (2) those which are connected with long-term investment operations; (3) those which minister to the need of small-scale enterprise, urban and rural—sometimes called people's banks; and (4) those whose chief function is to furnish credit to consumers. However, the larger banks of Japan, like those of other countries, are not highly specialized, engaging commonly in both short-term and long-term credit operations.

The commercial institutions may be divided into three groups: (a) the three central banks—of Japan, of Taiwan, and of Chosen; (b) a "special" bank known as the Yokohama Specie Bank, which engages chiefly in the foreign exchange business; and (c) the ordinary commercial banks which supply credit to private enterprises. The commercial banks of Japan, like those of Germany, have been closely associated with industrial and commercial enterprise. Indeed, a few great family enterprises, notably the Mitsui and the Mitsibishi, have largely controlled the commercial, industrial, and financial development of Japan.

The investment banking institutions consist of a series of "special banks," namely, The Hypothec Bank of Japan and the subsidiary agricultural and industrial institutions; the Industrial Bank of Japan; the Hokkaido Colonial Bank; the Chosen Industrial Bank; and the Oriental Development Company. There are no investment houses of the American variety, the nearest approach being some recently developed "installment sale" security dealers.

The Bank of Japan was established in 1882 for the primary purpose of unifying the currency system. The bank has a monopoly of the note issue function and, as the central repository of funds, provides the necessary elasticity of credit in time of crisis. It also serves as the fiscal agency of the Government, having charge of the funds of the Treasury, and of the administration of government bonds. The stock is owned by miscellaneous individuals, banks, and corporations. The directorate consists of one governor, one vice-governor, and four directors, the governor and vice-governor being appointed by the Government, while each director is appointed by the Finance Minister from two candidates nominated by the shareholders. The bank has sixteen branches. To facilitate the management of government funds and bonds, agency arrangements are maintained with a large number of banks widely distributed over the country.

The Bank of Japan is effectively controlled by the Government. As we have elsewhere indicated,[3] the Bank is now financing huge government deficits through the process of exchanging bank notes, payable on demand, for the time obligations of the Treasury.

5. Other Countries

While space does not permit consideration in specific terms of the credit systems of other countries, their essential features may be briefly indicated. Most European countries have followed the German rather than the British model. As a result, the so-called commercial banking institutions have conducted a combination of commercial and investment operations and have maintained close associations with industry. In most cases there has developed a high degree of banking concentration, a few large banks controlling the major part of the financial resources of the nation, and each operating an extensive branch banking system.

Most countries throughout Europe have developed central mortgage banks similar to the Crédit Foncier of France. These institutions granted long-term loans not only to agriculture and industry but also to local governments, financing their operations through the sale of bonds based on mortgages. In general these operations have been conducted with care, and in consequence, the bonds of these mortgage banks gradually attained a high financial position. In fact, in most countries the spread in the yield between the bonds of the central mortgage banks and of the government itself has been very small.

The difficulties encountered by the large commercial banking institutions during the depression had widespread effects upon the financial structure. For example, the failure of the Austrian Credit Anstalt not only impaired the economic life of the nation but also destroyed the credit of the Government itself. The result of the breakdown of these institutions was a complete change in government policy with respect to private banking institutions. In the pre-war period governments had adopted few regulations with respect to private bank-

[3] See p. 96.

ing operations. In recent years, however, there has been a rapid extension of government regulations pertaining to capital requirements and the character of credit extensions. In some cases, moreover, there has been a separation of commercial and investment banking operations.

Moreover, the financial crises of the depression period made it necessary for governments to make extensive grants of funds in order to restore the depleted capital of private banks. In some countries special government corporations, similar to the American Reconstruction Finance Corporation, were organized for the purpose of supporting the impaired banking structure. In some cases also it was necessary to establish entirely new machinery for commercial and investment banking. The Italian Government not only granted liberal assistance to the Italian banks, but established the Institute Mobiliera Italiana, as a government institution, for the purpose of granting long-term loans to finance Italian industry. Belgium established a National Industrial Bank to take over the long-term mortgage business.

The substitution of public for private banking institutions reached the extreme form in the case of Russia. The banking system of the late Russian Imperial Government was destroyed with the coming of the Soviet regime. In time, the Soviet Government came to realize the necessity for a banking system, and in due course a number of institutions were established. These include the Gosbank, or State bank, the Prombank, or Industrial bank, and the State Savings Bank. The first institution operates through a large number of branches, and receives the short-term deposits of the industrial enterprises operated by the Government. The Prombank receives the long-term deposits of the state industries, which also turn a large proportion of their profits into the capital funds of the Bank. For a time the Soviet Government tried to operate without a capital market; but the indifferent success of this experiment finally led to a complete reversal of policy. Learning by experience that capital was essential for its operations and that capital accumulation had to be encouraged, the Government established the State Savings Bank, which through a vast network of branches has played an important part in recent years in mobilizing the savings of the nation.

II. CENTRAL BANKING EXPERIENCE AND TRENDS

All of the older central banks of the world were originally organized chiefly for the purpose of providing a uniform bank note currency. With the passage of time, however, they became the credit reservoirs for the deposit currency system and assumed responsibility for controlling the credit system as a whole. It is noteworthy that although Euro-

FINANCIAL ORGANIZATION

pean countries suffered periodic economic crises comparable in severity with those of the United States, they largely escaped the banking panics which accompanied such crises in this country. The large reserve accumulations of the central banks, and the well developed system of rediscounting served to cushion the shock of business recessions and to provide the essential elasticity of currency.

Foreign central banks have not, however, been able to control the business cycle. The discount rate was, indeed, continuously utilized as a means of credit adjustment. The key to central bank policy was not the control of business conditions but the safeguarding of the money market, and the principal index was the flow of gold into and out of the bank reserves of a country. It was assumed that if the central bank protected the reserves of the banking system against undue strain it had performed its primary service. This end was accomplished by the adjustment of interest rates or by open market operations. If there were an outflow of gold and the reserves were in consequence declining, the situation could be rectified by an increase in the interest rate; and, vice versa, if there was an inflow of gold, a reduction in interest rates would reverse the trend.

It was, however, necessary to gauge whether the outflow or inflow of specie was due to a temporary situation which would presently correct itself, or to a more permanent change in the business and financial situation. The orthodox central bank policy in this connection has been well summarized as follows:[4]

If it appeared that a gold outflow was due to a mere seasonal strain which carried no threat of future trouble, or to a financial crisis abroad, the central bank would put credit into the market by purchasing bills or government securities to offset the loss of gold, and withdraw it again when the strain was past. On the other hand, in cases where the pressure appeared to be due to speculative expansion of credit on the part of commercial banks which threatened to grow cumulatively greater, sound policy required the central bank to tighten the market without waiting for the movement to deplete the reserves and thereby compel contraction. In the one case the objective was to enable the commercial banks to ignore the gold movement; in the other case it was to hasten the contraction of credit which must result from the outflow of gold and thereby to shorten the period of adjustment.

Vice versa, if a gold inflow was due to seasonal conditions and hence was not likely to last long, central banking policy aimed to prevent this reserve from being built into the credit structure through an expansion of credit operations. But if it was believed that an inflow was the result of a balance of payments favorable for more permanent reasons, approved central banking

[4] See Charles O. Hardy, *Credit Policies of the Federal Reserve System*, pp. 12–13.

policy was to permit the increased stock of gold to support an increased supply of credit.

Without a central bank, the decisive factor determining the effect of a gold inflow or outflow on the money market was the more or less accidental amount of slack in the reserves; with a central bank the crucial question was not the size of the reserves but the cause and the anticipated duration of any flow of gold into or out of them. Loss or gain of gold was regarded as a symptom of the state of the balance of payments rather than as a thing of immediate importance on its own account.

It will be observed that this method of control, which is best exemplified by the English experience, revolved around an international flow of currency. To ease the reserve strain in Great Britain, it was necessary to attract funds from abroad; to tighten the money market, it was necessary to induce funds to flow out. This could readily be accomplished by raising and lowering the rates of interest above and below those prevailing in other markets. As long as other countries were not simultaneously matching rates, it was thus possible to attract or to expel liquid funds. But if rates should move concurrently in all countries, no such shifting of reserves would be possible.

While the manipulation of the British rate did unquestionably affect the condition of the money market, it has never been able to promote quick recovery in periods of depression. The experience of the seventies and the nineties,[5] not to mention the 1930's, shows conclusively that low discount rates have been no more effective in bringing quick recovery in Great Britain than they have been in the experience of the United States. This is because the interest rate constitutes only one of the factors in the general business situation which business men must take into account in gauging the possibilities of making profits.

During the last twenty years central banks everywhere have become increasingly linked with government fiscal operations. In nearly every country there has been a decline in the proportion of credit granted to trade and industry as compared with that granted to the state. While the charters of most central banks contain restrictions with respect to state loans, such limitations have been impossible of enforcement in the face of the financial exigencies of recent times. Commercial banks are not only very large holders of government issues, but in the majority of cases they are under the practical necessity of underwriting huge current deficits.

In pre-war times the general tradition was that the central bank should be free of political control, but, as we have already noted, the

[5] See pp. 402–404.

financial exigencies of the World War led to a considerable reduction in the independence of the central banking institutions. In the years immediately following the war an effort was made to restore the independence of central banks. The League of Nations, in establishing such banks in the newly formed countries, sought to follow this ideal. Moreover, the Commission on Currency Exchange at the Brussels Conference of 1920 adopted a resolution stating that "a bank of issue should be free from political pressure and should be conducted solely on the lines of prudent finance." The hope was expressed that banks would be regarded as public trusts, responsive to the requirements of business enterprise, and not as departments of the government. The issuance of notes by national governments was especially criticized. In the words of one banking commission:

> Mindful as it is of the disasters of past years in all countries where currency was issued by the Government, and recognizing the hazards which come from changes of Government, from the development of budget deficits and other evils from which no country has found itself immune, the Commission is definitely of the opinion that the management of the legal tender note issue should be placed in the hands of a non-political and independent body, which shall control the conditions of issue and shall have full control and custody of the securities it holds.[6]

However, with the coming of the world depression and the need of funds to support tottering banking institutions and relieve unemployment, control of government over the central banks once more increased everywhere. The extent of government control over the administration of banks varies considerably. In the case of state owned banks it is complete; in the case of the privately owned central banks the government commonly has representation on the Board. In most cases the presiding officer of the bank is appointed by, and is subject to removal by, the government. Thus the trend noted in the United States in preceding chapters is part of a universal phenomenon.

III. INTERNATIONAL ASPECTS OF FINANCIAL ORGANIZATION

No attempt has been made in this volume to indicate in any detailed way the connections between the financial systems of different countries and the relation of a world financial system to modern economic organization as a whole. At a few points, however, we have necessarily been drawn into a discussion of certain phases of the international financial system. In the chapter on the foreign exchanges we saw how

---

[6] *Report of the Irish Free State Banking Commission,* quotation cited in Kisch and Elkin, *Central Banks,* p. 74.

international commercial and financial obligations are largely canceled through the use of bills of exchange; how the world supply of metallic currency is ordinarily distributed among the various nations of the world in rough accordance with their relative needs; and how central banking institutions have on occasion collaborated in the redistribution of gold with a view to promoting world financial and economic stability.

We have also noted how the breakdown of credit and currency systems during the last 20 years has led to a series of disastrous repercussions upon the world financial structure. This system of interdependent credit relations, world-wide in scope, was, however, well developed long before the World War period. When in the decade of the eighties the great speculative mania in the Argentine, accompanied by the issue of vast quantities of irredeemable paper currency, collapsed in 1890, it resulted in the failure of one of the greatest international banking houses of England, all but precipitated a general financial panic in Europe, and led to a very serious unsettling of American financial conditions. Similarly, financial difficulties in Japan and Egypt in 1906 contributed to the forces that were bringing on the American panic of 1907, while the repercussions of this panic in the United States were felt in every market of the world. In a word, business cycles are world phenomena and the modern financial structure is essentially international in its scope.

The growing interdependence of the financial systems of different countries and the development of an international financial structure give rise to the suggestion that if the financial system is to perform effectively its functions in assisting and regulating the modern economic organization, some method of international control must ultimately be devised. Just as the growth of a national, as distinguished from a local, basis of economic organization destroyed the efficacy of local and state control of finance and business and required the development of a system of national supervision, so the evolution of a world economic and financial system requires the creation of some form of international banking organization—a federal reserve system, so to speak, for the world at large.

Progress in the evolution of an adequate banking organization, like progress in so many other directions, is often the outgrowth of some particular period of stress. The financial disorganization which followed the World War, and in particular the difficulties encountered in connection with the reparation problem, thus gave a real impetus to the movement for the establishment of some form of international banking agency. In due course the Young Plan for the settlement of the reparation problem provided for a Bank for International Settlements, intended to combine, with its primary function of serving as a transmitter of reparation installments, certain clearing-house, exchange, and banking operations.

The international bank located at Basle, Switzerland, was obviously conceived as an agency which would in good season become a grand central banking institution for the world as a whole—one which would exercise functions in the international field similar to those which the Federal Reserve system of the United States or the central banks of other countries exercise in their respective national fields. The opposition of existing financial institutions, and political controversy as to its proper location, resulted, however, in limiting materially the scope of the powers of this bank.

The capital of the bank is 500 million Swiss francs, equivalent to $96,500,000. Eighty per cent of the stock was allocated to the countries which founded the bank, namely, Belgium, France, Germany, Great Britain, Italy, Japan, and the United States. The balance of the stock was available for purchase by banks in other countries, but only in countries interested in reparations or in those whose currencies fulfilled the practical requirements of the gold or gold exchange standard. It was expected that the central bank of each country would subscribe to the capital stock. In the case of the United States, however, the Government held that it would not be lawful for the Federal Reserve system or banks to purchase the stock and therefore the American share was taken up by two banks in New York and one in Chicago. The allotment to Japan was not subscribed by its central bank because under the terms of the subscription one of its officers would have to attend the meetings of the Bank for International Settlements, which would entail either constant travelling or continuous absence from home. A private group of Japanese bankers consequently took up the subscription. Forty-four per cent of the total stock authorized remained after the founding countries subscribed and this was allocated to the central banks of other nations which at the time were on either the gold or gold exchange standard. In all, some 28 countries subscribed. Only one-fourth of the par value of the stock was called for payment.

The board of directors was to number 25 and consist of the following: (1) the governors of the central banks of Belgium, France, Germany, Great Britain, and Italy, and a Japanese and an American representative chosen by the five governors; (2) one business man from each of the seven countries, to be selected by the first group; (3) representatives of central banks of nine countries other than the seven founding nations. These nine were to be selected by the second group.

The primary functions of the bank in the early years were to facilitate reparation payments. It acted as a trustee or agent in receiving, administering, and distributing the annuities paid, and in supervising and assisting in the commercialization and mobilization of certain portions of the annual payments. Other operations of the bank conform in general with the policies of the central banks of the participating countries, which have the right of objection to any proposed transaction which concerns them. The bank may make advances to central banks, engage in open market operations in bankers' bills, and purchase and sell foreign exchange. It may not, however, make loans to governments, accept bills, issue notes, or own any real estate aside from its place of business.

With the cessation of reparation payments, the main function of the bank and one of its important sources of working capital vanished. The fall of the gold standard has likewise seriously limited the activity of the bank, since the original intention was that it should confine its activities wholly to countries on the gold or gold exchange standard. The future usefulness of the bank depends to a considerable extent upon the further development of international cooperation in general and the re-establishment of the gold standard throughout the world.

CHAPTER XXVI

AGRICULTURAL CREDIT INSTITUTIONS

The analysis of financial operations in all of the preceding chapters has related primarily to the financing of industry and commerce, with only incidental reference to the agricultural side of our economic life. In the present chapter we shall study the financial structure from the point of view of agriculture, noting in what ways the financial institutions which have already been considered are associated with agricultural finance, and discussing, particularly, the work of the numerous special financial agencies that have been evolved for facilitating the raising of capital for agricultural purposes. No small part of our task will be to describe the work of the various agencies which have arisen out of the emergency conditions of the depression period.

Agricultural credit is of three types: long-term, intermediate-term, and short-term. The lines between these types of credit, especially between intermediate- and short-term, are not sharply drawn. The first type is identical in nature with that of the fixed capital of industrial enterprises, while the third is directly analogous to working capital. From the point of view of the duration of loans, intermediate credit, as the term indicates, lies midway between short-term and long-term credit, running as a rule from six or nine months to three years. It is used chiefly for the purchase of farm machinery, live stock, and products having a life extending well beyond a single harvest period. Such products are of course analogous to equipment in the field of industry.

The chart on page 437 reveals in a general way the character of the agricultural credit structure that has been evolved. Before discussing the specific functions of the various institutions, a brief statement is necessary by way of explanation and amplification of the chart. The arrows on the diagram are intended to indicate the movement of credit instruments from the farm borrowers with whom they originate to the institutions or individuals furnishing the funds. Ultimately the funds are all derived from the sources indicated in the rectangles at the bottom of the chart, though in many instances the credit instruments find lodgment in intermediary credit agencies. The dotted connecting lines on the diagram indicate administrative relationships.

The large area in the center of the diagram includes a group of agencies that are under the supervision of the Farm Credit Administration, which was established in 1933 for the purpose of coordinating the activities and simplifying the administration of the permanent agricultural credit agencies. The four institutions shown inside the area—Federal Land Banks, Banks for Cooperatives, Federal Intermediate Credit Banks, and Production Credit Corporations, are permanent central credit institutions akin in their respective fields to the Federal Reserve banks. They do not make direct loans to farmers but operate through other institutions. The supervisory work of the Farm Credit Administration extends not only to these institutions but to the associated National Farm Loan Associations and Production Credit Associations, to Federal Credit Unions, and to the Emergency Crop and Feed Loan Section.[1] The Federal Farm Mortgage Corporation is an independent corporation; but utilizes the personnel, facilities, and services of the Farm Credit Administration, the expenses of which are borne by the Federal Government.

The work performed by all the various types of agencies listed in the diagram will be indicated in the ensuing discussion. Inasmuch as short-term agricultural institutions were the first to be developed, we shall begin our discussion with the right-hand section of the diagram.

I. SHORT-TERM CREDIT

The working or operating capital used in agriculture is derived from a variety of sources—from commercial banks, cattle loan companies, private individuals, implement manufacturers, canning factories, local merchants, wholesale dealers, etc. Such credit extensions are evidenced in a variety of ways, including open book or charge accounts, single-name promises to pay, notes bearing one or more endorsements, chattel mortgages, warehouse receipts, and notes secured by stock and bond collateral. In view of the discussion in preceding chapters, the character of these short-term credit operations needs only brief comment.

1. *Trade or mercantile credit.*—A substantial part of the credit received by farmers takes the form of what is commonly called trade credit. As the diagram suggests, trade credit is extended for both short-term and intermediate-term purposes. The latter is devoted entirely to productive uses but much of the former goes for consump-

[1] The Administration also supervises joint stock land banks and regional agricultural credit corporations, which are now in process of liquidation.

tion. Until comparatively recent times the farming communities have in fact borrowed the larger portion of their working capital from other than banking sources. For reasons which need not here be considered, the farmer typically purchased the supplies needed for current use on the farm from the local stores, paying for them in the autumn after the sale of the season's crops. Such credit was usually extended without the requirement of a promissory note; it was book credit, with the merchants as a rule keeping the only records. Since the risks were relatively large, collections being slow and uncertain, the merchants necessarily added a substantial amount to the price of the goods in order to cover the risks involved. The looseness of the system, moreover, opened the way for exorbitant or usurious charges.

The system of trade credit has had its most extensive development in the South, particularly in connection with the growing of cotton and tobacco by small landowners and tenants. Under this system a local merchant or dealer at the beginning of the crop-growing season extends a line of credit at the store to a cotton grower, for example, and takes a "lien" on the cotton crop, or a chattel mortgage on the crop plus any other property which the borrower may own. It has been the custom to grant a maximum trade allowance per month, the amount varying with the community and with the color of the tenant. The interest is nearly always deducted in advance, and it appears that the borrower has, as a rule, been greatly overcharged for his goods. Perhaps the worst evil of this system is the fact that the borrower is virtually at the mercy of the storekeeper.

The owner of the land, as well as the local merchant, frequently advances trade credit to the tenant. It is also sometimes furnished by a "cotton factor" acting as the agent of a large cotton dealer. In some cases, moreover, the advance takes the form of actual money rather than goods. Private individuals have in many communities also made money loans to cotton and tobacco growers.

A very interesting development in rural credit in recent years has been the furnishing of seed and supplies to farmers by fruit and produce dealers, wholesale grocers, canning factories, etc. It appears that in many cases the advances take the form of actual money—the amount of the loans being deducted from the price of the crops, which are sold to the concerns which have furnished the required capital.

While this trade credit is extended directly by the local merchants, dealers, etc., the banks nevertheless ordinarily play an important part in the process, for the local merchants and dealers meanwhile usually borrow the funds from the local banks, or are carried by wholesalers and dealers higher up in the trade; in this event the latter

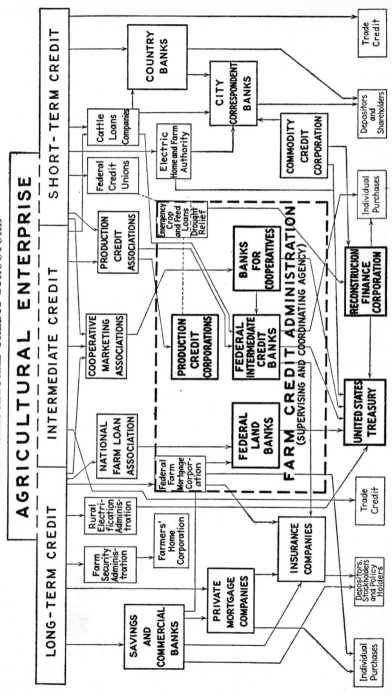

THE AGRICULTURAL CREDIT STRUCTURE

borrow heavily from the banks of the larger centers. In many cases, moreover, particularly in the farm-implement line, the credit is extended by the manufacturers, who borrow the necessary funds from the banks of the financial centers. Much of this credit is extended for a period of only six months, for the reason that many tools and supplies last for one season only. In the case of harvesting machines, however, the common practice has been for the manufacturer to allow three years for payment, one-third being paid in cash at the end of the first season, with promissory notes given for the balance. These notes are usually guaranteed by the retail dealer, who acts as the local agent for the manufacturer.

Although this system of selling farm implements still prevails to some extent, and while it is true that a large amount of trade credit is even now extended to farmers by local merchants, recent years have seen marked changes in agricultural credit methods. With the gradual application of business principles to the conduct of agriculture, which followed the passing of the frontier and the introduction of scientific methods, farmers came to see that paying cash for fertilizer, seed, and supplies saves money, even if the cash required has to be borrowed from the bank. The interest paid to the banks amounts to less than the discount on the price of the goods given for cash payment. The intermediate and emergency credit agencies to be discussed below have also served to modify the pattern of agricultural borrowing.

2. *Commercial banks.*—As the chart indicates, the operating capital used in agriculture, in so far as it takes the form of funds rather than goods, is borrowed largely from the commercial banks. As has been pointed out in other chapters, a substantial part of the business of the so-called country banks, both national and state, has been the extension of credit to agriculture. Such credit has, moreover, been extended not only for short-term uses but also for intermediate and even for fixed-capital purposes. Throughout their history the state banking institutions have made long-term loans on real estate mortgage securities. While the national banks were not permitted to make real estate loans as such prior to the passage of the Federal Reserve Act, they nevertheless made extensive agricultural loans for intermediate and fixed-capital purposes merely on the single-name or endorsed promissory notes of farmers. Although such loans normally ran for a year or less, they were, as has elsewhere been noted, repeatedly renewed.

In many cases, however, this constant renewal of loans merely indicated a more or less continuous need for borrowed working capital. Although unable to pay off a year's loan in full, the farmer was usually on the up-grade, financially speaking; and the banks were merely carrying him during the years of his adversity. In many other cases a bad year, or a series of them, necessitated continuous financial aid from the bankers. While one may reflect that such loose extension of credit constituted a very dangerous financial practice for commercial banks, it should be borne in mind as an extenuating circumstance that to the country bankers it seemed a duty to assist agricultural borrowers in hard times when they needed assistance most, quite as much as to extend them credit when their requirements were less.

As the chart indicates and as has been noted in earlier chapters, the country banks are connected with city correspondent banks with which they make deposits and from which they seek credit accommodation in case of need. Both directly and through their correspondent relations, country banks are articulated with the Federal Reserve system. The effects of changing agricultural conditions upon country banking institutions has been discussed in chapter XXII.

3. *Cattle Loan Companies.*—While this special type of financial institution should perhaps be classified rather as an intermediate than as a short-term credit agency, it will be convenient to discuss it at this place—for historically it has been closely connected with the commercial banking structure. The cattle loan company came into existence primarily to finance the growing of cattle, and to some extent sheep, on the ranges of the West. To a much smaller degree it served to finance the feeding of cattle on an extensive scale in the "corn belt" states. In brief, the reason for the development of the cattle loan company was the inability of local banks in the cattle growing and feeding regions to supply the large volume of loans required by the cattlemen. Unlike ordinary agricultural operations, cattle raising is typically conducted on a relatively large scale, and the borrower accordingly requires loans of large average size—large enough to absorb the entire lending resources of most local banks. Banking laws which restricted the volume of loans that might be made to any one borrower, and the fact that the financing of the cattle industry by the local banks would have resulted in an undue concentration of banking risks, made it necessary that the funds required be secured through financial institutions in the large money centers of the East. This the cattle loan company made possible, by acting as an intermediary between the borrowing cattlemen and the lending institutions in the financial centers.

There have been two main types of cattle loan companies—those organized and managed by individuals who make this their sole business, and those affiliated with state and national banks. The purpose of the second type of organization was chiefly to permit large banks, particularly in the livestock marketing centers, to expand the scope of their activity by means which, under the terms of their incorporation, they were not able to employ directly.

Cattle loans are of two distinct kinds, called respectively range loans and corn belt loans. The range loans, which have been by all odds of greatest importance, may in turn be subdivided into two classes—those on breeding herds and those on stockers. The corn belt loans and the loans on stockers are essentially short-term in character and are usually extended for less than a year. The breeding loans must of necessity run for a much longer period of time, and are properly classified as intermediate in type. Cattle loan paper is sold chiefly to the banks in the financial centers, the notes ranging in size from $1,000 to $500,000. Prior to 1920 the average loan was in the neighborhood of $25,000; but with changing conditions in the range country the average size of the loans has greatly diminished in recent years. The cattle loan companies usually hold for investment only a very small number of notes, the bulk of the paper being promptly sold to the bankers in financial centers.

In the period preceding the establishment of the Intermediate Credit system in 1923, the cattle loan companies performed a very important economic service. They filled a breach in the financial structure by enabling range operators to gain access to the credit resources of the financial centers, thus facilitating the growth of the livestock industry. After 1923 the cattle loan companies were accorded a new outlet for their paper through the rediscount privileges provided by the Federal Intermediate Credit system. However, the loan company developments of recent years have greatly reduced the field for the cattle loan companies, and at the present time only a few remain in operation.

4. *Commodity Credit Corporation.*—This emergency credit agency was created under authority of an executive order in 1933, for the purpose of extending loans to farmers on the security of staple agricultural products held in storage. Its capital stock was fixed at 100 million dollars, of which three millions are owned by the Treasury and 97 millions by the Reconstruction Finance Corporation. Additional funds are obtained by borrowing from the Reconstruction Finance Corporation as needed. An act of March 8, 1938 provides for an annual appraisal of the assets and liabilities of the Commodity Credit Corporation. If the net worth is shown to be less than 100 million dollars the Secretary of the Treasury is authorized to restore the amount of such capital impairment. The appraisal of that date showed the capital

to be impaired to the extent of $94,285,404.73; and this amount was appropriated in that year. The bulk of the Corporation's loans has been made upon the security of cotton—with small amounts upon corn, tobacco, peanuts, prunes, turpentine, dates, and figs. The principal of the loans outstanding on March 31, 1938 amounted to $213,795,981; the market value was appraised at $158,316,790. This Corporation, as the diagram indicates, is independent of the Farm Credit Administration. The amount of the loans per unit of product is fixed by the President of the United States. In some cases loans of this type are placed with commercial banks, under a commitment from the Commodity Credit Corporation to take them over on demand, a charge of one per cent being made for such guarantee. The life of this corporation has been twice extended, the terminal date now being June 30, 1939. There is little doubt, however, that it will continue to operate more or less indefinitely.

5. *Emergency Crop and Feed Loans "Section."*—These loans, which are of an essentially short-term character, are under the supervision of a section of the Farm Credit Administration. The director of the section is responsible to the Production Credit Commissioner. Loans of this general type were first authorized by acts of Congress as long ago as 1918. The scope of the program was greatly enlarged in 1931; and for the years 1931 to 1935 inclusive, approximately 490,000 loans were made annually, the average size being $135. Under an act of February 20, 1935, loans were authorized for the fallowing of land, the production and harvesting of crops, and the purchase and production of feed for livestock. Loans are restricted to applicants who have the necessary land and the equipment for cultivating it, or livestock for which feed is required, and who are unable to obtain credit from commercial sources or from production credit associations.

In addition to these loans, this section of the Farm Credit Administration also administers drought relief loans authorized by the Act of June 19, 1934. Most of these loans, which have been made on very liberal terms, are secured by crop liens. The funds for both the crop and feed loans and the drought loans are provided by the Reconstruction Finance Corporation.

6. *Federal Credit Unions.*—These cooperative credit agencies, which were authorized by an act of 1934, have already been mentioned in chapter XIX in connection with our discussion of urban credit unions. They are local cooperative credit associations, the stock of which is subscribed by the members. They make loans only to their own members. They receive their charters from, and are supervised by, a sectional director of the Farm Credit Administration, who is responsible

directly to the Governor of the Administration. No loan may exceed $200, and the length of maturity may not be greater than two years. The total volume of loans made to September 30, 1937 (by the 80 per cent of the unions which have made reports) was 40,655,209, and the amount outstanding on that date was $13,372,125. These cooperative agencies have received extensive aid from the Reconstruction Finance Corporation.

7. *Federal Crop Insurance Corporation.*—This new corporation was created by the Agricultural Adjustment Act of February 16, 1938. A capital stock of 100 million dollars was authorized, to be subscribed by the United States Treasury; but not more than 20 million dollars might be subscribed in the fiscal year 1939. The supervision of the Corporation is under the Department of Agriculture, the directors being appointed by the Secretary. The insurance feature is limited to wheat. While this corporation is not a lending agency, it is included here in order to round out the picture of the ways in which the Government is rendering financial assistance to agriculture.

II. LONG-TERM CREDIT

The credit problem with which farmers have been most continuously and insistently confronted has been that of long-term borrowing on the basis of mortgage securities. As has already been indicated, the great volume of long-term credit has been procured from banking institutions both with and without mortgage security. We are here concerned with the sale of mortgage securities in the general investment markets. The farm mortgage business became of large proportions in the years following the Civil War. According to the census report of 1890, out of a total number of 3,142,746 farms, cultivated by their owners, 886,957 were subject to incumbrance. There were in addition 1,624,433 tenant farms for which no data were collected. The aggregate value of the incumbered farms was over three billion dollars and the outstanding mortgages aggregated more than one million, the three states of New York, Iowa, and Illinois together having almost one-third of the total. The ratio of mortgage indebtedness to the value of the farm varied among the different states, ranging from 24 per cent in Utah to 55 in Mississippi, and averaging 36 per cent for the country as a whole. The great bulk of these mortgages was created for constructive purposes, less than three per cent going for farm and house and family operating expenses.[2]

---

[2] Data taken from report on "Farms and Homes: Proprietorship and Indebtedness," *Eleventh Census of the United States* (1890).

As a matter of fact, farm mortgages usually increase during periods of agricultural prosperity and have a tendency to decrease when the farmer is less prosperous. Strange as this may appear at the outset, the causes for it are easily understandable. The farmers, like other business men, are anxious to expand their operations when their business is profitable, and consequently they borrow more for such expansion during good times than in periods of depression. The census report of 1910 indicated that, notwithstanding the great improvement in agricultural conditions that came with the era of rising prices beginning in 1896, the total mortgage indebtedness on farms operated by their owners stood in 1910 at 1.7 billion dollars, an increase of 59 per cent in twenty years. In the same year the estimated mortgage indebtedness for all farms was 3.3 billion dollars. In 1920 the total mortgage indebtedness on farms operated by their owners was four billion dollars, while the estimate for all farm mortgages was 7.9 billions—an increase of 131 per cent during the ten most prosperous years in our agricultural history.

Before discussing the functions of the various types of farm credit agencies, it will be useful to note who are the ultimate investors in farm mortgages. The following table shows the distribution of farm mortgages, as far as institutional investors are concerned, in the year 1929 and from 1933 to 1935 inclusive.[3] Data with respect to individual holdings are not available for the country as a whole, but a detailed study of the State of New York indicates that individual purchasers usually absorb more than 50 per cent of farm mortgage loans made in the United States. The figures are in thousands of dollars.

	1929	1933	1934	1935
Life insurance companies	2,100	1,630	1,291	1,008
Federal Land banks	1,197	1,284	2,458	2,866
Joint stock land banks	627	392	256	177
Federal Reserve member banks	388	318	262	251
Total outstanding	9,241	7,855	7,770	7,500

1. *Private mortgage companies.*—Prior to the establishment of the Federal Farm Loan system in 1916 the bulk of the farm mortgage business was handled through local agencies, local banks, and private mortgage companies. The function of the local broker was simply to serve as an intermediary in bringing the farm borrower and the city lender together. This type of brokerage business has, however, been

[3] From *The Recovery Problem in the United States*, p. 337 (The Brookings Institution).

largely supplanted by the mortgage companies and by the insurance companies, which maintain their own agents in the agricultural areas.

Private mortgage companies conduct their operations on an extensive scale, many of them operating through subsidiary offices over large areas. In making a loan under this system the prospective borrower fills out an application blank furnished by the local agent, which requires the listing of all pertinent data with respect to the property to be mortgaged. Such mortgages have usually run from three to five years. The cost of credit to the borrower has been high, in part because of the size of the commissions, but more largely because of the frequent renewals, which always involve new commissions. These mortgage companies operate partly on the basis of their own capital and partly on funds derived from the sale of debenture bonds. The heyday of these companies was in the period preceding the World War, the development of the Federal Farm Loan system and other government credit agencies having greatly circumscribed their operations in recent years.

2. *Federal Land banks.*—An insistent agitation for a reduction of rates on agricultural loans and for an improvement in the general conditions on which credit is extended to farmers, began shortly before the World War. The establishment of a "panic-proof" commercial banking system naturally suggested the development of a complementary agricultural credit system. The ultimate outcome was the establishment in 1916 of a Farm Loan system under the auspices of the Federal Government.

In brief, the purpose of the law was, through an improved organization of credit facilities, to raise the credit standing of farm borrowers, to reduce commissions and legal fees, to lessen and equalize interest rates, and to enlarge the supply of funds available for agricultural development. In pursuance of this task the law provided for the organization of (1) Federal Land banks and national farm loan associations; and (2) joint stock land banks. The former constituted the distinctive feature of the new rural credit system; while the provision for the latter marked an attempt to develop private mortgage companies under constructive governmental supervision. The joint stock banks never proved very successful and many of them collapsed during the depression. In consequence of the development of the Federal Farm Mortgage Corporation these banks are now in process of liquidation.

The Federal Farm Loan Act, like the Federal Reserve Act, divided continental United States into twelve districts, in each of which was located a Federal Land bank. In creating these districts an attempt was made to group together, as far as possible, states of diverse character and development, as a means of minimizing the results of a crop failure in any one region. In determining the location of the Federal Land bank in each district the Board sought to secure (1) reasonable approximation to the geographical center of the district; (2) prompt and frequent train and mail service; (3) climatic conditions that would not impair the health of the officials; (4) congenial environment. As a rule, the largest cities were not selected, but rather those which had already shown an interest in agricultural development, or had been disappointed in not being selected as sites for Federal Reserve banks. The cities chosen were Springfield, Mass.; Baltimore; Columbia, S. C.; Louisville; New Orleans; St. Louis; St. Paul; Omaha; Wichita; Houston; Berkeley; and Spokane. Each district bank is controlled by a board of seven directors and a general agent representing the Farm Credit Administration. General supervision over the twelve banks is now exercised by the Land Bank Commissioner, an official provided for in the Farm Mortgage Act of 1933.

The capital stock of each Federal Land bank was originally set at $750,000. Since it did not prove attractive to investors, it was necessary for the Federal Treasury to subscribe virtually the entire amount. This capital was entirely repaid by 1934; but additional capital subscriptions were made by the Treasury in 1932 to the extent of 125 million dollars, of which $124,121,595 had been paid in on December 31, 1937. In addition, the Secretary of the Treasury has subscribed to paid-in surplus of the Federal Land banks in an amount equal to the extensions and deferments of loans made by the banks. Repayments of such contributions to surplus are held in the Treasury as a revolving fund for future use. At the end of December, 1937 the amount of this paid-in surplus was $160,426,168. The Government has not, however, furnished any capital funds to the national farm loan associations.

3. *National Farm Loan Associations.*—These associations, which were authorized by the Farm Loan Act, occupy a position analogous to the individual member banks of the Federal Reserve system. They are thus in an intermediate position between the Federal Land banks and farm borrowers. However, they differ in one very important respect from commercial banks in that they are cooperative associations organized by a group of farmers for the specific purpose of securing credit through the Federal Land banks.

The law provides that "ten or more natural persons who are the owners, or about to become the owners, of farm land qualified as security for a mortgage loan under this Act," may unite to form such a national farm loan association. No persons, except borrowers on farm loan mortgages, may become members thereof. The management of the association is vested in a board of five directors. The capital stock varies with the volume of loans secured, one share of stock being issued for every loan of $200 (or major portion thereof). Thus the borrowers may receive dividends in case any are earned by the association. The shareholders are "held individually responsible, equally and ratably, and not one for another," for all debts and obligations to double the amount of their stock holdings.

When an application for a loan is submitted to a national farm loan association, a loan committee of the association appraises the value of the property and makes a detailed report on the project. No loan may be approved by the directors of the farm loan association unless all three members of the loan committee recommend it; and before the loan is finally granted, it must also be approved by an appraiser of the Federal Land bank from which the funds are to be secured.

In case the loan is approved, the farm loan association subscribes for capital stock in the Federal Land bank of its district to an amount equal to five per cent of the loan desired; the stock is hypothecated with the Federal Land bank as partial collateral security for the loan. The farm loan association then indorses a first mortgage, which it has received from the borrowing member, over to the Federal Land bank, thus assuming a secondary liability for the payment of the obligation. The mortgage must always be a first lien on property owned by the borrower, and cannot exceed 50 per cent of the value of the land for agricultural purposes, and 20 per cent of the value of the permanent insured improvements.

The Federal Land bank advances the funds to the farm loan association and issues its own debentures, known as "farm loan bonds," for sale in the general investment market. These bonds are issued only under specific authorization of the Land Bank Commissioner. For purposes of administration each district has a Farm Loan Registrar (corresponding to the Federal Reserve Agent of the Federal Reserve system), appointed by the Commissioner. When any Federal Land bank desires to issue bonds, it must deposit the mortgages which have been taken from borrowers with the Registrar, to whom they are assigned in trust as collateral for the bonds.

These loans are made only on the amortization principle—by which both principal and interest are liquidated by a series of equal annual or semi-annual payments. They usually run for a long term of years. Every farm mortgage bond is an obligation not only of the Federal Land bank of the district but of the entire Federal Land bank system.

The maximum interest rate that may be charged by any Federal Land bank is six per cent; and in no event shall the rate be more than one per cent in excess of the rate on Federal Land bank bonds. The rates at the present time are around four per cent.

4. *Federal Farm Mortgage Corporation.*—The Farm Mortgage Act of 1933 authorized the Treasury to provide 200 million dollars for emergency mortgage loans, including second-mortgage loans, to be made on a more liberal basis than are those of the regular land banks. The administration of these loans was placed in charge of the Land Bank Commissioner, and the loans are accordingly known as "Land Bank Commissioner Loans." Later the Federal Farm Mortgage Corporation was organized, and was authorized to float bonds, guaranteed by the Federal Government, as a means of securing additional funds with which to make such loans. The outstanding land bank commissioner loans were taken over by the Farm Mortgage Corporation; but the term land bank commissioner loans is still used to designate all loans made by the Farm Mortgage Corporation. The directors of this corporation are the Governor of the Farm Credit Administration, the Secretary of the Treasury, and the Land Bank Commissioner. Its lending operations are carried on by the Federal Land banks and the Land Bank Commissioner.

All of the capital stock of the Federal Farm Mortgage Corporation, amounting to 200 million dollars, is owned by the United States Government. The Government also reimburses the Federal Farm Mortgage Corporation, and likewise the Federal Land banks, for statutory reductions of interest rates made on behalf of distressed borrowers. At the end of December 1937 the total amount of such reductions had been $109,459,660, practically all of which were, naturally, associated with the older loans of the Federal Land banks.

5. *Farm Security Administration.*—This agency, formerly known as the Resettlement Administration, has been given a detached position on the chart for the reason that it was set up as an independent agency. By an executive order of December 31, 1936, it was transferred to the Department of Agriculture. The funds are derived from relief appropriations. While loans are made for a variety of purposes, this agency should, on the whole, be classified as a long-term credit institution. It makes rehabilitation loans to farmers who do not qualify for loans through national farm loan associations or productive credit associations. Some of its loans have also been classified as emergency feed and crop loans and emergency drought loans. Most of them, however, are in the nature of relief loans. The loans are secured by chattel mortgages on property acquired by the borrower from the proceeds of

the loan, by assignments of the proceeds from the sale of produce, and in some cases by liens on other assets of the borrower, including real estate mortgages. Loans are also made to community and cooperative associations to establish, refinance, or extend the scope of cooperative facilities and services; and to individuals to enable them to purchase participating rights in community and cooperative associations. The essential difference between the credit advances of the Farm Security Administration and those of other agencies lies in the fact that they are regarded as part of a larger program for providing subsistence, and for developing on a systematic basis rural rehabilitation projects.

6. *Farmers' Home Corporation.*—An Act of July 22, 1937 authorized the Secretary of Agriculture to make loans enabling farm tenants, laborers, and share croppers to purchase farms, and the Farmers' Home Corporation was created to administer these loans. The board of directors of this agency consists of three persons employed in the Department of Agriculture and designated by the Secretary. However, the actual administration of the loans has since been placed under the Farm Security Administration. The funds are apparently derived from Agricultural Department appropriations. To June 30, 1938, the number of loans made was 1,879, aggregating $9,146,633. The interest rate is three per cent and the maturity is 40 years.

7. *Electric Home and Farm Authority.*—This agency was originally organized by authority of an executive order of January 17, 1934, to operate in connection with the Tennessee Valley Authority. The following year it was established as an independent agency under the control of a board of nine trustees appointed by the President. Its life has been periodically extended and now runs to June 30, 1939. Its purpose is to promote the electrification of homes and farm buildings, particularly in rural communities, and it rediscounts notes of individuals for the installation of electrical appliances and equipment and plumbing fixtures. It operates in some fifteen states and has consummated agreements with about one hundred manufacturers of appliances whereby certain types of electrical apparatus may be purchased at a substantial reduction in price. It works in cooperation with both private and municipal utility companies. The capital of the "Authority," amounting to $850,000, was furnished by the Treasury. Loans are procured from banks on unsecured notes. The agency is self-sustaining by virtue of the fact that it charges a five per cent discount on all notes purchased. The volume of business has not been large, the total contracts accepted to November 30, 1937 numbering only 49,582, representing a capital value of $7,880,062. The amount outstanding on November 30, 1937 was $4,986,508. Its administration is articulated

with the Reconstruction Finance Corporation and it works in close association with the Rural Electrification Administration.

8. *Rural Electrification Administration.*—The Rural Electrification Administration was established by the act of May 20, 1936. Its purpose is to initiate, formulate, administer, and supervise a ten-year program of approved projects for the generation, transmission, and distribution of electric energy. Loans for construction purposes are made to associations, cooperative organizations, public agencies, and private utilities in unserved rural areas, preference being given to public agencies and other non-profit organizations. It is specified that 25 per cent of each loan must be spent for labor. The agency is administered by a single executive officer responsible to the President. When a project is approved, a loan is made for a period not exceeding twenty-five years, to be liquidated from net revenues. The interest rate shall not exceed the average rate paid by the United States Government on obligations having a maturity of more than ten years. Loans are made both for the construction, operation, or enlargement of generating plants and for wiring home and farm buildings and installing plumbing fixtures.

Up to July 1, 1936 funds were allocated from the Emergency Relief appropriation. During the fiscal year 1937, 50 millions were borrowed from the Reconstruction Finance Corporation. The Rural Electrification Act of 1936 authorized an appropriation of 40 million dollars annually for a period of nine years. The contracts executed to November 15, 1937 amounted to $72,568,020, of which $70,847,470 was for line construction. The actual advances made to this date were $25,204,680. Very large outlays are planned for 1938–1939.

Mention should also be made here of the fact that the Tennessee Valley Authority has extended long-term credit not only to the electricity departments of municipalities but also to local cooperative power associations operating in the valley. These loans are secured by mortgage liens on electric properties. The loans to cooperative associations outstanding on June 30, 1937 amounted to $1,289,923.

III. INTERMEDIATE CREDIT

The development of the Federal Reserve system, on the one hand, and of the Federal Farm Loan system, on the other, naturally sharpened interest in the problem of intermediate credit. While, as we have seen, such requirements were being met after a fashion by commercial banks, by cattle loan companies, and by trade credit, the situation was far from satisfactory. Trade credit was costly and country bank charges were high. Moreover, renewals could not always be depended upon, for if loans fell due at times when the country banks were short of funds, the dealers were not infrequently seriously embarrassed in their operations. This was particularly the case during the severe agricultural depression of 1920–1921. The unnecessary losses during this period proved so great that agricultural interests insistently demanded the establishment of special rural credit institutions whose sole function would be to furnish intermediate credit to agriculture. The failure of the cattle loan companies to meet adequately the financial needs of the livestock industry contributed to this movement for rural credit reform. As a result of the agitation, Congress passed the Agricultural Credits Act of 1923, establishing the Federal Intermediate Credit system, designed to fill the gap between the fields occupied by commercial banks and by long-term investment institutions.

1. *Federal Intermediate Credit banks.*—The Federal Intermediate Credit system is patterned after the Federal Reserve system. The central institutions of this system are known as Federal Intermediate Credit banks. These banks are established in the same cities as the twelve Federal Land banks, and the districts for the Intermediate Credit banks are identical with those of the Federal Land banks. The officers and directors of the land banks are made ex officio officers and directors of the Intermediate Credit banks. In actual practice, however, special officers have been appointed to direct the work of the Intermediate Credit banks, and in every respect the accounts and records of the two institutions are kept separate. They are under the supervision of the Intermediate Credit Commissioner.

The stock of these banks, amounting to 70 million dollars (with a paid-up surplus of 30 millions) is owned by the Federal Government. They also raise funds through the sale of their debentures in the general investment market. These debentures, the maturities of which usually run from three to twelve months, are the joint liability of the twelve Federal Intermediate Credit banks.

The Federal Intermediate Credit banks rediscount agricultural paper held by private banks, Production Credit corporations, and Banks for Cooperatives; and in a few cases they make direct loans to cooperative marketing associations (see agency 5 below). Paper is not eligible for rediscount at the Intermediate Credit banks if its duration is over three years; and most of the loans rediscounted, in fact, run for from three to six months. The volume of credit extended by the Federal Intermediate Credit banks does not bulk large as compared with that extended by the old Federal Land banks and by the Federal Land Bank Commissioner.[4]

[4] See table, p. 453.

On the whole, the growth of the Federal Intermediate Credit system has been much slower than had been anticipated. In fact, the development of this system was along somewhat different lines than had been contemplated by its sponsors. It had been expected that it would provide a cheap and abundant source of funds, which were not available at either the commercial banks or the Federal Land banks. However, those charged with responsibility for administrating the system appear to have been as much concerned with building up permanent and sound banking institutions as with providing cheaper funds in the twilight zone between short-term and long-term credit operations. This attitude serves to explain the preponderance of short-term credits in the Intermediate bank portfolios.

The loan and discount rates were originally from five to six per cent, but since 1934 all credit has been extended on a two per cent basis—a reflection of the change in money market conditions. Prior to 1933, the business consisted of discounts for privately capitalized institutions, chiefly livestock loan companies, the regional agricultural credit corporations—now being liquidated—and cattle loan companies. Since 1933 the principal service of the Federal Intermediate Credit banks has been that of raising capital for the production credit associations and the Banks for Cooperatives.

2. *Banks for Cooperatives.*—The second permanent group of central credit agencies in this field are known as Banks for Cooperatives. These institutions were also authorized by the Farm Credit Act of June 16, 1933. The cooperative credit system consists of a Central Bank for Cooperatives in Washington and twelve district banks. They are supervised by the Cooperative Bank Commissioner. As in the case of the Intermediate Credit system, the districts are identical with those of the Federal Farm Loan system, and the boards of directors are the same. The contributions of the Government to capital stock amount to $149,-258,000. In addition a small portion is held by borrowing cooperatives.

The loans which are made to cooperative marketing associations (see 5 below) are of two classes: facility loans, which run from five to ten years and are intended to furnish permanent working capital and equipment; and commodity loans, which run from three to nine months and are connected with current marketing operations. At the end of 1937 the amount of loans outstanding was $87,633,166, of which practically one-fourth had been made by the central bank in Washington. Two-fifths of the loans have gone for operating capital, a little over one-third for storage purposes, and one-fourth for facility loans. About 27 per cent of the loans were made to cotton cooperatives and 22 per cent to those operating in the fruit and vegetable field. Dairy cooperatives accounted for nine per cent, and grain cooperatives for eight per cent.

3. *Production Credit Corporations.*—These agencies complete the list of central institutions authorized by the Farm Credit Act of June 16, 1933. Again, there are twelve corporations located in districts identical with those of the Federal Land banks and having the same boards of directors. General supervision of the system is exercised by a Production Credit Corporation Commissioner. The stock of these corporations, amounting to 120 million dollars, is furnished entirely by the Federal Government. These corporations make no loans, their activities being confined to the supervision of the operations of the production credit associations, to be described in the following section.

4. *Production Credit Associations.*—These associations are similar in character to the national farm loan associations but operate in the field of short- and intermediate-term credit. At the end of 1937 there were about 600, having a combined membership of 251,190 farmers and livestock growers. The stock of the associations is of two classes: Class A, subscribed by the Production Credit Corporation of the district; and Class B, subscribed by borrowers in an amount equal to five per cent of the loans. About four-fifths of the stock is Class A, the amount outstanding being $76,085,472. The directors of these associations are elected by Class B stockholders subject to approval by the Production Credit Corporation of the District.

5. *Cooperative Marketing Associations.*—It will be observed that in the diagram on page 437 we have included Cooperative Marketing Associations in a position parallel with that of the National Farm Loan Associations and the Production Credit Associations. They are unlike these associations in that they have been organized under private auspices; but they are similar to them in that they take over the credit operations of their members. These agencies, which had their first considerable development during the twenties, were always confronted with a difficult credit problem. While incorporated, they usually did not have capital stock, and as a rule they possessed meager financial resources. Hence it was necessary to borrow extensively on the security of the crops which they were marketing. However, their lack of resources, together with the risks inherent in the financing of agricultural products, made it difficult for them to obtain from commercial banks adequate credit for marketing purposes.

In the light of this situation the Agricultural Credit Act of 1923 authorized the Intermediate Credit banks to make loans to the cooperatives. For some years the Intermediate institutions performed an important function in this connection. But since the establishment of the Central Banks for Cooperatives, the cooperative marketing associations have transferred their borrowing to this source.

The extent of the credit operations of the various agencies which operate under the supervision of the Farm Credit Administration is indicated by the following table:

LOANS MADE BY FARM CREDIT ADMINISTRATION AGENCIES*

Institution	Loans made May 1, 1933 through March 31, 1938		Loans outstanding March 31, 1938[a]
	Number	Amount	Amount
Farm mortgage loans:			
Federal Land banks.........	331,093	$1,307,682,433	$2,025,706,968
Land Bank Commissioner.....	507,639	946,930,645	798,775,970
Total...................	838,732	2,254,613,078	2,824,482,938
Short-term credit:			
Production credit associations[b].	948,377[c]	899,078,746[c]	162,599,968
Emergency crop loans........	1,475,077	162,075,742	119,385,723
Drought relief loans..........	300,614	72,008,540	56,414,303
Regional agricultural credit corporations............	115,733	423,488,762[c]	15,164,087
Federal Intermediate Credit banks (loans to and discounts for private financing institutions).........	Not available	566,444,944	39,525,911
Total...................	....	2,123,096,734	393,089,992
Loans to cooperatives:			
Federal Intermediate Credit banks..................	Not available	136,210,214[c]	1,419,664
Banks for Cooperatives........	4,736	328,357,050	82,322,848
Agricultural Marketing Act revolving fund..........	218	80,047,059[c]	27,303,831
Total...................	....	526,818,976[d]	111,046,343
Grand total................	....	$4,904,528,788	$3,328,619,273

* Farm Credit Administration *Report on Loans and Discounts*, March, 1938.

[a] Includes loans made both prior and subsequent to May 1, 1933.

[b] Includes data for production credit associations which have been placed in liquidation.

[c] Includes renewals.

[d] Loans in the amount of $17,795,347 made from Agricultural Marketing Act revolving fund were refinanced by the banks for cooperatives during the period. The amount of such loans is excluded from this total in order to avoid duplication.

It will be seen that the mortgage loans constitute about 90 per cent of the total. The full extent of the loans made by the Federal Intermediate Credit institutions is not revealed in this table, since the funds furnished to production credit associations, Banks for Cooperatives, and regional agricultural credit corporations are not included. All told, the Federal Intermediate Credit loans on March 31, 1938 aggregated $225,662,000. Mention should be made of the fact that the Agricultural Marketing Act revolving fund is in process of liquidation.

IV. SIGNIFICANCE OF AGRICULTURAL CREDIT ORGANIZATION

The striking feature of this summary account of the evolution of the agricultural credit structure is of course the number and variety of agencies that have been devised. Since 1916 no less than fourteen new types of institution have been created under government auspices. A few are concerned definitely with long-term credit needs, but many blur the lines and advance credit more or less indiscriminately for short-term, intermediate, and even long-term purposes. Some of them are ostensibly still emergency institutions, but as the years pass they tend to become engrafted as permanent parts of the agricultural credit mechanism.

Genuine progress in organization was made in 1933 when the various permanent agencies were coordinated under the Farm Credit Administration. This development not only unified the overhead administration, but it made possible the administration of the several types of district banks under joint boards of directors. Moreover, it facilitated the development of the Federal Intermediate Credit banks as rediscounting agencies for the other new central banks. The supervision of the shorter term emergency crop and feed loans is, however, somewhat misplaced, and is, in fact, regarded by the Farm Credit Administration as an orphan child if not an ugly duckling. There is urgent need for considering the future of such loans in relation to those made by the Commodity Credit Corporation and other short- and intermediate-term lending agencies.

Because of the unstable conditions which have prevailed in American agriculture during the last twenty years, and the very short history of the agencies established since 1932, it is difficult to appraise the economic significance of our farm credit institutions. It is obvious that some of the emergency agencies were of great service during the depression in tiding distressed business over an exceedingly acute situation and in preventing a general collapse of the whole farm mortgage structure. It is not so clear that the multiplication and indefinite continuance of emergency agencies have had altogether beneficial results—unless we assume that permanent subsidization of a considerable part of the farm population has become essential to the national welfare.

The best test of the economic significance of the newer forms of agricultural institutions is of course the cost of credit to the farm borrowers. In this respect definite progress has been made since pre-war days. The Federal Land bank system materially reduced the costs of long-term borrowing, not only by means of lower rates but also through the elimination of frequent renewal charges. At the same time the introduction of the amortization principle facilitated and systematized the process of repayment; one can scarcely overestimate the importance of this change. Similarly, in the field of intermediate credit a reduction of rates was made possible by the development of a system which enabled farm borrowers to draw upon the general capital market through the medium of well financed credit institutions, that is, the Intermediate Credit banks. Again, the elimination of frequent renewals has served to reduce costs and to afford greater security to the borrower. In the case of many of the newer agencies the element of subsidy, or the underwriting of losses, is so great that the true costs of credit extension cannot be measured.

Notwithstanding the improvement in farm credit organization since 1916, it is interesting to note that the reduction in the cost of borrowing in recent years has not kept pace with the decline in the cost of credit to urban business enterprises. In 1917 the average rates charged on newly recorded farm-mortgage loans in the state of New York averaged 5.6 per cent. In the late twenties it was 5.8 per cent; and in 1935, in spite of the substantial decline in interest rates, it was still as high as 5.3 per cent. The national farm loan associations now charge four per cent, while the Land Bank Commission loans carry a five per cent rate. The Federal Intermediate Credit banks borrow at two per cent on their own debentures—which is substantially above the rate paid by the large discount corporations. They charge the Banks for Cooperatives three per cent for rediscounts, and the production credit associations five per cent. When one compares these rates with those that have prevailed in the general money market in recent years it is apparent that the cost of farm credit is still relatively high.

CHAPTER XXVII

FINANCING URBAN REAL ESTATE

The building and construction industry is one of the major divisions of economic activity in the United States. The industry as a whole includes the construction of residential, public work and public utility, industrial, commercial, educational, and institutional buildings. It is estimated that new construction for the period 1924–1929 averaged approximately 10 billion dollars a year, which does not include about 2.5 billions for ground value. This total was distributed as follows: residential construction, 3.3 billions; public works and utilities, 2 billions; industrial buildings 2 billions; commercial buildings, 1.5 billions; educational buildings, 600 millions; and hospitals and institutions, 400 millions. For the period 1930–1936 the average fell from 10 billions to one-fourth that amount, distributed as follows: residential construction 570 million dollars; public works and utilities 925 millions; industrial buildings 140 millions; commercial buildings, 245 millions; educational buildings 175 millions; and hospitals and institutions 275 millions. It is the residential construction with which we are here principally concerned, since most of the other types of building operations are financed by methods explained in earlier chapters.

The construction industry is financed in a variety of ways. In some cases the cost is borne entirely by the individual owner; in many instances the funds are provided in part by the owner or builder, and in part by the sale of a mortgage on the property. To a considerable extent, also, capital is provided through cooperative building and loan associations. With the coming of the apartment house era, however, the large amount of capital required for residential construction led to the extensive use of mortgages and mortgage bonds, which are marketed through both ordinary and special investment banking channels. As in the marketing of railroad, industrial, and other bonds, commercial banks, trust companies, savings banks, and insurance companies serve as financial intermediaries. The building and loan associations will be given first attention.

I. BUILDING AND LOAN ASSOCIATIONS

The building and loan association is the oldest form of cooperative credit institution in the United States, the first one having been organized in a suburb of Philadelphia in 1831. In the course of their evolution the building and loan associations have passed through several phases, a brief account of which will best serve to indicate both their purpose and the nature of their operations.

The original form of building and loan association was little more than a home-builders' club, where each individual paid into the common treasury a certain sum of money each month. The purpose was to secure enough members so that a moderate monthly payment by each would provide every month a fund sufficient to build a house for one of the group. For example, if there were one hundred members and each paid into the association twenty dollars per month, every month one member could begin the building of his house, to cost two thousand dollars; and at the end of one hundred months each would have a two-thousand dollar home. The club required each house-builder to give a mortgage on the home as security in case he failed to continue his monthly payments after receiving a loan from the association. When each member had acquired a house, the association, having accomplished its purpose, was dissolved.

A second step in the development of the building and loan association was marked by the introduction of shares, which enabled any individual who wished to build a better house than his fellows to do so by investing more money each month than did the others. In the foregoing illustration, if an individual invested $40 per month instead of $20, he could build a $4,000 instead of a $2,000 house.

A third phase was the development of the depositing membership plan. A depositing member was one who joined the association, not with the expectation of borrowing funds with which to build a home, but merely for the returns which he might receive from the investment of his funds in the association. The profits of the association were derived from two sources: (1) the payment of interest on the money advanced for home-building, and (2) from premiums and fines. Each individual who borrowed funds for home-building was at first supposed to pay interest to the association at the current rate; but often so many members wished to build at the same time that there developed the practice of making the award to the one who bid the highest above the current rate of interest. The fines were levied against members who became delinquent in paying their dues. Both these sources of income have at times proved very fruitful. It should be added here, however, that the administration of the system of fines and premiums gave rise to various abuses, which were gradually eliminated.

The depositing member has played a very important part in the development of building and loan associations. In crowded industrial centers where the demand for loans from prospective home-builders has usually exceeded the ability of the ordinary members to furnish the funds, the depositing member has proved of great assistance. Since the depositor was, however, interested only as an investor, it was found necessary to extend him one privilege not possessed by the ordinary member; that of withdrawing his shares at any time in case he desired to use his funds elsewhere.

The fourth stage in the evolution of the loan association was the introduction of the serial plan. The original associations, as we have seen, were dissolved, or terminated, as soon as each borrowing member had acquired a home; but under the serial plan the association becomes virtually a perpetual organization. Under this plan additional members may be added to the original association at stated intervals, say, once a year, each new group of members constituting an independent series which terminates when all the members of the series have acquired homes. Thus the association lives as long as new series of members continue to be added.

A further step was the introduction of the so-called permanent plan, which originated in Dayton, Ohio, in 1870. The distinguishing feature of this plan is that it is unnecessary for an individual who wishes to join a permanent association to wait until the opening of a new series of memberships; he may take out an individual membership at any time and purchase as many shares of stock as he may desire. Each borrower is also permitted to pay off his debt as fast as he desires and retire from the association at his own convenience.

All of these types of loan associations are still in operation in the United States—though the serial and permanent plans have become the dominant forms. Many of the larger associations do business throughout a state, and some extend their operations over the territory of several states.

The management of building and loan associations is vested in a board of directors chosen by the members, while the routine administrative duties are performed by elected officials. The association makes two types of loans, known as "stock loans" and "real estate loans." Stock loans are secured by the individual's shares in the association, the loan being limited as a rule to 85 per cent, or less, of the book value of the shares at the time the loan is made. The real estate loans are made to members on the security of mortgages on the homes to be built, or purchased. The valuation of the property is made by the board of directors or by an appraisal committee appointed by the directors.

The interest rates charged now range from about 5.6 to seven per cent. In addition, there are certain loan fees, running from one to five per cent. The maturity dates are usually from 12 to 15 years. It is of interest that prior to 1930 the majority of associations made loans on income producing properties, chiefly apartment buildings, and that in consequence of exceptional losses during the depression period such loans have become much less numerous in recent years.

An interesting problem of management has always been the disposition of the accumulated property. In the early associations the earnings were kept in a common fund and were not distributed until the final dissolution of the association, losses meanwhile being paid out of the accumulated funds. But with the introduction of depositing members, who had the privilege of withdrawing before the dissolution of the association, and whose interest in the organization was solely that of an investment, it became necessary to apportion the profit from time to time as dividends. At present, it is the almost universal rule to pay dividends semiannually.

In recent years there has been an important change in the method of paying off loans. Since 1929 the so-called "direct reduction," or amortization plan, has been adopted, compulsorily by the federal associations, and voluntarily by a majority of the state associations. Its advantages have been summarized as follows:[1] (1) costs the borrowers less than the other two plans; (2) enables borrowers to own homes in less time; (3) is the easiest plan for all borrowers to understand; (4) is the most efficient plan since it eliminates many calculations and entries and tends to reduce errors; (5) eliminates borrowers' risk of loss of payments on home, as in other plans, if the association becomes insolvent; (6) has no share accounts, no accumulation of sinking fund, no record of dividend credits, and no uncertainty as to maturity dates.

The growth of building and loan associations in the United States was rapid during the decade of the twenties. In 1921 the total assets amounted to about two billion dollars, while by the end of 1927 they stood at more than seven billions. The number of associations in 1927 was 12,804 and the membership 11,308,061. In the ensuing depression many associations were closed and by 1936 the number was reduced to 10,243, with a total membership of 6,101,703 and total assets of 5.6 billion dollars. While Eastern and Central states have the largest number of associations, the distribution in proportion to population is fairly uniform throughout the country. An interesting recent development has been the establishment of savings departments, thus placing the building and loan companies in direct competition with banks.

[1] Report of the Committee on Trends of the United States Building and Loan League, 1938.

The building and loan associations have filled a real need in our financial system. The lack of investment banking institutions, equipped to provide funds for the builder of small homes, left a crying need for an institution such as the building and loan association. Moreover, the convenience and cheapness of the association method of acquiring and paying for property would under any circumstances make it an institution capable of rendering great service in promoting thrift and economic progress.

The earlier loan associations were not adequately supervised by governing authorities. For many years there was very little attempt at regulation; but with the rapid growth of associations since the World War there developed a movement for government regulation. At the present time, the majority of states have some measure of supervision over the building and loan associations doing business within their boundaries; but, in many cases, the regulation still leaves much to be desired. In 1936 the Federal Government assumed control over a group of federal building and loan associations and other home financing organizations. These associations, which number approximately 1,100, have been placed under the general supervision of the Home Loan Bank Board.[2]

II. FINANCING THROUGH THE "OLD LINE" MORTGAGE

The "old line" or "lump sum" mortgage long represented the standard method of raising funds on real estate security. It is used principally to finance single- and two-family residences and small business buildings, but occasionally it is employed in connection with apartment-house construction. The "old line" mortgage is usually relatively small in amount, since the intention is that it should be bought by an individual investor, either directly or through the intermediation of a mortgage company or the mortgage department of a commercial bank or trust company. Before considering the marketing of mortgages, however, attention must be given to their character and to the nature of the contract between the builder and the mortgage company.

Before agreeing to make a loan on mortgage security the company makes a credit analysis, involving a consideration of the character of the man seeking the loan, the part of the city in which the building is to be located, the probable direction of growth of the city, and the possible saturation point for residences in that vicinity. It also makes sure that the building is not too expensive for the vicinity in which it

[2] For further discussion see pp. 468–469.

is located, and carefully considers the possibility of a decline in real estate values in that neighborhood.

A margin of safety is always required by the mortgage company. The standard practice has been to grant a first-mortgage loan equal to only 50 per cent of the value of the property; but in recent years the percentage has tended to rise, and in the case of dwelling houses the loan is sometimes equal to 75 per cent of the cost of the building. The practice, however, varies considerably with different companies and in different sections of the country. As protection against loss in case of the premature demise of the owner, he is often required to take out life insurance as additional security for the loan.

The duration of a mortgage loan has commonly been from three to five years, although there has recently been a tendency to lengthen the period for which it may run. The selling commission, which is usually collected when the contract for the loan is closed, ordinarily ranges from 2 to $3\frac{1}{2}$ per cent. The other charges paid by the borrower include a fee for inspection, and very frequently another fee for a photograph of the property. The borrower also pays for the abstract of title or for title insurance. In some cases, however, mortgage companies charge a flat fee of 4 or 5 per cent, and then meet all the expenses, except those in connection with the title.

The mortgage company acts both as an underwriter of the project and as a distributor of securities. The commissions received are compensation, in part for the bank's service in discovering and investigating the project; in part, for the risks assumed as underwriter of the loan; and, in part, for the service performed in marketing the mortgage. The amount of the commissions is determined by general competitive conditions.

The mortgage company resembles the investment bank in that it seeks as rapid a turn-over of capital as possible. It does not desire to hold the mortgages as investments; it sells them as soon as opportunity offers. Since it is necessary for the mortgage company to advance the funds to the borrower before the mortgage is sold, it must—like the bond house and commercial paper house—borrow large sums from the commercial banks for short periods of time. The mortgage company may, of course, be able to procure funds from the commercial banks at a slightly lower rate than that at which the mortgage is floated; and thus a small incidental profit may sometimes be realized from the interest on the mortgage during the time it is held by the mortgage company.

The marketing of real estate mortgages involves no elaborate financial machinery. Since the mortgage is for a lump sum it must be sold to a single investor; and the main customers, therefore, are usually large institutions which can buy loans of substantial size and still apply the principle of diversification of investment. These include insurance companies, colleges, eleemosynary institutions, trustees of estates, commercial banks, and building and loan associations. There are also some individual investors. The life insurance companies are by far the most important purchasers.

Since few of the purchasers of real estate mortgages are willing to buy before the building has been constructed, the builders must finance the construction by short-time credit operations. As a matter of fact, they procure the needed funds chiefly from the commercial banks, on personal loans secured by collateral. They also secure mercantile credit advances by giving their notes to dealers from whom building materials and supplies and fixtures are purchased. These notes are made to mature at the date when it is expected that the mortgage can be sold.

Second-mortgage companies have been organized in numerous states. These companies have sometimes attempted to sell second mortgages to the public, but in the main their activities are confined to purchasing second mortgages outright for investment. Some of them also buy first mortgages at a discount and sell them to the public. The stock of these companies is usually subscribed by builders, building-material interests, banks, and real estate men.

The profits from dealing in second mortgages are derived in part from interest on the mortgage and in part from a discount on its purchase price. The nature of the profits may best be shown by a typical case. Suppose a contractor has sold a residence for $10,000. The home-buyer is required to pay cash for 20 per cent of the price, or $2,000. He gives a first mortgage for $5,000, which is sold to an investor through a mortgage company, and a second mortgage for the remaining $3,000. The second mortgage bears interest at, say, six per cent, and the principal must be paid off at the rate of $100 each month. The contractor who receives the mortgage from the home-buyer naturally wishes to get his capital out as soon as possible in order that he may undertake new operations. He therefore sells the mortgage to a second-mortgage company at a substantial discount. In the case before us the mortgage company buys the mortgage at a discount of five per cent, amounting to 12.5 per cent for the 2½-year period. The company would thus pay to the contractor $2,625 for a $3,000 mortgage. Since the mortgage is paid off in monthly instalments of $100, the total investment is returned to the company in twenty-six and one-quarter instead of in thirty months. The mortgage company thus receives in interest proper, 7.6 per cent on its average loan, and in addition to this it receives a discount profit amounting to $375, which is equivalent to 13.2 per cent on the average amount of the loan. The two combined make the cost to the contractor 20.8 per cent. It often works out that the profits of the second-mortgage company are even larger than this. Since most house-buyers are anxious to clear their homes of debt as soon as possible, they often retire the mortgage more rapidly than is stipulated in the contract. The more rapid the reduction in principal, the larger is the rate of return on the funds actually invested in the mortgage.

It will be seen that under this plan the home-owner nominally pays only six per cent on the second mortgage and that it is the contractor who pays the large discount. In figuring the cost of the building, however, the contractor counts the cost of the funds which he uses as a part of the cost of construction. Accordingly, it enters into the price which he asks for the house. During a period when there is a housing shortage, he can get his price; but in a period when the building industry has expanded too rapidly, it is of course not so easy to pass the burden along to the house-owner or renter.

The financing of building operations by means of the "old line" mortgage has several shortcomings. First, if the investor needs his funds before the mortgage matures he finds no ready market for the mortgage except at a substantial discount. Second, the mortgages run for relatively short periods and renewal charges often constitute an important additional financial burden. The investor is likewise often deterred from purchasing short-term mortgages because of the frequency with which he would have to make reinvestments. Finally, the mortgage is usually too large for the ordinary individual investor and thus the market from which funds may be drawn for real estate financial operations is unduly restricted.

III. FINANCING THROUGH THE FIRST-MORTGAGE BOND

The real estate bond was devised as a means of overcoming the weaknesses of the "old line" mortgage, particularly in the financing of large apartment house and hotel construction. This type of financing flourished in the post-war era up to 1929, and the following description applies to the conditions of that period. Practices are now somewhat more conservative.

Real estate mortgage bonds, which are very similar in character to "old line" mortgages, are secured by deeds of trust. These bonds have typically been handled by investment banking houses specializing in this field. The house acts as a dealer by issuing and selling bonds to the public. It usually assumes no legal liability for the bonds, but it may act in the capacity of a guarantor, and in this case it becomes legally liable for the bonds in the event that the mortgagor does not meet his obligation. A real estate bank may also act as an investment trust in issuing its own bonds based on real estate as collateral. In this case the investment trust is the primary obligor.

A significant feature of this business is that the mortgage companies typically advance funds for the actual construction of the building. That is to say, the bonds are usually put on the market before or during the construction of the building, rather than after the building is completed as is the case with the "old line" mortgage. The builder is, however, commonly required to furnish a bond guaranteeing the completion of the building according to specifications. This practice also differs from the familiar method employed by industries, public utilities, etc., which do their primary financing by means of stock issues, subsequently putting out bonds on the security of the property acquired or developed with the proceeds of the sale of stock.

The money derived from the sale of bonds is not turned over to the builder in a lump sum. It is advanced a little at a time as the construction progresses. It is also commonly required that the builder must himself have at each stage of the development a stake in the enterprise equal to at least 15 per cent of the total investment. Some companies stipulate that the owner must deposit with the company, before the beginning of construction, a sum equal to the difference between the amount of the mortgage loan and the cost of the building. This precaution is intended, of course, to safeguard the company and the investors in case the owner should meet with financial reverses or should attempt to divert his funds to other purposes.

The old principle of making loans up to only 50 per cent of the cost value of the property has not usually been adhered to in the case of real estate mortgage bonds. As already indicated, it is the common practice to give a trust deed equal to 75 per cent of the cost of the property; and not infrequently the property has been mortgaged at as much as 90 per cent of its cost. The security is not really measured by the margin between the amount of the mortgage and the cost of the building; it is measured by the excess of probable earnings over operating expenses and interest charges. The banker estimates as carefully as possible the probable net earnings available for interest charges, and a substantial margin of safety is commonly required. That is to say, the estimated earnings must be greatly in excess of the amount of the interest payments, after allowance has been made for depreciation and operating expenses. It is a common practice, moreover, to have the bonds mature serially. During the first two or three years, depreciation, repairs, and upkeep are relatively small, and at the same time the difficulties of renting the apartments and holding the tenants are commonly at a minimum. For this reason it is regarded as sound policy to have some of the bonds paid off during the first few years, leaving the amount of indebtedness smaller at a time when a shrinkage in earnings is most likely to begin.

For many years real estate bonds were among the safest and most conservative of investments. Such mortgage bonds appealed particularly to persons who were not interested in the appreciation of their investment, but rather in the safety of principal and in the assurance of a moderate return. Because of the attractiveness of the real estate bond in this respect the demand far exceeded the supply of conservative issues. Consequently real estate houses, in their effort to meet the almost insatiable public demand, began to issue bonds of lower and lower quality. Real estate bonds came to be placed on highly specialized properties such as theatres and apartment houses. The percentage of the mortgage to the appraised value of the property became larger and larger and the appraisal became less and less conservative. With the coming of the depression and a sharp reduction in the earnings of the underlying properties, interest payments on the real estate bonds could not be met, and widespread defaults followed. However, the excesses of the past should not impair the future usefulness of the real estate bond, for properties which were conservatively bonded proved safe and stable investments throughout the entire depression.

The real estate bond houses perform a number of incidental services for the investor. Before a bond is sold, the bond house sees that agreements covering the type of building are carried out; it assists in the laying out of the building project; and it periodically inspects the building during the process of construction. After the building has been constructed it sees that it is properly maintained, that fire insurance is periodically renewed, and that the taxes are regularly paid. In ordinary times the bond house will undertake, for a commission of one or two per cent, to resell the bond in case the investor needs funds, though in periods of monetary stringency it cannot guarantee a re-sale.

A real weakness in the financing of urban real estate has been the lack of ready marketability for the securities. Urban real estate mortgages and bonds have been purchased by building and loan associations, banks of various types, life insurance companies, and individuals. Of the 25 billion dollars of first-mortgage real estate bonds outstanding in 1925, it is estimated that about 18 billions were held by building and loan associations and the various types of banks, and the remainder by life insurance companies and individuals. Investments made by building and loan associations, banks, and individuals are largely confined to the securities issued by local borrowers, whereas the bulk of the insurance company holdings is of an intersectional character.

A real estate securities exchange was established in 1929. This institution is the result of a special investigation of real estate financial problems, conducted by the Real Estate Board of New York. In announcing the opening of this exchange, the president stated its functions as follows:

It is the purpose of the New York Real Estate Securities Exchange to make real estate securities liquid by providing a regular market where real estate stocks, bonds and other securities may be negotiated, sold and transferred. In addition it will urge banking institutions to arrange to finance real estate transactions and the transactions growing out of real estate.

The Exchange will direct its efforts also to safeguard the interests of both dealers and investors.

Proposed listings will be rigidly investigated. Their acceptance or rejection will be based on appraisals of property and examination of the financial condition, the records of past activities and the personnel of corporations and individuals offering securities. This information will be made available to prospective investors so that, if they wish, they may form independent opinions on the basis of responsible data.

Through the mutual benefits to the investing public, real estate men and the people whose interest in real estate is founded on their every day use of it, the Exchange will give new life to the real estate business.

Stabilization of the real estate market values will be an outstanding achievement through its tendency to curtail blind speculation and its strong emphasis of the aspect of sound investment.

Real estate men whose securities are accepted will gain sales prestige by having their securities bear the approval of the Exchange, and the public will be served both by the liquid market as well as by the Exchange's discouragement of unsound offers.

The necessity of launching the project under a sponsorship enjoying the firm confidence of the public has been acknowledged as a prerequisite to success. For this reason it was decided that the Real Estate Board of New York should be the sponsor. It stands responsible for the discharge of the duty assumed by real estate on its initiation into the field of organized financial markets.

The membership of the Exchange is restricted to members of the board, but this does not confine the membership to New York City real estate men to the exclusion of those in other cities, nor does it prevent listing of securities on property throughout the country. The various classes of membership permit memberships in other cities, and securities on property in Seattle, Washington, or Brownsville, Texas, may be listed if they pass the test of soundness.

The board pledges its character for the Exchange, but the Exchange, however, in order to carry out its function to the limit of its possibility for the benefit of investors and the real estate field, must earn and maintain confidence on its own merit of service.

Membership in the Exchange is limited to 500. The initial price of seats was $5,000. The unit of trading in bonds is $1,000. In the case of stocks selling at 50 cents a share and over, the unit of trading is 100 shares; and of stock selling below 50 cents, 1,000 shares. The listing requirements and the procedures in general are modeled closely after those of the New York Stock Exchange.

As has been pointed out in previous chapters, the commercial banks participated extensively in both agricultural and urban real estate financing. Since attention has been specifically called to the series of acts relaxing the restrictions on real estate loans by national banks, this development need only be mentioned at this place. In 1932 the volume of real estate loans made by central reserve and reserve city banks stood at a peak of 807.5 million dollars. The so-called country banks held another 800 millions of such loans, many of which were connected with small town real estate operations. The urban real estate loans of state banks cannot be segregated, but they undoubtedly exceeded those of the national institutions. In concluding this brief statement it should be noted that national banks may loan up to 60 per cent of the appraised value of the property, and the loan may run for a period of ten years, provided the contract calls for an amortization of at least 40 per cent of the loan within that period of time. If there is no amortization provision, the maturity is limited to 5 years and the amount of the loan to 50 per cent of the appraised value of the property.

IV. GOVERNMENT PARTICIPATION IN URBAN REAL ESTATE FINANCING

In recent years the Federal Government has entered the field of urban real estate financing in a large way. This development is the outgrowth of (1) the need for assisting distressed private institutions operating in this field; (2) the desire to reduce rentals for the lower economic groups; and (3) the hope of stimulating, through activity in this industry, a revival of general business activity. These ends have been promoted, first, by means of various types of lending agencies; and, second, by means of an insurance scheme.

1. LENDING AGENCIES

The lending institutions consist of a group of agencies dealing with building and loan associations and distressed home owners, which operate under the general supervision of the Federal Home Loan Bank Board; three single institutions—the Reconstruction Finance Corporation Mortgage Company, the Disaster Loan Corporation; and the Federal Mortgage Association—which are affiliated with the Reconstruction Finance Corporation; and an independent agency known as the United States Housing Authority.

1. *Federal Home Loan Bank Board.*—This Board, which consists of five members appointed by the President, has supervision over a group of agencies including twelve Federal Home Loan Banks, the Home Owners' Loan Corporation, the Federal Savings and Loan Insurance Corporation, and the federal savings and loan associations. The organization in this field is analogous to that of the Federal Reserve system.

a) *Home Loan Banks.*—Each of these banks has under it a large number of member associations, including state building and loan associations, and also federal savings and loan associations of the type described below. The Home Loan banks make loans and advances to members on the security either of home mortgages or of United States bonds. Advances are also made to non-member mortgagees on the security of mortgages insured by the Federal Housing Administration. Funds of these banks may also be invested in United States government bonds.

The capital stock outstanding amounts to 161 million dollars, out of which 125 millions has been contributed by the Treasury and 36 millions by members of the system. The Home Loan banks have authority to issue debentures and bonds, which may be either the obligations of the individual bank or consolidated obligations of the twelve banks.

b) *Home Owners' Loan Corporation.*—This agency was organized to refinance the loans of distressed home owners, and its obligations are guaranteed by the United States Government. It ceased to accept new applications after June 13, 1936, and is now gradually liquidating its outstanding obligations. The total amount of loans at the peak was over three billion dollars. The capitalization of the Corporation is 200 million dollars, all of which is owned by the United States Government.

c) *Federal Savings and Loan Associations.*—As a result of the distress in which many building and loan associations found themselves, the Federal Government in 1936 undertook to supply needed capital resources. The Government was empowered by law to invest in the preferred stock of these companies up to a maximum of $100,000 for each association, subject to the provision that the subscription of the Government may not exceed that of the private shareholders. The

United States may also invest in full-paid "income shares." The total investment in any association may not exceed 75 per cent of the total share investment. On June 30, 1938 the capital shares aggregated about 938 million dollars, of which 48 millions was owned by the Treasury and 171 millions by the Home Owners' Loan Corporation.

d) *Federal Savings and Loan Insurance Corporation.*—The purpose of this Corporation is to guarantee the share liabilities of building and loan associations and similar home-financing organizations. The Corporation has 100 million dollars of capital, all of which was subscribed by the Home Owners' Loan Corporation. It is directed by a manager who is appointed by the Board. Federal savings and loan associations are required to insure their income shares with the Corporation, and state-chartered building and loan associations are permitted to do so. The maximum amount insured for any one shareholder is $5,000. The premium is one-eighth of one per cent on the combined shareholder and creditor liabilities of the insured associations.

The Corporation also has authority to purchase the assets of insured associations or to make contributions to restore them to normal operating capacity. The Corporation acts as conservator or receiver of all federal savings and loan associations in default; and it may accept appointment as conservator or receiver of state-chartered institutions.

2. *RFC Mortgage Company.*—This company, created by an Act of January 31, 1935, is a subsidiary of the Reconstruction Finance Corporation. It was authorized to make loans on types of properties and for purposes which were not adequately provided for by other government agencies. Loans are made on (1) income-producing business properties, including apartments, hotels, and business and office buildings on which mortgage loans are in default or about to mature; (2) to distressed individual holders of mortgage bonds and mortgage certificates; and (3) for the construction of new buildings "for which there is an economic need."

The stock of the corporation, which is limited to 100 million dollars, is subscribed by the Reconstruction Finance Corporation. By November 30, 1937, 25 millions had been subscribed. The company rediscounts its mortgages with the Reconstruction Finance Corporation, no limit being fixed on the amount of such discounts. The loans made to November 30, 1937 amounted to slightly over 83 million dollars.

3. *Disaster Loan Corporation.*—As a result of the widespread havoc wrought by floods, Congress created on February 11, 1937 the Disaster Loan Corporation with a capital stock not to exceed 20 million dollars, of which 10 million dollars has thus far been advanced by the Treasury. This corporation was authorized to "make such loans as it may determine to be necessary or appropriate because of floods or catas-

trophes." Originally limited to disasters in the year 1937, it was later amended to include those which had occurred in 1936 and which might occur in 1938. On November 30, 1937 the loans made amounted to $5,884,000, of which the great majority were for the purpose of rehabilitating urban property.

4. *Federal Mortgage Association.*—This association was organized on February 10, 1938 as a subsidiary of the Reconstruction Finance Corporation. Its purpose is to make real estate loans insured by the Federal Housing Administration under the provisions of an amendment to the National Housing Act, approved by Congress on February 3, 1938. The Federal Mortgage Association has a capital of 10 million dollars and a surplus of one million supplied by the Reconstruction Finance Corporation.

5. *United States Housing Authority.*—This latest addition to the group of federal agencies concerned with urban real estate financing was authorized by an act of September 1, 1937, which was extensively amended on June 21, 1938. It is directed by an administrator appointed by the President. Its capital stock, subscribed by the Treasury, is one million dollars.

The purpose of the Housing Authority is to promote adequate housing for the lowest income groups. In order to raise the necessary capital funds the Housing Authority may issue obligations in installments to an aggregate total of 800 million dollars. These obligations, which may run for a period of 60 years, are guaranteed by the United States as to payment of principal and interest.

The Housing Authority advances money to local public housing agencies, which construct and operate projects. It may advance as much as 90 per cent of the cost of such undertakings. The Authority also contracts with the local agencies to make annual contributions in order to subsidize the projects. Such contributions may be made to an aggregate amount of 28 million dollars per year. The Authority may also make direct grants not exceeding 25 per cent of the cost of a project, while an additional grant of 15 per cent for payment of labor may be made from unemployment relief funds. The total of capital grants is limited to 10 millions a year for the first three years. This agency should not be confused with the United States Housing Corporation, organized during the World War (see table page 481).

2. THE INSURANCE SYSTEM

The desire to stabilize the mortgage situation and to stimulate expansion in the building industry also led to the establishment of a credit insurance system under the auspices of the Government. The

Federal Housing Administration was established by the National Housing Act of June 27, 1934, which has been several times amended. This agency is directed by an administrator appointed by the President. Its important activities are as follows:

(1) To insure loans made by approved banks and other financial institutions for repairs and improvements on real property and the installation of fixed equipment. There is no premium charge. These are known as "modernization" credit loans. The total liability of the Administration, however, may not exceed 100 million dollars. Moreover, the liability is limited to 10 per cent of the total advances made by any one institution. Up to November 30, 1937 the total insurance written amounted to $560,598,912; on that date the estimated insured loans outstanding amounted to $197,097,595.

(2) To administer a mortgage insurance fund in connection with the guarantee of real estate mortgages on urban residences, excluding apartment buildings. The Act provides that loans on mortgage security may be insured to the extent of two billion dollars and, with the approval of the President, to three billions. The terms are exceptionally liberal: Loans of 90 per cent may be made on properties not exceeding $6,000 in value; on additional values up to $10,000 the loan is limited to 80 per cent; and on values over $10,000 the rate on the entire amount is 80 per cent. The maximum loan is $16,000. The premium charge is one-half of one per cent per annum. Loans made prior to July 1, 1939 must have a provision for amortization over a period not to exceed twenty-five years, and thereafter twenty years.

This Act is also applicable to farms having farm houses and other farm buildings. Moreover, it applies to low cost housing projects which involve outlays not in excess of five million dollars and which do not cost more than $1350 per room. Insurance may also be placed on multi-family dwellings or groups, limited to ten single-family dwellings costing not more than $1150 per room and aggregating a total value not in excess of $200,000.

The ultimate results of these efforts to decrease the cost of housing, to stabilize the industry, and to promote a great expansion of construction remain to be seen.

CHAPTER XXVIII

THE POSITION OF THE GOVERNMENT IN THE CREDIT SYSTEM

At various places throughout this volume, and especially in the chapters immediately preceding, we have seen that the United States Government has become in many ways intimately connected with the credit system. Its regulatory activities cover virtually every aspect of modern financial organization, while its direct participation in the furnishing of capital for both public and private enterprise extends over a substantial portion of the whole economic system. The influence of the Government is exercised through its control over money and deposit currency, via the Treasury, the Federal Reserve system, the Comptroller of the Currency, and the Federal Deposit Insurance Corporation; through the regulative activities of such agencies as public utility commissions, the Securities and Exchange Commission, and the Farm Credit Administration; and by means of a congeries of specially organized credit agencies, many of which have been called into existence by the emergency conditions of the last decade.

In former chapters this important aspect of financial organization has necessarily been considered in segments—the discussion covering one institution, or at the most one field of credit, at a time. Accordingly, an attempt should now be made to obtain a broader view, to envisage the position of the United States Government in the credit system as a whole. We shall first attempt to reveal the relation of the Treasury to the flow of money and credit throughout the economic system; and, second, we shall survey the extent to which the Treasury now furnishes funds for the operation of government credit agencies.

I. SOURCES OF TREASURY FUNDS

In the diagram on page 475 an attempt is made to indicate in a graphic way the flow of money and credit in relation to government fiscal operations. This diagram is analogous to that given on page 25, but it is focused upon government rather than upon private enterprise. The lower part of the diagram will therefore be ignored in the ensuing discussion. The arrows indicate the direction of movement of money and credit as it flows through government and other channels.   The dotted lines, with arrows, indicate the onward flow of money income as it is distributed anew in the form of wages, interest, rents and profits.

The revenues of the Government are of two types: (1) those derived from taxation and receipts from government enterprises; and (2) those obtained from borrowing operations.   Under normal conditions the latter are unimportant; indeed, there is sometimes a surplus which can be used for debt reduction.[1]   But in times of war and depression the revenues from government loans reach a magnitude comparable to those derived from taxation.   In the following discussion we shall be primarily concerned with these borrowing operations and the credit advances which they in turn make possible.

As the diagram indicates, the Government borrows from individuals, from savings and investment institutions, and from the commercial banks.   As has been revealed in chapter VII, the commercial banks and the Federal Reserve banks have constituted by far the most important sources of public credit during recent years. Owing to the restricted demand for commercial bank loans with which to finance ordinary private productive operations, the commercial banks have had available huge resources with which to purchase government issues. They can not only use idle reserves for this purpose, but, in case of need, they can also draw upon the resources of the Federal Reserve banks. In consequence of the enormous reserves of the banking system as a whole, the market for government securities has seemed to be almost limitless. In addition to the credit resources of the commercial banking system, the volume of individual and business savings available for the purchase of government securities has in recent years been exceptionally large—simply because of the dearth of investment opportunities elsewhere. From 1933 to 1937 inclusive the volume of new security flotations by private enterprises (refunding operations excluded) has averaged only about 620 million dollars as compared with 5,715 millions in the period 1925 to 1929.

The most striking financial phenomenon of recent years has been the extraordinarily low level of interest rates on government issues and in the money market generally.   It would seem as though the credit of the Government is in inverse ratio to the size of the Treasury deficits and the magnitude of the public debt—for the rates at which the Government has been able to borrow have steadily declined since 1933.   This phenomenon has been a source of endless confusion, and has beguiled many into the belief not only that the financial position

[1] See diagram, p. 91.

of the Government is as sound as the proverbial rock, but that the wells of public credit are endlessly deep. The fundamental explanation of this phenomenon is the extraordinary volume of loanable funds on the one hand and the lack of normal demand on the other, as pointed out in the preceding paragraph.

It has often been said that the low interest rates are wholly artificial, resulting simply from the Treasury policy of borrowing from the banks funds which, after they are disbursed through the agencies to which they are allocated, promptly give rise to new bank deposits. Such an explanation does not appear to be an adequate one. It is of course true that such a flow of funds operates to create new bank deposits. When banks purchase government securities they immediately set up a deposit account for the Treasury. From time to time, as needed, the Treasury transfers these funds to the Federal Reserve banks, and then in meeting its manifold requirement draws checks against these balances. Individuals or corporations receiving these government checks normally deposit them to their accounts in their respective banks; and, in due course, private checks are drawn against such accounts with the recipients thereof redepositing them in one bank or another. Thus the initial expansion of bank deposits arising out of the government loans is not liquidated; the checks become deposits somewhere in the banking system as a whole. With each succeeding government issue this process is repeated.

Such an expansion of bank deposits is, however, in no sense peculiarly related to government borrowing. It is precisely what happens when bank loans are being extended to private borrowers who open deposit accounts and draw against them checks, which in turn are redeposited somewhere in the banking system. Such an expansion of deposits continues as long as business expansion continues. It should be noted, however, that there is a marked difference in the character of the assets which the bank obtains in the process—in the one case government obligations and, in the other, loans directly related to commercial operations. Low interest rates, both on long-term securities and short-term loans, will continue until such time as business demands for commercial and investment loan accommodations are renewed on a large scale. As soon as the volume of new corporate flotations approximates former levels, long-term interest rates will rise; and the prices of high-grade securities, including government bonds, will accordingly decline. However, in view of the enormous credit resources of the banks at the present time, relatively low interest rates may well prevail for some years to come.

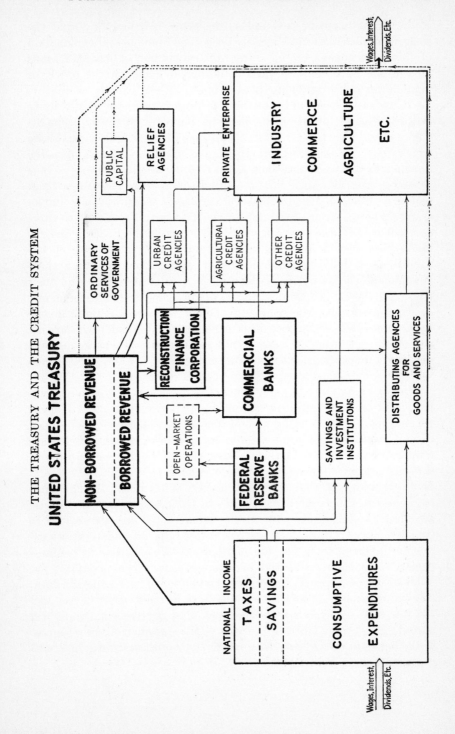

THE TREASURY AND THE CREDIT SYSTEM

II. THE USES OF GOVERNMENT FUNDS

We may now turn to the diagram on page 475 and note the purposes for which the Treasury disburses its income. A large part of the total naturally goes for the ordinary operations of government, incident to the administration of public business, the payment of interest on the public debt, meeting pension commitments, etc. A substantial amount also is spent for public capital projects, some of which are financed directly by bond issues, and others by direct appropriations from current revenues. The nature of such enterprises, both federal and state, is shown in the table on page 151. The disbursement of public money for relief purposes is also indicated in the upper right-hand area of the diagram.

Specific attention must be given to the Reconstruction Finance Corporation, which may be looked upon as a functioning arm of the Treasury in extending aid to varied types of business enterprise. The Reconstruction Finance Corporation was organized under the Hoover Administration, early in 1932, on the model of the old War Finance Corporation which had rendered an important service, particularly to the livestock industry, in the difficult years immediately following the World War. This corporation derives the great bulk of its funds in the form of direct advances from the Federal Treasury, only a small amount coming from the sale of notes in the investment market.

The Reconstruction Finance Corporation, as the name suggests, was organized for the purpose of tiding distressed economic institutions over a critical situation and of rehabilitating them on a sound financial basis. The larger part of such assistance has been given by making loans to, or purchasing the stock of, private enterprises. However, large allocations have also been made to other governmental agencies, particularly to farm and urban mortgage corporations operating under government auspices. The corporation has also made extensive advances for relief purposes and has purchased a large part of the securities received by the Public Works Administration in connection with its construction program.

The relative importance of these types of activities is indicated by the figures of total disbursements, which are as follows: Loans to private enterprise, 5,225 millions; relief advances, 1,382 millions; purchases of securities from the Public Works Administration, 571 millions; and allocations to other governmental agencies, 2,442 millions. A summary statement showing the types of enterprises to which aid has been given is presented on the following page.

RECONSTRUCTION FINANCE CORPORATION ACTIVITIES
FEBRUARY 2, 1932 TO MARCH 31, 1938[a]
(In dollars; 000 omitted)

	Disbursements	Repayments and Reductions	Outstanding March 31, 1938
Loans to Private Enterprise:			
Banks and Trust Companies[b].............	3,098,205	2,386,351	711,854
Building and Loan Associations............	117,935	115,609	2,326
Insurance Companies[c]....................	124,050	94,161	29,889
Mortgage Loan Companies[d]..............	447,431	279,959	167,472
Agricultural Financial Institutions.........	608,976	597,319	11,657
Rural Electrification.....................	31,757	2	31,755
Mining Industry........................	3,507	1,017	2,490
Drainage and Irrigation..................	79,820	2,298	77,522
Railroads..............................	550,659	182,188	368,471
Industrial and Commercial Business........	99,390	26,702	72,688
Fishing Industry........................	719	244	475
State Funds (insuring public deposits, etc.)..	13,065	13,065	
Public Schools..........................	22,450	22,300	150
Miscellaneous..........................	6,773	4,774	1,999
Relief advances:			
Self-Liquidating Projects.................	293,760	62,768	230,992
Agricultural Aid........................	799,845	703,825	96,020
Earthquakes, Cyclones, Fire, etc...........	8,529	4,351	4,178
Relief and Work Relief...................	299,985	299,985	
Purchases of Securities from P.W.A..........	570,737	429,740	140,997
Allocations to Other Governmental Agencies...	2,442,326[e]	2,422,326	
Total.................................	9,619,919	7,668,984	1,950,935
Commitments Outstanding March 31, 1938[a]...	....	....	163,087

[a] Compiled from Report of Reconstruction Finance Corporation, March 31, 1938.

[b] Including stock subscriptions and purchases of notes and debentures; the amount outstanding is $564,571,347.

[c] Including stock purchases; $100,000 outstanding.

[d] Including stock subscriptions; amount outstanding is $36,000,000.

[e] Amount allocated $2,540,567,000.

[f] Conditional agreements to make loans upon the performance of specified conditions.

It will be seen that out of total disbursements of 9,620 million dollars, only 1,951 millions remained outstanding on March 31, 1938 as assets of the corporation. It should be carefully noted, however, that the second column is headed "repayments and reductions." A reduction of 2,405 millions was made pursuant to the provisions of an act of Congress of February 24, 1928, which required the cancellation of corporation notes received from other governmental agencies to which funds had been allocated. It is obvious that notes from one govern-

mental agency to another do not constitute assets from the point of
view of the Government as a whole.

Among the loans to private enterprise, much the largest repayments
have been made by financial institutions. The fact is that a considerable
part of the advances made to financial institutions, as events proved,
was not really required. A substantial part of the purchases of securities from the Public Works Administration have also been paid off.

As has been pointed out in our discussions of agricultural and urban
credit, the Treasurer, either directly or through the intermediation of
the Reconstruction Finance Corporation, has provided large amounts
of capital for numerous mortgage credit agencies. There are also a
number of other credit agencies which derive their funds from the
Treasury. Accordingly, we have placed three rectangles on the
diagram representing respectively urban, rural, and other credit
agencies.

The table on pages 479, 480, and 481 summarizes the available data
with respect to the sources and ownership of capital of these numerous
institutions. The table, which has been compiled by the General
Accounting Office, is tentative in character. Since the figures are for
slightly varying dates it is impossible to give a precise total as of a
particular time; hence the figures in the following summary must be
regarded as rough approximations only.

These agencies as a whole have capital stock outstanding to the
extent of approximately 3,300 million dollars, of which the Federal
Government or its agencies own about 2,300 millions. They have issued
bonds, debentures, and notes aggregating approximately eight billion
dollars, of which roughly two billions are owned by the United States
Government or its agencies. It is impossible to give a figure showing the
extent to which the Government is empowered to furnish funds for
these corporations as a whole, since in some instances no definite limits
have been set by the law. The Government stands as guarantor for
over 3,500 millions on obligations now outstanding. The extent of the
potential contingent liability under present laws cannot be precisely
determined because of the indefinite character of some of the loan
authorizations.

It should be noted here that the table does not include all government corporations which have been furnished capital by the Government. For example, such government operating agencies as the Inland
Waterways Corporation, the Alaska Railway, the Panama Railroad,
and the Virgin Islands Company are not included. Nor does the table
cover all types of government outlays; the total expenditures of the
Government have been indicated in chapter VII. The purpose of this

SOURCES AND OWNERSHIP OF CAPITAL OF GOVERNMENT CREDIT AGENCIES
(In dollars; 000 omitted)

Agency	Date of Creation	Authorized Capital	Issued and Outstanding	Owned by	Bonds Guaranteed?
Banks for Cooperatives (12)					
Stock........	June 16, 1933	Not specified	98,761	96,000 (Treasury) 2,761 (Public)	No
Central Bank for Cooperatives					
Stock........	June 16, 1933	Not specified	50,497	50,000 (F.C.A.)a 497 (Public)	Yes
Bonds........		To 5 times paid-in capital, surplus	......	......	
Commodity Credit Corporation					
Stock........	Oct. 16, 1933	100,000	100,000	Treasury	
Debentures, bonds, notes........		Not to exceed 500,000	200,000 (Notes)	Public	
Disaster Loan Corporation					
Stock........	Feb. 11, 1937	20,000	10,000	Treasury	
Electric Home and Farm Authority					
Stock........	Jan. 17, 1934	1,000	850	Treasury	
Notes........	Apr. 30, 1938	4,325	4,325	Commercial banks	
Export-Import Bank of Washington					
Common stock........	Feb. 2, 1934	1,000	1,000	Treasury	
Preferred stock........		10,000	20,000b	R.F.C.	
Farm Security Administration........	Dec. 31, 1936				
Farmers' Home Corporation........	July 22, 1937	Not specified			
Federal Crop Insurance Corporation........	Feb. 16, 1938				
Federal Deposit Insurance Corporation					
Stock........	June 16, 1933	A 150,000 B ½ of surplus of Fed. Res. banks To 3 times paid-in capitald	20,000 150,000 139,000	Treasury Treasury Federal Reserve banks	
Federal Public Works Administration					
Debentures, bonds, notes........					
....	June 16, 1933	e	29,384	P.W.A.	

a Funds furnished by Treasury; administered by Farm Credit Administration.
b As given in daily statement of U.S. Treasury for Feb. 28, 1938.
c Funds derived from relief appropriations.
d The R.F.C. and the Treasury are authorized to purchase obligations to the extent of $500,000,000; the Corporation can also sell approximately $415,000,000 of obligations to banking or investment houses.
e Funds derived from relief appropriations and sale of obligations received as security for loans. These are sold to the public and the R.F.C. (See table p. 477.)

SOURCES AND OWNERSHIP OF CAPITAL OF GOVERNMENT CREDIT AGENCIES.—(Continued)
((In dollars; 000 omitted))

Agency	Date of Creation	Authorized Capital	Issued and Outstanding	Owned by	Bonds Guaranteed?
Federal Farm Mortgage Corporation.					
Stock.	May 12, 1933	200,000	200,000	F.C.A.ᵃ	Yes
Bonds.		Up to 2,000,000	1,409,766	52,858 (F.C.A.)ᵃ / 11,102 (Prod. Credit Assns.)	
Federal Mortgage Association.					
Stock.	Feb. 10, 1938	At least 2,000	11,000	R.F.C.	No
Federal Home Loan Banks.					
Stock.	July 22, 1932	At least 60,000	160,580	{124,741 (Treasury) / 35,839 (Membs. of Sys.)}	Yes
Debentures.		Indefinite	76,500	Public	
Federal Housing Administration.					
Debentures, bonds, notes.	June 27, 1934	2,000,000ᵇ	570	Public	No
Federal Intermediate Credit Banks (12).					
Stock.	Mar. 4, 1923	60,000	70,000ᶜ	Treas. and F.C.A.ᵃ	No
Surplus.		Indefinite	30,000	Treas. and F.C.A.	
Debentures.		To 10 times [paid-in cap. and surplus	212,400	198,110 (Public) / 14,290 (F.C.A.)ᵃ	
Federal Land Banks (12).					
Stock.	1916; 1933	At least 9,000	238,551	{124,802 (F.C.A.)ᵃ / 113,749 (Public)}	No
Surplus.		Indefinite	164,382	Treasury	
Bonds.			1,782,959	{787,062 (F.C.A.)ᵃ / 75,268 (Prod. Cr. Assns.) / 920,629 (Public)}	
Notes.			{41,700 / 6,568 / 23,238}	Fed. Farm Mtge. Corp. / R.F.C. / Public	
Federal Savings and Loan Associations.	June 13, 1933	Indefinite	938,356	{47,803 (Treasury) / 170,764 (H.O.L.C.) / 719,789 (Public)}	No
Federal Savings and Loan Insurance Corporation.					
Stock.	June 27, 1934	100,000	100,000	H.O.L.C.	ᵈ
Debentures, bonds, notes.		Not specified	.....	.....	No

ᵃ Funds furnished by Treasury; administered by Farm Credit Administration.
ᵇ President authorized to increase to three billion dollars. There is also a liability up to 100 million dollars on account of "reconditioning" loans.
ᶜ Increase authorized Jan. 31, 1934.
ᵈ Associations' shares are guaranteed up to $5,000 for each shareholder.

SOURCES AND OWNERSHIP OF CAPITAL OF GOVERNMENT CREDIT AGENCIES.—(Continued)

(In dollars; 000 omitted)

Agency	Date of Creation	Authorized Capital	Issued and Outstanding	Owned by	Bonds Guaranteed?
Grain Stabilization Corporation...					
Notes...	June 15, 1929	Indefinite	67,759	F.C.A.[a]	Yes
Home Owners' Loan Corporation...					
Stock...	June 13, 1933	200,000	200,000	Treasury	Yes
Bonds, debentures, notes...		4,750,000	2,938,078	Various agencies and public	
Production Credit Associations...					
Stock...	June 16, 1933	Indefinite	About 95,000	76,085 (Prod. Cr. Corps.) 19,000 (Public)	
Production Credit Corporation...					
Stock...	June 16, 1933	Indefinite	120,000	F.C.A.[a]	
Reconstruction Finance Corporation...					
Stock...	Jan. 22, 1932	500,000	500,000	Treasury	
Bonds...		3,020,000	{ 854,723 298,573	Treasury[b] Public	Yes
RFC Mortgage Company...					
Stock...	Mar. 1935	25,000	25,000	R.F.C.	No
Bonds...			23,293	R.F.C.	
Rural Electrification Administration...	May 20, 1936	Unknown[c]			
Tennessee Valley Authority...	May 18, 1933				
Bonds...		50,000	None[d]		
United States Housing Authority...	Sept. 1, 1937				
Stock...		1,000	1,000	Treasury	
Bonds...		800,000		Treasury	Yes
United States Housing Corporation...	1916				
Stock...		100,000[f]	66,500	Treasury	
United States Maritime Commission...	June 29, 1936				
Ship Mortgage Insurance Fund...	June 23, 1938	200,000		Treasury	Yes

[a] Funds furnished by Treasury; administered by Farm Credit Administration.
[b] This amount is after write-off by Act of Congress Feb. 24, 1938 of 2,405 million dollars of unrecoverable assets.
[c] Funds derived from R.F.C. and appropriations.
[d] The Authority has received $114,900,000 from government appropriations.
[e] This corporation is concerned only with liquidation covering housing undertaken as an incident to the conduct of the World War.
[f] Funds derived from Treasury and operations.

table is simply to show the extent to which the Treasury has provided funds for government credit-granting agencies.

As has been pointed out in preceding chapters, a number of the credit institutions which have been established during the past decade or so were conceived as permanent parts of the American financial organization, while many others were set up as temporary agencies designed to meet the exigent problems arising from the great depression of 1929–1933. Still others, as the table indicates, have been organized since 1933, not so much to cope with emergency needs as to facilitate the Administration's program of economic and social reform. How many of these numerous and varied types of credit agencies will become permanently incorporated in the financial structure only time will tell.

It should be observed, however, that few of the emergency agencies have thus far shown any noteworthy tendency toward liquidation, notwithstanding the fact that since the date of their organization we have passed through a long period of economic expansion, culminating in a new business reaction. It is seldom realized that the recovery and prosperity period from the spring of 1933 to the early autumn of 1937 constituted the longest interval of expansion, without a substantial, if perhaps short-lived, recession, in our entire industrial history. On the other hand, however, the extent of economic recovery and growth between 1933 and 1937 was very much less than that of former periods of expansion. Whereas heretofore we have always quickly reached a level of production equal to that attained at the peak of the previous boom period, and then moved on to increased output and higher standards of living, in the present instance we failed at any time to equal the former volume of production. In the year 1937 the total national production—which determines national income—was only about 90 per cent as great as in 1929, notwithstanding a six per cent increase in population and an eight to nine per cent increase in the population of working age. Figured on a per capita basis, national production was only about 85 per cent as high as in 1929.

We are not interested in appraising the causes responsible for the situation. Our failure to reach former levels of production is pointed out here merely for the light it throws on our failure to liquidate emergency credit agencies, and on the persistent pressures for further extensions of credit—to provide for continuing relief requirements, and also to stimulate economic activity. The data presented in the preceding tables cover in the main only the period of the recovery movement, as they do not extend in most cases beyond the spring of 1938. The credit advances for the ensuing fiscal year are certain to show a great increase. The trend in subsequent years will of course depend upon economic conditions in general.

III. THE SHIFTING BALANCE OF POWER

In concluding this discussion a word should be said with reference to the effects of recent trends in the field of public credit upon the balance of power in the modern economic system. Beyond question—for good or for ill—control of the character of the economic life of the nation has in substantial measure been transferred from private to public hands. Government officials rather than directors of private banking corporations now occupy the positions of dominant importance in directing the flow of national income and thus allocating the productive energy of society. We are not referring so much to the supervisory and policing activities of government regulatory agencies as to the direct power which lies in control of the purse, and especially of the reservoirs of credit, whence flow the funds which continuously replenish the exchequers of government credit agencies.

Control and influence are exerted, not only directly by means of grants and subsidies, but, more subtly, by the threat of potential competition and coercion. To give but a single illustration, the Chairman of the Reconstruction Finance Corporation in an open letter[2] warned the bankers of the country that they must loosen up in their policies of credit extension or expect to see an important part of their natural business taken over by government lending agencies.

In the view of many the transfer of the control of credit from private to public hands seems a natural and a desirable step. Since the interest of the public is paramount—why should the granting of life-giving credit not be vested in government hands? Others, equally interested in the welfare of the people fear that such a transfer of power will result, not in life and health for the economic organism, but in persistent decay. They point to a long history of government credit-granting in this and other countries, which revealed the baneful influence of political pressure, and to a long and eventually successful struggle in the nineteenth century to remove the extension of credit and the creation of currency from political control—to the end that credit, and in consequence productive activity, might be allocated on the basis of economic merit, thereby promoting productive efficiency and the expansion of the wealth and income of the nation. Recent trends suggest that we may have traversed a cycle of time and may be returning to the conceptions which dominated the political and economic philosophy of the eighteenth century.

[2] July 1938.

CHAPTER XXIX
THE PECUNIARY SYSTEM AND PRICE MOVEMENTS

Our study of the numerous types of financial institutions which operate in the modern world has now been completed. It has been shown that each institution has been called into existence to meet some particular requirement of an evolving capitalistic system of wealth production and distribution, and that, taken together, these institutions constitute a financial system around which the entire economic mechanism largely revolves. In the light of this analysis we are now prepared to consider an issue which has necessarily been touched upon at various places in this treatise, namely, the causes of price fluctuations—as reflected in both commodity and security markets. Attention was given in chapter II to the effects of price fluctuations upon the different social groups; and in various chapters we have noted the repercussions of price changes upon the functioning of the economic system itself. Discussion of the forces responsible for, or the factors involved in, such price movements was, however, postponed, in order that the problem might be considered systematically in the light of the study as a whole.

The question with which we are concerned is one of the oldest in economic literature. Indeed, discussions of the relationship between money and prices long antedated the development of the modern capitalistic system. It was a matter of interest to observers in the ancient empires of Asia, and in Greece and Rome, while in the late Middle Ages there developed an extensive literature on the subject. A number of writers in the seventeenth century were concerned both with the relation of coinage debasement to prices, and with the effects of the increasing gold supplies resulting from the discovery of the New World. Beginning more than a century before the appearance of Adam Smith's "Wealth of Nations" in 1776, a series of writers had formulated in a preliminary way what came to be known as the quantity theory of money. As we shall presently see, practically all of the modern literature of money and prices has been constructed on the foundations laid by these earlier writers, and has embodied the same general approach to the problem.

Instead of tracing step by step the evolution of the theory of money, credit, and prices from these early beginnings to the more elaborate formulations of modern theorists, we shall endeavor to take a fresh look at the entire problem in the light of the analysis made in this volume of the evolution of the modern capitalistic system. Our first task will be to consider the general economic setting in which prices are determined.

I. THE ECONOMIC SETTING

In the highly complex pecuniary organization of the modern world the price-making process is an integral part of the operation of the whole economic system. The truth of this statement is suggested in a general way by the charts on pages 16, 226, and 342, which reveal respectively the movements of commodity prices, the movements of security prices, and the fluctuations of business activity. It is obvious from these diagrams that the oscillations of business and the movements of prices are in substantial degree associated phenomena. As a rule, though not always, periods of very active business are marked by rising commodity prices, while periods of business recession are accompanied by declining prices. Whether the fluctuations in business conditions are the result of changes in prices, or vice versa, or whether both are merely a reflection of common underlying causes, cannot, of course, be determined by a study of the charts themselves.

Under modern conditions practically all economic activity is organized and carried out through the use of money and credit instruments. As was pointed out in chapter III, money is employed, not merely in the exchange of consumption goods, but in connection with every phase of the productive and distributive process—in the production of raw materials and in the manufacturing process quite as much as in wholesaling and retailing operations. Moreover, it is essential to bear in mind that money is used to purchase labor as well as to purchase commodities. Indeed, as we have seen, all the factors of production are assembled by the offer of money payments; and, in turn, the distributive shares accruing to land, labor, and capital are disbursed in the form of money rents, wages, interest, and profits. The reader should refer again to the charts on pages 23 and 25, which reveal the all-pervasive flow of money income throughout the economic system.

In a highly developed pecuniary system the disbursements made by business enterprisers in connection with the employment of labor, the purchase of materials and supplies, the borrowing of capital, etc. constitute money costs of production, the magnitude of which necessarily has a direct bearing upon the prices at which the goods are offered for sale. On the other hand, the money income received by the various

participants in the productive process constitutes the means by which
the goods which are being produced are purchased in the markets.
The money costs of production relate, of course, to the supply side
of the price problem, while the money incomes received relate to the
demand side of the equation. In aggregate terms, the money costs of
production (including profits) must, of course, exactly equal the money
incomes received by the participants in the productive process—
though the magnitude of the demand for particular types of commodities will depend upon the way in which the money income is distributed.
We are not here interested, however, in discussing the distribution of
income, or in considering what factors in the complex process under
consideration may be of controlling importance.

The fundamental problem with which we are concerned is that of
the motivating forces in the movements of prices. What is the price-
changing-process—that is, how and why do prices in a complex
pecuniary system work from one level to another, now upward, now
downward? Is there some simple, all-embracing explanation, or may
the forces responsible for such fluctuations be of somewhat varying
character? In order to throw light on these issues we shall consider
separately certain long-term trends, and the shorter-term price changes
associated with cyclical movements and with factors affecting the
monetary standard itself.

II. LONG-TERM PRICE TRENDS AND ECONOMIC PROGRESS

Under a system of production and distribution operated without
the use of money, such as that of primitive societies and even of the
manorial economy of the feudal era, the benefits accruing from increasing productivity are distributed to the public directly in the form
of an increased supply of goods and services. But under a highly
developed pecuniary system, in which the masses of the people receive
money income for services rendered, and in which business enterprisers incur money costs which must be covered in the prices at which
goods are sold in the markets, the mechanism by which the benefits
of increasing productivity are disseminated is of a wholly different
character. The amount of goods which can be purchased by those who
receive wages, for example, will depend upon the relationship between
prices and wages. If we assume that employment remains stable, the
consuming power of labor over a period of years will be gauged directly
by the ratio of commodity prices to wage *rates*. If the wage earner
gets more dollars and prices remain unchanged, or, similarly, if he gets
the same number of dollars and prices decline, his purchasing power
will be increased. But it can be expanded only through the process of

increasing wage rates as compared to prices. A second principle needs to be borne in mind in this connection, namely, that an increase of wage rates relatively to prices depends upon increasing efficiency in production. Only thus will the means be available with which to pay higher real wages—that is, to provide more goods and services.

This conception of the process by which the benefits derived from increasing efficiency are disseminated under a capitalistic system has, of course, long found expression in economic literature. The traditional statement of the way in which competition among business enterprisers leads to economic progress for the masses may be briefly summarized as follows: First, each business manager will naturally gain if he increases efficiency and thereby reduces costs. He may accomplish this end by the construction of a larger and more efficient plant; by the installation of better equipment; by the introduction of superior internal management; by improved methods of marketing; or by a combination of these various methods.

Second, having reduced costs of production, he is in a position to increase his profits in one or the other of two ways. He may continue to sell at the same prices as before, enjoying the advantage of a wider margin between cost and selling price, or he may make price concessions in the hope of expanding the volume of his business. It is reasoned, that since the increase in efficiency, which is responsible for the reduction in costs, commonly involves an expansion of productive capacity, and since the maximum economies can be attained only when a plant is operating at full capacity, the greatest profit will result if sales are expanded by means of a reduction of prices. In short, increased efficiency makes lower prices possible, while an actual reduction of prices is insured by the profit incentive.

Third, the process naturally involves the gradual elimination of obsolescent and inefficient, high cost, establishments. The industrially fit—those who can sell at a minimum price—alone survive. Moreover, the efficient plant of today promptly becomes the inefficient one of tomorrow. A particular business man, firm, or corporation may indeed survive over a long period of years, but only if the production methods employed keep abreast of current improvements.

It is apparent that with a system thus operating, standards of living will steadily rise. The progressive reduction of prices as efficiency increases constantly expands the purchasing power of the masses, giving them an increasing volume of goods for the same money.

In analyzing the cost and price process in relation to living standards, writers on economics early directed attention to what appeared to be an essential difference between the so-called extractive industries and the manufacturing, transporting, and distributing industries. Agriculture, mining, and other natural resources were seen as operating under conditions of diminishing returns, or rising costs of production. Hence, as an expanding population pressed against limited resources, it was argued that the prices of foodstuffs and raw materials would necessarily rise. In the broad field of industry, on the other hand, division of labor, specialization, the expanding scale of enterprise, and the increasing power of capital instruments gave promise of operation for a long period of time under conditions of diminishing costs, which would make possible an improving ratio of prices to wages. It was believed, however, that eventually the rising costs of foodstuffs and raw materials might more than offset the continuing gains from technological progress.

Thus far, however, the expected rise in costs and prices in extractive industries has not occurred. This fact is attributable to the vast improvements in methods of production that have been introduced in agriculture and mining as well as in industry during the last fifty years. The prices of agricultural products and industrial raw materials, as compared with those of industrial products, have in fact fallen during recent years. In view of the restricted rate of population growth in recent years and the continuing applications of science to the extractive industries, it may turn out that rising costs may be indefinitely postponed.

But whatever the future trends may prove to be, it is evident that since the industrial revolution and the development of a full-fledged capitalistic system, we have had a more or less continuous reduction in the real costs of producing goods and services. Thanks to technological advances, the amount of human energy required to turn out a given amount of product has been greatly reduced; stated conversely, the output per man per hour has been greatly increased. In consequence of this increasing efficiency in production methods, we have had a vast improvement in standards of living.

It must be noted, however, that prices have not declined in proportion to the increase in productive efficiency. The explanation is to be found in the fact that a substantial part of the rise in standards of living among the laboring population has been obtained through increases in money wages rather than by means of price reductions. In fact, the improvement since 1800 in the ratio of wages to prices has on the whole resulted somewhat more from increasing wage rates than from falling prices. A comparison of the movements of wholesale prices and money wage rates in the United States from 1801 to 1937 will be found in the diagram on the next page. The line marked "real

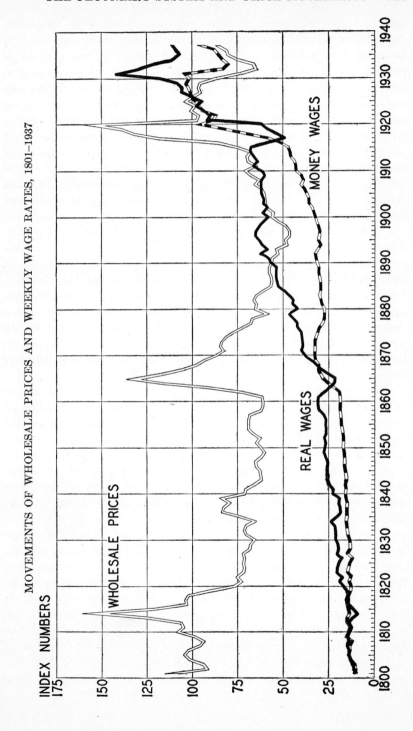

MOVEMENTS OF WHOLESALE PRICES AND WEEKLY WAGE RATES, 1801–1937

wages" indicates the rising purchasing power resulting from the changing ratio of wage rates to prices. At certain periods the advance achieved by labor has been due mainly to falling prices, while at other times it has been the result of rising wage rates. At times, indeed, it has come when both wages and prices were rising, but with the former increasing more rapidly. Moreover, there has often been a sharp improvement in periods of depression when the decline in prices was much greater than the reduction in wage rates. Since prices declined somewhat over the period as a whole, the rise in real wages was greater than the rise in money wages.[1]

It is thus apparent that the gains resulting from technological improvements may be distributed to the labor population either by reducing prices or by increasing wage rates. It is obvious, moreover, that to the extent that such gains are absorbed in paying higher wages, they cannot be employed in reducing prices. To state the matter another way, the increasing wages constitute a monetary cost of production which must be considered in the determination of prices.

In economic literature attention has also been repeatedly called to certain other factors which may affect the general level of prices. For example, discussions of the imposition of protective tariffs always point out that a horizontal increase in tariff rates will exert a powerful pressure in the direction of higher prices; indeed, it is usually contended that a 25 per cent increase in the prices of imported commodities, through its cumulative effects upon the cost structure, would doubtless result in a rise of much more than 25 per cent in the prices paid by the ultimate consumers. Similarly, it has repeatedly been argued that the levying of indirect taxes, particularly a universal sales tax, would promptly raise the general level of commodity prices.

It will of course have been observed in connection with the foregoing discussion, that nothing has been said about the available supply of money and credit. This is not because money and credit have no place in the picture, but simply because the motivating forces which we have been discussing are not of a monetary character. When business enterprisers reduce prices in order to meet existing competition or to expand sales at the expense of higher cost producers, they are in no wise influenced by consideration of the aggregate supply of available money and credit in the country. Similarly, when modern large-scale enterprisers, such as those operating in the automobile and

---

[1] While both price and wage data for the greater part of the nineteenth century are far from precise and adequate, the diagram nevertheless unquestionably gives an approximately correct view of the major trends. For a discussion of the data used, see the author's *Income and Economic Progress*, pp. 180–183.

mail order businesses, decide to reduce prices with a view to stimulating the greatest possible volume of sales,[2] they give no thought to the quantity of gold and other forms of money. In like manner, labor organizations have exerted a powerful influence in the direction of higher money wages—with consequent effects upon prices—without considering the volume of money and credit.

It is obvious, however, that the quantity of money and credit available in a country is none the less an integral part of the wage and price situation. For instance, if the supply of money and credit had remained stationary over the period covered by the chart on page 489, and if population and the volume of production had increased exactly as it did increase, we could not have had a level of wages and prices such as that indicated in the accompanying chart. In view of the enormous expansion in the volume of production over the course of the period covered by the chart, it is apparent that we had to have either an extraordinary increase in the total quantity of money and credit in use—or else an extraordinary decrease in the level of costs and prices at which business was actually being conducted.[3] It is self-evident that money and credit must have increased in line with production and price trends.

It will be of interest to inquire, however, whether at any time during the period under consideration a dearth of money proved a restricting factor. The answer is that on certain occasions an inadequate supply of money and credit served to check business expansion. As was pointed out in chapter XX, there were numerous occasions during the period between the Civil War and the World War when the available supplies of loanable funds in central reserve city banks fell so low that discount rates not only rose sharply, but actual curtailments of credit became necessary. As we have also seen, a final restriction of this sort occurred in conjunction with the inflation movement of 1919–1920. However, as a result of the great changes which have come in the post-war era, the possibility of another shortage in the supply of available money and credit—unless artificially produced through modification of reserve requirements—is remote.

In the discussion thus far we have been concerned solely with the long-run relationship between technological progress and the wage-

---

[2] For discussion of the price-making process in modern industry, see Edwin G. Nourse and Horace B. Drury, *Industrial Price Policies and Economic Progress*, the Brookings Institution, 1938.

[3] If the supply of money and credit had not expanded, it may of course be asked whether high money rates and the restriction of loans would not have so adversely affected business as to make business expansion impossible.

price ratio. No attention has been given to the major swings of prices
as revealed in the diagram on page 489. Before discussing these so-
called secular trends, it is desirable to consider the fluctuations of
prices arising out of the phenomena of the business cycle.

III. PRICE CHANGES AND THE BUSINESS CYCLE

It has been a general characteristic of the business cycle that prices
rise and fall with the alternating periods of prosperity and depression.
In the ensuing paragraphs an attempt will be made to indicate the
steps in the process by which prices rise on the upswing of a cycle and
fall in the ensuing period of recession. The analysis may advantageously
start with the situation existing at the beginning of a recovery movement, when there is a large volume of unused plant capacity and also
of unemployed labor.

When, for reasons which need not here be considered, the economic
outlook appears favorable, business managers begin to place orders
for additional quantities of goods. The accompanying increase in
production necessitates larger money outlays for both materials and
labor. For a time these requirements may be met through idle funds,
but sooner or later it will be necessary to seek credit accommodations
at the banks. As funds are disbursed, they flow through the channels
of industry and increase money wages, interest, and profits. As the
demand for commodities and for labor expands, prices and wage
rates show a tendency to rise; and thus costs, in the successive
stages of production, advance. In due course, also, the cost of money,
that is, interest rates, usually rises. If the general situation is such as
to create boom conditions, we enter upon a period which has been well
described as a vicious spiral of rising prices, rising costs, rising prices,
and again rising costs and prices.

It is apparent that the greater the volume of output, and the
higher the level of production costs, the greater will be the volume of
money and credit required in the productive process as a whole. The
increased quantity of money is derived chiefly from the expansion of
bank credit as business men seek ever-increasing accommodations
with which to meet their expanding requirements. The initiative in the
procurement of additional credit naturally lies with the borrowers,
although when conditions appear especially promising the bankers
may meet them fully half way. The truth of the matter seems to be
that when business conditions are favorable, business psychology
buoyant, and the supply of loanable funds abundant, credit is sometimes so liberally extended that the boom, and in consequence the
advance of prices, is greatly accentuated.

It must now be noted that, inasmuch as wage rates constitute only one of the elements of cost, we may have a situation in which the advance in prices greatly exceeds the advance in wage rates—thus adversely affecting the wage-price ratio. At first glance it would seem that such a development would immediately so reduce the buying power of the labor population that the price advance itself would be halted. Such an effect is, however, prevented for a time by virtue of the fact that *total wages* may be increasing relatively to prices. This situation is made possible by the great increase in total employment and by extra pay for overtime work. The rapid increase in aggregate wages may not only sustain but even increase the buying power of the laboring population as a whole. Ultimately, however, such an advance in prices, if uninterrupted, will inevitably restrict the buying power of the labor population—for after the slack in the labor market has been taken up the relation between the movements of wage rates and prices becomes of decisive importance. A conspicuous illustration is found in the boom of 1919–1920,[4] when prices rose very much faster than wage rates, and eventually brought on a buyers' strike.

To guard against misunderstanding at this point, it must be emphasized that the foregoing analysis has not been set forth as a general theory of business cycles.[5] The purpose has been merely to reveal the price changing process in a period when prices are advancing, and particularly to show how credit finds its way into the channels of circulation by means of bank loans and disbursements in connection with productive operations.[6]

The process of price deflation in a period of depression is simply the reverse of the process of price inflation during a period of expansion. Instead of a rising spiral of costs and prices we have a downward spiral of prices and costs. The volume of new orders and commitments is sharply curtailed, production schedules are reduced, and employees are discharged or placed upon a part-time basis. The shrinkage of

[4] See chart on p. 489.

[5] The truth is that commodity prices do not always rise on the upswing of a business cycle. For example, in the late twenties price and wage relationships were wholly different from those in 1919–1920, wage rates showing a moderate rise and wholesale prices a moderate decline. (See chart on p. 489). The depression of 1937 came at a time when wage rates were advancing much more rapidly than were prices.

[6] The vicious spiral of rising costs and rising prices which we have been describing finds its most striking illustration in the period of the World War when in two years the general level of prices rose more than 100 per cent. For the successive steps in the wartime advance in prices, the reader is referred to "War Finance and the Price Level" by the author in *The Journal of Political Economy*, October 1919.

disbursements by business enterprises, and the accompanying decrease in wages, profits, and to a lesser extent rents and interest, necessarily result in a sharp reduction in the demand for nearly every variety of product, and a consequent fall of prices. The curtailment of demand is in fact very much greater than the actual decrease in purchasing power, for the simple reason that buyers postpone purchases of unnecessary products, in order either to economize or to take advantage of the lower prices which are expected to prevail later. Thus the downward movement is greatly accentuated. As the volume of business shrinks, the need for bank credit declines and outstanding loans are paid off at maturity instead of being renewed. One of the most striking features of a protracted depression is the gradual accumulation of excess reserves. Unemployment of money becomes quite as marked as unemployment of labor or of plant and equipment.

IV. MODIFICATIONS OF THE STANDARD AND PRICE CHANGES

Thus far we have been considering price movements associated with developments in the field of business enterprise. We now pass to a consideration of a different type of price change—arising from modifications of the monetary standard itself. As has been indicated in earlier chapters, history is replete with illustrations of so-called inflationary price movements resulting from interferences with the standard of value. The two principal types of monetary derangement are (1) the replacement of a metallic standard by irredeemable paper currency, and (2) a reduction in the weight of the monetary unit. The former, as we have seen, usually arises out of fiscal exigencies in time of war or depression, while the latter is usually an outgrowth of antecedent monetary disturbances.

The way in which a reduction in the weight of the monetary unit affects prices has already been indicated in the discussion of the devaluation of the dollar in 1933.[7] To recapitulate briefly, when a monetary unit is modified, its exchange value as compared with foreign currencies is immediately altered, and in consequence, the prices of goods entering into international trade are directly affected. There is, however, no similar effect upon the prices of domestic commodities—though in due course higher costs of imported materials which are used in domestic manufacture will exert an influence upon the prices of particular products. As we have seen, however, the devaluation of the dollar was not accompanied or followed by a proportional rise in prices—even though assisted by numerous other policies designed to restore prices to the 1926 level.

[7] See chap. V.

An issue of irredeemable paper currency affects prices in much the same way as does a devaluation of the monetary unit. When, during the Civil War, the United States Government issued irredeemable United States notes, or greenbacks, the paper currency gradually depreciated as compared with gold; to state the matter conversely, there was a premium on gold as compared with paper currency. Since the paper currency was legal tender, gold was driven from circulation, and greenbacks became the sole means of payment. Accordingly international trade quotations were promptly readjusted in line with the changing value of the actual medium of exchange.

If a depreciation of paper currency is of moderate proportions only, and if there is reason to believe that the emergency which occasioned the issue will soon be over, the extent of the price rise will be restrained. However, if the fiscal and international exchange situation is thoroughly demoralized, as was the case in Germany in the early post-war period, forces are set in operation which lead to a rapid and almost universal advance in prices. In the advancing stages of the German inflation, for example, with each new decline in the value of the mark internal prices as well as external were immediately advanced. Moreover, it became the established policy to advance wages monthly, weekly, and even daily in proportion to the rise in the cost of living index. Under such conditions, the rush to buy commodities "before the value of money should evaporate," served to accelerate the process.

V. THE TRADITIONAL APPROACH TO THE PRICE PROBLEM

We have now reached a point in the analysis at which consideration may advantageously be given to the general theory of prices as it has developed in economic literature. As was noted at the beginning of the chapter, formal discussions of the relation of money to prices began long before the industrial revolution and the emergence of a complex pecuniary system. Inasmuch as payments for labor were then made in kind and the productive process was conducted almost entirely without the use of money, it was only natural that the theory of prices should have been related solely to the process of exchange. The problem appeared to be simply that of considering the exchange ratio between consumptive commodities and the quantity of money available for their purchase.

Throughout the history of monetary discussions, however, there have been divergent approaches to this exchange problem. One line of analysis has run in terms of a simple comparison of the number of units of goods offered for sale with the number of units of money available for their purchase. The other approach has involved a comparison of *values*. Money was conceived as a commodity, which is subject, like other commodities, to changes in value as a result of fluctuations in supply and demand. Prices were thus regarded merely as an expression of the value of the monetary unit as compared with the values of other commodities. Both lines of approach, however, led to the same conclusion, namely, that the prices of commodities fluctuated with changes in the quantity of money.

The interpretative literature in any field of knowledge ordinarily tends to grow by a process of accretion. As new information, or insight, is acquired, the tentative generalizations of former scholars are elaborated and refined in the interests of a more comprehensive outlook and greater precision of statement. The evolution of the literature pertaining to the quantity theory of money affords a striking illustration of this process. It also reveals, as we shall show, the dangers involved in adhering too closely to an established groove, or framework, of thought.

It is unnecessary here to trace in detail the steps in the evolution of the so-called quantity theory of money and credit. It must suffice to state that in one form or another the theory that changes in the general level of prices are attributable to changes in the quantity of money and credit was accepted with little qualification by practically all of the economic writers of the eighteenth and nineteenth centuries. Some writers emphasized the value of the monetary unit in relation to the value of commodities, while others thought directly in terms of the volume of money in circulation as compared with the volume of goods offered in exchange.[8]

The quantity theory achieved added dignity when, in the 1880's, it was stated in mathematical form by the astronomer, Simon Newcomb. In due course Newcomb's statement was elaborated by Irving Fisher in a comprehensive equation of exchange which was designed to embrace all the factors involved in the relation of money, credit, and prices.[9] Since this was in a sense the culmination and the epitome of the classical line of approach extending back for several centuries, it is a convenient medium for illustrating the character of the thinking that had developed.

[8] It is not usually understood that J. Laurence Laughlin, who is regarded as perhaps the leading opponent of the quantity theory, was himself one type of quantity theorist. He was a strong adherent of the doctrine that if the value of gold falls, prices will rise proportionally and vice versa. He restricted the term "quantity theory" to the other conception, namely, that of exchange of the total quantity of money directly for the total quantity of goods; and it was this conception of the problem against which he directed his polemics.

[9] *The Purchasing Power of Money*, 1911.

The equation of exchange is stated most simply as follows:

$$\frac{\text{Money} \quad \text{velocity} \quad \text{credit currency} \quad \text{velocity}}{\text{Volume of trade}} = \text{Price level}$$

Velocity means the number of times the supply of money or credit currency is used in the course of a given time period, such as a year. From this equation it would follow that if a nation's supply of money and credit, multiplied by their respective velocities, amounted to 100 billion dollars, while the volume of trade amounted to 50 billions, the resulting quotient, or average of prices, would be two dollars. If, in the ensuing year, the volume of money and credit should double, while the quantity of trade remained the same, the level of prices would become four dollars; and, vice versa, if the quantity of trade should double while the number of units of money and credit remained the same, the level of prices would be cut in two.

It was argued by Fisher that there was normally a fixed ratio between the volume of money and the volume of credit outstanding, the ratio being determined by banking customs and reserve requirements. It was also held that the velocities of money and credit changed but gradually, as the habits of the people with respect to the use of money were modified. Hence the quantity of the basic money, gold, was the decisive factor in the monetary equation; if the supply of gold were increased by a given number of dollars, one could calculate the extent to which the total quantity of circulating media would be expanded, and—assuming that there were no offsetting changes in the volume of trade—the extent to which the price level would rise.

It was the implication of Fisher's analysis that there was no connection between money and credit, on the one side, and the volume of trade, on the other. The number of monetary units in circulation depends upon the productivity of the gold mines, while the number of units of goods to be exchanged depends upon the productivity of the rest of the economic system. Both the supply of money and the supply of goods find their way into the markets independently of one another. The level of prices is thus a mere arithmetical result, derived from dividing the one by the other. Fisher states that "The history of prices has in substance been the history of a race between the increase in media of exchange (money and credit) and the increase in trade. . . . Sometimes the circulating media shot ahead of trade and then prices rose . . . Sometimes, on the other hand, circulating media lagged behind trade and then prices fell."[10]

[10] *Op. cit.*, second edition, pp. 246–247.

It must next be noted that in Fisher's analysis it was assumed that money and credit are used only in the purchase of consumer goods. In illustrating the two sides of the equation by means of a pair of scales, Fisher put a bag of gold and a check book on the one side and a loaf of bread, a roll of cloth, and a scuttle of coal on the other. There was no intimation that the supply of money and credit was also utilized in the purchase of production goods, in the buying of securities constituting title to existing capital goods, in paying interest, rents, and profits, or in employing labor.[11] Both the illustration, and the implications of the entire analysis ran in terms of the conditions of a pre-capitalistic era.

When the quantity theory was first formulated, it was undoubtedly relevant to the economic conditions and processes of the time. Before the development of the wage system and the organization of production on the basis of the pecuniary calculus, goods did not enter the markets bearing price tags based upon costs of production, computed by elaborate accounting systems. It was expected that prices would be determined in the market by the interaction of the forces of supply and demand. Moreover, new supplies of gold and silver were usually exchanged directly for consumption goods. If the supply of money was increasing more rapidly than the supply of goods, the prices of the latter would inevitably rise; and vice versa.

Inasmuch as the use of money was confined almost entirely to the exchange of consumption goods, it was of course not to be expected that price theories formulated in the pre-capitalistic era would take account of the complex processes involved in the pecuniary organization of a later historical period. The early writers merely described the operation of economic forces in the particular world in which they lived. Nevertheless, once their conclusions had found a place in economic literature, successive generations of writers tended simply to follow the lead and to elaborate upon the original statement, meanwhile ignoring the revolutionary changes which were occurring in the economic organization of society. This fact is the more interesting in view of the gradual development, in other divisions of economic literature, of very different conceptions of the forces responsible for price trends, such as have been outlined in a preceding section of this chapter. One often finds the same writer expounding the quantity theory as the accepted explanation of price changes and elsewhere discussing price-making forces of an entirely different character.[12]

[11] Nor was it seen that the velocity with which money and credit circulates is necessarily connected with the tempo of business activity.

[12] In this connection reference should be made to the principle of currency *elasticity*, which was so much discussed in connection with the establishment of the

Numerous writers in recent years have pointed out that the equation of exchange merely expresses in graphic form a truism—namely, that the quantities of money and credit, multiplied by their velocities of circulation, must of necessity equal the total volume of trade multiplied by the prices at which commodities are sold; and that such a statement sheds no light upon the causal relationships among the various factors which make up the equation. A more fundamental weakness, however, lies in the conceptions and assumptions inherent in the entire approach, and its complete failure to envisage the actual processes of price-making in a pecuniary system such as we have today.

Before leaving the discussion of the evolution of the theory of money and prices, attention must be called to the fact that in late years increased consideration has been given to the process by which an enlarged supply of money enters the channels of circulation. The conception that a change in the level of prices was merely a reflection of an altered value relationship between the standard, gold, and other goods, was in no way concerned with the flow of money through the economic system. Similarly, in the exchange conception as embodied in Fisher's equation, it was not asked, How do increased supplies of gold and the credit currency based thereon, become a functioning part of the system of production and distribution? It was simply assumed that the increased currency supply was automatically present in the consumer goods market, constituting "counters" on the money side of the equation. Coming to recognize that such conceptions represented oversimplifications of the problem, numerous writers have in recent times undertaken to indicate the way in which a new supply of money, and potential credit, gets into the channels of circulation.

The controlling or motivating factor in the situation is held to be the rate of interest. An increased supply of gold promptly finds its way into bank reserves, where it becomes available as a basis for credit expansion. Increasing reserves mean declining interest rates; and a reduction in the cost of loanable funds induces an expansion of borrowing by business men. Until the last decade, roughly speaking, this analysis usually ran in terms of short-time discount rates at the commercial banks. But in the last few years attention has been shifted to long-term interest rates in the investment market as the controlling

---

Federal Reserve system. Currency should be "responsive to the needs of business," expanding and contracting to serve the varying requirements of the economic system. This conception is obviously at variance with the assumption that a new supply of money will always automatically become a part of the circulation medium and that once in circulation it will remain there permanently as a price-determining factor.

element in the situation.[13] The adequacy of this conception will be given consideration presently. It should be noted at this point, however, that this newer analysis embodies no essential change in general point of view, its adherents still being preoccupied with the monetary approach to the price problem and to the control of the business cycle.

In concluding this section of the discussion, a brief reference must be made to the evidence that has been cited in support of the theory that at least the secular trends of prices are directly related to major changes in the production of gold. Since the middle of the nineteenth century, there have been three periods in which a rapid increase in gold production has occurred. The first was from 1849 to 1870; the second from about 1890 to the World War; and the third from 1930 to the present time. The intervening periods were marked by moderate decreases in the *annual output* of gold, which meant not a decrease in the accumulated supply but only a declining rate of increase. It has long been contended that the major price movements— the secular trends—are closely articulated with these changes in gold production, thus strongly suggesting, if not proving, that the production of gold is the controlling factor in the situation.

The chart on page 489 does not, however, warrant the conclusion that there is always a close relationship between changes in gold production and changes in the level of prices. There does, indeed, appear to be a fairly close correspondence in the period between 1897 and the World War, though it should be noted that the gold supply was increasing rapidly from 1889 to 1897, during which time there was a major decline in prices. In the other periods under consideration no correlation of gold production and prices is apparent.

The level of wholesale prices in the United States in 1860 was nearly four points lower than in 1846–1847—though in the intervening years prices had advanced and then declined in connection with the cyclical fluctuations of the fifties. The movements of prices in other countries during this period show a similar trend.[14] During the period of rapid increase in gold production since 1829 the price level has declined. The relation of gold to prices in the United States during the whole period since 1922 will be considered in a subsequent section.

[13] The leading exponent of this point of view at the present time is J. M. Keynes; though it should be noted that Mr. Keynes also attaches great importance to disbursement of funds by way of the Treasury.

[14] See Rufus S. Tucker, "The Myth of 1849," in Charles O. Hardy, *Is There Enough Gold?* (Appendix A).

It will be observed from the chart that even during the periods of falling prices, between 1820 and 1850, and between 1870 and 1897, there were intervals of rising prices, associated with cycle movements. It is of special interest to note that, although the production of gold reached much its lowest level in the five years, 1880 to 1884, these years showed advancing prices. On the whole, therefore, the evidence does not support the view that either in short periods or in long periods there is any close correlation between gold production and price movements. While a shortage of bank reserves and rising interest rates, as we have already noted, sometimes checked business expansion, the drastic and persistent price declines of the late seventies and the early nineties were not forced by a dearth of currency. On the contrary, to use a common expression of the time, money and credit were redundant.

VI. LESSONS OF RECENT EXPERIENCE

The trends of the last fifteen years have shed much new light upon the factors which influence price movements. In the early post-war years it was confidently predicted by adherents of the quantity theory that the level of prices in the United States would permanently remain upon a plane very much higher than that of pre-war days. Fisher pointed out that we had had a price revolution and that in consequence of the great increase in the quantity of money and credit in circulation prices could not fall, except in so far as an increased volume of commodity production might gradually modify the equation of exchange.[15] In the early twenties it was observed by many students that in view of the greatly increased gold supplies of the United States (see chart, page 74) this country could look forward to rising prices as compared with those of other countries, the eventual result of which would be a modification of the balance of trade and a gradual redistribution of the world's gold supply. The collapse of world prices following 1929 was attributed by many to the declining rate of gold production during the period of the twenties.[16]

The experience of the post-war period conclusively demonstrates that the supply of gold bears no direct relation to prices, as far as a given country is concerned. The gold supply of the United States increased from about four billion dollars in 1922 to about 13 billions in July 1938.[17] The aggregate production of goods and services in

[15] Irving Fisher, *The New Price Revolution*, in a paper distributed by the United States Department of Labor, March 1919.

[16] It was this view which underlay the Warren program of devaluation.

[17] Had there been no devaluation, the supply on the latter date would have been 7.7 billion dollars.

1937 was approximately five per cent above that of the year 1923.[18] According to the strict interpretation of the quantity theory we should thus have had an enormous increase in prices, not only because of the increase in gold but also by virtue of an accompanying expansion of credit currency. The price index, however, has shown a decline of nearly 20 per cent.

The experience of this period has also proved that there is no fixed relation between the supply of gold and the supply of credit outstanding. Not only has there been no automatic expansion of credit on the basis of the increasing supplies of gold; but as we have seen in the preceding chapters in the discussion of the Federal Reserve system, the efforts to promote credit expansion have proved wholly unsuccessful.[19]

The third lesson of this period is that open market operations and low interest rates are powerless to create an expansion of credit currency and a rise of prices, in the face of adverse business trends, or beyond "the requirements of business" as determined by operating conditions at any given period. It will be recalled that open market purchases by the Federal Reserve banks merely result in the transference of funds from the Federal Reserve banks to the member banks, and that the latter cannot put the money into circulation except as business men are interested in borrowing. Even the lowest money market interest rates ever known have not been effective in stimulating appreciable expansion of bank loans. Nor have low rates on long-term investment money succeeded in stimulating expansion in the capital markets. There have been large refunding operations to reap the advantages of lower interest costs; but, as previously noted, the volume of new issues since 1933 has been of negligible proportions.

The inadequacy of the low interest rate conception, whether one has in mind the bank discount rate or the long-term investment rate, lies simply in the fact that the cost of credit is only one of many factors which the business manager must weigh in the balance in determining

[18] These particular years are chosen because both were years of active business.

[19] In explanation of the phenomena of the twenties some writers attributed the failure of credit to expand to a "sterilization" process which rendered the increased gold supply powerless to exert its normal influence on prices; but the record shows that no sterilization policy was adopted by the Reserve officials during this period. Others argued that the increased gold supply in the twenties at least affected prices *negatively*—that, in the absence of the increased volume of money and credit, prices would have fallen materially, in consequence of the increasing efficiency of production. This argument overlooks the fact that although productive efficiency was increasing, the effects were offset in substantial degree, as far as money costs of production were concerned, by rising money wages. Numerous other factors were also involved in the price trends of this period.

business policy. The advantage of cheap credit may be much more than offset by high costs of labor, by oppressive taxes, or by uncertainties in the economic and political situation as a whole. The truth is that for many businesses the cost of credit is of little or no importance in periods of slack. For some years now many, if not most, of the larger industrial enterprises of the United States have had large unused cash resources of their own; and hence are under no necessity of borrowing in order to expand the volume of current production or to construct new plant and equipment. Even under conditions when it is necessary to resort to the investment market for capital funds, the interest rate is, under present-day conditions, of minor importance. Much the greater part of the capital required by industrial enterprises is now raised by the sale of common stock. The time may indeed come when no capital is raised on the basis of a contractual interest rate.

Finally, the trends of the past fifteen years have indicated that, increasingly, money wage rates and hours of labor are becoming factors of positive importance in determining the level of commodity prices. The reduction in hours and the general advance in money wage rates promoted by the National Recovery Administration of 1933–1934 substantially raised the level of money costs in American industry as a whole.[20] In the ensuing period from about the middle of 1934 to the middle of 1936, the increase in productive efficiency in manufacturing industry was approximately offset by the continuing advance in wage rates. Meanwhile the prices of manufactured goods remained practically stationary. Between the early autumn of 1937 and June, 1938, wage rates in manufacturing industries were raised sharply, and the standard work day was further shortened. In consequence, one of the most important elements of cost was greatly increased (see chart, page 489); and the prices of manufactured goods were quickly advanced. It may also be observed that organized resistance to wage rate reductions in periods of depression tends to maintain a higher cost basis than would otherwise prevail. Looking forward, it would seem that wage policies may come to be of decisive importance in determining the trend of prices in major sectors of the economic system.

The essence of our analysis of price movements in a pecuniary society may be very simply recapitulated in the following terms. Under a capitalistic system, in which all the processes of wealth production and distribution are carried out through the medium of

[20] The restriction policies of the Agricultural Adjustment Administration of course worked in the same direction, in the field of agriculture.

money disbursements, the determination of prices is inextricably interwoven with the whole fabric of business enterprise. The forces which affect price movements are of varied character, relating not only to the supply of money and credit and to modifications of the monetary standard, but also to wage, fiscal, and other policies which react directly upon the structure of money costs, and to underlying technological developments which affect the efficiency of wealth production. It is impossible to weigh the relative importance of these numerous forces, since they vary at different periods and under changing conditions. In any case the economic mechanism is made up of such closely linked parts, and its processes are so interrelated, that a change, no matter where or how originating, exerts an influence throughout the entire price-cost-price structure.

In the light of this analysis of the factors and forces responsible for price movements in a pecuniary society, it seems apparent that the control of business and price fluctuations—if they are to be controlled—involves something more than the mere "management" of the currency supply, whether through modifications of the standard, the manipulation of interest rates, or the adjustment of bank reserves. The control must be envisaged in terms as broad as the nature of the problem which is to be controlled—that is, it must include all of the factors which influence prices in a financially organized economic system.

INDEX

A

Acceptance (*see* Bank acceptance; Trade acceptance)
Accommodation bill, 113
Accounts receivable, 112
  discount of, 269–270
Agricultural Adjustment Act, 45, 49, 51
Agricultural Credit Act, 452
Agricultural credit, significance of, 454–455
Agricultural credit institutions, 434–455
  chart, 437
  significance of, 454–455
Aldrich bill, 344
Aldrich-Vreeland Act, 343
Arbitrage, 66
Argentina, currency depreciation in, chart, 79
Assay commission, 30–31
Assay offices, 30–31
Australia, gold fields, 36
  public debt of, 95
Austria, adopts gold standard, 37
  breakdown of finances of, 76, 426
  exchange rates of, 71, 73
Automobile bank (*see* Discount companies)
Axias, 287

B

"Baby Bonds," 187
Balance of international payments of U.S., chart, 69
Balance of trade (*see* Balance of international payments)
Bank acceptances, amount of, 267
Bank checks, 114
Bank credit, 101
  (*See also* Deposit currency)

Bank draft, 112, 113
Bank examinations and reports by, clearing-house associations, 296–298
  under National banking system, 332
Bank failures and depreciable assets, 320–321
  causes of, in the twenties, 353–354
Bank loans (*see* Commercial bank loans)
Bank notes (*see* National bank notes; Federal Reserve bank notes; Federal Reserve notes)
Bank for International Settlements, 76, 431–433
Bank of England, 420
Bank of France, 422–423
Bank of Japan, 425–426
Bank reorganizations, 355–357
Bank suspensions, 355–357
Banking Act of 1933, 357–358
  and trust company examinations, 234
Banking Act of 1935, 357–358
  and Federal Reserve system, 383, 410
  and speculative issues, 233
Banking consolidation, in other countries, 418–427
  in U.S., 351–353
Banking panic of 1933, 44, 354–357
Banking reform, movement for, 341–345
Banking regulation, 325–361
Banks for Cooperatives, 451
  chart, 437
  loans by, table, 453
  table, 479
Barron, C. W., 317
Barter, inconvenience of, 20
Bear raids, 225
Belgium, 427
  adopts gold standard, 36

Belgium, currency depreciation of, chart, 79
exchange rates, 71, 73
Berle, Adolph A., 228
Bill of exchange, 262
bankers', 113
definition of, 112
Bill of lading, loans on, 257–258
Bill of Lading Act, 258
Bimetallism, abandonment of, by various countries, 36–37
and compensatory action, 33, 37–38
and Gresham's law, 31–36
suggested reestablishment of, 49
Bland-Allison Act, 37, 41
Blue Sky legislation, 235
Board of Governors of the Federal Reserve system, 367–368
power of, over economic system, 409–411
Bonds, real estate mortgage, 463–465
types of, 107–109
Book credit (book accounts) 102
(See also Accounts receivable)
Borrower's statement, illustration of, 250
Branch banking, 348–349
renewed impetus to, 358
Brokers, 216
Bryan, William Jennings, 38, 373
Bubble Act of 1719, 125
Building and loan associations, 456–460
Business booms (see Business cycles)
Business cycles, and Federal Reserve control, 377–382, 390–417
and price changes, 492–494

C

California gold fields, 36
Call loans, 255–256
Capital, types of, 137–138
Capital raising, the corporation and, 123–126
methods of, chart, 149
through promotion, 140–144
by public agencies, 149–152
stock exchange and, 212–227
Capital requirements, of governments, 149, 152

Capital requirements, of private business, 137, 149
and sources of capital, 137–152
Cashier's check, 114
Cattle loan companies, 439–440
chart, 437
Central banks, trends in foreign countries, 427–430
Central reserve cities, 307
Certified check, 114
Chain banking, 350–351
Chatters, Carl E., 231
Checks (see Bank checks; Deposit currency)
China and silver purchase program, 50
Clayton Act, 352
Clearing-house associations, 292–298
Clearing-house bank examinations, 296–298
Clearing-house certificates, 294
Clearings under Federal Reserve system, 300–303
Coinage, effects of bad system of, 28–30
a government function, 30
regulation in U.S., 30–31
Coins, abrasion of, 30
counterfeiting of, 30
debasing of, 28–30
(See also Copper; Nickel; Silver; Minor coins; Fractional coins)
Collateral loans, 253–257
Commercial bank investments, growth of, 312–316
Commercial bank loans, classification of, 314
and deposits compared, chart, 306
regulation of, 330–331
types of, 247–261
(See also Real estate loans)
Commercial banking, changing character of, 310–324
Commercial banking system, 292–309
Commercial banks, and agricultural credit, 438–439
chart, 437
dominant position of, 308–309
and foreign trade, 261, 263
importance of, charts, 333, 335
position of, in financial structure, charts, 133, 437, 475

Commercial banks, practical operations of, 239–263
Commercial credit, 99–101
Commercial credit companies (*see* Discount companies)
Commercial Credit Corporation, 440–441
  chart, 437
  table, 479
Commercial credit institutions, 264–276
Commercial credit instruments, 111–114
  (*See also* Credit instruments)
Commercial letters of credit (*see* Letters of credit)
Commercial paper, amount of, 266–267
Commercial paper houses, 264, 269
  chart, 133
Common denominator of value (*see* Pecuniary unit)
Common stock (*see* Stock)
Comstock lode, 37
Concentration of money and credit (*see* Banking consolidation)
Consumer goods, 26
Consumptive credit, definition of, 101, 277
  significance of, 290–291
Consumptive credit agencies, 277–291
Comptroller of the Currency, 329
Cook, W. W., 140
Cooperative credit unions, 285–287
  (*See also* Credit unions)
Cooperative marketing associations, 452
  chart, 437
Copper coins, 31
Corporation, as capital-raising device, 123–126
  "close," 134
  relation to financial structure, chart, 133
Corporations, regulation of, 228–230
Correspondent banks, 298–300
Country banks, failure of, 353–354
  reserves of, 336
Credit, 99–105
  basis of, 102–103
  kinds of, 100–102

Credit, significance of, 103–105
Credit currency (*see* Deposit currency)
  in relation to prices, 484–504
Credit institutions, evolution of, 123–136
Credit instrument, 106–122
Credit unions, amount of loans, 279
  (*See also* Federal credit unions)
Creditor class, 17
Crime of 1873, 37, 341
Crises (*see* Business cycles)
Curb market, 213–215
Currency Act of 1900, 38, 42
  banking provisions of, 343
Cyanide process, 38
Cycles (*see* Business cycles)

D

Davis, Joseph H., 128
Deferred payments (*see* Standard for deferred payments)
Denmark, abandons gold standard, 78
  adopts gold standard, 36
Department-store finance (*see* Financial integration)
Deposit currency, elasticity of, under Federal Reserve system, 368–374
  manufacture of, 303–308
Deposit insurance, 359–360
Depositary banks, for government funds, 385–389
  table, 388
Deposits of national banks, table, 316
  (*See also* Federal Deposit Insurance Corporation)
Depression of 1929–1933, underlying reasons for, 406–407
Depressions (*see* Business cycles)
Disaster Loan Corporation, 469–470
  table, 479
Discount companies, 270–276
  chart, 133
  paper of, 267–268
Discount market, 269, 420–421
Discount rates, 328–329
  and control of credit, 499–500, 502–503
  as a control device, 402–404, 410
Discounting receivables (*see* Accounts receivable)

Double liability of bank shareholders, 330

Draft (*see* Bills of exchange)

Drury, Horace B., 491

E

Elastic currency, 498
   under Federal Reserve system, 368–374

Electric Home and Farm Authority, 275, 448–449
   chart, 437
   table, 479

Emergency Crop and Feed Loans, 441
   chart, 437
   table, 453

Equation of exchange, 497–498

Escrow, 198

European debt to the U.S., 230

Exchange, foreign (*see* Foreign exchange)

Exchange stabilization, 81–82

F

Farm Credit Administration, 435
   chart, 437
   (*see also* Federal Land banks)

Farm mortgage companies, 443–444
   chart, 437

Farm Security Administration, 447–448
   chart, 437
   table, 479

Farmers' Home Corporation, 448
   chart, 437
   table, 479

Federal Advisory Council, 368

Federal credit unions, 441
   chart, 437

Federal Crop Insurance Corporation, 442

Federal Deposit Insurance system, 360
   table, 476

Federal Farm Loan Act, 444

Federal Farm Mortgage Corporation, 447
   chart, 437
   table, 480

Federal Home Loan Bank, 468–470
   table, 480

Federal Home Loan Bank Board, 468–470

Federal Housing Administration, 470–471
   table, 480

Federal Intermediate Credit banks, 450–451
   and cattle loan companies, 440
   chart, 437
   loans by, table, 453
   table, 480

Federal Land banks, 444–445
   loans by, table, 453
   table, 480

Federal Mortgage Association, 470
   table, 480

Federal Open Market Committee, 410

Federal Public Utility Act, 229

Federal Reserve Act, 362
   regulation of bank note currency by, 368–374

Federal Reserve Agent, 364, 371, 375

Federal Reserve bank notes, 40, 42
   regulation of, 370

Federal Reserve banks, assets and liabilities of, table, 384
   organization of, 363–367
   position in financial structure, chart, 475
   reserve position of, chart, 398

Federal Reserve districts, map of, 366

Federal Reserve notes, 42, 370–374
   amount of, 39
   in circulation, 40

Federal Reserve system, 362–417
   Board of Governors of (*see* Board of Governors)
   evolution of policy of, 397–400
   and international cooperation, 404–405
   methods of control by, 400–404
   operations of, table, 383
   organization of, chart, 365
   policies of, 411–417
   reserve position of member banks of, chart, 411
   reserve requirements of, 410
   and war-time finance, 390–392

Federal Savings and Loan Insurance Corporation, 469

Federal Savings and Loan Insurance Corporation, table, 480
Fiduciary services of trust companies, 195–196
Finance companies (*see* Discount companies)
(*See also* Personal finance companies)
Financial consolidation (*see* Banking consolidation)
Financial crises (*see* Business cycles)
Financial integration, process of, 336–340
Financial panics (*see* Business cycles)
Financial structure, 132–136
charts of, 133, 437, 474
Financial system, interrelations of, 97
charts, 133, 437
(*See also* Pecuniary system)
Finland adopts gold standard, 37
First Bank of the U.S., 326
Fiscal agent, 204–206
Fisher, Irving, 497–498, 501
Flow of money, charts showing, 23, 25
Foreign banking and credit systems, 418–433
Foreign branch banks, 349
Foreign exchange, 62–83
breakdown of, during depression, 75–80
restoration of stable, 73–75
war-time disruption of, 70–73
Fort Knox, Ky., gold stored at, 49
Fractional coins, amount of, in U.S., table, 39
in circulation, table, 41
France, adopts gold standard, 36
exchange rates, 71, 73
financial system of, 422–423
public debt of, 95
value of franc, chart, 72
"Free banking" law of New York, 327
Free silver agitation, 37–38, 49–50

G

German zollverein, and silver standard, 36
Germany, breakdown of finances, 76
currency inflation of, 88–90

Germany, exchange rates of, 71, 73
Federal Reserve cooperation with, 404
financial system of, 423–425
public debt of, 95
Gold, adoption of, in U.S., 36–38
amount of, in U.S., 38–39
chart, 35
in circulation, 40
commercial ratio to silver, 32–33
embargo on, 45
exports of, 44
hoarding of, 44
holdings of leading nations, chart, 74
price of, 48, 53
production of, table, 34
qualities of, 12
why chosen as standard, 12–14
Gold bloc, 81
Gold certificates, 38, 40
redemption of, 60
"Gold clause" cases, 53–60
Gold contracts, 46
Gold devaluation, 49
chart, 52
and price level, 51–53
Gold dollar, definition of, 3, 14
"Gold exchange" standard, 75
Gold points, 63–65
Gold reserves of U.S., 49
Gold standard, 12–14
abandonment of, by U.S., 45
adoption of, in U.S., 36–38
in various countries, 36–37
disintegration of, 78–79
law of 1900, 38
at present in U.S., 60–61
Gold supply, distribution of world supply of, chart, 74
future distribution of, 82–83
Government finance and monetary stability, 84–98
Great Britain, currency depreciation of, chart, 79
exchange rates, 71, 73
Federal Reserve cooperation with, 404
financial system of, 418–422
public debt of, 95
Greenback currency, 39

Greenback currency, depreciation of, 46
　original issue of, 42
Gresham's Law, 31–32
　and bimetallism, 31–36
Grobben, Margaret, 279
Group banking, 350–351

H

Harris, N. W., and Co., 156
Henderson, Leon, 281
Holding companies, regulation of, 29–2 230
Holland (see Netherlands)
Home Owners Loan Corporation, 468
　table, 481
Hoover moratorium, 76
Hungary, adopts gold standard, 37
　exchange rates of, 71–73
　public debt of, 95

I

Illegal lenders, 280–282
　(See also Loan sharks)
Independent banking, 328
Independent treasury, 386
　(See also Depositary banks)
Index numbers, 15, 19
Industrial banks, 288, 289
　amount of loans, 279
Inflation, in Germany, 88–90, 96
　in Revolutionary France, 86–87
　types of, 95–96
Installment credit (see Installment sales)
Installment sales, financing of, 270–274
　significance of, 274–275
　by stores, 281–282
Insurance companies, 188–190
　assets of, 189
　charts, 133, 437
　policy loans of, 280
　regulation of, 233
Insurance of deposits (see Deposit insurance)
Integration (see Financial integration)

Interest rates, low level at present, 93–94
　(See also Discount rates)
Interlocking directorates, system of, declared illegal, 352
Intermediate credit, 137–138
　agricultural, 449–454
　chart, 437
　(See also Federal Intermediate Credit banks)
International Bank, 76
　(See also Bank for International Settlements)
International finance, 430–433
　(See also Foreign exchange; Bank for International Settlements)
International monetary system, 42–43, 430–433
Interstate Commerce Commission, regulation of securities by, 232
Investment banking, 153–174
　chart, 133
　and economic organization, 171–174
　function of distribution, 166–168
　function of investigation and analysis, 157–162
　function of underwriting (see Underwriting)
　history of, 153–156
　syndicates, 163–166
Investment counsel, 181
Investment credit, 101
　instruments of, 106–111
Investment institutions, 175–193
Investment trusts, 175–181
Italy, 427
　adopts gold standard, 36
　exchange rates of, 71–73
　public debt of, 95

J

Japan, adopts gold standard, 37
　currency depreciation of, chart, 79
　finances of, 96
　financial system of, 425–426
　public debt of, 95
Joint stock banks of England, 419
Joint stock land banks, 435
　table, 443

K

Kendrick, F. Slade, 144
Keynes, J. M., 500
Klondike gold mines, 13, 38

L

Labor banks, 279
Lamke, Edwin, 357
Land Bank Commissioner, loans, 447
    table, 453
    (*See also* Federal Land Banks)
Latin monetary union, 36
Laughlin, J. Laurence, 311, 496
League of Nations, and central bank
    policies, 430
Legal tender, 42
Letters of credit, 262
Liberalization of credit policies in
    1938, 323–324
Limited liability, advantages of, 125
Liquidity, the problem of, 316–320
"Living trusts," 198
Loan sharks, 280–282
    amount of loans, 279
London Conference (*see* World Eco-
    nomic and Monetary Conference)
London stock exchange, 212–213

M

Macaulay, 28, 127, 128
McFadden Act, 348–349, 351, 358
"Margin" trading, 220, 224, 256
Means, Gardiner C., 228
Medium of exchange, function of, 20–21
Mercantile credit, 100
Mexico currency, depreciation of, chart,
    79
    and silver purchase program, 50
Minor coins, 39, 40, 41
    redemption provisions, 60
Mints, gold stored at, 49
    tolerance of, 31
    of United States, 30–31
Monetary Act of 1792, 32
Monetary Act of 1834, 3, 32, 37
Monetary Act of 1934, 3, 48
Monetary management, by govern-
    ment, 47

Monetary regulation, recent changes in,
    44–61
Monetary system, evolution of, 28–43
    international, 42–43
    recent changes in, in America, 44–61
Monetary unit (*see* Pecuniary unit)
Money, in circulation, table, 40
    and economic origin, 24–27
    forms of, in U.S., 38–42
    functions and services of, 20–27
    as medium of exchange, 20–21
    in relation to prices, 484–504
    in relation to production, 21–24
    as store of value, 21
Money income, flow of, charts, 23–25
    of U.S., 26
Money rates (*see* Interest rates)
Money savings, 24–27
Morgan, J. P., and Co., 155, 156, 357
Morgan, Stanley, and Co., 157
Morris Plan Bank, 288
Mortgage, "old line," 460–463
Mortgage companies, 443–444
Multiple standard, 19
Municipal governments, debt of, 151
    limitations of security issues of,
    231

N

National bank notes, 42
    amount of, 39, 40
    under Federal Reserve system, 369
    retirement of, 48
National banking system, 327–334
National banks, demand and time
    deposits of, 316
    growth and importance of, charts,
    333–335
    loans and investments of, 315
    chart, 314
National Farm Loan associations, 445–
    447
    chart, 437
National Industrial Recovery Act, 51
National Monetary Commission, of
    1910, 344
National Municipal Bankruptcy Act,
    231
Negotiability, principles of, 115–122

Netherlands, The, adopts gold standard, 36
exchange rates of, 71, 73
New York Curb, (see Curb market)
New York Stock Exchange, history of, 213–216
Newcomb, Simon, 19, 496
Norway, adopts gold standard, 36
public debt of, 95
Note brokerage (see Commercial paper houses)
Nourse, Edwin G., 491
Noyes, Alexander D., 352
Nugent, Rolf, 281

O

Odd-lot dealers, 217
Open accounts (see Accounts receivable)
Open Market Committee, 368
Open market operations, 400–402, 410
Open market paper (see Commercial paper)
Overcertification, 257
Overdrafts, 245
Over-the-counter market, 215

P

Panic of 1907, 343
of 1933, 355–357
Paper currency, of confederate states, 87–88
continental, 86–87
forms of, 38–42
France, 86, 87
German (illustration of) 90
Par collections, 302–303
Pawnbrokers, amount of loans, 279
business of, 282–283
Pecuniary system, and price movements, 484–504
Pecuniary unit, 3–11
and family budget, 7–8
as index for business policies, 4–7
number of grains in, 3, 48
and price changes, 494–495
and social standards, 10–11
Personal credit, 100
Personal finance companies, 283–285
amount of loans, 279

Personal loan department of commercial banks, 289–290
amount of loans, 279
Poland, exchange rates, 71, 73
public debt of, 95
Portugal, abandonment of bimetallism, 36
Preferred stock (see Stock)
Price changes, 14–16, 20, 484–485
and the business cycle, 492–494
charts of, 16, 490
after Civil War, 17
and creditor class, 17
and debtor class, 16
economic consequences of, 16–19
and gold devaluation, 51–53
and modification of the standard, 405–406
Price level and gold devaluation, 51–53
(See also Price changes)
Price movements and the pecuniary system, 484–504
Price trends, and economic progress, 486–492
Prices, relation of money to, 19, 51–53
and wage rates, chart, 489, 503–504
traditional approach to, 494
Private banks, 329, 506
Production credit associations, 452
chart, 437
table, 481
Production credit corporations, 452
chart, 437
loans by, table, 453
table, 481
Promissory note, 112
double name, 252
as collateral, 253
Promotion, methods of, 140–144
Prosperity, periods of (see Business cycles)
Public credit, 100, 472–474
Public Works Administration, table, 479
Pujo Investigation, 352

Q

Quantity theory of money, 484–504

R

Real estate, financing urban, 456–471
Real estate exchange of New York, 466–467
Real estate loans, 458–459
Real estate mortgage bonds, 463–465
Reconstruction Finance Corporation, activities of, table, 477
and agricultural credit, 434–455
financing of urban real estate, 468–470
organization and purpose of, 476
table, 481
RFC Mortgage Co., 469
table, 481
Reichsbank, 424–425
Reichsbank note, illustration of, 90
Remedial loan societies, 283–284
Reorganization, agreement and trust companies, 203
Reserve cities, 307
Reserves, control of member banks by Federal Reserve official, 410
of Federal Reserve system, charts, 398, 411
mobilization of, 374–376
redepositing of, 307–308
regulation of, 332
requirements under Federal Reserve system, 382
under National Banking system, 336
sterilization of, 412
Rural credit (see Agricultural credit)
Rural Electrification Administration, 449
chart, 437
table, 481
Russell Sage Foundation, 281, 284
Russia, adopts gold standard, 37
financial system of, 427

S

Savings, 24–27
Savings and Loan Associations, 468–469
table, 480
Savings institutions, 181–188

Savings institutions, chart, 133, 437
cooperative, 181
departments in commercial banks, 182–184
economic significance of, 190–193
"guaranty," 182
management of, 184–185
mutual, 181–182
postal, 185–188
regulation of, 233
stock, 182
Scandinavian monetary union, 36
Second bank of the United States, 326
Secrist, Horace, 231
Section 77B, 230
Securities, fluctuations in prices of, 226
marketing of, 153–174
regulations of marketing of, 235–237
by types of business, 148
Securities and Exchange Commission, 234–238
Seigniorage, 41
profits on silver, 50
Settlement fund, 302
Sherman Silver Purchase Act, 37, 41
Short selling, 220, 224
Short-term credits and world depression, 76–77
Short-term note, 109
Silver, bullion in U.S., 39
commercial ratio to gold, chart, 35
fractional coins (see Copper; Nickel; Minor coins)
price of, 50
production of, 34
Silver certificates, 39, 41
Silver dollar, 31, 39, 41
Silver Purchase Act of 1934, 50
Sixteen to one, ratio of silver to gold, 32, 37, 38
suggested return to ratio of, 50
South African gold fields, 38
South Sea bubble, 212
Small loan companies (see Personal finance companies)
Smith, Adam, 484
Speculation, in 1688, 125, 128
in 1719, 125

Speculation, in 1929, 467
(*See also* Margin trading; Short selling)
Stabilization fund, 48
Standard for deferred payments, 12–19
why gold was chosen, 12–14
Standard of value (*see* Pecuniary unit)
State and local governments, debt of, 151
limitations on security issues of, 231
State banks, after Civil War, 334–340
before Civil War, 327
growth and importance of, charts, 333, 335
Sterling area, 81
Stock, types of, 109–111
Stock exchange and capital raising, 212–217
chart, 133
economic functions of, 221–227
fluctuations on, chart, 226
listing requirements, 218
organization of, 216–221
regulation of, 237–238
Stockholders' rights, 111
Subsidiary silver, 31
and Act of 1853, 41
redemption provisions of, 60
Supreme Court and Gold Clause cases, 53–60
Surplus, accumulation of required, 329–330
Sweden, adopts gold standard, 36
currency depreciation in, chart, 79
exchange rates, 71, 73
public debt of, 95
Switzerland, 36
currency depreciation in, chart, 79
exchange rates of, 71, 73
Syndicate (*see* Underwriting)

T

Tabular standard (*see* Multiple standard)
Taylor, F. M., 20
Thomas amendment to Agricultural Adjustment Act, 45, 50
Token coins, 41

Trade acceptance, definition of, 113, 252–253
Trade credit, in agriculture, 435–438
chart, 437
Trade drafts (*see* Trade acceptance)
Transfer agent, 195
Treasury notes of 1890, 40, 41
Trial of the Pyx, 30
Trust agreement, 197
Trust companies, 334–340
chart, 133
examinations of, 234
and the financial system, 194–211
growth and importance of, charts, 333, 335
regulation of, 234–235
Trust indentures, regulation of, 234
Trust receipt, 261

U

Underwriting, 162–166
diagrams, 156
syndicates, investment banking, 163–166
Unification of the banking system, 346–348
Unit banking, 328
United States, abandons gold standard, 45
adopts gold standard, 37, 38
United States Government, capital expenditures of, 151
finances, 84–98
chart, 475
debt of, chart, 93
participation in financing of urban real estate, 467–471
position of, in the credit system, 472–483
receipts and expenditures of, chart, 91
revenues of, 473
uses of funds of, 476–478
United States Government credit agencies, sources and ownership of capital of, table, 479–481
United States Housing Authority, 470
table, 481
United States notes (*see* Greenback currency)

United States Treasury, and the credit
system, charts, 437, 475
and Federal Reserve system, 412–417
(*See also* United States government finances)
Upham, Cyril B., 357
Urban mortgage companies, 460–463

V

Veterans, loans to, 280

W

Wage rates, and prices, chart, 489,
503
War Finance Corporation, 476
Warehouse Act, of United States, 259
Warehouse receipts, loans on, 258–260
West Point, silver stored at, 49
World Economic and Monetary Con-
ference of London, 45–47, 80, 83
World War debts, 76